COGNITION

FIFTH EDITION
COGNITION

DANIEL SMILEK · **SCOTT SINNETT** · **ALAN KINGSTONE**

OXFORD
UNIVERSITY PRESS

OXFORD
UNIVERSITY PRESS

Oxford University Press is a department of the University of Oxford.
It furthers the University's objective of excellence in research, scholarship,
and education by publishing worldwide. Oxford is a registered trade mark of
Oxford University Press in the UK and in certain other countries.

Published in Canada by
Oxford University Press
8 Sampson Mews, Suite 204,
Don Mills, Ontario M3C 0H5 Canada

www.oupcanada.com

Third Edition published in 2007
Fourth Edition published in 2010

Library and Archives Canada Cataloguing in Publication
Smilek, Daniel, 1974–
Cognition / Daniel Smilek, Scott Sinnett & Alan Kingstone. — 5th ed.

Includes bibliographical references and index.
ISBN 978–0–19–544749–1

1. Cognition—Textbooks. 2. Cognitive psychology—Textbooks.
I. Sinnett, Scott II. Kingstone, Alan, 1941– III. Title.

BF311.B45 2013   153   C2012-906483-1

Cover image © Digital Storm/Shutterstock

Contents

From the Publisher

What do we know, and how do we know it? What is the relation between the mind and the brain? How does memory work? What is intelligence? How do we learn language, acquire concepts, solve problems?

These are just a few of the fundamental questions that frame this fifth edition of *Cognition:* the essential text for introductory courses in cognitive psychology.

Building on the strengths of the previous edition, in which Alan Kingstone and Daniel Smilek joined John Benjafield to update and expand his original text, this fifth edition has the significant benefit of Scott Sinnett's contributions. While preserving the clear, straightforward style, fascinating research examples, and easy-to-navigate organization of the earlier editions, the new three-author team presents a wealth of up-to-date information and research, useful learning tools, and student-oriented examples, including (for the first time) case studies that highlight key issues in each chapter. The result is a well-rounded, current, and comprehensive text that is both accessible to students and a pleasure to teach from.

Cognition, **fifth edition, retains all the hallmarks of previous editions:**

- Broad, balanced treatment of major theories and controversies;
- Clear, focused writing that makes even the most difficult concepts accessible without oversimplification;
- Historical perspectives on key issues and phenomena; and
- Abundant citations of both classic and current research from Canada and around the world.

Highlights of the Fifth Edition

- **New** case studies open each chapter with an account of a real-world situation that illustrates one or more of the concepts to be explored in the text that follows.

Case Study   Head Office

Let's take a moment to think about our heads and all they do for us. First of all, the head houses the nose and mouth, both of which are crucial to life itself. For the purposes of cognitive psychology, however, eyes and ears are equally important, for they are what enable us to see and hear the world around us. The simple fact that the head is centred at the top of the body means that it is ideally situated for the reception of information from the environment, which ultimately leads to perception and behaviour. These are all fairly obvious observations. Less obvious, perhaps, is the significance of the fact that your head is hard—really hard. Why is that so important? Your brain knows why: because it is the star of the show that is your life, and it needs all the protection it can get.

Although it accounts for only about 2 per cent of your body weight, your brain manages to claim about 20 per cent of all the blood supply in your body. If you didn't have a brain you wouldn't have a thought, and without thought there is no cognition. Yet we often take the brain for granted—at least until something goes wrong.

You may know someone whose life has been changed profoundly because of a brain disease or injury. If not, you almost certainly know of some prominent person who has suffered a brain injury, whether as a result of a stroke, a tumour, or some kind of trauma. For instance, consider the boxer Muhammad Ali. One of the most famous athletes in the world, as a fighter he would "float like a butterfly and sting like a bee" (to borrow his own phrase), and he commanded as much respect for his quick intelligence and verbal skills as for his abilities in the ring. Now this most beloved and dignified man is barely able to move or speak. Or consider Ronald Reagan and Margaret Thatcher, the two most powerful people in the Western world in the 1980s (Figure 2.1). By the time of his death in 2004, Reagan had lived with Alzheimer's disease for a decade, and today Thatcher as well is said to be battling dementia.

Virtually everyone who has ever taken an introductory psychology course will know the name of Phineas Gage, a young railroad foreman who in 1848 survived an explosion that drove an iron bar through his head. Although he suffered bouts of depression and epileptic seizures following the accident, his cognitive abilities seemed remarkably unaffected. As amazing as the Gage story is, it appears to have been replicated in Brazil in August 2012. Eduardo Leite was working on a construction site when a falling 1.8-metre iron bar pierced his hard hat, entered his skull, and came out between his eyes (see Figure 2.2). The surgery to remove the bar took five hours. Although it is still too soon to be certain, doctors report that Leite shows few if any cognitive deficits.

FIGURE 2.1   Muhammad Ali, Ronald Reagan, and Margaret Thatcher

Case Study Wrap-Up

We began this chapter by considering how easy it is to take the brain for granted, even though it is indispensable to all thought and behaviour. The life-altering consequences of brain injury were recently driven home by the case of Congresswoman Giffords, who survived a bullet in the head but then faced significant difficulties in understanding and producing speech. Based on what you have read in this chapter, which side of her brain do you think was injured?

We have considered three convergent lines of evidence suggesting that the injury must have been in the left hemisphere: brain lesion studies (e.g., the research conducted by Broca and Wernicke), surgical intervention (e.g., the split-brain work of Sperry and colleagues), and the fMRI studies involving healthy individuals. In fact, it was the left hemisphere of Giffords' brain that was damaged.

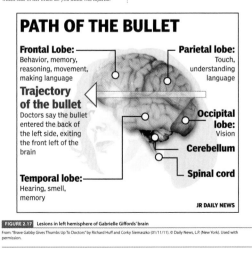

PATH OF THE BULLET

Frontal Lobe:
Behavior, memory, reasoning, movement, making language

Trajectory of the bullet
Doctors say the bullet entered the back of the left side, exiting the front left of the brain

Temporal lobe:
Hearing, smell, memory

Parietal lobe:
Touch, understanding language

Occipital lobe:
Vision

Cerebellum

Spinal cord

JR DAILY NEWS

FIGURE 2.17   Lesions in left hemisphere of Gabrielle Giffords' brain

From: "Brave Gabby Gives Thumbs Up To Doctors" by Richard Huff and Corky Siemaszko (01/11/11). © Daily News, L.P. (New York). Used with permission.

- **New** case-study "wrap-ups" at the end of each chapter revisit those cases in the light of the chapter discussion.

- **New** four-colour, single-column design includes dozens of new illustrations.

FIGURE 5.5 Flashbulb memories: Terrorist attacks on the World Trade Center, New York City

other tests designed to measure additional aspects of the flashbulb phenomenon, such as the intensity of the emotion felt when the events were recalled. They then divided the 54 participants into three groups of 18 each and re-tested each group once. The first group was tested one week later; the second, six weeks later; and the third, 32 weeks later. The major variable of interest was the consistency of the account given at the three different intervals. For example, if a participant said on 12 September that "Fred" was with him when the event occurred and later said that "Alice" was with him, but not "Fred," that response was scored as inconsistent. Each participant's recall was given a consistency score based on the number of details consistently recalled, as well as an inconsistency score. Figure 5.6 shows the change in consistency and inconsistency scores as a function of time. Notice that both flashbulb and everyday memories show a decline in consistency and an increase in inconsistency. Although the flashbulb memories had more emotion associated with them, in terms of their actual content they were certainly no more accurate than "ordinary" memories. However, participants erroneously believed that their flashbulb memories were more accurate than their "ordinary" memories. Talarico and Rubin concluded that although a flashbulb event "reliably enhances memory characteristics such as vividness and confidence," people should not put that much faith "in the accuracy of their flashbulb memories" (2003, p. 460).

FIGURE 6.10 Fragment of a semantic network

From: Collins, A.M., and & Loftus, E.F. (1975). A spreading-activation theory of semantic processing. *Psychological Review, 82,* 407–428. Copyright 1975 by the American Psychological Association.

Kvavilashvili and Mandler (2004) reported on diary and questionnaire studies designed to probe the mind-popping phenomenon. Kvavilashvili kept two diaries of her semantic "mind pops" for 19 and 18 weeks, when she was 35 and 37 years old, respectively. She logged a total of 428 memories, which tended to be either words (e.g., *rummage*) or images (e.g., *a view of a road and a small church in Cardiff*). She had no episodic information accompanying these involuntary semantic memories. Most of the mind pops occurred while she was engaged in routine activities not requiring a lot of attention, and at first they appeared unrelated to the current activity. However, Kvavilashvili was often able to retrospectively find cues that had triggered the memories without her awareness. For example, one pop-up was *Itchy and Scratchy*, the names of two characters from *The Simpsons* television show. Kvavilashvili noticed she was scratching her back when the pop-up occurred. Examples like this suggest that involuntary semantic memories are primed by events of which we are typically unaware.

Kvavilashvili and Mandler's (2004) study shows how their ecologically valid research complements and extends laboratory work. We will return to the effect of ongoing activations on the way we think in Chapters 10 and 12, on problem-solving and creativity.

Working memory
The system that allows for the temporary storage and manipulation of information that is necessary for various cognitive activities.

Working Memory

The concept of **working memory** has been at the centre of Alan Baddeley's (1986, 1989, 2000a, 2001, 2002a, 2002b; Baddeley & Hitch, 1974; N. Morris & Jones, 1990; Parkin & Hunkin, 2001) influential research program. Working memory "involves the temporary storage and manipulation of information that is assumed to be necessary

Enhanced Pedagogy

- More text boxes are now included in every chapter:

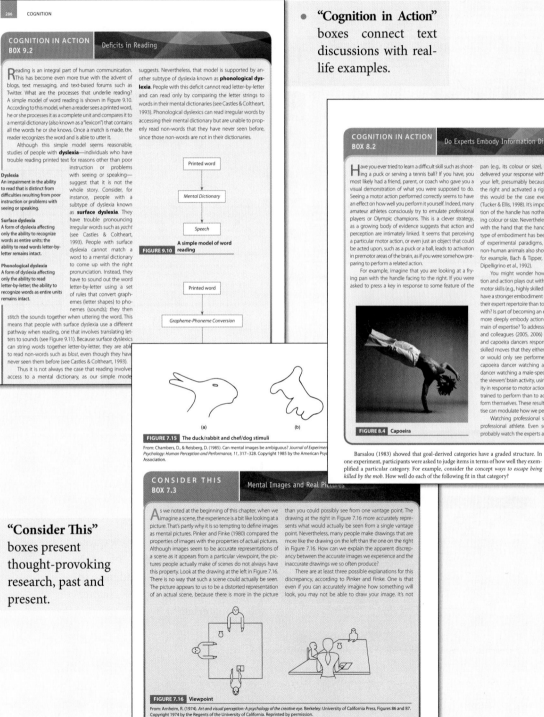

- **"Cognition in Action"** boxes connect text discussions with real-life examples.

- **"Consider This"** boxes present thought-provoking research, past and present.

- **"Think Twice"** boxes invite students to engage personally with ideas and issues raised in the chapter.

- **"In the Know"** review questions at the end of each chapter allow students to test their grasp of chapter material.

- Key terms are defined at first use in a **running glossary**, and all definitions can be found in a standard glossary at the end of the text.

Supplements

Cognition, fifth edition, is supported by an outstanding array of ancillary materials for both instructors and students, all available on the companion website: **www.oupcanada.com/ Cognition5e**.

FOR THE INSTRUCTOR

- An **instructor's manual** includes comprehensive chapter overviews, topics for classroom discussion or debate, recommended readings, web links, homework assignments with sample answers, suggestions for research paper topics, and a sample syllabus.

- A **test generator** offers a comprehensive set of multiple-choice, true/false, short-answer, and essay questions, with suggested answers, for every chapter.

- **PowerPoint® slides** summarize key points from each chapter and incorporate figures, tables, and images from the textbook.

FOR THE STUDENT

Available at **www.oupcanada.com/Cognition5e.**

The **student study guide** offers additional review questions linked to each chapter; practice quizzes, including one final examination practice quiz; an answer key for review questions and quizzes, with page references to help students find the answers in the text; key terms and definitions; chapter summaries; and study tips for mid-term and final examinations.

DISCOVERY LAB (ISBN 9780195447774)

by Carolyn Ensley, Department of Psychology, Wilfrid Laurier University

Cognition, fifth edition, is accompanied by *Discovery Lab*, which offers a wide variety of interactive experiments, exercises, and animations designed to help students understand important concepts and principles. *Discovery Lab* brings cognition topics to life by allowing students to act as researchers and test subjects and by giving them the ability to analyze and share results.

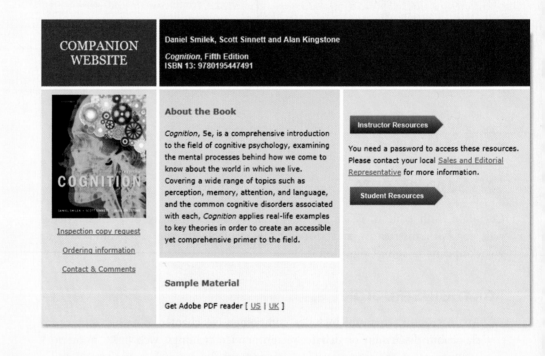

A Final Word of Thanks

We gratefully acknowledge the contributions of the following individuals whose efforts and thoughtful review comments and suggestions have helped to shape this book and its ancillaries:

Robert Cassidy, Condordia University
Todd Ferretti, Wilfrid Laurier University
Deanna Friesen, York University
Sandra Hessels, Concordia University
Dan Hufnagle, University of Calgary
Karin Humphreys, McMaster University
Jason Ivanoff, Simon Fraser University
Harvey H.C. Marmurek, University of Guelph
Patricia McMullen, Dalhousie University
Jean Paul Minda, University of Western Ontario
Penny M. Pexman, University of Calgary
Michael Picard, University of Victoria
Catherine Plowright, University of Ottawa
Gillian Rowe, University of Toronto

Preface

We could not be more excited about this fifth edition! So much of it is new and fresh. Each chapter has been carefully combed for material that was outdated or unnecessary, and new studies have been incorporated that bring readers up to speed on the latest and greatest in the study of human cognition. In addition, each chapter now has a similar format, beginning with a case study designed to whet readers' appetites and ground the issues to be discussed in the text that follows. Those familiar with the book will also notice the addition of Dr Scott Sinnett (University of Hawaii) to the authorial team, replacing John G. Benjafield, who was the sole author of the first three editions.

Acknowledgements

In fewer than four years we have managed to revise this textbook twice, and we are extraordinarily pleased with the result. We are supremely grateful to Oxford University Press in general, and to our developmental editor, Lisa Peterson, and editor, Sally Livingston, in particular. We would also like to thank the reviewers whose thoughtful comments and suggestions helped to shape this textbook.

Finally, and most importantly, we would like to thank our wives, Shelley Smilek, Cindy Sinnett, and Erica Levy, for their incredible support and encouragement. Without their efforts this book would not have been possible, and without their patience, we might all now be single.

Daniel Smilek, Scott Sinnett, and Alan Kingstone
September 2012

List of Boxes

Case Studies

CONSIDER THIS

COGNITION IN ACTION

THINK TWICE

Case Study Wrap-Up

COGNITION

Introduction

Chapter Contents

Chapter Objectives

- To identify the concepts associated with the field of cognition, beginning with information-processing.
- To outline the essentials of information theory.
- To distinguish among different models of the information-processing approach to cognition.
- To explain the advantages and limitations of the information-processing approach.
- To review experimental evidence for the information-processing approach.
- To identify different research methods in cognitive psychology.

The year is 2054, and you are sleeping peacefully when suddenly, out of nowhere, Captain John Anderton and three associate members of the "PreCrime" police force crash through your skylight, yank you out of your bed, put you in handcuffs, and place you under arrest. Why? A small group of "PreCogs"—mutated individuals with pre-cognitive abilities—working for the PreCrime Unit have looked into the future and witnessed you committing a horrific murder later that morning. For the past six years, the PreCogs' visions have allowed the PreCrime Unit to arrest "killers" before they have had the chance to kill. And directly as a result of these PreCog visions, depicted in the futuristic movie thriller *Minority Report*, the city of Washington, DC, has been homicide-free for six years.

Folk psychology
An umbrella term for various assumptions and theories based on the everyday behaviour of ourselves and others.

Even though it has no basis in reality, the *Minority Report* scenario raises a number of fundamental questions, including the classic philosophical question of free will vs. determinism: do people have the freedom to choose what they do, or are they fated to carry out certain actions? With respect to cognition, the scenario also raises the question of whether any one person's perception—whether a PreCog's vision of the future or an ordinary human's perception of the present or memory of the past—can be accepted as an accurate and truthful (i.e., veridical) reflection of the world.

But we are getting ahead of ourselves. First we should consider why the mutant visionaries are called "PreCogs." Well, the *pre* obviously means "before in time" or "prior to." And *cog* is short for "cognitive," the adjective formed from the noun *cognition*—a word that, as we shall see, has an extraordinarily rich and wonderfully complex set of meanings.

As a starting point, let's look at the way the word *cognition* is understood in everyday life. Although scientific psychology usually seeks to refine the "common-sense" assumptions of **folk psychology**, a quick look at the concepts typically associated with cognition may give us an idea of the range of topics that cognitive psychology might cover.

For example, *The New Oxford American Dictionary* defines *cognition* as "the mental action or process of acquiring knowledge and understanding through thought, experience, and the senses." This definition underscores a key point: that cognition is the mental *action* of knowing. How we come to know is the domain of cognition and the focus of this textbook.

FIGURE 1.1   "PreCogs" from *Minority Report*

Cognitive Psychology and Information Processing

The study of human cognition has advanced in three stages (Van Kleeck & Kosslyn, 1991). The first stage, from the late 1950s to early 1960s, was one of rapid progression propelled by the methods of traditional psychophysics (the scientific investigation of the relationship between sensation and stimulus) and experimental psychology. The second stage, under way by the mid-1970s, was fuelled by computational analysis and marked the arrival of cognitive science. The third phase, which began in the mid-1980s, has incorporated evidence from neuropsychology and animal neurophysiology, and most recently an ever-increasing array of imaging techniques that allow us to observe the brain in action.

Foundational to all of cognitive psychology is the idea that the world contains information that is available for humans to process. The amount of information provided by a given event can be quantified in terms of **bits** (short for "binary digits"). Imagine a situation in which one of two equally likely events is about to occur: a coin toss, for instance. You are uncertain of the outcome until the coin falls, but when it does it gives you one bit of information: either heads or tails. Every time the number of equally likely outcomes doubles, the number of information bits you receive increases by one. A common illustration of this process is the old guessing game in which I think of a number and you try to guess it by asking me questions (Garner, 1962, p. 5). The number of information bits in play corresponds to the number of questions you need to ask. Your best strategy is to reduce the number of possibilities by half with each question. For example, if the number I'm thinking of is between 1 and 8, you need to ask at most three questions. First, ask if it's above 4. If the answer is "yes," then ask if it's above 6. If the answer is "yes" again, then ask if it's above 7. If the answer is "yes," then the number is 8; if it's "no," then the number is 7.

Every day we take in and act on information in countless ways. As we drive down the street we take in information about location, direction, the traffic, the weather, the people on the sidewalk. When we're learning a new computer system, we try to understand and remember the procedures and commands that we'll need to use later. And every time we count our change or balance our chequebook we rely on our knowledge of how to add and subtract. To many people, these everyday activities—attending, comprehending, remembering, manipulating numerical information—fall under the general heading of "thinking." To psychologists, they are aspects of information processing—the subject matter of cognitive psychology.

Bit
Short for "binary digit"; the most basic unit of information. Every event that occurs in a situation with two equally likely outcomes provides one "bit" of information.

Information Theory

Basic to the concept of information-processing is the idea that information reduces uncertainty in the mind of the receiver. Suppose you and I are exchanging addresses over the phone and I'm spelling the name of my street, but the connection is bad and you don't hear me well enough to make out one of the letters. The best you can do is guess that it was one of the 26 letters that make up the alphabet. Clearly, your uncertainty here is a function of the number of possibilities. Now let's suppose that I pronounce the letter again, and this time you can tell that it's either *A* or *K*. Your uncertainty is much less now: a function of 2 rather than 26.

FIGURE 1.2   **There is a lot of information in our world**

The amount of information provided by a given message is proportional to the probability that that particular message will occur. If you greet a friend with the query "How are you?" and receive the reply "Absolutely awful—I must have picked up a flu bug" rather than a standard "Fine, thanks," the former reply is much more informative than the latter because it is much less probable. The idea underlying information-processing theory is that the information provided by a particular message is not determined solely by its content, but rather by the whole array of possible messages of which this particular message is just one. To put it more succinctly, the amount of information a message conveys is an increasing function of the number of possible messages from which that particular message could have been selected. In other words, **information theory** posits that the information provided by a particular message is inversely related to the probability of its occurrence: the less likely it is, the more information it conveys.

Information theory
The theory that the information provided by a particular event is inversely related to the probability of its occurrence.

EARLY TESTS OF INFORMATION THEORY

Hick (1952) measured the time it took participants to react appropriately to the occurrence of one of a set of possible signals. The stimuli were one to ten lights arranged in a nearly circular display, and the responses were delivered by pressing keys located under the participants' fingers. The time taken to respond to a stimulus was found to vary as a function of the number of possible stimuli, with response time slowing down as the number of stimulus alternatives increased. This result suggested to Hick that stimulus

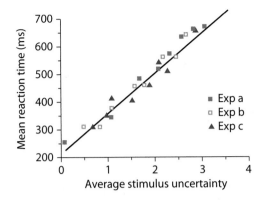

FIGURE 1.3 **Hyman's data showing mean reaction times for one subject**

Hyman used small lights as stimuli and vocal responses. The three experiments varied stimulus uncertainty by (a) different numbers of equally frequent stimuli, (b) different relative frequencies of a fixed number of alternatives, and (c) different first-order conditional probabilities subject to equal relative frequencies.

From: Hyman, Ray. Stimulus information as a determinant of reaction time. *Journal of Experimental Psychology, 45*: 188–196, 1953, p. 192. http://www.apa.org/.

information is tightly linked with processing time: the more information a signal provides, the more time it takes a subject to produce the appropriate response.

Other investigators were quick to extend this idea. For example, Hyman (1953) asked participants to make an appropriate verbal response to a varying number of lights. Increasing the number of equally probable alternatives from one to eight produced an increase in response time, confirming Hick's observations. In a second condition, Hyman made the occurrence of some signals more frequent than that of others. The result was that response time to frequent signals was reduced for all four participants, while for all but one of them response time to infrequent signals increased. In a third condition, Hyman introduced sequential dependencies into the presentation of signals (e.g., certain lights were followed by others at specific frequencies), while keeping the overall probability of each signal the same. For example, in a situation with two alternatives, the probability of change from one alternative on trial "n" to the other on trial "n+1" was 0.80; thus the probability that the same signal would be repeated on successive trials was 0.20. Again, responses became faster as a signal's probability increased and slower as it decreased (Figure 1.3). These results showed that the time it took a participant to react to any one stimulus was not determined solely by the stimulus itself, but rather by the entire complex of situations of which that particular signal was just one. Thus it takes longer to react to an improbable stimulus (which conveys more information) than to a probable one (which conveys less information).

LIMITATIONS ON INFORMATION-PROCESSING

The classic experiments by Hick and Hyman demonstrate that it takes time to translate a visual signal to either a key-press or a verbal response. The amount of time it takes for information to flow through the nervous system is one limitation on information-processing capacity, but the amount of visual information that a person can process at any one time has limits as well. The more information a visual signal conveys, the longer it takes for the viewer to make an appropriate response. Thus, in addition to a

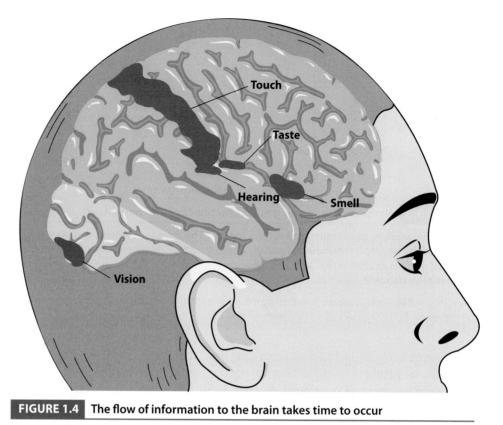

FIGURE 1.4   The flow of information to the brain takes time to occur

Based on: research.yale.edu/ysm/images/77.4/articles-synesthesia-brain.jpg.

time limitation, the nervous system exhibits a capacity limitation for the amount of information that it can handle within a fixed period of time.

Experimental paradigms using simultaneous auditory messages suggest a similar conclusion. In an early experiment, Webster and Thompson (1953) had airport control tower operators listen to recorded voice transmissions simulating messages from pilots. A pilot-to-tower communication consisted of the aircraft's call signal and a sequence of three unrelated words. For example, a typical message might be "Tower, this is BA 427, Pencil, Beard, Camera, over" or "Tower, this is WW 618, Rage, Wire, Coffee, over." The call signals (BA 427, WW 618) were drawn from a set of 10 possible signals, whereas the word messages (e.g., "Pencil, Beard, Camera)" were drawn from a set of 1152 possi-bilities. Clearly, the amount of information (in a technical sense) conveyed by each call signal was much less than that contributed by each word message because the traffic controllers had a fairly good idea of what the call signal would be, but almost no idea of what the word message would be. Although they were able to identify the call signals from two airplanes arriving simultaneously, they could not identify more than one of two simultaneous word messages (Figure 1.5).

This finding suggests that there are limits to the nervous system's capacity for information-processing. When two messages arrive simultaneously, the amount of interference between them depends on the amount of information they convey. The limit is, as Broadbent (1957) would say, one of information rather than stimulation. For example, Hick and Hyman showed that people respond faster to an expected stimulus than to one that is unexpected.

FIGURE 1.5   Dichotic listening

In dichotic listening, as in the instance of an air traffic controller, two different messages are received simultaneously.

Based on: http://penta.ufrgs.br/edu/telelab/2/dochotic.jpg.

The importance of these findings lies in their suggestion that people deal with overload of their capacity to process information by attending to only some of the available signal information. Humans are not merely passive receivers and transformers of signal information: they are active selectors of information from the environment. Only some of the information is selected for processing; only some is responded to; only some is remembered. The amount of information available in any individual's perceptual world is clearly much greater than he or she can handle. For instance, as Hick (1952) found, there is a fixed upper limit to the amount of information that a person can process in unit time (i.e., at a given moment).

Models of Information-Processing

Cognitive psychologists have suggested several models of the relations between different cognitive processes. We will consider two classic models here.

BROADBENT'S FILTER MODEL

Studies of human attention have focused on the limitations of the capacity to process information and the selective processes that are used to deal with those limitations. How much control do we have over which information we select and which we reject? What are the costs and the benefits of expecting one particular type of information rather than another? The first complete theory of attention was Broadbent's (1958) **filter model** (Figure 1.6). The idea on which it was based—that information-processing is restricted by **channel capacity**—was originally suggested by Shannon (1948) and Shannon and Weaver (1949).

Filter model
A theory based on the idea that information-processing is restricted by channel capacity.

Channel capacity
The maximum amount of information that can be transmitted by an information-processing device.

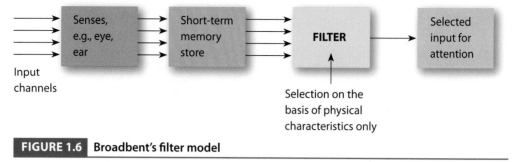

Based on: www.simplypsychology.pwp.blueyonder.co.uk/broadbent.jpg.

FIGURE 1.6   Broadbent's filter model

Broadbent (1958) argues convincingly that the whole nervous system can be regarded as a single channel with limits to the rate at which it can transmit stimulus information. Overloading of this limited capacity channel is prevented by a selective device or filter, which allows only some of the available incoming information to enter the system. Preceding the filter is a capacity-free sensory buffer or temporary store.

When two or more signals or messages occur at one time, they enter the sensory buffer together. The buffer then extracts such simple stimulus characteristics as colour (vision), voice (hearing), or spatial location. The filter operates by selecting messages that share some basic physical characteristic (e.g., location in space) and passing them along to the limited capacity system that is responsible for the analysis of "higher-order" stimulus attributes, such as form and meaning. Meanwhile, any messages that were not selected are held, in parallel (i.e., simultaneously), in the sensory buffer, where they are subject to decay with the passage of time.

This filter theory represented a strong account of the data on attention that were available at the time (cf. Broadbent, 1956; Cherry, 1953; Hick, 1952; Hyman, 1953; Webster & Thompson, 1953, 1954). A classic example comes from Broadbent (1954), who asked his participants to listen to three pairs of digits. One member of each pair arrived at one ear at the same time that the other member of the pair arrived at the other ear. For instance, if the sequence was "73–42–15" the participant would hear "7, 4, 1" in the left ear, and simultaneously "3, 2, 5" in the right ear. The pairs were separated by a half-second interval, and the participants were asked to recall the digits in whatever order they wished. They were able to recall 65 per cent of the lists correctly, and in almost every case the correct responses followed the same pattern: participants would recall all the digits presented to one ear, followed by all the digits presented to the other ear (e.g., "741–325" or "325–741"). In a second condition, participants were asked to recall the items in the sequence in which they were presented. Since the participants were hearing two digits at the same time, one in each ear, they were allowed to report either member of the pair first, but were required to report both digits before continuing through the sequence (e.g., either "73–42–15" or "37–24–51"). In this condition participants were able to report only 20 per cent of the lists correctly.

Broadbent interpreted this difference in recall performance to mean that the ears function as separate channels for information input. The different physical locations for the two messages are initially entered and preserved in the short-term sensory buffer. Selective attention, represented by the filter, operates to determine which channel is recalled first. Switching attention between ears requires time. Performance is poorer for recall by presentation order because more attentional switching is required.

THINK TWICE BOX 1.1

Distracted Driving

Are you a good driver? Can you manoeuvre your vehicle through traffic while drinking a coffee and listening to the radio? We suspect that most of you would say "yes" (many people overestimate their driving skills). Are you also aware that many jurisdictions have recently made it illegal to use a cell phone while driving? Do you think such legislation is needed?

Before you answer, let's consider another question. Is it safe to drive with a blindfold over your eyes? Every time you take your eyes off the road, whatever the reason, you are essentially putting a blindfold on. That's why texting while driving is so dangerous. You might think that just talking on your phone would be no problem, since you can still keep your eyes on the road, but you would be wrong. Obviously, reading a text requires you to physically move your eyes away from the road to look at the screen; this is an overt attention shift. But the same thing happens when a conversation directs your attention away from the road, even if your eyes don't move. The only difference is that this attention shift is covert (we will discuss the distinction between overt and covert

attention in more detail in Chapter 4). The truth is that any distraction can compromise your ability to use the information that your eyes take in: you might look but fail to see.

To demonstrate this, Strayer, Drews, and Johnston (2003) placed participants in a driving simulator and asked them to complete a driving course, keeping pace with the traffic, staying in their own lane, and braking for obstacles. What they found was that conversing on a cell phone led to significantly poorer driving performance. Amazingly, it made no difference if the phone was hands-free (Strayer & Johnston, 2001)! In a subsequent experiment the same authors (2003) used an eye tracker to register where the eyes were looking and for how long. It showed that drivers who were engaged in a cell phone conversation were roughly half as likely as the phone-less control group to remember details from the course (e.g., billboards), even though their eyes had rested on those details for the same length of time. In short, using a cell phone while driving can be deadly even if you never take your eyes off the road because it can affect what you see.

Meanwhile, as attention is switching between locations (ears), the information in the sensory buffer continues to decay, and thus becomes less and less available with the passage of time. In the first condition, where participants recalled all the items from one ear and then all the items from the other ear, only one switch of attention was required—from one input location to the other. In the second condition, where participants had to recall the items in the order of presentation, at least three switches of attention were required—for example, from left to right, from right to left, and once more from left to right.

WAUGH AND NORMAN'S MODEL OF INFORMATION-PROCESSING

Figure 1.7 comes from an early but still important paper by Waugh and Norman (1965). The flow of information is indicated by the arrows. Upon being stimulated, we may have an experience called a primary memory, a concept derived from the highly influential American psychologist William James (1890/1983). This is noteworthy because the approach that James relied on for many of his major insights and hypotheses was one that few if any cognitive psychologists today would use: **introspection** (see Box 1.2). **Primary memory** consists of the "immediately present moment" (James,

Introspection
"Looking inward" to observe one's own thoughts and feelings.

Primary memory
What we are aware of in the "immediately present moment"; often termed "immediate memory" or "short-term memory."

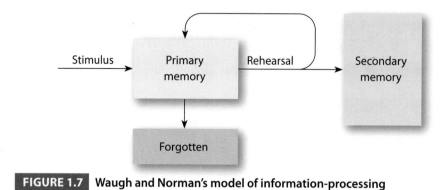

FIGURE 1.7 Waugh and Norman's model of information-processing

From: Waugh, N.C., & Norman, D.A. (1965). Primary memory. *Psychological Review, 72*, pp. 89–104. Copyright 1965 by the American Psychological Association. http://www.apa.org/

Secondary memory
Knowledge acquired at an earlier time that is stored indefinitely, and is absent from awareness; also called "long-term memory."

Brown–Peterson task
An experimental paradigm in which subjects are given a set of items and then a number. Subjects immediately begin counting backward by threes from the number and, after a specific interval, are asked to recall the original items.

1890/1983, p. 608), and is thus also known as "immediate memory." The arrow labelled "rehearsal" refers to the fact that primary memories tend to be quickly forgotten unless they are repeated, as you might repeat a telephone number to yourself after looking it up. Whereas primary memory belongs to the present, **secondary memory** belongs to the past.

Waugh and Norman (1965) noted that James's distinction between primary and secondary memory was based on introspective evidence. Such evidence is seldom treated as definitive in cognitive psychology. However, the subjective reports of participants are often used in conjunction with more objective evidence such as that provided by well-designed experiments (Jack & Shallice, 2001; see Figure 1.8). Experimental evidence for the primary–secondary memory distinction came from analysis of the **Brown–Peterson task** (J. Brown, 1958; Peterson & Peterson, 1959)— one of the most widely used experimental tasks in memory research. In the typical Brown–Peterson experiment, participants are given a set of items to remember (e.g., the letters B, Q, R), and then a number from which they immediately begin counting backward by threes. Thus a participant given the number "107" would start counting ("104, 101, 98, . . ." and so on) and after a specific interval (say, 6, 9, 12, 15, or 18 seconds), would be asked to recall the specified items (in this case, the letters B, Q, R). Because the interval is filled with the counting exercise, the participant is presumably prevented from rehearsing the letters and therefore unable to retain them in his or her primary memory. An unfilled interval, by contrast, would allow the participant to rehearse the items and keep them in primary memory. Waugh and Norman's analysis showed that participants' ability to recall letters declined as the number of interfering items increased (Figure 1.10).

INTROSPECTION	EXPERIMENTAL
Subjective	Objective
Individual thoughts/perspectives	Group data averaged
Non-statistical	Statistical

FIGURE 1.8 Introspection vs experimental method

From: http://www.apa.org/

Waugh and Norman (1965) pointed out that primary memory makes it possible for us to immediately and accurately recall our most recent experiences. For example, we are able "to recall verbatim the most recent few words in a sentence [we are] hearing or speaking" (p. 102), provided that no distraction intervenes. Although we take primary memory for granted, it is extremely important to us.

Students of literature might know of William James as the older brother (by a year) of Henry James, the famous American realist novelist of manners and personal psychology, yet today William is widely recognized as one of the most eminent psychologists the world has known. Born in New York to a wealthy family with liberal ideals and wide interests, James studied medicine at Harvard, where he later taught. His two-volume, 1200-page masterwork, *The Principles of Psychology* (1890), exemplifies James's holistic thinking, embracing not only psychology, physiology, and philosophy, but a wealth of personal observation, introspection, and opinion. For example, James described the infant's perception of the observed world "as one great blooming, buzzing confusion" (is that your recollection of earliest infancy?); introduced the idea of "the stream of consciousness"; pointed out the importance of habit in human life; and warned against the "psychologist's fallacy" whereby researchers too often allow their own personal experience and views to intrude on their rational understanding of the phenomena they are analyzing.

FIGURE 1.9   **William James**

Ecological Validity

In standard information-processing models such as Broadbent's or Waugh and Norman's, a lot of interest is focused on the processing required to make a stimulus meaningful. However, such models may not say very much about the information available in the stimulus itself. Other psychologists, such as J.J. Gibson (1904–79) (Figure 1.11), took more interest in the richness of the information provided by the

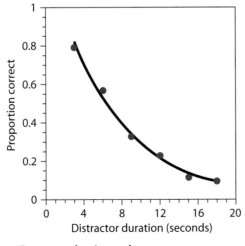

FIGURE 1.10   **Brown–Peterson classic result**

From: Peterson, L.R., & Peterson, M.J. (1959). Short-term retention of individual verbal items. *Journal of Experimental Psychology, 58*, 193–198.

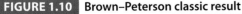

Gibson's theory of visual perception emphasized an ecological perspective on stimuli that was missing from other accounts of the way perception and attention function (e.g., Broadbent's filter theory).

Ecological approach
A form of psychological inquiry that reflects conditions in the real world.

Affordances
The potential functions or uses of stimuli (i.e., objects and events) in the real world.

Information pickup
The process whereby we perceive information directly.

Schema
An expectation concerning what we are likely to find as we explore the world (plural *schemas* or *schemata*).

Perceptual cycle
The process whereby our schemata guide our exploration of the world and in turn are shaped by what we find there.

environment in which people find themselves. Gibson (1950, 1966) argued that the stimuli used by information-processing psychologists in their experiments were often impoverished in comparison with the information available in the real world. He argued for the development of an **ecological approach** to perception that would describe environmental stimulation at the appropriate level. Gibson believed that the meaning of objects and events can be perceived through what he called their **affordances**, which he defined as "simply what things furnish, for good or ill" (1966, p. 285): thus food affords the possibility of eating, stairs afford the possibility of climbing, ice affords the possibility of skating, and so on. Of course, knowledge of those affordances is not innate: we have to learn what can (and can't) be done with items in the world. Thus Gibson's theory is one of **information pickup**, in which learning means becoming progressively more attuned to what the environment affords us.

By contrast, Neisser (1976, p. 21) proposed a cyclical model of cognition in which the perceiver possesses a **schema** that represents what he or she expects to find in the environment and that directs his or her exploration of it. In the course of that exploration, however, the perceiver encounters not only the expected information but also some that is unexpected (Figure 1.12). This unexpected information is capable of modifying the schema so as to increase the accuracy with which it represents the environment. Thus the **perceptual cycle** (Figure 1.13) begins with a schema that brings the person into contact with new information that he or she can use to correct the schema, and so on.

To see how this perceptual cycle might work, consider Figures 1.14a and 1.14b. Halper (1997) noticed a building in Manhattan with balconies that appeared to tilt upward. Obviously, it would be absurd to build balconies like that, so what was going on? In terms of the perceptual cycle, we might describe the process as follows. Our schema is our cognitive model of the environment, constructed over time through our interactions with that environment. Our schema provides us with a set of general expectations and assumptions regarding what we are likely to find in the environment, although we need not be aware of them. One of our expectations is that balconies will be either square or rectangular (i.e., bounded by right angles). We automatically impose this expectation on the buildings in Figures 1.14a and 1.14b. As a consequence we perceive the balconies of the building in the foreground to be tilting upward, as they would have to be if they were rectangular. When we explore this building from a different angle, our expectations may even lead us to perceive the balconies as tilting downward, as in Figure 1.14c! If we continue to explore the situation, however, we can come to understand it. In fact, "the balconies are parallelograms vertically perpendicular to the face of the building" (Halper, 1997, p. 1322), as can be seen in Figure 1.14d. Now our schema for buildings has been modified to include the possibility that some balconies will be built at angles that are other than right. In general, the perceptual cycle allows us to become increasingly sophisticated in our dealings with the environment.

The relative virtues of laboratory-based and ecological approaches to cognitive research have been hotly debated (e.g., Anderson & Bushman, 1997; Chayter & Schmitter-Edgecomb, 2003; Loftus, 1991; Neisser, 1978; Schmuckler, 2001; Kingstone, Smilek, Ristic, Friesen, & Eastwood, 2003). Kingstone, Smilek, and Eastwood (2008)

FIGURE 1.12   Lucy and Desi

Comedienne Lucille Ball in her 1950s television series *I Love Lucy*. Unexpected events force us to adjust our perceptions of the environment. As expectations change, we must change our schemas.

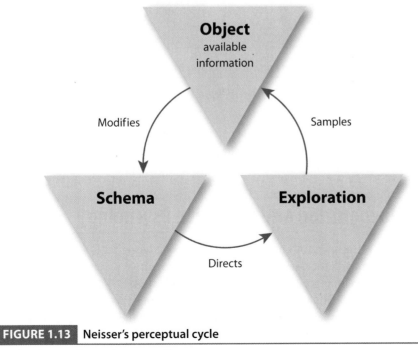

FIGURE 1.13   Neisser's perceptual cycle

Based on: huwi.org/images/image001.gif.

FIGURE 1.14   Balconies on *The Future*, a building in New York City.

From: Halper, F. (1997). The illusion of *The Future*. *Perception, 26*, pp. 1321–1322. Reprinted with permission of the author.

have recently outlined an approach that may resolve this dispute. **Cognitive ethology** (see Box 1.3) offers concrete and specific suggestions for carrying out studies in the real world in a way that will complement laboratory-based research.

Metacognition and Cognitive Psychology

Cognitive ethology
A new research approach that links real-world observations with laboratory-based studies.

Metacognition
Knowledge about the way that cognitive processes work; understanding of our own cognitive processes.

Metacognition is the term for knowledge about knowledge—that is, knowledge about the way that cognitive processes work. The study of cognitive psychology can be seen as a process of developing our metacognition (Rebok, 1987). We all begin in pretty much the same place, with a common-sense understanding of cognition, and our goal in studying cognitive psychology is to develop this understanding further. Sometimes that means changing our beliefs about how cognition takes place, or giving them up altogether. Often it means accepting some uncertainty regarding what we can assert

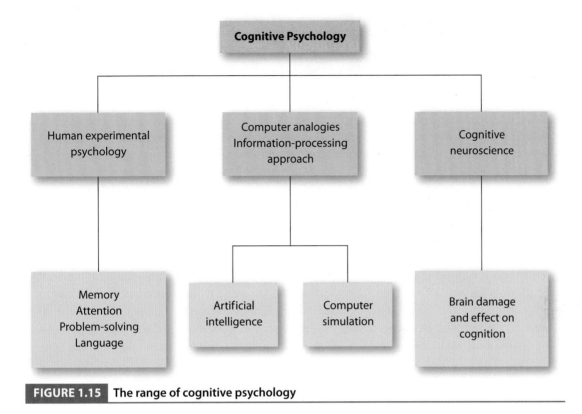

FIGURE 1.15   The range of cognitive psychology

about cognition at a particular point. Cognitive psychology is not a complete body of knowledge, but an actively developing area of inquiry (see Figure 1.15). What it offers is not so much a set of definitive answers as a series of hypotheses about the way the mind works. In the next chapter we will review some of the better-known approaches to the field, to get a better idea of the "lay of the land."

The biggest challenge for a beginning student of cognitive psychology may be to get over the feeling that thinking about thinking is an impossibly abstract skill that only a select few can master. The truth is that you probably already have a pretty elaborate way of thinking about thinking. As you work through this book, try to relate the concepts and hypotheses you encounter to the concepts and hypotheses you already have. Of course, this means that you will need to work out what it is that you think at this point. You may occasionally discover that you've generated a hypothesis that seems to offer an interesting alternative to the theories that cognitive psychologists have already developed. When that happens, you are becoming a cognitive psychologist yourself. Try to think of ways of testing the hypotheses that you come up with. As many psychologists have observed (e.g., Kuhn, 1989), formulating and testing hypotheses about how the mind works is one of the ways in which personal observations can develop into scientific knowledge.

The Range of Cognitive Psychology

Cognitive psychology provides important tools for the analysis of problems of all kinds. Throughout this book you will find not only concrete, practical examples of the application of cognitive psychology but also discussions of the social and emotional aspects of cognition. The study of those topics has been greatly influenced by cognitive psychology, but they

COGNITION IN ACTION BOX 1.3 — Cognitive Ethology

Research into human cognition, like research in general, often begins when researchers notice something interesting in the world. Cognitive researchers then create a lab-based experiment that controls for everything except what they believe is the core mental process in question, and run experiments to understand that process. When all the experiments have been done, they conclude that they now have a fundamental understanding of the mental process that causes the real-world phenomenon they initially wanted to understand.

A new research approach, called cognitive ethology, recognizes that this standard research approach operates on the flawed assumption that cognitive processes, like off-the-shelf tools, always do the same job regardless of the situation (Kingstone, Smilek, & Eastwood, 2008). This is patently untrue. By the mid-1970s it had become very clear that most statements about cognition were true if, and only if, particular laboratory conditions were met; when those conditions were not met, the relationships between factors became unpredictable. **"If A then B" in the lab does not necessarily mean "If A then B" in the world.**

So, for example, memory experiments found that what research subjects remembered depended on factors such as (a) what processing they performed on the stimulus materials, (b) what stimulus materials they expected to receive, (c) what materials were actually presented, (d) what they were doing before their memory was measured, (e) how their memory was measured, and so on. The take-home messages were that cognitive processes vary; that they are affected by what is happening elsewhere within the cognitive system; and therefore that they depend critically on the specific situational context in which the subject is embedded.

The fact that cognitive processes are fluid, adapting to the situation and goals of each individual, means that many of our psychological theories could be flawed if not downright wrong. It also means that the justification behind traditional lab-based cognitive research—the assumption that we can isolate and test the same mental process in different environments—may no longer hold, and that we need to broaden the ways in which we do our work.

Cognitive ethology proposes the following alternative approach:

1. Carefully observe and describe behaviour as it naturally occurs.
2. Then move it into the laboratory and gradually simplify relevant factors.
3. Test to find out whether lab findings predict, as well as explain, real-world phenomena.

are not always covered in cognition texts. Now cognitive psychology has developed to the point that it is integral to most other forms of psychology, and it's important that you become aware of how it may be applied, both in other areas of psychology and in the real world.

▌ Summary

In this chapter we have introduced several of the key concepts covered by the term *cognition*, beginning with information-processing. Central to the information-processing approach to cognition is the idea that the information provided by a particular message is not determined solely by the message itself, but rather by the whole array of possible messages of which this particular one is just a single instance. The less likely it is that a particular signal will occur, the more information it will convey and the more time it will take to process. Hick and Hyman have produced experimental evidence using visual stimuli to support the notion that people respond more slowly to less likely signals. The slow reaction times suggest that there are limits to the amount of information that the nervous system can handle within a fixed period of time, whether the information signal is visual or auditory. To prevent overloading of our capacity to process information, we select only some of the available signal information to process, respond to, and remember. In other words, we are not merely passive receivers of information from our perceptual world: we are *active selectors* of information.

Several classic models dominate the study of information-processing. First, Broadbent's *filter model* is based on the idea that information-processing is restricted by the *capacity* of the *channel* that is the nervous system. When multiple messages arrive at the same time, Broadbent's model suggests that a filtering device chooses among them on the basis of common physical characteristics. By contrast, Norman and Waugh's model distinguishes between primary and secondary memory. Primary memories are created in the immediately present moment and tend to be quickly forgotten unless they are rehearsed or repeated. We will extend our exploration of memory to more recent concepts in Chapter 6.

Also noteworthy is Gibson's ecological approach to information-processing. His theory of *information pickup* focuses on the wealth of information available through the stimulus itself, rather than the processing required to make a stimulus meaningful. In this model, learning is less about the processing of information and more about becoming attuned to what the environment affords us.

One thing these varied models have in common is their reliance on the standard lab-based research approach, which assumes that the same mental processes can be isolated and tested in different environments. An alternative research approach is *cognitive ethology*, which acknowledges that cognitive processes are fluid, adapting to the situation and goals of an individual. Whichever approach is employed, the study of cognitive psychology can be understood as a matter of *metacognition*—in other words, "thinking about thinking."

Case Study Wrap-Up

We began this chapter with a scenario in which the PreCogs' perceptions of the future led to your arrest for a murder that you had yet to commit. In the context of that scenario we raised the question of how veridical cognition can be. Can the PreCogs' vision be taken as an accurate reflection of something that was actually going to occur? Or is there some uncertainty in play? Based on what we have seen in this chapter, and what we will see in the chapters that follow, it seems that cognition always involves some element of uncertainty. Indeed, much of the research discussed in this chapter was designed to come to grips with this apparent fact. From the beginning, researchers recognized that there was a connection between the amount of information conveyed by any given event and the probability of that event: the less likely the event, the more information it conveys. Furthermore, because people are limited in the amount of information they can process at any one moment in time, a lot of information is going to be lost.

And there's the rub. There is no single reality for any of us. What we see, what we attend to, what we think about, and what we remember is a complex combination of the situation within which we receive information and the actions that we perform on the basis of that information; and those actions of course will reflect who we are. Thus my cognition in a given situation will almost certainly be different from yours. So, can the PreCogs' visions be trusted? Could the PreCrime Unit have made a grave error when they arrested you?

? In the Know: Review Questions

1. Cognitive psychology draws heavily on the idea that humans are information processors. What are some advantages of this approach? What are some limitations?

2. Folk psychology and introspection are two possible sources of knowledge about cognition, based on everyday observation and personal reflection, respectively. How valuable do you think they are? How does the knowledge derived from those sources relate to the knowledge produced by the controlled studies of researchers like Hick, Hyman, and Broadbent?

Key Concepts

What follows here is a list of some of the most influential ideas in the area we have just reviewed, which made their first appearance above in boldface; a similar list will be included in each of the chapters to follow. Some concepts are quite general and not associated with any particular psychologist. Others are accompanied by the names of the psychologists with whom they are identified. If any of the names or concepts seem unfamiliar, reread the appropriate section of the chapter. You should be able to define each concept and discuss the research that is relevant to it. Brief definitions are included in the margins where the terms are introduced, as well as in the Glossary at the end of the book.

affordances
bit
Brown–Peterson task
channel capacity
cognitive ethology
ecological approach
filter model (Broadbent)
folk psychology
information pickup

information theory
introspection
metacognition
perceptual cycle
primary memory (Waugh and Norman)
schema
secondary memory (Waugh and Norman)

Links to Other Chapters

affordances
Chapter 8 (prototypicality)

ecological approach and ecological validity
Chapter 4 (inattentional blindness)
Chapter 5 (ecological approaches to memory)
Chapter 6 (involuntary semantic memories)

Chapter 7 (criticisms of classical concept research)
Chapter 10 (*in vivo* and *in vitro* methods)
Chapter 11 (ecological rationality)
Chapter 12 (practical intelligence)

metacognition
Chapter 5 (elaboration and distinctiveness)
Chapter 10 (feeling of knowing)

perceptual cycle
Chapter 4 (attention capture and inattentional blindness)
Chapter 7 (images as anticipations)

schema
Chapter 4 (task switching)
Chapter 5 (schema theories, Bartlett, body schema, phantom limbs, scripts)

primary memory
Chapter 3 (pattern recognition)
Chapter 5 (levels of processing)

Further Reading

A history of early developments in cognitive psychology can be found in Chapter 14 of Benjafield (2005). For a particularly well-informed analysis of those developments, see Mandler (2002).

Analyses of folk psychology—people's beliefs about how the mind works—include Rips and Conrad (1989) and Fellbaum and Miller (1990). Additional elaboration on folk psychology can be found in D'Andrade (1987) and Vendler (1972). Stich (1983) is a classic critique of folk psychology. For a more appreciative survey of the pervasiveness and variability of folk psychology see Lillard (1998).

We review the large literature on metacognition at various places in this book. Flavell (1979) is a good place to start; he was one of the pioneers in this area. For a more recent perspective see Sternberg (1998).

Winograd, Fivush, and Hirst (1999) is a collection of papers presented in appreciation of Neisser's contribution to ecologically valid studies.

Benjafield, J. (2005). *A history of psychology*. Toronto: Oxford University Press.

D'Andrade, R. (1987). A folk model of the mind. In D. Holland & N. Quinn (Eds.), *Cultural models in language and thought* (pp. 112–148). Cambridge: Cambridge University Press.

Fellbaum, C., & Miller, G.A. (1990). Folk psychology or semantic entailment? *Psychological Review 97*: 565–570.

Flavell, J. (1979). Metacognition and cognitive monitoring. *American Psychologist 34*: 906–911.

Lillard, A. (1998). Ethnopsychologies: Cultural variations in theories of mind. *Psychological Bulletin 123*: 3–32.

Mandler, G. (2002). Origins of the cognitive (r)evolution. *Journal of the History of the Behavioral Sciences 38*: 339–353.

Rips, L.J., & Conrad, F.G. (1989). Folk psychology of mental activities. *Psychological Review 96*: 187–207.

Sternberg, R.J. (1998). Metacognition, abilities, and developing expertise. *Instructional Science 26*: 127–140.

Stich, S. (1983). *From folk psychology to cognitive science: The case against belief*. Cambridge, Mass.: MIT Press.

Vendler, Z. (1972). *Res cogitans: An essay in rational psychology*. Ithaca, NY: Cornell University Press.

Winograd, E., Fivush, R., & Hirst, W. (Eds.). (1999). *Ecological approaches to cognition*. Mahwah, NJ: Erlbaum.

CHAPTER 2

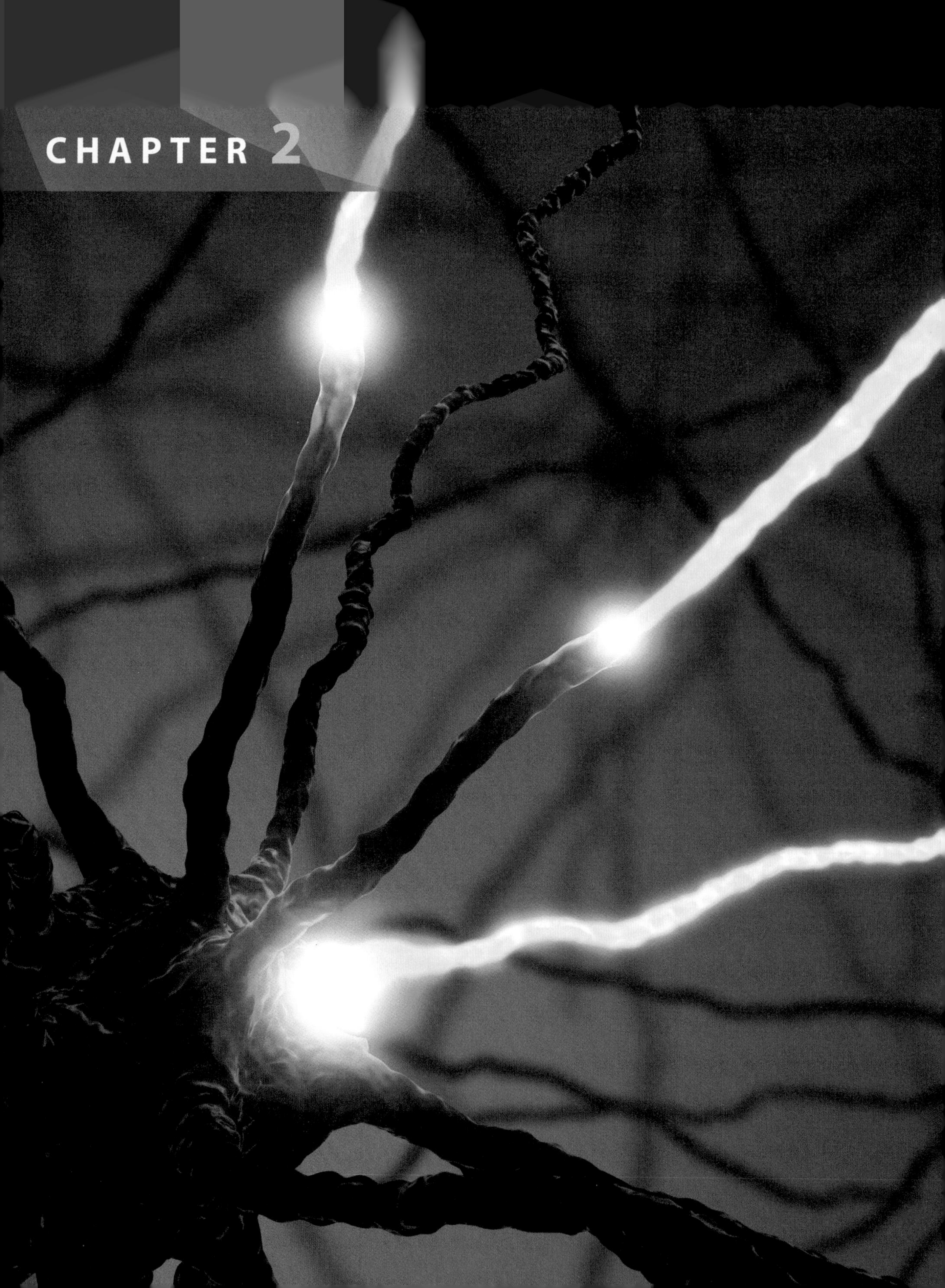

Cognitive Neuroscience

Chapter Contents

Chapter Objectives

- To examine the key issues in the localization of function debate.
- To outline the theoretical issues surrounding the relationship between the mind and the brain.
- To explain approaches to studying that relationship.
- To identify the advantages and limitations of the various methods used to localize cognitive processes in the brain.

Case Study Head Office

Let's take a moment to think about our heads and all they do for us. First of all, the head houses the nose and mouth, both of which are crucial to life itself. For the purposes of cognitive psychology, however, eyes and ears are equally important, for they are what enable us to see and hear the world around us. The simple fact that the head is centred at the top of the body means that it is ideally situated for the reception of information from the environment, which ultimately leads to perception and behaviour. These are all fairly obvious observations. Less obvious, perhaps, is the significance of the fact that your head is hard—really hard. Why is that so important? Your brain knows why: because it is the star of the show that is your life, and it needs all the protection it can get.

Although it accounts for only about 2 per cent of your body weight, your brain manages to claim about 20 per cent of all the blood supply in your body. If you didn't have a brain you wouldn't have a thought, and without thought there is no cognition. Yet we often take the brain for granted—at least until something goes wrong.

You may know someone whose life has been changed profoundly because of a brain disease or injury. If not, you almost certainly know of some prominent person who has suffered a brain injury, whether as a result of a stroke, a tumour, or some kind of trauma. For instance, consider the boxer Muhammad Ali. One of the most famous athletes in the world, as a fighter he would "float like a butterfly and sting like a bee" (to borrow his own phrase), and he commanded as much respect for his quick intelligence and verbal skills as for his abilities in the ring. Now this most beloved and dignified man is barely able to move or speak. Or consider Ronald Reagan and Margaret Thatcher, the two most powerful people in the Western world in the 1980s (Figure 2.1). By the time of his death in 2004, Reagan had lived with Alzheimer's disease for a decade, and today Thatcher as well is said to be battling dementia.

Virtually everyone who has ever taken an introductory psychology course will know the name of Phineas Gage, a young railroad foreman who in 1848 survived an explosion that drove an iron bar through his head. Although he suffered bouts of depression and epileptic seizures following the accident, his cognitive abilities seemed remarkably unaffected. As amazing as the Gage story is, it appears to have been replicated in Brazil in August 2012. Eduardo Leite was working on a construction site when a falling 1.8-metre iron bar pierced his hard hat, entered his skull, and came out between his eyes (see Figure 2.2). The surgery to remove the bar took five hours. Although it is still too soon to be certain, doctors report that Leite shows few if any cognitive deficits.

FIGURE 2.1   Muhammad Ali, Ronald Reagan, and Margaret Thatcher

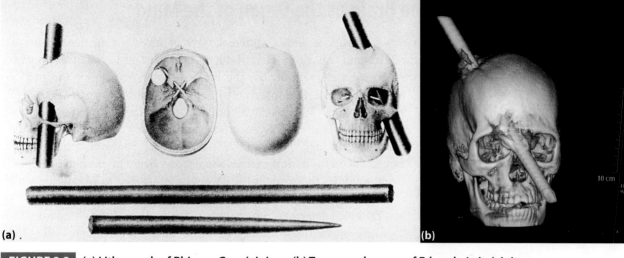

(a)   **(b)**

FIGURE 2.2   (a) Lithograph of Phineas Gage's injury; (b) Tomography scan of Eduardo Leite's injury

Almost as recent is the story of US Congresswoman Gabrielle Giffords. On the morning of 8 January 2010 she was holding a "Congress on your corner" session, meeting and answering questions from members of her Arizona constituency, when suddenly a gunman appeared and shot her along with more than a dozen other people. The bullet entered Giffords' head just above her ear and ripped through her brain. But she was not killed. Surgeons removed part of her skull to allow the injured brain to swell without pressure on the regions that are critical for life functions.

Fast forward to five months after the shooting. As the swelling subsided, the surgeons replaced the part of the skull that had been removed, and 180 days after the shooting Giffords was released from hospital. Her cognitive abilities, however, are not yet what they were before she was shot. In particular, she has difficulty speaking and understanding speech.

Let's pause here for a moment and ask why it was Giffords' language abilities that were compromised rather than, say, her ability to remember past events. What might this tell us about the relationship between specific forms of cognition and the brain? One thing it suggests is that specific cognitive mechanisms are associated with specific brain areas. The area of research concerned with this relationship is cognitive neuroscience. A combination of cognitive psychology and neuroscience, cognitive neuroscience seeks to discover the brain mechanisms that give rise to mental functions such as language, memory, and attention. This is an ambitious goal, and one that cannot be reached via any single research approach. In fact, cognitive neuroscience is both defined and fuelled by its interdisciplinary emphasis.

FIGURE 2.3   Gabrielle Giffords

The Brain as the Organ of the Mind

This chapter will introduce several different ways of investigating the relationship between the brain and behaviour. First, though, it's important to note that cognitive neuroscientists assume that the brain is composed of specific parts or **modules** (Fodor, 1983), each of which is responsible for particular cognitive operations. Whether it is completely modular is a matter of debate, and there have been differences of opinion over the number of modules that may exist (e.g., Pinker, 1997; Sperber, 2002). However, there is general agreement on the basic principle, and once we begin to speculate about how many modules there might be, it's only a short step to wondering which cognitive functions each of them might be responsible for.

Efforts to determine which parts of the brain are specialized for which cognitive operations go back at least as far as Franz Joseph Gall (1758–1828) and his student J.G. Spurzheim (1776–1832). Gall and Spurzheim promoted **phrenology**. Phrenological charts like the one in Figure 2.4 purport to show where various psychological functions are located in the brain. Although Gall and Spurzheim's theories are not taken seriously today their underlying premises still deserve consideration:

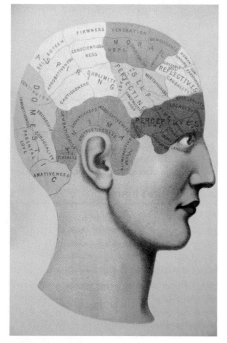

FIGURE 2.4   A phrenological chart

Their argument reduced to three basic principles: (1) The brain is the sole organ of the mind. (2) Basic character and intellectual traits are innately determined. (3) Since there are differences in character and intellectual traits among individuals as well as differences in various intellectual capacities within a single individual, there must exist differentially developed areas in the brain, responsible for these differences! Where there is variation in *function* there must be variation in the controlling *structures*. (Krech, 1962, p. 33)

Modules
Different parts of the brain, each of which is responsible for particular cognitive operations.

Phrenology
The study of the shape, size, and protrusions of the cranium in an attempt to discover the relationships between parts of the brain and various mental activities and abilities.

Localization of function
The idea that there is a direct correspondence between specific cognitive functions and specific parts of the brain.

Gall and Spurzheim's method for locating functions in the brain was highly speculative. They believed that the more highly developed a function was, the larger it would be, and that the larger the function, the more clearly it would manifest itself as a protrusion on the skull. On the basis of these assumptions they reasoned that they could divine a person's strengths and weaknesses by examining the shape of his or her skull. Their theory had a powerful impact on nineteenth-century cultural practices, and many paying customers came to rely on the advice of phrenologists (Sokal, 2001). The weakness of their method is now obvious. Still, their underlying hypothesis—that specific functions are localized in specific parts of the brain—has guided much subsequent research (e.g., Gardner, 1983; Sarter, Berntson, & Cacioppo, 1996), even though not all those involved have agreed that there is a direct correspondence between specific cognitive functions and specific parts of the brain.

A landmark in the history of the **localization of function** debate was the work of Shepherd Ivory Franz (1874–1933). Franz was an expert in the technique of ablation, whereby parts of the cortex (the outer layer of the brain, which plays a significant role in cognitive functions such as memory, attention, perception, and language) of an animal are destroyed and the consequences for behaviour are observed. If functions were localized in the cortex, then the effect of ablation should depend on the area destroyed. However, this was not what his observations showed.

Franz and his student Karl Lashley (1890–1958) studied the effects of ablation of the frontal lobes in rats. Instead of opening up the animal's skull, they would make small holes in it and then observe the effect of the lesions on the retention of a simple learned maze habit; only later would they examine the animal's brain to see "precisely where the lesions had occurred" (Bruce, 1986, p. 38). Their results persuaded them that as long as sufficient tissue remained after the operation, the location of that tissue was irrelevant. Franz (1912) concluded that "mental processes are not due to the independent activities of individual parts of the brain, but to the activities of the brain as a whole" and that "it would appear best and most scientific that we should not adhere to any of the phrenological systems" (p. 328).

Lashley subsequently published a work that became a classic in the area of localization of function, called *Brain Mechanisms and Intelligence* (1929). This research developed further the procedures he had learned from Franz. Lashley lesioned the cortex of rats in different places and to different degrees. He reasoned that "if there were reflex paths transversing the cortex . . . then surgery would destroy them" (Weidman, 1994, p. 166). Lashley (1929, p. 74) observed the ability of rats to learn or remember tasks such as finding their way through mazes of different levels of difficulty, and found that performance in simple mazes was not greatly affected by limited brain damage (Figure 2.5). However, performance declined as the difficulty of the task increased and/or the amount of brain damage increased. Lashley (1930/1978) summarized the implications of his results as follows.

> Small lesions either produce no symptoms or very transient ones, so that it is clear that the mechanisms for habits are not closely grouped within small areas. When larger areas are involved, there are usually amnesias for many activities. . . . After injuries to the brain, the rate of formation of some habits is directly proportional to the extent of the injury and independent of the position within any part of the cortex. (p. 271)

FIGURE 2.5   Rat in a maze

There was no evidence in the brain for specialized connections developed as a result of learning. Neither learning nor memory was "dependent upon the properties of individual cells"; rather, both were functions of "the total mass of tissue" (Lashley, 1930/1978, p. 271). These results came to be formulated as two laws: the **law of mass action** (learning and memory depend on the total mass of brain tissue remaining) and the **law of equipotentiality** (even though some areas of the cortex may become specialized for certain tasks, any part of an area can, within limits, do the job of any other part of that area). To explain his findings, Lashley (1930, p. 271) compared the cortex to an electric sign: the "functional organization plays over" cortical cells "just as the pattern of letters plays over the bank of lamps in an electric sign." A single bank of lights can be used to display any number of messages; similarly, the cortex can be organized in any number of ways depending on circumstances.

The Relation between Mind and Brain

Cognitive neuroscience draws on several disciplines, including biology, linguistics, philosophy, and psychology, in its efforts to arrive at an integrated understanding of the mind and the brain (Gold & Stoljar, 1999). We will begin this section by examining the attempts of four classic efforts toward that end: interactionism, epiphenomenalism, parallelism, and isomorphism. First, however, it's important to note that, although the brain is often considered the "organ of the mind," specifying the exact relation between mind and brain is far from easy, and debate on this issue is ongoing (e.g., Noë & Thompson, 2004). It's also important to distinguish between "consciousness" and "mind." Consciousness is the narrower concept, often taken to mean what we are aware of at any point in time. Mind is the broader concept. It includes consciousness, but also encompasses processes that may take place outside of our awareness. Both of these concepts are the focus of intense research activity, and consequently neither of them has a universally accepted definition.

Interactionism is associated with Descartes (1596–1650), who believed mind and brain to be separate substances that interacted and influenced each other. He even specified the particular place in the brain where he thought this interaction took place—a site in the centre of the brain called the pineal gland (Finger, 1994, p. 26). Ingenious though it was, Descartes' answer to the mind/brain problem was not widely adopted by subsequent investigators (Finger, 2000, p. 80). More recently, though, some eminent psychologists have taken interactionist positions. Among them is Nobel Prize winner Roger Sperry, whose work will be discussed later.

Epiphenomenalism maintains that the mind is simply a by-product of brain processes and has no causal role in determining behaviour. T.H. Huxley (1825–95) used an analogy to illustrate the epiphenomenal position: the mind is to the brain as the steam from a steam whistle is to a coal-powered locomotive. Just as you would not discover much about the locomotive by studying the steam from the whistle, so you would not discover much about the brain by examining what goes on in the mind. Many twentieth-century psychologists adopted positions similar to epiphenomenalism, believing that consciousness was irrelevant to an understanding of behaviour (e.g., Skinner, 1989).

Parallelism found its purest expression in the work of G.T. Fechner (1801–87), whose studies of the relationships between events in the external world and the

---

Law of mass action
Learning and memory depend on the total mass of brain tissue remaining rather than the properties of individual cells.

Law of equipotentiality
Even though some areas of the cortex may become specialized for certain tasks, any part of an area can (within limits) do the job of any other part of that area.

Interactionism
Mind and brain are separate substances that interact with and influence each other.

Epiphenomenalism
"Mind" is a superfluous by-product of bodily functioning.

Parallelism
"Mind" and brain are two aspects of the same reality and flow in parallel.

mind and brain have not lost any of their relevance (Dehaene, 2003; Link, 1994; Murray, 1993). For the parallelist, mind and brain are two aspects of the same reality, and every event in the mind is accompanied by a corresponding event in the brain. If this supposed correlation is true, then studying mental events might reveal something of value about the brain. For example, one might ask research subjects to introspect and then record events in their brains as they are doing so (Jack & Roepstorff, 2002).

Isomorphism can be traced to Gestalt psychologists such as Wolfgang Köhler (1887–1967); the term *Gestalt* means form or configuration. These psychologists argued that consciousness tends to be organized into a coherent whole. Some still maintain that this is a fundamental property of consciousness (e.g., Searle, 2000, p. 9). The doctrine of isomorphism holds that an experience and its corresponding brain process share the same pattern (e.g., Lehar, 2003). The difference between parallelism and isomorphism is that the latter envisions more than a simple point-for-point correspondence between mental events and brain events: as Köhler put it, "psychological facts and the underlying events in the brain resemble each other in all their structural characteristics" (Köhler, 1969, p. 64).

To illustrate this hypothesis, a Necker cube (Figure 2.6) is often used; it was named after Louis Albert Necker (1832/1964), who was the first to remark on this psychologically interesting phenomenon. When you focus on the cube face labelled ABCD, then that face seems to be in the foreground. However, the figure can reverse itself in the viewer's focus so that the face labelled EFGH comes to the foreground. This is an important example because the "external stimulus is constant but . . . the internal subjective experience varies" (Searle, 2000, p. 15). For each subjective experience the parts of the cube are organized differently. When the cube switches from one organization to the other, there must be a corresponding change in the structure of the underlying brain process. Köhler's idea was that such alterations were produced as a result of prolonged inspection of a figure. The area in the brain that is responsible for processing and creating a representation of the figure becomes fatigued, or only weakly capable of supporting electrical fields, and so another part of the cortex then begins to take over the task. As the cortical representation changes, so too does one's perception of it. Although Köhler's specific hypothesis was discredited, the relation between such "Gestalt switches" and the underlying brain organization remains the focus of considerable research interest (e.g., Kornmeier & Bach, 2004; Long & Toppino, 2004; Parker, Krug, & Cumming, 2003; Toppino, 2003).

Numerous alternatives to and variations on the preceding formulations have appeared more recently (e.g., Baars, 2002), and we will consider some of them as we go along. However, we should not expect solutions to such a longstanding and difficult problem to come easily. The following quotation from the neuroanatomist Larry Swanson (2003) underlines what we are up against:

> Gram for gram, the brain is far and away the most complex object we know of in the universe, and we simply haven't figured out its basic plan yet—despite its supreme importance and a great deal of effort. There is nothing equivalent to the periodic table of the elements, relativity, or the theory of evolution for organizing and explaining a large (but still woefully

Isomorphism
Mental events and neural events share the same structure.

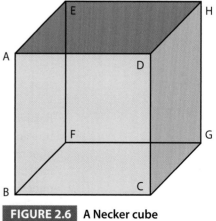

FIGURE 2.6 A Necker cube

incomplete and often contradictory) body of information about brain structure and function. No Mendeleyev, Einstein, or Darwin has succeeded in grasping and articulating the general principles of its architecture; no one has presented a coherent theory or model of its functional organization. (p. 2)

Given the magnitude of the challenge, it's fortunate that there is no need to decide the mind/brain issue in order to discover extremely interesting and suggestive correlations between psychological functions and brain activity. In what follows we will outline some of the ways in which the study of the brain can facilitate the inquiries of cognitive psychologists.

Methods in Cognitive Neuroscience

ANIMAL MODELS

An indirect route to investigating brain mechanisms in humans is provided by animal models. The human brain is largely inaccessible to the invasive approaches allowed by animal models, such as experimental brain lesioning and the measurement of cell activity in a specific area (i.e., single cell or multiple unit recordings). Experiments that track the response of cell units as an animal is required to change the focus of its attention show how attention may control the processing of some visual stimuli (Moran & Desimone, 1985; Spitzer, Desimone, & Moran, 1988) or enhance the processing of others (cf. Colby, 1991, for a review). The use of carefully controlled lesions, including reversible lesions produced by procedures such as cooling, makes it possible to specify the relationship between cognition and different brain regions. Almost everything we currently know about the micro-organization of brain structure and function is derived from the study of animal brains. A complete description of human brain structure and function may ultimately rest on our understanding of animal neuroanatomy and physiology.

However, even a full understanding of brain operations in another organism will not lead us to a complete understanding of human brain operations. A mouse brain is not a monkey brain, and a monkey brain is not a human brain (Figure 2.7). Differences across species in terms of structure and function place strong limitations on our ability to generalize from one species to another and from animal models to humans. Homologous structures can be very difficult to identify across species, and the specializations of different animals lead to large differences in their neuroanatomy and neurophysiology. For example, much of the rat brain is dedicated to olfactory input, while much of the human brain is dedicated to visual input. Understanding human psychological states of mind must ultimately require study of the human brain at work.

BEHAVIOURAL STUDIES

Behavioural investigations of healthy human subjects can tell us a lot about the structure and function of the human brain. This second approach combines our knowledge of normal sensory systems with precise stimulus presentation and response recording. However, behavioural studies alone cannot draw a specific link between behaviour and underlying brain mechanisms. For example, many experiments have shown that we move our eyes from point A to point B faster when the item fixated at point A disappears from view. Through careful behavioural research involving the timing of when points

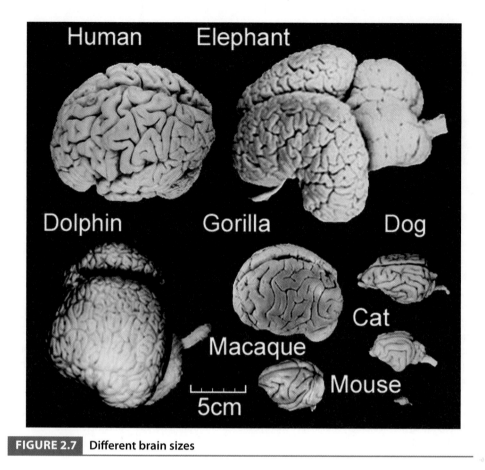

FIGURE 2.7   Different brain sizes

A and B disappear and appear, researchers such as Saslow (1967) and Kingstone and Klein (1993) concluded that the disappearance of an item at point A triggers a disinhibition of the eye movement system, and that a small midbrain structure called the superior colliculus (SC) plays a critical role in this response. Importantly, they had no direct evidence that the SC was involved, but had to rely on studies (cf. Munoz & Wurtz, 1992) of non-human primates. The study of eye movements is illustrated in Figure 2.8.

The Study of Brain Injuries

Brain injuries can serve as a kind of substitute for experiments that provide evidence for the localization of one or more functions. It may be possible to relate the symptoms displayed by brain-injured patients to the parts of the brain that have been damaged. The study of cases involving brain injury is seldom neat and tidy, and it is difficult for such studies to yield definitive evidence concerning localization of function. Even so, they are certainly more informative than the phrenological studies of the early nineteenth century.

A classic study of the consequences of brain injury is the investigation by Paul Broca (1824–80) of the loss of the ability to express ideas by means of speech. The plight of people who have lost that ability is that they often know what it is they want to say. Most of us have at some time or another been dissatisfied with our ability to put our thoughts into speech; just imagine how frustrating it would be to lose that ability

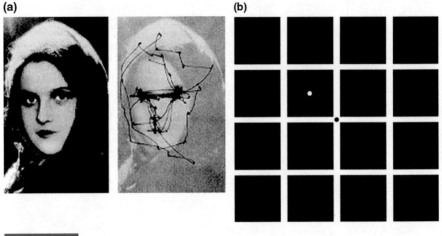

(a)   **(b)**

FIGURE 2.8 | **Eye movements**

(a) An observer views a picture (left) while eye positions are monitored (right) for one minute. The eyes jump and then seem to fixate or rest momentarily, producing a small dot on the trace, before jumping to a new region of fixation. Even during the fixation or "rest" times, however, the eyes are continuously moving, never still. (b) Pattern for showing fixational eye movements. Look at the central black dot for about a minute, then look at the white dot in the adjacent dark square. The dark after-image of the white line pattern should be seen in constant motion owing to fixational eye movements.

Sources: (a) Yarbus, A.L. (1967). Eye movements and vision. Trans. L.A. Riggs. New York: Plenum Press. With kind permission from Springer Science+Business Media B.V. (b) Verheijen, F. J. A simple after image method demonstrating the involuntary multidirectional eye movements during fixation. Optica Acta (London) 8, 309–312 (1961)

Broca's aphasia
A deficit in the ability to produce speech as a result of damage to Broca's area.

Broca's area
The area of the brain's left hemisphere that is responsible for how words are spoken.

Wernicke's area
Area of the brain's left hemisphere that is responsible for processing the meaning of words.

Wernicke's aphasia
A deficit in the ability to comprehend speech as a result of damage to Wernicke's area.

more or less entirely. This disability is often called **Broca's aphasia**. Broca (1861/1966) described a patient who was unable to speak, but who still apparently was able to understand what was said to him. An autopsy showed severe damage to a part of the left hemisphere that has since come to be known as **Broca's area** (Figure 2.9). Broca, as well as others, was able to observe similar deficiencies in similarly aphasic brains at autopsy.

Another class of patients, who are able to speak but unable to comprehend what is said to them or to produce coherent speech, was identified by Karl Wernicke (1848–1905). In extreme cases, these patients may ramble incoherently, their words bearing no obvious relation to thought. Wernicke studied 10 such cases and found that the lesions apparently responsible for their symptoms were located in the left hemisphere in the area that became known as **Wernicke's area** (Figure 2.9). The corresponding disorder is called **Wernicke's aphasia**.

Although Broca and Wernicke made lasting contributions to the study of localization of function, discoveries such as theirs cannot be interpreted in any straightforward way. It may be tempting to believe that Broca's area is responsible for speech production and Wernicke's area for speech comprehension, but such a simple conclusion is not justified. For one thing, the aphasias are not particularly well defined, and it is recognized "that clinical aphasic syndromes are comprised of variable clusters of symptoms" (Poeppel & Hickock, 2004, p. 4). It's difficult to see how such ill-defined phenomena could be regulated by a precisely located part of the brain. More important, the exact location of (for example) Wernicke's area is difficult to determine on the basis of anatomy alone (Cacioppo et al., 2003, p. 654). Even more important,

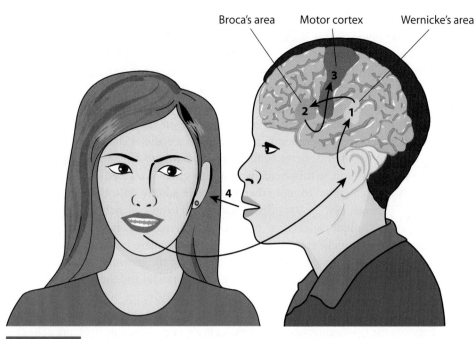

Broca's area   Motor cortex   Wernicke's area

FIGURE 2.9 Traditional illustration of language comprehension and production

The meaning of words is processed in Wernicke's area (1). That information is then passed to Broca's area (2), which determines how words will be spoken. That information in turn is passed to the motor cortex (3), which controls the movement of the mouth and tongue, ultimately resulting in the production of speech (4).

Based on: www.gazzaro.it/g/Language%20in%20the%20brain_fi le/broca_wernicke_speak.gif.

"modern work has identified areas outside of the classical regions that are implicated in language processing" (Poeppel & Hickock, 2004, p. 5). Although Broca's and Wernicke's areas together form "an image with iconic status in neuroscience, [that] forms the basis of a neurolinguistic model that has informed research for almost 150 years and constitutes the canonical model of brain and language taught across disciplines" (Poeppel & Hickock, 2004, p. 1), they cannot bear the full weight of explanation. The general lesson to be learned from studies of the relationship between the loss of psychological functions and brain damage is that such studies can be a very suggestive source of evidence, but are seldom definitive or complete (Marshall & Fink, 2003).

Surgical Intervention

We discussed earlier in this chapter how Lashley used ablation to investigate localization of function. Roger Sperry (1913–94) also used surgical techniques, but in a more precise manner. Sperry received the Nobel Prize in 1981, in part for his research on **interhemispheric transfer**. This work was conducted on cats and initially involved severing the optic chiasm (the area in the brain where the optic nerves that transmit information from the eyes to the visual cortex cross), with the result that information coming from the right eye was projected only onto the visual areas of the right hemisphere, and information from the left eye projected only onto the visual areas of the left hemisphere. Eventually Sperry also severed the corpus callosum, and in so doing showed that it "plays the dominant role in interhemispheric interaction" (Hoptman &

Interhemispheric transfer Communication between the brain's hemispheres, enabled in large part by the corpus callosum.

Davidson, 1994, p. 2). When the corpus callosum is severed, information transfer between the hemispheres is disrupted. Under these conditions, each hemisphere appeared to be "a separate mental domain operating with complete disregard—indeed with a complete lack of awareness—of what went on in the other. The **split brain** animal behaved . . . as if it had two entirely separate brains" (Sperry, 1964, p. 43).

Sperry's work broadened considerably when he was able to study humans whose corpus callosum had been severed by neurosurgeons in the hope of alleviating epilepsy. In a series of clever experiments, Sperry and his associates claimed to have shown not only that "the two hemispheres of the brain had unique capabilities" but also that "the combination of both hemispheres working together produced a unified state of consciousness that amounted to more than the simple additive effects of the two hemispheres alone" (Puente, 1995, p. 941). Sperry's work led to an avalanche of research seeking to discover the "unique capabilities" of each hemisphere. As we have already seen, the work of Broca and Wernicke suggested that the left hemisphere was typically associated with linguistic functions. Split-brain research led many to the general conclusion that the left hemisphere managed "analytic" (e.g., verbal, rational) tasks; and the right hemisphere, "holistic" (e.g., non-verbal, intuitive) tasks; (e.g., Jaynes, 1976, pp. 100–125; Martindale, 1981, pp. 286–287). However, it later became clear that there was no simple division of labour between the two hemispheres in an intact brain (e.g., Gardner, 1982, pp. 278–285; Hoptman & Davidson, 1994). Indeed, "because of their complexity, the actual organization of intracerebral connections may well lie beyond the limits of human comprehension" (Swanson, 2003, p. 166). While the split brain (Figure 2.10) is a fascinating object of study, there are naturally limits to the conclusions that can be drawn from such atypical cases.

In the final phase of his career, Sperry turned his attention to broad issues such as the nature of consciousness (Erdmann & Stover, 1991/2000; Stover & Erdmann, 2000). He argued that consciousness was an **emergent property** of the brain, meaning that it is not reducible to or predictable from other features of the brain. Once consciousness emerges, then, it can have an influence on lower-level functions, a process that may be termed **emergent causation** (Erdmann & Stover, 1991/2000, p. 50). Sperry (1987, p. 165) recognized a "mutual interaction between neural and mental events" such that "the brain physiology determines the mental events" but is in turn "governed by the higher subjective properties of the enveloping mental events." Describing the mind as **supervenient**, he argued that mental states may "exert downward control over their constituent neuronal events—at the same time that they are being determined by them" (Sperry, 1988, p. 609). Although Sperry's speculations on the mind/brain relation were greeted with skepticism, they were an important part of the discussion that led to a more open consideration of the problem of consciousness.

Event-Related Potentials

The earliest imaging technique, computed tomography (CT), provided detailed anatomical data that revolutionized neurology and experimental neuropsychology. Magnetic resonance imaging (MRI) provides similar images but with greater spatial resolution. Both produce high-quality "snapshots" of human brain structures and thus make it possible to localize brain lesions, tumours, and developmental abnormalities. However, neither provides images of brain activity. To measure the time course of the flow of sensory information and response-related processes, the electrical

Split brain
A condition created by severing the corpus callosum.

Emergent property
In Sperry's sense, a property that "emerges" as a result of brain processes, but is not itself a component of the brain. In the case of the mind, this means that consciousness is neither reducible to, nor a property of, a particular brain structure or region.

Emergent causation
In Sperry's sense, causation brought about by an emergent property. Once the "mind" emerges from the brain, it has the power to influence lower-level processes.

Supervenient
In Sperry's sense, describes mental states that may simultaneously influence neuronal events and be influenced by them.

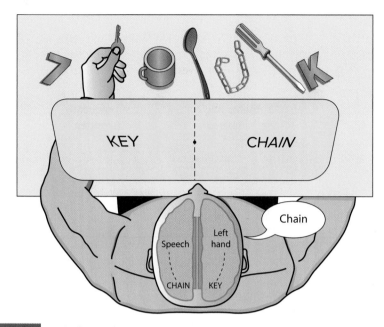

FIGURE 2.10   Split-brain operations

There is no way to communicate between the right and left hemispheres once the corpus callosum has been severed. For this reason, patients who have had such operations provide scientists with valuable information about the lateralization of the human brain: in particular, the dominance of the left hemisphere for language and the right hemisphere for visual–spatial tasks.

Based on: erraticwisdom.com/images/38.gif.

signals emitted by the brain can be recorded using electrodes placed on the scalp (electroencephalography, or EEG). The electrical signals that occur after the onset of a stimulus, such as a word, make up a pattern of electrical activity called an **event-related potential (ERP)** and can be represented by waveforms such as those shown in Figure 2.11. A single trial is not enough to provide unambiguous information, but when the electrical responses to a stimulus are averaged over a great many trials, interesting patterns may emerge. One such pattern can be seen in Figure 2.11, which shows the results of studies reviewed by Rugg (1995). In these studies, participants were initially presented with a series of items (e.g., words, labelled S1, S2, S3, and S4 in Figure 2.11) and the ERP associated with each one was recorded. Note the waveform arising after each of the items in Figure 2.11. Subsequently, the participants were asked to recall the items. The experimenter then sorted the items into those that were recalled and those that were not, and looked for differences in the ERPs for each class of item. Figure 2.11 suggests that the waveform for items that will be remembered is different from the waveform for items that will be forgotten. So far, so good: it looks as if the ERP can predict the subsequent recall of items. However, it's not easy to interpret ERPs in terms of the cognitive processes that underlie them. In this case, perhaps the different waveforms simply indicate that the participants paid attention to some items and ignored others (Rugg, Otten, & Henson, 2003, p. 213); or perhaps they represent more complex processes. In general, although event-related potentials can provide suggestive information, additional techniques must be used in order to gain a more complete picture of brain processes.

Event-related potential (ERP)
An electrical signal emitted by the brain after the onset of a stimulus.

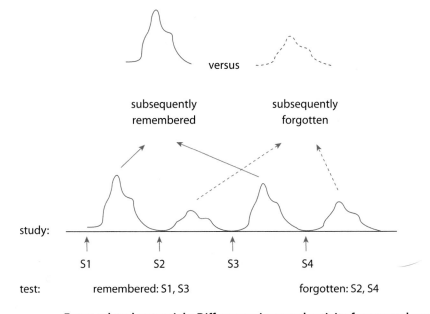

versus

subsequently
remembered

subsequently
forgotten

study:

S1   S2   S3   S4

test: remembered: S1, S3   forgotten: S2, S4

FIGURE 2.11   **Event-related potentials: Differences in neural activity for remembered versus forgotten items**

From: *The Physiology of Cognitive Processes* by Andrew Parker, Andrew Derrington and Colin Blakemore (2003); Chapter 10 "The Neural Basis of Episodic Memory: Evidence from functional neuroimaging" by Michael D. Rugg, Leun J. Otten, and Richard N. A Henson; fig. 10.1 p.213. By permission of Oxford University Press.

Positron Emission Tomography

One assumption underlying **positron emission tomography** (PET) is that when a specific psychological function is engaged, then only those parts of the brain responsible for that function will also be engaged (Papanicolaou, 1998, p. 23). If a participant is given a specific cognitive task, the parts of the brain responsible for that task will "work harder" than when the participant is not performing that task. When a part of the brain is active in this way, it will use up oxygen at a faster rate than when it is inactive, and the need to replenish that oxygen in turn will lead to an increase in blood flow to the area. PET takes advantage of this chain of events. The participant in a PET study is first given a radioactive substance that mingles with the blood and thus circulates to the brain. This procedure allows for the detection of blood flow to particular areas of the brain and makes it possible to construct images showing which parts of the brain are particularly active in relation to the performance of different tasks (Figure 2.12).

One problem with PET methodology is that there are limits to the amount of radiation to which a participant may be exposed, and therefore limits to the amount of information that can be obtained from each participant. Although PET was extremely popular until the mid-1990s, functional magnetic resonance imaging has now replaced it as the method of choice (Rugg, 2002, p. 59).

Functional Magnetic Resonance Imaging (fMRI)

While standard MRI can be extremely useful in viewing the structure of the brain, it does not indicate what areas of the brain are involved in any specific behaviour.

CONSIDER THIS
BOX 2.1

"Mind Reading"

Can brain imaging be used to read minds? Some scientists believe that it can. In 2007, for instance, Dr Marco Iacoboni of the University of California, Los Angeles, and colleagues published an article in *The New York Times* called "This Is Your Brain on Politics." Accompanying the article was a series of images of the brains of swing voters recorded as they responded to photos and videos of several potential candidates for the presidency in the 2008 US election. Iacoboni and colleagues said the findings were clear-cut. Activity in the amygdala in response to Mitt Romney revealed voter anxiety; activity in the insula indicated disgust with John Edwards, while the patterns of brain activity elicited by photos of Barack Obama and John McCain suggested no powerful reaction, either positive or negative.

Unfortunately, Iacoboni and colleagues (2007) made a mistake that many consumers of science make: they assumed a one-to-one correlation between brain regions and mental states: in this case, that amygdala activation meant anxiety, that activity in the insula meant disgust, and so on. In fact, such one-to-one mapping is simply not possible. For instance, we know that the amygdala is activated not only by anxiety but also by anger, arousal, happiness, and sexual excitement. And activation of the insula may just as easily indicate a sense of unfairness, or pain, or pleasure as disgust. As for Obama and McCain failing to spark any strong emotions, we now know that this was far from the case.

Overly simplistic interpretations of brain-imaging results are far too common. For instance, a difference in brain activation for faces that differ in attractiveness is taken to indicate the activation of a neural mechanism that computes attractiveness; yet the same effect might be caused by mechanisms associated with feelings of familiarity, or the assessment of social status. A difference in brain activation for white and black faces is interpreted to mean that certain brain regions are associated with racism when it could just as well indicate feelings of social injustice or inequality. These fundamental limitations aside, there remains the issue of whether brain activations generated in a lab-based environment can tell us anything about behaviour in real-world settings; currently there is no evidence whatsoever that brain activations are predictive of performance in everyday life. These are important points to keep in mind whenever a study claims to have found that a particular brain region is associated with a specific mental state or behaviour.

However, **functional magnetic resonance imaging (fMRI)** does measure blood flow (actually, the flow of oxygen in the blood) while the subject completes some sort of task, and is capable of correlating the location of brain activity with the cognitive behaviour. One advantage of fMRI is that it does not depend on a radioactive signal. Another is that data can be acquired more rapidly using fMRI than is possible using PET (Rugg, 1999, p. 22). The fMRI technique involves placing the subject's head inside a very large magnetic field and having him or her view some sort of stimuli, or perform some sort of cognitive task. This allows for neurological measurement of activity associated with the functioning of some aspect of cognition. The magnetic field of the machine causes atoms in the brain to become aligned with it (Papanicolaou, 1998, p. 49). Changes in the flow of oxygenated blood can then be picked up as alterations in the magnetic field, and this information can be used to construct an image of cortical activity.

An experiment conducted by Bavalier et al. (1997) is an example of an fMRI study involving Broca's and Wernicke's areas. The tasks used in that study were sentence reading and the viewing of consonant strings. Sentence reading "has been acknowledged

Functional magnetic resonance imaging (fMRI)
A non-radioactive, magnetic procedure for detecting the flow of oxygenated blood to various parts of the brain.

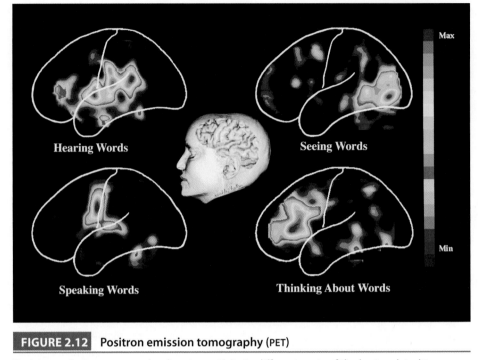

Hearing Words

Seeing Words

Speaking Words

Thinking About Words

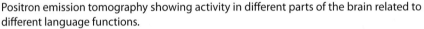

FIGURE 2.12   **Positron emission tomography (PET)**

Positron emission tomography showing activity in different parts of the brain related to different language functions.

to invoke many different aspects of language processing," while "the presentation of consonant strings is believed to activate only basic visual recognition routines. . . . The comparison of these two conditions should reveal brain areas concerned with . . . language processing" (Bavalier et al., 1997, p. 667). The results revealed wide individual differences in the patterns of activation shown by each of the eight participants. Examination of the pattern of activation that best characterized the entire group of participants did show that Broca's and Wernicke's areas were more activated by the sentence-reading task than by the viewing of consonant strings. However, other areas were also consistently more activated by sentence reading than by consonant viewing. Bavalier et al. (1997, p. 678) concluded that language is not simply localized "in a few cortically well-circumscribed areas" (see Figure 2.13).

It's tempting to wish for a "magic bullet" technique that would reveal the precise cortical locations for all psychological functions. If brain-imaging techniques did constitute such a "magic bullet," however, they would be "no more than a modern and extraordinarily expensive version of 19th century phrenology" (Raichle, 2003, p. 3959). In fact, the view of the brain that seems to be emerging is not at all phrenological. According to Marshall and Fink (2003), "recent work [suggests] that functional localization is not such a fixed property of brain regions as either lesion studies or early neuroimaging work might have suggested" (p. 56). They illustrate this point with respect to Broca's area. Neuroimaging studies have found that it plays "a role in natural language syntactic processing (Caplan, Alpert, Waters, & Olivieri, 2000; Heim, Opitz, & Freiderichi, 2003), in processing musical syntax (Maess, Koelsch, Gunter, & Friederichi (2001), in the perception of rhythmic motion

Sentences vs Consonant Strings

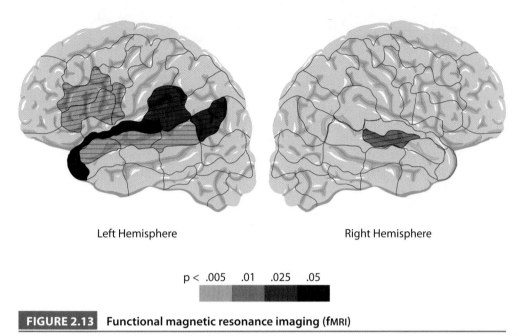

Left Hemisphere   Right Hemisphere

p < .005 .01 .025 .05

FIGURE 2.13   **Functional magnetic resonance imaging (fMRI)**

Showing the difference in activity of language processing in the left and right hemispheres between sentence reading (the darker shaded areas in Broca's and Wernicke's areas of the left hemisphere) and the viewing of consonant strings (the fine lines throughout both hemispheres).

From: Bavalier, D., et al. (1997). Sentence reading: A functional MRI study at 4 Tesla. *Journal of Cognitive Neuroscience, 9,* 664–686.

(Schubotz & von Cramon, 2001), in imaging movement trajectories (Binkofski et al., 2000)," and so on. Marshall and Fink conclude that "it is difficult to see how a single common function (localized in Broca's area) could underlie such a disparate collection of effects" (p. 56), and suggest that, at least to some extent, the interaction of different areas of the brain determines their function on a particular occasion. This point is reinforced by Cabeza and Nyberg (2003, p. 241), who observe that "the vast majority of functional neuroimaging studies have investigated a single cognitive function. Yet, with the accumulation of functional neuroimaging data, it has become obvious that . . . the neural correlates of cognitive functions overlap considerably, with most brain regions being involved in a variety of cognitive functions." Marshall and Fink (2003, p. 56) anticipate the development of "new methods of measuring the functional integration of different brain regions" that will improve our current models of the brain.

Magnetoencephalography (MEG)

While the spatial resolution of fMRI is very good, the temporal resolution is quite poor compared to ERP. **Magnetoencephalography (MEG)** is a noninvasive brain imaging technique that seeks to marry the significant spatial resolution of fMRI with the outstanding temporal resolution of ERP. While the spatial resolution of MEG might not be quite as good as fMRI, it does have significantly better temporal resolution (10 milliseconds or faster vs hundreds of msecs for fMRI) because MEG measures the magnetic

Magnetoencephalography (MEG)
A non-invasive brain imaging technique that directly measures neural activity.

THINK TWICE BOX 2.2

The Ethics of Brain Imaging

Let's make the reasonable assumption that you're a good person—that you don't cheat or steal, that you recycle as best you can, and that you believe in treating everyone equally, regardless of skin colour. Yet you have recently taken part in a brain imaging study that suggested you could be an unconscious racist. What does this mean? Do you accept that brain imaging has advanced to the point where it can detect your unconscious attitudes, even if those attitudes are in direct conflict with what you consciously believe and do? Even if imaging had advanced to that point, do interior, unconscious attitudes matter more than overt actions? These are the types of issues that neuroscientists, specifically those in the field of neuroethics, are now grappling with. Do people who have never behaved in a racist manner but who show brain activation that suggests racial prejudice deserve to be treated as racists? Do people who have never stolen anything but who show heightened activation in regions of the brain associated with the need to exert cognitive control deserve to be treated as if they were predisposed to steal? What do you think? The "Cognition in Action" box on p. 43 may help you to work through this issue.

Connectionism
A theory that focuses on the way cognitive processes work at the physiological/neurological (as opposed to information-processing) level. It holds that the brain consists of an enormous number of interconnected neurons and attempts to model cognition as an emergent process of networks of simple units (e.g., neurons) communicating with one another.

Diffusion tensor imaging (DTI)
An MRI-based neuroimaging technique that makes it possible to visualize the white-matter tracts within the brain.

fields produced by electrical activity in the brain. An additional advantage of MEG is that it provides a direct measurement of neural activity rather than the indirect measurement offered by fMRI or PET, which are intimately tied to changes in blood flow in the brain. A third advantage of MEG is that irregularities in the head itself (e.g., the skull) do not have much effect on the magnetic fields produced by neural activity, unlike the electrical fields used by ERP. Nevertheless, MEG has two limitations. First, the decay of signal as a function of distance is pronounced for magnetic fields (as anyone who has tried to push two magnets together will know) and therefore MEG is really good only for detecting activity near the cortical surface of the brain. Second, MEG devices are not widely available (unlike fMRI) and therefore their cost effectiveness is relatively poor (see Figure 2.14).

Connectionist Models

It's not intuitively obvious that the information-processing flow-chart models we have looked at so far could also be models of how the brain works. For instance, Herbert Simon acknowledged that "explanation of cognitive processes at the information-processing (symbolic) level is largely independent of explanation at the physiological (neurological) level that shows how processes are implemented" (Simon, 1992, p. 153). **Connectionism** is an example of the latter: an alternative to the more traditional approaches focused on information-processing (Schneider, 1987) that focuses on the physiological/neurological level. Connectionist theory holds that the brain consists of an enormous number of interconnected neurons, and that a model of the networks formed by these neurons might help us to understand how cognitive processes work. Using modern brain imaging techniques such as **diffusion tensor imaging (DTI)**, researchers can understand the organization of the neural interactions within the brain (e.g., how information flows between and within brain regions; see Figure 2.16).

The two basic connectionist ideas are that (a) information can be broken down into elementary units (neurons) and (b) there are connections between these units.

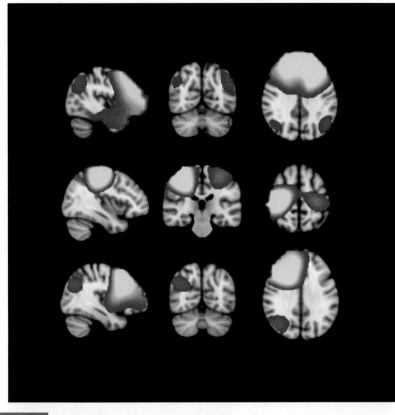

FIGURE 2.14   **Magnetoencephalography (MEG)**

Scans of the magnetic fields produced by the networks of electrical currents resulting from neuronal activity within the brain. The gradient of activity runs from low (red) to high (yellow). The top row shows the network involved when the brain is at rest; this network disappears when the subject is performing a task. The second row shows the sensory–motor network, which appears when the subject performs a motor task (e.g., tapping fingers). The bottom row shows the right lateral frontoparietal network.

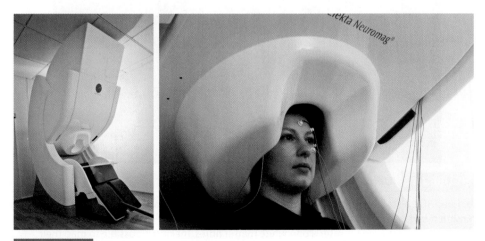

FIGURE 2.15   **Magnetoencephalograph scanner**

Neural network
Neurons that are functionally related or connected.

Hebb rule
A connection between two neurons takes place only if both neurons are firing at approximately the same time.

Parallel processing
Many neural connections may be active at the same time.

Serial processing
Only one neural activity may take place at any one time.

These connections can have different strengths, and a **neural network** learns by modifying the strength of connections between elements so that the proper output occurs in response to a particular input. Among the assumptions made concerning the way connections between neurons are formed and strengthened is the **Hebb rule**, named after the Canadian D.O. Hebb, one of the founders of neuropsychology. The Hebb rule states that "when an axon of cell A is near enough to excite a cell B and repeatedly or persistently takes part in firing it, some growth process or metabolic change takes place in one or both cells such that A's efficiency, as one of the cells firing B, is increased" (Hebb, 1949, p. 62). This "idea that a connection between two neurons takes place only if both neurons are firing at about the same time" has greatly influenced subsequent theorizing (Milner, 2003, p. 5).

Another assumption of connectionist models is that many connections can be active at the same time. This is an example of **parallel processing** as opposed to **serial processing**, in which only one connection operates at a time. Thus connectionist models may also be described as *parallel distributed processing* models (McClelland & Rumelhart, 1986a, 1988).

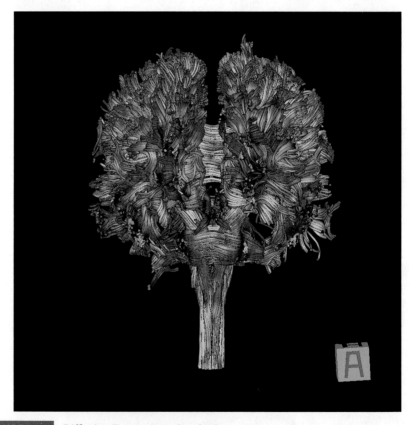

FIGURE 2.16   **Diffusion Tensor Imaging (DTI)**

Coloured 3D DTI scan of the brain, showing the bundles of white matter nerve fibres that transmit nerve signals between brain regions and between the brain and the spinal cord. DTI scans show the diffusion of water along white matter fibres, making it possible to map their orientations and the connections between brain regions.

COGNITION IN ACTION BOX 2.3 — The Implicit Association Test

In a ground-breaking study, Richeson and colleagues (2003) found that some people need to exert additional cognitive control to avoid behaving in a racist manner. They also found that the same people showed a unique pattern of brain activation when presented with pictures of black faces. Participants first completed a task called the implicit association testx (IAT). The IAT seeks to measure hidden biases by requiring participants to respond to two categories of words with a single button press, for instance, press the left key if a word is positive (e.g., LOVE) or a name typically associated with white people; and press the right key if the word is negative (e.g., HATE) or a name typically associated with black people. In a separate run of trials the positive–negative and black–white associations were reversed. The IAT effect is the difference between the two conditions (e.g., longer response times for the positive–black pairing than for the positive–white pairing). Richeson et al. found that the more racial bias participants showed on the IAT, the more difficulty they had on a cognitive control task that for they were asked to perform after interacting with a black experimenter. According to the researchers' interpretation, the participants with the higher IAT scores had to make a special effort to exercise cognitive control when interacting with the black experimenter, and this strain affected their ability to perform the task (specifically, the Stroop task; see Chapter 4). Critically, fMRI revealed that those participants also showed greater activity in brain regions associated with cognitive control when looking at pictures of black faces that were irrelevant to their task.

Does this mean that the IAT is a valid measure of racial bias and prejudice, or that people must be prejudiced if, when presented with pictures of black faces, they show heightened activation in the areas of the cortex associated with cognitive control? Both conclusions must be treated with caution, for two reasons. First, the IAT measures a relative difference, so even if we accept that it taps into unconscious attitudes toward whites and blacks, a large effect could be observed in people who have positive associations with blacks if their associations with whites are *more* positive. Second, most blacks (and all whites) show an IAT effect, suggesting that what the test measures is environmental associations with whites and blacks (i.e., familiarity with stereotypes) rather than the individual's personal endorsement of those associations. Either of these alternative scenarios would produce the same pattern of results that Richeson et al. reported.

A big difference between connectionism and older information-processing approaches is that knowledge is embodied in the connections that make up the network rather than in a series of information-processing stages. Connectionist models are quite good at simulating many cognitive processes; we will examine some of these models in succeeding chapters.

COMBINING METHODS

At its best, cognitive neuroscience melds theories and methods from all the approaches described in this chapter. Hypotheses about brain mechanisms in animal models are constructed through careful control of behaviour using paradigms developed through research on both animals and humans. Data from human behavioural studies can be interpreted in the context of findings provided by animal studies, allowing direct observation of neural functioning at a local level. Data from either or both of these sources can be used when designing and interpreting experiments using functional imaging methods or looking at patients who have had some sort of brain lesion. For instance, by combining behavioural measures with *static* brain-imaging techniques such as CT or

MRI, strong links can be made between behaviour and brain structure. With *dynamic* imaging techniques such as ERP, PET, fMRI, or MEG, these links can be expanded to map the connections between behaviour and function.

Fendrich, Wessinger, and Gazzaniga (1992) used the latter approach to study a patient with a condition known as "blindsight." As we will see in Chapter 3, some people who have suffered lesions to the primary visual cortex are able to make accurate judgments about the location of visual stimuli that they claim they cannot see. This "blindsight" has been attributed to visual pathways that bypass the primary cortex (for reviews, see Weiskrantz, 1990; Cowey & Stoerig, 1991). However, others have argued that it could be the result of spared functioning in the primary cortex (Poppel, Held, & Frost, 1973; Campion, Latto, & Smith, 1983). Using psychophysical tests and an image stabilizer that allows for extended and repetitive stimulus presentations to a very small area of the retina, Fendrich, Wessinger, and Gazzaniga (1992) discovered a small and isolated island of blindsight in a hemianopic patient (i.e., one who was functionally blind on one side of the visual field). This behavioural result suggested that a region of cortex within the lesioned area had been spared. MRI images confirmed that there was indeed cortical sparing, and a subsequent PET investigation revealed that the spared cortex was metabolically active. Based on this combination of behavioural and neuroimaging data, Fendrich et al. (1992) were able to conclude that blindsight can result from cortical sparing within a lesioned area (see also Gazzaniga, Fendrich, & Wessinger, 1994).

One final comment on the methods of cognitive neuroscience is in order. This section has looked at various methods of localizing cognitive processes in the brain. As researchers we generally operate as if our task were simply to find the brain correlates of those processes. If we're honest, however, we have to admit that there is no universal agreement even on what the basic cognitive processes are (Fodor, 2000; Marshall & Fink, 2003, p. 54; Uttal, 2001). One of our most important goals in this text is to present current perspectives on cognitive processes. We should expect that our understanding of cognitive processes and their relation to the brain may never be set once and for all. It is in the nature of science that our theories are always evolving and hence always provisional.

▊ Summary

In this chapter we have introduced cognitive neuroscience, the field that studies the brain mechanisms that give rise to human cognition and behaviour. A major research question for this field is which parts of the brain are specialized for specific cognitive operations. From the speculative methods of phrenology to the lesion studies of Lashley (*law of mass action; law of equipotentiality*) to the behavioural work of Gauthier, Skudlarski, Gore, and Anderson (2000), research has explored the strictness of the correspondence between specific cognitive functions and specific parts of the brain (*localization of function*).

Another major research question in cognitive neuroscience is the relationship between the mind and the brain. Some traditional approaches to the mind/brain problem include *interactionism, epiphenomenalism, parallelism,* and *isomorphism*. A significant distinction emerging from these approaches is that between "consciousness" and "mind." "Consciousness" refers to what we are aware of at any point in time. "Mind" is a broader phenomenon that includes consciousness but also a number of other processes that may take place outside our awareness. These concepts and their meaning are the subject of continuing research and debate.

Interestingly, the fact that the mind/body question has not been resolved has not prevented the discovery of either correlations between psychological functions and brain activity or methods for localizing cognitive processes in the brain. An indirect route to investigating brain mechanisms in humans is through the study of animal neuroanatomy and physiology using invasive techniques that cannot be used on humans. However, even a full understanding of another organism's brain operations will not lead us to a complete understanding of human brain operations.

A second approach focuses on behavioural investigations of healthy human subjects. This approach combines our knowledge of normal sensory systems with precise stimulus presentation and response recording. The shortcoming of this approach is that it can only infer a relation between behaviour and underlying brain mechanisms: it cannot establish a specific link.

A third approach is based on case studies of brain-injured patients. By relating patients' symptoms to the parts of the brain that have been damaged, these studies can provide evidence of localization of function (Broca's aphasia; Wernicke's aphasia). However, because individual cases differ, brain injuries can at best provide only incomplete evidence. In some cases of brain injury, surgical intervention is necessary. One outcome of such intervention can be greater understanding of the relationship between brain function and behaviour (*interhemispheric transfer*; *split brain*).

Recent technological advances have enabled us to observe the brain structures directly through both *static* brain-imaging techniques such as CT or MRI and *dynamic* imaging techniques such as ERP, PET, fMRI, and MEG. Each has its own specific strengths and limitations. Generally, dynamic or functional neuroimaging studies provide images not only of brain structures but also of brain activity. However, many of these investigations focus on a single cognitive function and thus do not capture the overlap of brain regions involved in a variety of functions. Furthermore, it is questionable whether brain activations generated in a lab-based environment can tell us anything about behaviour in real-world settings.

Finally, a fourth approach to understanding cognitive processes reflects the theory known as *connectionism*: that cognition can be modelled as a network of interconnected units (e.g., neurons). Connectionist models operate on a set of specific assumptions (*Hebb rule*, *serial processing*, *parallel processing*) about the formation and strengthening of neural network connections.

Case Study Wrap-Up

We began this chapter by considering how easy it is to take the brain for granted, even though it is indispensable to all thought and behaviour. The life-altering consequences of brain injury were recently driven home by the case of Congresswoman Giffords, who survived a bullet in the head but then faced significant difficulties in understanding and producing speech. Based on what you have read in this chapter, which side of her brain do you think was injured?

We have considered three convergent lines of evidence suggesting that the injury must have been in the left hemisphere: brain lesion studies (e.g., the research conducted by Broca and Wernicke), surgical intervention (e.g., the split-brain work of Sperry and colleagues), and the fMRI studies involving healthy individuals. In fact, it was the left hemisphere of Giffords' brain that was damaged.

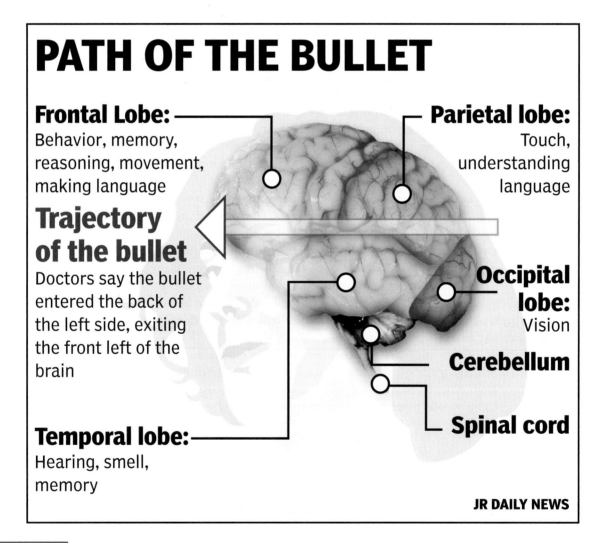

PATH OF THE BULLET

Frontal Lobe:
Behavior, memory, reasoning, movement, making language

Trajectory of the bullet
Doctors say the bullet entered the back of the left side, exiting the front left of the brain

Temporal lobe:
Hearing, smell, memory

Parietal lobe:
Touch, understanding language

Occipital lobe:
Vision

Cerebellum

Spinal cord

JR DAILY NEWS

FIGURE 2.17   Lesions in left hemisphere of Gabrielle Giffords' brain

? In the Know: Review Questions

1. How important do you think the physical localization of cognitive processes is to the study of human cognition?

2. Review the approaches to the mind/brain issue outlined in the text (including Sperry). Which of these approaches (if any) do you prefer? If you don't favour any of them, what is your alternative?

3. Explain the major differences between ERP, PET, MRI, fMRI, MEG, and DTI. How do they differ functionally? What are their limitations?

Key Concepts

Broca's aphasia
Broca's area
connectionism
diffusion tensor imaging (DTI)
emergent causation
emergent property
epiphenomenalism
event-related potential (ERP)
functional magnetic resonance imaging (fMRI)
Hebb rule
interactionism
interhemispheric transfer
isomorphism
law of equipotentiality

law of mass action
localization of function
magnetoencephalography (MEG)
modules
neural networks
parallelism
parallel processing
phrenology
positron emission tomography (PET)
serial processing
split brain
supervenient
Wernicke's aphasia
Wernicke's area

Links to Other Chapters

blindsight
Chapter 3

Broca's area
Chapter 9 (evolution of language)

connectionism
Chapter 6 (connectionist models of memory)

event-related potential (ERP)
Chapter 7 (mental rotation)
Chapter 10 (insight)
Chapter 11 (negativity bias)

functional magnetic resonance imaging (fMRI)
Chapter 4 (preattentive processes, Stroop task)
Chapter 5 (levels of processing)
Chapter 7 (dual coding)
Chapter 11 (perception of streaks)
Chapter 12 (expertise)

left and right hemispheres
Chapter 7 (mental rotation)

positron emission tomography (PET)
Chapter 4 (Stroop task)

Further Reading

Three excellent histories of the emergence of cognitive psychology are Baars (1986), Gardner (1985), and Hilgard (1987).

Searle (1980) includes a famous critical discussion of computer simulation. For a very readable account of some of his views, see Searle (1999). Green (1996) offers a sophisticated analysis of many of the issues surrounding computer simulation.

For a basic introduction to neural networks see Hinton (1992). Smith (1996) is another introduction to connectionism that also shows some of its broader implications.

An influential book by an enthusiast of connectionism is Churchland (1996). Rock and Palmer (1990) is a suggestive review of the contributions of Gestalt psychology that shows its similarity to some aspects of connectionism.

For overviews of the mind/brain issue by four eminent scientists and one philosopher see Crick and Koch (2003), Edelman (2004), LeDoux (2002), and Chalmers (1996).

Not everyone is enthusiastic about the achievements of cognitive neuroscience. For a well-informed critique see Bennett and Hacker (2003). They argue that, as Wittgenstein (1953, p. 232) put it, "problem and method pass one another by" in cognitive neuroscience: in other words, that neuroscience is not addressing the problems it thinks it is addressing. To appreciate their line of argument, you might want to become acquainted with Wittgenstein, although understanding him is no mean achievement.

For a basic introduction to event-related potentials, see Begleiter (1977). Finally, Logothetis (2003) is a demanding but worthwhile discussion by one of the most highly respected researchers in the field of fMRI.

Baars, B.J. (1986). *The cognitive revolution in psychology*. New York: Guilford Press.

Begleiter, H. (1977). *Evoked brain potentials and behavior*. New York: Plenum.

Bennett, M.R., & Hacker, P.M.S. (2003). *Philosophical foundations of neuroscience*. Oxford: Blackwell.

Chalmers, D.J. (1996). *The conscious mind: In search of a fundamental theory*. New York: Oxford University Press.

Churchland, P.M. (1996). *The engine of reason, the seat of the soul*. Chichester: Wiley.

Crick, F., & Koch, C. (2003). A framework for consciousness. *Nature Neuroscience, 6*, 119–126.

Edelman, G.M. (2004). *Wider than the sky: The phenomenal gift of consciousness*. New Haven: Yale University Press.

Gardner, H. (1985). *The mind's new science*. New York: Basic Books.

Green, C.D. (1996). Fodor, functions, physics, and fantasyland: Is AI a Mickey Mouse discipline? *Journal of Experimental and Theoretical Artificial Intelligence, 8*, 95–106.

Hilgard, E.R. (1987). *Psychology in America: An historical survey*. New York: Harcourt Brace Jovanovich.

Hinton, G.E. (1992). How neural networks learn from experience. *Scientific American, 267* (Sept.), 144–151.

LeDoux, J. (2002). *Synaptic self: How our brains become who we are*. New York: Penguin.

Logothetis, N.K. (2003). The neural basis of the blood-oxygen-level-dependent functional magnetic resonance imaging signal. In A. Parker, A. Derrington, & C. Blakemore (Eds.), *The physiology of cognitive processes* (pp. 62–116). Oxford: Oxford University Press.

Rock, I., & Palmer, S. (1990). The legacy of Gestalt psychology. *Scientific American, 263* (December), 84–90.

Searle, J.R. (1980). Minds, brains, and programs. *Behavioral and Brain Sciences, 3,* 417–424.

Searle, J.R. (1999). I married a computer. *New York Review of Books* (Apr. 8), pp. 34–38.

Smith, E.R. (1996). What do connectionism and social psychology have to offer each other? *Journal of Personality and Social Psychology, 79,* 893–912.

CHAPTER 3

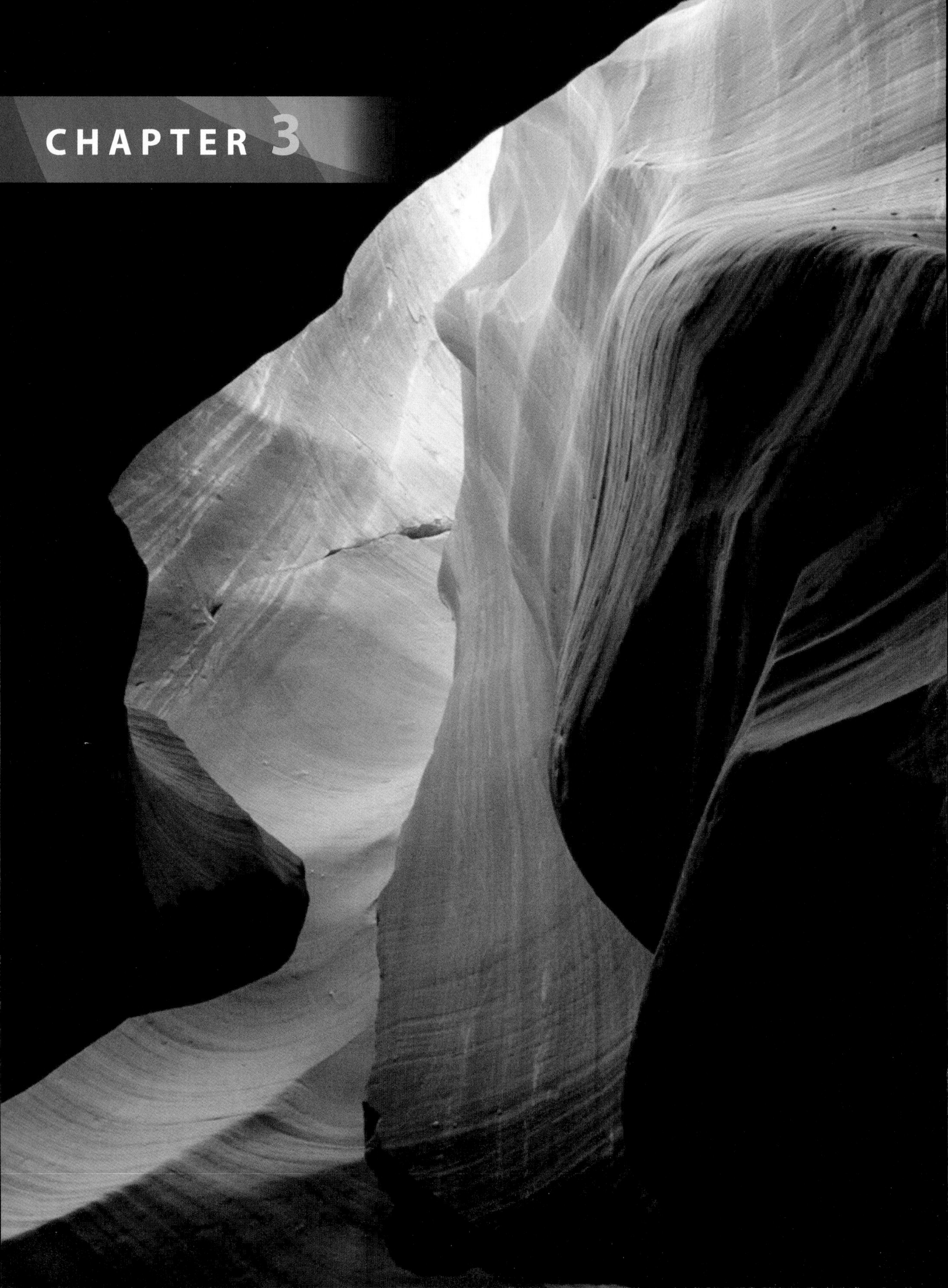

Perception

Chapter Contents

Chapter Objectives

- To review studies of subliminal perception.
- To describe Gibson's theory of vision.
- To illustrate the importance of context in theories of vision.
- To discuss how the limitations of the visual system prevent us from having a detailed internal representation of the world.
- To examine the contributions of Gestalt psychologists to the study of vision.
- To outline how perception breaks down, with specific reference to patients with visual deficits.

Imagine for a moment that you have just woken up in a hospital bed after suffering a head injury or a stroke that has blocked the blood flow to a part of your brain. As the scene around you slowly comes into focus, you are horrified to realize that you can't attach a name to any of the things you see. Someone comes over to your bed and holds up a series of objects, which she asks you to identify. You can't do it. Finally you reach out and grab one of the objects, and on feeling it you immediately recognize it as a hairbrush and name it correctly. But you still can't identify any of the objects that you haven't touched.

A very similar situation was described more than a century ago by H. Lissauer (1888/2001). An 80-year-old patient who was experiencing perceptual deficits as a result of damage to the brain was presented with a number of simple visual objects and asked to identify them. His responses are reported in quotation marks here, interspersed with the interviewer's questions and comments:

Object Presented	Patient's Response
A lamp containing a light:	"A figure." What does it represent? "That, I can't guess." After a pause: "It could be a man. But the figure only goes up to there" (shows the length of the light). "The other (shows the lamp) is something fixed, a base." Is it really a man and not perhaps a column? "No, here are his head and his legs." "Here is even (shows the bent wick of the light) a bent leg."
Clothes brush:	"That is the earlier figure which was a cat." What was it really? "I have forgotten." The movement of brushing is demonstrated on his jacket. "Oh, of course, a brush."
A large wall mirror:	"That is a lamp made of glass I think." "A lamp." He steps close up to it. Where does the light go? "Here." He points to a corner of the mirror. What is inside it? (the reflection of the patient himself): "Seems to have a horse in it."
Umbrella (2 feet long):	"A lamp." How large do you estimate it to be? "8 inches." Shows on request both ends of the umbrella correctly. How long is 8 inches? Marks with his hands approximately the length of the umbrella. The umbrella is put up. Is it really a lamp? "Yes, yes, there (near the top) the light is put there." (. . .)

A sheet of paper with illustrations of animals is shown (not in colour):

Donkey:	"That's Napoleon." Is it a picture? "Yes, it's a painting of Napoleon."
Horse:	"Horse." Shows head and tail correctly.
Parrot:	"Seems to be a donkey."
Swan:	"A giraffe."
Cat:	"Cat or monkey." The sheet of paper is turned over so that its reverse is shown: Do you see any pictures here? "No."

Amusing as it is to imagine mistaking a donkey for Napoleon, it's worth noting that the patient did identify some of the objects correctly, including the horse and (after briefly second-guessing himself) the cat. This condition, characterized by impairment in visual identification of objects, is known as **visual agnosia**.

Now imagine you don't have visual agnosia (thankfully!) but are suffering from excruciating migraine headaches. The pain is so bad that you have to see a neurosurgeon. The doctor conducts a series of tests and concludes that you have a problem with some blood vessels at the back of your brain, near an area involved in visual perception. Since the only hope of relief lies in surgery to remove the blood vessels and a small amount of brain tissue serviced by them, you agree to go under the knife. When you wake up after the surgery, the migraine is mostly gone, but you are unable to see anything in the lower left quadrant of the visual field. Although the area affected becomes somewhat smaller over time,

Visual agnosia
An inability to identify objects visually even though they can be identified using other senses (e.g., touch).

the problem does not go away. Sometime later, while examining your perception, your doctor places a series of objects in the blind area of your visual field and asks you to identify their orientation. Certain that you don't see anything, you can only guess. However, to your astonishment, the doctor tells you that most of your "guesses" were correct. In what now is considered to be a classic case study, Weiskrantz (1986) describes just such a patient. D.B. had undergone a surgery that left him with a blind area in his lower visual field. What was striking about D.B.'s case was that even though he could not consciously see the objects presented in his blind area, his guesses about their properties were impressively accurate. For instance, Weiskrantz (1986, p. 26) reported that D.B. was able to point to and reach for objects presented in his blind area with a high degree of accuracy. As another example, Weiskrantz (1986) described an informal test in which D.B. was shown a short stick in his blind area. Of course, he reported not seeing anything. Yet when asked to guess at the stick's orientation, his answers were very accurate. Weiskrantz (1986, p. 24) reports the following discussion with D.B., which took place after he had correctly identified the orientation of the stick on multiple trials without seeing the stick itself:

> "Did you know how well you had done?" he was asked. "No," he replied, "I didn't—because I couldn't see anything; I couldn't see a darn thing."
> "Can you say how you guessed—what it was that allowed you to say whether it was vertical or horizontal?" "No, I could not because I did not see anything; I just don't know." Finally, he was asked, "So you really did not know you were getting them right?" "No," he replied, still with something of an air of incredulity.

Weiskrantz and his colleagues dubbed this condition **blindsight**.

How can these fascinating conditions be explained? In this chapter we will take a closer look at some of the major ways in which cognitive psychologists have studied and theorized about **perception**. At the most general level, researchers investigate how sensory information is processed, how we become conscious of information received through the senses, and how information from the environment guides action in the world. One of the exciting aspects of visual perception from a student's perspective is that it's so easy to test; you can learn a lot about visual perception by "seeing" how it works for yourself.

Blindsight
A condition in which patients with damage to the primary visual cortex are able to make accurate judgments about objects presented to their blind area even though they report no conscious experience of the objects and believe they are only guessing.

Perception
The processing of sensory information in such a way that it produces conscious experiences and guides action in the world.

Perception and Awareness

Weiskrantz's (1986) studies of blindsight suggest that we may be able to perceive visual objects even when we have no conscious experience of them. Indeed, the well-known psychologist William James (1890/1983, p. 275) made the point that people are not actually aware of all the things in their environment of which they could be aware. Lots of things are going on of which we appear to be unconscious. James talked about how different travellers visiting the same place will bring back very different accounts of what they have seen. Today we might say that people encode events in different ways. A code is "a set of rules or operations that transforms items, objects or data from one systematic form into another. . . . Thus, for example, the hearer of a sentence will code the sequence of physical, acoustic events into a meaningful form" (Reber, 1985). The words you hear arrive at your ear as physical, acoustic events; then you encode these events as words. Thus **encoding** refers to the process of transforming information into one or more forms of representation.

Encoding
The process of transforming information into one or more forms of representation.

How do we encode information? There are several ways. Consider how we might encode a word. In an influential paper, D.D. Wickens (1970) used this example: "When a person hears the word horse, it is encoded into the broader categories of beasts of burden, four-legged creatures, mammals, warm blooded animals, and finally of animals in general" (p. 1). How does this encoding process take place? Wickens suggested that it was largely automatic: in a world with so much information available at any moment, the task of encoding it would be impossibly complex if we had to be aware of what we were doing. Wickens drew the analogy of a major league baseball player who is able to hit or catch a ball without paying attention to what he is doing. In fact, there is evidence that if highly skilled performers do try to pay attention to what they are doing, their performance declines (Baumeister, 1984; Bielock, 2002; Grey, 2004; Schlenker & Leary, 1982).

Wickens suggested that the process of encoding was not only unconscious but also very fast. Moreover, an event can be encoded along several different dimensions simultaneously. Thus a single word might be encoded in terms of multiple dimensions: frequency of occurrence, how we feel about it, as well as its physical characteristics, such as its size, shape, and so on. This process is called multidimensional encoding.

SUBLIMINAL PERCEPTION

Subliminal perception
Also known as unconscious perception, subliminal perception occurs when an observer is unaware of perceiving a stimulus, yet the stimulus can still have an impact on his or her behaviour.

Stimulus
An entity in the external environment that can be perceived by an observer.

Limen
Threshold.

Wickens's point of view is consistent with the existence of a phenomenon called **subliminal perception** (N.F. Dixon, 1971; Lazarus & McCleary, 1951). Subliminal perception operates when a **stimulus** has an effect on behaviour even though it has been exposed too rapidly or at too low an intensity for the person to be able to identify it. For example, suppose that a word (the stimulus) is presented to a participant for such a short interval that it is below the participant's threshold for reporting the occurrence of an event. Another word for threshold is **limen**, and so a stimulus that is "below threshold" is called *subliminal*. Even when the participant does not identify the stimulus, it may still have an effect. Wickens reviewed experiments in which participants have been able to say whether the stimulus word is pleasant or unpleasant, without reporting that they have actually seen it (e.g., Eriksen, Azuma, & Hicks, 1959).

Subliminal perception effects often involve semantics—the study of meaning. Two words that are similar in meaning are said to be semantically related. Thus *duck* and *swan* are semantically related in that both refer to water birds (Eagle, Wolitzky, & Klein, 1966). In some early subliminal perception experiments, participants would report seeing a word that was semantically related to the stimulus word but would not report seeing the word they were actually shown (Postman, Bruner, & McGinnis, 1948).

Experiments like the ones we have just described were often criticized. For one thing, they appear to have serious methodological problems. How can we be sure that a stimulus presented below the threshold of awareness was not actually seen? If the stimulus was attended to, however briefly, then we should not be surprised if it had some effect on behaviour. In the late 1970s and early 1980s, however, novel experimental techniques revived the notion that information is extensively encoded below the threshold of awareness. Among the most influential studies were those that employed a technique called "backward masking."

BACKWARD MASKING

Backward masking involves presenting a stimulus, called the target, to the participant and then covering, or masking, the target with another stimulus. The time difference between the first stimulus and the masking stimulus is called the **stimulus onset asynchrony**, or **SOA**.

In one early experiment (Marcel, Katz, & Smith, 1974), participants were briefly shown a single word that was then masked by a pattern. The participants were asked to report whatever they could. Sometimes participants reported words that they had not been shown but that were semantically related to the stimulus word (e.g., *queen* instead of *king*, or *apple* instead of *orange*). This phenomenon is sometimes called **priming**, by analogy with the activity of priming a pump. The stimulus acts as a *prime* that makes a semantically related response more likely.

Other studies done by Marcel used a time difference between the first stimulus and the masking stimulus (SOA), which was apparently too brief to allow detection of the stimulus. In one study, after a target word was presented and masked, a colour patch was presented. For example, the target might be the word *blue*, and the colour patch might be red. Some trials had target words and colours that were congruent (e.g., the target word was *red* and the colour patch was red), whereas in other trials the target words were incongruent (e.g., the target word was *blue*, and the colour patch was red). In one condition, participants were required to name the colour of the patch. Even when participants were not able to say anything about the word they were shown (the target) before the mask appeared, they still responded more quickly in congruent than in incongruent trials. This suggests that the target stimulus had an effect on colour-naming latency (response time) even when the participants were not aware of it.

Marcel thought that these studies lent support to the idea that "[w]hen an indirect measure of perceptual processing is used, such as associative effects of the undetected word on a subsequent task, all participants show effect of undetected stimuli" (Marcel, 1983a, p. 232). To determine whether or not a stimulus has affected cognitive processes, then, it might not be necessary to rely on **direct measures** of cognitive processes, such as participants' verbal reports that they have not seen the stimulus; **indirect measures** of perceptual processes could be used instead. Masking a stimulus so that it is not reported by the participant does not mean that it has no effect: it may be processed anyway and thus influence that person's subsequent behaviour.

OBJECTIVE AND SUBJECTIVE THRESHOLDS

Experiments such as Marcel's are examples of the **dissociation paradigm**: an experimental strategy designed "to demonstrate that it is possible to perceive stimuli in the complete absence of any conscious awareness of these stimuli" (Merikle & Reingold, 1998, p. 304). This experimental design is intended to show that **perception without awareness** is a real phenomenon. Merikle (1992) described its general form:

> First, a measure of conscious perceptual experience (C) is selected. Second, a measure that is sensitive to unconscious perceptual processes (U) is identified. Third, experimental procedures are initiated to ensure that C exhibits no sensitivity to the

Backward masking
Presenting a stimulus, called the target, to the participant and then covering, or masking, the target with another stimulus.

Stimulus onset asynchrony (SOA)
The temporal delay between the first stimulus and a masking stimulus.

Priming
The tendency for some initial stimuli to make subsequent responses to related stimuli more likely.

Direct vs indirect measures
Participants' reports that they have seen a stimulus, as opposed to the effects of an undetected stimulus on a subsequent task.

Dissociation paradigm
An experimental strategy designed to show that it is possible to perceive stimuli in the absence of any conscious awareness of them.

Perception without awareness
A stimulus has an effect even though it is below the participant's subjective threshold of awareness.

critical perceptual information. If U can then be shown to exhibit some sensitivity to the same perceptual information that C is insensitive to, then it is concluded that perception without awareness has been demonstrated. (p. 792)

However, this paradigm still does not eliminate the threshold problem. Merikle and his colleagues (Cheesman and Merikle, 1986; Merikle, Smilek, & Eastwood, 2001) have pointed out the importance of distinguishing between **objective** and **subjective thresholds**. The objective threshold is the level at which people detect a target stimulus no more often than would be expected by chance. For example, suppose that participants are presented with a series of stimuli and asked to indicate in each case whether or not they have detected the stimulus: if someone is correct only half the time, then it seems reasonable to conclude that he or she is only guessing and is not in fact aware of the presence or absence of the stimulus. The participant's results are no better than "would be obtained by a blind observer" (Erdelyi, 2004, p. 75). The subjective threshold can be determined by degrading "the stimulus conditions until the quality of the stimulus information is so poor that observers claim not to be able to perceive the stimuli" (Merikle & Daneman, 2000, p. 1296). In other words, the stimulus may be presented so quickly, or at such a low intensity, that participants will *say* they have not perceived it.

In backward-masking experiments, the objective threshold refers to an SOA at which a participant can detect the target stimulus only at a chance level. The subjective threshold refers to an SOA at which a participant claims not to be able to detect the stimulus. The subjective threshold has been used to distinguish between conscious and unconscious processes. However, it is far from obvious that perception without awareness has in fact occurred when participants "do not believe any useful stimulus information was perceived" (Merikle & Joordens, 1997, p. 111). One problem is the impossibility of demonstrating "in a completely convincing fashion" that "no relevant information was consciously perceived" (Merikle & Joordens, 1997, p. 111). To rule out this possibility would require a complete assessment of the contents of the participants' consciousness (Merikle & Reingold, 1998). Rather than try to make a sharp distinction between conscious and unconscious effects, a better research strategy might be to investigate the relative contributions of each (Merikle & Joordens, 1997, p. 112).

One study often cited as an example of just such a strategy was conducted by Debner and Jacoby (1994), who used a **process dissociation procedure**. This technique requires participants *not* to respond to items they have seen previously. If participants are aware of having previously seen an item, then they can exclude it. If they are not aware of having previously seen an item, however, there is no reason for them to exclude it. Items were masked and presented for short (50 milliseconds) or long (500 milliseconds) durations. Then a word stem appeared on the screen, consisting of the first three letters of a five-letter word. An example would be *tab– –*, which could be completed with different letter combinations such as *table*, *tabby*, or *taboo* (Debner & Jacobi, 1994, p. 308). Participants were easily able to exclude the items they had seen for the longer duration. Thus, shown *table* for 500 milliseconds and then shown *tab– –*, they chose a word other than *table* to complete the word stem. This shows that participants had perceived the item and were able to control their response on the stem-completion task.

However, if participants were shown *table* for only 50 milliseconds, they were much less likely to exclude it as a solution to the stem-completion task. In fact, they

Objective and subjective thresholds
The point at which participants can detect a stimulus at a chance level versus the point at which they say they did not perceive it.

Process dissociation procedure
An experimental technique that requires participants *not* to respond with items they have observed previously.

were much more likely to choose *table* than they would have been by chance alone. The fact that they were unable to exclude the word *table* suggests that they did not perceive the word when it was shown to them. However, it also suggests that their behaviour was influenced by an event of which they were unaware. In short, participants were not in conscious control of their own behaviour.

Mindful of the controversies surrounding perception without awareness, Kihlstrom (2004) proposed using the term **implicit perception** for the phenomenon we have reviewed in this section. "Implicit perception" refers to "the effect on the subject's experience, thought or action of an object in the current stimulus environment in the absence of, or independently of, conscious perception of that event" (Kihlstrom, 2004, p. 94). This definition is intended to link unconscious perception to similar phenomena in other areas of cognition. We will examine some of these in Chapter 6, on memory systems.

Implicit perception
The effect on a person's experience, thought, or action of an object in the current stimulus environment in the absence of, or independent of, conscious perception of that event.

CONSCIOUS AND UNCONSCIOUS PROCESSES: SUMMARY AND CONCLUSION

Although Marcel's (1983a, 1983b) experiments have been superseded, the conclusions he drew from them are still valuable. His studies and the others we have reviewed point to the importance of the distinction between conscious and unconscious mental processes. People are not always aware of perceptual processes. Importantly, what studies of unconscious perception reveal is that a conscious **percept** is not always the goal of perception. Recall the blindsight patient D.B., who was unable to consciously perceive an object presented in his blind area, but was nevertheless able to accurately point at it. This suggests that one key aspect of perception is that it allows us to act and behave appropriately in our environment. We next consider a theory of perception focused not on how we consciously perceive objects, but on how stimuli in the environment lead to action.

Percept
The visual experience of sensory information.

Perception as a Function of the Environment

An influential conceptualization of perception that relied heavily on the nature of the external environment and its ability to guide action was offered by J.J. Gibson (1961, 1966). His **theory of ecological optics** (see Gibson, 1961) focused on the idea that in real-world situations, the sensory organs are stimulated by energy coming from the environment, and that this energy contains systematic information which can be used to guide action. Gibson articulated the strong link between the environment and perception as follows: "perception is the function of stimulation and stimulation is a function of the environment; hence perception is a function of the environment" (Gibson, 1959, p. 459). He also believed that "all processes for explaining the conversion to sensory data into percepts are superfluous. No process of conversion is assumed" (Gibson, 1959, p. 460). This suggests that Gibson believed perception to be accomplished mainly by the sensory organs themselves, without any extensive internal processing of the incoming information. The point is captured nicely by the title of one of his influential books: *The Senses Considered as Perceptual Systems* (Gibson, 1966).

As an example of the information in the environment that can be directly apprehended, Gibson pointed to the patterns in light that are reflected from surfaces and

Theory of ecological optics
The proposition that perception is based on direct contact of the sensory organs with stimulus energy emanating from the environment and that an important goal of perception is action.

the objects around us. He referred to the panorama of visual information available as we look out at the world from any given position as the **ambient optical array (AOA)**, or the ambient array (see Gibson, 1966). Gibson noted that from every individual viewing point, a unique pattern of light enters the eyes because it is reflected from and emitted by a unique combination of surfaces. Much of Gibson's work was devoted to examining how structures in the world are manifested in the AOA, and to showing that these manifestations are sufficient for us to unambiguously perceive those structures.

For example, if you look at your current environment, you will likely notice that many of the surfaces around you are composed of systematic patterns. Note, for instance, the pattern made by the cobblestones shown in Figure 3.1 (see also Gibson, 1950). As an observer standing on a cobblestone road and looking down at your feet you will notice that the cobblestones are all rectangles of roughly equal size. Looking away from you, however, you notice that the rectangles slowly morph into progressively smaller parallelograms. Gibson (1950) noted that as you look at elements (i.e., cobblestones) of the road farther away from you, the density of the elements increases. The incremental change in the density of the cobblestones is referred to as a **gradient of texture density** (Gibson, 1950, see also Rosenholtz & Malik, 1997). As you walk forward along the road, the dense parallelograms that were some distance in front of you now appear as larger, less dense rectangles under your feet. This tells the visual system that the cobblestones on the surface are actually equal in size and that the density gradient conveys important information regarding the slant of the surface. Gibson also noted that when two different textures intersect, they create a discontinuity in the pattern, which he called a **topological breakage** (see Figure 3.2). Topological breakage gives us useful information about the edges of objects (Gibson, 1966).

To directly evaluate whether the slant of a surface could be judged on the basis of gradients of texture density, Gibson (1950) compared how well different people were

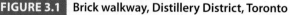

FIGURE 3.1   Brick walkway, Distillery District, Toronto

able to judge the slants of surfaces consisting of irregular and regular textures. The two types of textures used are shown in Figure 3.3. As you can see, the irregular texture consists of elements that are not very regular or clearly defined, whereas the regular texture is composed of very clearly discernible repeating elements. Observers were

FIGURE 3.2   Topological breakage at the intersection of two converging textures

FIGURE 3.3   The irregular (left) and regular (right) textures used by Gibson (1950)

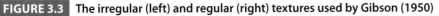

shown photographs of these surfaces at different slants and asked to judge the angle of each slant. Gibson's conjecture was that if people use the gradients of texture density to judge the slant of surfaces as, then (1) they should be able to judge the slants of these surfaces quite well based only on texture information, and (2) their judgments should be more accurate with more regularly textured surfaces as these would provide clearer information about the gradient of texture density at various slants. The results showed that observers were able to judge the relative slants of all the surfaces reasonably well. However, the assessments were more accurate for the regular surface than for the irregular textured one.

Gibson (1966) observed that surfaces of different degrees of smoothness reflect light in different ways and that the nature of the reflected light thus provides useful information about the smoothness of the surface. For instance, a rough surface reflects light more widely than a smooth surface. This is illustrated in Figure 3.4, where the solid lines indicate rays coming from a light source and the dashed lines indicate rays that have been reflected from two surfaces that differ in smoothness. The degree of **scatter-reflection** (i.e., how widely light scatters) from objects tells us a lot about the nature of the object's surface.

A critical aspect of Gibson's paradigm was that he included motion on the part of both observer and environment as a fundamental component of perception. Gibson argued that much of the classical theories and classical experiments—particularly those studying illusions—assumed a fixed, monocular perspective. For instance, from the appropriate vantage point, a trapezoidal frame can be made to appear rectangular; this type of illusion has been argued to demonstrate the ambiguity of visual information. However, as Gibson pointed out, the moment you allow the observer to move about, even slightly, the illusion vanishes. Gibson believed that the entire optical array undergoes a change as the observer moves. This change in the way all surfaces project light on the retina is referred to as a **transformation** of the optic array (Gibson, 1966). The focus on movement led to the concept of the **optic flow field**—the continually changing (i.e., transforming) pattern of information in the AOA that results from the movement of objects or the observer through an environment (see Lee, 1980). Perhaps the simplest way of representing an optic flow field is by generating moving dots on a computer display. Observers viewing this type of display can accurately identify the direction of motion relative to a target object even with very few dots, or with only brief presentation times.

Scatter-reflection
The degree to which light scatters when reflected from a surface.

Transformation
In the theory proposed by Gibson (1966), the change of optical information hitting the eye when the observer moves through the environment.

Optic flow field
The continually changing (i.e., transforming) pattern of information that results from the movement of either objects or the observer through the environment.

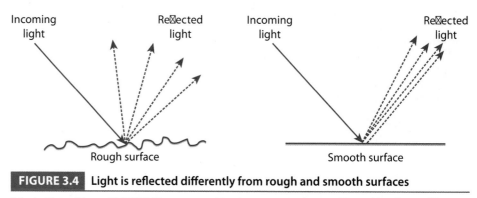

FIGURE 3.4   Light is reflected differently from rough and smooth surfaces

Adapted from: Gibson, J.J. (1966). *The senses considered as a perceptual system.* Boston: Houghton Mifflin.

An everyday example is the view you see from your car while driving. Figure 3.5 shows a photograph taken (by the passenger, not the driver!) from the side window of a car travelling on the highway. The car was moving quite fast (but still below the speed limit!) and the camera was set at a relatively slow shutter speed, which caused the objects in the scene to appear blurred in the photograph. However, if you look closely you will see that the bushes in the foreground are more blurred than the trees in the background. This is because objects that are relatively close to the moving camera (i.e., the observer) appear to be moving faster than objects that are farther away. Thus the perceived speed of object motion can be used as a guide to judge the relative distance between the object and the observer. McLean and Hoffman (1973) have shown that drivers use this information when navigating through bends in the road.

In some ways, Gibson was reacting against studies that relied on visual illusions to learn about perception. He wrote that his theory was "concerned in the first place with veridical perception and only in the second place with illusions and errors" (Gibson, 1959, p. 459). He believed that illusions reveal aspects of vision that are not particularly relevant for everyday life. He was more interested in studying situations where an individual is moving and directly picking up information from a complex, changing world.

Gibson's arguments for the importance of ecological considerations in cognition are persuasive, and they have certainly remained influential. Many of today's more successful theories are best seen as hybrids sitting somewhere between the purely internal mechanisms of classical cognition theory and the environment-driven mechanisms emphasized by Gibson. Gibson's contributions were vital in pulling attention away

FIGURE 3.5   Photo taken from the side window of a car travelling on a highway

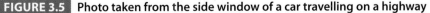

from the simplified, reductionist stimuli of his time and directing it towards the dynamic, meaning-laden environment of the real world, spurring radical new approaches to understanding the relations between environment, perception, and behaviour.

Pattern Recognition

As we noted above, Gibson's theory was based on the idea that perception is a function of stimulation from the environment. Now we will turn to other theories of perception based on pattern recognition. These theories also emphasize the characteristics of the stimulus, but they differ from Gibson's theory in at least two ways. First, they do not consider the complex array of light information reflecting from all surfaces and objects, as Gibson's theory does; the focus is primarily on specific objects or patterns. Second, they focus on how it is that we build internal representation of objects during the process of identification, whereas Gibson focused on how information is directly perceived.

The phrase **pattern recognition** comes from computer science, where it refers to a computer's ability to identify configurations such as the account numbers on bank cheques. In an analogous manner, people are able to identify many of the configurations they encounter. For example, you recognize the components of this sentence as words rather than meaningless squiggles. To take another example, when we are confronted with a small cylindrical object with a handle, we recognize it as a *coffee mug*. Currently, machines outperform humans in "highly constrained" situations such as ensuring the alignment of printed labels on medicine bottles, but humans outperform machines in "real-world tasks" such as face recognition (Sinha, 2002).

Recognizing a configuration involves contact between the emerging percept and memory. This process is sketched in Figure 3.6. We can imagine that at some point in your early childhood you were shown the letter *A*. At that time you would have formed first a percept of *A* and then a **memory trace** of that experience. The phrase "memory trace" simply refers to the trace of an experience that is left in memory (Rock & Ceraso, 1964). In order to *recognize* the letter *A* on some later occasion, your emerging perception of *A* must somehow make contact with its memory trace. The process whereby an emerging perception makes contact with a memory trace is called the **Höffding function**, named after a nineteenth-century Danish psychologist (Neisser, 1967, p. 50).

Pattern recognition
The ability to recognize an event as an instance of a particular category of event.

Memory trace
The trace that an experience leaves behind in memory.

Höffding function
The process whereby an experience makes contact with a memory trace, resulting in recognition.

	Time 1	Time 2
Stimulus	A	A
Perception	A	A
Memory Trace	A	

FIGURE 3.6   **The Höffding function**

From: Asch, S. (1969). A reformulation of the problem of associations. *American Psychologist, 24*, pp. 92–102. Copyright 1969 by the American Psychological Association.

TEMPLATE MATCHING

According to the *Oxford English Dictionary*, the word *template* originally meant a "gauge or a guide to be used in bringing a piece of work to its desired shape." Such a guide might have edges corresponding to the outline of the finished product. For example, if you were painting a sign, you might make a cut-out, or stencil, of the letters you wanted to use. The cut-out is a **template**. It's possible that we store templates in memory that correspond to the standard forms of the configurations we see. The process of template matching would involve comparing the current configuration with the standard or **prototypical** forms that we have in memory. Thus a letter can take any one of many different forms. Here is the first letter of the alphabet in lower-case printed in several different fonts:

$$a \ \mathrm{a} \ \alpha \ \mathrm{a} \ \mathbf{a} \ \mathbf{\alpha} \ \mathrm{a}$$

According to a **template-matching theory**, we would *compare* each *a* with the prototypical *a* that we have in memory; then, if the match is good enough, we would recognize the letter.

Although superficially plausible, template matching is a difficult process to spell out in detail (e.g., Hofstadter, 1982). The prototypical pattern must differ somewhat from the particular patterns we perceive, just as each *a* in the example above differs from the others. As Uhr (1966, pp. 372ff.) observed, the problem is to specify how a template can match not only patterns that are identical to it, but also patterns that are *similar enough* to it. It's not easy to spell out the characteristics that a pattern must have to qualify as a "similar enough" match to a template. For this reason template models have often been criticized. Nevertheless, the hypothesis that we see things as similar to one another because they resemble an underlying prototype is one that, in various forms, has been extensively investigated.

One approach to the role of prototypes in recognition comes from Hintzman (1986; Hintzman, Curran, & Oppy, 1992), who proposed a **multiple-trace memory model** that accounts for prototype effects in an interesting way. Hintzman's multiple-trace model assumes that traces of each individual experience are recorded in memory. No matter how often a particular kind of event is experienced, a memory trace of the event is recorded every time it is experienced.

Hintzman's approach distinguishes between primary and secondary memory. As we saw in Chapter 1, primary memory is what we are aware of at any point in time, whereas secondary memory refers to all the memory traces created out of all the experiences we have had. Secondary memory can be activated by means of a **probe** from primary memory. According to Hintzman (1986, p. 412), "The probe is an active representation of an experience" in primary memory. When a probe goes out from primary to secondary memory, memory traces are activated to the extent that they are similar to the probe. The activated memory traces are said to return an **echo** to primary memory. The echo is made up of contributions from all the activated memory traces.

Hintzman suggested that one way to understand what he meant by the term *echo* would be to think of listening to a choir. Instead of hearing only one voice in response to a probe of memory, we may hear an entire chorus of voices if many memory traces are similar to the current experience. In such a chorus, the properties of individual memory traces will tend to be lost, and only a general impression of what they all have in common will remain.

Hintzman used his theory to explain the results of classic studies by Posner and various colleagues (Posner, Goldsmith, & Welton, 1967; Posner & Keele, 1968, 1970). In these experiments, participants were shown distortions of several different prototypical patterns (for examples of the prototypes see Figure 3.7). These distortions were formed by randomly moving the dots away from their positions in the prototype (Figure 3.8). Posner and Keele (1968, p. 359) referred to each set of the distortions

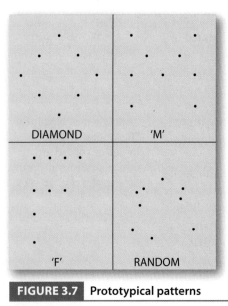

FIGURE 3.7   **Prototypical patterns**

From: Posner, M.I., Goldsmith, R., & Welton, K.E. (1967). Perceived distance and the classification of distorted patterns. *Journal of Experimental Psychology, 73,* 28–38. Copyright 1967 by the American Psychological Association.

derived from a given prototype as a "concept." Participants were shown the "concepts" (i.e., the distortions of the various prototypes) but did not see the prototypes themselves. Later they were required to classify another set of patterns into the various "concepts." This time, however, the patterns consisted of the prototypes, the original distortions, and some new distortions of the prototypes. The interesting result was that the prototypical patterns were quite well classified, even though they had never been seen before. In another experiment, Posner (1969) showed that participants sometimes misidentified the prototype as a pattern they had seen before, even though they had previously seen only distortions of it.

Hintzman explained Posner's findings as follows. The memory traces of the set of distorted patterns produce an echo based on what the different distortions have in common, rather than the peculiarities of each individual distortion. Therefore the prototype is recognized even though it has never been seen before. An interesting implication of this approach is that once an echo has been experienced in primary memory, it can leave a memory trace of itself in secondary memory. In this way, relatively abstract experiences can later be directly remembered as "echoes of echoes" (cf. Goldinger, 1998).

FEATURE DETECTION

Feature detection theory
Detecting patterns on the basis of their features or properties.

Pandemonium
A model of pattern recognition consisting of three levels: data, cognitive demons, and decision demon.

Feature
A component or characteristic of a stimulus.

Cognitive demon
A feature detector in the pandemonium model that decides whether the stimulus matches its pattern.

Decision demon
A feature detector in the pandemonium model that determines which pattern is being recognized.

Another approach to pattern recognition had its origin in the **feature detection theory** of Selfridge (1959; Neisser, 1967, p. 71). A simple version of his pattern recognition model is called **pandemonium**. It consists of three levels and has a whimsical quality. At the bottom level is the image, or cluster of data, in which a pattern of features is represented. These **features** might include properties such as size, colour, shape, and so on. The next level consists of so-called **cognitive demons** who examine the pattern of features in the image. Each demon is looking to detect a particular pattern. Thus there might be a demon for detecting apples, one for detecting oranges, one for detecting baseballs, and so on. If a cognitive demon thinks that it detects the pattern it has been waiting for, then it shouts. The more similar the pattern in the image is to the one it is looking for, the louder the demon shouts. All the demons may be shouting at the same time with different levels of intensity, depending on the similarity of what they have found to the data in the image. It's because of the ruckus these shouting demons create that the model is called "pandemonium." Sitting above all the hullabaloo is the **decision demon**, who selects the cognitive demon that is shouting loudest. This choice constitutes the pattern that is recognized.

In practice, of course, the process would be much more complicated than this. However, the basic ideas behind Selfridge's model, and others like it, have been very influential. The notion that objects and events are made up of clusters of features, and that we use those clusters to identify them, has been embedded in many theories of pattern recognition.

A study by Pelli, Farell, and Moore (2003) is relevant to the feature detection stage of models such as Selfridge's. They investigated the effect of the contrast between the letters in a word and the background on which they are printed. For

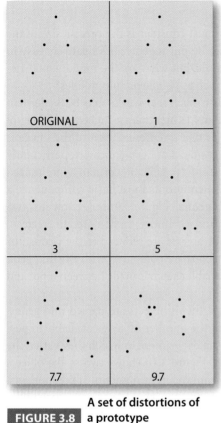

ORIGINAL | 1

3 | 5

7.7 | 9.7

FIGURE 3.8 A set of distortions of a prototype

From: Posner, M.I., Goldsmith, R., & Welton, K.E. (1967). Perceived distance and the classification of distorted patterns. *Journal of Experimental Psychology, 73*, 28–38. Copyright 1967 by the American Psychological Association.

example, a grey letter printed on a grey background would be unreadable, a grey letter printed on a white background would be readable, and a black letter on a white background would be more readable still. As Pelli et al. put it, black letters on a white background have more **contrast energy** than grey letters on the same background do. Pelli et al. reported a study in which they varied both contrast energy and word length (the number of letters in a word). Participants were shown common English words varying in length between 2 and 16 letters. Each word was shown on a screen for 200 milliseconds. After each word was shown, the participants were presented with a list of 26 words of the same length as that word and asked to pick out the one they had just seen. All told, the participants were exposed to 26 words for each word length between 2 and 16 letters. Within each set of 26 words, contrast energy was varied, allowing the experimenters to determine how much contrast energy was required for each word length. They found that the contrast energy required for a participant to identify a word was closely related to the word's length: the more letters, the greater the contrast energy required.

Contrast energy
The relative ease with which a stimulus can be distinguished from the background against which it is displayed.

According to Pelli et al., their results showed that letters are crucial features that the visual system attempts to detect during the process of word recognition. Remember that participants were shown a word for only 200 milliseconds. The longer the word, the more letters had to be detected per unit of time. For high contrast-energy words, the signal presented by each letter was strong enough to enable detection even when the presentation was very brief. However, if the contrast energy of individual letters was too low, identifying a large number of them in a short time became too difficult, and the process of word recognition ground to a halt. Letters with low contrast energy are weak signals that the visual system will tend to "squelch," preventing any further processing of features that are not clearly present. **Squelching** is a reflection of the visual system's preference for rigour in the detection of figures. In refusing to "guess" when it is not sure, the system "achieves reliability at the expense of efficiency. . . . The human visual system has a vast number of feature detectors, each of which can raise a false alarm, mistaking noise for signal. Squelching blocks the intrusion of countless false features that would besiege us if weak features were not suppressed" (Pelli, Farell, & Moore, 2003, p. 754).

Squelching
The tendency of the nervous system to inhibit the processing of unclear features.

RECOGNITION BY COMPONENTS

A critical issue that feature detection theories must consider is the precise size of the finite set of features from which all objects can be put together. It's relatively easy to compile a list of basic features for letters or words, but what are the fundamental elements for complex three-dimensional objects such as people or automobiles?

To explain how feature analysis could apply to such real-world objects, Biederman (1987) proposed the **recognition by components (RBC)** theory: "when an image of an object is painted on the retina, RBC assumes that a representation of the image is segmented—or parsed—into separate regions at points of deep concavity, particularly at cusps where there are discontinuities in curvature" (p. 117). Biederman hypothesized that this parsing ultimately breaks the object down into its most basic components: a set of three-dimensional shapes that he called "**geons**." Figure 3.9 shows how just two of the set of 36 fundamental geons (a rectangle and a cylinder) can be used to create an image of an object as complex as a tractor. Once objects are reduced to their constituent geons, the theory states that the resulting geons are compared with existing geon configurations stored in memory. When a reasonable match is made between input and memory, you recognize the object.

Biederman and his colleagues hypothesized that if objects are parsed into geons, then object recognition should be a function of the number of geons available to perceive. To verify this hypothesis they conducted an experiment in which they varied the *number* of geons used to depict a given object. Figure 3.10 shows two of the objects they constructed (a penguin and a flashlight) from different numbers of components. In addition, they varied the *complexity* of the objects. More complex objects, such as the penguin on the right, needed more geons (nine, in this case) than less complex ones, such as the three-geon flashlight. The objects were flashed for only 100 milliseconds and then covered up to interrupt perceptual processing. Participants were then asked to name the object as quickly and accurately as possible.

Recognition by components (RBC)
The theory that we recognize objects by breaking them down into their fundamental geometric shapes.

Geons
The set of 36 basic three-dimensional shapes from which all real-world objects can be constructed.

FIGURE 3.9   A tractor made from two geons (a cylinder and rectangle) for an annual fall fair near Fergus, Ontario

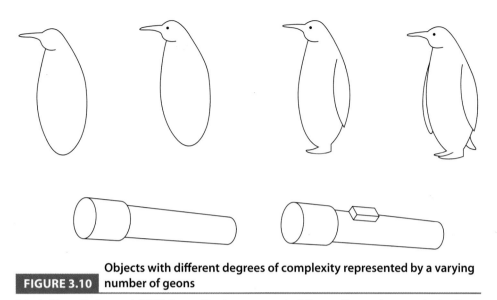

FIGURE 3.10 | Objects with different degrees of complexity represented by a varying number of geons

Adapted from: Biederman, I. (1987). Recognition-by-components: A theory of human image understanding. *Psychological Review, 24*, 2, pp. 122–123. Copyright © 1987 the American Psychological Association.

Overall, the results showed that people were quite good at recognizing objects represented by only two or three geons; accuracy was around 80 per cent at the worst. It also turned out that recognition ability improved progressively when more geons were used to add detail. Thus accuracy increased for the more detailed penguin images. In addition, contrary to what intuition might suggest, Biederman found that more complex objects (e.g., penguin) were recognized more efficiently than less complex ones (e.g., flashlight). It seems reasonable that more complex objects, since they contain more information, should require more processing and hence more time, but obviously this is not the case. What complexity and detail provide is more geons, and more geons lead to better recognition. With this and many other studies, Biederman and his colleagues made a strong case that deconstructing objects into geons is a critical component of object recognition.

Context and Knowledge

The detection of individual features is obviously important. But there is considerable evidence now that the context in which objects appear is also important. Bar (2004) suggests that **context effects** are likely very common:

> Recognizing someone's hand, for instance, significantly limits the possible interpretations of the object on that person's wrist to either a watch or a bracelet; it is not likely to be a chair or an elephant. This *a priori* knowledge allows the visual system to sensitize the corresponding visual representations of a watch and a bracelet so that it is easier to recognize the surrounding objects when we attend to them. (p. 617)

In this section we consider several classic demonstrations of the impact that context and knowledge can have on perception. One interesting example of context altering perception is the phenomenon known as the **moon illusion** (Box 3.1).

Context effects
The influence of proximate stimuli and the situation on the perceptual experience of a stimulus.

Moon illusion
The tendency for the moon to appear different in size depending on where it is in the sky.

COGNITION IN ACTION BOX 3.1

The Moon Illusion

Children are often amazed at how large the moon looks when it is close to the horizon. The surprise is likely because they usually see the moon high up in the sky, where it seems much smaller. When parents are asked to explain this apparent difference in moon size, they are often caught off guard, and many will make up an explanation—that the atmosphere somehow distorts the size of the moon, or that the moon moves closer and farther away from the earth in the course of an elliptical orbit. You can prove to yourself that these explanations are incorrect simply by taking photos of the moon at different positions in the sky. When you look at the photos you will find that the moon is always the same size (see Enns, 2004; Rock & Kaufman, 1962). And don't be tricked by professional photos with large-looking moons: those are created by overlaying a zoomed shot of the moon onto a photo of a landscape taken with a wider angle lens. It turns out that the notion of a moon that changes size depending on where it is in the sky is a perceptual error referred to as the moon illusion.

Apparent-distance theory An explanation for the moon illusion; it posits that the moon on the horizon appears larger because "distance" cues lead the observer to perceive it as being farther away than the zenith moon.

One promising explanation of the moon illusion takes into account the visual context in which the moon appears (see Enns, 2004; Rock & Kaufman, 1962; Kaufman & Kaufman, 1999). When it's near the horizon, the moon is close to various objects that we can use to judge distance. When the horizon moon is compared to the objects on the earth, the visual system assumes that it is very far away—much farther than when it is at its zenith, high in the sky. The visual system further assumes that if the horizon moon is farther away than the zenith moon, but the images projected into your eye (as on the sensor of a camera) are the same size, the horizon moon must in reality be substantially bigger. With these assumptions in mind, your visual system compensates and makes the horizon moon seem a lot bigger. This explanation is known as the **apparent-distance theory** (see Kaufman & Rock, 1962; Kaufman & Kaufman, 1999) and is illustrated in Figure 3.11. There is a quick experiment you can do that may convince you the apparent-distance theory is likely correct (see Kaufman & Rock, 1962; Kaufman & Kaufman, 1999). The next time you see a large moon at the horizon, just occlude the objects on the earth from view and you will likely see the moon illusion disappear. The moon illusion is an excellent example of how context affects perception.

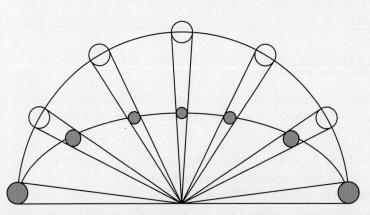

The actual (white circles) and perceived (green circles) distance and size of the moon according to the apparent-distance theory

FIGURE 3.11

From: Kaufman, L., & Kaufman, J.H. (1999). Explaining the moon illusion. *Proceedings of the National Academy of Sciences, 97*, 1, 500–505. Copyright 1999, National Academy of Sciences, USA.

LETTERS IN CONTEXT

A profound example of the effect of context on word and letter perception is the **jumbled word effect** (Grainger & Whitney, 2004). Conisder soemhting lkie tihs senetnece. Even though the letters are mixed up within the words, you can easily read the words and make sense of the sentence. Does this mean that all the time you spent learning to spell was wasted? How is this possible? You may have thought of one of the reasons already: your expectations regarding what the words in the sentence will be help you to determine what the words actually are.

Another well-documented example of how letter perception is affected by context is the **word superiority effect** (Reicher, 1969): the finding that it is easier to correctly perceive a letter when it appears in a real word than when it appears in a non-word. Remarkably, it is even easier to perceive a letter in a word than a letter alone. This effect might occur because after "years of fast reading" we are able to "more efficiently map strings of tentatively identified letters to real words" (Pelli, Farell, & Moore, 2003, p. 755).

Context effects on letter perception have been extensively modelled using connectionist approaches to pattern recognition. Connectionist approaches make use of **parallel distributed processing (PDP)**. PDP models are based on the assumption "that information processing takes place through the interactions of a large number of simple processing elements called units, each sending excitatory and inhibitory signals to other units" (McClelland, Rumelhart, & Hinton, 1986).

PDP researchers seek to specify the microstructure of cognition by working out detailed, highly specific models of the ways in which processes like pattern recognition work (McClelland & Rumelhart, 1986a, 1986b; Rumelhart & McClelland, 1986). For example, Figure 3.12 shows a part of McClelland and Rumelhart's (1981) model of context

Jumbled word effect
The ability to raed wdors in steentnces dsepite hvinag mexid-up ltteers in teh mlidde of smoe of the wrods. (The ability to read words in sentences even when the letters in the middle of some of the words are mixed up.)

Word superiority effect
It's easier to identify a letter (e.g., "P") if it appears in a word (e.g., "WARP") than if it appears alone.

Parallel distributed processing (PDP)
A model of perception according to which different features are processed at the same time by different "units" (simple processing elements) connected together in a network.

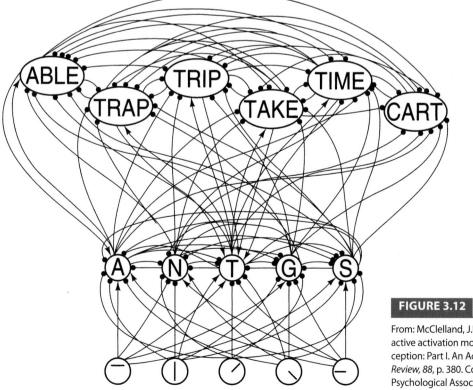

FIGURE 3.12 | McClelland and Rumelhart's pattern recognition model

From: McClelland, J.L., & Rumelhart, D.E. (1981). An interactive activation model of context effects in letter perception: Part I. An Account of basic findings. *Psychological Review, 88*, p. 380. Copyright 1981 by the American Psychological Association.

Examples of ambiguous letter strings

FIGURE 3.13

From: Rumelhart, D.E., & McClelland, J.L. (Eds.). (1986). *Parallel distributed processing: Explorations in the microstructure of cognition: Vol. 1.* Cambridge, Mass.: MIT Press, p. 8. Copyright 1986 by the Massachusetts Institute of Technology. Reprinted by permission.

effects in letter perception. This model is designed to explain context effects such as the word superiority effect and how we are able to perceive and interpret ambiguous letter strings such as those shown in Figure 3.13. Notice that all the units in the model are very richly interconnected.

At the bottom of the model (Figure 3.12) are units that correspond to basic features of letters. A unit is activated by being present in the letter being perceived. Suppose you are shown a four-letter word, such as *trap*. The first unit, which is a horizontal line at the top of a letter, is consistent with the hypothesis that the first letter is a *t*. This hypothesis is also consistent with the possibility that the word is *trap*, but inconsistent with the possibility that the word is *able*. If the first letter is taken to be a *t*, that will facilitate the hypothesis that the word is *trap*, but inhibit the hypothesis that the word is *able*. The hypothesis that the word is *trap* will in turn facilitate the perception that the second letter is *r*, while inhibiting the perception that the second letter is *b*. Excitatory and inhibitory connections between units determine what you end up seeing. When you look at one of the degraded words in Figure 3.15, therefore, you see a particular set of letters even though one or more of them may be ambiguous. This occurs because all the connections between units in the word recognition system influence one another to produce a stable pattern.

COLOURS IN CONTEXT

It's tempting to think that when we look at objects in the world, the colours we see are determined completely by the wavelengths of light that are reflected from a surface. Contrary to this intuition, however, colour vision is another domain in which context can have an interesting impact on what you see. Many good examples of contextual effects on colour vision have been provided by Purves and Lotto (2003) and can be seen on Dr Purves's lab website: http://www.purveslab.net/seeforyourself/. Here we will consider just one of his examples. Take a look at the top two cubes shown in Figure 3.14, which has been adopted from the website. The cube on the left appears to be bathed in yellow light; the cube on the right, in blue light. Each cube is covered with squares in a wide variety of colours: red, green, blue, yellow, brown, and white. Crucially, however, none of the squares on the top two cubes are grey. Now shift your attention to the two cubes at the bottom of the figure. These cubes have been created by covering the cubes from the top of the figure with white cubes that occlude all but a few of the squares from the original cubes. Surprisingly, the squares that show through all appear grey. And yes, these are exactly the same squares shown in the top of the figure. The only difference is that the surrounding colour information has been removed by the occluders. You may also have noticed that the colours of the squares that look grey when surrounding colours are removed appear to vary slightly in shade, depending on the colour of the light they appear to be bathed in (yellow or blue). The main point here is that the perception of colour is influenced by the perceptual context in which an object appears. To convince yourself that this is the case, take a piece of paper and cut out small rectangles or parallelograms, as in the bottom of the figure, and then superimpose it on the cubes shown in the top of the figure. Or just go to the Purves website and, as the URL puts it, "see for yourself"!

FIGURE 3.14	Perception of colour is determined both by the wavelength of light coming into the eye and by the context in which an object appears

Adapted from: Purves, D., & Lotto, R.B. (2003). *Why we see what we do: An empirical theory of vision*. Sunderland, Mass.: Sinaur Associates, Inc.

To explain colour illusions such as this, Purves and Lotto (2003) developed a theory of the context effects on colour perception that they call an **empirical theory of colour vision**. The basic idea is that our perception of colour depends on our prior experience with how objects look when they are viewed among different objects and under various lighting conditions. This implies that colour perception is not solely the result of the patterns of light reflected from objects; context and prior experience are part of the equation as well, and all these factors together create the final percept.

CROSS-MODAL CONTEXT

Thus far we have considered contextual factors only in the visual modality, but contextual influences can also cross modalities. Shams, Kamitani, and Shimojo (2004) point to a familiar real-world example of cross-modal context effects on perception, namely ventriloquism. Anyone who has seen a good ventriloquist will surely agree that the voice that originates from the mouth of the human performer appears to come from the mouth of his or her puppet. Here we perceive something different from what actually is because of our prior expectations: we expect voices to come from moving mouths and so we attribute the voice to the wrong visual source. Critically, in this case

Empirical theory of colour vision
The theory that colour perception involves not only the processing of wavelengths of light but also the influence of prior experiences with the way different surrounding objects and different lighting conditions affect the appearance of objects.

the context is visual (i.e., the movement of mouths) but the stimulus affected by the context is auditory (i.e., the voice is heard as coming from the puppet's mouth); in other words, the context effect is cross-modal.

Shams et al. (2004) also discuss a compelling example—originally reported by McGurk and MacDonald (1976)—of the extent to which auditory information can be affected by visual processing. You can easily simulate their study by asking two friends to stand one behind the other so that you see only the one in front. You then have the person in front (the one you can see) make mouth movements corresponding to the syllable "ga" but without actually making any sound. Simultaneously (you can synchronize your actors by counting to three) you have the occluded person clearly say the syllable "ba." What do you hear? You might want to ask another person who is familiar with this experiment, since you may be biased by knowing what each actor is doing. Chances are that you and/or the naive observer will actually hear the sound "da," which was neither the syllable mouthed by the person you saw nor the syllable said by the person who spoke. The perception of the sound in this case is altered by the visual cues made by the mouth movements of the visible person. The closing of the mouth needed to initiate the sound "ba" is inconsistent with the open mouth required to make the sound "ga." As a result, the perceptual system creates the experience of something in between—a syllable that sounds like "ba" but can be created with an open mouth. This **McGurk effect** is another example of how context affects perception. In recent years there has been considerable interest in cross-modal perception. This research is showing that far from being independent entities, the various modalities interact in complex and fascinating ways (see Shams, Kamitani, & Shimojo, 2004).

SUMMARY

Some important conclusions can be drawn from our discussion so far. On the one hand, the processes involved in feature detection provide the data for perception. On the other hand, perception is influenced by our expectations for what we are likely to find in a given context. In most cases, the outcome is determined by neither the data nor the context alone. Perception, like "[m]ost human behavior[,] would seem to lie in between these two extremes, reflecting the joint impact of high-level goals (so-called **top-down influences**) and recent stimuli (so-called **bottom-up influences**)" (Pashler, Johnston, & Ruthruff, 2001, p. 630). Next we will consider a profound example of the effects of knowledge on our conscious experiences.

▌ The Grand Illusion

When we look at the world around us, it seems as though we have a sharp, detailed, and picture-like image of our visual environment. But what if this was an illusion? What if, instead of having a true and accurate visual representation of the world, we were actually processing only fragments of our visual field and representing only one or at most two objects in detail at a time? Though this sounds far-fetched, there is considerable evidence that it may be the case.

McGurk effect
The auditory experience of the syllable "da" when seeing a mouth silently saying "ga" while at the same time hearing a voice say "ba."

Top-down influences
The influence of context and an observer's knowledge, expectations, and high-level goals on perceptual experience.

Bottom-up influences
The influence of the stimulus on the resulting perceptual experience.

CHANGE DETECTION

A compelling change detection study conducted by Rensink, O'Regan, and Clark (1997) demonstrates that our experience of a picture-like visual world may be an illusion. Rensink and colleagues showed participants two pictures of the same scene on a computer screen. The two pictures were identical with the exception of one object or region, which was altered in one of the pictures. For instance, the engine of an airplane was present in one view of an airport scene and missing in another. The original and the changed photographs were alternated back and forth on the computer screen with a brief blank interval inserted between the photographs. Each of the photographs was presented only briefly, for about a quarter of a second, and the blank screen was presented for a few hundred milliseconds. As the two photos switched back and forth (with the blank screen in between), participants had to detect the change. The result that surprised many researchers in the field was that people had a very difficult time seeing the change. In most cases, it took many alternations of the photos before the change was finally detected. You can experience the same effect just by looking at an original photo and an altered version of it presented side by side, as in Figure 3.15. Can you see the difference? Shifting your eyes back and forth between images simulates the condition (alternating images with a brief interval in between) that Rensink and colleagues created on their computer screen.

One of the main points raised by **change blindness** is that our internal representation of the world is not as rich as we think. We feel that we perceive all the information in our visual field with high resolution. However, the fact that we fail to detect very large changes across scenes suggests that this feeling may be largely an illusion. In fact, the illusion of a rich and detailed representation of the external world is known as the **grand illusion of perception** (see Enns, 2004a; Noë, Pessoa, & Thompson, 2000). Rensink and colleagues (1997) argued that, contrary to our subjective experience, we likely process only one or two objects in detail at any given moment. It seems that the grand illusion is the result of a considerable amount of top-down interpretation of very fragmentary visual information.

In light of the research on change blindness, one might wonder how it is that we are able to get around in the world safely and efficiently. The change detection experiment reported by Rensink and colleagues suggests one possible answer to that question.

Change blindness
The failure to consciously detect an obvious change in a scene.

Grand illusion of perception
The illusion that what we see in our visual field is a clear and detailed picture of the world.

FIGURE 3.15   **An original image and a slightly altered version of it**

Can you see the difference? Hint: focus on the pumpkins.

In addition to presenting two photographs with a brief temporal interval in between (the condition that led to change blindness), they included a condition in which they removed the brief temporal interval and presented the photographs back-to-back. They found that under this condition the change was often noted immediately. The change was easily detectable in this case because switching directly from one image to the other, without a temporal interval, created a flicker or motion signal that attracted the participants' attention. The same mechanism likely operates in the real world. We become aware of important changes that occur while we are driving, for example, because they create motion signals that draw our attention to them.

Change blindness is not restricted to static images (for a review of the literature on this subject, see Simons & Rensink, 2005). In fact, people often fail to perceive change in everyday life, as Simons and Levin (1998) have shown. To appreciate how their experiment worked, you can put yourself in the shoes of the participant. You begin by having no idea that you are actually taking part in a study. You are simply walking across the campus to get from one class to another. Along the way you are stopped by a young man with a map of the campus asking you for directions. Agreeing to help, you try to determine where he wants to go and how you could best direct him. All of a sudden, two men carrying a door nudge their way between the two of you, briefly occluding your conversation partner from your view. After the door has passed by, you resume your conversation. Unbeknownst to you, however, the young man you are talking to is not the one who originally asked for directions. The interruption was staged, and while the door was between you and your conversation partner (an experimenter), the conversation partner was switched for one of the men carrying the door (another experimenter)—and you never noticed! The critical moments of the experiment reported by Simons and Levin (1998) are shown in Figure 3.16. The researchers found that roughly half of their participants failed to notice that their conversation partner had been switched. A growing body of literature is now showing change detection failures such as this in both laboratory and real-world settings (see Simons & Levin, 1997, for a review). These studies suggest that our experience of a detailed perceptual world may indeed be an illusion, and a grand one at that.

FEATURE INTEGRATION THEORY

One of the main conclusions drawn from studies of change blindness is that what we perceive is not a faithful and detailed view of the world but an assortment of mostly disconnected features. In some ways this conclusion was implied by an earlier model of vision introduced by Anne Treisman and called the **feature integration theory (FIT)** (Treisman, 1986; Treisman & Gelade, 1980; Treisman & Gormican, 1988). This theory is based on the assumption that when we initially view objects in our field of vision we unconsciously extract their features (e.g., colour, orientation) across the whole scene being viewed through a process called **preattentive processing**. Like theories based on studies of change blindness, FIT assumes that for an object to be consciously perceived as a whole object, its features must be "bound" together. This **feature binding** takes place when attention is applied to the features in a given region of the visual field. Since attention can be directed at only one location at any one time, this processing operates in a serial manner. Thus of everything we see at a given moment, only one or two objects can be "bound" and experienced as a whole. Everything else is just a gooey mess of features.

Feature integration theory (FIT)
Before we can attend to objects in the world we must extract the features that constitute them.

Preattentive processing
The unconscious extraction of features that must take place before we can perceive an object.

Feature binding
The combining of visual features to form whole objects; a process that takes place when attention is directed at a particular location.

FIGURE 3.16 | Frames from an experiment in change blindness

Frame (a) shows the experimenter and the naive participant discussing directions. Frame (b) shows the change of the experimenters during the interruption. Frame (c) shows the second experimenter now discussing directions with the participant. Frame (d) shows that the two experimenters were very similar.

From: Simons, D.J., & Levin, D.T. (1998). Failure to detect changes to people during a real-world interaction. *Psychonomic Bulletin & Review, 5,* 644–649.

But what are all those features that we process in locations we are not attending to? In order to identify the basic features that we extract early in the perception process, Treisman relied on a clever series of demonstrations. If a feature *pops out* of a display (i.e., immediately grabs your attention), then that feature is a good candidate for being a basic property out of which we construct perceived objects. For example, in Figure 3.17 the boundary between the upright and tilted Ts *pops out* at you. However, you may not notice the boundary between the upright Ts and the rotated Ls until it is pointed out to you. This suggests that a property such as the orientation of a line is extracted preattentively.

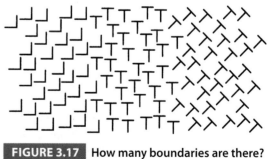

FIGURE 3.17 | How many boundaries are there?

From: Beck, J. (1966). Effect of orientation and shape of similarity on perceptual grouping. *Perception and Psychophysics, 11,* 300–301. Copyright Psychonomic Society, Inc. Reprinted by permission.

THE CONSTRAINTS OF THE VISUAL SYSTEM

If you still don't believe that your experience of a detailed and complete visual world is an illusion, consider the characteristics of the primary visual system and the physical limits of the eye. In an influential paper published in the *Canadian Journal of*

Psychology, vision researcher Kevin O'Regan (1992) made a strong case for the idea that a high-fidelity percept of the world is not possible because (1) visual information is degraded as it moves through the visual organs to the brain and (2) information from all areas of viewed space is not equally represented in the brain. This means that your visual acuity is not going to be the same across your whole field of vision.

At the levels of both the retina at the back of the eye, which is by no means uniform, and the visual cortex of the brain there is a decrease in visual processing for peripheral information. As we will see in Figure 4.10, for example, letter size must increase substantially when presented outside the central field of vision if our processing capacity is to remain constant. Even at a physiological level, then, we can process detailed information from only a very small region of visual space. The experience of uniform detail across our field of view appears to be nothing more than an illusion.

PERCEPTUAL FILLING-IN

One might think that a non-uniform retina would be problematic enough for our experience of a perfectly clear percept, but it turns out that each eye has a region in which there are no photoreceptors (light receptors) at all. This area is at the back of the eye, where the neurons from the retina exit the eye and go to the brain, and is called the **blind spot** (see Pessoa, Thompson, & Noe, 1998; Palmer, 1999). Because there are no light receptors in this area of the retina, the visual light that falls on this region is not processed, making you essentially blind to stimuli presented in that area of your visual field. "But," you say, "I don't experience an empty hole in my field of view!" Although the blind spot is there, you typically do not experience it because your brain compensates for the missing information with the information it receives both from the receptors surrounding the blind spot and from the other eye; this process is called **filling-in**. Pessoa, Thompson, and Noë (1998, p. 723) define filling-in as the subjective experience that "something is present in a particular region of visual space when it is actually absent from that region, but present in the surrounding area." Another term Pessoa et al. (1998) use for this process is "**perceptual completion**."

Demonstrations of change blindness, the nature of the eye and the primary visual system, and the filling-in phenomenon illustrate that much of our subjective visual experience is a construction. The evidence suggests that we have a clear, detailed view of at most a couple of the objects in our visual field at any one time. Thus the idea that we experience a richly detailed world of perceptual objects seems to be a grand illusion. What allows us to function effectively in the world even though we see only one or two objects at a time is the fact that we have built-in mechanisms (such as rapid detection of motion signals) that direct our attention to important objects and events around us. We will discuss these attention mechanisms in greater detail in Chapter 4.

Perceiving Whole Objects: Gestalt Psychology

Having noted that we likely do not have a completely detailed perceptual rendition of the visual world, we can now turn to another puzzling aspect of visual experience. In addition to experiencing the visual world as if it were a complete picture, we tend to experience the visual stimulation that comes from the world as consisting of whole

Blind spot
A region in the eye that does not contain any photoreceptors and so the visual system cannot process visual stimulation that falls in that region.

Perceptual completion (filling-in)
The incorrect impression that a stimulus occupies a section of the visual scene when in fact it occupies only the surrounding region.

THINK TWICE
BOX 3.2

Can You Find Your Blind Spot?

In his book *Vision Science: Photons to Phenomenology*, vision scientist Stephen Palmer (1999, p. 34) outlines an excellent exercise that you can do to detect your blind spot. A version of this exercise is reproduced in Figure 3.18. To experience your blind spot, focus your left eye on the "X" and shut the other one. Keeping your right eye closed, slowly move the page towards or away from you. As you move the page and the dot enters the area of your blind spot, it will suddenly vanish. You might have to try this several times to get the desired effect. As you move the page back and forth, you will notice that the dot vanishes only when the page is a specific distance away from your face. Moving the page too close or too far away from your face will move the dot out of your blind spot, revealing it to your peripheral vision. For a demonstration of the blind spot in both eyes see Pessoa et al. (1998, p. 725).

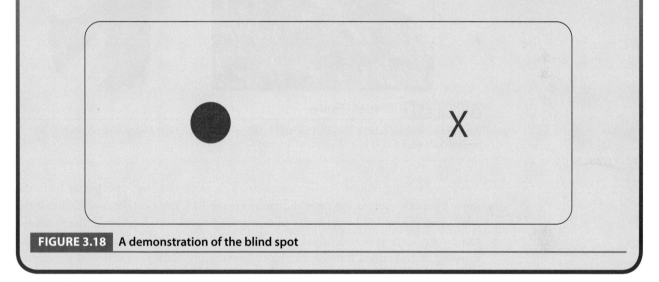

FIGURE 3.18   **A demonstration of the blind spot**

objects rather than a sea of undifferentiated features. Why is this so? What are the principles by which we combine the features in such a way as to experience the specific objects we see and not the many other possible configurations?

This critical issue was highlighted and addressed by a research movement that came to be known as **Gestalt psychology** (e.g., Koffka, 1922; Köhler, 1969). One of the main propositions put forward by the Gestalters was that a percept is not simply a straightforward function of the elements in the visual field. As an example, take a look at the image shown in Figure 3.19a. At first glance you might see either an older woman with large nose and thin straight lips or a young woman looking over her right shoulder and wearing a necklace. If you still can't see the young woman, think of the old woman's mouth as the young woman's necklace and the old woman's nose as the young woman's chin. Images such as this are called **bi-stable figures** since there are two different stable percepts that can be formed from the same image. Whether you saw an old woman or a young one, the image remains exactly the same; yet the perceptions are substantially different. Another example is shown in Figure 3.19b, where you may see either a man playing a saxophone (black in foreground) or a silhouette of a face against a black background.

Gestalt psychology
A branch of psychology that focuses on wholes as opposed to parts.

Bi-stable figures
Images from which two separate percepts can be formed.

(a)

(b)

FIGURE 3.19 Bi-stable figures

From: www.mitologica.com.br/joomla/images/gestalt/gestalt%20(1).gif and www.nwlink.com/~donclark/hrd/history/gestalt.gif.

Based on many now classic demonstrations of competing experiences from the same stimulus, such as the ones shown in Figure 3.19, the Gestalters argued that the whole that is perceived is an entity in its own right and therefore cannot be predicted just by considering its individual parts. This point is further made by demonstrations showing that identical features can be recombined to form very different perceptual objects. Consider another example shown in Figures 3.20a and 3.20b. Both figures have identical features (lines and circles). Yet they seem to depict very different objects: a person and something like a birdhouse.

The Gestalt movement derived its name from the German noun *gestalt*, which has no simple equivalent in the English language. Wolfgang Köhler (1929, p.192), a prominent figure in the movement, defined it as follows: "in *gestalt theorie* the word 'gestalt' means any segregated whole." Gaetano Kanizsa (1979, p. 56), a later member of the movement, offered a more precise definition:

> "Gestalt" ought to be translated as "organized structure," as distinguished from "aggregate," "heap," or simply "summation." When it is appropriately translated, the accent is on the concept of "organization" and of a "whole" that is *orderly, rule-governed, nonrandom.*

As Kanizsa's definition suggests, the Gestalt movement believed that perception is **holistic** (focusing on whole objects) in nature rather than **atomistic** (focusing on features or elements) and that the **grouping** of visual elements to form a whole follows certain fundamental **organizational principles** (i.e., rules or laws).

Holistic
Focusing on the whole configuration of an object.

Atomistic
Focusing on the features or components of objects.

Grouping
The combination of individual elements to form a perceptual whole.

Organizational principles
The rules (or laws) that govern how whole objects or events are perceived from a collection of individual elements.

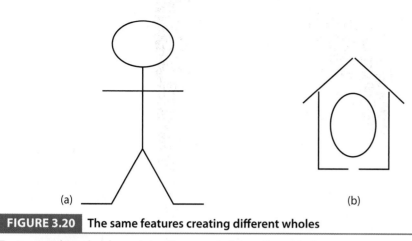

(a)   (b)

FIGURE 3.20   **The same features creating different wholes**

Try to recombine the elements in other ways to form other objects.

ORGANIZATIONAL PRINCIPLES

Katz (1951) reviews six basic principles of organization that emerged from the Gestalt movement. We will discuss each of these principles in turn, starting with the **principle of experience**, even though early Gestalters put less emphasis on it than later ones did. According to this principle, we tend to group and perceive objects based on our prior experience with objects in the world. The principle may explain how someone can see the shape of a polar bear in a lump of butter based on prior experience of viewing pictures of polar bears (or seeing them at the zoo). Chances are that people who have never seen or heard of a polar bear would have an entirely different perception. They may simply see a lump of butter.

Experience may also be important for perceptually distinguishing the object in a scene (i.e., the figure) from the background (i.e., the ground). This process, often referred to as **figure–ground segmentation**, comes into in the bi-stable image in Figure 3.19b, where, depending on focal point, you see either a black saxophone player (figure) against a white backdrop (the ground) or the white silhouette of a face (figure) against a black backdrop (the ground). But what would happen if only one of the regions (black or white) formed a recognizable object and the other did not? Would the recognizable region, the one known from prior experience, be more likely to become the figure?

These questions were addressed in a clever study reported by Peterson and Gibson (1993), in which participants were shown images that could be interpreted as having a figure and a ground; a set of six samples are shown in Figure 3.21. As you can see in the figure, each of the panels includes an area that forms a recognizable object and an area that does not. Because the former were both more meaningful and more familiar than the latter, Peterson and Gibson used the concept of **denotivity** to differentiate them. They described the regions forming a recognizable shape as *high in denotivity* (i.e., high in meaning and familiarity) and the regions making unrecognizable shapes as *low in denotivity* (i.e., low in meaning and familiarity). The concept of denotivity is relevant to our discussion of the principle of experience because, clearly, both meaning and familiarity depend on an individual's prior experience with an object. A series of perceptual tests with the images shown in Figure 3.21 showed that the region typically judged to

Principle of experience
Visual elements are grouped together based on the prior experience and knowledge of the observer.

Figure–ground segmentation
Perceptual organization of a scene such that one element becomes the foreground (figure) and the other element(s) become(s) the background (ground).

Denotivity
The degree to which an object is meaningful and familiar to an individual observer.

FIGURE 3.21   **Denotivity stimuli used by Peterson and Gibson (1993)**

The top three panels show stimuli in which the black regions are high in denotivity and the bottom three panels show stimuli in which the white regions are high in denotivity.

From: Peterson, M.A., & Gibson, B.S. (1993). Shape recognition inputs to figure–ground organization in three-dimensional displays. *Cognitive Psychology, 25*, 383–429.

be the figure was the highly denotative (recognizable) region. These findings illustrate that, in accord with the principle of experience, an individual's prior experience with shapes, which determines their meaning and degree of familiarity, can influence figure–ground organization or segmentation.

Although the early Gestalters acknowledged the role of prior experience, they quite often downplayed its role. As Köhler (1928, p. 208) observed more than 80 years ago:

> That meaning automatically produces a form where beforehand there is none, has not been shown experimentally in a single case, as far as I know. It may be that in a very *unstable* constellation, in which a certain form can be seen or organized, past experience of such a form will tend to produce it really, whereas without that previous experience, this would not happen. Even in this case, however, we would still have to explain what factors produced that form in previous life.

Gestalters such as Köhler were interested in much more *fundamental* laws or principles of perceptual organization, ones that ultimately give rise to recognizable objects. To illustrate these, they often used very simple and meaningless elements and showed that their grouping depends on how they are organized. Such explorations have led to five fundamental principles of grouping (Katz, 1951; see also Palmer, 1999).

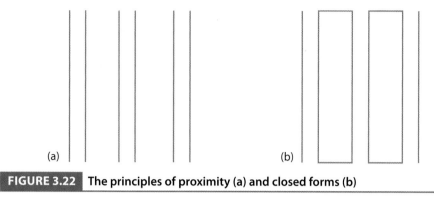

(a)　　　　　　　　　　(b)

FIGURE 3.22 The principles of proximity (a) and closed forms (b)

Adapted from: Katz, D. (1951). *Gestalt psychology: Its nature and significance*. London: Methuen.

Figure 3.22a illustrates our tendency to group elements based on how close they are to each other; this is known as the **principle of proximity**. Thus in the figure the lines that are close to one another seem to be paired, whereas the lines spaced more widely apart do not. Figure 3.22b illustrates the **principle of closed forms**, which leads us to group together items "which enclose a surface" (Katz, 1951, p. 25). Notice that the vertical lines spaced more widely apart are now grouped because horizontal lines have been added on the top and bottom, making them into closed rectangles.

Why do we perceive the elements in Figure 3.23a as three overlapping shapes (square, circle, and triangle) rather than a larger number of odd geometric shapes (e.g., semicircles, a rectangle with a concave contour)? The reason involves the **principle of good contour**: we tend to group together elements that appear to have a "common destiny" (Katz, 1951, p. 26), forming the most direct continuation of each other. If a figure can be seen as either a series of sharp, jagged components or as smooth, continuous lines, we tend to perceive the latter. In Figure 3.23b you likely perceive the pattern as consisting of groups of four letters (Xs and Os) making a checkerboard pattern. This demonstrates the **principle of similarity**, according to which we tend to group similar-looking elements together. It's easy to find examples of this principle in everyday life. For instance, when you're leaving a party and go to look for your shoes in the pile by the door, chances are that you will perceptually group the similar-looking shoes together.

Principle of proximity
Visual elements that are close to one another are grouped to form a whole.

Principle of closed forms
Visual elements that form the edges of closed shapes are grouped to form a whole.

Principle of good contour
Visual elements that form the most direct continuation of each other are grouped together.

Principle of similarity
Visual elements that are similar are grouped together.

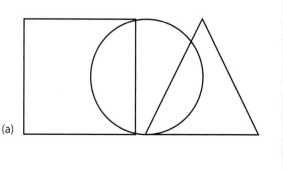

(a)

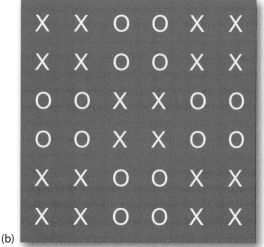

(b)

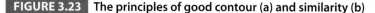

FIGURE 3.23 The principles of good contour (a) and similarity (b)

Principle of common movement

Visual elements that move simultaneously and in the same way are grouped to form a whole.

Gestalt psychologists also considered how we apply perceptual organization to dynamic, moving items. They developed the **principle of common movement**: we tend to group together items that are "moving simultaneously and in a similar manner" (Katz, 1951, p. 27). A good example of the influence of this principle in action has recently been reported by a team of researchers from the University of Western Ontario led by Susanne Ferber (Ferber, Humphrey, & Vilis, 2003). They showed participants images such as the one in Figure 3.24b, which looks like a jumble of random line elements. However, embedded among the random line elements was a meaningful shape such as the bear shown in Figure 3.24a. After participants had looked at the composite image (as in Figure 3.24b), the elements forming the object (e.g., the bear) were rotated around the centre of the image while the random elements remained in their place. This separated the elements of the object from the random elements, grouping them together and making the object readily identifiable (see also Regan, 2000). This grouping reflects the principle of common fate. Interestingly, the percept of the object remained for some time *after* the elements ceased to move. By measuring brain activation as the participants viewed the images, Ferber and colleagues showed that parts of the brain associated with object recognition were active when the critical object could be segregated from the random elements both during the movement, when they were grouped by common fate, and for a short while after the movement had stopped. These findings also lend credence to one assumption underlying the Gestalt movement, which was that the principles of grouping are fundamental, rooted in basic neural functions (see Kanizsa, 1979; Katz, 1951).

LIMITATIONS OF GESTALT PERCEPTION

Of course, no movement or theory is without limitations. One limitation concerns the role of the grouping principles in everyday situations. It's easy to see how the Gestalt principles of grouping operate in the simple displays often used to illustrate

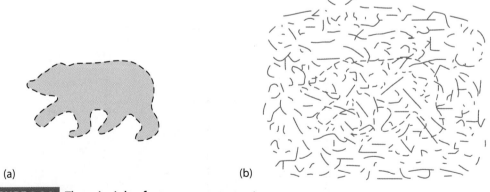

(a)   (b)

FIGURE 3.24   **The principle of common movement**

This example of the stimuli used by Ferber, Humphrey, and Vilis (2003) shows an object made of broken line segments (a) and the object placed in a display of random line elements (b) so that the object is no longer recognizable.

Adapted from: Ferber, S., Humphrey, G.K., & Vilis, T. (2003). The lateral occipital complex subserves the perceptual persistence of motion-defined groupings. *Cerebral Cortex, 13*, 716–721.

them. They are said to function ***ceteris paribus***: that is, they determine how we group items when everything other than the principle in question is held constant (see Palmer, 1992, 1999). When defining the Gestalt principles or laws of grouping, Katz (1951, p. 25) often began his definitions with the words "Other things being equal. . . ." In the real world, however, different factors are constantly interacting with each other, and Gestalt theory did not specify how people will or will not group objects under these uncontrolled conditions. A complex grouping of elements into figure and ground can be seen in Figure 3.25. When people first look at the image, they often see a woman at the edge of a forest. But after people look at the image for a while, they often see that the forest features make up the image of a man playing a wind instrument. Which grouping principles, in what combinations, might create this effect?

A second problem with the Gestalt theory, noted by Kanizsa (1979), is that it essentially treated the principles of grouping as laws, assuming that they would hold in every instance of perception. Kanizsa referred to this assumption as the **Gestaltist's error** and provided several examples of situations in which predictions made by Gestalt theory are not borne out: for example, see Figure 3.26 (see Kanizsa, 1979, p. 84–86). Gestalt theory would consider the overall grid pattern to be the "whole" of which the individual squares are the "parts." But take a look at the areas occluded by the circles. In these areas the overall pattern seems to break down, so that under the circles you see a partly occluded cross (top right) and a large square (bottom left). This effect is inconsistent with the hard-core Gestalter belief that the percept will always be determined by the whole pattern, not by any specific part of it. In fact, it seems that local elements can sometimes override the whole pattern and determine what we perceive.

Another challenge to the Gestalt theory of perception can be seen in Box 3.3, on the work of the American artist Chuck Close. In Close's portraits, both the percept and the interpretation of it change with the distance between the observer and the image.

Ceteris paribus
A Latin phrase meaning "other things being equal."

Gestaltist's error
The assumption that whole objects will always dominate over the elements of an image.

| **FIGURE 3.25** | Bev Doolittle's *Music in the Wind* |

This work provides a good example of grouping in a complex scene and the overlapping of figure and ground.

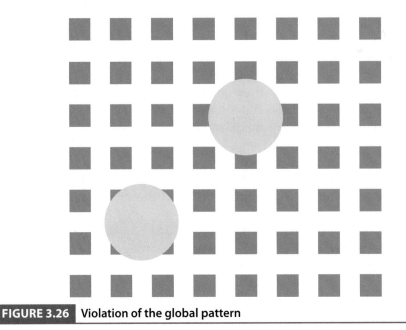

FIGURE 3.26   **Violation of the global pattern**

Notice that the squares under the circles lead to the perception of a partly occluded cross (top right) and a large square (bottom left) rather than a continuous pattern of small squares.

Adapted from: Kanizsa, G. (1979). *Organization in vision: Essays on Gestalt perception*. New York: Praeger.

▌ Summary

We began our discussion with the concept of unconscious perception and a review of the experimental evidence supporting the conclusion that stimuli can be processed and have an influence on behaviour even when the observer is not aware of perceiving them. The research on masking suggests that what we are aware of and what we perceive are two different things. Although we encode many aspects of the stimuli that impinge on us, very little of what we encode reaches awareness.

We then explored J.J. Gibson's theory of ecological optics, which postulates that complex information in the light hitting our eyes can be used to guide behaviour in the world. According to Gibson, cues such as topological breakage and scatter reflection give us information about the surfaces of objects that enables us to act on them appropriately. In addition, Gibson highlighted the important role of observer and object motion during the act of perception.

We also discussed theories of pattern recognition. One way that we recognize objects is by matching them to templates in memory; the multiple-trace memory model is an example of template matching theory. Another way is by processing the individual features of objects. The pandemonium model is a good example of such a feature-detection theory. However, object perception depends not only on the object itself, but also on the context in which it appears. The jumbled word effect and the word superiority effect indicate the importance of context in object perception. When

CONSIDER THIS BOX 3.3

Art and Perception: How Perception of Shape Depends on Viewing Size

The work of the painter Chuck Close has attracted viewers from all over the world. Imagine you are at an art gallery looking at one of Close's paintings. As you approach from across the room you see a very large (floor-to-ceiling) image of a face. You also notice that the image seems to be pixelated, with each "pixel" consisting of a small, individually painted block. Moving closer to the towering canvas, you pass a critical point and suddenly the face disappears: now all you can see are the component blocks, each of which is a unique abstract painting in itself. An example of one of these block portraits, *Bill II*, is shown in Figure 3.27.

New York University vision scientist Denis Pelli (1999) conducted a systematic investigation into how far people had to be from one of Close's portraits in order to perceive the face (specifically the nose). He found that, once the relative size of the blocks was taken into account, this distance was very similar not only across viewers but across paintings. He also found that when the face is perceptible, the individual blocks are perfectly visible as well; this indicated that seeing the face is not just a matter of the blocks' being blurry or imperceptible. At the critical distance, the perceived size of the blocks relative to the size of the face is such that the face emerges from the many small blocks. This finding is surprising because it is often believed that the perceived shape of an object is not determined by its perceived size. Apparently this belief is false: size does matter after all.

FIGURE 3.27 Chuck Close block portrait titled *Bill II*

Photograph © Chuck Close, courtesy Pace Gallery.

we look out at the world around us, we generally feel we have a detailed percept of it, but studies of change blindness show that this is just an illusion, often referred to as the "grand illusion of perception."

An account of how we perceive whole objects comes from Gestalt psychology. Gestalt theory maintains that the elements that make up a given display can be experienced as very different wholes, depending on how they are grouped together. Gestalt psychologists believe that we follow a number of fundamental organizational *principles* when we group visual elements in order to perceive a whole object.

Case Study Wrap-Up

Now let us return to the two cases we described at the beginning of this chapter. Lissauer's patient was unable to recognize objects presented to him visually, while Weiskrantz's patient D.B. was unable to consciously see objects in his lower visual field. Their case studies illustrate several of the concepts at the core of this chapter.

First, they highlight the distinction between the processing of visual features and the perception of meaningful whole objects. Specifically, Lissauer's patient had a particular subtype of *visual agnosia* in which the individual is able to perceive visual *features* but unable to use *Gestalt grouping principles* to group the features together into meaningful wholes. Proponents of the *feature integration theory* would suggest that Lissauer's patient had trouble with *feature binding*. This suggests that different mechanisms and even different areas of the brain might be responsible for feature detection and Gestalt grouping.

Second, the case studies illustrate the distinction between two kinds of perception: one with and one without awareness. Patient D.B., for instance, could not consciously "see" objects presented in his blind area. However, he was able to judge the orientation of those objects at above-chance levels. You could think of D.B.'s subjective report of awareness as a *direct measure* of consciousness and his judgment of orientation as an *indirect measure* of it. As you were reading the chapter, you might have noticed that Weiskrantz's original demonstration made use of the *dissociation paradigm* to illustrate perception without awareness in D.B.'s blind area.

Optic ataxia
Patients with this condition can identify objects but are unable to successfully reach for them, especially when the object is presented to their peripheral vision.

Third, cases of visual agnosia nicely illustrate the difference between perception for the purpose of conscious identification and perception for the purpose of action. University of Western Ontario researcher Melvyn Goodale and his colleagues (Goodale et al., 1991; Milner & Goodale, 1995) have conducted extensive studies of a patient with a type of visual agnosia similar to the one that Lissauer described. They found that while their patient was unable to identify the orientation of an object, she was able to correctly orient her hand when reaching for the object. Thus her capacity for conscious object identification was impaired (visual agnosia), but perception for the purpose of action remained intact. We can relate this phenomenon to Gibson's *theory of ecological optics*, which focuses on how humans use the complex array of visual stimuli provided by the environment to guide their action in the world. Some patients with visual agnosia are apparently able to use information in the *ambient optic array* to guide action even when they can't identify the object they are acting on. Interestingly, patients with a condition known as **optic ataxia** (Damasio & Benton, 1979) have the opposite problem: they have no trouble identifying objects, but are unable to reach for them properly!

Finally, the case study section suggests just how complex perception is. Before taking this course you probably never imagined that visual perception would involve so many distinct cognitive processes. Even today, researchers are only beginning to scratch the surface of this fascinating topic.

? In the Know: Review Questions

1. Describe the experimental evidence for the existence of subliminal (unconscious) perception.

2. Compare and contrast feature-detection and template-matching approaches to pattern recognition.

3. How does Gibson's theory of vision differ from theories focused on pattern recognition?

4. What important contributions did the Gestalt psychologists make to the study of vision?

5. What is change blindness and what does it tell us about perception?

Key Concepts

ambient optical array (AOA)
apparent-distance theory
atomistic
backward masking
bi-stable figures
blind spot
bottom-up influences
ceteris paribus
change blindness
cognitive demon
context effects
contrast energy
decision demon
denotivity
direct versus indirect measures
dissociation paradigm
echo
empirical theory of colour vision
encoding
feature
feature binding
feature detection theory
feature integration theory (FIT)
   (Treisman)
figure–ground segmentation
filling-in (perceptual completion)
geons
Gestaltist's error
Gestalt psychology
gradient of texture density

grand illusion of perception
grouping
Höffding function
holistic
implicit perception
jumbled word effect
limen
McGurk effect
memory trace
moon illusion
multiple-trace memory model
   (Hintzman)
objective and subjective threshold
optic ataxia
optic flow field
organizational principles
pandemonium (Selfridge)
parallel distributed processing (PDP)
pattern recognition
percept
perception
perception without awareness
perceptual completion (filling-in)
preattentive processing
priming
principle of closed forms
principle of common movement
principle of experience
principle of good contour
principle of proximity

principle of similarity
probe
process dissociation procedure
prototype
recognition by components (RBC)
scatter-reflection
squelching
stimulus
stimulus onset asynchrony (SOA)

subliminal perception
template
template-matching theory
theory of ecological optics
top-down influences
topological breakage
transformation
visual agnosia
word superiority effect

Links to Other Chapters

memory trace
Chapter 5 (consolidation)
Chapter 6 (encoding specificity)

bottom-up processing
Chapter 4 (Stroop task)
Chapter 10 (flexibility-rigidity and
the brain)

template matching
Chapter 8 (prototypicality)

direct perception
Chapter 11 (perception and intuition)

priming
Chapter 6 (implicit memory)

Further Reading

So-called subliminal perception has great commercial potential, as Kihlstrom (1987) observes. One way of exploiting that potential has been through the marketing of self-help audiotapes designed to improve memory or self-esteem by means of subliminal messages. Greenwald, Spangenberg, Pratkanis, and Eskenazi (1991) devised a clever study to determine the actual effects of such products. They found that participants believed the labels (e.g., "improves memory") on the tapes they were given, even when they had been deliberately mislabelled. After five weeks of listening to them, all participants, including those who had actually received self-esteem tapes, believed that their memories had improved; however, tests showed no change whatever in their performance. Studies such as this suggest that we should be skeptical about the claims made by manufacturers of such aids. See also Moore (1995).

Palmer (1999) is an excellent and comprehensive overview of vision science that deals with all aspects of perception from the time that light energy hits the retina to the time when a visual object is fully recognized.

Purves and Lotto (2003) is a detailed account of the empirical theory of colour vision that includes discussions of numerous fascinating and provocative illusions.

For a comprehensive description of visual agnosia see Farah (1990).

Finally, for an interesting critique of feature integration theory (FIT) see Enns and Rensink (1990). Their findings suggest that preattentive processing involves not only basic features of objects but also more complex scene-based properties of objects, such as their perceived direction of illumination.

Enns, J.T., & Rensink, R.A. (1990). Scene-based properties influence visual search. *Science, 247*, 721–723.

Farah, M.J. (1990). *Visual agnosia: Disorders of object recognition and what they tell us about normal vision.* Cambridge, MA: MIT Press.

Greenwald, A.G., Spangenberg, E.R., Pratkanis, A.R., & Eskanazi, J. (1991). Double-blind tests of subliminal self-help audiotapes. *Psychological Science, 2*, 119–122.

Kihlstrom, J.F. (1987). The cognitive unconscious. *Science, 237*, 1445–52.

Moore, T.E. (1995). Subliminal self-help audiotapes: An empirical test of auditory consequences. *Canadian Journal of Behavioural Science, 27*, 9–20.

Palmer, S.E. (1999). *Vision science: Photons to phenomenology.* Cambridge, MA: MIT Press.

Purves, D., & Lotto, R.B. (2003). *Why we see what we do: An empirical theory of vision.* Sunderland, MA.: Sinaur Associates, Inc.

CHAPTER 4

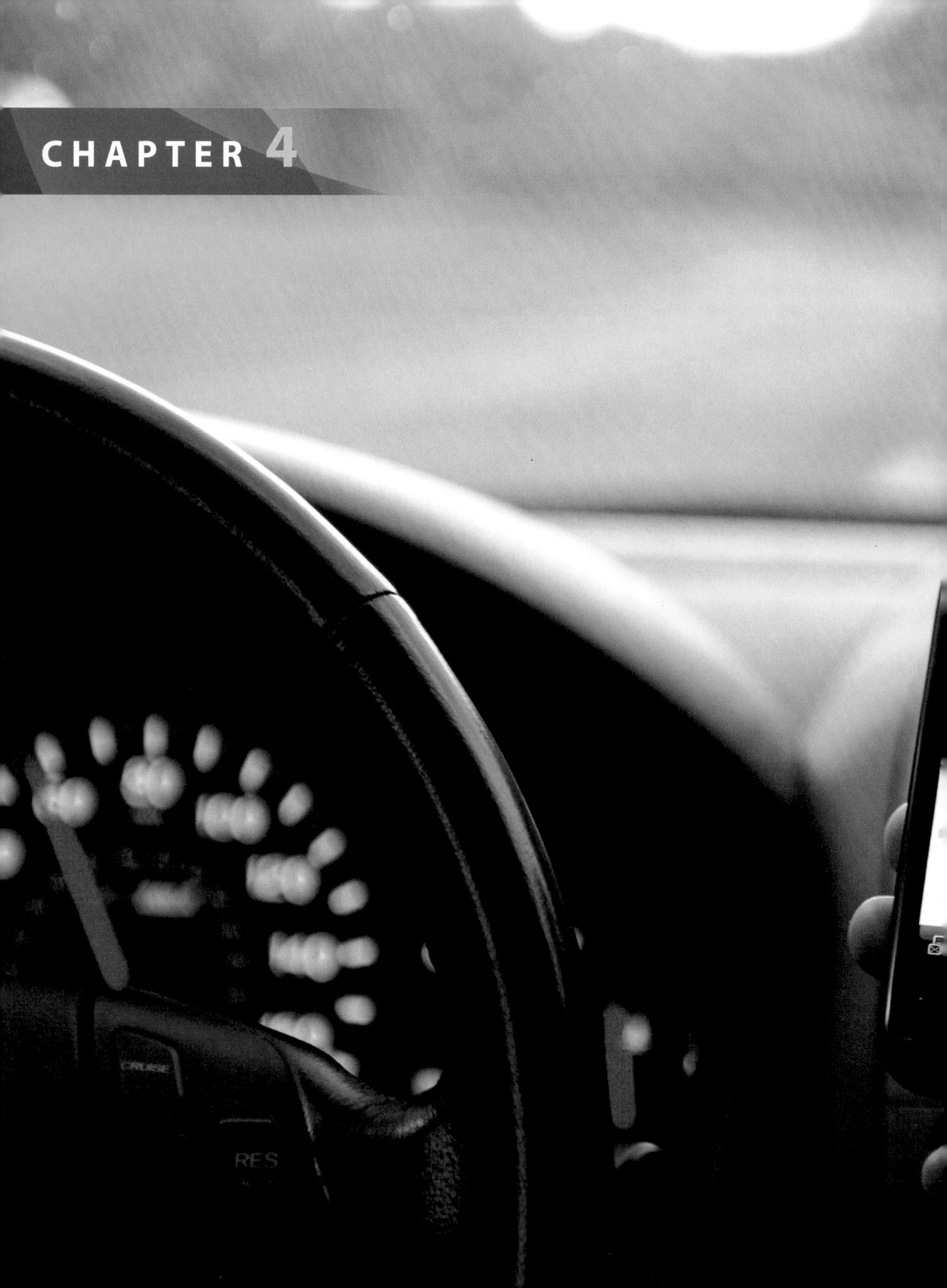

The Varieties of Attention

Chapter Objectives

- To distinguish between theories of early and late selection and review experimental evidence for each.
- To discuss the concepts of attentional capture and inattentional blindness as complementary aspects of cognition.
- To review experimental studies investigating divided attention.
- To explain why mind wandering reduces attention to the primary task.
- To distinguish between covert and overt visual attention.

Case Study   A Total Train Wreck

The town of Golden, British Columbia, is a hotbed for enthusiasts of extreme sports like paragliding and heli-skiing (see http://www.hellobc.com/). While the area has long been known as a premiere outdoor destination, in March 2010 it made headlines in connection with a major train collision that led to the spillage of more than 12,000 litres of diesel fuel into the picturesque valleys and meandering rivers that surround Golden (Transportation Safety Board of Canada (TSB), RIOVOO38, 2010). Fortunately, both trains were carrying freight rather than passengers and no one died, but the environmental damage was substantial.

How could such an accident happen? Was it a matter of equipment failure? A problem with the signalling system? According to the Railway Investigation Report released by the Transportation Safety Board there were no problems with the brakes on either train, and the signalling system—a series of lights that warn the trains' engineers that a stop signal is approaching—was in perfect working order. If there were no mechanical problems, why did the crew of the eastbound train pass two advance warning signals, acknowledge those signals over the radio, yet fail to stop at the subsequent red signal, ultimately plowing into a westbound train occupying the main track just past the red signal?

According to the investigators, the primary cause of the accident was human error on the part of the eastbound crew. As they approached the red signal, the engineer and conductor were preoccupied, focused on evaluating the temperature of the wheels of a car on their train. Worse, the evidence suggested that they were using their cell phones, both texting and talking, minutes before the accident. As a result of these distractions, they failed to notice the warning signals and the clearly visible red signal telling them to stop. At the heart of the Golden crash was the failure of human attention.

This was hardly the first train accident caused by attention-related error. A similar but much more serious accident had happened in September 2008, when a train carrying over a hundred passengers ran a red signal and crashed into an oncoming freight train near Chatsworth, California (Figure 4.1). According to the report issued by the US National Transportation Safety Board, 25 people died and roughly 100 more were injured, and the equipment damages totalled more than $12 million. Interestingly, as with the Golden incident, the investigation of the Chatsworth accident found no problems with either the signalling systems or the commuter train. So what went wrong? Well, you can probably guess: the engineer was distracted by his

FIGURE 4.1   Train crash in Chatsworth, California, 2008

cell phone and wasn't paying attention to the upcoming red signal. In fact, analysis of cell phone records revealed that a text message was transmitted by the engineer's phone roughly 20 seconds before his train hit the oncoming freight train; both trains were travelling at roughly 65 km/h and the commuter train showed no sign of slowing before the crash (Nation Transportation Safety Board, Accident Report, 2010). This is another example of a tragic accident caused by a failure of human attention.

Railway safety expert Randall Jamieson believes that these and other types of attention failures are a relatively common cause of rule violations such as excessive speed and running red signals in the railway and public transportation industries (personal communication). According to Mr Jamieson's calculations, in some situations as many as 60 per cent of rule violations could be attention-related, and these are caused not by cell-phone use, but by distractions such as radio chatter and absorption in internal thoughts. Yet many people in the transportation industry seem to be unaware of the critical role that human attention plays in the safety of railway and public transportation operations.

Accidents such as the ones at Golden and Chatsworth have led to substantial reform of the regulations relating to cell-phone use during the operation of trains. In both Canada and the US, cell phones are banned from the cabs of locomotives. Things are changing, but many people still underestimate the limits of human attention and therefore put themselves in dangerous situations. If you are honest with yourself, you probably have to admit that you've peeked at your cell phone at one time or another while driving a car.

In this chapter we will explore cognitive theories and studies of human attention. As you read it, ask yourself how the various theories and studies we discuss might apply to real-world situations such as the accidents at Golden and Chatsworth.

James's Description of Attention

At the turn of the twentieth century, Harvard's William James was the leading American psychologist (Cattell, 1903). His great textbook *Principles of Psychology* (1890/1983) contains a chapter on attention that many psychologists still cite (e.g., Johnston & Dark, 1986; LaBerge, 1990; Fernandez-Duque & Johnson, 2002). Here is one of James's (1890/1983) most famous passages concerning attention:

> Everyone knows what attention is. It is the taking possession by the mind, in clear and vivid form, of one out of what seem several simultaneously possible objects or trains of thought. . . . It implies withdrawal from some things in order to deal effectively with others, and is a condition which has a real opposite in the confused, dazed, scatterbrained state which . . . is called distraction. (pp. 381–382)

A century later, not everyone is as confident as James was concerning the definition of attention. Harold Pashler (1998), an eminent contemporary cognitive psychologist, has gone so far as to say that "No one knows what attention is, and . . . there may even not be an 'it' there to be known about (although of course there might be)" (p. 1). Pashler's statement exemplifies just how complex attention appears to be. We no longer think that just because we have a word like *attention* there must be one particular phenomenon that it corresponds to. In fact, *attention* has a variety of meanings. Even James acknowledged this when he called a section of his chapter "The Varieties of Attention." Among the variations on the theme of attention that we will address in this chapter are selecting what to attend to; not attending to what we could attend to; involuntary attention; attempting to attend to more than one thing at a time; switching our attention between tasks; and the possibility of perceiving without attention or awareness.

Selective Attention

Dichotic listening
Participants are exposed to two verbal messages simultaneously and are required to answer questions posed in only one of the messages.

Selective attention
Attending to relevant information and ignoring irrelevant information.

Cocktail party phenomenon
The ability to attend to one conversation when many other conversations are going on around you.

Shadowing task
A task in which the subject is exposed to two messages simultaneously and must repeat one of them.

Filter
A hypothetical mechanism that would admit certain messages and block others.

Selective looking
Occurs when we are exposed to two events simultaneously, but attend to only one of them.

Early selection
The hypothesis that attention prevents early perceptual processing of distractors.

Late selection
The hypothesis that we perceive both relevant and irrelevant stimuli, and therefore must actively ignore the irrelevant stimuli in order to focus on the relevant ones.

Early research on attention was driven by practical problems experienced by armed forces personnel. One of those problems arose "in communication centers, where many different streams of speech reached the person at the same time" (Broadbent, 1980, p. 54). Investigation of this problem led to the development of an experiment in which the participant was required to "answer one of two messages which start at the same point in time, but one of which is irrelevant" (Broadbent, 1952/1992, p. 125). The experimental technique that Broadbent used, which we introduced in Chapter 1, is called **dichotic listening**. Participants were presented with two previously recorded verbal messages simultaneously and were required to answer questions posed in only one of the messages. When participants knew in advance which of two different voices contained the required message, then performance on this task was very good. In other words, they were good at **selective attention**—able to select the information that was relevant to their task and ignore the information that was not.

Broadbent also worked closely with Colin Cherry (1953), who identified what came to be known as the **cocktail party phenomenon** and invented a seminal technique for investigating attention (Wood & Cowan, 1995). The cocktail party phenomenon occurs when you are able to attend to one conversation in a crowded room where many other conversations are going on. Cherry studied the ability to attend to one message while ignoring another by using a **shadowing task**, in which participants wear headphones and are given two messages, one in each ear. The participants shadow one of the two messages by repeating it as they hear it. Early information-processing theories suggested that people must *filter out* information they do not wish to attend to (Treisman, 1969). Thus one of the stages of information-processing might involve a kind of **filter** that would admit some messages and block others.

A study by Neisser and Becklen (1975) used a visual analogue of dichotic listening called **selective looking**. Suppose you take videotapes of two different sequences of events, such as a hand-slapping game and a game involving throwing a basketball. What happens if you show the two videotapes overlapping? This would be like watching two television channels on the same screen. In the Neisser and Becklen study, people were able to attend to either sequence quite easily. They saw only the attended-to sequence and were not distracted by the unattended sequence.

The studies of dichotic listening and selective looking both produced results consistent with what is called the **early selection** view of attention. This view holds that "attention can effectively prevent early perceptual processing of irrelevant distractors" (Lavie, Hirst, Fockert, & Viding, 2004). On this account, the participant literally does not see or hear the irrelevant information. However, other tasks have produced results that appear to be more consistent with a **late selection** view of attention, according to which both relevant and irrelevant stimuli are perceived and participants must actively ignore the irrelevant stimuli in order to focus on the relevant ones. Late selection is often illustrated by the Stroop task.

THE STROOP TASK

Consider the following series of colour names: red, green, blue, green, red, yellow, blue, yellow, blue, green. It's easy to read those names in black and white. But suppose they were printed in colours different from the colours they name. For example, suppose the word *red* was printed in *blue*; the word *green*, in *yellow*, and so on. This is called a **Stroop task** (Stroop, 1935/1992), after John R. Stroop (1897–1973), the psychologist who invented it. (There are several demonstrations of the Stroop task on the Internet: you should try at least one of them. You'll find that naming the colours of the words takes longer than reading the colour words themselves.) Reading the colour names and naming the colours are strikingly different experiences. When you try to name the colours, it's as if you were constantly being distracted by the tendency to read the names. We could say that the tendency to read the names interferes with the attempt to name the colours. There are several variants of this task. For example, suppose you show someone a picture of a bird that is labelled "camel": if you then ask the person to name the picture, the tendency to say "camel" will interfere with the correct response, "bird" (MacLeod & MacDonald, 2000, p. 384).

One of the most useful research tools ever invented, the Stroop task has been employed in thousands of experiments (MacLeod, 1991, 1992; MacLeod & MacDonald, 2000). A typical Stroop experiment compares performance in an incongruent condition (e.g., the word *red* is printed in green and the participant's task is to name the colour that the word is printed in) with control conditions (e.g., the letters XXX are printed in green and the participant's task is to name the colour of the letters). It is reliably found that the incongruent condition takes more time than the control condition does.

If a process has been overlearned, there is often be a tendency to carry it out whether we wish to or not. For example, if you have learned how to read and you are presented with a list of words, you will find it hard not to read them. This may help to explain what happens in a Stroop task, which requires the participant to deliberately inhibit the reading of the words in order to accomplish the goal of naming the colours.

The results of Stroop experiments have often been taken to illustrate **controlled versus automatic processes**. Some processes may pick up information more or less automatically. A truly *automatic process* is autonomous; it runs itself without requiring us to pay attention to it. By contrast, with other processes we must pay attention if we are to execute them properly. Such processes are often called *controlled processes* (Shiffrin & Schneider, 1977). Although the distinction between automatic and controlled processes is still widely recognized (Birnboim, 2003; Schneider & Chein, 2003), there is another family of constructs that captures similar distinctions. Thus so-called automatic processes may also be described as bottom-up, stimulus-driven, or involuntary, while so-called controlled processes may also be called top-down, goal-directed, or voluntary (cf. Pashler, Johnston, & Ruthruff, 2001, p. 641). In the Stroop situation, an incongruent condition requires you to keep the goal of naming colours in mind even though you have an involuntary tendency to read the words.

Some intriguing investigations of the Stroop phenomenon have used hypnosis (MacLeod & Sheehan, 2003; Raz et al., 2003). People vary in their susceptibility to hypnosis. A standard test used to measure suggestibility is the Stanford Hypnotic Susceptibility Scale (Weitzenhoffer & Hilgard, 1962; available on the Internet). Raz and his colleagues gave English-speaking participants who scored high on the scale two post-hypnotic suggestions: first, that any letter strings they saw would appear to be in an unknown foreign language, and, second, that the participants would "not attempt to attribute any meaning to them" (Raz et al., 2003, p. 337). The participants' sole task was to name the colours in which the "meaningless" letter strings were displayed. Of course, they were actually given a standard Stroop task using English words. The interesting

Stroop task
A naming task in which colour names are printed in colours other than the colours they name.

Controlled vs automatic processes
Processes that demand attention if we are to carry them out properly versus processes that operate without requiring us to pay attention to them.

result was that the highly suggestible participants did not show the typical Stroop effect, whereas those who were less suggestible did.

This result has been replicated both by Raz and by MacLeod and Sheehan (2003). One possible explanation is that the reading of words is suppressed in those who are highly suggestible, allowing them to name the colour in which the word is printed with ease. This would mean that even an apparently automatic process such as word reading can be controlled by means of hypnosis. More generally, it suggests that cognitive processes normally considered to be automatic are nonetheless susceptible to "top-down influences exerted by suggestion at the neural level" (Raz et al., 2003, p. 343).

Several PET and fMRI studies have been designed to shed light on the brain processes underlying Stroop task performance (MacLeod & MacDonald, 2000, pp. 386–390). These studies compare blood flows to different regions of the brain for performance in incongruent and control conditions. Among the brain regions most often identified in these studies are the **dorsolateral prefrontal cortex (DLPFC)** and the **anterior cingulate cortex (ACC)**. The relative locations of these areas are shown in Figure 4.2. The DLPFC is called *dorso* (short for *dorsal*), meaning that it is towards the top of the cortex as opposed to the bottom (*ventral*). *Lateral* refers to the outside as opposed to the inside (*medial*) part of the cortex. *Prefrontal* means that it is located at the front of the frontal lobes. So the *dorsolateral prefrontal cortex* is located towards the

Dorsolateral prefrontal cortex (DLPFC)
An area of the brain that may exert a top-down bias that favours the selection of task-relevant information.

Anterior cingulate cortex (ACC)
An area of the brain that may detect conflicting response tendencies of the sort that the Stroop task elicits.

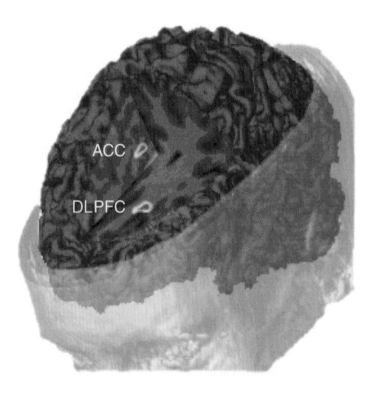

FIGURE 4.2 The dorsolateral prefrontal cortex and the anterior cingulate cortex

From: MacLeod, C.M., & MacDonald, P.A. (2000). Interdimensional interference in the Stroop effect: Uncovering the cognitive and neural anatomy of attention. *Trends in Cognitive Science, 4*, 382–391. Reprinted by permission of Elsevier.

top, outside part of the front of the frontal lobes (Harrison, 2001, p. 160). The ACC is called *anterior*, meaning towards the front as opposed to the back (*posterior*). *Cingulate* means "arch-shaped."

In general, the prefrontal areas are thought to exert "a top-down bias that favours the selection of task-relevant information. . . . [S]uch a bias is especially important for exerting control when task-irrelevant information can effectively compete with task-relevant information for priority in processing" (Milham, Banich, & Barad, 2004, p. 212). Both the DLPFC and the ACC may be "activated among some tasks that require processes to resolve among competing responses. We also know that these brain regions are not necessarily involved in all such tasks, but that other regions may be recruited instead" (Jonides, Badre, Curtis, Thompson-Schill, & Smith, 2002, p. 243).

A great deal of speculation has centred on the role of the ACC. One possibility is that it detects conflicting response tendencies of the sort that the Stroop task elicits. It's also possible that heightened ACC activity is accompanied by heightened awareness of such conflicts (Mayr, 2004). However, the precise role of the ACC may change depending on the specific task with which the person is dealing (Kéri, Decety, Roland, & Gulyás, 2003, p. 31). The ACC should probably be seen as one part of a network responsible for attentional control, "communicating with other equally essential components within this network . . . [and having] multiple functions depending on the content and origin of the signals from other components in the attentional network" (Tibbetts, 2001, p. 329).

ATTENTION CAPTURE AND INATTENTIONAL BLINDNESS

If you're walking down the hall and someone behind you says your name, chances are that you will attend to that voice and turn around. This is an example of **attention capture**: the diversion of attention by a stimulus so powerful that it compels us to notice it even when our attention is focused on something else. Intuitively, attention capture would appear to be "ecologically useful . . . [because it enables] attention to be drawn to new objects in the field [that] may well represent either an important threat to be avoided (like a predator) or an important opportunity to be sought out (like prey)" (Pashler, Johnston, & Ruthruff, 2001, p. 632). It's possible that we are "tuned" to pick up useful information even when our attention is directed elsewhere.

The reverse of attention capture is **inattentional blindness**: failure to attend to events that we might be expected to notice. "Imagine an experienced pilot attempting to land an airplane on a busy runway. He pays close attention to his display console, carefully watching the airspeed indicator on his windshield to make sure he does not stall, yet he never sees that another airplane is blocking his runway" (Mack, 2003, p. 180). According to Mack, Haines (1991) found that some experienced pilots using flight simulators did just that, failing to notice the second plane until it was too late to abort the landing. A great many accidents may be due to inattentional blindness.

Although attention capture and inattentional blindness might appear to be contradictory, they actually go hand in hand. Let's begin with inattentional blindness. Recall the Neisser and Becklen (1975) experiment on selective looking that we discussed in the section on selective attention. Participants who were shown two overlapping videos of different sequences of events were able to attend to one sequence without being distracted by the other. In a subsequent study using the selective looking paradigm,

Attention capture
The diversion of attention by a stimulus so powerful that it compels us to notice it even when our attention is focused on something else.

Inattentional blindness
Failure to attend to events that we might be expected to notice.

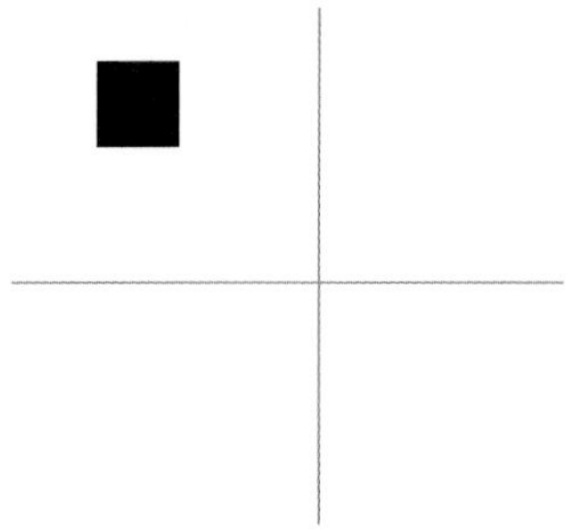

FIGURE 4.3 **Asymmetrical crosses and inattentional blindness**

The participant judges the relative line lengths of the cross and may fail to see the black square.

Simons (2000; Simons & Chabris, 1999) showed participants overlapping videos of two teams playing basketball and asked them to count the passes made by one of the teams. Accordingly, the participants paid close attention to one or the other of the teams, and 73 per cent of them failed to notice a gorilla walk across the screen. Even when the gorilla stopped and pounded its chest, only 50 per cent of the participants noticed it!

Mack and Rock (1998; Mack, 2003) used a different experimental paradigm to investigate inattentional blindness. Participants were shown a series of asymmetrical crosses and on each trial were asked to judge which arm of the cross was longer. On the fourth trial the display included a new feature: a small black square located in one of the quadrants defined by the cross. Thus the critical fourth trial looked something like Figure 4.3. When the participants were asked if they had seen anything other than the cross, many said they had not. Paying attention to the cross, they had failed to perceive the unexpected intrusion.

Among the issues addressed by Mack and Rock's paradigm is the question of whether unattended stimuli are nevertheless registered by the system and able to influence behaviour. This question is closely related to the idea of subliminal perception discussed in Chapter 3. To address it, Mack and Rock presented a word in one of the quadrants defined by the cross and later asked participants to perform a word completion task. They hypothesized that if a priming effect was observed for a word to which participants were inattentionally blind, that "would indicate that the unseen word was registered and encoded below the level of conscious awareness" (p. 176).

For example, Mack and Rock would present a word such as *chart* in one of the quadrants of the cross and sometime later they would ask participants to complete the word stem *cha– –*. The fact that so many common words begin with *cha—chair*, *chase*, *charm*, and so on—made it very unlikely that anyone would choose to create the word *chart* by chance. However, participants who had been shown the word *chart* and claimed not to have seen it were much more likely than those who had not been shown it to use the letters *rt* to complete the word-stem. These results were evidence "of the processing, registration and encoding of the unseen and unidentified words presented under conditions of inattention" (Mack & Rock, 1998, p. 179).

Merikle, Smilek, and Eastwood (2001) observed that Mack and Rock's technique for studying attention is more **ecologically valid** than techniques used to investigate unconscious perception that rely on masking or manipulation of the quality of the stimulus. The Mack and Rock paradigm reflects the very common situation in which

Ecologically valid
Generalizable to conditions in the real world.

there are many unattended stimuli outside [an individual's] immediate focus of attention which are not consciously experienced. In these situations, the unattended stimuli could be consciously experienced if the person's focus of attention changed so that it was directed toward the relevant spatial locations. For this reason, the experimental conditions in studies in which unattended stimuli are presented at spatial locations removed from the current focus of attention more closely resemble the conditions under which visual stimuli are perceived in everyday situations. (p. 121)

Mack and Rock's (1998) paradigm has also been used to find out what types of stimuli capture attention. In one variation of the experiment, Mack and Rock (1998) used a happy cartoon face rather than small black squares. The happy faces were detected 85 per cent of the time. Other stimulus categories such as simple circles were

COGNITION IN ACTION
BOX 4.1

Déjà Vu

This is a common experience in which you have the impression of having previously experienced the situation in which you find yourself, accompanied by the sense that this may not in fact be the case. **Déjà vu** has been studied by psychologists for at least 100 years. As Brown (2003) observed, it's unfortunate that déjà vu has typically been associated with paranormal and pathological experiences, because this has hindered its investigation as a common experience for "ordinary" people. In fact, the results of more than 41 surveys together suggest that approximately two-thirds of us have had at least one déjà vu experience (Brown, 2003, p. 397). Are you one of those people? If so, you have lots of company.

Interesting demographics are associated with the experience of déjà vu. For one thing, people over the age of 60 are less likely to report having had a déjà vu experience than are people in their twenties. As Brown observes, this is an illogical outcome, since everyone who reaches the age of 60 was once 20. The explanation seems to be that social attitudes have changed, and people today are more willing to report déjà vu experiences than they might have been in the 1960s (Brown, 2003, p. 400). Although there are no reliable gender differences in the frequency of déjà vu experiences, there are socio-economic, educational, and travel differences. Those who are higher on the socio-economic scale, the better-educated, and the well-travelled are more likely than others to report déjà vu experiences. Such differences may occur because wealthy, well-educated, and worldly people are more likely to experience the novel situations that may provide the occasion for a déjà vu experience.

Brown reviews several possible explanations of déjà vu. One plausible candidate centres on priming associated with inattentional blindness. As we have seen, Mack and Rock's studies showed that people often fail to perceive something right in front of them, "hiding in plain sight" as it were; yet what they did not see can still register below the level of awareness and influence the way they structure their subsequent experience. "For example, one may enter a room talking on a cell phone while looking directly at a particular stimulus, and moments later this same stimulus is consciously perceived and elicits a déjà vu" (Brown, 2003, p. 407).

Déjà vu
The impression of having previously experienced the situation in which one finds oneself, accompanied by the sense that this is not actually the case.

---

detected as rarely as 15 per cent of the time. This result suggests that faces may be special. Indeed, Lavie and her colleagues (Lavie, Ro, & Russell, 2003; Ro, Russell, & Lavie, 2001) have provided evidence for the hypothesis that faces are more likely to attract attention than other classes of stimuli. In one experiment they used a version of a so-called **flanker task**: participants had to search the computer screen for the name of a famous person and then indicate whether that person was a show-business personality (e.g., Michael Jackson) or politician (e.g., Bill Clinton). The name might appear in any of several locations on the screen, sometimes by itself and sometimes within a list of letter strings (e.g., Csiprmy Qhplrt). Meanwhile, on the periphery of the screen was a picture of either the person whose name was being sought (congruent condition) or a person from the opposite category (incongruent condition). One screen from this task is presented in Figure 4.4. Thus a congruent condition would be to search for Bill Clinton's name while his picture was being shown, while an incongruent condition would be to search for Michael Jackson's name while Clinton's picture was shown. Participants were told to ignore the face and, when they found the name, to press a key indicating whether it belonged to a celebrity or to a politician. Of course, it took longer to identify the name correctly as the number of alternatives on the name list increased

Flanker task
An experiment in which participants may be influenced by an irrelevant stimulus beside the target.

Cslprmy Qhplrt
Bmpt Vrtjkslcg
Gtklsd Njplrtdn
Sfhgjc Xnkprkm
Michael Jackson
Lsjflym Gslpkn

FIGURE 4.4   **Example of a flanker task**

This example shows an incongruent condition. The target name (Michael Jackson) could appear in any of the six positions in the list of names, and the face could appear on either the left or the right.

From: Lavie, N., Ro, T, & Russell, C. (2003). The role of perceptual load in processing distractor faces. *Psychological Science, 14,* 510–515.

from 1 to 2 to 4 to 6 (i.e., the more alternatives through which the participant must search). Incongruent conditions also took longer than congruent ones, indicating that the faces were not ignored but in fact interfered with reaction time. Importantly, the size of this distractor effect was the same at all list lengths.

This finding stood in contrast to the results of a parallel study in which participants searched for the names of either musical instruments or fruits while pictures of musical instruments or fruits were the distractor items. Here again, there was an effect of list length and a congruence effect, with incongruent trials generally taking longer. However, the congruence effect was reduced and eventually disappeared as the list got longer. If we compare the two studies, we see that as task difficulty increased, faces continued to distract the participants, but fruits and musical instruments did not. In other words, faces were always attended to, no matter what else the participants were supposed to be doing. By contrast, participants "gave up" on attending to musical instruments when the overall task became too difficult. Lavie, Ro, and Russell (2003, p. 510) concluded that "face processing may be mandatory." It seems that attention to faces is involuntary: we can't help noticing them, even when we try to ignore them.

Faces are not the only things that capture our attention. It turns out that representations of the human body do as well. Downing, Bray, Rogers, and Childs (2004) used the same technique that Mack and Rock (1998) did in their attentional blindness study, placing silhouettes of whole human bodies as well as other objects in different quadrants of the cross. The bodies were detected at a much higher rate than were the other objects (e.g., telephones, guns, or even human hands).

Downing and his colleagues discussed their findings in relation to the suggestion that there may be **domain-specific modules** in the brain that automatically process faces (e.g., Farah, 1996; Kanwisher, McDermott, & Chun, 1997). The existence of such a module would mean that in the presence of a face we can't help but attend to it. Does the finding that human bodies capture attention mean that there may also be a module specialized for detecting bodies? Downing and colleagues conclude that there may indeed be "independent neural systems for a few object types" (2003, p. B28). However,

Domain-specific modules
The hypothesis that parts of the brain may be specialized for particular tasks, such as recognizing faces.

such modules need not be innate. Rather, it may be that over time we gain expertise in dealing with particular categories of stimuli, such as faces and bodies. If modules for faces and bodies are not innate, it's possible that certain brain areas may be recruited to process stimuli of this kind (Gauthier, Skudlarski, Gore, & Anderson, 2000). This issue is likely to be a focus of research for some time (Gauthier, Curran, Curby, & Collins, 2003; Rhodes, Byatt, Michie, & Puce, 2004).

A related issue involves the heightened ability of particular stimuli to capture attention. For example, it has been known for a long time that a person's own name has the power to capture that person's attention (e.g., Moray, 1959). Mack and his colleagues (Mack, Pappas, Silverman, & Gay, 2002, p. 504), who considered this finding in conjunction with other studies of attention capture, have suggested that highly meaningful stimuli are able to capture our attention; this would explain why a mother will awake to her child's cry while others remain asleep. "[M]eaning is the primary determinant of selective attention and therefore of the content of perceptual consciousness. We see what interests us, what we are looking for and what we are expecting."

Finally, Horstmann (2002) has placed the discussion of attention capture in the context of the perceptual cycle (Neisser, 1976). As we noted in Chapter 1, this is the cycle in which our expectations (i.e., schemata) guide our exploration of the environment, but the environment itself can also influence our experience of it. "If attentional capture were always conditional on an intention, organisms would perceive only what they intended to see; other events would rarely be recognized, and threats would be frequently overlooked" (Horstmann, 2002, p. 504). Although we often see only what we are looking for, if something meaningful happens that we were not expecting, we recognize it very quickly. What examples from your own experience can you think of?

Dual Tasks and the Limits of Attention

One obvious question about attention concerns its capacity. How many things can we attend to at once? The answer to this question may depend on what sorts of things we are trying to do and how skilled we are at doing them. Although it's easy to see how we are able to perform a voluntary task in conjunction with an automatic one, such as carrying on a conversation while walking, it's not so easy to imagine doing two goal-directed things at once. We can do more than one simple task at a time, but as the tasks become more complex they begin to interfere with one another. An example often used to make this point involves the task of driving a car (e.g., C.D. Wickens, 1984). If you are a skilled driver and you are driving a route you know well, then your task is relatively simple. Under these conditions, you may also be able to carry on a lively conversation as you drive. However, should something out of the ordinary happen—if it starts snowing heavily, for example—then driving is likely to become a more complex task.

As Hirst (1986; Hirst & Kalmar, 1987) pointed out, the notion that attention is limited might be conceptualized in different ways. It might mean that attention is like a power supply (Kahneman, 1973) or a reservoir of fuel. If you try to do too much, you will simply run out of gas. Performance on a task has a limit imposed by the capacity of the fuel tank that powers attention. For obvious reasons, this model of attention is called a **capacity model**.

Capacity model
The hypothesis that attention is like a power supply that can support only a limited amount of attentional activity.

Structural limits
The hypothesis that attentional tasks interfere with one another to the extent that they involve similar activities.

Central bottleneck
The hypothesis that there is only one path along which information can travel, and it is so narrow that the most it can handle at any one time is the information relevant to one task.

Divided attention
The ability to attend to more than one thing at a time.

Another possibility is that attention has **structural limits**. If two tasks require the same kind of activity, then they may interfere with each other more than they would if each required a different kind of activity. For example, we can make a distinction between auditory and visual processes. You might very well be able to have a visual image of your living room and describe it in words at the same time. However, suppose you were asked to think of (without writing down) the sentence "A bird in the hand is worth two in the bush" and then categorize each word as either a noun or not a noun by saying yes or no (L.R. Brooks, 1968). The correct sequence would be "no, yes, no, no, yes, no, no, yes, no, no, yes."

This task turns out to be quite hard. Try it yourself for the sentence, "Wise men make proverbs and fools repeat them." The problem is that you are trying to do two highly verbal tasks at the same time: imagining a sentence may require you to say it to yourself, and categorizing the words requires you to say yes and no. Saying two things at once is not easy. If you perform the same task by tapping with your left hand for a noun and tapping with your right hand for a non-noun, then it's easier. This is because the two tasks are quite different: tapping is a non-verbal process and therefore interferes less with a verbal task. From this viewpoint, interference between tasks is more likely to occur if they both draw on the same processing resources (e.g., both visual or both verbal) (Kahneman & Treisman, 1984).

Some theories see attention as requiring a central processor (e.g., Broadbent, 1984). If that is the case, then we can't pay attention to more than one thing at a time. This is because the central processor will be able to handle only one task at a time, and if another task is added, then the processor will have to switch from one task to another. It's as if there is a **central bottleneck** through which information relevant to only one task at a time can pass (Pashler, 1994). Doing two things at once will require you to alternate your attention between the two tasks and selectively attend to only one at a time. Can we learn to attend to more than one thing at a time? If so, we would have mastered the skill of **divided attention**. If we were able to successfully divide our attention, then perhaps with practice our attention could improve beyond normal limits.

An influential study of divided attention was conducted by Spelke, Hirst, and Neisser (1976). Few students would attempt to read and take lecture notes at the same time. Yet this is essentially what these researchers taught their participants to do. In their first study, they trained two participants, named Diane and John, to read short stories while copying dictated words; the participants were then given comprehension tests regarding what they had read while taking dictation. This dual task was very difficult at first, but after roughly six weeks of practice their comprehension was as good as it had been for reading stories alone. However, at this stage Diane and John were not picking up information about the words being dictated to them; for instance, they did not notice that some of the words in the lists came from the same category (e.g., vehicles). They were then told to try to notice any special characteristics of the dictated words. The two participants were soon able to recognize the relationships between the dictated words even while reading with comprehension. In another experiment with new participants, comprehension and speed of reading did not suffer even when the difficulty of the material to be read was increased; performance when doing both tasks was equal to performance when reading alone.

In a follow-up study, Hirst, Spelke, Reaves, Caharack, and Neisser (1980) trained two participants, Arlene and Mary, to simultaneously read and copy complete sentences. Here are examples of some of the dictated sentences:

> The rope broke.
> Spot got free.
> Father chased him.

The participants were tested to see if they could recognize sentences that had been dictated to them. Here are examples of some of the test sentences:

> Father chased him.
> Spot chased Father.
> Spot's rope broke.

The first of the test sentences should be recognized as one of the originally dictated sentences. The second sentence should not be recognized. The third sentence might be falsely recognized if the participants were paying attention to the dictated sentences. The reason for this is that people will often make inferences on the basis of what they hear (Bransford & Franks, 1971). They will then often falsely recognize these inferences as sentences they actually heard. This is in fact what happened in the study by Hirst et al. This result can be taken as demonstrating that the participants genuinely understood the sentences they were writing while they were reading. In other words, they were not taking the dictation mechanically, without paying attention, any more than they were reading mechanically, without paying attention.

Perhaps people can learn to genuinely divide their attention between two tasks, rather than just switch it rapidly back and forth between two tasks. Perhaps so-called "simultaneous" translators, who listen to a speaker in one language and very quickly translate that speech into another language, have perfected this skill as well (Hirst, Neisser, & Spelke, 1978, p. 61). However, the studies we have just reviewed do not disprove the hypothesis that people who seem to be doing two things at once are actually switching very rapidly from one to the other. "It is quite possible that critical mental operations on the two tasks never proceed at the same time, but [participants] are nonetheless able to smoothly switch back and forth between the two tasks" (Pashler, Johnston, & Ruthruff, 2001, p. 644).

Do bottlenecks still exist with highly practised tasks? Experiments on this subject typically involve figuring out what response goes with what stimulus; this is called "stimulus response mapping." For example, participants might be presented with one of three tones—low, middle, or high—and asked to say "one" for the low, "two" for the middle, and "three" for the high tone. This task maps auditory stimuli onto verbal responses. Another task might map visual stimuli onto manual responses. For example, the participant might see a stimulus appear in one of three locations on a computer screen and respond by pressing a key with one of three fingers (index, middle, or ring). We can think of these tasks as consisting of three stages (Hazeltine, Teague, & Ivry, 2002, p. 532). The first stage is identification of the stimulus, the second would be use of central processor to select of the appropriate response (this is where the attentional bottleneck comes in), and the third would be the execution of the response.

One of the experiments reported by Hazeltine, Teague, and Ivry (2002) used the tasks described in the previous paragraph. Participants were trained on each task

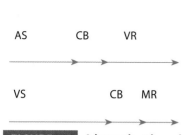

FIGURE 4.5 **A latent bottleneck**

AS = auditory stimulus; VS = visual stimulus; CB = central bottleneck; VR = verbal response; MR = motor response. The processing stages for AS and VS end at different times, allowing each to be processed separately by the central bottleneck.

separately and then asked to execute them simultaneously. That is, the visual and auditory stimuli were presented at the same time, and participants were instructed to execute both tasks as fast as they could. The conclusion was that "participants were able to achieve levels of performance under dual task conditions that were similar to those obtained under single task conditions" (Hazeltine, Teague, & Ivry, 2002, p. 530). The experimenters found no evidence of a central bottleneck that could not be overcome through practice. They also pointed out that the ability to perform two tasks simultaneously without interference (i.e., to perform them as well together as separately) may require that the stimulus and response phases of each process involve different modalities (e.g., auditory and visual stimuli, verbal and motor responses).

You might think that would be the end of the matter, but Ruthruff, Johnston, Van Selst, Whitsell, and Remington (2003) observed that it is still logically possible for a "latent" bottleneck to exist even for highly practised tasks. This possibility is represented in Figure 4.5. Notice that the "pre-bottleneck" stages finish at different times. This allows each task to pass through the bottleneck separately. You can see how many logical possibilities there are even in an apparently simple situation such as the dual-task experiment. That is one reason why research in cognition seldom progresses rapidly. Since it's necessary to examine all the logical possibilities before definitive conclusions can be drawn, the process is both labour-intensive and time-consuming.

MIND WANDERING AND DUAL TASKS

Typically, when we talk about "dual task" situations, we are referring to conditions under which an individual is given two tasks that must be performed at the same time. For instance, we have already discussed how Spelke and colleagues (1976) had participants read stories and take dictation at the same time. Another example would be a railway engineer who has to perform at least two tasks at a time while operating a train. Remember the reason the engineers discussed in the case study at the beginning of this chapter crashed their trains: they were trying simultaneously to monitor signals and use their cell phones. Since both tasks draw on the limited pool of attentional resources, they simply cannot be done effectively at the same time (see Box 4.2).

But let's consider for a moment a different kind of "dual task" situation, illustrated by a near-accident involving two commuter trains. Railway safety investigator Randy Jamieson (personal communication) tells of an incident in which a veteran engineer with a perfect performance record ran a red light and almost smashed his train right into an oncoming train. It would have been another Chatsworth, and possibly worse. Fortunately, the engineer noticed the red signal in time to radio an emergency call to the oncoming train, engage his emergency brakes, and stop the train. Onboard cameras from the cab of the offending train show that as it left the preceding station, the engineer was agitated, pacing around the cab and audibly talking to himself. At times he was shaking his head and moving his fingers as if counting something. As the train progressed, and between these agitated behaviours, the engineer called into the radio (as stipulated by the rules) both of the yellow lights that preceded the red light. Yet even though he acknowledged the yellow lights, he didn't slow his train: instead, he sped up. The train was moving quite quickly when the red light came into view, at which point the engineer initiated emergency manoeuvres, stopping the train just in time. A post-incident

CONSIDER THIS
BOX 4.2

Are You Resistant to Dual-Task Interference?

There is considerable evidence that using a cell phone while driving can hurt driving performance, even if the phone is hands-free (see Strayer & Drews, 2007, for a review). As we saw in Chapter 1, using a cell phone not only slows driving-related responses (Strayer & Johnston, 2001) but impairs memory for signs on the side of the road (Strayer, Drews & Johnston, 2003). Yet it seems that there are some people for whom performing a secondary task while driving does not measurably reduce driving performance. Could you be one of those people, the ones Watson and Strayer (2010) call "supertaskers"? Watson and Strayer (2010) had a larger number of university students do a driving task in a simulator either as a single task, or while solving math problems (a dual-task situation). The driving performance of most of the participants suffered when they had to simultaneously complete a secondary task. Strikingly, however, 2.5 per cent of the participants seemed to be completely unaffected by the secondary task. Figure 4.6 shows this pattern of results for the time it takes to initiate braking when an obstacle appeared; the only people who weren't affected by the dual task were the supertaskers. If you're tempted to think that you might be one of them, don't be surprised if you find out you're not: remember, only about 2.5 per cent of the people in any population fall into that category.

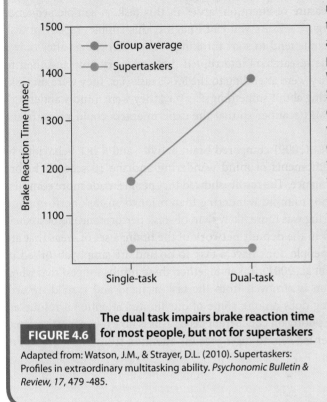

FIGURE 4.6 The dual task impairs brake reaction time for most people, but not for supertaskers

Adapted from: Watson, J.M., & Strayer, D.L. (2010). Supertaskers: Profiles in extraordinary multitasking ability. *Psychonomic Bulletin & Review, 17,* 479 -485.

interview with the engineer revealed that he had been having problems with the train and had got into an argument with his supervisor at the preceding station. As he left that station, therefore, he was preoccupied, ruminating on the mechanical problems he had experienced and replaying the argument with his supervisor over and over in his mind. In Mr Jamieson's opinion, the engineer's attentional resources had been absorbed in his thoughts and so diverted away from the safe operation of the train. In effect, it was as if the engineer's thoughts were an internally imposed secondary task that had placed him in a "dual task" situation of sorts. Could this really be the case? Can **mind wandering** take attention away from the task at hand?

The answer appears to be a resounding "yes." According to a recent study by a research group at the University of British Columbia, both task performance and brain activity clearly showed that mind wandering was associated with reduced attention to the primary task (Christoff, Gordon, Smallwood, Smith & Schooler, 2009).

Mind wandering
A shift of mental resources away from the task at hand and towards internal thoughts.

Sustained attention to response task (SART)
A continuous response task in which digits (e.g., 0 to 9) are sequentially presented on a computer screen and participants are asked to press a button in response to all but one of them (e.g., the infrequent digit 3); response to this infrequent digit is supposed to be withheld (see Robertson et al., 1997).

Commission error
Failure to withhold a response to the infrequent digit in the SART.

Default network
A set of brain areas that are active when an individual does not have a specific task to do and is absorbed in internal thought.

The participants in this study were required to perform a version of the **sustained attention to response task** (SART), which involves pressing a response button (e.g., the spacebar) when a digit is presented on a computer screen and withholding a response when an infrequent "critical digit" is presented (see Robertson, et al., 1997). In this particular case, the digits 0 to 9 were presented every two seconds and the critical digit requiring a non-response was 3, which occurred roughly five per cent of the time. Since withholding a response to the infrequent critical digit requires attention, failure to do so is a good indicator that attention is disengaged from the task; thus **commission errors** are the primary measure of attention lapses in this task. A sample sequence of trials is illustrated in Figure 4.7. As you can imagine, this simple, repetitive task is very boring, and thus people tend to start thinking about other things after only a short time. Importantly, the researchers interrupted the task every now and then to ask participants whether they were attending to the SART task (i.e., they were on task) or whether they were thinking about something else (i.e., they were mind wandering). The task was done in an fMRI scanner so that the experimenters could measure the brain activity in each case.

Christoff and colleagues (2009) compared brain activity and SART behaviour in the 10 seconds preceding moments of mind wandering and the 10 seconds before moments of on-task performance. The results showed that people made more commission errors on the SART prior to mind wandering than prior to on-task performance. Furthermore, mind wandering was more likely than on-task performance to be associated with increased activity in the **default network** of the brain: a set of areas that are known to be active when people don't have a task to do and are simply absorbed in their thoughts (see Raichle et al., 2001). Taken together, these results suggest that when the mind wanders, attention is removed from the task at hand and turned inward. Apparently, mind wandering does require some of our limited attentional resources, leading us to perform more poorly on concurrent tasks. This is how the mental ruminations of the railway engineer led him to disengage his attention from the operation of the train and run a red light.

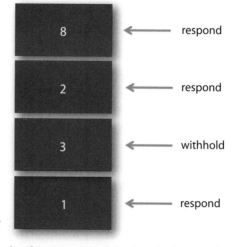

An example of a sequence of displays in the sustained attention to response task (SART)

FIGURE 4.7

FIGURE 4.8 An action slip: Putting a plastic coffee lid on a porcelain mug

Have you ever started walking down the street and noticed that you still had your slippers on? Or absent-mindedly tried to fit a plastic coffee lid on your porcelain mug? Or put the cereal box in the fridge and the milk in the cupboard? If you know what it's like to make this kind of mistake, you're in good company. In fact, according to James Reason (1979; 1984; see also Norman, 1981) these **action slips** are quite common, especially when we are preoccupied with "**parallel mental activity**" (Reason, 1979, p. 76)—a fancy term for "mind wandering."

Reason (1979; 1984) described a series of diary studies in which participants were asked to keep a record of every silly (and not so silly) error they made. Interestingly, Reason found that these errors are often attention- and memory-related, and that they tend to occur more at certain times of the day than at others. To keep track of your own everyday mistakes, use a diary or your smart phone to record the error, the circumstances surrounding it, and the time of day. After doing this for several weeks, look to see if there are any patterns.

Action slips
The kind of behavioural errors that often occur in everyday life.

Parallel mental activity
Thinking about something other than the task at hand.

THE ATTENTIONAL BLINK

Another fascinating demonstration of the limits of human attention is known as the **attentional blink** or **AB** (Shapiro, Arnell, & Raymond, 1997). Suppose you present a series of letters in the centre of a screen and ask participants to identify them. The attentional blink occurs when two of these stimuli are presented within 550 milliseconds of each other. During that very short interval, the probability that the second letter will be reported is much less than it would be for a longer interval. In such cases it's as if participants' attention "blinks" and leaves them with nothing to report. One interpretation of these results is that participants apply their attentional resources to the first letter and then don't have enough attentional resources left to apply to the second letter. Since awareness of the letters requires that you allocate sufficient attentional resources to them, you are aware of the first one but completely unaware of the second.

Olivers and Nieuwenhuis (2005) have reported some very counterintuitive findings, which suggest there is something you can do to reduce the attentional blink. They presented participants with a rapid stream of roughly 15 letters and two numbers. The letters were to be ignored and the two numbers were targets. While this procedure might seem very similar to the SART task described earlier, the AB task is quite different with regard to the speed of presentation. In the SART the items are presented every 2 seconds and each item is considered to be a single trial. By contrast, in the AB task the items are presented about every 120 ms and each stream of 17 items constitutes a single trial. The quick presentation of successive stimuli is often referred to as **rapid serial visual presentation (RSVP)**. An example of an RSVP stream is shown in Panel A of Figure 4.9. After the RSVP stream, participants are asked to report the first number and then the second number.

Attentional blink
Failure to notice the second of two stimuli presented within 550 milliseconds of each other.

Rapid serial visual presentation (RSVP)
The presentation of a series of stimuli in quick succession.

Olivers and Nieuwenhuis varied the number of letters intervening between the two target digits. When there is one intervening item between the first digit (Target One: T1) and the second digit (Target Two: T2), T2 is said to be presented at Lag 2 because T2 is the second item after T1. At Lag 3 there are two intervening letters between T1 and T2, and so on. Because the attentional blink typically occurs only when two targets are presented in close temporal proximity, one would expect the most blinking to occur at short lags and for performance to improve at longer lags.

More important, Olivers and Nieuwenhuis also included a condition in which participants completed the AB task in silence, and a condition in which they listened to music while completing the AB task. We will refer to these two conditions as the "no-music" and "music" conditions, respectively. The music in the music condition was meant to function as a concurrent, though irrelevant, task that might engage some attentional resources. How would this secondary task influence performance in the AB? Based on the studies we have discussed thus far, you might think that the music would deplete attentional resources, making the attentional blink larger.

The results of the Olivers and Nieuwenhuis study are shown in Panel B of Figure 4.9. The figure shows the accuracy with which participants were able to identify the second digit (T2) as a function of Lag between T1 and T2, as well as whether or not participants listened to music while doing the task. Strikingly, the results showed that playing music actually reduced the magnitude of the attentional blink, leading to very high accuracy of T2 identification! Olivers and Nieuwenhuis (2005, p. 268) concluded that "performance on an attentionally demanding visual detection task may improve when the task is accompanied by task-irrelevant mental activity." So at least in some cases, it appears that allocating some attention to a secondary task may actually improve performance in the primary task.

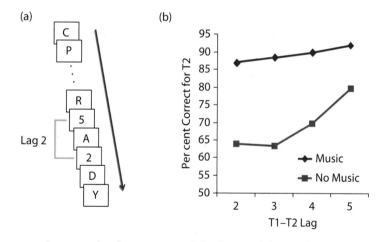

FIGURE 4.9 An example of a sequence of displays and the results of an attentional blink study reported by Olivers and Nieuwenhuis (2005)

Panel A: A sequence of displays illustrating T1 and T2 separated by a Lag of 2. The dots illustrate other intervening letter displays. *Panel B*: The accuracy with which T2 is identified. Notice that there is a substantial attentional blink in the No Music condition, which is largely absent in the Music condition.

Adapted from: Olivers, N. L. & Nieuwenhuis, S. (2005). The beneficial effect of concurrent task-irrelevant mental activity on temporal attention. *Psychological Science*, 16, 265–269. Only some of the conditions in the actual study are represented in the figure.

The attentional blink has also been used to address other issues related to attention and perception. Shapiro, Arnell, and Raymond (1997) explored whether the second target, which is not perceived consciously because it occurs shortly after the first target (i.e., T2 is in the attentional blink), could nevertheless be processed unconsciously and still have a priming effect. Suppose you presented *three* targets in a row, with the second and third being semantically related words (e.g., *lawyer*, *judge*). Suppose further that the second word (*lawyer*) is "blinked." It turns out that the third word (*judge*) is more likely to be correctly identified than it would be if the second word had been semantically unrelated to it (e.g., *tree*) (Shapiro, Arnell, & Raymond, 1997, pp. 291–292). This elegant evidence for perception in the absence of attention further supports the existence of subliminal perception, which we discussed in Chapter 3.

Barnard, Scott, Taylor, May, and Knightley (2004) have used the attentional blink to reinforce the connection between attention and meaning. In one study they presented

> lists of 35 words . . . at a rate of 110 ms/item, with one word replacing another with no interstimulus interval. Most words referred to things or events occurring in natural environments (e.g., *island*, *snowstorm*). Participants were instructed to report a single target, a word that referred to a job or profession that people engage in for pay (e.g., *banker*, *shepherd*). On test trials, targets were preceded . . . by a potential distractor word and the semantic relationship between distractor and target was varied. (p. 179)

One class of distractor items included words referring to activities for which people are not paid, such as *shopper*, *coward*, and *witness*. Because these distractors are also properties of people, they are semantically related to the target. Another class of distractor was inanimate (e.g., *freezer*, *cupboard*, *wireless*), and thus less closely related to the target. When a semantically related word preceded a target word, there was a greater likelihood of an attentional blink than when an inanimate word preceded the target. That is, people were less likely to report the target when it followed a semantically related word than when it followed an inanimate word.

One important feature of this study was that the targets and distractors differed only in meaning, not in characteristics such as colour (Barnard et al., 2004, p. 179). The participants were set to attend to *jobs that people do for pay*. The more meaningfully the item was related to the target, the more it was attended to. Barnard et al. (2004, p. 185) conceived of this process as involving an initial "glance" at an item, followed by a closer "look" if it seemed to be a possible target. The more time was spent looking at an item, the less likely it was that the next item would receive even a "glance." The result was an attentional blink. This account of the attentional blink harks back to Mack's point that highly meaningful stimuli capture our attention. It also recalls the notion that much of cognition involves what Bartlett (1932) called an "effort after meaning." We will consider this point in detail in the next chapter.

▌ Task Switching

The concept of the **set** was reintroduced into psychology after a prolonged absence (Allport, Styles, & Hsieh, 1994). One of the reasons it had fallen into disuse was that some considered it too vague to be useful (e.g., J.J. Gibson, 1941). However, many others, such as R.S. Woodworth (1869–1962), found sets to be essential for explaining human behaviour. One example of a set is the way "an individual often prepares to

Set
A temporary, top-down organization in the brain that facilitates some responses while inhibiting others in order to achieve a certain goal; also referred to as a "mental set."

act before beginning the overt effective action," as when sprinters take their mark on the starting line (Woodworth, 1940, p. 29). Woodworth argued that there are many different kinds of sets. For example, in addition to the preparatory sets illustrated by sprinters there are executive sets that guide us through a sequence of responses, as when driving a car; and goal sets that represent what we aim to achieve. Woodworth described sets as temporary organizations in the brain that act "by facilitating some responses, while preventing or inhibiting others. . . . While looking eagerly for a lost object you do not notice sounds that at other times would surely attract your attention. Readiness for one act is at the same time unreadiness for other acts" (Woodworth, 1940, p. 33). In the context of the distinctions we have been using throughout this chapter, a set is a top-down process that organizes our action to meet a particular goal.

Task switching is one of the research contexts that have led to the revival of the "set" concept. The first systematic investigation of task switching is usually attributed to Jersild (1927). Monsell (2003, p. 134) gives a good example, of which the following is a modified version. Suppose you are at your computer, trying to finish an essay, when an email arrives from the registrar's office, reminding you that today is the deadline for paying the remainder of your fees. You are annoyed at the interruption, but recognize the importance of the message. You look around for your bank card, find it, and head off to the registrar's office. Along the way, you stop and talk with some friends. Each of these tasks—writing an essay, reading an email, finding your bank card, going to the registrar's office, talking to friends—"requires an appropriate configuration of mental resources, a procedural 'schema' . . . or 'task-set.' . . . We exercise intentional 'executive' control to select and implement the task-set, or the combination of task-sets, that are appropriate to our dominant goals . . . , resisting temptations to satisfy other goals" (p. 134).

Closely associated with task switching is the phenomenon known as **switch cost** (Monsell, 2003, p. 135). This cost is a reflection of the fact that performance on a task immediately after a switch is worse than typical performance on the same task. To continue with the example from the previous paragraph, when you return from the registrar's office and start working on your essay again, you may not be able to pick up smoothly where you left off. You may need to reconstruct exactly what you were doing before you switched to the task of reading the email from the registrar. Sometimes switching back to a task can lead you to feel as if you need to start all over again. This may be due to the time required to reset the cognitive system so that the behaviours appropriate to the current task are engaged once again and behaviours appropriate to the previous task are inhibited (Leung & Monsell, 2003, p. 919).

Usually experiments on this topic require participants to switch tasks when given a certain cue by the experimenter. For example, they may be shown a series of letter–number pairs, such as "H 3" (Yeung & Monsell, 2003, p. 923). Participants are required to perform one of two tasks on each trial. In the "alphabet arithmetic" task, they must "add" the number to the letter. In this case the participant would say *K* because *K* is the third letter in the alphabet from *H*. In the "perceptual comparison task" the participant must say "yes" if the letter and the number both contain curved lines or both contain only straight lines. For a pair such as "H 3" the answer would be "no" because the letter has only straight lines while the number has only curved lines (Yeung & Monsell, 2003, p. 922). When cued to do so, participants must switch from whatever task they are currently doing to the other task. A switch cost is reliably observed under such conditions.

Task switching
Changing from working on one task to working on another; usually studied in situations in which the switch is involuntary.

Switch cost
The finding that performance declines immediately on switching tasks.

Arrington and Logan (2004) did a clever experiment that shed light on task switching when the participant, rather than the experimenter, controls precisely when the task switch occurs. Voluntary task switching was initiated by telling the participants that they had to decide which tasks to perform on each trial. The participants' goal was to perform each task about half the time and to try to switch randomly between them, without either counting the number of times they had performed each task or simply alternating between them (Arrington & Logan, 2004, p. 611). On each trial the participants were shown a single digit between 1 and 9. The two tasks consisted of indicating whether the digit was even or odd and indicating whether it was larger or smaller than 5.

Even though the task switching was voluntary, there was still a switch cost for each task. The participants did perform each task approximately half the time. However, although the participants had been instructed to try to switch randomly, they did not in fact do so. Rather, they tended to produce a series of runs on one task, then switch to a series of runs on the other task, then switch back to a series of runs on the first task, and so on. This suggests that once participants are used to one task they may be reluctant to incur the cost of switching to the other. Notice that these participants were not completely free to choose which task to perform but were constrained to try to perform each task about half the time. It's possible that, in a situation where we are completely free to choose which task to perform, we may persist with one task until boredom sets in and we are prepared to pay the switch cost. We will consider the important role that boredom plays in directing our attention in Chapter 13, on personal cognition.

Like other topics we have examined in this chapter, task switching research suggests that top-down processes play an important role in regulating our attention. Indeed, Pashler, Johnston, and Ruthruff (2001) have concluded that one of the "main themes to emerge from" recent research "is the idea that the effects of mental set are more pervasive than had been previously thought" (p. 648). It is also true that recent research has reached "a rather broad consensus that higher level control operations—those operations that implement task sets by selecting, ordering, and chaining lower level task execution processes—are intimately linked to conscious awareness" (Meiran, Hommel, Bibi, & Lev, 2001, p. 10). Task switching requires us to change our set—just the sort of operation that might be expected to show a correlation with awareness. Thus we might assume that people are aware of achieving a preparatory set and know when they are ready to perform the next task. Meiran et al. (2001) tested this assumption by asking participants in a task-switching experiment to indicate for each trial when they were ready. The fact that longer preparation times were not associated with better performance suggested that they were *not* actually aware of whether they were ready or not.

All of this is consistent with earlier research, reviewed by Humphrey (1951/1963, Ch. 2), suggesting that people may be aware of the goal they are trying to achieve, but not of the operations required to achieve it. Although we have reviewed many studies suggesting that we often do have control of our attention, we may still wonder about the extent to which we are aware of, and thus in control of, our attentional processes. This leads directly to our next topic.

Overt Visual Attention

Embodied
Existing within a body; the term reflects the general view that cognition depends not only on the mind but also on the physical constraints of the body in which the mind exists.

Overt attention
Attending to something with eye movement.

Covert attention
Attending to something without eye movement.

Sequential attention hypothesis
A hypothesis about the relationship between overt and covert attention that posits a tight relationship between the two whereby covert attention is shifted first and overt eye movement follows.

Retina
Tissue at the back of the eye that is filled with photoreceptors.

Photoreceptors
Receptor cells in the retina that help transform energy from photons (light) into neural signals.

Fovea
The central region of the retina where photoreceptors are most densely packed.

Based on what we have learned about attention so far, you may be tempted to think that attention has been conceived of only as an internal mental process. Indeed, many models of visual attention construe it as a mental capacity or limited resource. In this section we will see that attention can also be understood as something that is **embodied** and therefore constrained by the nature and limitations of our physical body. In the case of visual attention, this implies considering attention in the context of the physical nature of the eyes, the light receptors in the eye, the nature of the primary visual cortex of the brain, and how the eyes move. The process of attending to objects by moving the eyes to look at them is referred to as **overt attention** and can be contrasted with the process of attending to an object while holding the eyes stationary, which is referred to as **covert attention** (see Findlay & Gilchrist, 2003; Klein & Pontefract, 1994).

The available evidence suggests that the two forms of attention often work closely together. If you choose to attend to another person in the room, for instance, you will likely shift your eyes to wherever that person is. First, however, it's likely that your covert attention will already have moved to that location. Studies using controlled laboratory stimuli have suggested that when new objects are about to be viewed, covert attention shifts to the location first and then is followed by the eyes. This has been referred to as the **sequential attention hypothesis** (Henderson, Pollatsek, & Rayner, 1989; see Findlay & Gilchrist, 2003, for a review). This hypothesis suggests a tight connection between covert and overt attention (Findlay & Gilchrist, 2003).

But the two forms of attention are not always so tightly coupled (Findlay & Gilchrist, 2003). Recall, for instance, the studies of inattentional blindness discussed earlier. In these studies, an object was presented exactly where the person was looking but the latter failed to notice it. If covert attention was focused exactly where the person was looking, how could this happen? Another example of a separation between the two forms of attention occurs when you "look" at something "from the corner of your eye." To experience this, just look straight ahead and, holding your eyes still, try to see what a person in the periphery of your vision is doing. In this case, overt attention is focused straight ahead and covert attention is focused to the side of your line of sight. This is hard to keep up, however; after a few minutes, you may notice that it takes some effort to maintain the dissociation between your covert and overt attention.

Despite the possibility that the eyes and covert attention sometimes move separately, Findlay and Gilchrist (2003) make the strong claim that overt and covert attention in most cases move together and that researchers should focus on studying overt attention because of its critical role in everyday attending. According to Findlay and Gilchrist (2003), the importance of overt attention is related to the physical constraints of the eye. Light enters the eye and hits the tissue at the back, known as the **retina**. Among other things, the retina contains **photoreceptors**, which play a role in the initial steps of turning light energy into a neural signal (see Palmer, 1999). Importantly, the photoreceptors are not evenly spaced across the retina: there is a relatively small area with densely packed photoreceptors surrounded by a region in which the photoreceptors are more widely spaced.

The small area with more photoreceptors is known as the **fovea**. Because of the distribution of photoreceptors, light falling on the fovea is processed with high resolution and so is associated with perception of high acuity, while light falling on the surrounding area is processed with less resolution and therefore is associated with

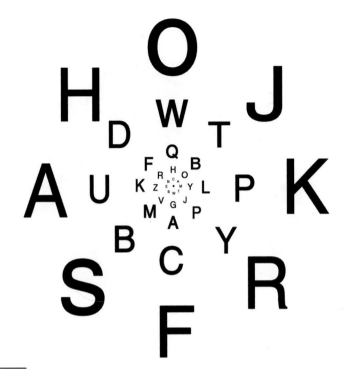

FIGURE 4.10   **How objects would have to vary in size in order to be equally discriminable**

This is assuming that the observer is looking right at the dot in the centre.

From: Anstis, S.M. (1974). A chart demonstrating variations in acuity with retinal position. *Vision Research, 14,* 589–592, by Elsevier Science Publishers. Reprinted by permission.

lower visual acuity. This decline in visual acuity is demonstrated in Figure 4.10. Here we see that when letters are presented outside the fovea, their size must increase rapidly if the amount of visual processing capacity dedicated to them is to be held constant. This means that if you want to see something with good resolution, you have to move your eyes so that information falls on that specific location of the retina. In what follows, we will discuss how overt attention shifts (i.e., how the eyes move) during several everyday tasks such as reading and viewing objects and scenes.

OVERT ATTENTION DURING READING

How do you think your eyes are moving as you read this text? Most people might think their eyes move smoothly along the letters as they read. To accurately measure the behaviour of the eyes, researchers use complicated eye-tracking technology. An example of a modern eye-tracking device is shown in Figure 4.11. This device works by aiming a camera and a small infrared light at the eye and then locating both a reflection of this light off the cornea and the location of the pupil, which is the point where the most light is absorbed. By tracking the bright corneal reflection and dark pupil over time the system is able to determine accurately the current location of a person's gaze.

Although while reading you may subjectively feel that your eyes are moving smoothly from left to right across the page, studies using eye-tracking devices have shown that they are doing quite the opposite. The eyes make a seemingly chaotic series

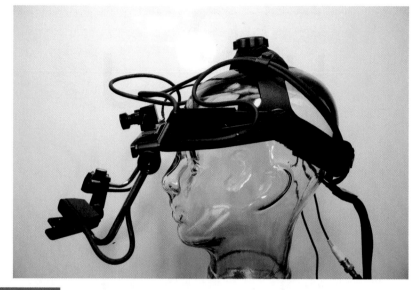

FIGURE 4.11   A modern eye-tracking system

This is an EyeLink II system developed by Canadian-based SR Research. The device is placed on the head and two cameras positioned below the eyes track the location of eye gaze.

Saccades
The rapid, jerky movements made as the eye scans an image.

Fixation
Holding the eye relatively still in order to maintain an image on the fovea.

Nystagmus
Small but continuous movements made by the eye during fixation.

of rapid movements called **saccades** interspersed by moments when they are relatively still, known as **fixations** (see Findlay & Gilchrist, 2003; Palmer, 1999; and Rayner, 1998, for reviews). During fixation the eye is relatively stationary in order to optimize the transmittal of visual information to the brain, while during saccades the eyes move very rapidly and visual information is essentially cut off. The typical fixation duration is between 200 and 300 milliseconds, but times can vary widely depending on the word being fixated, the position where the eye falls within the word, and how well the word has been interpreted (see Rayner, 1998). It's worth keeping in mind that during fixations the eyes are not perfectly stationary. In fact, they are constantly making very minute movements known as **nystagmus** (Rayner, 1998; Palmer, 1999). Typically, eye-tracking programs have an algorithm that uses the velocity and distance of the eye movements to determine whether the eye is in a state of fixation: if the movements are very small, the program assumes that the eye is in a state of fixation; if the movements are larger, it assumes that the eye is making a saccade.

Figure 4.12 shows an example of the eye movements made by someone reading a selection from the book *A Short History of Nearly Everything* by Bill Bryson (2003). The very first fixation made following the appearance of this page of text is indicated with the number "1" and is just below the end of the first paragraph. In this figure circles are drawn at the location of eye fixations made while reading. Average fixations are shown with medium-sized circles while particularly short fixations have smaller circles and, conversely, particularly long fixations are shown with larger ones. As is evident from the circles, most of the time the eyes fixate on a word only once, and for a consistent period, before moving on to the next word perhaps six or more letters on down the line. At other times, though, fixations come in clusters, and a small section of text may receive multiple fixations of varying duration until the reader has come to understand it and is ready to move on. That all of this goes on without our conscious awareness of it—indeed, without any particular intentional control—is quite remarkable.

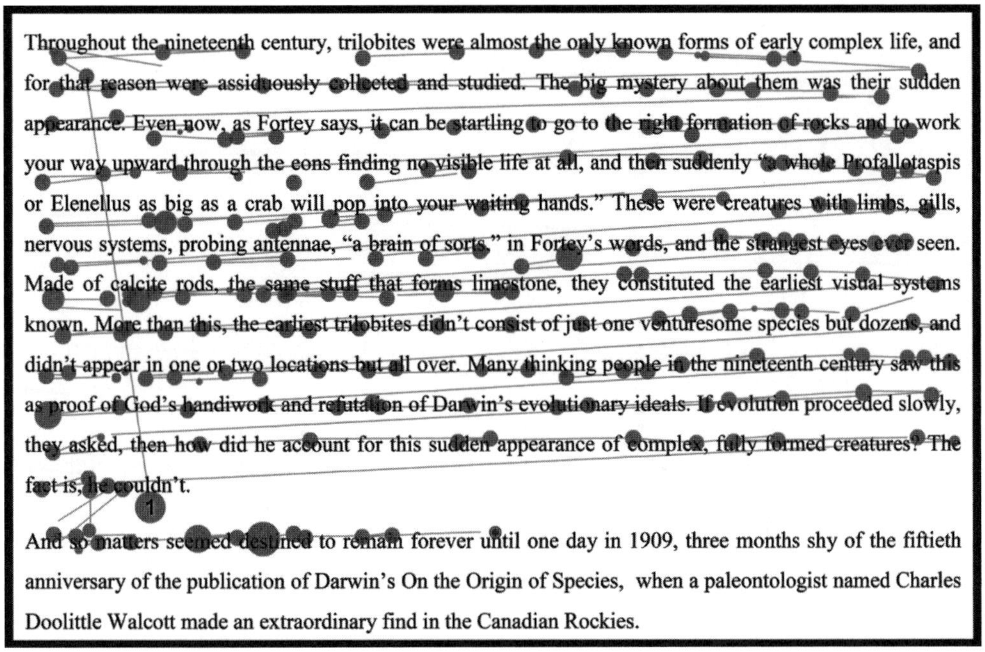

Throughout the nineteenth century, trilobites were almost the only known forms of early complex life, and for that reason were assiduously collected and studied. The big mystery about them was their sudden appearance. Even now, as Fortey says, it can be startling to go to the right formation of rocks and to work your way upward through the eons finding no visible life at all, and then suddenly "a whole Profallotaspis or Elenellus as big as a crab will pop into your waiting hands." These were creatures with limbs, gills, nervous systems, probing antennae, "a brain of sorts," in Fortey's words, and the strangest eyes ever seen. Made of calcite rods, the same stuff that forms limestone, they constituted the earliest visual systems known. More than this, the earliest trilobites didn't consist of just one venturesome species but dozens, and didn't appear in one or two locations but all over. Many thinking people in the nineteenth century saw this as proof of God's handiwork and refutation of Darwin's evolutionary ideals. If evolution proceeded slowly, they asked, then how did he account for this sudden appearance of complex, fully formed creatures? The fact is, he couldn't.

And so matters seemed destined to remain forever until one day in 1909, three months shy of the fiftieth anniversary of the publication of Darwin's On the Origin of Species, when a paleontologist named Charles Doolittle Walcott made an extraordinary find in the Canadian Rockies.

FIGURE 4.12 **An example of eye movement behaviour when reading an extended passage**

Fixations are indicated by circles (circle size reflects fixation duration) and lines indicate the saccades that connect successive fixations.

Figure 4.12 shows that the motion of the reading eye is anything but smooth, but it doesn't quite show the direction of the saccades. If it did, it would reveal a further illusion at work in our subjective experience of reading: the feeling that our eyes are moving consistently from left to right. If this impression were true and we put arrows on the saccade lines indicating directions, nearly all the arrows would point to the right, with the exception of the one long saccade back from the end of one line to the beginning of the next. But this is not the case. Figure 4.13 shows an enlarged portion of the left half of a page so that you can see the eye movements in more detail. Inspection of the figure reveals a large number of leftward saccades, most of which represent reorientations within or between words while reading. These are referred to as **regressions** (Rayner, 1998). In addition, notice that some leftward saccades terminate to the left of the vertical dotted line; these are primarily the result of expected transitions from the end of one line to the beginning of the next. Interestingly, in every case this transition requires two saccades, not one: the first, longer saccade does the majority of the work in transitioning between lines, but it stops short of the beginning of the line, and a second, smaller saccade is necessary to reach the desired starting point.

One question that emerged early in the study of overt attention during reading was how much information an individual processes from the periphery of vision. In other words, when the eye fixates on a word, how many letters or words to the left or right are processed and influence what is understood? McConkie and Rayner (1975; see Rayner, 1998, and Findlay & Gilchrist, 2003, for reviews) developed a clever method called the **moving window technique** to answer this question. This technique involves obscuring information in the periphery of vision while an individual is reading. For instance, most of

Regressions
Right to left movements of the eyes during reading, directing them to previously read text.

Moving window technique
A method of determining how much visual information can be taken in during a fixation, in which the reader is prevented from seeing information beyond a certain distance from the current fixation.

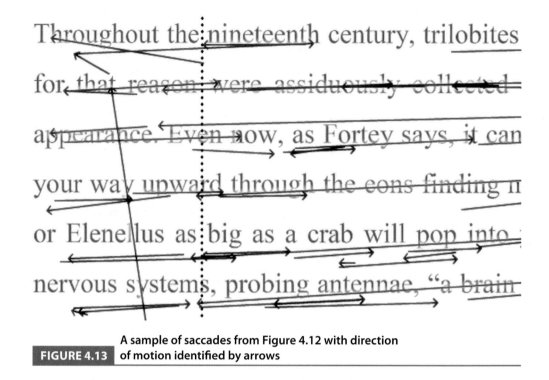

FIGURE 4.13   A sample of saccades from Figure 4.12 with direction of motion identified by arrows

the letters on each side of a person's current fixation might be changed to *Xs*, leaving only six legible letters on either side of that point. Then, every time the eyes move to a different location, the person would be able to see six letters on either side of the fixation but all letters farther away would again be changed to *Xs*. This is done with sophisticated eye-tracking technology that changes the reading material on the fly, depending on where an individual is looking. The results showed that reading is hindered when the person sees fewer than 17 to 20 characters; as long as that much is visible, reading seems to be unaffected.

Thus far we have considered how people move their eyes while reading material consisting of printed text. However, a growing body of research is now considering more complex situations, such as reading a page that contains both text and images. For instance, Rayner and colleagues (2001) evaluated how the eyes move when people are asked to evaluate visual advertisements. You can imagine how informative such research would be for the advertising industry! Consistent with what we have discussed thus far, the eyes move in very systematic ways in the context of advertisement viewing. Specifically, we tend to look first at the words and then at the pictures. Overall, more fixations are made on the text than on the picture. And although the pictures are fixated on less often, the average fixation on pictures is longer than the average fixation on the words in the ad.

Eye movements have even been measured while people engage with more complex material such as newspapers. Newspapers are an interesting medium because each page contains a number of articles, which often include large headings and pictures. Recently, Holmberg, Holsanova, and Holmqvist (2006) studied how people view newspaper pages. As you might expect, the results showed that most people begin by searching for places—**entry points**—to start reading. An entry point might be a heading or a picture. After finding an entry point, people will often read a section of text for some period of

Entry points
The locations to which we direct our eyes before starting to read a section in a piece of complex material such as a newspaper.

time and then begin looking for another entry point. This research also found individual differences with regard to (1) how much of an article people will read before moving on and (2) the extent to which people look at the pictures. At present, researchers are only scratching the surface of how overt attention is deployed when viewing complex reading materials. It's quite possible that studies of eye movements during reading will change the way text is formatted and laid out, so that it allows for faster reading and optimal comprehension.

OBJECT AND SCENE VIEWING

One of the main conclusions drawn from the research on the movement of overt attention during reading is that the eyes move in very systematic ways. You might say that this makes sense because the visual organization of text is very systematic: words are organized in horizontal lines, and to extract meaning we have to read from left to right. But how do the eyes move when people view more complex objects and scenes? Some of the initial work addressing this question was conducted by Alfred L. Yarbus (1967). At a time when eye-tracking technology was still in its infancy, Yarbus was able to measure eye movements with relatively high accuracy as his participants viewed pictures of objects and natural scenes.

You have already encountered one example of the sorts of eye-tracking records that Yarbus collected. Figure 2.8 shows that when people look at a face, whether of a person or an animal, they tend to focus primarily on the eyes and the mouth. In Figure 4.14 the face was viewed for three minutes. If we compare this figure with Figure 2.8, where the viewing was for one minute, we can see that this tendency to fixate on the eyes and mouth is especially pronounced at the beginning of the viewing process, while other areas are explored somewhat later. Based on his research, Yarbus (1967, p. 190) concluded that an "observer's attention is usually held only by certain elements of the picture." That is, the eye fixations are not just randomly or evenly spaced but seem to focus on important information. Indeed, Yarbus noted that the eyes and mouth tell us a lot about an individual and so it makes sense that people focus on those parts of the face.

The eye-tracking record shown in Figure 4.14 also makes another interesting point about the nature of eye movements. The record is not just a combination of dots (fixations) and straight lines (eye movements). In addition, there are some lines that are curved in various ways with dot-like discontinuities.

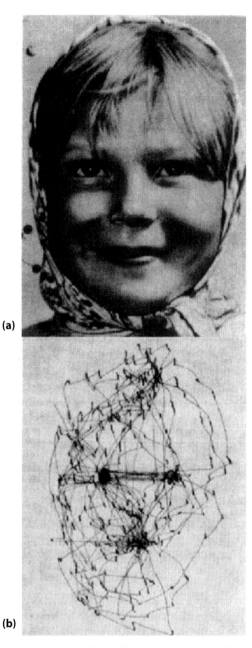

(a)

(b)

FIGURE 4.14 Recorded eye movements (b) while viewing a photograph of a face (a) over a three-minute period

Compare these tracings with those shown in Figure 2.8.

From: Yarbus, A.L. (1967). *Eye movements and vision*. Trans. L.A. Riggs. New York: Plenum Press. With kind permission from Springer Science+Business Media B.V.

This is because the eyes don't always move in perfectly straight lines. Yarbus drew the moment-to-moment positions of the eyes during ballistic (rapid) movement to give a better idea of what the eyes are actually doing when they move quickly. The discontinuities in Yarbus's eye-tracking records are fixations, and, as we noted, these discontinuities seem to aggregate in certain meaningful locations of the image.

As an aside, we should mention that the eyes can be made to move smoothly, without interrupting fixations, when they are following a smoothly moving target. You can observe this by having a friend face you and follow your finger with her or his eyes as you move it from left to right. As you look at the person's eyes you will notice that the movements are not jerky but smooth. These are called **smooth pursuit movements** (Robinson, 1965). Interestingly, according to Robinson (1965, p. 569), these "[s]mooth pursuit movements . . . constitute a large portion of ocular activity."

Yarbus also conducted numerous studies of how people shift their gaze when looking at scenes. From them he drew some important conclusions. Here we will illustrate these conclusions with recently collected eye movement records. Take a look at the photo in the upper half of Figure 4.15. As you can see, it shows a number of people sitting outside a coffee shop. Below it is the eye-tracking record of a viewer who was asked to look at that image for 15 seconds and then *describe the people* in it. In this instance, the viewer's eyes fixated almost exclusively on the people. When the same experiment was conducted with a different viewer (results not shown here), most of the fixations again fell on the people, although the background also received a few. This evidence of similarity in the way different individuals move their eyes when given the same viewing task is consistent with one of the conclusions reached by Yarbus. Finding these commonalities across individuals (when they have the same goals) is exciting for researchers because they indicate that eye movements are systematic behaviours that generalize across individuals.

Another important conclusion drawn by Yarbus (1967) regarding how the eyes move in complex scenes is illustrated in Figure 4.16, which shows the eye fixation pattern of an individual who was asked to view the image in Figure 4.15a with the purpose of describing the *location* rather than the people. In this case the eyes fixated not only on the people, but also on the sign beside the door and on items in the window and on the wall. Looking back at Figure 4.15b you will see that the sign on the coffee shop was never fixated on when the participant's task was to describe the people in the scene. This illustrates that the deployment of overt attention depends not only on the nature of the image viewed, but also on the *goals* of the viewer. This conclusion, originally drawn by Yarbus, is consistent with a large body of scene-viewing literature reviewed by Henderson (2003). Henderson refers to eye guidance based on the task goals of the observer as guidance by **task-related knowledge**. Of course, it's worth noting that salient visual features, such as bright or uniquely coloured portions of an image, may also influence how overt attention is deployed in a scene (see Henderson, 2003). However, our prior knowledge, our goals, and our biases seem to account for a substantial portion of our viewing behaviour.

Taken together, studies of eye movement during real-world tasks such as reading and scene viewing have substantially improved our understanding of how visual attention is deployed in more complex situations (see Box 4.4 for another example). With the advent of newer portable eye-tracking technology, the technique of indexing attention by monitoring the eyes has proven very useful in studies of attention both in the

Smooth pursuit movements
Movements of the eye that, because they are not jerky, enable the viewer to maintain fixation on a moving object.

Task-related knowledge
An observer's knowledge of the goals and the task at hand as it guides the eyes during a visual task.

laboratory and in everyday life. Indeed, it may be one way to link the sorts of research paradigms used in the lab with the ways in which attention operates in everyday situations (see Kingstone et al., 2008).

(a)

(b)

FIGURE 4.15   A scene from the Distillery District, Toronto (a), and the eye fixations (black dots) of a participant (b) asked to view the image and describe the people

The participant's objective was to be able to describe, at a later time, the people in the image.

FIGURE 4.16 | The eye fixations of an individual asked to view the image in order to later describe the location of the scene

The fixations are depicted by black circles.

Eye Movements in Sports: The Quiet Eye

Have you ever marvelled at the professional basketball player as he effortlessly makes his free-throw shot or the golf pro who putts with incredible precision? Anyone who has played these sports is familiar with the conventional wisdom of "picking your spot" concentrating, or drawing that imaginary line between ball and target destination. But exactly how do the experts direct their overt visual attention when playing sports? How does vision guide the body's movements to achieve the necessary hand–eye coordination? Recent research suggests that expert athletes use their gaze differently than non-experts do. It appears that the key to an expert's success lies in the ability to keep the gaze on a critical location for just the right amount of time, a technique known as the **Quiet Eye** (Vickers, 1996, 2004; Harle & Vickers, 2001).

Quiet Eye
Sustained and steady eye gaze prior to an action or behaviour.

Joan Vickers, a researcher at the University of Calgary, and her colleagues explored the gaze behaviour of basketball players who varied in their shooting ability (Vickers, 1996; Harle & Vickers, 2001). The players were divided into two groups based on their free-throw performance. Here we will refer to them as experts of high and moderate proficiency. While each of the players performed free throws, Vickers and her colleagues recorded (1) the scene the player was looking at, (2) his eye position in relation to the objects in the scene, and (3) his body posture and movement. The recording equipment used was specially designed for these studies. The results of the study were striking. Among other things, the researchers found that, compared to moderately proficient experts, the highly proficient experts gazed at the rim of the basket sooner and for a longer period of time before beginning the body movements associated with the free throw. Thus the really good players appeared to use the Quiet Eye. Highly proficient experts would also tend to direct their eyes away from the front of the hoop while shooting, to effectively suppress further processing of relevant visual cues so that, once initiated, the shot process would not be disrupted. By contrast, moderately proficient players tended to keep looking at the hoop during the action, thus possibly continuing to modify their shots as they released the ball. The fact that excellent players benefit by not looking at the hoop while shooting may explain why they can often make shots even when their view is blocked by members of the opposing team. In fact, by preventing the shooter from seeing the basket during the shot, the defender may inadvertently be helping the shooter! The idea that free-throw performance is improved by (1) using the Quiet Eye before shooting the ball to effectively locate the target and (2) looking away from the basket while actually shooting the ball to suppress unwanted cues is known as the **location-suppression hypothesis**.

Perhaps you're asking yourself whether you could score more often in basketball if you mimicked the eye movements of experts. Harle and Vickers (2001) conducted a fascinating study to answer this very question. They found that training a basketball team in how to use the Quiet Eye improved free-throw performance substantially, and that the improvement was greater than that shown by other teams not trained with the technique.

If you're interested in sports such as volleyball, hockey, or golf, you may also be interested to know that variants of the Quiet Eye have been shown to operate in those sports as well. Overall, it seems that the Quiet Eye involves:

1. Focusing the eyes on the optimal location of the critical target(s) in the sport.
2. Beginning and ending the Quiet Eye at the optimal times, corresponding to action initiation.
3. Holding the eyes on the optimal location for an extended period of time.

Of course, the details differ across sports. For example, an accurate putt in golf requires, among other things, that the golfer co-ordinate the position of the ball and the position of the hole. The eye movements of good and poor putters are shown in Figure 4.17. As you can see, good putters (1) focus their gaze on the back of the ball for several seconds, (2) then move their eyes quickly and accurately to the front of the hole, and (3) hold their gaze on the resting location of the ball even after the

ball leaves that spot. The good news for aspiring amateurs is that training the Quiet Eye can substantially improve performance in many sports (Harle & Vickers, 2001). Try it for yourself: next time you're out on the golf course or in the gym playing basketball, apply the Quiet Eye and see if your performance improves.

Location-suppression hypothesis
A two-stage explanation for the Quiet Eye phenomenon: in the preparation stage, the Quiet Eye maximizes information about the target object; then, during the location stage, vision is suppressed to optimize the execution of an action or behaviour.

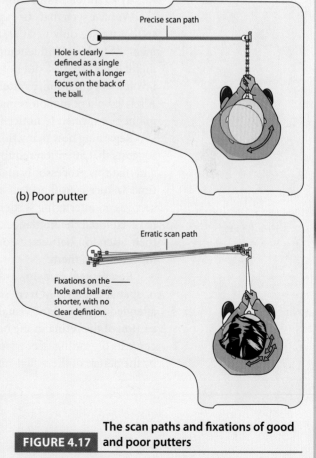

(a) Good putter

Precise scan path

Hole is clearly defined as a single target, with a longer focus on the back of the ball.

(b) Poor putter

Erratic scan path

Fixations on the hole and ball are shorter, with no clear defintion.

| **FIGURE 4.17** | **The scan paths and fixations of good and poor putters** |

From: Vickers, J.N. (2004). The Quiet Eye: It's the difference between a good putter and a poor one, here's proof. *Golf Digest* (Jan.), 96–101.

▊ Summary

In this chapter we learned that "attention" is a sophisticated concept encompassing a number of processes, including selective attention and inattention, involuntary attention, divided attention and task switching.

Early studies of selective attention by cognitive psychologists emphasized *filter* theories of information-processing. These theories suggested that people must filter out information to which they do not wish to attend. Dominating the filter theory literature is an important distinction between early and late selection. With early selection, attention prevents the perception of irrelevant information, as evidenced by dichotic listening and selective looking tasks. In late selection, both relevant and irrelevant stimuli are perceived, so that the person must actively ignore the irrelevant stimuli in order to focus on the relevant ones (e.g., Stroop task). Another distinction identified in the early information-processing theories is the one between automatic and controlled processes. Automatic processes are described as "bottom-up," stimulus-driven, or involuntary: they run without our having to pay attention to them. By contrast, controlled processes are more "top-down," goal-directed, and voluntary. Controlled activities require that we pay attention to them in order to execute them properly.

We have seen that our expectations often guide our exploration of our environment, so that we see only what we're looking for. On some occasions, though, our environment is capable of influencing our experience of it, making us suddenly aware of meaningful events that we did not expect. Cognitive psychologists refer to such instances of involuntary attention, or attention without intention, as episodes of attentional capture. A related phenomenon is inattentional blindness, or failure to attend to events that we might be expected to notice (demonstrated by the flanker task).

Regarding how many things we can attend to at once, the central bottleneck theory suggests that attention requires a central processor to handle the relevant information, and that this processor is unable to handle the information for more than one task at a time. In turns out that even mind wandering requires the central processor and so can serve as an interfering secondary task. Studies on divided attention and task switching have explored the bottleneck theory by examining whether people can learn to divide their attention between two tasks, as opposed to simply switching rapidly back and forth between them.

Researchers studying attention have distinguished between covert and overt shifts of spatial attention. Overt shifts of attention involve movement of the eyes to fixate attended regions of the visual field so that they can be processed by the high resolution section of the retina in the back of the eye (the fovea). Studies of eye movement in the contexts of reading, scene viewing, and sports suggest that the eyes are guided not only by the nature of the visual stimuli but also by the goals of the observer.

Case Study Wrap-up

How can we apply the contents of this chapter to the train accidents described in the case study? Well, one central point is that the concept of attention is relevant for almost all of the tasks that we do. This is especially the case in settings where errors can have drastic consequences. Railway and public transportation operations are excellent examples of such safety-critical settings. And as these industries are beginning to find out, many of the puzzling accidents that have occurred in the past could have been caused by failures of attention.

Engineers and bus drivers may be prone to making mistakes in situations where they are required to juggle multiple tasks at the same time—answering the radio, monitoring intersections, looking for yellow or red signals or adjusting their speed. In these moments of *divided attention*, engineers could make mistakes because their attention is so divided that they have insufficient attentional *capacity* to successfully perform one or more of the critical tasks (e.g., looking for yellow or red signals). As we have seen, the evidence also suggests that *task switching* leads to a *switch cost*: so even trying to quickly switch between tasks could lead to delayed responses.

Railroad engineers may also be at risk of making errors in those situations that are relatively uneventful. In such situations, engineers might begin *mind wandering* and rely on *automatic processes* rather than *controlled processes*. Relying on automatic processes can cause serious problems when they conflict with what the engineer actually wants to do, just as word reading interferes with colour naming in the *Stroop task*. During mind wandering (and multi-tasking, for that matter), engineers could suffer from *inattentional blindness*, and therefore completely miss important signals.

Finally, there are the limits of *overt attention* to consider. If an engineer or bus driver becomes tired and stops regularly scanning the track or roadway ahead, s/he might fail to *fixate* important information and thus completely miss it. Given how many limits attention is subject to, it's surprising that major accidents don't happen more often.

? In the Know: Review Questions

1. Why has the Stroop task been such a popular research tool?
2. Discuss the ways in which inattentional blindness and attention reveal complementary aspects of cognition.
3. Can we attend to two things at once? Discuss research relating to this question.
4. What is the difference between overt and covert shifts of attention?

Key Concepts

action slips
anterior cingulate cortex (ACC)
attentional blink
attention capture
capacity model
central bottleneck
cocktail party phenomenon
commission errors

controlled vs automatic processes
covert attention
default network
déjà vu
dichotic listening
divided attention
domain-specific modules
dorsolateral prefrontal cortex (DLPFC)

early selection
ecologically valid
embodied
entry points
filter
fixation
flanker task
fovea
inattentional blindness
late selection
location-suppression hypothesis
mind wandering
moving window technique
nystagmus
overt attention
parallel mental activity
photoreceptors
Quiet Eye

rapid serial visual presentation (RSVP)
regressions
retina
saccade
selective attention
selective looking
sequential attention hypothesis
set
shadowing task
smooth pursuit movements
Stroop task
structural limits
sustained attention to response task
    (SART)
switch cost
task-related knowledge
task switching

Links to Other Chapters

anterior cingulate cortex (ACC)
Chapter 10 (insight and the brain)
Chapter 13 (cognition and emotion)

domain specificity
Chapter 6 (teaching domain-specific
    knowledge)
Chapter 8 (folk biology)
Chapter 11 (the selection task and
    domain-specific reasoning, training in
    statistical reasoning)

Chapter 12 (evolution of g)

dorsolateral prefrontal cortex (DLPFC)
Chapter 6 (working memory)
Chapter 10 (flexibility–rigidity and the
    brain)

selective attention
Chapter 8 (perceptual symbol systems)

Stroop task
Chapter 11 (negativity bias)

Further Reading

People are able to discriminate between human and computer voices very early in the process of attention, according to Lattner et al. (2003).

A connectionist model of Stroop performance can be found in Cohen, Dunbar, and McClelland (1990).

Attention is sometimes characterized as a limited resource; for a discussion see Norman and Bobrow (1975). However, it's not easy to specify precisely what kind of resource it is, as Allport (1980) shows.

For more on inattentional blindness, see Most et al. (2001).

Finally, some preliminary findings in the neuropsychology of task switching are reviewed by Gurd, Weiss, Amunts, and Fink (2003).

Allport, D.A. (1980). Attention and performance. In G. Claxton (Ed.), *New directions in cognitive psychology* (pp. 26–64). London: Routledge & Kegan Paul.

Cohen, J.D., Dunbar, K., & McClelland, J.L. (1990). On the control of automatic processes: A parallel distributed processing account of the Stroop effect. *Psychological Review, 97,* 332–361.

Gurd, J.M., Weiss, P.H., Amunts, K., & Fink, G.R. (2003). Within-task switching in the verbal domain. *NeuroImage, 20,* S50–S57.

Lattner, S., Maess, B., Wang, Y., Schauer, M., Alter, K., & Friederici, A.D. (2003). Dissociation of human and computer voices in the brain: Evidence for a pre-attentive Gestalt-like perception. *Human Brain Mapping, 20,* 13–21.

Most, S.B., Simons, D.J., Scholl, B.J., Jimenez, R., Clifford, E., & Chabris, C.F. (2001). How not to be seen: The contribution of similarity and selective ignoring to sustained inattentional blindness. *Psychological Science, 12,* 9–17.

Norman, D.A., & Bobrow, D.G. (1975). On data limited and resource limited processes. *Cognitive Psychology, 7,* 44–64.

CHAPTER 5

Memory Traces and Memory Schemas

Chapter Contents

Learning Objectives

- To distinguish between memory traces and memory schemas.
- To outline the concept of flashbulb memories.
- To examine schema theory and review experimental evidence supporting it.
- To review research into eyewitness testimony and false memories.
- To identify the strengths and weaknesses of the "levels of processing" framework.

Case Study   Picking Cotton

The ability to accurately recall information—that is, to remember—is perhaps one of the most important cognitive processes that humans (and most animals) use. Remembering something as basic as "red means 'stop' and green means 'go'" could make the difference between life and death. This simple example demonstrates that the ability to assimilate information, commit it to memory, and access it quickly is foundational to both everyday existence and long-term survival. This of course holds true for complex information as well. For instance, we typically trust that our medical providers will prescribe the correct medicine based on knowledge that they have stored in long-term memory, perhaps decades in the past (depending, of course, on how old your doctor is). The next two chapters will describe many different concepts regarding how memory functions, how it can fail, and numerous approaches, past and present, to investigating and modelling memory that have contributed greatly to our scientific understanding of this crucial cognitive process. First, though, let's turn our attention to a case study that highlights the importance of memory and the dire consequences that can follow when memory fails.

In July 1984 a college student named Jennifer Thompson woke up and saw a man with a knife beside her bed. When she screamed, he held the knife to her throat and said he would kill her if she didn't keep quiet. She offered him her wallet, even her car, but he told her he didn't want those things. Realizing what he was there for, she made a conscious effort to study his face, looking for details she could remember later and use to identify him. Eventually she escaped to a neighbour's by persuading the rapist to let her get him a drink.

Thompson worked closely with the police to create a composite sketch. When she was shown a photo lineup she studied it carefully before deciding she recognized the man that the police had identified as the suspect. She picked out the same man, Ronald Cotton, in a physical lineup, and when the case went to court she swore that he was the one who had raped her. Cotton, 22, was sentenced to life.

FIGURE 5.1   Jennifer Thompson and Ronald Cotton

In prison Cotton met someone who looked so much like him that other prisoners sometimes mistook one for the other. Bobby Poole had been living in the same North Carolina town as Cotton and Thompson, and was serving time for a series of rapes. When Cotton asked if he had raped Thompson he denied it, but another inmate told Cotton that Poole told him he had. Finally, in 1995 a DNA test was conducted and confirmed Poole's guilt. Cotton was exonerated, and Thompson was overwhelmed with remorse. How could she have made a mistake that cost an innocent man more than 10 years of his life?

In fact, eyewitnesses are very often mistaken. As of 2009, DNA tests had led to the exoneration of more than 230 convicted men in the US alone, and in 79 per cent of those cases faulty eyewitness testimony had been involved (Innocence Project, 2009, Appendix A). Why are eyewitnesses so often wrong? How are false memories created? How is it that the people who hold them believe them to be true? These are among the many questions that this chapter will explore.

Memory doesn't work the way a video camera does: you can't turn it on and off, it doesn't simply record whatever is going on in front of its lens, and it can't be rewound and replayed at will. Rather, it seems that we capture the gist of incoming messages, assimilate that information with schemas that are already stored in our long-term memory, and then use those schemas to "fill in the blanks" when we're missing important bits and pieces of information.

Schema-based Theories of Memory

Probably no idea is more important in cognitive psychology generally, and in theories of memory in particular, than the idea of the schema. When we first encountered the schema, in Chapter 1, we defined it in terms of what we expect to find as we explore the world. However, we could also say that a schema is something that helps us to organize the information we receive. We will begin this chapter by considering how the concept of a memory schema differs from the concept of a memory trace, which was introduced in Chapter 3. Both Paul (1967) and Erdelyi (1985) suggest that Freud's (1925/1961) **mystic writing pad model** might be a good place to start.

The mystic writing pad is a common children's toy consisting of a sheet of waxed paper sandwiched between a layer of black wax and a sheet of clear plastic (celluloid). When you write on the plastic with a stylus, you can see what you've written because the waxed paper sticks to the wax wherever you have pressed on it. When you lift the waxed paper and plastic, the writing disappears from the overlay, but the imprint of the stylus remains visible on the black wax.

The overlay is like our perception of an event. Such perceptions are transitory; we pass from one experience to the next. Memories are similar to what remains on the wax tablet after we lift the plastic—after-effects of perception. The problem is that over time they tend to run together. Thus, if you examine the black wax layer after using the pad for a while, you will see numerous lines overlapping, as in Figure 5.2. How can you tell what was originally written? The only way would be by making inferences on the basis of whatever evidence was available. Thus given a clear *p* followed by a slightly less clear *e*, two straight descending lines, what looks like another *e*, and a clear *r*, you might infer that the word written was *pepper* and that the letters *ppe* had simply been written over.

The mystic writing pad analogy is imperfect. It's unlikely that memory has the truly haphazard structure of the fragments that remain on a wax tablet, and (as we will see) schemas may be quite well-organized. However, the analogy helps to clarify the distinction between a memory schema

Mystic writing pad model
A model of memory based on a toy writing tablet that retains fragments of old messages even after they have been "erased." In time, these fragments accumulate and begin to overlap, so that they become increasingly hard to read.

FIGURE 5.2 **The mystic writing pad**

From: Erdelyi, M.H. (1985). *Psychoanalysis: Freud's cognitive psychology*. San Francisco: Freeman, p. 119. Copyright 1985 by Matthew Hugh Erdelyi. Used with permission.

and a memory trace. The latter could be compared to a video recording that can be preserved indefinitely and replayed over and over. If memory is entirely a matter of recalling memory traces, then remembering would be like re-experiencing the past. This notion is what Neisser (1967) called the **reappearance hypothesis**: "that the same 'memory' . . . can disappear and reappear over and over again" (p. 282). By contrast, if we do not have "stored copies of finished mental events," then memory must be schematic, relying on "fragments . . . to support a new construction" (p. 286).

In the following section we will consider the evidence for the trace theory of memory.

The Trace Theory

FLASHBULB MEMORIES

Do we have any memories that are especially clear and distinct? Some psychologists have argued that memories for particularly important events can be exceptionally clear and vivid. For example, a great many people who were of school age or older when John F. Kennedy was assassinated, in 1963, claimed to be able to remember exactly the circumstances under which they learned of his death. Such memories were first investigated by R. Brown and Kulik (1977). In the mid-1970s they asked 80 Harvard undergraduates to try to recall the circumstances under which they heard of the assassination. The participants wrote a "free recall" account of what they remembered. In addition they estimated how consequential they felt the event was at the time, and how frequently they had talked about it. A similar procedure was used to study memories of the assassinations or attempted assassinations of some other prominent figures, such as Martin Luther King, Jr.

The students' accounts typically included information on five specific subjects:

1. Where they were when they learned of the assassination;
2. What they were doing at the time;
3. The person who told them;
4. Their affect (how they felt at the time); and
5. The aftermath: what they did immediately after hearing the news.

The results showed that almost every participant had what appeared to be vivid, detailed memories not only of the Kennedy assassination, but often of the others, and the more consequential the event was felt to be, the more often it had been rehearsed (i.e., discussed with others).

The term that Brown and Kulik (1977) coined to refer to such unusually vivid and detailed accounts was **flashbulb memories**. To explain how such memories are produced, they took Livingston's (1967) **Now Print! theory**—that especially significant experiences are immediately "photocopied" and preserved in long-term memory—and elaborated on it to create the model illustrated in Figure 5.3.

The sequence that Brown and Kulik proposed has five stages. First, the stimulus event is tested for "surprisingness." If it is completely ordinary, then we will pay no attention to it at all. If it is sufficiently traumatic, we will respond with "retrograde amnesia" and not process it at all. However, if the event is extraordinary (as

Reappearance hypothesis
The hypothesis that the same memory can reappear, unchanged, again and again.

Flashbulb memories
Vivid, detailed memories of significant events.

Now Print! theory
The theory that especially significant experiences are immediately "photocopied" and preserved in long-term memory.

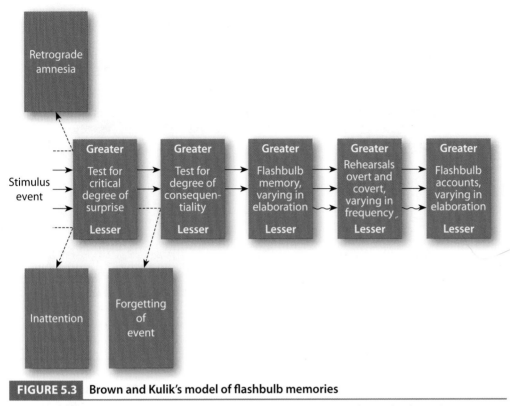

FIGURE 5.3 **Brown and Kulik's model of flashbulb memories**

From: Brown, R., & Kulik, J. (1977). Flashbulb memories. *Cognition, 5*, 73–99. Copyright 1977 by Elsevier Science Publishers. Reprinted by permission.

assassinations were in the early 1960s), then we will pay very close attention to it. In the second stage the event is tested for consequentiality. Events that fail this test will be forgotten, but those we consider important as well as surprising will move on to the third stage, in which flashbulb memories are formed. Flashbulb memories will vary in vividness and completeness depending on how surprising and consequential they are. The fourth stage is rehearsal, in which we think about those memories and develop verbal accounts of them. Finally, in the fifth stage we tell and retell those accounts to other people.

Now Print! theory focuses on the third stage, in which the surprising and consequential experience is preserved in long-term memory. The process as Livingston (1967) envisioned it resembled the production of a photocopy: just press the Print button and the machine makes a faithful reproduction of everything on the page, including the context in which the experience occurred. In short, flashbulb memories would be examples of highly detailed memory traces.

Investigating the Flashbulb Hypothesis

Brown and Kulik's work attracted a great deal of attention, and a number of historically important events were eventually investigated as possible sources of "flashbulbs." Among them was the *Challenger* space shuttle explosion (Figure 5.4) in January 1986 (Bohannon, 1988; Bohannon & Symons, 1992; McCloskey, Wible, & Cohen, 1988). Three days after the disaster, McCloskey and his co-workers collected questionnaire

FIGURE 5.4 Flashbulb memories: The *Challenger* explosion

data from 45 people. Then, approximately nine months later, 27 of those people completed a follow-up questionnaire, as did 31 new people who had not seen the first questionnaire. The questionnaires included four questions:

1. Where were you when you first learned of the *Challenger* explosion?
2. What were you doing?
3. Did you see the event as it was actually happening, or did you learn about it later?
4. What were your first thoughts on hearing the news?

All participants remembered something about the circumstances in which they had heard about the disaster. However, comparison of the immediate and nine-month questionnaire data showed that quite a bit of information had been lost over the interval, and that the details were not always consistent. Although seven of the nine-month accounts were more specific than the immediate accounts, 20 were more general (less specific). For example, someone who had initially named the person he heard the news from might only refer to "a friend" nine months later. In addition, seven of the nine-month accounts were inconsistent with the original reports on matters such as where the respondents were when they heard the news (e.g., sitting at the desk versus walking out the office door).

Even so, it's important to note that none of the nine-month accounts were wildly inconsistent with the earlier versions. Rather, the inconsistencies were "the same sort of reconstructive errors that seem to occur frequently for 'ordinary' memories." In both cases, "inaccuracies may be introduced when information that cannot be retrieved from memory is filled in through inference or guesswork" (McCloskey et al., 1988, p. 175).

THINK TWICE BOX 5.1

Do We Necessarily See What's in Front of Our Eyes?

Imagine that you have just been attacked on the street by three people. Fortunately, in the midst of the attack you see a police officer racing towards you. But he runs right past! The officer later says he was chasing someone else and did not recall seeing what was happening to you. Do you believe him? Remember your answer.

This very scenario played out in Boston in 1995. Around 2:00 a.m. police officer Kenneth Conley responded to a call about a shooting and ultimately gave chase to the suspect. During the chase he ran right past three fellow police officers who were beating a man they mistakenly believed to be the suspect (in fact, he was an undercover police officer). Conley, the officer who ran past the assault, claimed he never saw it, but the jury rejected his story. He was later convicted of perjury and obstruction of justice and sentenced to 34 months in jail. As unlikely as this scenario seems, it raises a serious question. Could Conley really not have seen a brutal assault that was taking place right in front of his eyes?

This real-world example should remind you of the Chapter 1 box on the use of cell phones while driving (Box 1.1) and the discussion of inattentional blindness in Chapter 4. In both cases, the point was that people whose attention is distracted can sometimes fail to consciously perceive things that are right in front of their eyes. This obviously has a direct impact on their ability to remember those things. If Conley never had any conscious perception of the assault, how could he have had any recollection of it?

Conley's conviction was eventually overturned on technical grounds. Recently, though, a group of researchers at Union College in New York set out to determine if his story could in fact have been true (see Chabris, Weinberger, Fontaine, & Simons, 2011). In their study they asked participants to run behind a confederate (someone helping with the experiment), while three other confederates staged a fight along the route. Amazingly, a post-experiment questionnaire revealed that only 35 per cent of the participants recalled noticing the fight when the experiment was conducted at night (the Conley incident took place in the dead of night). Although this percentage jumped to 56 per cent in daylight, even under ideal conditions almost half the participants failed to notice the fight. This experiment highlights the importance of attention and conscious perception for memory. If the event was not even perceived, then the memory of it will be degraded if it exists at all. After reading the previous three chapters you should be aware of how interconnected many cognitive processes are. That is, it should be apparent that sensation, perception, and attention all play significant roles in how and what we remember. Now recall your answer to the question we asked in the first paragraph above. Would you have believed Conley? Do you think he should have been convicted?

McCloskey et al. concluded that so-called flashbulb memories are not necessarily more accurate than normal memories, and that there is no need for a special flashbulb mechanism to account for them. They concluded that if these type of memories seem easier to recall in vivid detail than ordinary memories, it's only because we have replayed them so often and thought about them so much.

A number of studies have explored flashbulb memories concerning the destruction of the World Trade Center in New York City on 11 September 2001 (see Figure 5.5) (e.g., Greenberg, 2004; Neisser, 2003). Talarico and Rubin's (2003) study was particularly well designed. On 12 September 2001, they tested 54 Duke University students using an open-ended questionnaire similar to Brown and Kulik's to get descriptions not only of the momentous events of the previous day, but also of an ordinary event, such as a party, that each participant had recently experienced. Talarico and Rubin added

FIGURE 5.5 **Flashbulb memories: Terrorist attacks on the World Trade Center, New York City**

other tests designed to measure additional aspects of the flashbulb phenomenon, such as the intensity of the emotion felt when the events were recalled. They then divided the 54 participants into three groups of 18 each and re-tested each group once. The first group was tested one week later; the second, six weeks later; and the third, 32 weeks later. The major variable of interest was the consistency of the account given at the three different intervals. For example, if a participant said on 12 September that "Fred" was with him when the event occurred and later said that "Alice" was with him, but not "Fred," that response was scored as inconsistent. Each participant's recall was given a consistency score based on the number of details consistently recalled, as well as an inconsistency score. Figure 5.6 shows the change in consistency and inconsistency scores as a function of time. Notice that both flashbulb and everyday memories show a decline in consistency and an increase in inconsistency. Although the flashbulb memories had more emotion associated with them, in terms of their actual content they were certainly no more accurate than "ordinary" memories. However, participants erroneously believed that their flashbulb memories were more accurate than their "ordinary" memories. Talarico and Rubin concluded that although a flashbulb event "reliably enhances memory characteristics such as vividness and confidence," people should not put that much faith "in the accuracy of their flashbulb memories" (2003, p. 460).

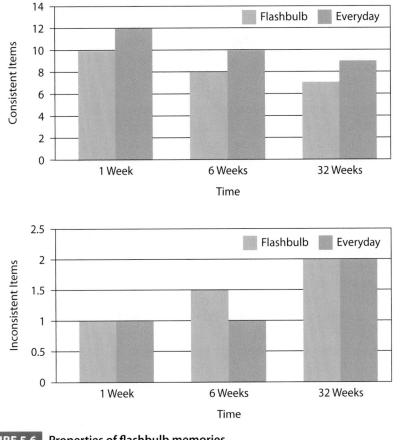

FIGURE 5.6 **Properties of flashbulb memories**

Notice that the y-axes of the two graphs are not to the same scale.

Data from: Talarico, J.M., & Rubin, D.C. (2003). Confidence, not consistency, characterizes flashbulb memories. *Psychological Science, 14,* 455–461.

ARE MEMORY TRACES PERMANENT?

These flashbulb memory experiments have led many to question the idea that memory traces persist unchanged over time. As a result, the theory of memory traces has been undergoing considerable modification (Dudai, 2004; Nader, 2003; Wixted, 2004a). According to the classic **consolidation theory** (Woodworth, 1938, p. 51), memory traces of an event are not fully formed immediately after that event, but take some time to consolidate. This process of consolidation can be disrupted by events that occur after the event to be remembered; such disruption is called **retroactive interference**. Woodworth's (1938, p. 227) review of the classic literature (e.g., Jenkins & Dallenbach, 1924) concluded that "rest immediately after learning . . . allows for full consolidation of the traces, while strenuous mental work just at this time . . . leaves the traces weak." This conclusion is echoed in the recent literature. For example, Wixted (2004a, p. 247) argued that "even if the intervening study material is not related to the original learning in any obvious way, the new learning draws on a limited pool of resources that may have otherwise been available to consolidate the original learning. As a result, memory for the original material suffers."

Consolidation theory
The classic theory that memory traces of an event are not fully formed immediately after that event, but take some time to consolidate.

Retroactive interference
A decline in the recall of one event as a result of a later event.

Hippocampus
A site in the brain that plays a crucial role in the consolidation of memory traces.

It is known that the **hippocampus** is a crucial site for the consolidation of memory traces, converting immediate memories into long-term memories (Figure 5.7). "If the hippocampal formation is damaged before the consolidation process is complete, recently formed memories that are still undergoing the consolidation process will be impaired" (Wixted, 2004a, p. 242). It is likely that retroactive interference occurs because "ordinary mental exertion and memory formation" detract from an ongoing process of [hippocampal] consolidation" (Wixted, 2004a, p. 264).

It was long believed that once the consolidation process was complete, then the memory trace in question was fixed and permanent. However, it now appears likely that when the stored trace is re-activated, it becomes labile (i.e., changeable) (Dudai, 2004; Nader, 2003). Thus recalling a previous experience places it in working memory, where it comes into contact with other experiences. For example, the context in which you recall a flashbulb event may be quite different from the context in which you originally experienced it. This provides an opportunity for revision of the memory trace, although the *extent* of such revision is controversial. In any case, the revised trace would then undergo **reconsolidation** in the hippocampus (Nader, 2003, p. 66). Furthermore, there is nothing to say that this process cannot become a cycle whereby a memory trace is reactivated and reconsolidated indefinitely. Thus we have no reason to believe that a memory trace is necessarily a faithful rendition of the original experience.

Reconsolidation
The hypothetical process whereby a memory trace is revised and reconsolidated.

Nader (2003, p. 70) reviewed the memory reconsolidation literature, and his conclusion is extremely important: "There can be no doubt at this point that memories are fundamentally dynamic processes, as first explicitly demonstrated by Bartlett (1932). They are not snapshots of events that are passively read out but, rather, are constructive in nature and always changing (Tulving & Thomson, 1973; Loftus & Yuille, 1984; Schacter, 1999)." In reaching this conclusion, Nader pays tribute to Frederic Bartlett (1886–1969) and in particular his 1932 book *Remembering*. It is to an examination of that work and its influence on cognitive psychology that we will now turn.

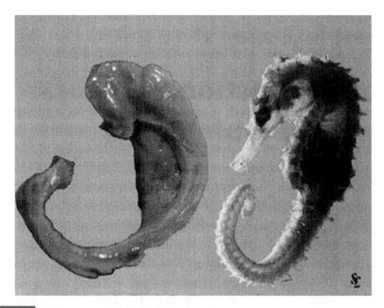

FIGURE 5.7   **A hippocampus looks like a sea horse**

BARTLETT AND THE CONCEPT OF THE SCHEMA

It was Bartlett who made the schema concept central to the psychology of memory (Roediger, 1997; Thompson, 1997; Weiskrantz, 2000; Zangwill, 1972). His best-known experimental techniques were the **method of repeated reproduction** and the **method of serial reproduction**. In the former, a participant, A, is given a story to read and then attempts to reproduce it, first 15 minutes later and then at longer intervals. The latter begins the same way, but A's version is then given to a second participant, B, who reads it and then writes down what he or she can recall of it. B's version in turn is given to C, and so on (if you ever played "telephone" in elementary school, you'll recognize the principle). Thus each participant tries to reproduce the previous participant's version of the original story based solely on what he or she can recall. The results showed the same pattern in both cases, but were particularly dramatic with the method of serial reproduction. The story to be reproduced was the following North American folktale:

The War of the Ghosts

One night two young men from Egulac went down to the river to hunt seals, and while they were there it became foggy and calm. Then they heard war-cries, and they thought: "Maybe this is a war party." They escaped to the shore and hid behind a log. Now canoes came up, and they heard the noise of paddles and saw one canoe coming up to them. There were five men in the canoe, and they said:

"What do you think? We wish to take you along. We are going up the river to make war on the people."

One of the young men said: "I have no arrows."

"Arrows are in the canoe," they said.

"I will not go along. I might get killed. My relatives do not know where I have gone. But you," he said, turning to the other, "may go with them."

So one of the men went, but the other returned home.

And the warriors went on up the river to a town on the other side of Kalama. The people came down to the water, and they began to fight, and many were killed. But presently the young man heard one of the warriors say: "Quick, let us go home: that Indian has been hit." Now he thought: "Oh, they are ghosts." He did not feel sick, but he said he had been shot.

So the canoes went back to Egulac, and the young man went ashore to his house and made a fire. And he told everybody and said: "Behold I accompanied the ghosts, and we went to fight. Many of our fellows were killed, and many of those who attacked us were killed. They said I was hit, and I did not feel sick."

He told it all, and then became quiet. When the sun rose he fell down. Something black came out of his mouth. His face became contorted. The people jumped up and cried.

He was dead. (Bartlett, 1932, p. 65)

To test your own recall, stop reading now and wait 15 minutes; then try to reproduce the story.

In Bartlett's serial experiment, successive reproductions became increasingly different from the original. By the tenth person the story had become the following:

Method of repeated reproduction
One participant is given multiple opportunities to recall a story over time.

Method of serial reproduction
One participant, A, writes down what he or she can recall of a previously read story. A's version is given to a second participant, B, who reads it and then tries to reproduce it. B's version in turn is given to C, and so on.

The War of the Ghosts (2)

Two Indians were out fishing for seals in the Bay of Manpapan, when along came five other Indians in a war canoe. They were going fighting.

"Come with us," said the five to the two, "and fight."

"I cannot come," was the answer of the one, "for I have an old mother at home who is dependent upon me." The other also said he could not come, because he had no arms. "That is no difficulty," the others replied, "for we have plenty in the canoe with us"; so he got into the canoe and went with them.

In a fight soon afterwards this Indian received a mortal wound. Finding that his hour was come, he cried out that he was about to die. "Nonsense," said one of the others, "you will not die." But he did. (Bartlett, 1932, p. 124)

Bartlett believed that this experiment showed what happens to memory over time. Obviously, several parts of the original were dropped along the way, so that the story was simplified. Although the title was reported correctly in reproduction 10, there was no longer any mention of ghosts. Participants tended to select some material to remember and omit other material. These omissions reflect a process of **rationalization** as each participant tried to make the story as coherent and sensible as possible, from his or her viewpoint. Material that did not seem to fit tended to drop out of the narrative. Recall the death of the Indian in the original version: "When the sun rose he fell down. Something black came out of his mouth. His face became contorted." Over successive reproductions this passage changed substantially—a "black thing rushed from his mouth," "his soul fled black from his mouth," "his spirit fled"—until finally, by version 10, these details had disappeared altogether. The mysterious blackness became conventionalized as a soul and then was dropped altogether. Bartlett noted that unfamiliar material was transformed over time to conform to more familiar patterns.

On the basis of his experiments, Bartlett concluded that

remembering is not the re-excitation of innumerable fixed, lifeless and fragmentary traces. It is imaginative reconstruction, or construction, built out of the relation of our attitude towards a whole active mass of organized past reactions or experience, and to a little outstanding detail which commonly appears in image or in language form. (1932, p. 213)

This "active mass of organized past reactions" is what Bartlett meant by the term **schema**. Thus a schema in Bartlett's sense is an organized setting that guides our behaviour, a standard that can be adjusted to fit changing circumstances.

As an example Bartlett used the ability to make the proper stroke in a ball game such as tennis. You must adjust your posture and bodily movements to fit the current situation. You don't simply repeat a stroke you have performed before, because the ball is not likely to be in exactly the same place twice, and neither are you. A schema is a flexible organization, and that is what makes it useful. If our memory were just a collection of traces, it would too rigid to be useful. A schema is a more abstract and general setting within which memory traces have meaning.

It's important to note that Bartlett never denied the existence of memory traces (Ost & Costall, 2002). The case of Professor Aitken (Hunter, 1977) is a very good example of the way memory traces and memory schemas can work together; see Box 5.2.

Rationalization
The attempt to make memory as coherent and sensible as possible.

Schema (Bartlett)
An active mass of organized past reactions that provides a setting that guides our behaviour.

COGNITION IN ACTION
BOX 5.2
An Exceptional Memory

Professor A.C. Aitken (1895–1967) was a "brilliant mathematician . . . and an accomplished violinist" whose phenomenal memory was studied for decades by psychologists (Hunter, 1977). Often people with an extraordinary memory are said to have a correspondingly poor ability to think abstractly, but that was not the case with Aitken. In fact, it was precisely because of his ability to rapidly schematize information that his memory was so prodigious. According to Hunter (1977, p. 157), the process whereby Aitken would take even the most mundane events and weave them into an "unusually rich densely structured gestalt of properties" that still preserved the uniqueness of each event exemplified what Bartlett (as we noted in Chapter 4) called "effort after meaning." Typically, Aitken's ability to remember was an unintended consequence of his desire to make things meaningful. He never wanted to "memorize" anything merely by rote.

Aitken felt that the most important thing was to relax and become absorbed in the material to be learned. Once you allow yourself to become interested in it, then you will begin to comprehend it in deeper and deeper ways. The more deeply you comprehend something, the better you will remember it. (This is a theme that will recur towards the end of this chapter when we discuss the "levels of processing" approach to memory.) Aitken observed that "the thing to do is to learn by heart, not because one has to, but because one loves the thing and is interested in it" (Hunter, 1977, p. 158).

Because he was interested in his own mental processes, Aitken agreed to be a participant in a variety of experiments. In 1933 he was asked to memorize 25 unrelated words. Twenty-seven years later, in 1960, he attempted to recall them, and succeeded. However, Aitken did not repeat even this "meaningless" list of words by rote. Rather, he proceeded by inference to reconstruct the list. Aitken's memory operated in a schematic way even for a list of words. We will examine some very different techniques for memorizing large amounts of material in our discussion of imagery, in Chapter 7.

More typical of Aitken's memory was his knowledge of music. He believed that musical memory could be both rich and precise because music has so many different aspects, including "a metre and a rhythm, a tune, . . . the harmony, the instrumental colour, a particular emotion, . . . a meaning, . . . perhaps a human interest in the composer" (Hunter, 1977, p. 157). All these elements combine to create a framework within which the act of recall can take place. You may be reminded of Aitken's musical memory later in this chapter, when we discuss how actors learn their lines.

FIGURE 5.8 Professor A.C. Aitken

PHANTOM LIMBS AND THE BODY SCHEMA

Bartlett (1958, p. 146) began using the schema concept as a result of his work with the great neurologist Sir Henry Head. Head wanted to understand how it is that people generally have a very good sense of their posture and are able to alter it so as to successfully move around in the world. That is, without thinking about it, we "know" where our arms, legs, and the rest of our body parts are positioned at any time and smoothly coordinate them so as to walk, sit down, turn around, and so on. Head proposed the word *schema* to mean the

> standard against which all subsequent changes of posture are measured before they enter consciousness. . . . By means of perpetual alterations in position we are constantly building up a postural model of ourselves which constantly changes. Every new posture of movement is recorded on this plastic schema, and the activity of the cortex brings every fresh group of sensations evoked by altered posture into relation with it. (Bartlett, 1932, pp. 199–200)

Head was talking about what we call our **body schema**, or **body image**.

How the body schema works is well illustrated by the phenomenon known as the **phantom limb**. A phantom limb occurs when a body part, such as an arm or a leg, is suddenly lost (e.g., through amputation). The person *feels* that the missing body part is "still there" even though he knows that it is not (Simmel, 1956). "Many patients awake from an anaesthetic after an amputation feeling certain that the operation has not been performed. They feel the lost limb so vividly that only when they reach out to touch it, or peer beneath the bed sheets to see it, do they realize that it has been cut off" (Katz, 1993, p. 336). The phantom limb is a vivid but in a certain sense false memory (a concept that we'll discuss shortly). The phantom develops immediately after an amputation in approximately 75 per cent of patients, and incidence rises to 85 per cent eight days after such surgery (Katz, 1993; Ramachandran & Hirstein, 1998). There is often intense pain associated with the phantom limb, and "more than 70 per cent of amputees continue to experience phantom limb pain of considerable intensity as long as 25 years after amputation" (Katz, 1993, p. 336).

Phantom limbs occur as a consequence of the way the body schema represents the parts of our bodies and their relationships. If the loss of a body part, such as a finger, occurs slowly, as it does in people with leprosy, then there is much less likelihood of experiencing a phantom (Simmel, 1956; Ramachandran & Hirstein, 1998, p. 1625); perhaps it's easier for the schema to adjust when the change is gradual. In any event, the schema does change, even in cases of sudden and devastating loss.

To understand how the schema changes, however, we must first look at how the various parts of the body are represented in the sensory cortex under normal conditions. The image in Figure 5.9 is a version of the **Penfield homunculus**. Named after Wilder Penfield, the neuroscientist who developed the concept, the "homunculus" is a map of the sensory cortex that shows where the various parts of the body are represented. The area of each body part in the map is proportional to the area of the cortex that represents it. Notice that the hands are represented next to the face.

The significance of this location can be seen in the case of a man who had his arm amputated just above the left elbow and developed a phantom limb (Ramachandran (2004, p. 10; Ramachandran, 1993; Ramachandran, Rodgers-Ramachandran, & Cobb, 1995). Amazingly, when stimulated with a cotton swab on the surface of his face he felt as if parts of his missing hand were being stimulated. There have been several reports of cases similar to this one. Why does this happen? Recall that the face is next to the hand in the Penfield homunculus. Ramachandran explains the phenomenon as follows:

Body schema or body image
The individual's schematic representation of his or her body.

Phantom limb
The feeling, following the sudden loss of a body part, that it is still present.

Penfield homunculus
A map of the sensory cortex that shows where the various parts of the body are represented; the size of each part is proportional to the area of the cortex that represents it.

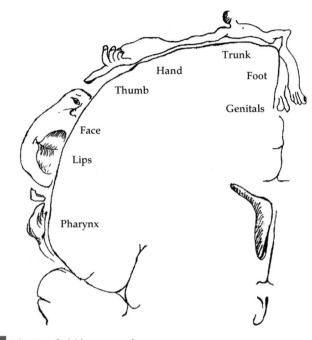

FIGURE 5.9 The Penfield homunculus

From: Ramachandran, V.S., & Hirstein, W. (1998). The perception of phantom limbs. *Brain, 121*, 1603–1630. Reprinted by permission of Oxford University Press and the authors.

When an arm is amputated, no signals are received by the part of the brain's cortex corresponding to the hand. It becomes hungry for sensory input and the sensory input from the facial skin now invades the adjacent vacated territory corresponding to the missing hand. (Ramachandran, 2004, p. 13)

Brain-imaging techniques have supported this hypothesis, showing that for the sort of patient just described, "input from the face and upper arm could now activate the hand area" of the brain (Ramachandran & Hirstein, 1998, p. 1616). The body schema is not fixed, but shows considerable **plasticity** (i.e., flexibility). This flexibility is well illustrated by an ingenious technique used to ameliorate phantom pain. Sometimes a patient feels as if the phantom hand is clenching, with the fingernails painfully digging into the skin. If the person could unclench the phantom hand, perhaps the pain would go away. Now look at Figure 5.10. This apparatus allows the patient to see the mirror image of the remaining hand in such a way that the missing hand appears to have returned. If the patient unclenches the real hand, the phantom hand will feel as if it too is unclenching; in fact, the pain goes away in many patients (Jackson & Simpson, 2004). Nothing could better demonstrate the dynamic way in which the body schema, and schemata generally, are organized and reorganized (Ramachandran & Hirstein, 1998, p. 1622).

You can experience an analog of a phantom limb by setting up a variant of the procedure illustrated in Figure 5.10. You will need a plastic hand or a glove. Put your left hand in your lap, and your right hand flat on a table. Your right hand must be hidden from your view by some sort of screen (e.g., a pile of books). Then put the fake hand on the table in front of you, as shown in Figure 5.10. Have a confederate "repeatedly tap and

Plasticity
Flexibility.

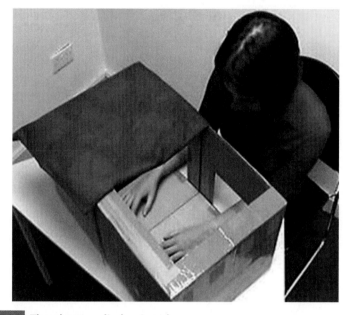

FIGURE 5.10   **The phantom limb mirror box**

Selection
The hypothesis that we select information both as we receive it and as we recall it.

Abstraction
The hypothesis that we tend to remember only the gist, not the specifics, of what we experience.

Interpretation
The hypothesis that we interpret information by making inferences, and then remember the inferences as part of the original information.

Integration
The hypothesis that we abstract the meaning of an event and then put that meaning together with the rest of our knowledge to form a coherent, consistent whole.

stroke your concealed right hand in a random sequence. Tap, tap, tap, stroke, stroke, tap, stroke, stroke. At the same time, while you watch, he must also tap and stroke the visible dummy in perfect synchrony" (Ramachandran & Rogers-Ramachandran, 2005). After a while, you will feel as if *you* are being touched on the dummy hand.

▌ Research Based on Schema Theory

Over the years, it has been noted that many studies have employed the schema concept in the same general way that Bartlett did. Several reviews (e.g., Alba & Hasher, 1983, p. 204; Koriat, Goldsmith, & Pansky, 2000, pp. 494–495) suggest that most schema theories discuss memory in terms of four processes: **selection**, **abstraction**, **interpretation**, and **integration**. The schema selects information consistent with our interests at the time. We then convert that information into a more abstract form. In other words, instead of trying to preserve the specifics of the event in its entirety we extract its gist, or meaning. We then interpret that information in terms of other information in our memory. Finally, we integrate the information in such a way as to make it consistent with the schema. Koriat, Goldsmith, and Pansky (2000) add a fifth process, reconstruction, whereby the act of recall blends general knowledge and individual experiences in order to "imaginatively reconstruct" the past.

Thus when you are finished reading this chapter, it's unlikely that you will remember every word of it. You will probably have selected some points to remember and let others go, depending on your interests and concerns at the time of reading. If someone asks you what the chapter is about, you will more likely give them a selective abstract than a literal recap. Over time, you may realize that you did not simply interpret the ideas in this chapter: you also integrated them with other ideas that you had already taken in. For example, the idea that the schema is selective may remind you that the last chapter made a similar point about attention. Moreover, the processes we are now discussing may reflect the way information is encoded—another process that we considered in Chapter 4. Of course, these connections may seem somewhat vague (i.e., schematic), and you may need to reread those sections in order to fully remember the concepts discussed earlier. Finally, years from now, if you set out to reconstruct what you learned from this chapter, you may have only fragmentary clues to work with. You may even have trouble remembering when you took this course, what grade you got for it, or who was in your class at the time.

EYEWITNESS TESTIMONY

Loftus and Palmer (1974) did a classic study of eyewitness testimony. Participants were shown a film depicting a traffic accident. Some were asked, "About how fast were the cars going when they hit each other?" Others were asked the same question, but with the word *hit* replaced by *smashed, collided, bumped,* or *contacted.* The results are given in Figure 5.11. Notice that the estimate of the cars' speed is a function of the intensity of the verb in the question. If the question used the word *smashed,* then the cars were reported to have been going faster than if they had merely came into "contact" with one another.

In another experiment, participants were also shown a film of a collision and then asked one of two questions: either "How fast were the cars going when they hit each other?" or "How fast were the cars going when they smashed into each other?" One week later, participants were asked some additional questions about the accident they had seen on film the week before. One of the questions was "Did you see any broken glass?" The participants who had earlier been asked if the cars "had smashed into each other" were more likely to report seeing broken glass than were the participants who had been asked if the cars "had hit each other" (Figure 5.12). Loftus and Palmer (1974) interpreted these results as follows:

> We would like to propose that two kinds of information go into one's memory for some complex occurrence. The first is information gleaned during the perception of the original event; the second is external information supplied after the fact. Over time, information from these two sources may be integrated in such a way that we

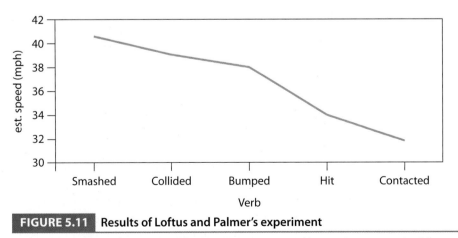

FIGURE 5.11   **Results of Loftus and Palmer's experiment**

From: Loftus, E.F., & Palmer, J.C. (1974). Reconstruction of automobile destruction: An example of the interaction between language and memory. *Journal of Verbal Learning and Verbal Behavior, 13,* 585–589.

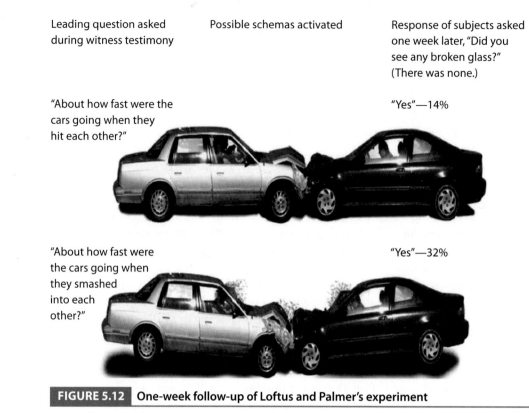

Leading question asked during witness testimony	Possible schemas activated	Response of subjects asked one week later, "Did you see any broken glass?" (There was none.)
"About how fast were the cars going when they hit each other?"		"Yes"—14%
"About how fast were the cars going when they smashed into each other?"		"Yes"—32%

FIGURE 5.12   **One-week follow-up of Loftus and Palmer's experiment**

From: Loftus, E.F., & Palmer, J.C. (1974). Reconstruction of automobile destruction: An example of the interaction between language and memory. *Journal of Verbal Learning and Verbal Behavior, 13*, 585–589.

are unable to tell from which source some specific detail is recalled. All we have is one "memory." (p. 588)

In several subsequent publications, Loftus and others provided a great deal of evidence that misleading post-event information often becomes integrated with the original information (e.g., Cole & Loftus, 1979; Loftus, 1992, 2003; Loftus & Loftus, 1980). This has been termed the **misinformation effect** (Loftus, 2004, p. 868; Loftus & Hoffman, 1989). According to Loftus (2004, p. 145), recent research strongly suggests that more can be changed than "a detail in memory for a previously experienced event." Indeed, it appears quite possible to "plant an entirely false memory into the mind."

> **Misinformation effect**
> The hypothesis that misleading post-event information can become integrated with memory for the original event.

FALSE MEMORIES

A key aspect of Loftus and Palmer's original argument was that people cannot always identify the source of misleading post-event information. We may not recognize that the source is something other than the event itself. In short, we may not be very good at discriminating between memory of real events and memory of imagined events (Johnson, Hashtroudi, & Lindsay, 1993; Johnson & Raye, 1981; Lindsay, 1993). If we imagine an event in a particularly vivid way, we may later have the illusion that the event actually happened. The idea that people can fail to identify the true source of their memories was investigated by D.S. Lindsay and Johnson (1989).

Lindsay and Johnson's experiment was typical of studies of source monitoring. Participants were shown a picture of four people in an office containing a variety of objects (e.g., coffee cup, pencil holder). After seeing the picture some participants also read a text describing the office. Sometimes the text contained misleading descriptions (e.g., "There is a filing cabinet behind the women on the right," when there was no filing cabinet). Participants were tested in two ways. One test simply asked them to read a list of items and indicate whether or not each item (e.g., filing cabinet) occurred in the picture. This was called the recognition test. Another test asked participants to indicate whether or not each item was in the picture, in the text, or in both. This last test was called the source-monitoring test.

The results of the recognition test showed evidence of suggestibility, as had been found in similar experiments of this type. That is, participants attributed suggested items to the picture when they had in fact appeared only in the text. However, the source-monitoring test resulted in fewer errors of this sort. On the basis of these data Lindsay and Johnson argued that the mistakes people make when they try to recall an event are often due to faulty source monitoring. In general, the theoretical framework within which Johnson and others have investigated such phenomena is called the **source monitoring framework** (e.g., Johnson & Raye, 1998; Lindsay & Johnson, 2000; Mitchell & Johnson, 2000).

> **Source monitoring framework**
> A theory of the reason people sometimes fail to distinguish between a real and an imagined event.

LOFTUS ON BARTLETT

The aspects of memory that we have examined here are often explained using a general schema theory. The last word on this topic should go to Elizabeth Loftus, who has done more than anyone else to expose the vagaries of memory:

> A half century ago, Frederic C. Bartlett . . . posited that remembering is "imaginative reconstruction, or construction," and "it is thus hardly ever exact" (Bartlett, 1932, p. 213). His insights link up directly with contemporary research on memory distortion, although even he might have been surprised to find out just how inexact memory can be. . . . Bartlett died in 1969, just missing the beginning of a vast effort to investigate the memory processes that he so intelligently foreshadowed, and that show unequivocally how humans are the authors or creators of their own memories. They can also be the authors or creators of someone else's memory. (Loftus, 2004, p. 147)

▌ Scripts

As we have seen, the schema concept has been used to explain a great deal. Some other approaches are quite similar to it, but are sufficiently distinctive to merit separate discussion. The concept of the script, for example, can be used to do much the same work as the schema concept.

A **script** has been defined as a "structure that describes an appropriate sequence of events in a particular context" or "a predetermined stereotyped sequence of actions that defines a well-known situation" (Schank, 1982a, p. 170). The use of this concept in memory research can be traced to the work of Schank and Abelson (1975, 1977; Schank, 1982a, 1982b). Originally, these authors focused on scripts for particular situations, such as going to a restaurant. If people are asked to describe what typically happens when they go to a restaurant, their stories will usually include a common sequence of events: ordering food, eating it, paying the bill, and so on. Although the particulars of the stories will vary, there will still be quite a bit of common ground across situations and people (Bower, Black, & Turner, 1979).

> **Script**
> A set of expectations concerning the actions and events that are appropriate in a particular situation.

CONSIDER THIS
BOX 5.3

Implanting False Memories

A particularly effective demonstration of the implant-ing of false memories was conducted by Lindsay, Hagen, Read, Wade, and Garry (2004). It was based on the assumption that viewing photographs from their child-hood could elicit vivid accounts of events from their own lives that may or may not have actually happened. The participants in the study were undergraduate students whose parents had supplied the researchers with a class photo from Grade 1 or 2. The parents had also provided descriptions of true episodes from each student's pri-mary school experience in Grades 3–5. The participants were presented with written accounts of both the true episodes and a false episode that described "putting Slime, a brightly colored gelatinous compound manu-factured by Mattel as a toy, on the teacher's desk" in either Grade 1 or Grade 2 (p. 150). Approximately half the participants were given photos of their Grade 1 or 2 class and all were given a written description of the "Slime" event. The participants were encouraged to try to remember the earliest of the episodes, namely the false one. A week later they were asked if they had remem-bered the "Slime" event. Amazingly, two-thirds of the stu-dents who had been given class photos "remembered" the "Slime" event, compared with 23 per cent who had not been given photos.

The fact that even the no-photo condition elicited a fair number of false memories is worth noting. However, the photos stimulated significantly more of them. As the authors observe, it's common for psychotherapists to suggest that patients seeking to recover lost childhood memories look at pictures from their youth while rumi-nating about their past. The implication of the "Slime" study is that this practice may encourage false memories.

Lindsay et al. (2004) note that their results may be understood within the framework of source monitoring theory. If looking at a childhood photo encourages active imagining of what might have been, it may lead to confu-sion between what actually happened and what never did.

Life script
A cultural narrative that guides autobiographical memories and prescribes the age norms for important events in an individual's life.

Berntsen and Rubin (2004) have drawn attention to the importance of **life scripts**: "culturally shared expectations as to the order and timing of life events in a proto-typical life course" (p. 427). Life scripts are more abstract than the scripts described by Schank and Abelson. Whereas the latter deal with prototypical situations such as going to a restaurant, life scripts involve the age norms that each society uses to "structure expectations and regulate behavior" (p. 429). Life scripts are prescriptive, not descrip-tive. That is, instead of simply describing an individual's life, they prescribe what the sequence of important events in that life should be. Thus life scripts contain events that the culture judges to be important, such as marriage. They are not concerned with events that are biologically rather than culturally cued, such as menopause. Life scripts are not abstracted from personal experiences, as a restaurant script is, but are "handed down from older generations, from stories, and from observations of the behavior of other, typically older, people within the same culture" (p. 429).

In one of their experiments, Berntsen and Rubin (2004, p. 435) asked Danish undergraduates to imagine a "quite ordinary infant" and list the seven most important events that are likely to take place in that infant's life. The participants also estimated the age at which these events would occur. The 10 most commonly listed events and the ages at which they were predicted to occur are given in Figure 5.13. While particu-lar cultures may associate different ages with each event, the sequence of events is likely to be quite similar for many Western countries. Research into life scripts in other cultures would be a useful undertaking. If you are from a non-European and/

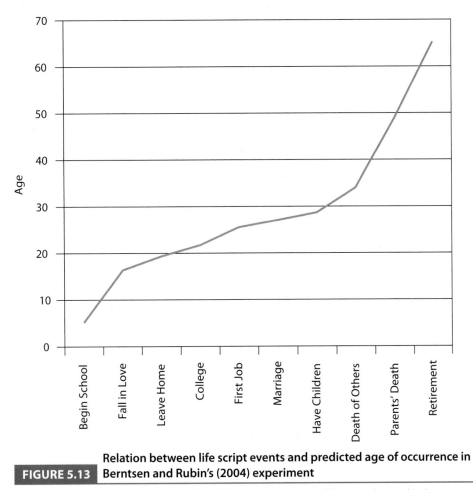

FIGURE 5.13   Relation between life script events and predicted age of occurrence in Berntsen and Rubin's (2004) experiment

From: Berntsen, D., & Rubin, D.C. (2004). Cultural life scripts structure recall from autobiographical memory. *Memory & Cognition, 32*, 427–442.

or non-English-speaking country, how do you think your life script might differ from the illustration?

Notice that the curve for the period between the ages of roughly 15 and 30 is relatively flat. This is because there are more culturally prescribed events during this period than during others (Berntsen & Rubin, 2004, p. 438). We will return to this phenomenon and its connections with autobiographical memory in Chapter 13, on personal cognition. For now, we will simply note that in Berntsen and Rubin's study the order in which participants listed life-script events was correlated with the age at which they were expected to occur. That is, events predicted to come early in life were listed before events predicted to come later in life. The life script does indeed prescribe the order in which events are expected to occur. As we shall see in more detail in Chapter 13,

> events that fit into the life script are more easily recalled than events that do not. Life scripts are likely to also influence encoding and retention by endowing events that match the life script with an importance and consequentiality that is socially agreed upon and by providing a shared background for rehearsing such events in social settings. (Berntsen & Rubin, 2004, p. 440)

Levels of Processing

Think back to our discussion of the information-processing tradition in Chapter 1. Craik (1980) noted that the early models were more concerned with the *structure* of cognition than with the *process* of cognition. That is, early information-processing approaches were preoccupied with the various components of the cognitive system. As we have already seen, these components were identified by labels such as "primary memory" and "secondary memory" (Waugh & Norman, 1965), or "short-term memory" and "long-term memory" (Atkinson & Shiffrin, 1971). To remind yourself of the sort of model that Craik criticized, look again at the diagram of the Waugh and Norman model in Figure 1.7 (p. 12). Waugh and Norman emphasized the structure of memory, dividing it into "primary" and "secondary" components.

Craik criticized models such as Waugh and Norman's because they don't tell us very much about the processes that determine what will be remembered (i.e., what exactly it is that leads us to remember certain kinds of information better than others). The capacity of structures such as primary memory depends on the process used to deal with the information to be remembered, and the process in turn depends on the nature of the information. As Craik pointed out, if the items to be remembered are unrelated (e.g., a random group of digits) primary memory will be unable to retain more than four or five of them. However, that capacity will be much higher if the items are related in some way. Thus if I ask you to remember 10 words that form a sentence—say, "The lazy brown dog ran over the energetic green turtle"—you will have no problem doing it. This suggests that it would be more fruitful to focus on the *process* of remembering, rather than the structures that might underlie memory. Primary memory, as Lockhart and Craik (1990) conceived of it, is a "processing activity and not a structure"; it is not located in any one place, but is a way of "paying attention to different types of information" (p. 105).

Craik and Lockhart (1972) presented an approach to memory research that did indeed focus on the processes that influence memory. This approach begins by distinguishing between shallow and deep **levels of processing**. For example, consider the word *TRAIN*. A relatively shallow way of processing that word is to observe that it is printed in capital letters. This is shallow because it deals only with the word's physical characteristics. A deeper way of processing the word would be to observe that it refers to a form of transportation. Now you are processing the word in terms of its meaning. The more meaning you extract from an event, the more deeply you are processing it. In other words, according to Craik and Lockhart, cognition is a system designed for perception and understanding. The more deeply we process an event, the more we will have comprehended it. The more important an event is to us, the more we will try to comprehend it. Thus depth of processing is a continuum that ranges from registering an event purely in terms of its physical characteristics to analyzing it in terms of its meaning and relationship to other things that you know. These relationships are illustrated in Figure 5.14.

ELABORATION AND DISTINCTIVENESS

As Lockhart and Craik (1990; Craik, 2002) observed, the notion that there are different levels of processing has been refined with development of the concepts of elaboration

Levels of processing
A continuum that ranges from registering an event purely in terms of its physical characteristics to analyzing it in terms of its relationship to other things that you know.

Level of processing	Type of encoding	Example of questions used to elicit appropriate encoding
Shallow processing	*Structural encoding:* emphasizes the physical structure of the stimulus	Is the word written in capital letters?
Intermediate processing	*Phonemic encoding:* emphasizes what a word sounds like	Does the word rhyme with *weight*?
Deep processing	*Semantic encoding:* emphasizes the meaning of verbal input	Would the word fit in the sentence: "He met a _____ on the street"?

Depth of procesing →

FIGURE 5.14   **Depth of processing**

and distinctiveness. **Elaboration** may be defined as "extra processing . . . that results in additional, related or redundant" material (Reder, 1980, p. 7), while **distinctiveness** refers to the precision with which an item is encoded. For example, to encode the word *cabbage* as a "food" is less distinctive than to encode it as a "vegetable" (Frase & Kamman, 1974).

There is evidence that the more distinctively an item is elaborated, the better it will be remembered. For example, Stein et al. (1982) compared the elaborations produced by two groups of students, one academically successful and the other less so. In one experiment the students were given short statements on the model of "The hungry man got into his car" (in which the fact that the man is hungry has no obvious bearing on the fact that he got into his car) and had to write continuations for them. The academically successful students tended to write precise elaborations that connected the formerly unrelated elements: for example, "The hungry man got into his car to go to the restaurant." This elaboration is precise because the information it adds is directly related to the fact that the man is hungry. By contrast, the elaborations produced by the less academically successful students tended to be less precise: for example, "The hungry man got into his car and drove away." This is a less precise elaboration because the additional material doesn't explain why the man got into his car. It also turned out that the academically successful students were able to recall more statements than were their less successful colleagues.

The authors concluded that, unlike the more successful students, the less academically successful group did not spontaneously use precise elaboration on the material they were attempting to learn. They also suggested that academically successful students may have a better understanding of the importance of elaborating information in a meaningful way. Knowing what strategies to use in order to facilitate cognitive processes is another example of metacognition. Training students how to use elaboration may

Elaboration
Adding to or enriching information by relating it to other information.

Distinctiveness
The precision with which an item is encoded.

be an important way of improving their performance. In Chapter 7, on imagery, we will review additional work on the role of distinctiveness in facilitating memory.

The importance of elaboration in memory has been further demonstrated in a series of studies of the way professional actors learn their lines. Noice (1991, 1992, 1993) showed that professional actors do not memorize scripts by rote. In a study comparing the way that professional actors and novices learned a six-page scene, Noice (1991) found that the professionals made many more elaborations of the material they needed to learn. These elaborations included considering the perspective of the character and asking questions about motivation. In another study (1992) she had professional actors describe their strategies for learning a part. They said they did not use rote memory, and stressed the importance of "finding reasons why [a] character says each line and performs each action." Noice concluded that when people talk about an actor "creating" a character, "it is literally true. The author supplies the words but the actor ferrets out the meaning" (Noice, 1992, p. 425). A by-product of actors' relentless search for meaning is that they end up memorizing the part without rote repetition. This should remind you of Aitken's musical memory, discussed in Box 5.2.

LEVELS OF PROCESSING AND AGING

Craik (2002) has suggested that it may be helpful to distinguish between **specific** and **general levels of representation**, particularly in connection with age-related changes in memory performance. Among those changes is a loss of the ability to remember specifics such as names, even when the people concerned are close acquaintances. Another change is a tendency to retell the same stories to the same audience. Craik argues that names are relatively superficial details and that even if you forget someone's name, you may still have a deep knowledge and understanding of the person in question. Similarly, the ability to remember the occasions on which you have told a particular story pales in comparison to the importance of the story itself. With advancing age, the specific details of events may be forgotten, but their deeper meaning may still be retained.

Specific and general levels of representation
As people age they tend to forget specific details but to remember deeper, more general meanings.

LEVELS OF PROCESSING AND THE BRAIN

As Roediger, Gallo, and Geraci (2002) observed, one implication of the "levels of processing" approach is that there is no particular place in the brain where memories are stored. Rather, the same parts of the brain used to comprehend an event will be activated when the event is recalled. They describe an MRI study done by Wheeler, Petersen, and Buckner (2002) in which participants were shown a word (e.g., *dog*) and then presented with either a compatible sound (e.g., barking) or a compatible picture (e.g., of a dog). Subsequently, participants were shown the word and asked to recall what went with it. When recall was successful, the predicted area of the brain was activated. Thus if the person had heard a dog barking, then at recall the auditory cortex was more activated, while if the person had seen a picture, then the visual cortex was more activated. The conclusion was that "the type of processing during test recruits the same brain regions as engaged during study" (Roediger, Gallo, & Geraci, 2002, p. 328). Evidence supporting a similar conclusion is reported by Nyberg (2002).

EVALUATION OF THE LEVELS OF PROCESSING APPROACH

The "levels of processing" approach has had an enduring influence on memory research. This influence was reviewed by Lockhart and Craik (1990) and in a set of papers looking back over 30 years of levels of processing research (Clifford, 2004). A persistent criticism has been that the concept of levels of processing is too vague (Baddeley, 1978). Although there is general agreement on what constitutes deep as opposed to shallow processing, there is still no objective measure of depth (Craik, 2002, p. 308). At its most superficial, levels of processing research has simply extended Bartlett's point that the effort after meaning is a crucial determinant of what is remembered (Craik, 2002, p. 312). However, as Lockhart and Craik (1990; Craik, 2002) pointed out, the levels of processing framework has generated and is still generating important research. Its heuristic value is undeniable.

Two Approaches to Memory Research

There are two contrasting approaches to memory research. Both seek to uncover the general principles regulating memory, but one is lab-based and emphasizes experimental control, while the other incorporates real-world complexities.

THE LAB-BASED APPROACH

For several decades, most memory research has focused on laboratory experiments. This **lab-based approach to memory research**, which Bruce (1985) called the general principles tradition, goes back at least to Ebbinghaus (1885/1964), whose work has been enormously influential (Gorfein & Hoffman, 1987; Slamecka, 1985).

Ebbinghaus pioneered the use of **nonsense syllables**—a consonant followed by a vowel followed by a consonant, such as PIB or WOL—in memory research. In one experiment he read and re-read lists of 13 nonsense syllables each until he could recite them perfectly twice from memory. After various intervals, he then determined how long it took him to relearn a list. Naturally, the longer the time since the original learning, the longer it took to relearn a list. On the basis of these experiments he was able to estimate how much had been forgotten after different periods of time. In general, memory loss was greatest immediately after learning; then the rate of decline became more gradual. Ebbinghaus's results were replicated by other experimenters, and can be summarized in the famous **forgetting curve**, an example of which is shown in Figure 5.15.

One general principle that has fared very well over time is **Jost's law of forgetting**, which was first published in 1897. This law states that of two memory traces of equal strength, the younger trace will decay faster than the older one (Wixted, 2004b). Another way of putting it is to say that the rate at which forgetting occurs will become slower over time. Figure 5.15 illustrates this nicely. Notice that more than 70 per cent of the material is lost in the first two days, but that there is only a very slow decline in the subsequent four days. Although the specific amount of forgetting that takes place during a particular interval will depend on many factors, including the nature of the material learned, the general finding that the rate of forgetting slows with the passage of time is extremely robust.

Lab-based approach to memory research
An approach that emphasizes controlled laboratory (as opposed to real-world) research in the search for general principles.

Nonsense syllables
Nonsense "words" consisting of a consonant followed by a vowel followed by a consonant.

Forgetting curve
Ebbinghaus's finding that the rate at which information is forgotten is greatest immediately after the information has been acquired, and declines more gradually over time.

Jost's law of forgetting
Of two memory traces of equal strength, the younger trace will decay faster than the older one.

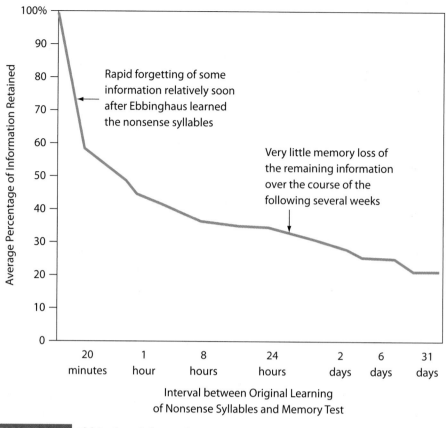

Rapid forgetting of some information relatively soon after Ebbinghaus learned the nonsense syllables

Very little memory loss of the remaining information over the course of the following several weeks

FIGURE 5.15   **Ebbinghaus's forgetting curve**

Ribot's law of retrograde amnesia
Older memories are less likely to be lost as a result of brain damage than are newer memories.

Law of progressions and pathologies
A "last in, first out" principle referring to the possibility that the last system to emerge is the first to show the effects of degeneration.

Ecological approach to the study of memory
An approach that emphasizes real-world complexities in its investigations to discover general principles.

A likely explanation of Jost's law involves the process of consolidation, which we referred to earlier in this chapter. We noted that over time memories tend to become more resistant to interference from more recently acquired information. This suggests that "as a result of the process of consolidation . . . forgetting functions would be expected to exhibit an ever-decreasing rate of decay and Jost's law of forgetting would follow naturally" (Wixted, 2004b, p. 877). Another implication of Jost's law is **Ribot's law of retrograde amnesia**: that older memories are less likely to be lost as a result of brain damage than are newer memories. Ribot's law illustrates a very general tendency that R. Brown (1958, p. 297) called the **law of progressions and pathologies**. This is a "last in, first out" principle suggesting that the last system to develop is the first to show the effects of degeneration. Whether this law is truly general remains unclear, but we will refer to it again when we discuss the effects of age on memory.

THE ECOLOGICAL APPROACH

The lab-based approach can be contrasted with the **ecological approach to the study of memory** (Loftus, 1991; see also the discussion in Chapter 3 above). Proponents of the ecological approach have often argued that lab-based approaches do not come to grips with the complexity of memory as it operates in everyday life (Neisser, 1978b, 1982b). An ecological approach would examine memory in natural settings

(Neisser, 1985) and explore how it functions in complex real-world situations (Hirst & Levine, 1985).

For its part, the ecological approach has been criticized precisely because it can sacrifice experimental control in its search for general principles. Proponents (e.g., Neisser, 1991) have replied that the kind of field studies done by those with an ecological orientation are an important part of other sciences, such as biology, and should be central to the scientific study of memory as well.

Neisser (1997) sounded a conciliatory note in this dispute (see Banagi & Crowder, 1989). Drawing on Koriat and Goldsmith (1996), he recast the issue as a debate between those who investigate how memory is stored (e.g., Ebbinghaus) and those who investigate how it is used (e.g., Bartlett). "Memories are not so much retrieved as they are constructed, usually with a specific goal in mind" (Neisser, 1997, p. 1697). If the goal changes, the memory that is reconstructed may change as well.

Neisser described those who study how memory is used as "ecologically oriented" because they are concerned with the way it operates in the real world. However, he noted that lab-based approaches can provide us with an understanding of "the neural systems that preserve information in the brain," and that both types of studies are necessary "if we are ever to understand the exquisitely human activity of remembering in an adequate way" (Neisser, 1997, p. 170).

BAHRICK AND THE PERMASTORE

Studies of flashbulb memories, which we reviewed earlier in the chapter, are often cited as models of ecologically valid research. Also singled out in this regard are Bahrick's (1984, 2000; Bahrick & Hall, 1991) studies of long-term memory focusing on the practical question of how long we remember what we learned in school. Because Bahrick's studies focus on retention of real material, as opposed to nonsense words, they stand in sharp contrast to Ebbinghaus's lab-based studies. Writing in 1984, Bahrick pointed out that while there had been many laboratory studies of learning, few studies had been conducted to see how well people remember what they actually learned in school. In the late 1970s Neisser (1978b, p. 5) had questioned why, since higher education "depends heavily on the assumption that students remember something valuable from their educational experience," psychologists had not taken "the opportunity to study a critical memory problem so close to hand, but they never do." Thanks in large part to Bahrick's work, we now know much more than we did about what we remember from our schooling.

Bahrick (2000, p. 347) observed that since the 1980s a consensus had gradually developed according to which "important questions about memory should not be ignored just because they are not amenable to laboratory exploration." Although there are serious methodological problems involved in studying long-term retention of school learning, researchers simply must do the best they can under the constraints of real-world environments. In studying learning in school, the investigator needs to know such things as how well something was originally learned, and how often it has been rehearsed in the interval. Acquiring this kind of information is difficult and very time-consuming. Bahrick (1984) attempted to overcome these problems in a naturalistic study of Spanish learned in school.

With 773 participants, Bahrick's study was very large. Some participants were current students of Spanish at the high school or college level. Others had studied it in the past, anytime between 1 and 50 years earlier. All participants were classified in terms of the number and level of Spanish courses they had taken in high school and college.

Participants were asked for information concerning the grades they had received in their Spanish courses and how often they had been able to use Spanish since they had last studied it. They also took a comprehensive test of their knowledge of Spanish, which included measures of reading comprehension, vocabulary, grammar, and knowledge of idioms and word order. In the reading comprehension test participants were asked to read a passage in Spanish and then answer questions about it. The vocabulary test, in part, required participants to write the English meaning of a Spanish word, and vice versa. Grammar items required the participants to write the proper form of a verb to use in a sentence. Knowledge of idioms was tapped by asking participants to identify the English meaning of Spanish idioms such as *desde luego* ("of course") and knowledge of Spanish word order was measured by giving participants a random sequence of Spanish words to reorder to make a proper sentence.

The first point to note is that the absolute level of performance varied with the number of Spanish courses taken and the grade level obtained. The more Spanish participants had studied and the higher their grades, the better they performed when their knowledge was tested later on. Responses to a question about rehearsal indicated that very few participants had spoken, read, written, or listened to Spanish after the end of their studies. The most striking finding was the consistency of the pattern of language loss over time. For the first three to six years after stopping the study of Spanish, there was a continuous loss of knowledge. However, after that initial period there was a period of roughly 25 years during which no further loss occurred. The general shape of the curve describing levels of knowledge at different times is shown in Figure 5.16. Of course, the absolute level of knowledge will vary with the amount and quality of prior learning, but the shape of the curve tends to be similar for everyone.

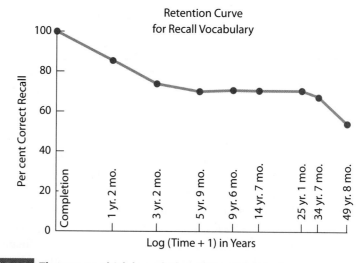

FIGURE 5.16   **The rate at which knowledge of Spanish is lost**

From: Bahrick, H.P. (1984). Semantic memory in permastore: Fifty years of memory for Spanish learned in school. *Journal of Experimental Psychology, 113*, 1–31. Copyright 1984 by the American Psychological Association.

Bahrick argued for the existence of what he called a **permastore**. It's important to note that by "permastore" Bahrick did not mean a particular place where memories are stored, but the state of relative permanence in which some kinds of memory may continue to exist after the initial period of decay comes to an end. Because Bahrick's study found so little evidence of Spanish rehearsal after studies had ended, it appears that rehearsing material after it is learned does not affect the transfer of information to permastore. Whether material ends up in permastore appears to be determined at the time the material is learned. However, the precise mechanism through which the transferal of information to permastore takes place remains unclear.

> **Permastore**
> Bahrick's term for the state of relative permanence in which he found that some kinds of memory can be retained over very long periods of time.

ADDITIONAL DEMONSTRATIONS OF LONG-TERM RETENTION OF EDUCATIONAL MATERIAL

Bahrick and Hall (1991) also looked at long-term retention for mathematics, in a study in which they enrolled 1726 participants. They sampled items from standardized tests of algebra and geometry from high school mathematics courses taught between 1937 and 1986. Participants ranged in age from 19 to 84 and varied in terms of the amount of mathematical training they had received, from no algebra or geometry courses at all to university-level studies.

It turned out that long-term retention of knowledge from participants' first algebra course was influenced most by their subsequent exposure to or practice with algebra. "When exposure to mathematics is extended over several years, performance levels remain stable for half a century without the further benefit of practice. . . . [People] who took three or more college-level math courses, with the highest of these above calculus, show[ed]" virtually no loss of high school algebra knowledge during 50 years, even if there was no measurable rehearsal in the interim (Bahrick & Hall, 1991, p. 24). Whether a student got A's or C's mattered less than how many courses were taken. There were similar findings for geometry knowledge. In short, the study suggested that subsequent learning reinforced and consolidated prior learning.

PRACTICAL IMPLICATIONS OF LONG-TERM MEMORY RESEARCH

Bahrick (2000; Bahrick & Hall, 1991) argued that his work had several practical implications. For example, since retention seemed to be "much more influenced by . . . variables pertaining to the curriculum and schedule of instruction" than by "individual differences [in] aptitude and achievement," the "life span of knowledge" could be extended by introducing "[c]hanges that increase the duration of acquisition or exposure and require maintenance and relearning of content during an extended period" (Bahrick & Hall, 1991, p. 32). Among the "curricular interventions [that] could produce such changes" were a longer course duration so that the same number of hours were spread out over a longer time; "cumulative re-examinations at the end of a program of several years; and . . . capstone review courses at the end of programs" (Bahrick & Hall, 1991, p. 32).

Bahrick's studies suggest that how well students do in a subject is far from the only thing that determines how much they will remember in the long run. Rather, the data suggest that, regardless of their grades, students who are prepared to take several courses in a discipline will forget less of the material they studied even after several years have gone by. In order to prevent long-term forgetting of information learned in school, it appears to be very important to spread courses in a particular subject over several years, with lots of repetition of central concepts, rather than to take a short, concentrated course. It appears to be entirely possible for students to learn at least some aspects of a subject and never forget them. They would be permanently stored in memory, and recallable when required. (You might like to have a look at one of your old exams. You may be surprised at how much you can still remember from courses you took in the past.) In fact, Conway, Cohen, and Stanhope (1991) have shown that students in a cognitive psychology course may retain general factual knowledge from the course for at least 12 years.

▌▌ Summary

In this chapter we have considered the development of different concepts and supporting research for understanding memory as a cognitive process. Central to our understanding is the distinction between memory traces and memory schemas. Generally speaking, *memory traces* are permanent and complete copies of previous experiences. When we recall memory traces, we can re-experience the past (*reappearance hypothesis*). By contrast, *memory schemas* are organizational frameworks that support new constructions of past experiences from fragments of information.

Both concepts have generated a number of interesting research questions. Regarding the accuracy of memory traces, researchers R. Brown and J. Kulik (1977) investigated a class of memories called *flashbulb memories*. These are clear, distinct, and detailed types of memory traces that lay down enduring records of experience. They theorize that flashbulb memories are produced by a unique mechanism consisting of a sequence of information-processing events (*Now Print! theory*).

By contrast, when McCloskey et al. (1988; the *Challenger* experiment) compared changes in ordinary and flashbulb memories over time, they found that flashbulb memories were no more accurate than ordinary memories and that their formation did not require a special mechanism.

The dominant idea in the "memory trace" literature is that memory is a dynamic process and hence that memories change over time. Memory traces of an event are not fully formed immediately after that event, but take some time to become complete (*consolidation theory*). Consolidation occurs in a part of the brain known as the *hippocampus*. The consolidation process can be disrupted by events occurring immediately after the event-to-be-remembered (*retroactive interference*). Also, once consolidation is complete, the memory trace is still susceptible to revision through *reconsolidation*.

With his *method of serial and repeated reproductions*, Bartlett demonstrates that memory production involves both the selection and the omission of material. Both processes are guided by a general, abstract setting within which the memory traces have meaning, known as a *schema*. The general assumption in much of the memory schema literature is that memory involves four processes: selection, abstraction, interpretation, and integration. However, a couple of key studies have shown disruptions in this process. Loftus and Palmer's study of eyewitness testimony showed that misleading post-event information can become integrated with the original information-to-be-remembered (the *misinformation effect*). Lindsay and Johnson's study of false memory investigated failure to monitor the sources of their memories.

A less traditional approach to memory research focuses not on the structures of memory but on levels of processing. Craik and Lockhart (1972) distinguished between *shallow* and *deep processing*, as well as *general* and *specific* levels of processing. Their approach also accounted for extra processing of related material (*elaboration*) and how precisely an item is encoded (*distinctiveness*). However, with no objective measure of depth, the "levels of processing" concept of memory has been criticized for being too vague.

Finally, *ecological approaches* focus on memory in real-world situations. Researchers such as Bahrick (2000; Bahrick & Hall, 1991) study the complexity of memory in everyday life by looking at the long-term retention of educational experiences (the *permastore*).

Case Study Wrap-Up

Jennifer Thompson was devastated to realize how her mistaken testimony had harmed Ronald Cotton, and eventually she arranged to meet with him. To her amazement he not only forgave her but became her friend and, eventually, co-author. Their joint memoir, *Picking Cotton* (co-written with Erin Torneo), was published in 2009. Thompson is now an advocate for the wrongfully convicted, calling for legal reform and, in particular, better understanding of why eyewitness testimony is so unreliable.

Several elements of the Cotton case can be related to the material in this chapter. Loftus and Palmer demonstrated how easily memory for an event can be modulated by post-event information. Furthermore, Thompson appears to have had a particular script or schema in mind when she picked Cotton out of the photo lineup. She told NBC she was "consciously . . . trying to figure out the person in the photographic lineup that most closely resemble[d] the [police] sketch, as opposed to the actual attacker" (NBC News, 2009), and in an interview with CBS she explained how her expectations influenced her behaviour: "When you're sittin'

in front of a photo lineup, you just assume one of these guys is the suspect" (CBS News, 2009). For their part, the police had already chosen Cotton as a suspect, so their bias was confirmed when Thompson chose him out of the photo lineup, and this initial confirmation may have led them to disregard other evidence. It's possible that Thompson would have identified Bobby Poole if she had seen his picture early enough in the investigation. Unfortunately for Ronald Cotton, she did not. By the time the case went to trial, the only face she remembered was his.

Finally, the Cotton case highlights one of the most important take-home messages from this chapter. To put it simply, memory is far from perfect. Eyewitnesses are not the only ones whose testimony may be fallible: all of us are prone to errors of memory, whether because of post-event misinformation, decay, or interference. This is not necessarily a bad thing. After all, if we were required to remember every detail of every daily encounter, our thoughts might well be preoccupied with them, severely limiting our ability to function in the present.

? In the Know: Review Questions

1. Discuss the differences between memory traces and memory schemas. How might they be related?

2. What are flashbulb memories? Discuss alternative explanations of their nature. Do you have any memories that fall into this category? Is there any way for you to check on their accuracy?

3. Discuss research relevant to the general form of schema theory as outlined by Alba and Hasher as well as Koriat, Goldsmith, and Pansky.

4. Review the research on eyewitness testimony and false memories discussed in this chapter. How does misinformation acceptance work?

5. Summarize the strengths and weaknesses of Craik and Lockhart's "levels of processing" framework.

Key Concepts

abstraction
body schema (body image)
consolidation theory
ecological approach to the study of memory
elaboration and distinctiveness
flashbulb memories
forgetting curve
hippocampus
integration
interpretation
Jost's law of forgetting
lab-based approach to memory research
law of progressions and pathologies
levels of processing
life scripts
method of repeated reproduction (Bartlett)
method of serial reproduction (Bartlett)
misinformation effect (Loftus)

mystic writing pad model (Freud)
nonsense syllables
Now Print! theory
Penfield homunculus
permastore (Bahrick)
phantom limb
plasticity
rationalization (Bartlett)
reappearance hypothesis
reconsolidation
retroactive interference
Ribot's law of retrograde amnesia
schema (Bartlett)
script
selection
source monitoring framework
specific and general levels of representation

Links to Other Chapters

consolidation theory
Chapter 10 (insight and the brain)

hippocampus
Chapter 7 (cognitive maps and the hippocampus)

Chapter 10 (insight and the brain)
Chapter 12 (expertise)

plasticity
Chapter 12 (neural plasticity and *g*)

scripts
Chapter 13 (autobiographical memory)

levels of processing
Chapter 9 (literacy)

distinctiveness
Chapter 7 (imagery and distinctiveness)
Chapter 13 (autobiographical memory)

Further Reading

For a useful collection of papers on so-called flashbulb memories see Winograd and Neisser (1992).

Arbib and Hesse (1986) argue that schema theory may be applied to just about everything.

Bartlett's emphasis on the social nature of remembering is discussed in Weldon and Bellinger's (1997) study of collective memory.

For a fascinating review of the factors that influence eyewitnesses' identification of suspects in contexts such as police lineups, see Wells and Olson (2003). On the importance of interviewing witnesses as close to the time of the crime as possible, see Tuckey and Brewer (2003).

There has been a great deal of additional work with the script concept. If you are interested in deepening your knowledge of this topic, you should read Mandler (1984) and Mandler and Murphy (1983). See also Thorndyke (1984).

For more on forgetting curves, see Rubin and Wenzel (1996). Noice and Noice (2002) studied long-term memory retention among professional actors and reached conclusions similar to those of Bahrick.

Ecological approaches to memory are well-illustrated by Herrmann and Neisser (1979). In the same edited volume, Hunter (1979) discusses memory in everyday life. Perhaps the tour de force on ecological approaches to memory is Rubin (1995).

Arbib, M.A., & Hesse, M.B. (1986). *The construction of reality*. Cambridge: Cambridge University Press.

Herrmann, D.J., & Neisser, U. (1979). An inventory of everyday memory experiences. In M.M. Gruneberg & P.E. Morris (Eds.), *Applied problems in memory*. London: Academic Press.

Hunter, I.M.L. (1979). Memory in everyday life. In J.R. Anderson & S.M. Kosslyn (Eds.), *Tutorials in learning and memory* (pp. 167–191). San Francisco: Freeman.

Mandler, J.M. (1984). *Stories, scripts and scenes*. Hillsdale, NJ: Erlbaum.

Mandler, J.M., & Murphy, C.M. (1983). Subjective judgements of script structure. *Journal of Experimental Psychology: Learning, Memory, and Cognition 9*, 534–543.

Noice, T., & Noice, H. (2002). Very long-term recall and recognition of well-learned material. *Applied Cognitive Psychology 16*, 259–272.

Rubin, D.C. (1995). *Memory in oral tradition: The cognitive psychology of epic, ballads, and counting out rhymes*. New York: Oxford University Press.

Rubin, D.C., & Wenzel, A.E. (1996). One hundred years of forgetting: A quantitative description of retention. *Psychological Review 103*, 734–760.

Thorndyke, P.W. (1984). Applications of schema theory in cognitive research. In J.R. Anderson & S.M. Kosslyn (Eds.), *Tutorials in learning and memory* (pp. 167–191). San Francisco: Freeman.

Tuckey, M.R., & Brewer, N. (2003). The influence of schemas, stimulus ambiguity, and interview schedule on eyewitness memory over time. *Journal of Experimental Psychology: General 9*, 101–118.

Weldon, M.S., & Bellinger, K.D. (1997). Collective memory: Collaborative and individual processes in remembering. *Journal of Experimental Psychology: Learning, Memory, and Cognition 23*, 1160–1175.

CHAPTER 6

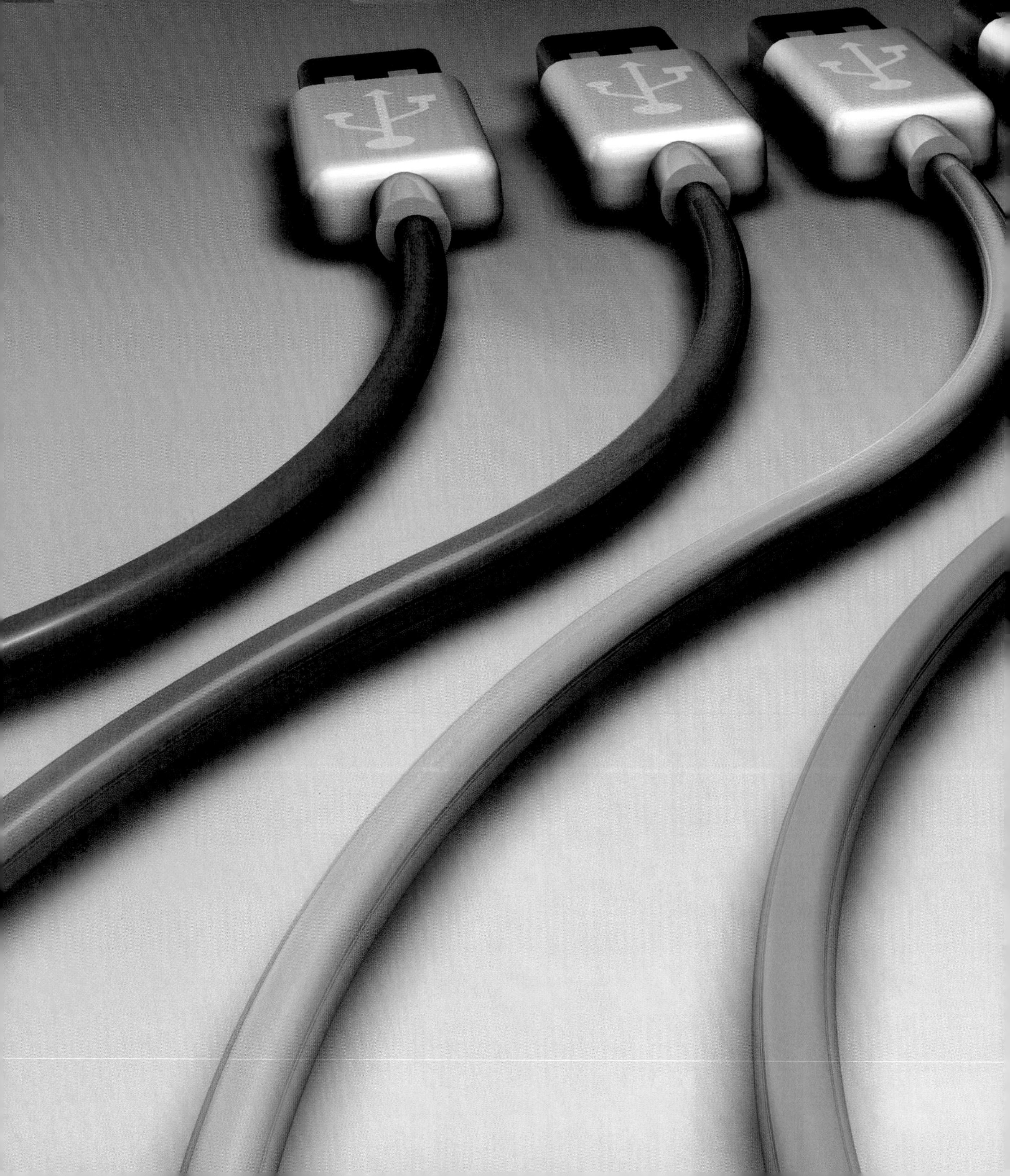

Memory Systems

Chapter Contents

Chapter Objectives

- To distinguish between various memory systems.
- To outline Tulving's approach to memory.
- To look at various models of semantic memory.
- To review experimental evidence for the role of spreading activation in semantic memory.
- To examine the concept of working memory.
- To identify what the study of older individuals and people with memory deficits tells us about the nature of memory.

Quick! What was the movie with Drew Barrymore and Adam Sandler where Adam's character (Henry Roth) fell in love with Drew's, even though she woke up every day with no recollection of the previous day's events? Lucy was effectively trapped in time, unable to retain any new memories after suffering brain damage in a car accident.

Although the plot line is obviously far-fetched, it brings up many questions about how human memory operates. Is memory just a big black box where all the information we have ever taken in is stored? Are there different types of memory? If so, are there different areas in the brain dedicated to each type? Are they distinct from one another neurologically? Is it possible that one type of memory can be damaged while other types of memories are spared? These are just some of the questions that will be discussed in this chapter.

Before we start, were you able to remember the film's title? If you said *50 First Dates*, you were correct. This simple exercise is actually a good introduction to the subject of memory. If you were able to answer the question, you must have had the information stored in long-term memory. But how did you access it? Was there a mechanism that selected this information and effectively "pulled" it from memory so that you could answer the question? As we will see later in this chapter, this may in fact be the way we access an accurate memory.

FIGURE 6.1   Drew Barrymore (Lucy Whitmore) and Adam Sandler (Henry Roth)

Tulving and the Theory of Memory Systems

By now you will have realized that there are different ways of thinking about how memory works. Each approach highlights different aspects of memory. Memory theorists, like all scientists, try (as Plato put it) to "carve nature at her joints" (Ghiselin, 1981; Gould, 1985). Because memory is so complex, there are many possible ways of dividing it up, and we must be careful not to "hack off parts like a clumsy butcher" (Plato, *Phaedo*, 265). One very influential way of carving up memory was devised by Endel Tulving, who has explored in depth the question of how many memory systems there are and what each of them does.

ENCODING SPECIFICITY

Tulving's early experimental work concerned the **principle of encoding specificity** (e.g., Tulving & Thomson, 1973). This principle states that a cue is more likely to lead to the recall of a particular item if the cue was initially encoded along with that item: "a critical condition for effective retrieval is the extent to which the processing that occurs during retrieval reinstates the processing that took place during encoding" (Koriat, 2000, p. 337). For example, "if the word POKER is encoded as a metal rod" then it is less likely to be recalled by a cue such as *card game* than by a cue such as *prod* (Brown & Craik, 2000, p. 99).

As this example demonstrates, items can be stored in different ways. The word POKER can be understood, or encoded, as either a metal prod or a card game. In Tulving and Thomson's (1973) classic experiments, they exploited this fact. Participants learned a list of 24 pairs of words. The words that made up the pairs were only weakly associated, and they were printed differently, one of them in lower case and the other

> **Principle of encoding specificity**
> The way an item is retrieved from memory depends on the way it was stored in memory.

FIGURE 6.2   Endel Tulving

in upper case. For example, *plant* might be paired with BUG. The fact that a BUG is unlikely to be among the first things you think of when you think of a plant means that the two words are weakly associated. The same is true for a pair such as *ground* and COLD. The first word of each pair is called the weak cue word, and the second word of each pair is called the target word.

After learning a list of these weakly associated pairs, participants were given a series of tasks. In one case they were shown a list of 24 words, each of which was strongly associated with one of 24 target words on the original list. For example, *insect* was strongly associated with BUG, and *hot* was strongly associated with COLD. The words on this new list can be called *strong cue words*. Participants were asked to free-associate to the entire set of strong cue words and write up to six words that came to mind for each of the strong cue words. On average, participants came up with about 18 of the original 24 target words in this way. Participants were then asked to examine the lists of words they had generated. The question was: How many of those words would they recognize as target words from the original list? If they were able to recognize all of them, they would have recognized about 18 words on average. However, they were only able to recognize about four of the words they had generated. In other words, participants came up with target words without recognizing them as target words. Finally, participants were given the original 24 weak cue words and asked to recall the target words. This time they were able to recall about 15 of the target words.

There are several interesting points to be made about these results. First, and most important, the words generated in response to the strong cues were the same words that the participants had learned in response to the weak cues. However, the participants in many cases were not able to recognize those words. Thus, "conditions can be created in which information about a word event is available in . . . memory . . . in a form sufficient for the production of the appropriate response and yet a literal copy of the word is not recognized" (Tulving & Thomson, 1973). This phenomenon is called "recognition failure of recallable words," and has been extensively investigated (e.g., Tulving & Wiseman, 1975).

Tulving argued that the ability to remember a given item depends on how that item was encoded at input. In other words, the nature of the encoding will influence the memory trace. In the Tulving and Thomson experiments, participants learned the target words in the context of the weak cues. This meant that the weak cues were more effective retrieval tools than the strong cues were, because the latter were not present when the participant learned the original list of word pairs: only the weak cues were present and therefore became part of the memories formed at that time. The strong cues are associated with the target words because those relationships are part of people's general knowledge about words. Because general knowledge is not very helpful in remembering specifically what was learned in the experiment, one might conclude that these are examples of two different kinds of memory.

EPISODIC AND SEMANTIC MEMORY

Episodic memory
The memory system concerned with personally experienced events.

Semantic memory
The memory system concerned with knowledge of words, concepts, and their relationships.

Experiments such as the one just described support the important distinction between episodic and semantic memory (Tulving, 1972). **Episodic memory** refers to the "storage and retrieval of temporally dated, spatially located, and personally experienced events or episodes," whereas **semantic memory** refers to the "storage and utilization of knowledge about words and concepts, their properties and interrelations" (Tulving &

**THINK TWICE
BOX 6.1**   The Sense of Smell

Many people believe that our sense of smell is intimately connected with memory. In this case, the people are right: even though our perceptual experiences tend to be dominated by sight and sound, smell can often trigger a memory that is decades old. It's likely that many of you have had the experience of a distinctive scent sparking a fond (or not) memory of something from years past. Perhaps, for instance, the smell of apple pie takes you back to your grandmother's kitchen.

How is it that smell can trigger a memory? Addressing this question is relatively easy. After an odour molecule enters your nose and is recognized by olfactory sensors, this information is sent first to the olfactory bulb and ultimately to the cortex and the limbic system of your brain. As you may have learned in other classes, the limbic system is an area of the brain that includes a number of structures associated with memory. The hippocampus is especially important for the consolidation of long-term memories.

On the other hand, the sensory neurons in the epithelium (where smells are first registered) survive for only about 60 days. So how can a smell trigger a memory of something that happened years ago? It turns out that once a particular connection has been established between neuronal units in the epithelium and the hippocampus, it remains in place even as new olfactory neurons are generated to replace those that have died. Because the connections of the neurons always go to the same place in the hippocampus, the memories associated with a particular smell survive.

Thomson, 1973, p. 354). Examples of episodic memories given by Tulving (1972) included the following:

> I remember seeing a flash of light a short while ago, followed by a loud sound a few seconds later.
>
> Last year, while on my summer vacation, I met a retired sea captain who knew more jokes than any other person I have ever met.
>
> I remember that I have an appointment with a student at 9:30 tomorrow morning. (Tulving, 1972, p. 386)

Tulving proposed that an event could be stored purely as an episodic memory, that is, as an autobiographical event. By contrast, consider the following examples of semantic memories, which are also taken from Tulving (1972):

> I remember that the chemical formula for common table salt is NaCl.
> I know that the name of the month that follows June is July. (p. 387)

Tulving (1972) observed that such examples are unlike episodic memories because they are general knowledge, not "personally experienced unique episodes" (p. 387).

NEUROPSYCHOLOGICAL EVIDENCE FOR THE INDEPENDENCE OF EPISODIC AND SEMANTIC MEMORY

Studies of brain-injured persons have provided compelling evidence for the distinction between episodic and semantic memory. A good example is a study by Klein, Loftus, and Kihlstrom (1996) concerning self-knowledge of an amnesic patient. These authors discovered a patient, identified as WJ, who suffered retrograde amnesia—the inability to recall events prior to the injury—following a closed head injury (one in which the skull remains intact) that impaired her episodic memory. The issue that this case addresses is whether episodic memory is necessary in order to have a sense of personal identity. "Is it possible for someone who cannot recall any personal experiences—and therefore cannot know how he or she behaved—to know what he or she is like?" (Klein, Loftus, & Kihlstrom, 1996, p. 250).

How would semantic personal knowledge and episodic personal knowledge differ? Semantic personal knowledge "might include the facts that the person is kind, outgoing or lazy. . . . Episodic personal knowledge, by contrast, consists of memories of specific events involving the self [and] could include memories of instances in which one was kind, outgoing or lazy," for example (Klein, Loftus, & Kihlstrom, 1996, pp. 250–51). If semantic personal memory and episodic personal memory were truly independent of one another, then damage to one system should not affect the other system.

WJ was 18 years old, a female undergraduate who fell and sustained a concussion. When she was initially tested, about five days after the injury, she had no episodic memories for the preceding six or seven months. However, her general knowledge was good. She knew which classes she was enrolled in, although she could not remember attending a single one. She also knew names of teachers and friends, although she could not recall any personal experiences involving them. In most cases of closed head injury retrograde amnesia is temporary and the patient recovers within a few weeks. Three weeks after the event, WJ's memory for events prior to the accident had returned to normal.

A technique invented by Crovitz and Schiffman (1974) was used to evaluate WJ's episodic memory during the period in which she was amnesic. WJ was given a list of 24 words, each of which was a picturable noun such as *oven*. The task was to recall a personal event in relation to each word from any time in the past, and then date the memory in terms of when it occurred. Thus someone might recall putting bread in the *oven* this morning. When tested five days after her injury, WJ produced a very different pattern of results than did a control group of three undergraduate women of approximately her age. Figure 6.3 shows that the control participants had a **recency bias** in that they tended to recall experiences from the previous 12 months. By contrast, WJ showed a **primacy bias** in that she tended to recall experiences that were in the relatively distant past. However, when WJ recovered four weeks later, her pattern of episodic memory was similar to that of the control participants.

While still amnesic, WJ was asked to rate herself in terms of 80 personality traits in order to test her semantic personal memory. For example, she judged the extent to which she was *agreeable* or *dominant* and so on. She repeated this exercise after her amnesia had lifted. There was strong agreement between her ratings on these two occasions. The consistency of her ratings was similar to that for control participants. While amnesic, WJ was also asked to rate her personality as if she were in high school. The fact these ratings differed from her current ratings indicated awareness that she had changed while at college. "WJ knew something about what she had been like at college, which was different from what she was like in high school; but she knew this despite the fact that she could not recall anything from her time in college" (Klein, Loftus, & Kihlstrom, 1996, p. 256). These results are consistent with the hypothesis that

Recency bias vs primacy bias
A tendency to recall experiences from the recent past versus a tendency to recall experiences from the relatively distant past.

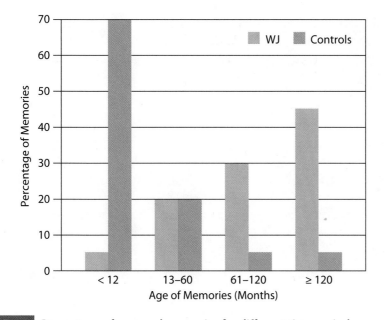

FIGURE 6.3   **Percentage of personal memories for different time periods**

Data from: Klein, S.B., Loftus, J., & Kihlstrom, J.F. (1996). Self-knowledge of an amnesic patient: Toward a neuropsychology of personality and social psychology. *Journal of Experimental Psychology: General*, 125, p. 255.

episodic and semantic memory are represented separately, and that we can have access to semantic knowledge without having access to episodic memory.

Another case of amnesia that Tulving (1985, 2002) reported on has been studied for many years and also supports the dissociation between episodic and semantic memory. This individual was born in 1951 and suffered a closed head injury when he was 30 as a result of a motorcycle accident (Figure 6.4). With "extensive brain lesions in multiple cortical and subcortical brain regions" (Tulving, 2002, p. 130), he never recovered his episodic memory. However, his other intellectual skills remained intact. For example, he was able to outline a standard restaurant script of the sort we considered in the previous chapter—evidence that semantic memory was still functioning. However, he could neither recall individual events from his past nor imagine what he might do in the future. Tulving (1985) reported a fragment of an interview he (ET) conducted with this patient, who was known as NN at the time (KC in later publications; see Tulving, 2002a).

ET: Let's try the question again about the future. What will you be doing tomorrow?
(There is a 15-second pause)
NN: smiles faintly, and says, "I don't know."
ET: Do you remember the question?
NN: About what I'll be doing tomorrow?
ET: Yes. How would you describe your state of mind when you try to think about it?
(A 5-second pause)
NN: A blank I guess. (p. 4)

FIGURE 6.4   Patient KC

At various points NN described his blank state of mind as "like being asleep," like "being in a room with nothing there and having a guy tell you to go find a chair, and there's nothing there," or "like swimming in the middle of a lake [with] nothing there to hold you up or do anything with" (Tulving, 1985, p. 4). While NN has retained his semantic memory systems, then, his episodic memory system is drastically impaired.

■■ The Development of the Theory of Memory Systems

For more than three decades, a great deal of work has been stimulated by Tulving's distinction between episodic and semantic memory. Over such a long period of time, there will inevitably be changes in any theory as it responds to new research. Tulving himself has published a series of changes to his basic theory (e.g., Tulving, 1983, 1984, 1985, 1986, 2000, 2001a, 2001b, 2002a, 2002b). Some researchers have suggested that in all there may be as many as five memory systems (Schacter & Tulving, 1994; Schacter, Wagner, & Buckner, 2000): episodic memory, semantic memory, procedural memory, perceptual representation system, and working memory.

PROCEDURAL MEMORY

Procedural memory (J.R. Anderson, 1976) underlies learned skills, such as riding a bike, playing a musical instrument, or even reading. One way of thinking about the distinction between procedural memory and other forms of memory is in terms of the distinction between **tacit** and **explicit knowledge**. Polanyi (1958) pointed out that

Procedural memory
The memory system concerned with knowing how to do things.

Tacit knowledge
Knowing how to do something without being able to say exactly what it is that you know.

Explicit knowledge
Knowing that something is the case.

"the aim of a skilled performance is achieved by the observance of a set of rules which are not known as such to the person following them" (p. 49).

Procedural knowledge is a form of tacit knowledge in that we have it without necessarily being aware of what it is that we know. I can ride a bike even if I can't tell you how I do it. If I were to outline the principles that regulate bicycling, I would be converting my tacit knowledge into explicit knowledge. Doing this would require semantic memory. Semantic memory contains whatever explicit knowledge we have about bike-riding. Procedural memory is what we actually rely on to ride. Finally, episodic memory would contain particular experiences of bicycling, as in, "Remember that time we rode from Campbellford to Belleville and it rained all day, and we ran out of food...?"

Procedural memory was the first additional system to be identified after the initial distinction had been made between episodic and semantic memory. Tulving's (1985) view of the relation between these three memory systems is presented in Table 6.1.

TABLE 6.1	The relation between memory systems and consciousness

MEMORY SYSTEM	CONSCIOUSNESS
Episodic	Autonoetic
Semantic	Noetic
Procedural	Anoetic

From: Tulving, E. (1985). Memory and consciousness. *Canadian Psychology*, 26, 1–12. Copyright 1985 by the Canadian Psychology Association. Reprinted by permission.

Episodic Memory and Autonoetic Consciousness

As the table indicates, Tulving (1985) suggested that each of the three systems is associated with a different kind of consciousness. **Anoetic** means "non-knowing." To describe procedural memory as anoetic is to say that when we use it we are concerned only with our immediate situation. Procedural memory does not go beyond itself; it stays in the here and now. When I'm riding a bike, I'm focusing on responding appropriately to a particular vehicle (the one I am on) in a particular situation (the one I am in) at a particular time (now).

By contrast, **noetic** means "knowing." Semantic memory is noetic because when we use it we are aware not only of our immediate surroundings, but also of things that lie beyond it. If I'm riding my bike and remember that Polanyi wrote about the sort of skill that bike-riding requires, then my memory will be accompanied by noetic consciousness. Finally, **autonoetic** means "self-knowing." Episodic memory is autonoetic because it involves remembering personal experiences.

Tulving (2001, 2002a, 2002b) has been especially interested in episodic memory and autonoetic consciousness. Normal adults are able to see themselves as having a past and a future as well as a present. Their individual experiences are located in time, and they are able to engage in "mental time travel" (Tulving, 2002a, p. 2). Although remembering a personal past is a crucial aspect of episodic memory, so is the ability to project ourselves into the future and imagine what we might find there. It is this ability that enables us to set goals and plan future actions (Atance & O'Neill, 2001).

Autonoetic awareness requires healthy functioning of the frontal lobe. Among the most important sources of evidence for this relationship was the now-abandoned medical practice of **prefrontal leucotomy** (also known as prefrontal lobotomy; see Figure 6.5). This was a surgical procedure, invented by Moniz (1954/1968; Freeman & Watts, 1950/1968), in which the connections between the prefrontal lobes and other parts of the brain were severed. One goal of the procedure was to calm patients who ruminated excessively about themselves and their problems: "Frontal leucotomies

Anoetic, noetic, and autonoetic
Three levels of consciousness corresponding to the procedural, semantic, and episodic memory systems.

Prefrontal leucotomy
A surgical procedure, now abandoned, in which the connections between the prefrontal lobes and other parts of the brain were severed; also known as prefrontal lobotomy.

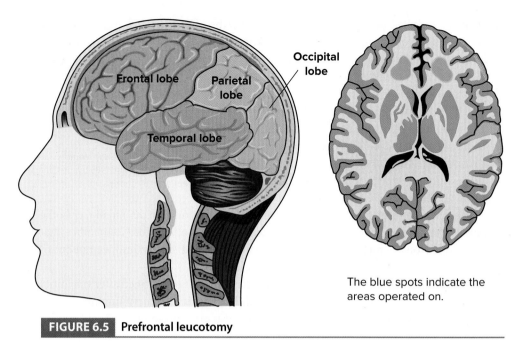

The blue spots indicate the areas operated on.

FIGURE 6.5   Prefrontal leucotomy

This procedure was used to control symptoms such as excessive anxiety and self-absorption, but was discontinued because of side effects such as apathy and listlessness.

change patients so that they are no longer interested in the sorts of past, present, and future problems that were so absorbing and incapacitating before the operations" (Wheeler, 2000, p. 602).

Tulving (2002b) has argued that autonoetic consciousness is not only uniquely human, but a crucial factor in the evolution of human culture and civilization. He has called our sense of subjective time **chronesthesia**, and considers it a cognitive capacity as important in its own way as the capacity to see or hear. "The development of civilization and culture was, and its continuation is, critically dependent on human beings' awareness of their own and their progeny's *continued existence* in time that includes not only the past and the present but also the future" (Tulving, 2002b, p. 321). Given this capacity, people have been able to contemplate changing the environment to suit them better, rather than simply adapting to it. The consequence has been the emergence of a human culture that has altered the environment in many ways. Autonoesis and chronesthesia depend on the prefrontal lobes, as we have seen. "The conclusion follows that the human prefrontal cortex, undoubtedly in collaboration with other areas of the brain, is directly responsible for the cultured world as it exists today" (Tulving, 2002b, p. 321).

Not everyone agrees that autonoesis is a uniquely human characteristic. For example, Clayton and Dickinson (1998) claim to have observed "episodic-like" memory in scrub jays. The birds they studied would store insect larvae (which the jays valued highly as food but which spoil quickly) and peanuts (which they valued less highly as food, but which remain edible for a long time) in different locations. When the birds were allowed to retrieve stored food, their choices depended on the length of

Chronesthesia
Our subjective sense of time.

the interval between storage and retrieval. If the interval was short they would retrieve the larvae, but if the interval was long they would go for the peanuts instead. This was taken as evidence that the birds remembered particular episodes and located those episodes in time, recalling that the larvae were stored too long ago to have remained edible. The counter-argument is that these results do not show that the birds were able to anticipate the future—only that they know something about the past (Suddendorf & Busby, 2003). What they know may not be experienced subjectively as anything resembling a human episodic memory. "It could be that episodic memory represents a sharp discontinuity in evolution, and humans are unique in possessing it" (Hampton & Schwartz, 2004, p. 195).

EPISODIC MEMORY AND DEVELOPMENT

Tulving (1985) argued that children acquire episodic memory relatively late compared with other kinds of memory. In this connection, Tulving cited the work of authors as diverse as Neisser (1978a) and K. Nelson and Gruendel (1981), who suggested that very young children do not experience anything that adults would call episodic memory. The hypothesis is that episodic memory develops out of semantic memory (Kinsbourne & Wood, 1975). Although small children are prodigious learners, most of their learning may involve the acquisition of general knowledge, rather than the accumulation of individual experience.

Perner (2000, p. 301) suggested that episodic memory does not emerge until roughly four to six years of age. It is then that children are able to discriminate between things they have known for a long time and things they have learned recently. In a similar vein, four-year-olds are able to discriminate between events they have observed and events they have been told about, while younger children can seldom make that distinction. Wheeler, Stuss, and Tulving (1997, p. 345) conclude that "the self-knowledge necessary for episodic remembering is not reached until around age 4 or later."

THE DISTINCTION BETWEEN REMEMBERING AND KNOWING

A central distinction made by Tulving (1985) is that between remembering and knowing. He wanted to reserve the term *remembering* for autonoetic experiences (i.e., episodic memory). He noted that "even when a person does not remember an event, she may know something about it" (1985, p. 6). Thus I may not remember the experience of eating a specific meal in a particular restaurant on a specific occasion, but still know that I ate a meal in that restaurant. The feeling of knowing in the absence of episodic memory has been called the **butcher-on-the-bus phenomenon** (Yovel & Paller, 2004). The term refers to the experience of running into someone who looks familiar (the butcher) in an unexpected place (on the bus). You might feel that you know the person, but not be "able to remember the circumstances of any previous meeting or anything else about" him (Yovel & Paller, 2004, p. 789).

Tulving's distinction has been made in various forms by other memory researchers (e.g., Gardiner, 2001; Gardiner & Richardson-Klavehn, 2000; Squire, 2004) and has stimulated quite a bit of ingenious research. A good example is research on implicit memory.

Butcher-on-the-bus phenomenon
The feeling of knowing a person without being able to remember the circumstances of any previous meeting or anything else about him or her.

IMPLICIT MEMORY

There are many situations in which a person remembers something without being aware of doing so (e.g., Jacoby & Dallas, 1981; Jacoby & Witherspoon, 1982). "It is possible to distinguish the effects of memory for prior episodes or experiences on a person's current behaviour from the person's awareness that he or she is remembering events of the past" (Eich, 1984, p. 105). Schacter (1987, 1992) proposed the phrase **implicit memory** for such phenomena. Implicit memory comes into play when "information that was encoded during a particular episode is subsequently expressed without conscious or deliberate recollection" (Schacter, 1987, p. 501). It is often demonstrated by means of priming experiments similar to those discussed in Chapter 4 on attention (see, for example, the Mack and Rock experiment outlined on p. 98).

A demonstration of the practical consequences of participating in priming experiments is a study by Jacoby and Hollingshead (1990) in which participants read incorrectly spelled words. This experience subsequently increased the likelihood that the participants would unintentionally make the same spelling mistakes themselves. As Jacoby and Hollingshead observe, this kind of research may be unethical, because it can impair performance in an important area (spelling) and the people involved will not necessarily be aware of this impairment. In the same way, "reading student essays may be hazardous" to professors' spelling accuracy (Jacoby & Hollingshead, 1990, p. 345), if those essays contain spelling errors. An unintended consequence of this research was described by Jacoby and Hollingshead (1990), who noted that the second author of that paper herself "lost confidence in her spelling accuracy [and could] no longer judge spelling accuracy on the basis of a word 'looking right'. The word might look right because it was one of our incorrectly spelled words" (p. 356). This finding makes us wonder about many of the shortcuts we use today when texting on our smart phones!

Implicit memory has also been studied using a fame judgment task (Jacoby & Kelley, 1992; Kelley & Jacoby, 2000). Participants were divided into two groups and given a series of non-famous names (e.g., *Sebastian Weisdorf*) to read. As the names appeared on a computer screen, one group read them with full attention (i.e., no distractions) and one with divided attention (achieved by adding a task such as listening to a series of numbers and pressing a key if there were three odd numbers in a row). Then names from the first trial (old non-famous names) were mixed with new names, some famous and some non-famous, and the participants were asked to judge whether or not they were famous. Participants were also told that all the names on the first list were non-famous. Consequently, anyone who recognized a name as coming from the first list was aware that it was non-famous. Now examine Figure 6.6, in which the vertical axis is the percentage of non-famous names judged to be famous. The higher the number, the more non-famous names that group judged to be famous. Under conditions of full attention people tended to recognize names from the first list, and to say that fewer names from the first list were famous. However, participants from

> **Implicit memory**
> Memory without episodic awareness; the expression of previous experience without conscious recollection of the prior episode.

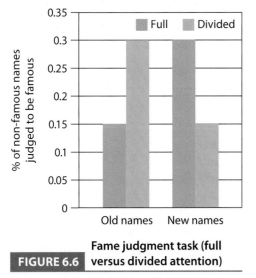

FIGURE 6.6 Fame judgment task (full versus divided attention)

Data from: Jacoby, L.L., & Kelley, C.M. (1992). A process-dissociation framework for investigating unconscious influences: Freudian slips, projective tests, subliminal perception, and signal direction theory. *Current Directions in Psychological Science, 1*, p. 175.

the divided attention group had implicit memories of the old names without explicitly recognizing them as coming from the first list. Therefore the divided-attention participants were more likely to categorize names from the first list as famous because they seemed familiar. It's as if they said to themselves, "Oh, I've heard that name before, but I don't remember where—it must be famous." In this way *Sebastian Weisdorf* became famous.

Studies of fragmented words are another way of showing unconscious influences in memory (Jacoby, 1998; Jacoby & Kelley, 1992; Toth, 2000). Like the Debner and Jacoby (1994) study we reviewed in Chapter 3, such studies use the **method of opposition** (Curran, 2001), which pits conscious (explicit) and unconscious (implicit) tendencies against one another. Participants are shown a number of words (e.g., *motel*) under conditions of either full or divided attention. They are then given a number of word stems (e.g., *mot– –*). Half the participants in each condition (full and divided attention) are asked to complete the word stems using either a word from the list previously seen or, if they could not remember one, the first word they thought of. The other half are asked to complete the word stems by *not* using a word from the list previously seen. Thus if *motel* was on the previous list, they should not complete the stem with mot*el*, but with another word, like mot*or*. The first instruction is the *inclusion* condition, while the second is the *exclusion* condition.

> **Method of opposition**
> Pits conscious (explicit) and unconscious (implicit) tendencies against one another.

Now examine Figure 6.7. The vertical axis is the percentage of stems completed with words from the first list. Under the full attention condition, participants performed well on both the inclusion and exclusion tasks. When told to include words from the first list, they completed the word stems with words from the first list 61 per cent of the time. When they were told to exclude words from the first list, the number of stem completions using words from the first list dropped to 36 per cent. This difference indicates that these people had a degree of conscious control over the process of stem completion. However, in the divided attention condition there is no difference between the inclusion and exclusion tasks. These participants complete the stems with words from the first list equally often, whether they are trying to do so or trying not to. Thus they do not demonstrate any conscious control over their behaviour in these tasks.

Conscious control is reflected in differences between performance when one is trying to do something, and performance when one is trying *not* to do it (Jacoby & Kelley, 1992, p. 177). A good analogy to the memory experiments we have been reviewing might be the various real-world attempts we make *not* to do something. For example, when we diet we try not to eat as much, or when we quit smoking we try not to smoke. If there is a difference between our behaviour when we are trying *not* to do something and our "ordinary" behaviour, then we are demonstrating that we can consciously control that behaviour. However, if our behaviour when we are trying *not* to do something is the same as it always has been, then we are demonstrating that we are unable to consciously control that behaviour.

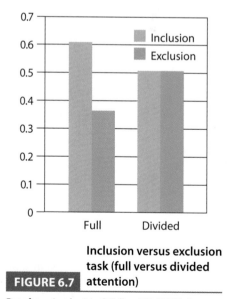

Inclusion versus exclusion task (full versus divided attention)

FIGURE 6.7

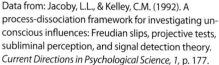

Data from: Jacoby, L.L., & Kelley, C.M. (1992). A process-dissociation framework for investigating unconscious influences: Freudian slips, projective tests, subliminal perception, and signal detection theory. *Current Directions in Psychological Science, 1*, p. 177.

The Perceptual Representation System

The results of experiments on implicit memory are consistent with the notion that there is a memory system called the **perceptual representation system** or PRS (Hayman & Tulving, 1989; Tulving & Schacter, 1990; Schacter, Wagner, & Buckner, 2000). This system would be responsible for priming effects. The important distinction is between "systems concerned with explicit recollection of past events" as opposed to "primed identification of previously encountered objects" (p. 247). The PRS contains very specific representations of previously encountered events. Thus if you had been shown the word fragment M–S–OU–I, only that fragment would be in your PRS: the complete word (*MISSOURI*) would not. The episodic memory system and the PRS would be driven by different processes. The episodic memory system operates with a deeper understanding of information, whereas the PRS deals with information on a more superficial level. Amnesiacs have an impaired episodic memory system, but their PRS may be relatively intact. Precisely how the PRS relates to other memory systems, such as semantic memory, is still unclear. As Berry and Dienes (1991) observed, there may be similarities between the processes responsible for implicit memory and those underlying implicit learning—a topic we will consider in Chapter 8 on concepts.

Semantic Memory

As we have already seen, "semantic memory" refers to general knowledge. Tulving (1972) compared semantic memory to a mental thesaurus, containing words, concepts, and their relations. You use your semantic memory when you try to remember someone's name. When (as often happens) you can't quite come up with that name, you experience the **tip-of-the-tongue phenomenon**. James (1890) referred to it as a "gap" and noted that it is highly specific: when incorrect names are suggested, they are immediately rejected because "[t]hey do not fit into its mold." Further, the "gap of one word does not feel like the gap of another. . . . When I try vainly to recall the name of Spalding, my consciousness is far removed from what it is when I vainly try to recall the name of Bowles" (p. 251).

THE TIP-OF-THE-TONGUE PHENOMENON

R. Brown and McNeill (1966) conducted a famous study in which they gathered data on the properties of tip-of-the-tongue phenomena (TOT). First, they observed this state when it occurred in themselves. For example, one of them was trying to remember the name of the street on which a relative lived. He kept coming up with names like *Congress*, *Corinth*, and *Concord*. When he looked up the street name, it turned out to be *Cornish*. This example illustrates several properties of the TOT state that Brown and McNeill subsequently found in an experiment.

In that experiment Brown and McNeill gave participants the definitions of 49 low-frequency words, such as *apse*, *nepotism*, *cloaca*, *ambergris*, and *sampan*, and asked them to identify the words. When participants found themselves in a TOT state, they were often able to identify some aspects of the target word such as its first letter or the number of syllables it contained. In addition participants were often able to make judgments about words that came to mind while they searched for the target word. Sometimes they knew that their incorrect guesses were similar in sound or meaning to the target. For example, while searching for *sampan*, some participants knew that *Siam* and *sarong* had a similar sound, and that *barge* and *houseboat* had a similar meaning. Thus they had access to quite a bit of information about the target word before they were actually able to recall it. *Generic recall* is the term used by Brown and McNeill for this ability to recall parts and attributes of a word without explicitly recalling the word itself.

Several different experimental techniques have been used to elicit the TOT state. If you want to experience it yourself, try naming the seven dwarfs from the film *Snow White and the Seven Dwarfs* (Meyer & Hilterbrand, 1984). A.S. Brown (1991) described a study exploring the relation between TOTs and stress. He surveyed 79 undergraduate psychology majors, 75 per cent of whom said that TOTs occurred more often under stress (e.g., during exams). Studies of the frequency with which TOTs occur find that adults generally experience about one a week, although the frequency tends to be somewhat greater in older people.

Several studies have replicated Brown and McNeill's finding that when people are experiencing a TOT, they are likely to recall words that are similar either in sound or in meaning. They are often able to guess the first letter of the desired word with a high degree of accuracy (e.g., Rubin, 1975). They may also know the last letter, though to a lesser extent than the first (A.S. Brown, 1991, p. 212). One of the most intriguing aspects of the TOT phenomenon is the often-reported experience of recalling the desired word only after we have stopped trying to recall it: "1 hour and 39 minutes after the start of the recall attempt, the word came . . . hours prior to the solution, there was no recollection of thought on the topic" (Norman and Bobrow, 1976, p. 116).

Burke, McKay, Worthley, and Wade (1991) believe that TOTs occur mainly with words that the person concerned has not used very often or has not used very recently, with the result that the link between its meaning and its pronunciation may have atrophied because of disuse. Consequently, other words that have a similar sound and/or meaning may be elicited along with the correct word. For example, consider *charity* and *chastity*. These words not only sound similar but may be considered related in that both are associated with virtue; furthermore, neither of them is used very often. Thus they may interfere with one another, causing a TOT state. Burke et al. (1991) also reported the interesting result that the names of famous people are particularly likely to lead to TOTs in older people. It's possible that this effect comes about because older people learned these names longer ago than did younger people. As a result, the names may be fresher in the memory of younger people and less prone to interference.

Brown and McNeill (1966) suggested that memory for words and their definitions (usually considered a central part of semantic memory) is organized like a dictionary. However, they realized that the structure of a mental dictionary was unlikely to be the same as that of a standard dictionary. Since the 1960s a great deal of work has gone into trying to determine how the mental store of words is organized and how we go about searching through it to find the information we need.

QUILLIAN'S TEACHABLE LANGUAGE COMPREHENDER

Teachable language comprehender (TLC) A computer program that is a model of semantic memory.

The first semantic memory models were developed by Quillian (1969), who wanted to create a computer program that would understand natural language. His program was called the **teachable language comprehender**, or **TLC**. Because such a program must contain information about concepts and their relations to one another, the TLC was not only a computer program but also a model of semantic memory.

Quillian's model represented semantic memory as having the structure of a network; for an example, see Figure 6.8. The network consists of three types of elements: units, properties, and pointers. Units are usually sets of objects, and they are the nodes of the network. They are typically labelled by nouns, such as *fish* or *shark*. Properties are often described by adjectives or verbs, such as *yellow* or *sing*. Pointers specify the relations between different units, and between units and properties, and represent verbs such as *is*, *has*, or *can*. Thus the network in Figure 6.8 conveys information such as *A canary is a bird*; *A canary can sing*; *A bird is an animal*; and *A bird has wings*.

Quillian's model assumes that using semantic memory means searching the network for the information you are seeking. A basic type of search would be to verify a sentence as either true or false. Thus if you were asked whether it is true that *A canary is a bird*, you would search the paths of the network to see if such a relationship exists. Then, since the information corresponding to *A canary is a bird* is in fact in the network, you would conclude that the statement is true. By contrast, if you could not find information corresponding to the statement *A canary is a machine*, you would judge that statement to be false. As we shall see, however, the actual mechanism for rejecting false statements is complex.

Collins and Quillian (1972) assumed that searching through a semantic network takes time. Although this seems an obvious assumption, it is an essential one, because

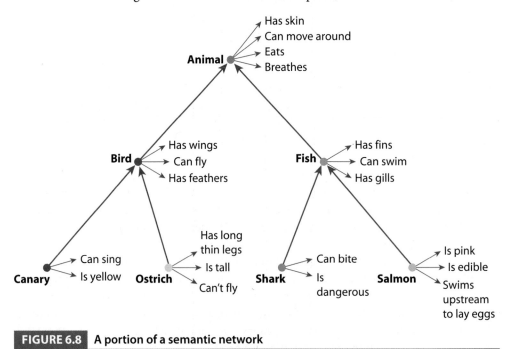

FIGURE 6.8   **A portion of a semantic network**

From: Collins, A.M., & Quillian, M.R. (1969). Retrieval time from semantic memory. *Journal of Verbal Learning and Verbal Behavior, 8*, 240–248. Copyright 1969 by Academic Press. Reprinted by permission.

measuring how long it takes to conduct searches through semantic networks is a basic way of getting data about their structure. This approach to the study of psychological structures is called **mental chronometry** (e.g., Posner, 1986). The experimenter gives participants different tasks that, on theoretical grounds, should take different times to complete. Measuring how long it takes the participants to complete the various tasks is a way of testing the theory. For example, one implication of the semantic memory model in Figure 6.8 is that it will take longer to verify sentences specifying relationships that are located far apart in the network than it would to verify sentences specifying relationships that are close together.

Now examine the paths leading from *Canary* in Figure 6.8. *Canary* is directly connected to *can sing*, but there are two pointers between *Canary* and *Can fly*. Thus it should take longer to verify the sentence *A canary can fly* than it does to verify the sentence *A canary can sing*. A similar prediction would be made about the difference between the sentences *A canary is a bird* and *A canary is an animal*. The former requires one step; the latter requires two. Collins and Quillian (1972) presented data that were more or less consistent with predictions from their model.

Subsequent research uncovered several difficulties with the Quillian model and others like it (Chang, 1986; Johnson-Laird, Herrmann, & Chafin, 1984). One problem is that such models do not specify very clearly the procedure used to tell if a sentence is false. A suggestion made by Collins and Quillian (1972) was called the *conditional stopping hypothesis*. Consider a false sentence such as *A polar bear has hands*. According to the conditional stopping hypothesis, a search would be conducted for paths connecting *polar bear* and *hands*. The search can be terminated if it arrives at a contradiction. A contradiction would occur if the property specified by the sentence and the property specified in memory were inconsistent—for example, if you found a path leading from *polar bear* to *paws*. The information in memory that *A polar bear has paws* contradicts the information given by the sentence *A polar bear has hands*. However, it is not clear what happens if no paths leading to a contradiction can be found.

In spite of difficulties with the Collins and Quillian (1972) model, the experimental procedure of asking participants to search their semantic memories for the answers to questions has been extremely productive. A good example can be seen in what has been referred to as the **Moses illusion** (Erickson & Matson, 1981; Reder & Kusbit, 1991). The term "Moses illusion" refers to the tendency to respond to the question *How many animals of each kind did Moses take on the Ark?* by saying *Two*, even though Moses did not take any animals on the Ark (it was Noah who did).

The Moses illusion is a very robust phenomenon, and has been demonstrated with a variety of other questions, as the following examples, from Reder and Kusbit (1991), show. If asked *What country was Margaret Thatcher president of?* people will answer *England*, even though Thatcher was prime minister, not president. When asked *Who found the glass slipper left at the ball by Snow White?* people will answer *The Prince*, even though it was Cinderella, not Snow White, who lost the slipper. Finally, when asked *What superhero does Clark Kent become when he changes in a toll booth?* people will answer *Superman*, even though Clark Kent always changes in a phone booth, not a toll booth.

People typically fail to notice the mistake in the question and answer it anyway. Why do they not notice the mistake? Why do they respond instead to a "corrected" version of the question? Shafto and MacKay (2000) have suggested that the Moses

Mental chronometry
Measuring how long cognitive processes take.

Moses illusion
The tendency to answer the question *How many animals of each kind did Moses take on the Ark?* with *Two*, either because you assume that the person who posed the question meant to say *Noah* rather than *Moses*, or because you didn't notice the error.

illusion occurs for two main reasons. First, the correct term (*Noah*) and the lure (*Moses*) are semantically related (i.e., have some shared meaning) in that both are Old Testament male figures. A second possible reason is that the two names *Moses* and *Noah* are phonologically related (i.e., they sound similar) in that both are two-syllable words with *o* as their initial vowel sound. Apparently people are less likely to answer the question *How many animals did Abraham take on the Ark?* by saying *Two* (Erickson & Mattson, 1981). The reason is that, while *Abraham and Noah* are semantically related (both are Old Testament male figures), they are not phonologically related (they do not share the same first vowel and do not have the same number of syllables). Thus participants are less likely to confuse *Abraham* and *Noah* than they are to confuse *Moses* and *Noah*.

SPREADING ACTIVATION

An important notion to emerge from the study of semantic memory is the concept of **spreading activation** (J.R. Anderson, 1984). Spreading activation was proposed by Quillian (1969) and elaborated by Collins and Loftus (1975). The idea is that when you search a semantic network, you activate the paths where the search takes place. This activation spreads from the node at which the search begins. "The spread of activation constantly expands, first to all the nodes linked to the first node, then to all the nodes linked to each of these nodes, and so on" (Collins & Loftus, 1975, p. 408). The more active a node is, the more easily its information can be processed. Thus information from active nodes can be retrieved more quickly than information from less active ones. Now let's see how the idea of spreading activation can help to explain how priming works.

Several experiments on priming have been done within the framework of the study of semantic memory; for a review of some of the best-known, see Meyer and Schvaneveldt (1976). One experiment on word recognition followed the procedure outlined in Figure 6.9. Participants looked at a screen with two dots, one above the other. Then a string of letters appeared at the top dot. Sometimes the letter string was an English word such as *wine* and sometimes it was a non-word such as *plame*. The participants were required to complete a **lexical decision task**, which is simply to decide whether or not the letter string was a word, and to respond "yes" if it was a word and "no" if it was a non-word. The time it took to make this response was recorded. Then another string of letters appeared at the bottom dot and participants had to decide if this second string of letters was a word.

Sometimes the first letter string was a word semantically related to the second letter string. For example, the first word might be *bus* and the second word *truck*; or the first word might be *sunset* and the second *sunrise*. These are pairs of words that you might expect to be close together in a semantic network. By contrast, if the first word was *sunset* and the second word was *truck*, then this pair would be semantically unrelated. You would not expect these two words to be close together in a semantic network.

This study found that the time it took to correctly recognize the second word was partly determined by the nature of the first word. If the first word was semantically related to the second word, then the time it took to recognize the second word was less than if the first word was semantically unrelated to it. That is, if the first word was semantically related to the second word (*sunset–sunrise*), then the first word

Spreading activation
The idea that activation of the paths that make up a semantic network spreads from the node at which the search begins.

Lexical decision task
A task requiring participants to determine if a presented string of letters is a word or not.

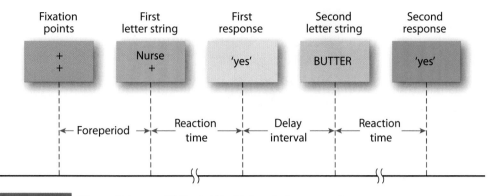

FIGURE 6.9 | **Meyer, Schvaneveldt, and Ruddy's priming procedure**

From: Meyer, D.F., Schvaneveldt, R.W., and Ruddy, M.G. (1975). Loci of contextual effects on visual recognition. In P.M.A. Rabbitt & S. Dornie (Eds.), *Attention and performance V* (p. 100). London: Academic Press.

primed recognition of the second word. This priming effect did not occur if the two words were semantically unrelated (*sunset–truck*).

One way of understanding this finding is in terms of the spreading activation theory outlined above. Consider the fragment of a semantic network in Figure 6.10. In this diagram, the greater the distance between any two concepts, the less closely they are related to one another. Thus *cherries* and *apples* are directly connected, but the connection between *street* and *flowers* is indirect, running through several paths. The closer together concepts are, the more easily activation will spread from one concept to another. If *clouds* is activated, it will in turn activate (or prime) *sunrises* and *sunsets*, but several more activations would be required to prime *vehicle*.

Now let's consider Meyer and Schvaneveldt's results in relation to Figure 6.10. Suppose that *bus* and *truck* and *sunset* and *sunrise* are connected in a semantic network in the way depicted in that figure. When the word *bus* is seen, activation quickly spreads to the *truck* node. The nodes for *sunrise* and *sunset* are much farther away in the network and so will be less activated. Consequently, *truck* will be primed by *bus* much more so than by either *sunset* or *sunrise*. Conversely, if the participant sees *sunset* first, then *sunrise* will be primed much more than either *bus* or *truck*. In this way, the semantic network model can explain the priming effect.

The precise mechanisms governing spreading activation still need to be worked out (Bodner & Masson, 2003; Chwilla & Kolk, 2002; McRae & Boisvert, 1998). However, the concept of spreading activation has proven to be quite durable (McNamara, 1992), and continues to be a useful explanatory tool for studies of semantic memory. A good example is a study of **involuntary semantic memory** by Kvavilashvili and Mandler (2004).

Involuntary semantic memory ("mind popping") A semantic memory that pops into your mind without episodic context.

INVOLUNTARY SEMANTIC MEMORIES

An involuntary semantic memory occurs whenever a semantic memory (e.g., a tune) pops into your mind without any episodic context. That is, you don't recall any auto-biographical information that might have triggered the semantic memory; it just pops up by itself and appears to be irrelevant to what you are currently thinking about. Kvavilashvili and Mandler (2004) call this *mind popping*.

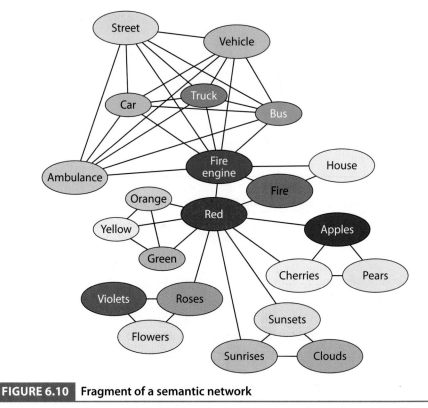

FIGURE 6.10   **Fragment of a semantic network**

From: Collins, A.M., and & Loftus, E.F. (1975). A spreading-activation theory of semantic processing. *Psychological Review*, 82, 407–428. Copyright 1975 by the American Psychological Association.

Kvavilashvili and Mandler (2004) reported on diary and questionnaire studies designed to probe the mind-popping phenomenon. Kvavilashvili kept two diaries of her semantic "mind pops" for 19 and 18 weeks, when she was 35 and 37 years old, respectively. She logged a total of 428 memories, which tended to be either words (e.g., *rummage*) or images (e.g., *a view of a road and a small church in Cardiff*). She had no episodic information accompanying these involuntary semantic memories. Most of the mind pops occurred while she was engaged in routine activities not requiring a lot of attention, and at first they appeared unrelated to the current activity. However, Kvavilashvili was often able to retrospectively find cues that had triggered the memories without her awareness. For example, one pop-up was *Itchy and Scratchy*, the names of two characters from *The Simpsons* television show. Kvavilashvili noticed she was scratching her back when the pop-up occurred. Examples like this suggest that involuntary semantic memories are primed by events of which we are typically unaware.

Kvavilashvili and Mandler's (2004) study shows how their ecologically valid research complements and extends laboratory work. We will return to the effect of ongoing activations on the way we think in Chapters 10 and 12, on problem-solving and creativity.

Working memory
The system that allows for the temporary storage and manipulation of information that is necessary for various cognitive activities.

Working Memory

The concept of **working memory** has been at the centre of Alan Baddeley's (1986, 1989, 2000a, 2001, 2002a, 2002b; Baddeley & Hitch, 1974; N. Morris & Jones, 1990; Parkin & Hunkin, 2001) influential research program. Working memory "involves the temporary storage and manipulation of information that is assumed to be necessary for a wide range of complex cognitive activities" (Baddeley, 2003a, p. 189). It is the system that pulls all the other memory systems together, and it has four components (Figure 6.11). The **central executive** coordinates information from among three subsystems: the **phonological loop**, the **visuo-spatial sketchpad**, and the **episodic buffer**. Both the phonological loop and the visuo-spatial sketchpad can interact with long-term memory, the former drawing on language (linguistically encoded knowledge) and the latter on imagery (non-verbal general knowledge), while the episodic buffer is used to move information to and from episodic and long-term memory. Its most important function is to organize information "from the phonological and visuo-spatial subsystems of [working memory] with information from [long-term memory]" (Baddeley, 2001, p. 1349). All three of these subsystems have a limited capacity and hold information only temporarily (Baddeley, 2000b, p. 421).

The central executive selects and integrates information from across the three subsystems. It is intimately associated with consciousness, constituting a workspace within which solutions are formulated (Baars, 2002). Finally, notice the distinction in Figure 6.11 between **fluid systems** and **crystallized systems**. The former are cognitive processes that manipulate information but are "themselves unchanged by learning," while the latter are "cognitive systems capable of accumulating long-term knowledge" (Baddeley, 2000b, p. 421).

To illustrate how some of the components of working memory interact, Baddeley (1989, p. 36) used the following simple example, which has also been used by Shepard (1966) and Neisser (1970). Suppose you were asked to recall the number of windows in your house or apartment. You would probably form a mental image of the building, using the visuo-spatial sketchpad, and imagine walking around

Central executive
The component of working memory that coordinates information from among the three subsystems.

Phonological loop and visuo-spatial sketchpad
Temporary stores of linguistic and non-verbal information, respectively.

Episodic buffer
The mechanism that moves information to and from episodic and long-term memory.

Fluid systems
Cognitive processes that manipulate information.

Crystallized systems
Cognitive systems that accumulate long-term knowledge.

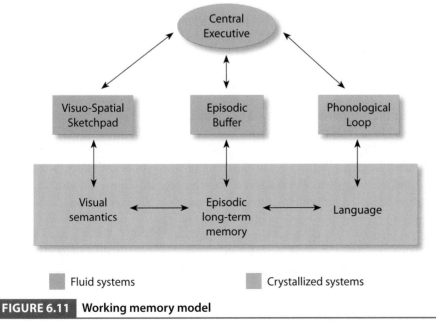

Fluid systems   Crystallized systems

FIGURE 6.11   **Working memory model**

From: *Principles of frontal lobe function* by Donald T. Stuss and Robert T. Knight (2002); Figure 16.4 p.256, Oxford University Press. Based on: *Trends in Cognitive Sciences*, Vol. 4, Issue 11, pp. 417-423: "The episodic buffer: a new component of working memory?" by Alan Baddeley.

COGNITION IN ACTION BOX 6.2

Context-Dependent Learning

The principle of encoding specificity, discussed earlier, is related to the concept of context-dependent learning. "Context-dependent learning" refers to the idea that we are most likely to recall something we have learned if the environment in which that information was encoded is replicated during retrieval. You may have experienced this yourself. For instance, have you ever completely forgotten about a homework assignment only to remember it the moment you walked into the classroom? Examples from daily life aside, there are many intriguing experimental findings that demonstrate this phenomenon. Perhaps one of the most extreme examples was a study conducted by Godden and Baddeley (1975). These researchers required scuba divers to learn lists of words either underwater or on the shore. Memory recall was then tested in either a congruent or incongruent condition. That is, half the divers who had learned the words underwater were tested underwater (congruent) and half on shore (incongruent). As you can probably imagine, the divers' ability to recall the words was best in the congruent condition. Could you incorporate this principle into your own studying? Studying in the same room where the exam will be held might help you score a few extra points.

A closely related concept is known as state-dependent learning: the idea that recall is best when the mental (Eich, 1995) or physiological (Goodwin, Powell, Bremer, Hoine, & Stern, 1969) state of the learner is consistent across encoding and retrieval. The idea that that retrieval can be facilitated when the learner is in the matching physiological state has even been found to extend to marijuana use (Eich, Weingartner, Stillman, & Gillin, 1975). However, it should be emphasized that at times drug use has been observed to reduce overall learning by half (Rickles, Cohen, Whitaker, & McIntyre, 1973). Thus we strongly recommend that you always come sober to both class and exams!

There are other areas for which this research could have important implications. Recall the case of Officer Conley reported in Chapter 5. Would he have been more likely to recall seeing the assault if he had been taken to the place where it occurred? The research suggests that he might have been; at the very least he would have had a better chance of remembering it. For instance, Wong and Read (2011) had participants view a video of a theft and then return a week later to identify the culprit in either the same or a different environment. Their findings suggested that accuracy was greater in the congruent than the incongruent condition. However, the improvement in accuracy came with another, more concerning finding. While recall was indeed better for many participants in the congruent condition, confidence levels were also much higher, even among those who were wrong.

it, counting the windows as you go. The counting is done by the phonological (or articulatory) loop, and the entire process is coordinated by the central executive.

Baddeley (2003b) suggested that the phonological loop evolved as an aid in the acquisition of language, facilitating the learning of words by allowing us to temporarily store and rehearse them. Once learned, speech becomes a powerful tool, capable of influencing the behaviour both of others and of ourselves. Sub-vocal speech can be used to articulate our plans and is an important aspect of self-control. This is a topic we will explore at length in Chapter 9, on language. Baddeley (2003b) also suggested that the visuo-spatial sketchpad evolved in order to facilitate the representation of things and their relations. Thus it aids in tasks as diverse as planning a route (e.g., how to get to a novel location) or figuring out how to put the parts of something together (e.g., assembling furniture components). Processes of this kind will be explored in the chapters on imagery (7), problem-solving (10), reasoning (11), and creativity (12).

WORKING MEMORY AND THE BRAIN

Baddeley (2002a) observed that working memory is a complex system and hence

> unlikely to map in a simple way onto an anatomical structure such as the frontal lobes. However, it is clear that the frontal lobes play an important role in integrating information from many other areas of the brain, and are crucially involved in its manipulation for purposes such as learning, comprehension, and reasoning. . . . [T]hese are precisely the roles attributed to working memory. (p. 258)

One frontal area that has been singled out as particularly important role for working memory (Figure 6.12) is the dorsolateral prefrontal cortex (DLPFC). When we reviewed Stroop research in Chapter 4, on attention, we noted that the DLPFC was believed to play a role in selecting between alternative response tendencies. This is an important function of working memory, in particular of the central executive. Curtis and D'Esposito (2003) have suggested that the DLPFC is an integral part of working memory, acting to monitor and control alternative courses of action.

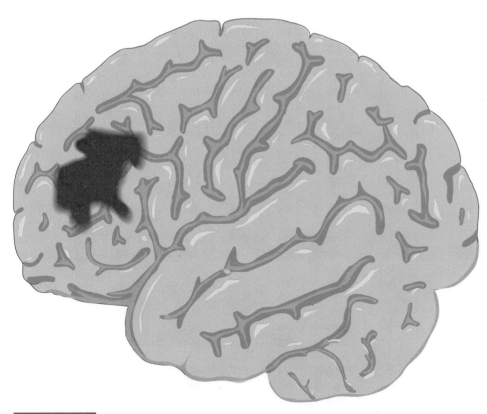

FIGURE 6.12   **The dorsolateral prefrontal cortex**

The dorsolateral prefrontal cortex is thought to play an especially important role in working memory.

Connectionist Models of Memory

When we introduced connectionist models in Chapter 3, we noted that they were designed to represent neural networks as they might exist in the brain. McClelland (2000, p. 583) observed that from a connectionist viewpoint individual items are not "stored in memory": rather, memories consist of certain patterns of activity. Nor are copies of particular experiences stored as memory traces; rather, neuron-like units representing each of the properties of an experience are connected to other neuron-like units. McClelland et al. (1986) pointed out that some experiences will have the same properties, and so the unit for a particular property will tend to be connected with several different experiences. Every time one property is activated, all the units to which it is connected will tend to be activated as well. In order to accurately recall previous experiences, therefore, the system needs to **excite** some connections and **inhibit** others.

Excitatory and inhibitory connections
Connections that either enhance or diminish the associations between the units that make up a neural network.

The Jets and the Sharks

Name	Gang	Age	Edu.	Mar.	Occupation
Art	Jets	40s	J.H.	Sing.	Pusher
Al	Jets	30s	J.H.	Mar.	Burglar
Sam	Jets	20s	J.H.	Sing.	Burglar
Clyde	Jets	40s	J.H.	Sing.	Bookie
Mike	Jets	30s	J.H.	Sing.	Bookie
Jim	Jets	20s	J.H.	Div.	Burglar
Greg	Jets	20s	H.S.	Mar.	Pusher
John	Jets	20s	J.H.	Mar.	Burglar
Doug	Jets	30s	H.S.	Sing.	Bookie
Lance	Jets	20s	COL.	Mar.	Bookie
George	Jets	20s	J.H.	Div.	Burglar
Pete	Jets	20s	H.S.	Sing.	Bookie
Fred	Jets	20s	H.S.	Sing.	Pusher
Gene	Jets	20s	COL.	Sing.	Pusher
Ralph	Jets	30s	J.H.	Sing.	Pusher
Phil	Sharks	30s	COL.	Mar.	Pusher
Ike	Sharks	30s	J.H.	Sing.	Bookie
Nick	Sharks	30s	H.S.	Sing.	Pusher
Don	Sharks	30s	COL.	Mar.	Burglar
Ned	Sharks	30s	COL.	Mar.	Bookie
Karl	Sharks	40s	H.S.	Mar.	Bookie
Ken	Sharks	20s	H.S.	Sing.	Burglar
Earl	Sharks	40s	H.S.	Mar.	Burglar
Rick	Sharks	30s	H.S.	Div.	Burglar
Ol	Sharks	30s	COL.	Mar.	Pusher
Neal	Sharks	30s	H.S.	Sing.	Bookie
Dave	Sharks	30s	H.S.	Div.	Pusher

FIGURE 6.13   **Some properties of gang members**

Adapted from: McClelland, J.L. Retrieving general and specific knowledge from stored knowledge of specifics. Proceedings of the Third Annual Conference of the Cognitive Science Society, Berkeley, Calif., p. 27. Copyright 1981 by J.L. McClelland.

McClelland (1981) and McClelland et al. (1986, pp. 27ff.) have demonstrated how a simple connectionist system might work. Figure 6.13 lists the members of two gangs, the Jets and the Sharks, with some of their properties: name, gang affiliation, age, education, marital status, and occupation. Some of the units that would be required to represent these individuals in memory are then presented in Figure 6.14. In the centre of the diagram are units representing shared properties for each of the persons listed in Figure 6.14. These individual units are connected to the appropriate property units. For convenience, the property units are grouped within different "clouds," and units within a particular cloud inhibit each other. Thus an individual cannot be called both *Lance* and *Art* at the same time.

Imagine that you have met all these individuals at one time or another. Imagine also that you find yourself in a conversation about the individual whose name is *Art*. When you try to remember what *Art* is like, what happens? Initially, when you hear the name *Art*, the name unit for *Art* will be activated. This name unit is connected to the individual unit for *Art*. The individual unit for *Art* is connected to all the property units that *Art* possesses. Activation of all of these property units corresponds to remembering *Art*. This model can be seen as an extension of the spreading activation models we considered earlier.

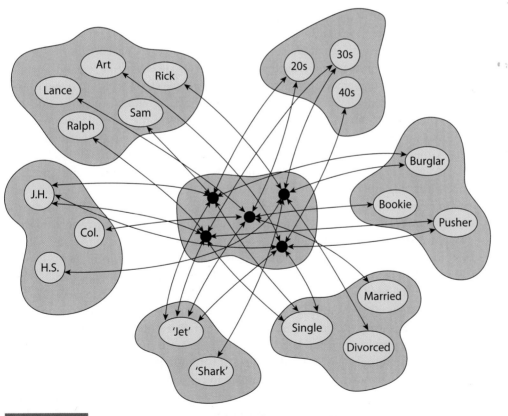

FIGURE 6.14 A connectionist model of the information in Figure 6.13

Of course, the act of remembering is not always so straightforward. If you hear someone talking about a gang member who is single, that information is not enough to enable you to identify the person in question, since several individual units are connected to the "single" property. However a combination of properties might serve to specify the individual more or less completely. Thus if you also hear that the single person in question is a *burglar* in his twenties with only a junior-high education, all four of those properties will point to the *Sam* unit, causing more activation there than in any of the other units. Activating the *Sam* unit will also activate the property units associated with *Sam*, and make you think that the person being talked about is a member of the *Jets*.

In this memory model, information about individual experiences is derived from the state of the entire system at a particular time. The pattern of excitation and inhibition in the system as a whole determines what you will remember.

Aging and Memory Disorders

MEMORY AND AGING

Folk wisdom says that memory declines with age. In fact, some forms of memory are relatively unscathed by advancing years. It is episodic memory in particular that shows a strong age effect (Craik & Grady, 2002, p. 529). A good illustration can be found in a study by Mitchell (1989) that explored differences in the ways *episodic* and *semantic* memories decline with age. Remembering that *I put salt on my food at lunch yesterday* is an episodic memory; remembering that *the formula for salt is NaCl* is a semantic memory. Mitchell tested the memories of a group of young people (19–32 years old) and a group of older people (63–80 years old). The young people clearly outperformed the older ones on the episodic memory tasks, but this was not the case on the semantic memory tasks. Although older people may sometimes have trouble recollecting recent personal experiences, their memory for general knowledge can continue to function well.

As we observed in the last chapter, in the section on levels of processing and aging, one frustrating aspect of getting older is a deterioration in the ability to recognize people and/or recall their names. In one study by Schweich, van der Linden, Bredart, Bruyer, Nelles, and Schils (1992), three groups of participants kept diaries of occasions on which they had experienced such difficulties. Group 1 contained young university students (19–25 years old) who reported no previous difficulties in recognizing faces; Group 2 contained young university students (19–25) who claimed they were often embarrassed by their inability to recognize faces; and Group 3 consisted of older people (54–73) also attending university. Over a one-month period, Group 2 reported the greatest incidence of difficulties; Groups 1 and 3 reported significantly fewer. In fact, the incidence of difficulty was identical for the two latter groups. Group 2, not surprisingly, had the greatest difficulty with recognizing faces, while most of Group 3's problems centred on attaching names to faces they recognized. The inability to consciously retrieve a name, given the face, is similar to the inability to directly remember episodic associations. Given enough time, however, most of the older participants in the diary study were able to recall the names they were looking for.

Naveh-Benjamin (2000; Naveh-Benjamin, Hussain, Guez, & Bar-on, 2003) has shown that older people's problems with names and faces may have the same

CONSIDER THIS
BOX 6.3

Memory and the Internet

Many readers will be too young to remember it, but there was a time not too long ago when humans' access to information was much more limited than it is today. When the authors of this book were growing up they had to resort to books, libraries, or experts with specific knowledge just to complete homework or figure out which movie won the Oscar for Best Picture in 1976 (Google says it was *Rocky*—which demonstrates the point). Today information is never farther away than the nearest computer or smart phone. Indeed, the company name Google is now an official word in the dictionary, and is regularly used as a verb. However, recent research has suggested that even though it is virtually indispensable in our daily lives, the ability to "google" whatever information we need could have consequences for our memory.

Sparrow, Liu, and Wegner (2011) devised an interesting experiment to explore whether having easy access to information can have an impact on how such information is encoded. In one of the experimental conditions participants were given a number of trivia statements that they had to type into a computer to verify. For example, a participant would read "An ostrich's eye is bigger than its brain" and then make that statement the subject of an Internet search. The key manipulation was that half of the participants believed the computer was saving whatever they typed, whereas the other half were led to believe it was not, and therefore that the statements would not be accessible at a later time. In a subsequent test of their ability to remember the trivia statements, participants performed better if they had thought that their search queries were being deleted.

This could indicate that we will put less effort into encoding and storing information if we think we will have easy access to it at a later date than we will if we think we won't have that access. Indeed, in another experiment Sparrow, Liu, and Wegner found that memory for where to find the information (e.g., which website was best) was better than memory for the information itself. By extension, although "googling it" can often give us instant answers, we may not remember those answers as well as we might wish.

FIGURE 6.15 **Google Search Engine**

source as their more general difficulty with episodic memory. According to his **associative deficit hypothesis**, older adults have a "deficiency in creating and retrieving links between single units of information" (Naveh-Benjamin, Guez, Kilb, & Reedy, 2004, p. 541). In one experiment, the ability to recall face–name associations was examined for two groups of men, one with a mean age of about 21 and the other with a mean age of about 72. All participants were shown 40 pairs of names and faces for three seconds per pair and were told to try to learn not only the faces and names, but also their pairings. They were then given a name recognition test, a face recognition test, and a face–name association test. In the first test, they were shown a name they had seen in the first part

Associative deficit hypothesis
The hypothesis that older adults have a deficiency in creating and retrieving links between single units of information.

of the experiment, paired with one they had not seen, and asked to name the one they had seen before. They were shown 16 such pairs in all. The face recognition test was the same, except that the pairs were faces. Finally, in the face–name association test participants were shown eight names they had seen before, each one paired with two faces, one they had seen previously and one they had not. They were also shown eight faces they had seen before, each paired with two names, one seen previously and one not. The task was to identify the names and faces they had seen before.

In general, the older participants were less able than the younger ones to correctly identify names or faces when they were presented by themselves; however, the difference was quite small. The big difference associated with age became apparent when participants had to correctly identify the name that went with a face, or the face that went with a name (Figure 6.16). In this task the older participants were considerably less successful than the younger participants. Thus the problem was not so much that the older people don't recognize names or faces as it is that they don't bind them together as easily as younger people do. Older adults have trouble in situations requiring the "merging of different aspects of an episode into a cohesive unit" (Naveh-Benjamin, Guez, Kilb, & Reedy, 2004, p. 541). Recalling previous episodes becomes difficult because the parts of a previous experience have not been bound together to form a coherent whole.

While older people may have difficulty consciously recalling recently experienced events, Howard, Fry, and Brune (1991, Experiment 2) found that they can still demonstrate knowledge of those events when tested more subtly. Younger (18–24 years) and older (62–75) people were asked to learn new associations. They were shown pairs of words (e.g., *queen–stairs*, *author–project*) and asked to make up a sentence containing them. When participants were given the first member of a pair and asked to recall the second member, the younger people tended to do better than the older one. However, older people did just as well as the younger ones on a more indirect test of memory. The indirect test was a word fragment completion task similar to those we mentioned earlier in the section on implicit memory. Participants were shown the first word of a pair plus a fragment of the second. Sometimes the word-fragment pairs corresponded to pairs shown in the first phase of the experiment (e.g., *queen–sta— —*, *author–pro— —*) but sometimes the pairs were mixed up (e.g., *queen–pro— —*, *author–sta— —*). Participants were asked to complete the stem with the first word that came to mind. Notice that in each case there are several words that could come to mind besides the one given (*star*, *process*, etc.). However, if the pair-stem combination corresponded to one they had seen before (e.g., *queen–sta——*), then both younger and older participants tended to choose the word originally shown (*stairs*), an effect that was not present if the word fragment pair had not been seen before (e.g., *queen–pro— —*). This demonstrated that the older participants had implicitly learned the new associations, even though they may not have realized it. Howard, Fry, and Brune concluded that you *can* teach old dogs new tricks—though only if they are given as much time as they want to learn those tricks. Self-pacing appears to be very important.

In a review of studies such as that of Howard, Fry, and Brune (1991), Mitchell and Bruss (2003) confirmed that older adults do seem

FIGURE 6.16 Young and old meeting: Which one is better at remembering names?

to be able to form implicit memories just as easily as younger people. They also respond to priming just as readily as younger people. Implicit memory appears to be stable across age.

Thus memory deficits in older people tend not to be general (Rabbitt, 1990). Not only may there be great individual differences in the rate at which memory declines, but a given memory deficit may be determined by the context in which it is tested. Rabbitt (1990, p. 230) suggested that repeated testing may improve the performance of older people to the point that age differences are eliminated.

THE AMNESIC SYNDROME

Both Schacter (1987) and Baddeley (1987a) pointed out the relevance of **Korsakoff's syndrome** for the study of memory. A form of amnesia affecting the ability to form new long-term memories (see Figure 6.17), Korsakoff's syndrome is attributed to the atrophy of brain tissue resulting from malnutrition, particularly thiamine deficiency (Brokate, Hildebrandt, Eling, Fuchtner, Runge, & Timm, 2003) and is often (though not exclusively) seen in chronic alcoholics. Edouard Claparède (1873–1940) was a pioneer in the investigation of this syndrome (Kihlstrom, 1995). Here is Claparède's (1911/1951) famous description of a 47-year-old Korsakoff's patient:

> Her old memories remained intact. She could correctly name the capitals of Europe, make mental calculations, and so on. But she did not know where she was, though she had been at the asylum five years. She did not recognize the doctors whom she saw every day, nor her nurse who had been with her for six months. When the latter asked the patient whether she knew her, the patient said: "No Madame, with whom have I the honor of speaking?" She forgot from one minute to the next what she was told, or the events that took place. She did not know what year, month, and day it was, though she was being told constantly. (p. 68)

Schacter (1987) also reviewed research on the so-called *amnesic syndrome*. This is a disorder produced by brain lesions, and includes patients with Korsakoff's syndrome, as well as Tulving's patient NN, whose case we mentioned earlier in this chapter. Amnesic patients may be able to operate normally in many areas, but unable to remember events that have occurred since the beginning of their affliction. Talland (1968) described this kind of patient:

> If time has come to a stop for the amnesic patient it is because he remembers virtually none of the events that he has witnessed since the onset of his illness. The days go by and none seems to be different from the others. Staff members and fellow patients reappear looking no more familiar than complete strangers. A story gives as much satisfaction on the tenth as it did on the first reading, its novelty never seems to wear off. If the patient recognizes a new figure in his environment, his doctor for example, as someone familiar, he may easily confuse him with another figure encountered in the same environment or name him correctly but as diffidently as if it were a wild guess. In the literature there are several accounts of the medical examination that had to be interrupted for a few minutes, in which the patient greeted the doctor on his return as someone he had not met for a long time. (p. 123)

Korsakoff 's syndrome
A form of amnesia affecting the ability to form new memories, attributed to thiamine deficiency and often (though not exclusively) seen in chronic alcoholics.

Warrington and Weiskrantz (1982) suggest that these amnesic patients have a **disconnection syndrome**: they may be able to acquire new information and yet not be aware that learning has taken place. It's as if there are at least two memory systems (Tulving, 1985) that normally interact but have become disconnected. This interpretation is reinforced by studies using the *famous name paradigm* we considered earlier. Squire and McKee (1992) showed lists of names to both amnesiacs and normals. Some of the names were of famous people (e.g., *Olga Korbut*, a famous Olympic athlete at the time) while others were not (e.g., *Emia Lekovic*). After seeing the names, all participants were shown another set of famous and non-famous names, some of which had been on the previous list and some of which had not. Participants were asked to rate these names as famous or non-famous. Both normals and amnesiacs tended to rate a name as famous if it had appeared on the first list, even if it was not really famous. Thus simply having been exposed to a name tends to influence participants' judgments. However, while normals were usually able to recognize a name as one that had appeared on the first list, amnesiacs were much less able to do so. They could judge a non-famous name to be famous because they had just seen it on the previous list, and yet not know that they had seen it.

Together, several studies reviewed by Warrington and Weiskrantz (1982) strongly suggest that amnesic patients do poorly on tasks requiring explicit memory, but much better on those requiring implicit memory. Graf and Schacter (1985) were able to further demonstrate this in a word-fragment completion experiment conducted with both normals and amnesiacs. Participants were presented with pairs of words. Some of the pairs were related by existing associations (e.g., *buttoned shirt*), whereas others were not (e.g., *window shirt*). In one part of the experiment, participants were required to make up a sentence that related the words "in a meaningful manner." Thus, given the word pair *ripe/apple*, a participant might generate the sentence, "He ate the ripe apple." Participants were then allowed to study each pair of words once.

Each participant was given two tests: a word completion test for implicit memory, and a cued recall test for explicit memory. In the former, participants were shown the first member of a word pair and the first three letters of the second member of the pair (the "word fragment") and asked to complete the word. The interesting question was whether they would complete the fragment with the word they were shown initially. Both amnesiacs and normals tended to do so. However, on the cued recall test, in which participants were given the first half of a word pair and had to recall the second, the amnesiacs were much less successful than the normals.

Levy, Stark, and Squire (2004) also observed that amnesiacs and normals showed similar performance on an implicit memory task, even though the amnesiacs' performance on an explicit memory task was far below normal levels. Amnesiacs may be able to form associations, and thus learn

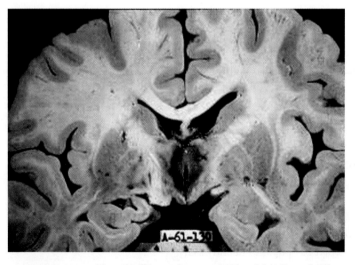

FIGURE 6.17 Korsakoff's syndrome, or Wernicke-Korsakoff encephalopathy

Note the pigmentation of grey matter, which occurs with thiamine (vitamin B$_1$) deficiency, most often in chronic alcoholics.

new material (Schacter & Graf, 1986; Kihlstrom, Schacter, Cork, Hurt, & Behr, 1990). However, this learning would be available to them only in implicit, not explicit, form. Korsakoff himself (1899, pp. 512, 518, cited in Schacter, 1987, p. 503) described this phenomenon as follows:

> Although the patient was not aware that he preserved traces of impressions that he received, those traces however probably existed and had an influence in one way or another on the course of ideas, at least in unconscious intellectual activity.
>
> We notice that a whole series of traces which could in no way be restored to consciousness, neither actively or passively, continue to exist in unconscious life, continue to direct the course of ideas of the patient, suggesting to him some or other inferences and decisions. That seems to me to be one of the most interesting peculiarities of the disturbance about which we are speaking.

ALZHEIMER'S DISEASE

Alzheimer's disease is among the most feared memory disorders (see Figure 6.18). In an American survey conducted in 2002, 95 per cent of respondents agreed that Alzheimer's was a "serious problem facing the whole nation," and 64 per cent of those between 35 and 49 years of age said they were afraid of getting it themselves (Halpern, 2002, p. 16). "Four million Americans already have the disease, a number that is expected to grow to fourteen million by mid-century" (Halpern, 2002, p. 16). Similar rates are likely in other industrialized countries (DiCarlo et al., 2002).

The diagnosis of Alzheimer's disease has become much better differentiated since the first case was recorded by Alois Alzheimer in 1907. The disease is progressive, beginning with a deterioration of episodic memory. A decline in the ability to retain recently acquired information is characteristic of the early stages (Hodges, 2000, p. 443). An example given by Jacoby (1999) illustrates how frustrating Alzheimer's can be for caregivers. He describes a woman diagnosed with Alzheimer's who was taken to visit a nursing home before moving there. She was introduced to the customs of the nursing home, one of which was that there was no tipping in the dining room. This fact was repeated several times. When the visit was drawing to a close, the prospective resident was asked if she had any questions. At that point she asked if she should tip in the dining room. "[R]epeated asking of questions is one of the most striking and frustrating symptoms of memory impairment resulting from Alzheimer's disease" (Jacoby, 1999, p. 3).

Not everyone who is unable to learn new material will go on to develop Alzheimer's. "It is . . . necessary to follow such patients for years in order to determine that they do indeed have" it (Hodges, 2000, p. 445). As the disease progresses, Alzheimer's patients will show impaired semantic memory (Glosser & Friedman, 1991; Hodges, 2000, p. 445). For example, Hodges, Salmon, and Butters (1992) gave a group of Alzheimer's patients a battery of semantic memory tests: asking them to name as many exemplars of a category (e.g., *animals*) as possible; to identify the objects in drawings; to generate definitions of words (e.g., *alligator*) that could be understood by "someone from a different country who has never seen or heard of such a thing"; and so on (p. 305). On all tests the Alzheimer's patients performed less well than normal controls. Moreover, performance on one test was correlated with performance on others: for example, failure to identify the animal in a drawing

Although a definitive diagnosis of Alzheimer's still requires an autopsy, the symptoms are better understood today than they were when this form of dementia was first identified, more than a century ago.

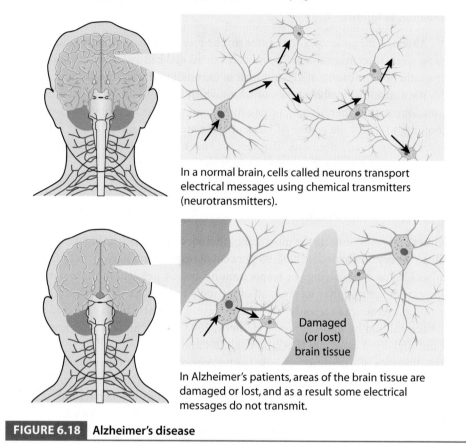

In a normal brain, cells called neurons transport electrical messages using chemical transmitters (neurotransmitters).

Damaged (or lost) brain tissue

In Alzheimer's patients, areas of the brain tissue are damaged or lost, and as a result some electrical messages do not transmit.

FIGURE 6.18   Alzheimer's disease

From: www.alzheimersmemoryloss.info/alzheimers-disease.jpg

as an alligator went along with an inability to define an alligator. This suggests that what Alzheimer's disease involves is not so much the inability to retrieve existing knowledge as the deterioration of knowledge that once existed. Hodges, Salmon, and Butters (1992, p. 312) observe that the definitions given by the Alzheimer's patients were particularly instructive. They included very general, non-specific characteristics (defining a *land animal* as *four-legged*), as well as inappropriate intrusions (defining a *rhinoceros* in terms appropriate for an *elephant*).

Salmon, Butters, and Chan (1999), in a review of a large number of studies, concluded that the evidence supported the hypothesis of semantic memory deterioration in Alzheimer's patients:

> The normal organization of semantic memory is disrupted by this loss of semantic knowledge and the semantic network appears to deteriorate as the disease progresses. Although the neuroanatomical basis of the deterioration of semantic memory in patients with [Alzheimer's] is currently unknown, it is likely that it results from synapse loss, neuron loss, and other neurodegenerative changes in the association cortices that presumably store semantic representations. (p. 115)

THE RETRAINING OF MEMORY

Efforts to rehabilitate memory have usually been based on intuition rather than adequate theories of memory disorders. B.A. Wilson and her colleagues (Kapur, Glisky, & Wilson, 2002; Wilson, 2002; Wilson & Moffat, 1984; Wilson & Patterson, 1990) have tried to identify treatment approaches that have a history of working and/or are based on a sound theoretical foundation.

Environmental Adaptations

Minimizing the number of situations requiring memory can be helpful. A written time-table, located where the patient can't miss it, can serve as a guide, helping the patient move from activity to activity. Simply posting signs that tell patients which room they are in can be valuable (Giles & Clark-Wilson, 1988). In general, environments should be designed so that they elicit the desired behaviour.

External Memory Aids

Prospective memory comes into play when we need to remember to do something at some future time. Older people in general, as well as those with memory disorders specifically, may forget not only when to do something, but also whether or not they have previously performed the required action. For example, people may not only forget to take their medication on time: they may also forget that they have taken it and so take it again (Einstein, McDaniel, Smith, & Shaw, 1998). An electronic diary that sounds an alarm when it's time to perform a particular task and that keeps track of the patient's behaviour may work around this problem to some extent (Harris, 1984). Electronic organizers such as the Palm Pilot may be useful too, serving as "prosthetic memories" with "a built in camera, handwriting recognition system and diary" (Abraham, 2004). The patient can take pictures of people as an aid to future recognition. These devices can also be programmed with a week's "to do" list and prompt the user to "remember" on each occasion. Of course, teaching patients how to use the device is a long and painstaking process, because most must rely on implicit rather than explicit memory. Sheer repetition makes a difference, and it's important that the teacher help the patient avoid errors. **Errorless learning** is widely believed to maximize patients' ability to use whatever memory resources they still have. Patients learn to do only what should be done and never learn to do things incorrectly (Wilson, 2002, p. 667).

Teaching Domain-Specific Knowledge

Learning in amnesiacs is unlikely to be generalizable to contexts very different from the one in which the original learning took place. Indeed, there is no evidence that attempting to restore "general memory ability" through practice actually accomplishes anything for the patient (Kapur, Glisky, & Wilson, 2002, p. 772). A more realistic goal is to attempt to teach amnesiacs specific skills that might be useful to them. To this end, Glisky and Schacter (1989) reported on what they called the **method of vanishing cues**. Amnesic participants were taught the meaning of computer commands by being presented with definitions of the commands and fragments of their names (e.g., S—— for the command SAVE). Additional letters were presented

Prospective memory
The intention to remember to do something at some future time.

Errorless learning
Subjects in a learning situation are taught in such a way that they never have the opportunity to make errors.

Method of vanishing cues
Amnesic patients learned the meaning of computer commands by being presented with definitions of the commands and fragments of the commands' names. Additional letters were presented until the patient guessed the word. Then letters were progressively removed until the patient was able to give the name of the command when presented with its definition.

until the participant guessed the word. Then letters were progressively removed until the patient was able to give the name of the command upon being presented with its definition. Glisky and Schacter report that this technique allowed amnesic patients to successfully perform basic computer operations. In such situations it's important that the material to be learned be concrete and specific and that the patient not be required to generalize very far from the original learning context.

Summary

In this chapter we have examined memory systems. The classification of the various systems is a result of the influential work of Endel Tulving. In their classic experiments on strong and weak cue words, Tulving and Thomson explored how we encode specific information about items (*encoding specificity*) and the influence of this encoding on memory.

These experiments were also significant for the distinction they revealed between episodic and semantic memory. *Episodic memory* is a type of long-term storage for personal experiences and events, whereas *semantic memory* stores factual information and general knowledge about the world. This distinction between two independent memory systems finds further support in studies of brain-injured persons, especially those with amnesia.

The last 30 years have seen a lot of research on phenomena associated with semantic and episodic memory, including tip-of-the-tongue phenomenon, spreading activation, and involuntary semantic memory. The more recent literature suggests that there may be as many as five memory systems in all. *Procedural memory* contains our knowledge of how to do things that involve a sequence of operations, such as riding a bicycle. Such knowledge is *tacit* rather than *explicit* because we aren't necessarily aware of how we perform those operations. The *perceptual representation* system contains specific representations of previously encountered events. It is responsible for priming *implicit memory*—that is, unintentional or unconscious recollection of a prior episode (for example, experiments by Jacoby and Hollingshead). Finally, *working memory*—the system that provides temporary storage and manipulation of the information necessary for many cognitive activities—pulls all the other memory systems together. Baddeley's working memory model has four components: the *central executive*, the *phonological loop*, the *visuo-spatial sketchpad*, and the *episodic buffer*.

The *connectionist model* of memory provides an alternative to the idea of memory as a stored memory trace. In this model neuron-like units representing the various properties of an experience are connected to other neuron-like units. The excitation or inhibition of specific connections between units creates a pattern of activity that constitutes memory.

In evolutionary terms, procedural memory is considered the oldest system and episodic the most recent. In terms of development, Tulving argues that we begin to develop episodic memory relatively late, at around 4–6 years. Furthermore, Tulving suggests there are three types of consciousness or levels of awareness associated with memory systems: procedural memory's awareness of the here and now is *anoetic*; semantic memory's awareness of what may be missing from our immediate surroundings is *noetic*; and episodic memory, as a type of "self-knowing," is *autonoetic*. These differing levels of conscious awareness are central to Tulving's distinction between *remembering* and *knowing* (the *butcher-on-the-bus phenomenon*).

Do all forms of memory decline with age? A large body of research suggests that they do not. Studies by Howard, Fry, and Brune (1991) and Mitchell and Bruss (2003) show that even though older adults often have difficulty recalling recent events, they form implicit memories just as readily as younger people do. Similarly, amnesic patients do not differ from normals on implicit memory tasks; however, their performance on explicit memory tasks is below normal. Patients with Alzheimer's disease experience a loss of semantic knowledge and a disruption in the organization of semantic memory. For the elderly and some amnesiacs, the rehabilitation of memory typically involves environmental adaptation, external memory aids, and instruction in domain-specific knowledge.

Case Study Wrap-Up

At the beginning of this chapter we briefly discussed the strange memory deficit of Lucy Whitmore, the young woman played by Drew Barrymore in the movie *50 First Dates*. After reading this chapter you should have a better idea of what Lucy's problem was. If you recall, a car accident had supposedly left her unable to retain new memories from one day to the next; however, all the memories she had formed before the accident were intact, and she was able to form new memories from moment to moment. In fact, all the forms of memory discussed in this chapter (semantic, episodic, tacit, explicit, implicit) appeared to operate normally for Lucy throughout any particular day: the only problem was that the new semantic and episodic memories disappeared overnight. Presumably Lucy would have been able to retain new implicit memories, as patients with disconnection syndrome do, although this wasn't demonstrated in the movie.

What type of real-world amnesia most closely resembles Lucy Whitmore's memory deficit? Earlier in the chapter we discussed Korsakoff's syndrome, a severe form of anterograde amnesia in which the individual is unable to form new memories. While this appears to describe exactly the deficit suffered by Drew Barrymore's character, there are is a key difference that separates fact from fiction.

Someone who suffers from Korsakoff's syndrome (or an equivalent anterograde amnesia) is unable to form new long-term memories. The components of working memory can often be intact, in which case the individual may be able to retain new information for 30 seconds or so. However, as soon as that information leaves working memory it is lost, apparently forever. Thus the real-life equivalent of Lucy Whitmore's memory problem is much more severe than the movie suggests. While the fictional character's memory functions normally until she falls asleep, in real life people with Korsakoff's syndrome (or an equivalent anterograde amnesia) have no normal moment-to-moment memory function. If you introduced yourself to a Korsakoff's patient and then left the room for 30 seconds, he or she might not recognize you when you came back.

If you enjoyed *50 First Dates* you might want to check out *Memento*, which presents a much more accurate (though still embellished) picture of this particular memory dysfunction.

? In the Know: Review Questions

1. Outline Tulving's approach to memory, emphasizing the distinctions between different memory systems.

2. Discuss the role of spreading activation in semantic memory, using relevant experiments to illustrate.

3. What do older people, people with the amnesic syndrome, and people with Alzheimer's disease tell us about the nature of memory? What kinds of treatments might be effective with such people? Why might these treatments be effective?

Key Concepts

anoetic, noetic, and autonoetic (Tulving)
associative deficit hypothesis
butcher-on-the-bus phenomenon
central executive
chronesthesia (Tulving)
crystallized systems
disconnection syndrome
episodic buffer
episodic memory (Tulving)
errorless learning
excitatory and inhibitory connections
explicit knowledge
fluid systems
implicit memory
involuntary semantic memory (mind popping)
Korsakoff's syndrome
mental chronometry

method of opposition
method of vanishing cues
Moses illusion
perceptual representation system
phonological loop and visuo-spatial sketchpad
prefrontal leucotomy
principle of encoding specificity (Tulving)
procedural memory
prospective memory
recency bias vs primacy bias
semantic memory (Tulving)
spreading activation
tacit knowledge
teachable language comprehender
tip-of-the-tongue phenomenon
working memory

Links to Other Chapters

episodic memory
Chapter 13 (autobiographical memory)

semantic memory
Chapter 7 (synaesthesia)

working memory
Chapter 3 (the modal model)
Chapter 5 (are memory traces permanent?)

Chapter 9 (social context of language, evolution of language)
Chapter 10 (flexibility-rigidity and the brain)
Chapter 11 (natural deduction systems)
Chapter 12 (working memory and g)

fluid and crystallized systems
Chapter 12 (fluid intelligence and g)

Further Reading

For additional angles on memory systems see Gaffan (2003), Moscovitch (2000), Roediger (1990), and Roediger and Blaxton (1987). A theoretical context for chronesthesia and a survey of chronesthetic experiences can be found in D'Argembeau and Van der Linden (2003).

Evidence from functional neuroimaging studies illustrating the variety of areas in the brain involved in semantic memory is discussed in Maguire and Frith (2004) and Thompson-Schill (2003). Tulving and his colleagues have presented a model suggesting that the left prefrontal cortex is more involved than the right prefrontal cortex in acquiring episodic memories, but that the reverse is true for recalling episodic memories. See Nyberg, Cabeza, and Tulving (1996) and Habib, Nyberg, and Tulving (2003). For a critique of this model see Owen (2003).

It's difficult for "normals" to imagine what learning is like for amnesiacs. An analogy might be the kind of learning that takes place while a normal person is unconscious. For example, Kihlstrom, Schacter, Cork, Hurt, and Behr (1990) investigated memory for events that occur while a (non-amnesic) patient is anesthetized. They pointed out that following surgical anesthesia, patients are typically not able to recall anything that took place while they were unconscious. However, there is also some evidence suggesting that events that take place during surgery can affect patients' subsequent behaviour, although these findings are controversial.

For a thorough review that supplements our discussion of the rehabilitation of cognitive deficits see Park and Ingles (2001).

D'Argembeau, A., & Van der Linden, M. (2003). Phenomenal characteristics associated with projecting oneself back into the past and forward into the future: Influence of valence and temporal distance. *Consciousness and Cognition, 13*, 844–858.

Gaffan, D. (2003). Against memory systems. In A. Parker, A. Derrington, & C. Blakemore (Eds.), *The physiology of cognitive processes* (pp. 234–51). Oxford: Oxford University Press.

Habib, R., Nyberg, L., & Tulving, E. (2003). Hemispheric asymmetries of memory: The HERA model revisited. *Trends in Cognitive Science, 7*, 241–244.

Kihlstrom, J.F., Schacter, D., Cork, R., Hurt, C., & Behr, S. (1990). Implicit and explicit memory following surgical anaesthesia. *Psychological Science, 1*, 303–306.

Maguire, E.A., & Frith, C.D. (2004). The brain network associated with acquiring semantic knowledge. *NeuroImage, 22*, 171–178.

Moscovitch, M. (2000). Theories of memory and consciousness. In E. Tulving & F.I.M. Craik (Eds.), *The Oxford handbook of memory* (pp. 609–25). New York: Oxford University Press.

Nyberg, L., Cabeza, R., & Tulving, E. (1996). PET studies of encoding and retrieval: The HERA model. *Psychonomic Bulletin and Review, 3*, 135–148.

Owen, A. (2003). HERA today, gone tomorrow? *Trends in Cognitive Sciences, 7*, 383–384.

Park, N.W., & Ingles, J.L. (2001). Effectiveness of attention rehabilitation after an acquired brain injury: A meta-analysis. *Neuropsychology, 15*, 199–210.

Roediger, H.L. (1990). Implicit memory: Retention without remembering. *American Psychologist, 45*, 1043–1056.

Roediger, H.L., & Blaxton, T.A. (1987). Retrieval modes produce dissociations in memory for surface information. In D. Gorfein & R.R. Hoffman (Eds.), *Memory and cognitive processes: The Ebbinghaus centennial conference* (pp. 349–377). Hillsdale, NJ: Erlbaum.

Thompson-Schill, S.L. (2003). Neuroimaging studies of semantic memory: Inferring 'how' from 'where'. *Neuropsychologia, 41*, 280–292.

CHAPTER 7

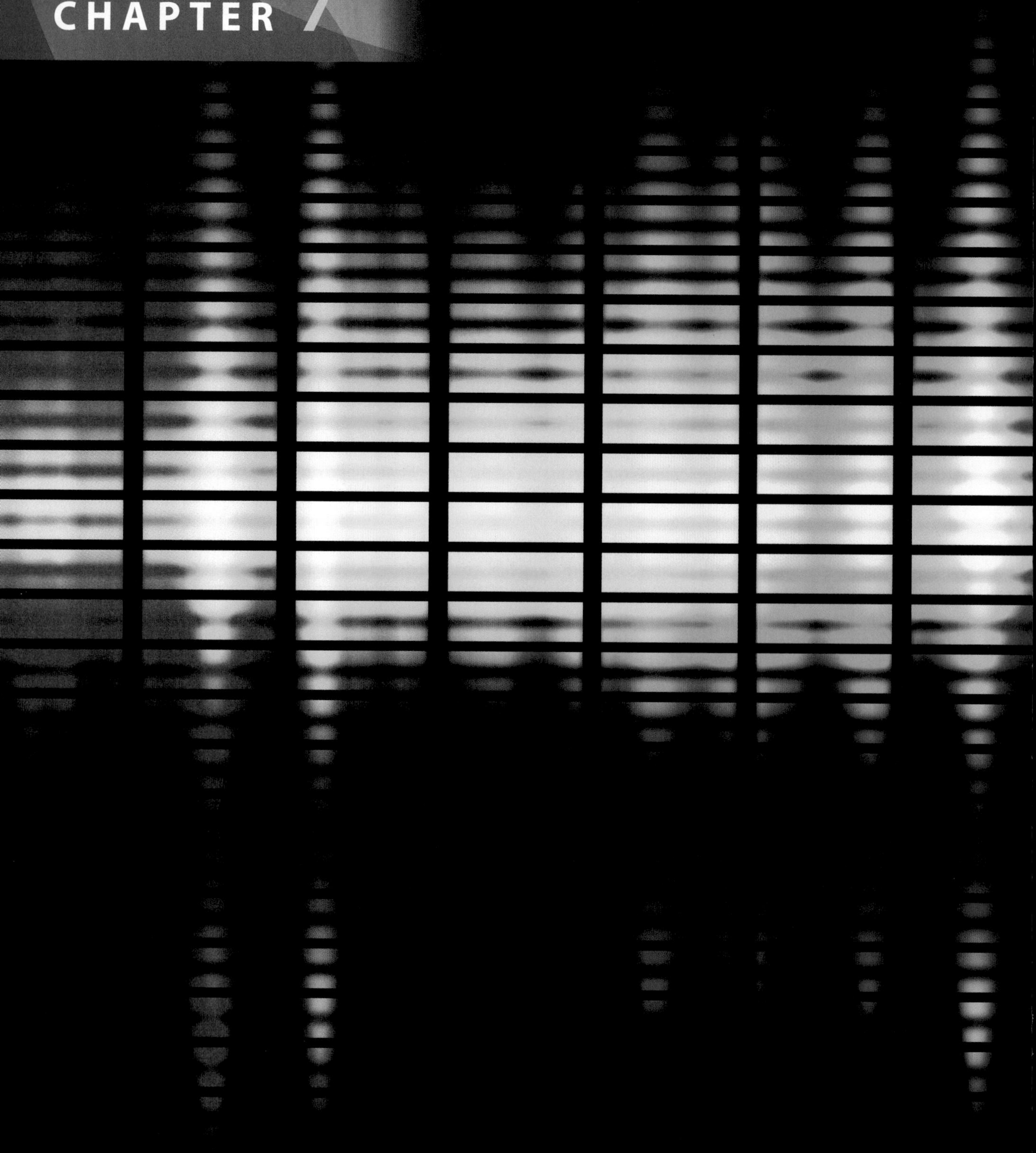

Imagery

Chapter Objectives

- To review experimental evidence for Paivio's dual-coding theory.
- To examine how synesthesia and eidetic imagery relate to ordinary imagery.
- To outline the role of distinctiveness in memory.
- To distinguish mental rotation, mental scanning, and egocentric perspectives.
- To identify the basic properties of cognitive maps.

Case Study   Time–Space Synesthesia and Number Forms

When we need to remember the time and date of an appointment or special occasion, most of us rely on our trusty day planners or smartphones. But imagine for a moment that instead of recording appointments in a book or electronic device, you could visualize a virtual calendar with each month, day, and hour in a specific location in space and simply place an appointment in the "right spot" on the space. In fact there are individuals who experience this kind of **time space**. When these people hear, see, or even just think of the names of various units of time such as days of the week (Monday, etc.), weeks, and months (January, etc.), they see them in spatial patterns external to themselves. Cases of this kind were described by several early investigators, including Sir Francis Galton (1908/1973). An example of one person's time space is shown in Figure 7.1. This person experiences the months of the year in an oval form, which appears about 30 cm in front of her face. Other individuals experience their time spaces as surrounding their bodies at about waist height. Some find that when they rotate their torso the space rotates with them; in fact, it goes with them wherever they go. An interesting aspect of these experiences is that they seem to occur automatically, which means that they cannot be consciously inhibited. People with time spaces often report using them as

Time spaces
The visual experience of time units such as days of the week or months of the year as occupying spatial locations outside the body.

Number forms
Automatically generated images of numbers in various spatial layouts external to an individual.

calendars to store important dates such as birthdays and due dates.

Some people also seem to be able to create vivid picture-like images of number sequences. Those who experience **number forms** see numbers organized in various geometric forms in front of them. Figure 7.2 shows a bird's eye view of the number form experienced by a woman known as "L" (see Jarick et al., 2009). She experiences single-digit numbers as if they were located to her left, the numbers from 10 to 20 in front of her, and the higher numbers to her right. As with time spaces, number forms are often experienced automatically: a number will simply appear, like a virtual picture, whenever it is thought of. Of course, it isn't really there: it's just a very vivid image.

Time spaces and number forms are relatively unusual forms of imagery. However, most of us can picture things in our minds, which is to say that we experience imagery of some sort or another. It's not easy to define precisely what an image is. The similarity between images and pictures has often been noted; in fact, *The Oxford English Dictionary* gives "To form a mental image of, to imagine" as one of the meanings of the verb *to picture*. Although a mental image can be defined as a "picture in the head," a number of qualifications must be added to this simple definition (Reber, 1985). This chapter is about those qualifications. In it we will examine how images arise, how they operate, and how they influence other psychological processes.

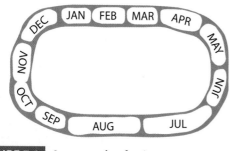

FIGURE 7.1   **An example of a time space**

From: Smilek, D., Callejas, A., Dixon, M.J., & Merikle, P.M. (2007). Ovals of time: Time-space associations in synaesthesia. *Consciousness and Cognition, 16,* 507–519.

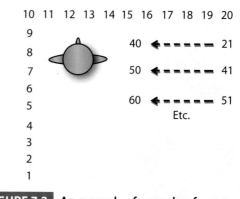

FIGURE 7.2   **An example of a number form**

Adapted from: Jarick, M., Dixon, M. J., Maxwell, E.C., Nicholls, M.E.R. and Smilek, D. (2009). The ups and downs (and lefts and rights) of synaesthetic number forms: Validation from spatial cueing and SNARC-type tasks. *Cortex, 45,* 1190–1199.

Memory and Imagery

PAIVIO'S DUAL-CODING THEORY

Images seem to be very subjective phenomena, and for a while during the twentieth century many psychologists considered them too subjective to be studied scientifically. However, interest in imagery began to revive during the 1960s. This revival was to an important extent sparked by Alan Paivio's (1971, 1986, 1991; Paivio & Begg, 1981) research into what came to be known as **dual-coding theory**. Paivio postulated that humans have two systems for representing events, verbal and non-verbal, each of which has its own code (Johnson, Paivio, & Clark, 1996, p. 115). For example, an event can be described in words using the verbal system, or it can be imagined without words, using the non-verbal system. Which system is used depends on the nature of the information.

The relations between the two systems are outlined in Figure 7.3. If you follow the diagram from the top down, you'll see that information arrives in either verbal or non-verbal form. After being picked up by the sensory systems, verbal information is represented in the verbal system and non-verbal information in the non-verbal system. The units that make up the verbal system are called **logogens** (a term borrowed from Morton, 1969). A logogen contains the information underlying our use of a particular word. The units that make up the non-verbal system are called **imagens** and

Dual-coding theory
The theory that that there are two ways of representing events, verbal and non-verbal.

Logogens
The units containing the information underlying our use of a word; the components of the verbal system.

Imagens
The units containing information that generate mental images; the components of the non-verbal system.

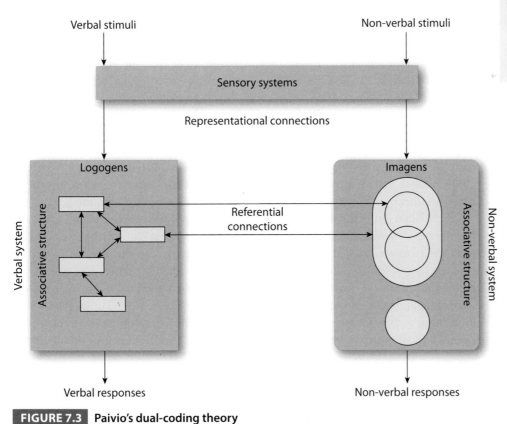

FIGURE 7.3   Paivio's dual-coding theory

From: *Mental Representations: A Dual Coding Approach* by Allan Paivio (1986); fig 4.1 p. 67. By permission of Oxford University Press.

contain the information that generates mental images. Imagens "correspond to natural objects, holistic parts of objects, and natural groupings of objects" (Paivio, 1986, p. 60). Imagens operate synchronously: the parts they contain are available for inspection simultaneously. This means that a variety of related mental images can be generated from imagens. For example, you can imagine a group of people, one person from the group, the face of that person, the nose on the face of that person, and so on. By contrast, logogens operate sequentially. When you listen to a sentence, for example, the words are not present all at once, but come one after the other.

Information contained in one system can give rise to a process in the other system. As an example, Paivio (1986, p. 62) used the experience of describing your dining-room table. If you are somewhere other than your dining room, you can probably still experience a mental image of the table. What you then describe is that image. This means that the two systems are linked by what Figure 7.3 calls "referential connections." A verbal description of something can elicit an image of it, and an image in turn can elicit a description. Paivio used the term **imagery** to refer to the ease with which something such as a word can elicit a *mental image*—that is, "a mental picture, or sound" (e.g., Toglia & Battig, 1978, p. 4).

According to Paivio's (1971) theory, words that easily elicit a mental image—that is, words with a high degree of *imagery*—tend to be concrete (e.g., *table*), whereas words that don't easily elicit a mental image tend to be abstract (e.g., *purpose*). **Concreteness** is defined as the degree to which a word refers to "concrete objects, persons, places, or things that can be heard, felt, smelled or tasted" (Toglia & Battig, 1978). In other words, *concreteness* is the degree to which a word refers to something that can be experienced by the senses. The notion that ideas have their origin in concrete sensory experience has a long tradition in the history of Western thought (see, for example, R. Brown, 1968; J.M. Clark & Paivio, 1989).

To measure imagery and concreteness, Paivio would give participants the definitions of those terms outlined above and have them rate words on seven-point scales anchored either with "low imagery" and "high imagery" or "low concreteness" and "high concreteness." In most cases he found imagery and concreteness to be very highly correlated (e.g., Paivio, Yuille, & Madigan, 1968). This led Paivio (e.g., Paivio & Begg, 1981) to argue that imagery and concreteness measure two aspects of the same process because our experience of concrete events is necessarily saturated with images.

Notice that one of the implications of the foregoing is that concepts such as *pain* and *love* are not concrete. If this seems puzzling, remember that "concreteness" in Paivio's sense refers to objects, persons, and places. Pain and love can certainly be caused by concrete things, but they themselves are not concrete events. Thus there are some words, such as *pain* and *love*, that are not concrete but still elicit vivid mental imagery. These words often refer to emotions (Benjafield, 1987; Paivio, 1971, p. 83; Yuille, 1968). Thus in addition to external sources of imagery there are internal, emotional sources. This is a point we will return to later on, when we discuss the effects of imagery on memory.

RESEARCH RELATED TO DUAL-CODING THEORY

One of Paivio's earliest studies (Paivio, 1965) focused on the role of imagery in learning. This study employed a paired-associate learning task. Four groups of participants each learned 16 pairs of words.

Imagery (Paivio's sense)
The ease with which something such as a word can elicit a mental image.

Concreteness (Paivio's sense)
The degree to which a word refers to something that can be experienced by the senses (i.e., heard, felt, smelled, or tasted).

Each group learned a different kind of stimulus–response pair. For the first group both words were concrete (e.g., *coffee/pencil*); for the second, the first word in each pair was concrete and the second abstract (e.g., *string/idea*); for the third, the first word was abstract and the second concrete (e.g., *virtue/chair*); and for the fourth, both words were abstract (e.g., *event/theory*). In the first learning trial, participants listened to the list of words, after which they were given the first (stimulus) word of each pair and asked to write down the second word. After four such trials, examination of the total number of correct responses revealed clear differences between the groups. These data are presented graphically in Figure 7.4.

Notice that learning is best when both words are concrete and worst when both are abstract. Notice also that the biggest difference between recall for concrete and abstract items is between concrete and abstract stimuli. A concrete stimulus led to much better recall of the response than an abstract stimulus. Paivio also had participants rate the image-ability of each word, and found that the concrete words were rated higher than the abstract ones. These results have been replicated many times (Marschark, Richman, Yuille, & Hunt, 1987; Paivio, 1983; Paivio, Khan, & Begg, 2000; Paivio, Walsh, & Bons, 1994).

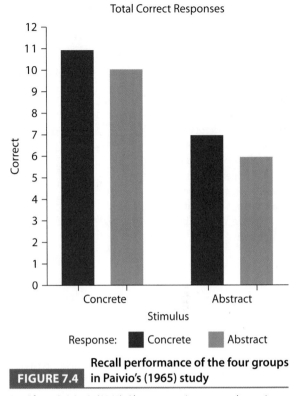

FIGURE 7.4 Recall performance of the four groups in Paivio's (1965) study

Data from: Paivio, A. (1965). Abstractness, imagery and meaningfulness in paired-associate learning. *Journal of Verbal Learning and Verbal Behavior, 4*, 32–38.

According to dual-coding theory (Paivio, 1969, 1971), these results can be explained as follows. A concrete word can be coded by both the verbal and non-verbal systems, whereas an abstract word will tend to be coded only by the verbal system because it is not likely to elicit much of an image. The fact that a concrete word is coded in two systems means that it is more easily available to memory than an abstract word that is coded in only the verbal system.

Paivio hypothesized that stimulus concreteness would be particularly important in learning pairs of words. Suppose you are given the stimulus-response pair *coffee/pencil* to learn. You might imagine a coffee cup with a pencil in it. Thus both words may give rise to a single image, and this imaginal code may be stored in memory. When the stimulus word *coffee* is later presented by itself, "its image arousing value would be particularly important, for the stimulus member must serve as a cue that reinstitutes the compound image from which the response component can be retrieved" (Paivio, 1969, p. 244). Abstract words would be less effective cues because they are not coded imaginally.

Paivio's dual-coding theory has been applied to various phenomena. For example, in addition to the findings on the relation between memory and imagery that we have already reviewed, dual-coding theory has been extended to the investigation of figurative language, such as metaphor (Katz, Paivio, Marschark, & Clark, 1988). It has also been used as a framework for understanding the mental processes involved in reading and writing (Sadoski & Paivio, 2001; Whitehead, 2003).

DUAL-CODING THEORY AND THE BRAIN

As we noted in Chapter 2, before the 1990s many researchers understood split-brain research to imply that the left hemisphere manages "analytic" (e.g., verbal, rational) tasks and the right hemisphere "holistic" (e.g., non-verbal, intuitive) tasks. Consistent with this viewpoint, Paivio (1991) argued that the verbal and non-verbal systems are

> dependent on different parts of the brain. The **left hemisphere** of most people controls speech and is more efficient than the **right hemisphere** at processing verbal material in such tasks as perceptual recognition, episodic memory, and comprehension. The right hemisphere has the advantage in such nonverbal tasks as face identification and discrimination, recognition of nonverbal sounds, and memory for faces and spatial patterns. The generalization holds for different sensory modalities, justifying the conclusion that the distinction is a verbal/nonverbal symbolic one that cuts across sensory modalities. (p. 272)

The hypothesis that imagery is mainly a right-hemisphere activity and verbal representation a left-hemisphere activity has been challenged by fMRI work done by Fiebach and Friederici (2003). A clear implication of dual-coding theory is that concrete words will trigger greater activity in the right hemisphere than will abstract words. After a review of the relevant neuroimaging research, Fiebach and Friederici (2003, p. 66) concluded that the evidence "does not fully support the assumption of a specific right-hemispheric involvement during the processing of concrete relative to abstract words."

Fiebach and Friederici (2003) conducted an fMRI study of their own in which participants were shown concrete words (e.g., *bike*, *church*, *basket*), abstract words (e.g., *norm*, *feature*, *status*), and pseudo words (words in which one or two letters have been randomly replaced). The participants were given a **lexical decision task** in which they had to indicate by a manual response whether or not each stimulus was a word. This task allows the experimenter to compare images of the brain activity triggered by abstract and concrete words even though the participants' response should be the same to both (i.e., both are words). Since the participants were not intentionally processing abstract and concrete words differently, any differences in brain activation could be attributed solely to the different properties of abstract and concrete words. The results showed that abstract and concrete words elicited different patterns of activity in the left hemisphere, but that concrete words did not elicit heightened activity in the right hemisphere. Thus the hypothesis that concrete words elicit greater left-hemisphere activation than abstract words was not supported (Fiebach and Friederici, 2003, p. 68). Commenting on these results, Scott (2004) suggested that linking imagery strongly with the right hemisphere is one example among many of "simplistic right brain/left brain attributions of cognitive functions, which in reality are supported by rather more complex bilateral systems" (p. 152).

IMAGERY AND MNEMONICS

Yates's *The Art of Memory* (1966) is a history of **mnemonic techniques**: techniques used to aid memory. According to Yates, imagery has been used as a mnemonic technique since ancient times. A second-century document called the *Ad Herennium*, for example, gave instructions for memorizing a great many items. This technique, usually called the **method of loci**, basically had two parts: places (*loci*) and images. The idea

---

Left and right hemispheres theory
The theory that the left hemisphere of the brain controls speech and is better at processing verbal material than the right hemisphere, which is better at non-verbal tasks.

Lexical decision task
A task in which participants must indicate whether or not a stimulus is a word.

Mnemonic techniques
Procedures used to aid memory.

Method of loci
A mnemonic technique based on places and images.

was to establish a cognitive map of a large building and place in each of its various *loci* an image representing one of the things to be remembered; then recalling those things would simply be a matter of mentally strolling through the building and collecting the images. It was recommended that the images be as distinctive as possible, even bizarre. For example, if you wanted to remember someone whose name was *Gorden* you might form an image of a garden and then "choose a prominent feature of the person's face and link the image of the name to it. Thus if Gorden has a large nose, an image could be formed of a garden growing over his nose" (P.E. Morris, Jones, & Hampson, 1978, p. 335). Yates reported that great feats of memory were accomplished using this technique; one adept was able to recite 2000 names in the order in which they were given, after hearing the list only once.

Yates's account of ancient mnemonic techniques stimulated quite a bit of contemporary research. Are these old methods really effective? There is some reason to believe that they are. Not only are similar methods promoted by professional teachers of mnemonic techniques (e.g., Lorayne & Lucas, 1976), but psychologists have shown that they really do aid memory. In an important account of the psychological principles behind mnemonics, Bower (1970a, 1970b) pointed out how you could use the method of *loci* to create a mental shopping list. First you would form images of various locations around the house, such as the living room and the bedroom; then you would form vivid images of the items to be bought (say, milk and bread) and relate those images to specific locations: for example, imagining someone milking a cow in the living room and a loaf of bread tucked into the bed. At the store you would remember what to buy by imagining each place and recalling the images located there.

Items interrelated to form units are easier to remember than individual items (Asch, 1969). The fact that imagery can be used to organize disparate items into meaningful units may be part of the reason it is so useful. However, a mental image can also make information distinctive (Begg, 1982). We have already observed, in our discussion of levels of processing in Chapter 5, that **distinctiveness** is an important aid to memory. The relation between imagery and distinctiveness has been the subject of some interesting research, to which we now turn.

> **Distinctiveness hypothesis**
> The hypothesis that the more distinctive the item is, the easier it will be to recall.

IMAGERY AND DISTINCTIVENESS

Yates (1966) noted that the author of the *Ad Herennium* recommended that the images used as memory aids be as striking as possible: "active, [with] exceptional beauty or singular ugliness," "ornamented 'with crowns or purple cloaks,'" "stained with blood or soiled with mud or smeared with red paint" (p. 10). The possibility that memory is facilitated by bizarre images has been extensively investigated. Initially, experiments did not demonstrate any effect of bizarreness (e.g., Nappe & Wollen, 1973). However, subsequent research showed that bizarreness can have an effect under certain circumstances (e.g., D. Anderson & Buyer, 1994; O'Brien & Wolford, 1982; Richman, 1994).

The specific conditions under which bizarreness has an effect have been explored in some detail (e.g., Einstein & McDaniel, 1987; Einstein, McDaniel, & Lackey, 1989; McDaniel, DeLosh, & Merritt, 2000; McDaniel, Einstein, DeLosh, May, & Brady, 1995). One of the more reliable findings has been that people remember bizarre items better when they occur along with common items. Thus if participants were given a list of sentences to learn, some of which were bizarre (e.g., *the maid licked ammonia off the table*) and some of which were not (e.g., *the maid spilled ammonia on the table*), then the bizarre items were remembered better. However, if the list consisted solely of bizarre items, then recall was generally no better than for a list composed entirely of common items.

The finding that bizarre items are memorable when they occur together with common items is reminiscent of a long-standing phenomenon called the **von Restorff effect** (von Restorff, 1933; Hunt, 1995), which holds that if one item in a set is different from the others then it is more likely to be recalled. It's important to realize that "being different" is a relative and not an absolute property (Hunt & Lamb, 2001). In a list of bizarre and common items, the bizarre items are more distinctive than the common items. This distinctiveness makes them memorable in a way that they are not when they appear in a list composed entirely of bizarre items. If a list is composed entirely of bizarre items, none of them will be distinctive.

> **Von Restorff effect**
> If one item in a set is different from the others, it will be more likely to be recalled.

HUMOUR AND DISTINCTIVENESS

Schmidt (2002; Schmidt & Williams, 2001) has observed that humour can have an effect similar to that of bizarreness. In a series of experiments he used as humorous items a set of cartoons by a well-known cartoonist; a set of literal items created by eliminating incongruous information in the cartoons, rendering them humourless; and a set of weird cartoons created by adding irrelevant elements to the original cartoons. In one study, participants were shown a set of cartoons and then unexpectedly asked to provide a brief description of each cartoon. When the cartoons shown were a mixture of the three types, the participants' descriptions of the humorous items were more accurate than those of either the literal or the weird ones. However, when all the items shown were humorous, the descriptions were generally no better than for all-literal or all-weird sets. These results paralleled those described above for bizarre items: the humorous items became more memorable only when contrasted with non-humorous items (both literal and weird). However, humorous items were apparently more memorable than weird items, and this raised the possibility of a connection with the effect of bizarreness: although bizarreness is less memorable than humour, the fact that it often strikes people as funny might help to explain why bizarre items can, under some circumstances, be easier to remember than common ones. Humour in itself may be a strong aid to memory, especially in situations where humorous material stands in contrast to neutral material (Schmidt, 2002, p. 135).

THE PROBLEM OF DISTINCTIVENESS

E. Winograd and Soloway (1986) noted that people often believe they can remember things better if they make the material to be remembered distinctive in some way. One strategy is to store things in special places. If we have something valuable to store, and we want to make sure we remember where it is, we will often put it in some special place. The problem with this strategy is that when you want to recover the item, you can't remember where that special place was. Winograd and Soloway (1986) pointed out that at first glance the special-place strategy may look similar to the method of loci that Yates (1966) described. However, there are important differences between the two.

Winograd and Soloway (1986) began with the observation that a special place to store an item is an unlikely place in which to find it. Some special places are chosen specifically to make sure that no one else, especially not a burglar, will find the item. Winograd and Soloway (1986, p. 371) commented that this is presumably why so many people store valuables such as cash in unlikely places, such as the freezer.

In one of Winograd and Soloway's experiments, participants were given sentences describing the locations of objects, such as "The milk is in the refrigerator" or "The tickets are in the freezer." Some participants rated these sentences for likelihood: how likely was it that somebody would store that particular object in that location? Some other participants also rated these sentences for memorability: how memorable would that location be as a place to store that item? A final group of participants were told to imagine putting each item in the location described, and then to rate each location for memorability. All groups were administered a recall test in which participants were given the name of the item and then asked to recall its location (e.g., "Where is the milk?" or "Where are the tickets?").

Winograd and Soloway compared recall for items of different levels of likelihood and memorability. It turned out that items from item-location pairings that were rated low in likelihood were remembered less well than items from item-location pairings that were rated high in likelihood, regardless of the level of rated memorability. To put this result a slightly different way: no matter how memorable we think a location will be, we will in fact remember it less well if it is unlikely than if it is likely. So the next time you decide to store your spare credit card in the medicine cabinet, perhaps you should think again.

Winograd and Soloway agreed with Begg's (1982) suggestion that distinctiveness is an effective aid for remembering individual items, but is not so useful for remembering the association between items. Consider why this difference is so important when you store an item in an unlikely place. When you want to retrieve it, you need to remember where you stored it: that is, you need to come up with an association between the object and the location. The problem is that the stored object is not an effective cue for remembering the location, and the distinctiveness of the location is irrelevant to the process of remembering.

This is where we can see how the "special places" storage method differs from the method of loci. When you use the method of loci, you begin with a set of places and then store items in them by forming an imaginative relationship between the two. Later, when you want to remember the item, you first recall the locus and then the object stored there. The process of recall goes from place to object. By contrast, when you store an object in a special place, the process of recall has to go from object to location, and there is usually no imaginative relationship between the two to serve as a memory cue.

Brown, Bracken, Zoccoli, and Douglas (2004, p. 650) have observed that the **special places strategy** is similar to a strategy that many of us use when creating passwords. We want a password that we can easily remember, but that others will be unable to discover. As we have just seen, it's very difficult to satisfy both these requirements simultaneously. Brown et al. (2004, p. 650) suggest using easily remembered (and therefore easily discovered) passwords in situations not requiring security, and creating distinctive passwords only when necessary. Finally, although you should certainly keep a written record of your passwords in a secure location, you should probably make sure the place you choose is not too special.

Special places strategy
Choosing a storage location that other people will not think of; the problem is that you may not think of it either when the time comes to retrieve the item.

Putting things in special places or creating unique passwords means relying on distinctiveness alone to be a sufficient aid to recall. Winograd and Soloway (1986) suggested that this is an example of a mistaken belief that we have about the way memory works. **Metamemory** is the name for our beliefs about how memory works. The decision to squirrel something away in an unusual location is an instance of metamemory failure.

Synesthesia and Eidetic Imagery

One of the most intriguing psychological states is **synesthesia**: a condition in which a stimulus appropriate to one sense (e.g., a sound) triggers an experience appropriate to another sense (e.g., a colour). Here is a report of an extreme synesthetic experience from a participant under the influence of mescaline (Werner, 1948/1961). "I think that I hear noises and see faces, and yet everything is one and the same. I cannot tell whether I am seeing or hearing. I feel, I taste, and smell the sound. It's all one. I, myself, am the tone" (p. 92). People who routinely have such experiences in everyday life are called *synesthetes*, and the most common experience that they report is **chromesthesia**, or *coloured hearing* (Harrison, 2001, p. 182). This is the experience of colour in response to an auditory stimulus. For example, a synesthete may experience a colour when hearing someone's name. The cue that elicits a synesthetic experience is called an **inducer**, and the synesthetic response itself is called the **concurrent** (Grossenbacher & Lovelace, 2001).

As many as one in 200 people may be synesthetes (Ramachandran, 2004, p. 19). Synesthesia appears to run in families and occurs more often in women than in men (Bailey & Johnson, 1997). Perhaps the most famous synesthete was the novelist Vladimir Nabokov, who routinely experienced coloured hearing, as did his wife and his mother (Harrison, 2001, p. 131).

Cytowic (2002) described several cases of synesthetes who believed that synesthesia improved their memory. Smilek, Dixon, Cudahy, and Merikle (2002) provided evidence that this may indeed be the case. They reported on a synesthete, known as C, who is possessed of an extraordinary memory. For example, when asked to remember four lists of nine digits each, she could recall them all, and after an interval of two months could recall all but two of the digits. In C's case, each digit consistently induces a particular colour. Thus the number 2 printed in black always induces the colour *red*, which is projected onto the number. Smilek et al. (2002) compared C's digit memory with that of a control group of non-synesthetes. Each participant was asked to memorize three displays of 50 numbers each. The first display had numbers printed in black. The second display had numbers printed in colours that were different from C's concurrents. For example, 2 induces *red* in C, but was printed in *purple*. This is called the *incongruent display*. The third display was composed of numbers printed in C's concurrents (e.g., 2 was printed in *red*). This is called the *congruent display*. C outperformed all other participants in the first, black-digit display. However, the incongruent display caused C's performance to plummet from 66 per cent correct in the first display to only 4 per cent correct in the second (see Figure 7.5). By contrast, the performance of other participants was similar on both displays. C found the incongruent display discombobulating, saying that she "had never had this happen" to her before, and that she had "all these numbers swirling around" in her head. It seems reasonable to think that the colours of the digits in the incongruent display

Metamemory
Beliefs about how memory works.

Synesthesia
The condition in which a stimulus appropriate to one sense (e.g., a sound) triggers an experience appropriate to another sense (e.g., a colour).

Chromesthesia
Coloured hearing.

Inducer
The cue that elicits a synesthetic experience.

Concurrent
The synesthetic response itself.

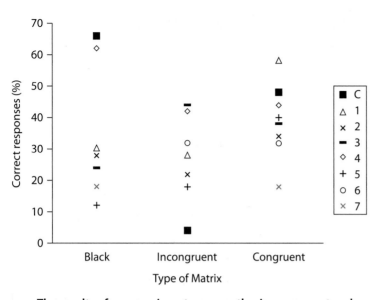

The results of an experiment on synesthesia: congruent and

FIGURE 7.5 incongruent number–colour matching and memory

The squares represent C's performance; the other symbols represent the performance of seven non-synesthetic control participants.

From: Smilek, D., Dixon, M.J., Cudhay, C., & Merikle, P.M. (2002). Synesthetic colour experiences influence memory. *Psychological Science, 13,* 548–552.

interfered with the colour she projected onto them. This interpretation is particularly likely since the congruent display did not adversely affect her performance (see Figure 7.5). Although C typically remembered digits extremely well, her memory for other kinds of material was similar to that of control participants. Thus it seems reasonable to conclude that synesthesia is an aid to memory in C's case, and perhaps in other synesthetes as well. In fact, recent studies of other synesthetes have shown very similar results (see Radvansky, Gibson, & McNerney, 2011). In his book *Embracing the Wide Sky: A Tour Across the Horizons of the Mind*, the synesthete Daniel Tammet (2009, 73–74) describes a study examining how his condition affected his memory performance:

> For me, the numbers 0 to 9 have different sizes ranging from 6 (the smallest) to 9 (the largest). The researchers [Shai Azoulai and Ed Hubbard] presented me with two 100-digit number matrices (each for three minutes); one that presented the numbers in sizes that conformed to my synesthetic perception of them, and another that did not. . . . Three days later I was able to remember 68 digits from the first but barely any from the second. I found the experience of being asked to read and later recall the numbers presented in "wrong" sizes extremely dizzying and uncomfortable—rather like asking someone to read and recite in a language he does not know!

THEORIES OF SYNESTHESIA

A traditional explanation of synesthesia is that it reveals the underlying unity of the senses (e.g., Werner, 1948/1961, p. 93). The idea is that our five senses evolved out of one primordial sense, and that synesthetic phenomena reflect this common origin. A more recent version of this theory was advanced by Maurer (1997), who suggested that "the newborn's senses are not well differentiated but are instead intermingled in a synesthetic confusion" (p. 227). This lack of differentiation could be due to inborn connections between different areas of the infant's brain, such as between "the visual and auditory areas of the immature cortex" (Kennedy, Batardière, Dehay, & Barone, 1997, p. 253). These are called *transient connections* because they are not permanent: over time they are gradually pruned, much as surplus branches are pruned from a tree. The pruning process, which allows the senses to become differentiated from each other, is called **apoptosis**, and is a form of programmed cell death. Perhaps adult synesthesia occurs when this pruning process fails to run its course, and what were supposed to be transient connections end up being permanent. It has been suggested that, in the case of synesthetes, "the 'pruning' gene is defective," resulting "in cross-activation between areas of the brain" (Ramachandran, 2004, p. 68).

Apoptosis
Programmed pruning of neurons.

Failure to weed out inter-sensory connections cannot be the whole story, however. It turns out that synesthetic responses can be elicited by concepts as well as percepts. Thinking about the number 7 is different from seeing the number 7 printed on a page. If simply thinking of a number can induce the same synesthetic response as perceiving the number, then cross-activation between sensory areas cannot be all there is to synesthesia. Dixon, Smilek, Cudahy, & Merikle (2000), in another study of C, had her perform the following task. After being shown two numbers (e.g., 5 + 2), she was shown a colour and asked to name it. It turned out that if the colour shown was incongruent with the sum of the two numbers then C took longer to name the colour than if the colour shown was congruent with that sum. For example, suppose C was shown 5 + 2. For C, 7 is the inducer for *yellow*. Thus C could then name the colour *yellow* faster than she could name the colour *red*. However, 2 is the inducer for *red*. When shown 1 + 1, therefore, C could name the colour *red* faster than she could name the colour *yellow*. Incongruent colours interfered with C's ability to name the concurrent induced by the sum of the two numbers. Notice that this sum was not shown to C: she had to calculate it herself. The fact that C's synesthesia did not depend on an external sensory stimulus, but could be induced by the sum of two numbers, is evidence that synesthesia need not be the result of connections between sensory systems, but can also be the outcome of a conceptual process.

Ward and Simner (2003) have further explored linguistic and conceptual factors in synesthesia. They reported on a man named JIW, who was a lifelong synesthete. In his case, the sounds of specific words induced particular tastes. For example, the word *Chicago* induces an *avocado* taste. Notice that *Chicago* sounds a bit like *avocado*, and some of the inducer words have this relationship to the taste concurrents. Thus *Virginia* induced *vinegar* and *Barbara* induced *rhubarb*. Some other word–taste links involved the meaning of the word. For example, *bar* induced *milk chocolate*. In general, the foods that JIW tasted on hearing words that recalled their names were ones he had known as a child. More recently acquired tastes, such as *coffee*, were rarely induced. Since the links between the names of foods and their tastes are obviously acquired, not inborn, they may properly be said to belong to semantic memory. These results "suggest a strong role for language and conceptual factors in the development of this type of synesthesia" (Ward & Simner, 2003, p. 254). In at

THINK TWICE
BOX 7.1

Can Anyone Become a Synesthete?

Non-synesthetes who wish they could experience synesthesia themselves often ask whether it is possible to induce the condition. If we were to train them on various letter and colour pairings, then perhaps over time they could begin to experience synesthesia. Although there is no solid evidence that such training would be effective, there is some evidence that synesthetic experiences can be induced through hypnosis. In a fascinating study reported by Cohen Kadosh and colleagues (2009), non-synesthetes were hypnotized and then told that each digit was associated with a particular colour. For instance, the digit "2" was associated with yellow and the digit "4" was associated with blue. Following the hypnotic session, these "posthypnotic suggestion" participants were interviewed and asked what they saw when they were shown a black digit. Promisingly, their responses were similar to those offered by synesthetes: they experienced the black digits they viewed as having coloured overlays. To objectively test these· reports, Cohen Kadosh and colleagues (2009) showed participants brief displays of a black digit against a background that was either congruent or incongruent with the colour hypnotically associated with the digit. Participants then had to name the digit. Strikingly, the participants with the hypnotically induced synesthesia actually made many errors when the background colour of the display was congruent with the colour associated with the digit. By contrast, they made very few errors when the digit and background colour were incongruent. Apparently the digits did elicit the hypnotically induced colour associations, and as a result they stood out from the background on incongruent trials, but blended in with the background on congruent trials. These results can be seen in Figure 7.6, which shows the error rate of digit identification on congruent and incongruent trials for two participants, one of whom received a posthypnotic suggestion (PHS) and one of whom (the control) did not (No PHS). Notice that the control group made virtually no errors in either the congruent or incongruent conditions because the black letters on a coloured background were easily perceptible. So it seems that synesthesia can be hypnotically induced. Still, before you run off to get yourself hypnotically induced with synesthesia, you should know that this method would work only for the small subset of the population who are highly hypnotizable; those of us who resist hypnotic suggestions are out of luck.

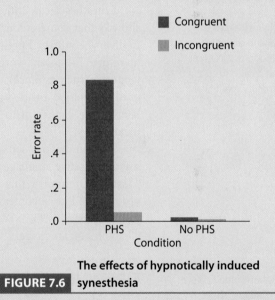

FIGURE 7.6 **The effects of hypnotically induced synesthesia**

Errors of digit identification on congruent and incongruent trials for two groups of participants: the PHS group had synesthesia induced through posthypnotic suggestion, while the No PHS group did not receive any posthypnotic suggestion.

From: Kadosh, R.C., Henik, A., Catena, A., Walsh, V., & Fuentes, L.J. (2009). Induced cross-modal synaesthetic experience without abnormal neuronal connections. *Psychological Science, 20,* 258–265.

least some cases, the experiences of synesthetes may be "entirely mediated by neural connections that exist in normal adult human brains" (Grossenbacher & Lovelace, 2001, p. 40).

STRONG AND WEAK SYNESTHESIA

Martino and Marks (2001) have distinguished between *strong* and *weak* forms of synesthesia. Strong forms are the "classic" instances involving an inducer in one sensory modality (e.g., a sound) and a concurrent image in another sensory modality (e.g., a colour). Martino and Marks give the example of Carol, who experienced colour (e.g., orange) in response to pain (e.g., as a result of a leg injury). The people we have discussed in the preceding section are **strong synesthetes**.

Even people who are not strong synesthetes may still show similar **cross-modal effects**. L.E. Marks (1982) observed that most people will judge *sneezes* to be brighter than *coughs*, and *sunlight* to be louder than *moonlight*. These and similar phenomena demonstrate that visual and auditory sensations share certain qualities for most people. For example, brightness and loudness seem to go together. Most of us are **weak synesthetes** in that we can appreciate these cross-modal associations without having strong synesthetic experiences. Martino and Marks (2001) suggested that these synesthetic associations "develop over childhood from experience with percepts and language" (p. 64).

Synesthesia can influence the way we label our experiences. McManus (1983) showed that some colour words are used more frequently than other colour words in diverse contexts: English and Chinese poetry, modern English novels, and popular literature. The colour words used most frequently are those that emerged earliest in the language (such as *black*). A word such as *black* has great synesthetic power; it can be used to describe a wide variety of experiences, while labels such as *pink* have emerged later in the history of the language and have a more restricted range of synesthetic meanings.

The fact that one sense can represent information from another sense facilitates the use of figurative language such as metaphor. Consider this line from Keats's "Isabella": "Taste the music of that pale vision." By uniting three senses (taste, audition, and vision), the line becomes especially memorable (Pollio, Barlow, Fine, & Pollio, 1977, p. 60; Ullmann, 1957). We will discuss some additional properties of colour words in Chapter 9 on language.

EIDETIC IMAGERY

An **icon** is a snapshot of the information contained in a visual stimulus. This information persists briefly even after the stimulus itself is no longer present. The icon's occurrence seems to depend on the eye's being stationary, a situation that seldom happens naturally (Haber, 1983). However, it is useful to compare the icon with a related phenomenon known as **eidetic imagery**. Like iconic images, eidetic images persist even after the stimulus, such as a picture, is removed. Unlike the icon, which decays rapidly, eidetic images may persist for a minute or more. Eidetic imagery is similar to synesthesia in that both are examples of **cognitive dedifferentiation** (Glicksohn, Steinbach, & Elimalac-Malmilyan, 1999), in which processes that typically function independently are fused instead. "For example, synesthesia entails the dedifferentiation of sense modalities, while eidetic imagery entails the dedifferentiation of imagery and perception" (Cytowic, 2002, p. 109). An eidetic image is a fusion of imagery and perception, such that the image is experienced as a percept.

Strong synesthetes
People who are susceptible to an inducer in one sensory modality (e.g., a sound) producing a concurrent image in another sensory modality (e.g., a colour).

Cross-modal effects
The ability to appreciate that the sensations of one modality can be similar to those in another modality.

Weak synesthetes
People who can appreciate cross-modal associations without having strong synesthetic experiences.

Icon
The initial, brief representation of the information contained in a visual stimulus.

Eidetic imagery
Images projected onto the external world that persist for a minute or more even after the stimulus (e.g., a picture) is removed.

Cognitive dedifferentiation
Fusion of perceptual processes that typically function independently.

Here are some of the features of eidetic images as identified by Haber (1979).

- Experiencing an eidetic image is not the same as having a vivid mental image: the image is perceived as being located "out there" rather than inside the person's head.
- The image can be scanned and its parts described.
- Descriptions of an eidetic image are quicker and more assured than reports from memory.
- Eidetic imagery is much more common in children than in adults.

Here is an excerpt from an 11-year-old's description of her eidetic image of a picture she had been shown for 30 seconds (Haber, 1979). The picture depicted a feast and contained many people, objects, and actions; it was no longer in front of her:

Experimenter: Tell me what you "see."

Participant: Up above it looks like stairs coming down and then there's a bench and a boy, then a girl and a couple of boys sitting on it, and then there's a very long table it looks like more plates without anything on them than food. There's a lady serving behind the table and then by the doorway it looks like children just gushing in and there's a clock by that—up in the left hand corner there's a china cabinet and a big hefty woman is putting dishes in there. (p. 587)

This excerpt represents only about one-quarter of the description the child provided. Despite the quantity of detail, however, it appears that descriptions of eidetic images are generally no more accurate than are ordinary memories collected from non-eidetic viewers of the same scene. Thus eidetic images are not *photographic* images, since they are not literal copies of the scene.

Jaynes (1979) made the intriguing suggestion that paleolithic cave paintings, such as those in France and Spain, are "tracings of eidetic images" (p. 606). That is, Cro-Magnon artists may have experienced eidetic images of significant objects, such as animals, and then drawn these images on cave walls. Among the factors that led Jaynes to this hypothesis was the fact that each image appeared to have been painted all at once (there is no evidence of repeated attempts at representation). Jaynes believes that describing an eidetic image may cause it to fade, and that Cro-Magnon eidetic images may have lasted longer than the images experienced in contemporary lab experiments partly because they were images of objects and events of great significance to the viewer and partly because they did not have to be put into words.

An excellent test for people who claim to have a photographic memory for pages in a text is to ask them to recall a page from the last word to the first. If they are actually "looking" at an image of the page, then they should be able to read it backwards as well as forwards. Most people are unable to do this; recall is much better in the forward direction (Neisser, 1967). However, Strohmeyer (1970/1982) reported the case of Elizabeth, an accomplished artist who claimed that she could write out a poem in a foreign language that she did not understand, and had seen only once, years before, from the last line to the first. Elizabeth's method was similar to the one used to create old-fashioned stereograms. In one test she was shown two dot patterns—one for each eye—that combined to form a three-dimensional image. Elizabeth would look at one pattern with one eye and form an eidetic image of it. Then she would look at the second pattern with the other eye and project an eidetic image of the first pattern onto the second. The result was an in-depth image. If you have an old stereoscope around the house, you could try using it this way; however, this kind of eidetic imagery ability is quite rare. In fact, there has not been another documented case resembling Elizabeth's, so although the results of Strohmeyer's experiment are suggestive, we should be cautious not to base any general conclusions on his findings.

VIVIDNESS OF VISUAL IMAGERY

Vividness of visual imagery
The degree to which images are clear and lively, resembling actual percepts.

Eidetic imagery seems to be an extraordinary form of imagery (Neisser, 1979), but it may only be an extreme form of an ability that is present in everyone (Paivio, 1986, p. 119). People vary in their experience of ordinary visual memory images (Harshman & Paivio, 1987). For example, **vividness of visual imagery** varies widely. This can be measured using the Vividness of Visual Imagery Questionnaire or VVIQ (D.F. Marks, 1972, 1999). Vividness is defined in terms of "clarity and liveliness" as well as similarity to an actual percept (D.F. Marks, 1999, p. 570). A clear and lively image is one in which colour is bright, form is well-defined, and so on. The current version of the VVIQ (D.F. Marks, 1999, p. 583) asks participants to imagine a series of people (e.g., relatives or friends) and scenes. Participants then rate the vividness of parts of the resulting image (e.g., the colours of a friend's clothes) on a scale ranging from "perfectly clear and as vivid as normal vision" to "No image at all." On the basis of these ratings, participants receive a VVIQ score.

The VVIQ has been used in a large number of studies, of which McKelvie (1995) reviewed more than 250. One of the obvious questions is whether people who score high on the VVIQ are better able to learn and remember than low scorers. The answer is that vividness of visual imagery does not appear to be a good predictor of superior performance on memory tasks. Baddeley and Andrade (2000) noted that the relation between vivid imagery and memory is complex. Participants examined pictures taken from a book of British and European birds after having judged their prior knowledge of birds as either "poor," "moderate," or "good." Participants were also given the name of each bird as it was presented. Then they were given the names again in the same order. Participants were asked to form an image of each bird as they heard its name and to rate the vividness of their image on a scale ranging from 0 (no image at all) to 10 (image as clear and vivid as normal vision). Those who rated their prior knowledge of birds as either "moderate" or "good" had higher vividness ratings than those who rated their prior knowledge as "poor." Baddeley and Andrade speculate that vividness of visual imagery is proportional to familiarity with the object envisioned. However, vividness is not an index of the accuracy of memory, only of its richness. It's possible to have very vivid imagery associated with events that are untrue (Gonsalves, Reber, Gitelman, Parrish, & Paller, 2004).

Another important issue is the relation between the vividness of imagery and perception. Can vivid imagery influence perception of external stimuli? This issue has been addressed in an interesting study reported by Cui, Jeter, Yang, Montague, and Eagleman (2007). On each trial of their study, participants were shown a sequence of displays depicted in Panel A of Figure 7.7. The critical display in the sequence contained a colour word (e.g., *orange*) presented in black against a coloured background that was either the same as (congruent with) or different from (incongruent with) the colour expressed by the colour word. The display was presented very briefly and followed by a

(a)

(b)

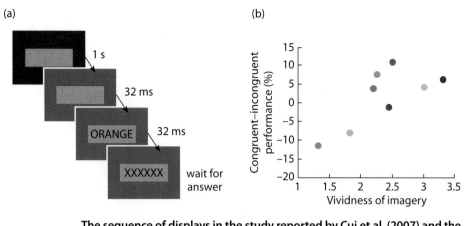

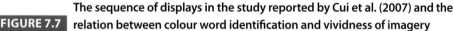

FIGURE 7.7 The sequence of displays in the study reported by Cui et al. (2007) and the relation between colour word identification and vividness of imagery

From: Cui, X., Cameron, B.J., Yang, D., Montague, P.R., & Eagleman, D. M. (2007). Vividness of mental imagery: Individual variability can be measured objectively. *Vision Research*, 47, 474-478.

pattern mask (a sequence of Xs) that made the colour word difficult to see. Participants were required to name the word on the display as accurately as possible. In addition, Cui et al. (2007) measured vividness of imagery using a version of the VVIQ in which low scores represent a high degree of vividness of imagery. Critically, they measured the difference in word identification accuracy between congruent and incongruent trials and related this to the participant's vividness of imagery as measured by the VVIQ. The results are shown in Panel B of Figure 7.7. Clearly, the difference in performance on congruent and incongruent trials correlated quite strongly with vividness of imagery scores. Interestingly, participants with a high degree of vividness of imagery (i.e., low VVIQ scores) were actually more accurate on incongruent trials than congruent ones. Cui et al. (2007, p. 477) suggest that "for more visual subjects, incongruent colors make it easier to see a color word. These findings imply an increased interaction between brain areas that code for color perception and color naming in highly visual individuals."

Mental Rotation

Thus far we have considered mental images only as static mental pictures. But of course we can also imagine objects in motion.

A canonical demonstration of the dynamic nature of mental images was conducted by Shepard and Metzler (1971). In their experiment, participants were presented with 1600 pairs of line drawings like those in Figure 7.8. Half the pairs showed the same object (as in Figures 7.8a and 7.8b) and half showed different objects (as in Figure 7.8c). The pairs of drawings of the same object varied in the angular rotation that would be required in order to bring the two images into alignment. The angular rotation required varied from 0° to 180° through 20° intervals. Some of the correct pairs required an angular rotation in the picture plane (as in Figure 7.8a), whereas others required an angular rotation in depth (Figure 7.8b).

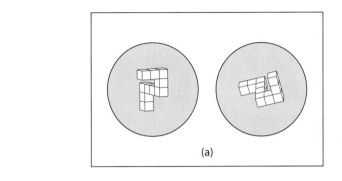

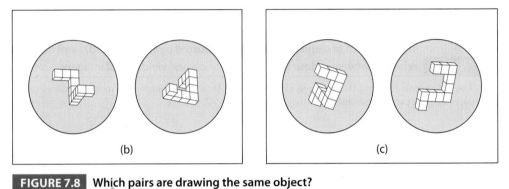

FIGURE 7.8   Which pairs are drawing the same object?

From: Shepard, R.N., & Metzler, J. (1971). Mental rotation of three-dimensional objects. *Science, 171*, 701–703. Copyright 1971 by the American Association for the Advancement of Science. Reprinted by permission.

For each pair, the participants had to decide whether the drawings depicted the same object or a different one and indicate their decision by pulling a lever with either the right hand or the left. Shepard and Metzler (1971) also measured the length of time it took to make each decision.

The most interesting findings concerned the relationship between angular rotation and reaction time for correct responses to drawings of the same object. This relationship is shown in Figure 7.9. For both picture-plane and depth pairs, the relationship between the two variables is almost perfect. The greater the angular rotation required, the longer it takes the participant to make a decision. Shepard and Metzler (1971) concluded that participants determined whether or not the drawings depicted the same object by means of a process called **mental rotation**. Perhaps participants were imagining the rotation of one of the pairs to determine if it matched the other member of the pair. The greater the angular rotation required, the longer it would take to imagine the rotation of one of the pairs until it came into alignment with the other. On the basis of Shepard and Metzler's (1971) data, it appears that the speed of mental rotation in this task was 60° per second.

There have been several subsequent demonstrations of the accuracy with which people are able to imagine the rotation of objects (Shepard, 1978; Shepard & Cooper, 1982). Shepard (e.g., 1984) has noted that the process of imagining an object seems quite similar to the process of perceiving an object. "What we imagine, as much as what we perceive, are external objects; although in imagining, these objects may be absent or even nonexistent" (Shepard, 1984, p. 420). As we shall see, considerable research has examined the apparent similarity between the processes of imagining and perceiving. Box 7.2 looks at some recent research related to video games and the perception of imagery.

Mental rotation
Imagining an object in motion and viewing it from different perspectives.

IS MENTAL ROTATION A RIGHT-HEMISPHERE PROCESS?

When we considered Paivio's theory, we concluded that imagery was not confined to the right hemisphere. However, mental rotation is a more dynamic process than static imagining of the sort elicited by concrete words. Mental rotation is a non-linguistic process, and for that reason may tend to be localized in the right hemisphere. However, the existing evidence is not decisive (Corballis, 1997). In an event-related potentials (ERP) study, Milivojevic, Johnson, Hamm, and Corballis (2003) further investigated the lateralization of mental rotation. They had participants perform two different tasks. One was a simple letter rotation task, in which letters were presented in normal or mirror-reversed orientation at varying degrees of tilt. For example, participants might see the letter *R* like this:

The participants' task was to say whether the letter was normal or mirror-reversed. What would you conclude about the letter above? How did you do it? The second task involved more complex folding tasks. For example:

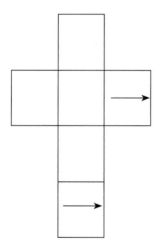

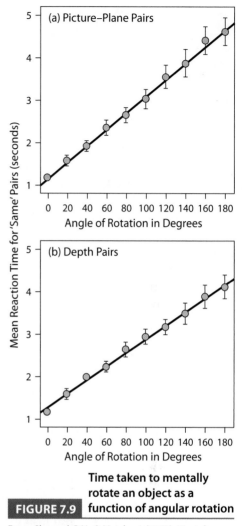

Time taken to mentally rotate an object as a

FIGURE 7.9 | **function of angular rotation**

From: Shepard, R.N., & Metzler, J. (1971). Mental rotation of three-dimensional objects. *Science, 171,* 701–703. Copyright 1971 by the American Association for the Advancement of Science. Reprinted by permission.

Participants had to decide whether or not the arrowheads would be aligned if the squares were folded to make a box. Again, what's your conclusion? How did you come to it? The first task required one mental transformation, while the second required a series of transformations. The second task took longer than the first, reflecting its greater difficulty. The ERP analysis showed that the mental rotation task tended to be carried out in the right hemisphere. However, the mental folding task was not lateralized, and both hemispheres were equally involved. Milivojevic et al. (2003, p. 1359) concluded that "the right hemisphere may be preferentially engaged when the task is simple" but "the left hemisphere is also engaged as the task becomes more complex."

COGNITION IN ACTION
BOX 7.2
Video Games and Imagery

If you are an avid video game player, you may have wondered whether all the hours you've spent playing amount to anything. Researchers at the University of Toronto (Feng, Spence and Pratt, 2007) reported a fascinating study exploring how action video games influence imagery abilities, and whether they affect males and females differently. The study tested two groups of participants. One group was asked to play a well-known violent game named "Medal of Honor." The second group, which served as the control group in this case, played a non-violent game named "Balance." The violent game was chosen because it demanded much more attention than the non-violent game. Importantly, the researchers

tested participants' mental rotation abilities (see Shepard and Metzler, 1971) both before and after 10 hours of playing the video games. They also looked at the performance of males and females separately. Initially, males performed better than females on the mental rotation task, but after 10 hours of play, the performance of all those playing the violent game improved, and the improvements were greater for females than males. The performance of those who had played the non-violent game did not show any enhancement. Thus playing action video games seems to improve spatial imagery and reduce pre-existing gender differences in this ability (for related results see De Lisi & Wolford, 2002).

SCANNING MENTAL IMAGES

In a series of experiments Kosslyn and his colleagues explored the relation between imagery and perception (e.g., Kosslyn, 1980, 1983; Denis & Kosslyn, 1999). In one such study (Kosslyn, Ball, & Reiser, 1978) participants were asked to memorize a map of an island that contained seven different locations (a tree, a beach, a hut, and so on; Figure 7.10). Some of the distances between the various locations were longer than others: for example, the distance from the hut to the beach was longer than the distance from the hut to the tree. The time it would take you to scan from one location to another on the real map would depend on the real distance: thus it would take longer to scan from the hut to the beach than from the hut to the tree.

What about the participant's memory image of the map? Does it take longer to scan between parts of the memory image that are far apart than between the parts that are close together? To answer this question, Kosslyn and his colleagues asked participants to imagine one of the locations on their memory image of the map. Then they were to imagine "a little black speck zipping in the shortest straight line" (Kosslyn et al., 1978, p. 52) from that location to another location. Sometimes they were asked to scan to locations that were not on the map. For example, they might imagine the hut and then be asked to scan from the hut to the beach (which is on the map) or from the hut to a location that is not on the map. If they could find the location, they pressed one button, and if they could not find it they pressed another button. The results showed that, for places actually on the map, the farther apart the two objects were, the longer it took to scan between them (Figure 7.11). This was interpreted by Kosslyn and his co-workers to mean that **objective distances** are preserved in our mental images of perceived scenes.

Rinck and Denis (2004) have shown that objective distance is not the only feature that determines how long it takes to scan from one part of a mental image to another. Another important variable is **categorical distance**: "the number of units that

Objective distance
The true distance between objects in the real world, which are preserved in our mental images.

Categorical distance
The number of units traversed during mental scanning: for instance, landmarks on an island map, rooms in a building, or counties in a state.

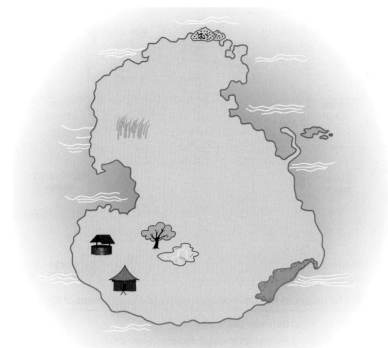

FIGURE 7.10   The map of the island used in a mental image scanning experiment

Participants mentally travelled over the locations on the island.

From: Kosslyn, S.M., Ball, T.M., & Reiser, B.J. (1978). Visual images preserve metric spatial information: Evidence from studies of image scanning. *Journal of Experimental Psychology: Human Perception and Performance, 4*, 47–60.

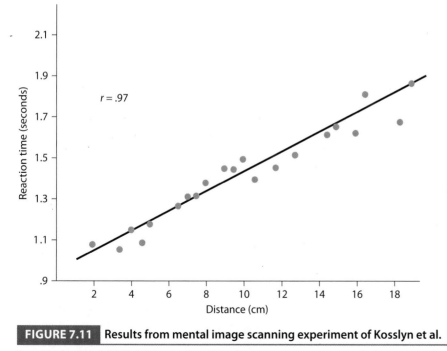

FIGURE 7.11   Results from mental image scanning experiment of Kosslyn et al.

From: Kosslyn, S.M., Ball, T.M., & Reiser, B.J. (1978). Visual images preserve metric spatial information: Evidence from studies of image scanning. *Journal of Experimental Psychology: Human Perception and Performance, 4*, 47–60.

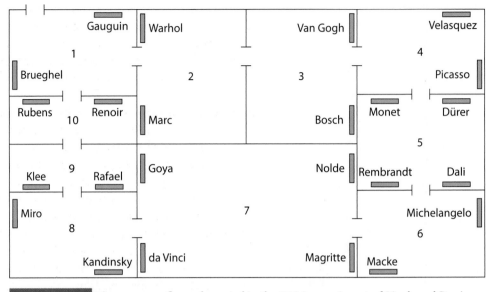

FIGURE 7.12   **The museum floor plan used in the 2004 experiment of Rinck and Denis**

Participants mentally travelled between paintings.

From: Rinck, M., & Denis, M. (2004). The metrics of spatial distance traversed during mental imagery. *Journal of Experimental Psychology: Learning, Memory, and Cognition, 30*, 1211–1218.

are traversed during mental scanning, for instance, landmarks on an island map, rooms in a building, or counties in a state" (Rinck & Denis, 2004, p. 1212). To investigate the relative influences of objective and categorical distances, participants were given a map of a museum floor to memorize. The floor was divided into rooms of different sizes, and each room contained paintings by various well-known artists, such as Van Gogh and Leonardo da Vinci (Figure 7.12). (At this point, in order to visualize the task, imagine the floor plan of your own dwelling, and imagine paintings by different artists in each room. Now imagine walking across a room from one painting to another. This would be an objective distance. Now imagine walking from a painting in one room to a painting in another room. This would involve not only an objective distance but also a categorical distance. This was the sort of task given to participants in this experiment.) Both the objective distance travelled and the categorical distance affected the amount of time it took to travel mentally between one painting and another. This result suggests that images may be structured hierarchically, with objective distances nested within categorical differences. We will return to this possibility in our discussion of cognitive maps, next.

IMAGES AS ANTICIPATIONS

Podgorny and Shepard (1978) did an experiment using grids like those in Figure 7.13. The participants' task was to imagine a letter superimposed on a grid, such as the letter F in Figure 7.13a. To try it yourself, imagine the F superimposed on the grid in Figure 7.13b. If you were a participant in this experiment, then a dot probe would appear in one of the squares in the grid, as in Figure 7.13c. Your task would be to decide, as quickly as possible, whether or not the dot was in a square covered by your imaginary F.

It turns out that this is a task that people can do both rapidly and accurately. In fact, performance on this particular task with imaginary letters is strikingly similar to performance when letters are actually present in the grid.

Farah (1989) used a similar task to demonstrate the role of **images as anticipations**. Participants imagined a letter superimposed on a grid, as in the Podgorny and Shepard experiment. However, the probe stimulus, an asterisk (*), was presented only for a very brief interval, and the participants had to detect its occurrence. The asterisk could fall either in a square covered by a participant's image, or in a square not covered by the participant's image. Probes were detected more often in the former case.

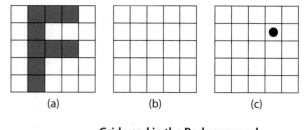

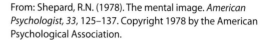

(a)   (b)   (c)

FIGURE 7.13 **Grid used in the Podgorny and Shepard experiment**

From: Shepard, R.N. (1978). The mental image. *American Psychologist, 33,* 125–137. Copyright 1978 by the American Psychological Association.

Farah also reported evidence suggesting that imagery lowers the participant's criterion for detecting a stimulus. It was not so much that participants were more sensitive to stimuli falling within the imaged region as it was that they were better prepared to pick up stimuli falling within the area of a projected image. Farah characterized this process in terms used by Ryle (1949) and Neisser (1976). Neisser defined an image as a readiness to perceive something (1976, p. 130; cited by Farah, 1989).

To understand what "a readiness to perceive something" means, remember our discussion of perceptual organization in Chapter 3. At any point in time, we anticipate picking up certain kinds of information and not others. When we anticipate something, the perceptual cycle is ready to pick up the information, but the information is not there yet. These anticipations are mental images (Neisser, 1978a). For example, if I imagine what is inside my desk drawer, I am anticipating what I would see if I opened the drawer. We pick up information that we anticipate more readily than information that we don't anticipate. In Farah's experiment, when participants projected an image onto the grid, they were anticipating seeing something in the squares covered by the image. That is, they were prepared to pick up a target that occurred in those squares.

Farah did another experiment that elaborated on the anticipatory nature of images. Participants were shown a pattern of shaded squares that could be seen as either an H or a T, as in Figure 7.14. They were told to attend to one letter or the other. Try this yourself. You can see the configuration in Figure 7.14 as an H if you attend only to those squares in the grid that make up an H; or you can see it as a T if you attend only to those squares that make up a T. Attending to one pattern or the other facilitates the pick-up of probes in that area, just as projecting an image does. That the results are the same for projecting and attending suggests that imagery is an active process that prepares you for perceiving information, and not just a passive representation of information.

Brockmole, Wang, and Irwin (2002) conducted a detailed investigation of the conditions under which images and percepts may be combined. They presented participants with a 4 x 4 grid in which several squares were filled with a dot. That grid disappeared and was replaced by another grid with dots in several other squares. One square only was not filled with a dot on either occasion, and the participant's task was to identify that square. Performance on this task was best when the interval between the first and second grid was about 1300 milliseconds. It's likely that participants required about that long to form an image of the first grid. The percept of the second grid could then be integrated with the image of the first grid to yield a representation that combined

Image as anticipation hypothesis
The hypothesis that an image is a readiness to perceive something.

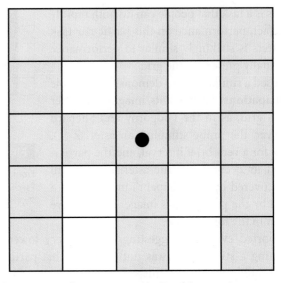

FIGURE 7.14   The pattern of squares used in Farah's experiment

From: Farah, M. (1989). Mechanisms of imagery-perception interaction. *Journal of Experimental Psychology: Human Perception and Performance, 15*, 203–211. Copyright 1989 by the American Psychological Association.

both grids and allowed the participant to identify the empty square. This integration of images and percepts shows that perception and imagery must share many of the same mechanisms (Kosslyn, Ganis, & Thompson, 2001). Box 7.3 explores how we construct real pictures out of what we see and imagine.

IMAGES AND AMBIGUOUS FIGURES

Farah's H or T figure is an example of an ambiguous figure. Some very interesting properties of images can be explored further through the use of drawings like these, other examples of which are presented in Figure 7.15. They are ambiguous figures in that they may be seen as representing either one thing or another (Shepard, 1978, p. 129). The drawing on the left can be seen as either a duck or a rabbit, and the drawing on the right can be seen as either a chef or a dog. An interesting question is whether ambiguous figures can be imagined as ambiguous. If imagining something is a bit like perceiving it, then it might be possible to shift from seeing one thing in an imaginary ambiguous figure to seeing something else. That is, perhaps I could imagine Figure 7.15a as a duck, and then imagine it as a rabbit, and then return to imagining it as a duck, and so on.

Chambers and Reisberg (1985) investigated this possibility. Participants were first shown some examples of ambiguous figures, and the experimenter made sure that each participant was able to see them reverse from one view to another. Then participants were shown a slide of the duck/rabbit in Figure 7.15a and asked to form a "mental picture of the slide so that they would be able to draw it later" (Chambers & Reisberg, 1985, p. 320). They were then shown the chef/dog picture in Figure 7.15b and told that they could see two different things by looking at different parts of the figure. (Try this yourself. If you look at the upper right you tend to see a dog, but if you look at the lower left you tend to see a chef.) Participants were asked to try to reverse their mental image

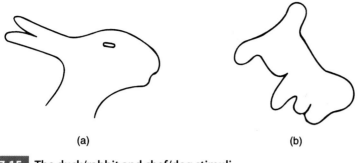

FIGURE 7.15 The duck/rabbit and chef/dog stimuli

From: Chambers, D., & Reisberg, D. (1985). Can mental images be ambiguous? *Journal of Experimental Psychology: Human Perception and Performance, 11*, 317–328. Copyright 1985 by the American Psychological Association.

CONSIDER THIS
BOX 7.3

Mental Images and Real Pictures

As we noted at the beginning of this chapter, when we imagine a scene, the experience is a bit like looking at a picture. That's partly why it is so tempting to define images as mental pictures. Pinker and Finke (1980) compared the properties of images with the properties of actual pictures. Although images seem to be accurate representations of a scene as it appears from a particular viewpoint, the pictures people actually make of scenes do not always have this property. Look at the drawing at the left in Figure 7.16. There is no way that such a scene could actually be seen. The picture appears to us to be a distorted representation of an actual scene, because there is more in the picture than you could possibly see from one vantage point. The drawing at the right in Figure 7.16 more accurately represents what would actually be seen from a single vantage point. Nevertheless, many people make drawings that are more like the drawing on the left than the one on the right in Figure 7.16. How can we explain the apparent discrepancy between the accurate images we experience and the inaccurate drawings we so often produce?

There are at least three possible explanations for this discrepancy, according to Pinker and Finke. One is that even if you can accurately imagine how something will look, you may not be able to draw your image. It's not

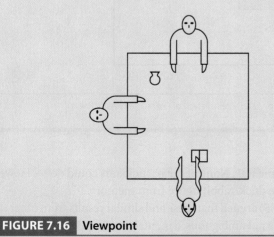

FIGURE 7.16 Viewpoint

From: Arnheim, R. (1974). *Art and visual perception: A psychology of the creative eye.* Berkeley: University of California Press, Figures 86 and 87. Copyright 1974 by the Regents of the University of California. Reprinted by permission.

continued

always easy to translate the image in your mind into a sequence of arm movements that will reproduce that image on the page. Another possibility is that you don't actually try to draw your image, but instead try to draw the object as you know it really is. This is a critical drawing error, as art historians have frequently observed (e.g., Edgerton, 1975). When you draw something the way you think it should be, the result will be a distorted representation that does not look at all like the object you actually see. This point is illustrated in Figure 7.17. What the artist represents on the picture plane is a projection of the surface of an object. The result is that objects depicted in a picture appear to lie behind the picture plane. The picture plane is like a window through which you are looking at objects in the distance. The eye can only be at one place when the picture is constructed. That position is called

the station point (Sedgwick, 1980, p. 40). The station point gives the spectator a point of view. Notice that a circle will appear as an ellipse on the picture plane when viewed from a particular station point. Changing the station point changes what will be represented in the picture, just as moving in relation to a window changes what you see through it. "As we approach a window we see more of the scene; as we move to the left, a portion of the scene on the left side becomes hidden by the window frame while more is revealed on the right, etc." (Sedgwick, 1980, p. 41). An artist using classical rules of perspective eliminates the third source of error mentioned by Pinker and Finke, which is attempting to draw parts of the scene from different vantage points, so that there is no consistent point of view.

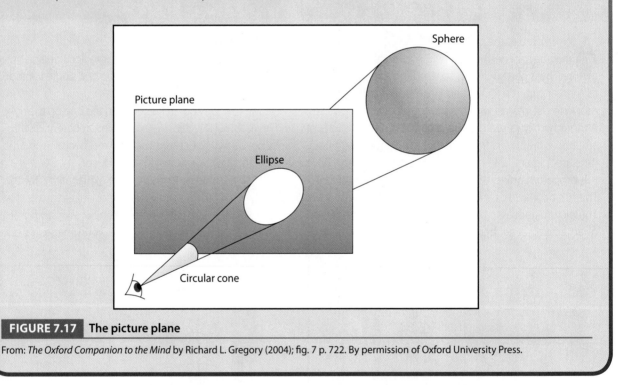

FIGURE 7.17   **The picture plane**

From: *The Oxford Companion to the Mind* by Richard L. Gregory (2004); fig. 7 p. 722. By permission of Oxford University Press.

of the duck/rabbit slide in the same way. None of the participants could do so. However, all of them were able to draw the duck/rabbit figure from memory.

Chambers and Reisberg (1985) argued that these and similar results from other studies suggest that mental images are not ambiguous: a mental image appears to be only one thing. If Chambers and Reisberg are right, then this would be one of the ways in which images differ from perceptions. However, Finke, Pinker, and Farah (1989) have questioned the generality of Chambers and Reisberg's results. They used a procedure whereby participants constructed images in stages. Here is an example of the process. First, participants would imagine the first figure (e.g., "Imagine a capital letter *H*"). Then they would be asked to imagine a capital letter *X* on top of the *H*. Follow these instructions yourself, and then inspect your image and see if you can detect any familiar forms in it. Participants often reported geometric shapes and letters such as *M* and *N*. This result is important because it means that more can be found in a mental image than whatever went into its construction (Shepard, 1978a). In the process of constructing an image, new properties may emerge. These are often referred to as **emergent properties** (e.g., Finke, 1996; Pinker & Finke, 1980).

Other researchers (e.g., Brandimonte & Gerbino, 1993; Hyman & Neisser, 1991; Peterson, Kihlstrom, Rose, & Glisky, 1992) have also found that images often can be reinterpreted. An insightful study by Mast and Kosslyn (2002; Lyddy, 2002) shows how mental rotation can lead to a new interpretation of an image. They constructed the configuration shown in Figure 7.18, which can be seen as a young woman when upright and an older woman when rotated 180 degrees. Participants were first shown the figure in one of the two orientations and memorized it so that they would be able to draw it from memory. Participants were not told that the figure was reversible. They then imagined the figure rotated to different angles. Several participants discovered the alternate figure when their image had been rotated 180 degrees. The conclusion was that "at least some people can detect a previously unrecognized interpretation" of a mental image (Mast & Kosslyn, 2002, p. 69).

It has often been argued that imagery is an **analog form of representation** (e.g., Shepard, 1978, p. 135). An analog embodies the essential relationships of the thing it represents. Spence (1973) gave the following example of an analog device. A carpenter who is building a picket fence wants to make sure that the spaces between the pickets are equal. The best way to do this is to cut a stick as long as the desired space. Then put up the first picket and use the stick to place the next one. The stick is an analog of the distance. Similarly, mental images may be analogs of situations in the external world, useful not only for capturing essential relationships between things in the external world, but also for discovering new relationships.

FIGURE 7.18   **A reversible figure**

From: Mast, F.W., & Kosslyn, S.M. (2002). Visual mental images can be ambiguous: Insights from individual differences in spatial transformation abilities. *Cognition, 86*, 57–70. Copyright 2002. Reprinted by permission of Elsevier.

Emergent properties
New properties that emerge when a mental image is constructed.

Analog form of representation hypothesis
The hypothesis that a mental image embodies the essential relationships of the thing it represents.

Egocentric Perspective Transformations

As Franklin and Tversky (1991) observed, reading a story produces a lot of mental imagery. To make their point, they quote the following passage from Ernest Hemingway's 1927 story "The Snows of Kilimanjaro":

> Out of the window of the hospital you could see a field with tumble weed coming out of the snow, and a bare clay butte. . . . From the other window, if the bed was

turned, you could see the town, with a little smoke above it, and the Dawson mountains looking like real mountains with the winter snow on them.

Did you experience any mental imagery while reading that passage? Did you imagine yourself located in the narrative? Could you locate the objects described relative to yourself?

Consider the relation of this kind of mental imagery to the Shepard and Metzler mental rotation task we considered earlier in this chapter. In that task, the participant saw something and then performed imaginary operations on it. When we read stories, we typically construct an imaginary representation of the environment the text describes. In such a representation, some things are in front of you, some behind, some above, some below, some to the right, some to the left. Does it matter where things are located? For example, could you imagine something behind you as quickly as something ahead of you? Such tasks require **egocentric perspective transformations**, in which your point of view changes. Rather than imaging an object rotated in space, as in the Shepard and Metzler task, you must imagine yourself moving while the objects in the environment remain still (Zacks, Mires, Tversky, & Hazeltine, 2000).

In one of their experiments, Franklin and Tversky (1991) had participants read different narratives. Here is a fragment of one of the stories:

> You are . . . at the opera. . . . you are standing next to the railing of a . . . balcony, overlooking the first floor. Directly behind you, at your eye level is . . . a lamp . . . mounted on a nearby wall beyond the balcony, you see a large bronze plaque . . . sitting on a shelf directly to your right is a beautiful bouquet of flowers. . . . (p. 65)

The story goes on quite a bit further, but you get the idea. If you had been a participant in this experiment, you would then have answered questions about the locations of the objects described. For example, was the lamp ahead of you, behind you, above you, below you, to your right, or to your left? Then you would have been asked to imagine yourself turned to face a different direction (e.g., 90 degrees to your left), and to answer the same questions.

All participants reported that they relied on mental imagery to recall the scene. Moreover, some questions are easier to answer than others. You can locate something quickly if it is above or below you. It takes longer to locate something behind you, perhaps because you have to imagine yourself turning around. Locating something that is to the right or left of you is also a relatively slow process. These results may be due to the fact that normally we imagine ourselves as being upright in a **spatial framework** that has one vertical (*above–below*) and two horizontal dimensions (*ahead–behind* and *left–right*) (Tversky, 2003). With respect to our bodies, *above–below* and *ahead–behind* are asymmetrical: our head is different from our feet, and our front is different from our back. However, our bodies are bilaterally symmetric: the left half of our body is the mirror image of the right half. Thus the two asymmetric dimensions are easily distinguished, but the symmetric dimension (*right–left*) is not. This symmetry may explain why we sometimes have so much difficulty remembering our right from our left (Bryant, Tversky, & Franklin, 1992; Franklin & Tversky, 1990, p. 74).

Egocentric perspective transformations
You imagine yourself moving, while the objects in the environment remain still.

Spatial framework
An imaginary space with one vertical (*above–below*) and two horizontal dimensions (*ahead–behind* and *left–right*).

Controversy Concerning the Nature of Mental Imagery

An enormous amount of research has been done on mental imagery, and some have felt that this work has overestimated the importance of the subject. Beginning with Pylyshyn (1973) there have been persistent criticisms of imagery research (e.g., Anderson, 1978). At the centre of this long-standing controversy is the issue of how knowledge is represented. In the last chapter we reviewed models of memory, such as J.R. Anderson's (1983), that hold knowledge about the world to be stored in memory in the form of propositions. If we accept this argument regarding **propositional knowledge** just to see where it leads, then what role do images have in cognition?

One possibility is that images are *epiphenomenal*. You should recall from our discussion of the mind–brain issue in Chapter 2 that an epiphenomenon is a by-product, or symptom, of something else. An example is the smoke that comes from a steam locomotive. The smoke is a by-product of the locomotive's operation, and serves no function itself. Similarly, imagery may serve no function. Images might be merely decorative, like pictures on the wall of your room, and not essential aspects of the mind's functioning.

Pylyshyn (2002, 2003a, 2003b) argued that it is a mistake to believe that images are "two-dimensional moving pictures" on "the surface of your visual cortex" (Pylyshyn, 2003a, p. 114), which we scan in order to extract information. Rather, you imagine something by "considering what it would look like if you saw it" (p. 114). Being able to imagine how objects look from other viewpoints requires inference and is susceptible to error. A similar argument was made by Rock, Wheeler, and Tudor (1989), who presented evidence that mental rotation is accurate only in highly practised tasks. When the task requires the rotation of unfamiliar objects, such as twisted wire shapes, then inaccuracy is the norm. Perhaps people find it harder to make the correct inferences concerning what an unfamiliar object will look like when it is rotated. Deciding how things will look from different perspectives requires thinking, and can be difficult in unfamiliar situations.

Naturally enough, those who are particularly intrigued by imagery find such criticisms unwarranted. They point out that imagery is interesting in its own right, regardless of its function (e.g., Kosslyn, 1980, p. 21; Kosslyn, Ganis, & Thompson, 2003; Kosslyn, Thomas, & Ganis, 2002, p. 201). Indeed, there is evidence that scores on the Vividness of Visual Imagery Scale reflect the degree to which people consider vividness of visual imagery to be worth investigating (Reisberg, Pearson, & Kosslyn, 2003). The more vivid your own imagery, the more interested in imagery you're likely to be. The debate over the nature and function of imagery is sure to continue.

Propositional knowledge hypothesis
The hypothesis that knowledge about the world is stored in memory in the form of propositions.

Cognitive Maps and Mental Models

BASIC PROPERTIES OF COGNITIVE MAPS

It was Tolman (1948) who put **cognitive maps** on the map, so to speak. Tolman believed that information from the environment was "worked over and elaborated . . . into a tentative, cognitive-like map of the environment. And it is this tentative map,

Cognitive map
Information from the environment that is "worked over and elaborated . . . into a tentative, cognitive-like map . . . indicating routes and paths and environmental relationships" (Tolman, 1948, p. 193).

indicating routes and paths and environmental relationships" (p. 193), that determines our behaviour. Tolman thought that broad and comprehensive cognitive maps were more useful than narrow maps. Narrow, overspecialized cognitive maps cannot contain information about more than a few routes through the environment. They may facilitate adaptation to specific environments, but they don't transfer well to new circumstances. For Tolman, a cognitive map was more useful if it gave its user a big picture of the environment and could be employed in a variety of situations.

The partial nature of our cognitive maps means that we are capable of making several interesting errors. For example, which of the following statements are true?

- Madrid (Spain) is farther north than Washington (District of Columbia).
- Seattle (US) is farther north than Montreal (Canada).
- The Pacific entrance of the Panama Canal is east of the Atlantic entrance.

In fact, *all* these statements are true (Stevens & Coupe, 1978, p. 423). The reason they may seem to be false can be seen by comparing the statements above with the following:

- Spain is farther north than the District of Columbia.
- The US is farther north than Canada.
- The Pacific Ocean is east of the Atlantic Ocean.

All the preceding statements are untrue. Large geographic units (such as countries, states, counties, etc.) can, in general, have one relationship to one another, while some of their members (e.g., cities) can bear the opposite relationship to one another. Because our cognitive maps are simplified, we can tend to assume that *all* members of a large geographic unit have the same relationship to *all* members of other large geographic units. Some people will totally reject the statement about the Atlantic and Pacific entrances of the Panama Canal until they have verified it for themselves on a map. Our cognitive maps are partly convenient fictions, designed to represent reality in a way that we think is useful but that may not be very accurate.

To illustrate this last point, draw a cognitive map of your campus. Then get some classmates to do the same. Pay attention to the various *landmarks* (e.g., important buildings), *paths* (e.g., roads), and *boundaries* (e.g., streams) that people show in their maps (Lynch, 1960). You may be surprised at how different various people's maps are. What accounts for the differences? For example, does it make a difference if one person has been at your campus for three years and another has been there only a few months?

COGNITIVE MAPS AND THE HIPPOCAMPUS

Cognitive maps have been linked with hippocampal activity at least since the classic work of O'Keefe and Nadel (1978; Nadel & Hardt, 2004). Among the most direct sources of evidence for hippocampal involvement are studies relating the relative size of the hippocampus to the amount of knowledge required to successfully navigate in a complex environment. A particularly dramatic example of this relationship has been observed in London taxi drivers. To qualify for a licence, drivers are required to learn the routes that connect thousands of places in London—a task that takes two years on average. Every London taxi driver has a highly complex, detailed cognitive map of the city. Maguire et al. (2000) compared MRI brain scans of licensed London taxi drivers with those of non-taxi drivers. Not only was the posterior part of the hippocampus larger in taxi drivers than in the control group, but the increase varied with the number of years spent driving a taxi in London. This finding indicated that it was the experience of driving a taxi that had led to the enlargement of the hippocampus, not an unusually large hippocampus that enabled the individual to become a taxi driver. In order to store the immense cognitive map required for the job, the posterior part of the hippocampus of taxi drivers becomes enlarged.

EGOCENTRIC FRAMES OF REFERENCE

There are at least two ways in which we can find our way through the environment. One is to use a cognitive map of the environment just as we would use a real map. When we navigate using a real map we locate our position on the map, then figure out how to proceed from there. This appears to be what London taxi drivers do. A second approach is to use an **egocentric frame of reference** (McNamara, Rump, & Werner, 2003). This means taking the sort of egocentric perspective that was discussed above. You imagine yourself at the centre of the action and use information available from your current perspective to orient yourself.

Some aspects of egocentric frames of reference can be illustrated as follows. Draw the following situation, which is taken from Hutchins (1983, p. 209): "Go at dawn to a high place and point directly to the centre of the rising sun. That defines a line. Return to that same high place at noon and point again to the centre of the sun. That defines a second line." Your drawing probably will look something like Figure 7.19. Notice that this drawing defines the position of the sun relative to your position on the earth. The drawing suggests that you stay still while the sun moves overhead. We both know better, of course. Yet it's natural to represent the situation that way. It corresponds to the situation from our egocentric perspective and allows us to think about it easily.

Wang and Spelke (2000, 2002) suggest that people often use egocentric frames of reference when they navigate. This process does not require an enduring cognitive map that you consult as you travel. All it requires is a temporary representation that is continuously updated. One example is a process known as **path integration**, whereby our position in relation to an important location (e.g., home) is continuously updated as we move through the environment. Other animals and insects also appear to use egocentric forms of navigation. For example, "desert ants forage by traveling on new and apparently random routes and then return home on a direct path once food is found" (Wang & Spelke, 2002, p. 376). Similarly, in principle you can explore a novel environment (e.g., a city you are visiting as a tourist) while keeping track of where you are in relation to some important landmark (e.g., your hotel).

Egocentric frame of reference
Using information available from our current perspective to orient ourselves.

Path integration
The process whereby our position in relation to an important location is continuously updated as we move through the environment.

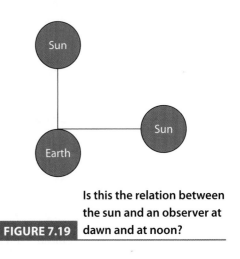

Is this the relation between the sun and an observer at dawn and at noon?

FIGURE 7.19

COGNITIVE MAPS AS MENTAL MODELS

Mental model theory
The theory that we construct a mental model of a given situation, on the basis of which we understand, reason, and draw conclusions about it.

A **mental model** is a representation of a situation that enables us to understand and reason about it (Gentner, 2002, p. 9683). We have mental models for a very wide range of situations, and we use them to describe, explain, and predict events (Rouse & Morris, 1986). For example, people often have mental models of the way a machine such as a vacuum cleaner works. DiSessa (1983) asked participants to "think of a vacuum cleaner whose nozzle you hold in your hand. If you put your hand over the nozzle, will the pitch of the sound you hear from the motor go up or down?" (p. 23). Ordinary people come up with different answers to this question. Some people think that the pitch will go down, and the speed of the motor will be reduced. This is because their mental model of the way a vacuum cleaner works suggests to them that placing a hand over the nozzle will interfere with the working of the motor and make it harder for the motor to run. Other people correctly say that the motor speed and the pitch will go up. The explanation they give is that, because the motor is being interfered with, it must put out more effort to overcome the resistance.

Notice that the vacuum cleaner models described above are quite anthropomorphic, attributing human characteristics to the machine (for example, the machine was represented as responding to interference by working harder). Mental models are often like this—"unscientific" and even "superstitious" (D.A. Norman, 1983, p. 8). However, they may still be useful for representing the world. One of their functions is to permit us to draw analogies between different domains (Gentner, 1983). Here is one person's mental model of how electricity works:

> Question: When you plug in a lamp and it lights up, how does it happen?

> Answer: . . . basically there is a pool of electricity that plug-in buys for you . . . the electricity goes into the cord for the appliance, for the lamp and flows up to—flows—I think of it as flowing because of the negative to positive images I have, and also because . . . a cord is a narrow contained entity like a river. (Gentner & Gentner, 1983, p. 99)

The virtue of mental models is that they give us a way of representing and drawing inferences about the behaviour of things in a wide range of contexts. Of course, our mental models do not always lead us to draw the correct inference about what will happen in a particular situation. The mental model in Figure 7.19, for example, is based on an erroneous assumption. Mental models can be a source of error as well as of insight. We will explore mental models further in Chapter 11, when we look at reasoning.

▌▌ Summary

In this chapter we have examined the subjective phenomenon of mental images and considered the role they play in cognitive processes such as perception, learning, and memory. Behind the rise of much current imagery research is the influential dual-coding theory of Alan Paivio. According to Paivio, imagery is a non-verbal system by which we represent events as mental images. It exists alongside and often in reference to a verbal system of representation.

We noted that mental images have the properties of *concreteness*, *distinctiveness*, and *vividness*. These properties enable imagery to organize incoming information into meaningful units and thereby aid learning and memory. Sometimes the common ability to form mental images takes extraordinary forms, as with individuals who experience eidetic imagery or synesthesia. A common form of synesthesia involves the experience of colour whenever achromatic letters or digits are presented. Unlike static pictures on a wall, though, mental images are dynamic. They can be *mentally rotated*, moved, or scanned, often from an egocentric spatial frame of reference. Furthermore, mental images differ from perceptions in that they are unambiguous, appearing to be only one thing. Nevertheless, that one thing may contain new emergent properties, resulting from the very process of constructing the mental image.

The functional importance of mental images is hotly debated in the imagery literature. There is some research to support the *anticipatory* use of mental images to ready us for perceiving certain kinds of information. Some research also supports the use of imagery in forming *cognitive maps* as a way of working out environmental relationships and aiding memory. Another contentious research question is whether or not imagery is a right-hemisphere process. To date, the evidence points to varied and complex levels of engagement in both right and left hemispheres.

Case Study Wrap-Up

In this chapter we have encountered several variations of an interesting condition known as synesthesia. We began with a description of time–space synesthesia, a subtype in which concepts of time take on external spatial locations. Later we described a subtype in which letters and numbers are associated with colour experiences (grapheme–colour synesthesia). At first glance, many of us may find these and other synesthetic experiences—like perceiving numbers in geometric forms or digits in very specific sizes (recall Daniel Tammet's experiences)—somewhat odd or even outright bizarre.

But if you think further about the intricacies of human imagery discussed in this chapter, perhaps synesthesia isn't so strange after all. The available evidence suggests that many people are able not only to create very *vivid* images in their minds, but even to *scan* them (recall Kosslyn's image scanning studies) and rotate them mentally (recall Shepard and Metzler's findings). Furthermore, just as synesthetes can use their synesthetic images to help them remember, say, a list of digits, most people can use image-based *mnemonic techniques* as memory aids. Finally, like time-spaces and number-forms, the *cognitive maps* that virtually all of us use have a clear spatial component.

Among the most striking characteristics of time–space synesthesia is the way some people with the condition experience time units as revolving around the body. But if you think about it, even that experience may not be so odd after all. As we have seen in this chapter, projection of an image onto external space is also characteristic of *eidetic imagery*, and may occur in people with a high degree of *vividness of visual imagery*. Finally, think about this: when you look out onto the world, you experience your visual perceptions as though they are "out there in space." How can that be? In the chapter on perception (Chapter 3) we learned that light information comes into our eyes and then is processed by the visual areas of our brain. If that is the case, why don't we experience what we perceive as being "in our heads" rather than "out there in space"? It seems that our brains fashion an internal model or "image" of the world and "project" it "out there." Could that mean that the projection of images is not odd at all, but rather an inherent part of perception?

? Know: Review Questions

1. Critique Paivio's dual-coding theory, paying attention to relevant experimental and neuropsychological evidence.
2. When it comes to memory, is distinctiveness always a good thing? Have you ever used the special places strategy? Have you ever failed to find something you hid in a special place?
3. What do synesthesia and eidetic imagery have in common? How is each process related to ordinary imagery?
4. Discuss the similarities and differences between mental rotation, mental scanning, and egocentric perspective.
5. Compare and contrast cognitive maps and egocentric frames of reference.

Key Concepts

analog form of representation
apoptosis
categorical distance
chromesthesia
cognitive dedifferentiation
cognitive map (Tolman)
concreteness
cross-modal effects
distinctiveness
dual-coding theory (Paivio)
egocentric frame of reference
egocentric perspective transformations
eidetic imagery
emergent properties
icon
imagens (Paivio)
imagery
images as anticipations
inducers and concurrents
left and right hemispheres

lexical decision task
logogens (Paivio)
mental models
mental rotation (Shepard)
metamemory
method of loci
mnemonic techniques
number forms
objective distances
path integration
propositional knowledge
spatial framework
special places strategy
strong synesthetes
synesthesia
time spaces
vividness of visual imagery
von Restorff effect
weak synesthetes

Links to Other Chapters

distinctiveness
Chapter 5 (levels of processing)
Chapter 13 (autobiographical memory)

emergent properties
Chapter 2 (Sperry)
Chapter 11 (mental models)

mental models
Chapter 11 (mental models and deductive reasoning)

vividness of visual imagery
Chapter 8 (perceptual symbol systems)

Further Reading

The Paivio, Yuille, and Madigan word norms are among the most widely used in psycholinguistic research. For an update of those norms, see Clark and Paivio (2004).

Halpern (1988) investigated mental scanning for the auditory imagery we associate with familiar songs. As she pointed out, an auditory image has different locations, just as a visual image does, and (like the songs you actually hear) imagined songs have a beginning, middle, and end. Try imagining the song *Happy Birthday to You*. You start at the beginning ("Happy birthday to you, Happy birthday to you . . ."), move to the next line ("Happy birthday, dear . . ."), and finish with the last line ("Happy birthday to you"). In other words, auditory imagery is extended in time just as visual imagery is extended in space. This point is developed further in Cupchik, Philips, and Hill (2001).

Another fascinating history of mnemonic techniques is Carruthers (1990). Eskritt, Lee, and Donald (2001) explore how the development of literacy has changed our strategies for remembering.

Under certain circumstances, our ability to recall things we have learned can actually improve as we attempt to recall them on successive occasions. This phenomenon is called *hypermnesia*. Defined by Payne (1987) as "improvements in net recall levels associated with increasing retention intervals," hypermnesia was discovered many years ago (Ballard, 1913), but M.H. Erdelyi rekindled interest in it. Erdelyi argued that imagery leads initially to better recall and later to hypermnesia. See, for example, Erdelyi and Becker (1974) and Erdelyi and Kleinbard (1978). However, the role of imagery in hypermnesia has also been called into question. See, for example, Mulligan (2002).

Shepherd (1978) explores mental imagery as an aid to creativity. For an autobiographical note on the convergence of the author's interests in drawing and the mind, see Shepard (1990).

A fascinating study of the ways in which blind people represent space can be found in Kennedy (1993).

Carruthers, M. (1990). *The book of memory: A study of memory in medieval culture.* New York: Cambridge University Press.

Clark, M. and Paivio, A. (2004). Extensions of the Paivio, Yuille, & Madigan (1968) norms, *Behavior Research Methods Instruments and Computers* (a special web-based archive of norms, stimuli, and data, which can be accessed at www.psychonomic.org/brm.htm).

Cupchik, G.C., Philips, K., & Hill, D.S. (2001). Shared processes in spatial rotation and musical permutation. *Brain and Cognition, 46,* 373–382.

Erdelyi, M.H., & Becker, J. (1974). Hypermnesia for pictures: Incremental memory for pictures but not for words in multiple recall trials. *Cognitive Psychology, 6,* 159–171.

Erdelyi, M.H., & Kleinbard, J. (1978). Has Ebbinghaus decayed with time? The growth of recall (hypermnesia) over days. *Journal of Experimental Psychology: Human Learning and Memory, 4,* 275–289.

Eskritt, M., Lee, K., & Donald, M. (2001). The influence of symbolic literacy on memory: Testing Plato's hypothesis. *Canadian Journal of Experimental Psychology, 55,* 39–41.

Halpern, A.R. (1988). Mental scanning in auditory imagery for songs. *Journal of Experimental Psychology: Learning, Memory, and Cognition, 14,* 434–443.

Kennedy, J.M. (1993). *Drawing & the blind: Pictures to touch.* New Haven: Yale University Press.

Mulligan, N.W. (2002). The emergent generation effect and hypermnesia: Influences of semantic and nonsemantic generation tasks. *Journal of Experimental Psychology: Learning, Memory, and Cognition, 28*, 541–554.

Payne, D.G. (1987). Hypermnesia and reminiscence in recall: A historical and empirical review. *Psychological Bulletin, 101*, 5–27.

Shepard, R.N. (1978). The externalization of mental images and the act of creation. In B.S. Randhawa & W.E. Coffman (Eds.), *Visual learning, thinking and communication* (pp. 133–187). New York: Academic Press.

Shepard, R.N. (1990). *Mind sights*. New York: Freeman.

CHAPTER 8

Concepts

Chapter Objectives

- To review and evaluate classical approaches to the study of concept attainment.
- To review experiments used to study complex rules.
- To describe vertical and horizontal dimensions of concept organization.
- To outline how cognition is embodied.
- To examine and provide evidence for the theory of idealized cognitive models.
- To consider how folk biology relates to concept attainment.

Case Study Grasping a New Concept

FIGURE 8.1 Steve Jobs

It was January 2010 and the hype had reached a fever pitch. Rumours had been circulating for weeks that Steve Jobs, founder and CEO of Apple Inc., was going to introduce a new product at a press event in San Francisco. Or was he? No one could be sure with Steve. And that was a big part of the appeal. Steve Jobs loved to surprise people with his revolutionary devices—from the original Apple 1 personal computer way back in 1976 to all the iPods, iPhones, and iPads that are now part of everyday life—often introducing them just before the end of a show with a tantalizing "Oh, and one more thing . . ."

Still, the excitement in 2010 felt different. It wasn't just that no one knew *if* Jobs would introduce the new product—a similar uncertainty had existed for the iPod and the iPhone. No, the difference was that in the past people had known what the product, if it was indeed introduced, *would* be. That's not to say that they knew exactly how it would look—not at all. But they knew how to conceptualize it. They had known that the iPod would be an MP3 player, for instance, and the iPhone a smartphone. But the new device—rumoured to be something between an iPhone and a laptop—had people flummoxed. What was it exactly? How should they *conceive* of it? Should they think of it as a laptop? Or as something more along the lines of a writing tablet, like the Microsoft Tablet PC, or the Newton MessagePad 100, which Apple had introduced many years before, and which had failed terribly?

Fast forward to the moment when Steve Jobs steps onstage. He introduces the iPad as offering the most extraordinary web browsing experience possible, claiming that it is better than any smart phone or laptop. Without a hint of exaggeration, he claims that it's like holding the Internet in your own hands. There is extensive coverage both in the mainstream media and in online blogs and reviews. But as the dust begins to settle, it seems that people are still unsure what the iPad is. Some hail it as the successor to the laptop, some think of it as an eReader for books. Others say it's for watching movies and playing games that pit angry birds against pigs, or plants against zombies. Others still predict that it is doomed to fail because people don't know what it is—that is, they don't know how to *conceptualize* it.

Incredibly, though we have moved quite far down the road since it was first introduced, people are still struggling with how best to conceptualize the iPad and the many products that have sought to emulate it. As you will see in this chapter, there are many theories about how people acquire new concepts. While you're reading it, ask yourself what these theories might have to say about the iPad. How would they go about conceptualizing it? Would they have predicted the uncertainty that surrounded its introduction?

The Classical Approach

A milestone in the study of cognition was the publication, in 1956, of Bruner, Goodnow, and Austin's book *A Study of Thinking*. It described a series of experiments exploring how people acquire concepts. All of us make use of concepts. We seldom see events as entirely unique. Rather, we tend to sort every event into a particular category—in other words, to see it as an instance of a particular concept. Thus the object you are looking at now clearly belongs to a category that you are familiar with: it's an instance of the concept *book*. It has a number of *attributes* in common with other instances of the concept *book*: pages, print, a cover, and so on. Each attribute can take on a number of *values*: thus print can be large or small, the cover can be hard or soft (paper), and so on.

Bruner et al. (1956) were concerned with the relations between attributes and concepts. Clearly, attributes could define a concept in several ways. Some concepts are simply conjunctions of attributes, but others are more complex. A *disjunctive concept* is one in which class membership is defined by one of two or more possible sets of attributes. For example, there are three ways of acquiring Canadian citizenship: by being born in Canada, *or* by being born abroad to a Canadian parent, *or* by becoming a naturalized citizen. Similarly, in baseball "[a] strike is a pitch that is across the plate and between the batter's knees and shoulders *or* it is any pitch at which the batter strikes but fails to send the ball into the field" (Bruner et al., 1956, p. 43). The third type of concept is *relational*. Here it is the relationship between attributes that determines the class to which an event will be assigned. The concept of marriage, for example, is a relationship between two people (Holloway, 1978).

A study of thinking inspired many experiments designed to explore how people acquire concepts based on the attributes that define membership in a category. The original experiments done by Bruner et al. made use of the cards shown in Figure 8.2. Suppose each card either is or is not an instance of a particular concept. If it *is* an instance of a particular concept, then it is a *positive instance*. Thus a simple *conjunctive concept* might be *black* and *square*. Any card with these two attributes would be a positive instance. This means that all the cards in column 6 in Figure 8.2 are positive instances. If a card does *not* contain the right attributes, then it is a *negative instance*. Thus the top leftmost card is a negative instance. In this example, attributes such as the number of figures on a card are irrelevant.

To understand why something is a positive instance of a simple conjunctive concept like the one in the preceding example, you need to know which attributes are critical for membership in the concept and which ones are not. You might try to figure this out by noting which attributes recur in positive instances. If an attribute is present in all positive instances, then you might conclude that it is a **criterial attribute**: its presence is required if something is to be considered a member of the concept. All attributes that do not recur in positive instances would be irrelevant.

Criterial attribute
An attribute that is required in order for something to qualify as an instance of a concept.

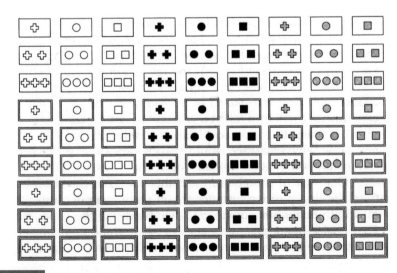

The process of including recurring attributes and excluding non-recurring ones is the process of *abstraction*. According to *The Oxford English Dictionary*, *to abstract* originally meant "to take away from." When you abstract the recurrent attributes from a set of positive instances you take them away from all the others. The recurrent attributes form a set that defines the concept.

Sometimes the process of abstraction is likened to a *composite photograph* (e.g., Galton, 1883). Imagine that you had negatives of photographs of everyone in your family for several generations and laid them one on top of the other. Then, if you held the pile of negatives up to the light, the recurrent attributes or features of the individual family members would stand out because they would be darker than the non-recurrent features. In this way you could abstract the recurrent features. This abstract set of features would not belong to any one person. Rather, it would define the concept of what a member of your family looks like. (Incidentally, composite photographs were quite popular in the nineteenth century. It was believed that a composite image showed what a "typical" family member would look like.)

The notion that concepts are like composite photographs is somewhat problematic. Ask yourself this: would all members of your family share some attributes, or would there be some family members without any of the others' characteristics? What does the idea of "family resemblance" really mean?

CONCEPT FORMATION TASKS

In their experiments Bruner et al. used two contrasting tasks to find out what strategies participants would use to acquire a simple conjunctive concept (e.g., "one black square"). In the first kind, known as a selection task, the experimenter would give you, the participant, one of the cards shown in Figure 8.2 (e.g., a card with one black square and a single border), tell you it was a positive instance of the concept, and challenge you to figure out what that concept was. Then you would be invited to choose any card you liked and the experimenter would tell you whether that card was a positive or a negative instance of the concept. This is called a **selection task**, because the participants select the instances they will use to figure out the concept that the experimenter has in mind. Which card would you choose next? What reason would you give for your choice?

One way of approaching this task is to choose an instance that differs from the first positive instance by only one feature. Thus you might choose a card with one white square and a single border. If the experimenter told you that your choice was a positive instance, what would you conclude? It must be that the attribute that has changed from the first positive instance is not included in the concept, because when it changes the instance remains positive. By contrast, if the experimenter told you that your choice was a negative instance, what would you know? Because the card you have chosen differs from the first positive instance in only one value of one attribute, that attribute must be criterial and "black" must be part of the concept. The colour of the figure is important because, when it changes, the instance changes from positive to negative.

Notice that the process we are describing is not a passive one in which the attributes that make up the concept are automatically abstracted after you have seen enough instances. Rather, you are actively formulating hypotheses and selecting instances to see if your hypotheses are correct. That is, you are using a strategy to try to discover what the concept is. The particular strategy we have been describing here is called **conservative focusing** because, when you use it, you focus on one attribute at a time and select instances that vary only in that particular attribute.

Selection task
A concept formation task in which the participant selects instances from those presented by the experimenter.

Conservative focusing
A concept formation strategy of actively formulating hypotheses and selecting instances to see if your hypotheses are correct by focusing on one attribute at a time and by selecting instances that vary only in that attribute.

This was not the only strategy that Bruner et al.'s participants used in this task. Among the others were focus gambling, simultaneous scanning, and successive scanning. In the case of **focus gambling**, you select instances that differ from the first positive instance in more than one attribute. You may get lucky and be able to eliminate a number of hypotheses quickly. Thus if, after being shown a card with one black square and one border, you choose two black squares with two borders and it turns out to be a positive instance, then you know that the number of squares and the number of borders are irrelevant. **Simultaneous scanning** involves keeping in mind all possible hypotheses and trying to eliminate as many as possible with each instance selection. This places a very great load on memory, because you must always keep in mind which hypotheses could be correct and which have been proven incorrect. **Successive scanning** is less demanding. The participant formulates a single hypothesis and tests it by selecting instances until the correct hypothesis emerges. Thus, if "black square" was your hypothesis, you would keep selecting cards consistent with that hypothesis until it was disconfirmed. Then you would formulate another hypothesis and carry on as before.

RECEPTION STRATEGIES

The second task used by Bruner et al. is called a **reception task**. Here the order in which instances are presented is under the control of the experimenter. Under this condition many of the participants in their study appeared to adopt one of two strategies, either wholist or partist.

With a **wholist strategy**, your first hypothesis is that all attributes in the first positive instance are included in the concept. If the next instance confirms that hypothesis, then you retain it. However, if the next positive instance is inconsistent with that hypothesis, then you form a new one that is consistent with whatever the old hypothesis and the current instance have in common.

With a **partist strategy**, your initial hypothesis includes only a part of the first positive instance. Then you maintain that hypothesis until you receive some disconfirming evidence. At that point you change your hypothesis to make it consistent with all the instances you have previously seen. This strategy, in its ideal form, places a heavy load on memory, because you must recall all previous instances in order to successfully revise your hypothesis.

The Bruner et al. study stimulated a great deal of research. Some of this work was concerned with the logical relations between different types of concepts (e.g., Hunt & Hovland, 1960; Neisser & Weene, 1962). There are some excellent reviews of this period of concept research (e.g., Bourne, 1966; Pikas, 1966). Nevertheless, psychologists gradually began to have doubts about the legitimacy of this kind of research.

CRITICISMS OF CLASSICAL CONCEPT RESEARCH

Experiments like the ones Bruner et al. did are reminiscent of certain kinds of games. In fact, there is a real similarity between the Bruner task and the popular game Mastermind (Best, 2001; Laughlin, Lange, & Adamopoulos, 1982). In Mastermind one player uses coloured pegs to create a code that another player must guess by proposing possible solutions, which are recorded with pegs on a board, and receiving feedback on how accurate the proposed solution is. Similarly, in the Bruner task the experimenter is the code-maker and the participants are the code-breakers. The participants try to read the

Focus gambling
The concept formation strategy of selecting instances that vary from the first positive instance in more than one attribute.

Simultaneous scanning
The concept formation strategy that keeps in mind all possible hypotheses and tries to eliminate as many as possible with each instance selection.

Successive scanning
The concept formation strategy that involves formulating a single hypothesis and testing it by selecting instances until the correct hypothesis emerges.

Reception task
A concept formation task in which the instances presented to the participant are chosen by the experimenter.

Wholist strategy
A concept formation strategy, used in reception tasks, in which you initially hypothesize that all attributes are members of the concept.

Partist strategy
A concept formation strategy, used in reception tasks, in which you initially hypothesize that only some attributes are members of the concept.

experimenter's mind and guess the code; then the experimenter provides feedback that the participants can use to tell how "warm" or "cold" their guesses are.

When the Bruner task is described in these terms, it begins to sound rather artificial. By the early 1970s many psychologists had begun to have serious doubts about this kind of laboratory study of concepts. Aren't real-world concepts more complex than the ones studied in a Bruner-type task? We saw in Chapter 4 that some techniques for studying attention have greater ecological validity than the kind that rely on contrived laboratory contexts. If you want to understand how people actually acquire and use concepts, perhaps there is a better way to go about it.

One way might be to continue studying artificial concepts (because that gives you more experimental control over their properties) but to try to make those concepts resemble real-world concepts in important ways. Another would be to give up studying artificial concepts and concentrate on studying concepts that people actually use.

Learning Complex Rules

Consider the diagram in Figure 8.3. It is an example of a *finite state grammar*. Such diagrams may also be called *railroad diagrams*. The reason for the latter name becomes clear if you imagine that each number in the diagram is a railroad station and each arrow is a track that you can follow from one station to another. The tracks go only one way, so you have to travel in the direction indicated by the arrow. All journeys begin at 1 and end at 4, 5, or 6. Each track is labelled by a particular letter, and some are even called by the same letter. Finally, some tracks are recursive: they go back to the place where they started.'

The finite state grammar in Figure 8.3 is really a set of rules for generating strings of letters. It's capable of generating all the strings of letters listed in the bottom of Figure 8.3 (and several others as well). These are letter strings that are consistent with this particular grammar. However, a string like VXRT would be inconsistent with this particular grammar.

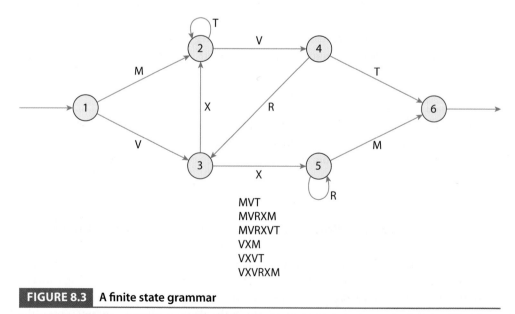

MVT
MVRXM
MVRXVT
VXM
VXVT
VXVRXM

FIGURE 8.3 A finite state grammar

From: Reber, A.S., & Allen, R. (1978). Analogic and abstraction strategies in synthetic grammar learning: A functionalist interpretation. *Cognition, 6*, 189–222. Copyright 1978 by Elsevier Science Publishers. Reprinted by permission.

Suppose you were asked to distinguish between those strings of letters that are consistent with the grammar (positive instances) and those that are inconsistent with it (negative instances). This concept task would require you to know the grammar in order to be able to make the proper distinctions.

As part of their investigation into the way people acquire knowledge about artificial grammars, Reber and his associates (1967; Allen & Reber, 1980; Reber & Allen, 1978; Reber, Allen, & Regan, 1985; Reber & Lewis, 1977) explored the distinction between **implicit** and **explicit learning**. For an illustration of implicit learning, suppose you show one group of participants some letter strings like those in Figure 8.3 and ask them to memorize as many of them as possible, but don't tell them that the strings follow certain rules. This group would represent the implicit learning condition. Now suppose you do tell a second group of participants that the letter strings follow certain rules and ask them to figure out what those rules are. This group would represent the explicit learning condition.

Which group do you think would do better at telling grammatical from non-grammatical letter strings? One way of finding out would be to show both groups a set containing both grammatical and ungrammatical letter strings and then ask them to identify the strings with the same structure as the first set of strings they had seen. It turns out that the implicit learning condition leads to a significant amount of rule-learning. Sometimes implicit learning even leads to better performance than explicit learning does.

This result is surprising because it suggests that people who are not trying to learn the rule structure can learn it at least as well as those who are consciously trying to learn it. Rather than actively forming and testing hypotheses, the people in the implicit learning group are unconsciously abstracting the structure of the grammar. Perhaps the implicit learning group is acquiring knowledge unconsciously and more efficiently than the explicit learning group.

According to Reber, people who learn implicitly have a vague sense of what is grammatical and what is not without being able to say specifically what the grammatical structure is. The higher the level of performance, the better the participants' ability to say what they have learned. However, their knowledge of what they have learned is largely *tacit*: they know it without being able to say exactly what it is.

Reber's work might tell us something about how people acquire other complex rule systems, such as those underlying natural (as opposed to artificial) languages. For example, when you were first acquiring your native tongue, your parents did not give you explicit instruction (e.g., grammar lessons) to ensure that you became proficient at generating grammatical sentences. You learned the structure of your language without knowing what that structure was, simply by listening to the people around you.

We know that children have already learned a great deal about the structure of the language before they start school because they are able to make more or less grammatical utterances. Preschool children are like participants in Reber's implicit learning condition. Of course, children may come equipped with powerful linguistic capabilities that allow them to acquire complex grammars quickly (we will consider the possibility that humans have an innate capacity for learning in Chapter 9, on language). In any case, it would appear that linguistic knowledge is largely tacit. According to Reber, Kassin, Lewis, and Cantor (1980), other forms of knowledge may work this way as well. Perhaps "complex structures, such as those underlying language, socialization, perception, and sophisticated games are acquired implicitly and unconsciously" (p. 492).

According to Reber (1989, 1990; Reber, Walkenfeld, & Hernstadt, 1991), his work shows that the **cognitive unconscious** plays an important role in cognition; he has also

Implicit vs explicit learning
Learning that takes place unintentionally versus learning that takes place intentionally.

Cognitive unconscious hypothesis
The hypothesis that implicit learning represents an evolutionarily primitive form of unconscious cognition.

suggested that "implicit and unconscious cognitive processes appeared early in our evolutionary history; consciousness is a late arriver on the phylogenetic scene" (Reber, 1990, p. 342). One implication of Reber's analysis is that conscious mental processes are associated with relatively recent forms of cognition. Reber, Walkenfeld, and Hernstadt (1991) argued that what we call "academic intelligence" is a form of cognition that has evolved relatively recently. Examples would include the ability to solve arithmetic problems and answer vocabulary questions of the kind used in standard IQ tests. These tests measure explicit, as opposed to implicit, cognitive abilities. Reber, Walkenfeld, and Hernstadt hypothesized that explicit cognitive abilities would predict performance on a task requiring explicit cognition, but not performance on a task requiring implicit cognition. To test this hypothesis, they gave participants a standard IQ test, as well as tests of implicit and explicit cognition. The implicit task was similar to the finite state grammar task we looked at above. The explicit task involved choosing the correct letter to complete a series of letters such as ABCBCDCDE (you can probably figure out that the right answer is D). As predicted, the correlation between scores on the IQ test and scores on the explicit task was much higher than the correlation between IQ scores and the implicit task. Moreover, there was only a small correlation between scores on the implicit and explicit tasks.

Reber (1997; Reber, Walkenfeld, & Hernstadt, 1991) concluded that the implicit cognitive system is very old in evolutionary terms and has not changed for a long time. "Once an adaptive, functional system evolves, and . . . the system is broadly operational in diverse environments, there is no adaptive value in change" (Reber, Walkenfeld, & Hernstadt, 1991, p. 894). Explicit cognition is more recent and less fixed by evolutionary processes. Consequently, although people differ widely in terms of explicit cognitive abilities, they do not differ very much in terms of implicit cognitive processes. Implicit cognition is a process in which we all share equally, according to Reber.

However, Dulany, Carlson, and Dewey (1984) argued that this interpretation was not justified. In a replication of an implicit learning experiment, they found that participants who had learned an artificial grammar implicitly were indeed able to formulate hypotheses about its underlying rules. Although their hypotheses were not perfect, the novel rules they consciously generated were in fact correlated with the actual rules. If their behaviour was under the control of those informal but nevertheless conscious rules, then Reber's emphasis on unconscious processes was mistaken.

Dulany, Carlson, and Dewey's argument has been refined and extended by others (e.g., Cleeremans, Destrebecqz, & Boyer, 1998). In a series of studies, Shanks and his colleagues (e.g., Kinder, Shanks, Cock, & Timney, 2003; Shanks, 2004; Tunney & Shanks, 2003) have presented additional evidence that implicit learning is accompanied by awareness (i.e., it is not unconscious). In one study, Tunney and Shanks (2003) had participants learn an artificial grammar implicitly, following a procedure similar to the one used by Reber above. However, in addition to judging whether a letter string was grammatical or ungrammatical, participants had to indicate how confident they were that their judgment was correct. In one measure of confidence, participants used a dichotomous rating scale to indicate whether or not they were confident in their judgment. If they had more confidence in their correct judgments than in their incorrect ones, then they must have had some awareness of the basis for their decisions. To put it another way, if they were aware of the reason for a particular decision, then they were confident, but if they were unsure, then they were not confident. If confidence ratings were unrelated to the correctness of their judgments, that would indicate that participants were unaware of what they had learned. It turned out that dichotomous confidence ratings were related to accuracy of judgment, suggesting that participants did indeed have some conscious awareness of the basis for their decisions.

This discussion of implicit learning should remind you of our discussions of *implicit perception* in Chapter 3 and *implicit memory* in Chapter 6. These three processes raise many of the same issues concerning the boundary between conscious and unconscious processes. As we have seen repeatedly, deciding whether a process is conscious or unconscious remains an extremely difficult methodological problem.

Wittgenstein's Analysis of Concepts

Up to this point we have considered concepts that have a definite rule structure. But how realistic is it to believe that the concepts we use in everyday life are as well-defined as those in the Bruner-type experiment? The philosopher Wittgenstein (1953) was interested in this type of question, and his approach to it was very influential both in philosophy and in psychology. In the following quotation, Wittgenstein is speaking to the question, "What do all members of a category have in common?" For example, what do all vegetables have in common that makes them all vegetables? Or what do all pieces of furniture have in common that makes them all furniture? Read his answer carefully:

I am saying that these phenomena have no one thing in common which makes us use the same word for all—but that they are related to one another in many different ways. Consider for example the proceedings we call "games." I mean board-games, card-games, ball-games, Olympic games, and so on. What is common to them all? Don't say: "There must be something common, or they would not be called 'games'"—but look and see whether there is anything common to all.—For if you look at them you will not see something that is common to all, but similarities, relationships, and a whole series of them at that. To repeat: don't think, but look!—Look for example at board-games, with their multifarious relationships. Now pass to card games; here you find many correspondences with the first group, but many common features drop out, and others appear. When we pass next to ball-games, much that is common is retained, but much is lost.—Are they all "amusing"? Compare chess with noughts and crosses [X's and O's]. Or is there always winning and losing, or competition between players? Think of patience. In ball games there is winning and losing; but when a child throws his ball at the wall and catches it again, this feature has disappeared. Look at the parts played by skill and luck; and at the difference between skill in chess and skill in tennis. Think now of games like ring-a-ring-a-roses; here is the element of amusement, but how many other characteristic features have disappeared! And we can go through the many, many other groups of games in the same way; can see how similarities crop up and disappear.

And the result of this examination is: we see a complicated network of similarities overlapping and criss-crossing: sometimes overall similarities, sometimes similarities of detail.

And I can think of no better expression to characterize these similarities than "family resemblances"; for the various resemblances between members of a family: build, features, color of eyes, gait, temperament, etc. etc. overlap and criss-cross in the same way.—And I shall say: "games form a family." (Wittgenstein, 1953, pp. 31–32)

Wittgenstein also compared the members of a category to the individual fibres that make up a thread or a rope. No single fibre runs the entire length of the thread. Rather, the individual fibres overlap with one another: "And the strength of the thread does not reside in the fact that some one fibre runs through its whole length, but in the overlapping of many fibres. . . . One might say that the concept of games is a concept with blurred edges" (pp. 32, 34).

Several ideas in this passage are worth noting. The most important is that the members of a category may not share any common features. Rather, their attributes may constitute a complicated network of overlapping features. This is a part of what we mean when we say that the members of a category bear a **family resemblance** to one another. Individual instances of a concept may shade into one another without any clearly definable boundary to the concept itself. Wittgenstein's example of the game concept illustrates this point nicely. Even if there were some activities that could not be considered games, it would still be difficult to say precisely where the concept of *game* begins and ends.

Wittgenstein's philosophical analysis is open to the criticism that it is based only on his intuitions and may not be true for everyone (Nichols, 2004). However, Wittgenstein held his philosophical observations to be a reflection of the way ordinary people use concepts. For that reason, some psychologists have wanted to explore Wittgenstein's insights by examining the way ordinary people use concepts. Eleanor Rosch is well known for having taken this next step.

> **Family resemblance**
> Instances of concepts that possess overlapping features, without any features being common to all.

▍ Rosch and Prototypicality

In some of her earliest studies, Rosch (née Heider) (Heider, 1971a, 1971b; Heider & Olivier, 1972) was interested in the structure of colour categories. Colour is a fascinating topic, and we will consider it again in Chapter 9, in relation to language. For now, we'll just note that some hues are better examples of a particular colour category than others. For example, some hues to which English-speakers apply the word *red* seem "redder" than others. In other words, some reds are more **prototypical** than others. Colour is not the only category in which this is true. Some breeds of dog (such as retrievers) are more representative of the category "dog" than others (such as Pekingese). Notice that, in this respect, natural concepts are unlike the artificial concepts with which we began this chapter. In the case of the Bruner cards, all cards with the attributes "black" and "square" are equally acceptable as examples of the concept "black square."

> **Prototypical**
> Representative of a pattern or category.

Rosch went on to develop a highly influential view of the nature of concepts. In doing so, she formulated two principles that she believed underlie the way we use concepts (Rosch, 1978): cognitive economy and perceived world structure.

Rosch's principle of cognitive economy refers to the constant effort to balance two opposing tendencies. One of these tendencies is to use our categories to maximize the amount of information they give us. This could be accomplished by having as many categories as possible. The more categories you have, the more distinctions you can make between "events." Taken to its logical conclusion, this tendency would lead to the creation of a separate category for every event in the world. On the other hand, if there were a one-to-one correspondence between your categories and events in the world, why have any categories at all?

One reason for having categories is to reduce the amount of information that we have to deal with. Although we want to be able to discriminate between events in the world, we also want to be able to group them together. In general, people try to make

CONSIDER THIS
BOX 8.1

The Downside of Categories

Suppose that at the beginning of the baseball season the Toronto Blue Jays are favoured to win the World Series. However, since there will also be a number of strong American-based teams with an excellent chance to win, and since Toronto is the only Canadian city with a team in the league, it would also be true that a team from an American city is likely to win the World Series. The reason for this apparent contradiction is that there are two different levels of category in this example, and the prediction we make will depend on the level we choose: the subordinate level of individual teams or the superordinate level of the countries to which these teams belong. If you're betting on which team will win, then Toronto is the best pick. However, if you're betting on which *country* will win, then you should put your money on an American team. This is an example of what Lagnado and Shanks (2003, p. 158) call **misaligned hierarchies**, in which a "judgment made with respect to one level of hierarchy" (Toronto will probably win) "may suggest one conclusion" (bet on Toronto) "whereas a . . . judgment made at a different level of hierarchy" (an American team will probably win) "may suggest a contrasting conclusion" (bet on an American team). Lagnado and Shanks (2003, p. 173) conclude that people

> do not just consider the most probable category, but commit in some way to its truth. We believe that this generalizes to many real world situations. Faced with uncertain information

about multiple categories, people adopt a short-cut strategy that focuses on just the most probable pathway, and neglects the less probable alternatives. This can empower their inferential capabilities, but will sometimes lead to error.

The title of this box is taken from an article by Murphy (2003), who drew out some of the implications of the Lagnado and Shanks study. He suggested that we may habitually use what Lagnado and Shanks call the **commitment heuristic** because we so often need to make decisions rapidly. Suppose you're speeding and see a car behind you in the distance on the highway. You think it may be a police car, but you aren't sure. If you decide that it is a police car and slow down, then you may avoid the ticket that you would have received if you'd waited until you knew for sure. Although the commitment heuristic may lead us into error in some situations, it may be of value in others. "One does not overuse a heuristic that is useless; one overuses one that has proved invaluable in the past" (Murphy, 2003, p. 514).

Misaligned hierarchies
Judgments made with respect to one level suggest one conclusion while judgments made at another level suggest a contrasting conclusion.

Commitment heuristic
A strategy in which we commit ourselves to the belief that something is true when it is only likely to be true.

concepts as simple as possible (Feldman, 2003). We can promote simplicity by ignoring differences between events and focusing on similarities. That way, many events that are different in some respects but similar in others can be treated as members of the same class. However, this tendency towards simplification has to be balanced against the necessity for differentiation. This tension between simplicity and complexity can create problems, as described in Box 8.1.

Rosch's second principle, perceived world structure, refers to the fact that some combinations of attributes tend to occur more frequently than other combinations. For example, animals that have wings also tend to have feathers and tend not to be covered with fur. Rosch contrasted this example with the sort of attribute relations used in artificial concept experiments. The Bruner cards in Figure 8.2, for example, do not have **correlated attributes**. Rather, the attributes of colour, form, number, and so on are orthogonal, or uncorrelated. Thus a black object is just as likely to be a square as it is to be a circle. This is another way in which artificial concepts differ from natural concepts. In the real world, attributes tend to cluster.

Correlated attributes
The hypothesis that some combinations of attributes tend to occur more frequently than other combinations.

VERTICAL AND HORIZONTAL DIMENSIONS

Rosch suggested that the principles of *cognitive economy* and *perceived world structure* lead us to organize concepts in a system that has both vertical and horizontal dimensions. The vertical dimension refers to the level of inclusiveness of the category: for example, *furniture* is a more inclusive category than *chair*, which is a more inclusive category than *kitchen chair*. Thus the vertical dimension refers to how general the concept is. By contrast, the horizontal dimension distinguishes between different concepts at the same level of inclusiveness: for example, *dog* and *cat* are concepts at roughly the same level of generality.

The Vertical Dimension

It's no accident that the example given above (*furniture, chair, kitchen chair*) has three levels of inclusiveness. This is just what Rosch found in her studies of concepts. The three levels are called **superordinate, basic,** and **subordinate**. For examples, see Table 8.1. There is considerable evidence to support the idea of three levels. For example, in one experiment, Rosch, Mervis, Gray, Johnson, and Boyes-Braem (1976) asked participants to list all the attributes for concepts such as those in Table 8.1. Basic-level concepts had more attributes in common than did those at the superordinate level. In another experiment, participants were asked to describe their body movements when interacting with objects. Objects in superordinate categories showed fewer common movements than did categories at the basic level. For example, what can you say about actions that go with clothing? Not much, right? But how about pants? You can probably imagine a fairly clear sequence of actions associated with pants. Subordinate categories, such as Levi's, have common movements as well, but they do not constitute an important difference over basic-level categories. Interestingly, Rosch also showed that children name basic-level categories accurately before they name superordinate categories. Thus words like *chair* are acquired earlier than words like *furniture*.

Basic-level concepts strike an important balance between the highly inclusive superordinate concepts and the highly differentiated subordinate concepts. "Basic objects should generally be the most useful level of classification. Universally, basic object categories should be the basic classifications made during perception, the first learned and first named by children, and the . . . most necessary in the language of any people" (Rosch, 1978, p. 435).

Rosch often noted that the level of a particular concept could change, depending on the sophistication of the person assigning the category. Thus *piano* is a basic-level object for most people. But what about musicians? Perhaps they perceive more differences among pianos, so that what is a basic-level object for a non-musician may be a superordinate-level object for a musician. Palmer, Jones, Hennessy, Unze, and Pick (1989) showed that something like this is, in fact, the case. Musicians and non-musicians were asked to list all the attributes they could think of for several instruments (e.g., *flute, violin, trumpet, piano, drum*). Musicians tended to give more distinctive descriptions for individual instruments. This suggests that our ability to perceive differences in the properties of individual objects becomes more refined as our experience of them increases.

Recall our discussion of J.J. Gibson's (1977; E.J. Gibson & Spelke, 1983) theory of perception in Chapter 3. Gibson's notion of *affordances* is relevant to the findings of Palmer et al. Objects afford particular actions. Thus a piano affords playing in a particular way that is different from what an organ affords. The more experience you have with a particular class of objects, the more aware you will be of its affordances. One consequence is, as Palmer et al. suggest, that the more expertise we have, the more subtle the distinctions we will make between categories.

Superordinate, basic, and subordinate levels
Levels of inclusiveness of a concept, as in *tree, oak*, and *live oak*.

TABLE 8.1	Different Levels of Concept of Objects	
SUPERORDINATE	**BASIC LEVEL**	**SUBORDINATES**
musical instrument	guitar	bass guitar, classical guitar
	piano	grand piano, upright piano
	drum	kettle drum, bass drum
fruit	apple	Delicious apple, Macintosh apple
	peach	freestone peach, cling peach
	grape	Concord grape, green seedless grape
tool	hammer	ball-peen hammer, claw hammer
	saw	hack hand saw, cross-cutting hand saw
	screwdriver	Phillips screwdriver, flat-head screwdriver
clothing	pants	Levi's, double-knit pants
	socks	knee socks, ankle socks
	shirt	dress shirt, knit shirt
furniture	table	coffee table, dining-room table
	lamp	floor lamp, desk lamp
	chair	kitchen chair, living-room chair
vehicle	car	sports car, four-door sedan
	bus	city bus, cross-country bus
	truck	pick-up truck, tractor-trailer truck

Adapted from: Rosch, E.H., Mervis, C.B., Gray, W.D., Johnson, D.M., & Boyes-Braem, P. (1976). Basic objects in natural categories. *Cognitive Psychology, 8,* 382–439. Copyright 1976 by Academic Press. Reprinted by permission of Elsevier.

The Horizontal Dimension

Within each category level some category members are more prototypical than others. This is the horizontal dimension of category structure. Rosch (1975) asked participants to rate category members according to how well they exemplified that category. The results probably won't surprise you. For example, in the furniture category *chair* is a better example than *telephone*; a *car* is a better example of a vehicle than *elevator* is; and *gun* is better than *shoes* as an example of the weapon category. People tend to have similar intuitions about how well a particular instance fits a particular category.

Rosch and Mervis (1975) showed that the more prototypical category members have more attributes in common than do those members that are judged atypical. Prototypical members also have the fewest attributes in common with members of other categories. This suggests that prototypical category members are the most representative of their own category and the least representative of other categories. Rosch and Mervis argued that this is what is meant by the phrase *family resemblance*. A category member has a strong family resemblance to the extent that it is a good example of the category to which it belongs and a poor example of any other category.

These findings with respect to the horizontal dimension of category structure can be summarized by saying that concepts have a **graded structure**. A concept is usually said to have a graded structure if some members of the category are better examples of it than others, and the boundaries of the category are unclear. However,

Graded structure
Describes a concept in which some members of the category are better examples of it than others and the boundaries of the category are vague.

Armstrong, Gleitman, and Gleitman (1983) showed that even some well-defined concepts show prototypicality effects. Consider the concept of *odd number*. It does not have a fuzzy boundary. A number is either odd or even. Armstrong et al. asked participants to rate examples of various well-defined categories, including odd and even numbers, for prototypicality. It turned out that participants rated certain numbers as better examples of their category than others. While these ratings do not alter the mathematical facts, participants felt that *three* was a better example of odd-numberedness than *fifty-seven* and, similarly, that *four* was better than *eight-hundred and six* as an example of even-numberedness. Thus a concept can have members that are "more prototypical" than others and yet still have a clear definition. This test shows that prototype effects are generalized subjectively and show up even in places where you might not expect them.

Embodied Cognition

In an important paper, Glenberg (1997) suggested that concepts should not be seen as disembodied abstract representations. Rather,

> the world is conceptualized (in part) as patterns of possible bodily interactions, that is, how can we move our hands and fingers, our legs and bodies, our eyes and ears, to deal with the world that presents itself? That is, to a particular person, the meaning of an object, event, or sentence is what that person can do with the object, event or sentence. (p. 3)

Embodied cognition
The role of cognition is to facilitate successful interaction with the environment.

We often ignore the fact that the brain/mind is situated in a body, and the "body requires a mind to make it function" (M. Wilson, 2002, p. 625). Cognition is **embodied**, and this means that its role is to facilitate successful interaction with the environment. Concepts must be understood as a part of the process whereby possible action patterns are determined. At any particular time, the environment affords many different actions. Concepts provide the bridge between our goals on the one hand, and the environmental possibilities on the other. For example, suppose I need a vase to put a flower in. I can select from among the objects in the environment those that would meet that need. A Coke bottle might do (Glenberg, 1997, p. 18). In this case, a Coke bottle would become a positive instance of the concept *vase* because it allows me to act in accordance with my current goal. If my goals change, then the meaning of a Coke bottle can change too. It can be a *doorstop* or even a *weapon*. "The meaning of a Coke bottle (how we interact with it) is not fixed, but infinitely varied depending on the context of use" (Glenberg, 1997, p. 18).

GOAL-DERIVED CATEGORIES

If your house caught fire, what would you try to save first? Presumably your list would include children, pets, computers, and so on. But suppose you had never thought of making such a list before. In fact, it is possible to construct on the spot a category of *things to save from home during a fire*. Such concepts are called *ad hoc* or **goal-derived categories** (Barsalou, 1983, 1987, 1999). A goal-derived category may contain members with no attributes in common, and may be something that most people have never thought of.

Goal-derived category
A category invented for a specific purpose on a particular occasion.

COGNITION IN ACTION
BOX 8.2

Do Experts Embody Information Differently?

Have you ever tried to learn a difficult skill such as shooting a puck or serving a tennis ball? If you have, you most likely had a friend, parent, or coach who gave you a visual demonstration of what you were supposed to do. Seeing a motor action performed correctly seems to have an effect on how well you perform it yourself. Indeed, many amateur athletes consciously try to emulate professional players or Olympic champions. This is a clever strategy, as a growing body of evidence suggests that action and perception are intimately linked. It seems that perceiving a particular motor action, or even just an object that could be acted upon, such as a puck or a ball, leads to activation in premotor areas of the brain, as if you were somehow preparing to perform a related action.

For example, imagine that you are looking at a frying pan with the handle facing to the right. If you were asked to press a key in response to some feature of the pan (e.g., its colour or size), you would be faster if you delivered your response with your right hand than with your left, presumably because the handle was facing to the right and activated a right-hand grasping response; this would be the case even if you were left-handed (Tucker & Ellis, 1998). It's important to note that the direction of the handle has nothing to do with a task involving colour or size. Nevertheless, response times are faster with the hand that the handle is pointing towards. This type of embodiment has been observed across a variety of experimental paradigms, stimuli, and even species: non-human animals also show embodiment effects (see, for example, Bach & Tipper, 2006; Beilock & Holt, 2007; Dipelligrino et al., 1992).

You might wonder how the link between perception and action plays out with experts in different types of motor skills (e.g., highly skilled athletes or dancers). Do they have a stronger embodiment response to motor actions in their expert repertoire than to actions they are less familiar with? Is part of becoming an expert related to an ability to more deeply embody action that is involved in that domain of expertise? To address this question, Calvo-Merino and colleagues (2005, 2006) explored how expert ballet and capoeira dancers responded to dancers performing skilled moves that they either would perform themselves or would only see performed by other dancers (e.g., a capoeira dancer watching a ballet dancer or a female dancer watching a male-specific move). Measurement of the viewers' brain activity, using fMRI, revealed more activity in response to motor actions that the experts had been trained to perform than to actions that they did not perform themselves. These results suggest that motor expertise can modulate how we perceive action.

Watching professional sports will not make you a professional athlete. Even so, aspiring athletes should probably watch the experts as closely as they can.

FIGURE 8.4 Capoeira

Barsalou (1983) showed that goal-derived categories have a graded structure. In one experiment, participants were asked to judge items in terms of how well they exemplified a particular category. For example, consider the concept *ways to escape being killed by the mob*. How well do each of the following fit in that category?

Change your identity and move to the mountains of South America.
Stay where you are presently living in New Jersey.

Barsalou (1983) found substantial agreement among participants concerning good and poor instances of goal-derived categories; this suggests that such categories have a graded structure. What determines how typical an item in a goal-derived category is? Barsalou suggested that the important determinant is how relevant the item is to the goal that the category serves. For example, imagine a category of *things not to eat on a diet*. The attribute "high in calories" is relevant to this category, but many other properties of foods that would ordinarily matter to us are irrelevant.

As Rosch suggested, people may initially prefer to classify an object using basic-level category names. Thus if you were asked to categorize a particular piece of furniture, your first response might be *chair*. However, as poverty-stricken aristocrats have occasionally discovered, when you run out of firewood you can burn a chair to keep warm, even if it is a priceless antique. As Barsalou (1987) noted, the goal-derived category of *emergency firewood* allows you to cross-classify a chair. The ability to cross-classify an object both in terms of its basic-level name and in terms of other goal-derived categories may be an important aspect of the ability to think creatively. "Perceiving these new organizations may be necessary to achieving new goals or to approaching old ones in novel ways" (Barsalou, 1987, p. 226).

A study by Ratneshwar, Barsalou, Pechmann, and Moore (2001) showed how a change in goals affects the extent to which objects are viewed as similar or different. People often construct categories based on personal goals: thus the category *healthy lunch substitutes* might include *sliced melon*, *green salad*, and *tuna sandwich*. But these personal goals will also be shaped by particular situational goals. For example, the situational goal of finding *things to eat while driving a car* should probably exclude *green salad*. In Ratneshwar et al.'s study participants were asked to judge the similarity of different pairs of food products (e.g., *apple-orange*). Their judgments were made as a function of different situational goals (e.g., *things to eat as snacks when in a hurry*). Notice that in this example the two foods (*apple-orange*) are similar with respect to nutritional value, but dissimilar in relation to the situational goal of *things to eat as snacks when in a hurry* (it takes some time to peel an orange). In the Ratneshwar et al. study, the judged similarity between foods was reduced (i.e., they were seen as more different) when one was consistent with the situational goal but the other was not. One advertising strategy that this research suggests would be to make situational goals more salient for consumers. Perhaps *soup* could come to be seen as a *breakfast food* if it were presented as satisfying the goal of *eating a hot and nutritious breakfast* (cf. Ratneshwar et al., 2001, p. 155).

PERCEPTUAL SYMBOL SYSTEMS

In the previous section we saw the enormous flexibility of the conceptual process. Barsalou (2003) argued that "there are no permanent or complete abstractions of a category in memory. Instead, abstraction is the skill to construct temporary . . . interpretations of a category's members" (p. 1177). This is why it is usually not possible to list all the criterial attributes that define a concept. As we saw when we discussed Wittgenstein, no matter how one defines a concept (e.g., *games*) there will be some members of the category to which that definition does not apply. Once we realize that concepts are usually temporary constructions designed to satisfy a specific goal in a particular situation, then their variability is no longer puzzling.

For Barsalou (1999, 2003), understanding how concepts are formed means studying the skills that enable us to construct temporary categories. These skills are rooted in perceptual experience. In the last chapter we observed that imagery and perception shared common mechanisms. Barsalou goes further, suggesting that perception and concept formation also have much in common. Recall our discussion of *selective attention* in Chapter 4, in which we noted that we perceive only a subset of all the information available. What perception delivers to memory are schematic instances of particular categories. For example, on many separate occasions we perceive different *cars*. Over time, these instances become integrated across all our senses and become a categorical representation. "For cars, such knowledge includes not only how they look but also how they sound, smell and feel, how to operate them, and emotions they arouse" (Barsalou, Simmons, Barbey, & Wilson, 2003, p. 88).

When knowledge of a particular category is distributed across all our senses it enables us to re-experience perceptual memories; for this reason such knowledge is called a *simulator*. The activity of conceptualization involves simulating sensory experiences. When we simulate sensory experiences we do not reconstruct all our previous perceptions. Rather, the simulation we conduct on a specific occasion is sensitive to the situation in which we find ourselves and our momentary goals. "On one occasion the . . . simulator might produce a simulation of travelling in a car, whereas on others it might produce simulations of repairing a car, seeing a car park and so forth" (Barsalou, 2003, p. 1180). We have no invariant concept of a *car*: rather, we construct different versions of *cars* on different occasions, each version focusing on different aspects of *cars*. Not every simulation of a car will include a *seatbelt*, or a *CD player*, or an *airbag*. Simulations represent those properties that are relevant for the task at hand.

The act of conceptualizing engages **perceptual symbols**: aspects of perceptual memories that "function symbolically, standing for referents in the world" (Barsalou, Solomon, & Wu, 1999, p. 210). Studies requiring participants to list the features of category members provide evidence for the perceptual nature of conception. For example, ask yourself what the features of a *watermelon* are. Now ask yourself what the features of a *half watermelon* are. Repeat this exercise for *computer* and *open computer*. If you are like the participants in the study conducted by Barsalou et al. (1999), the simulation of a *watermelon* or a *computer* is different from the simulation of a *half watermelon* or an *open computer*. The former brings to mind external properties, such as *surface colour*, while the latter reveals internal properties such as *seeds* or *wires*. It's likely that the object you imagine changes as its description changes. However, as we saw in the last chapter, people vary widely in the vividness of their visual imagery. Consequently, Barsalou made the point that we need not be aware of the activity of perceptual symbols, although we often will be. In essence, perceptual symbols represent brain states. "Most importantly, the basic definition of perceptual symbols resides at the neural level: unconscious neural representations—not conscious mental images—constitute the core content of perceptual symbols" (Barsalou, 1999, p. 583).

PERCEPTUAL SYMBOL SYSTEMS AND THE BRAIN

Like other approaches to embodied cognition (Wilson, 2003), the theory of perceptual symbol systems understands conceptualization as a process that connects our perceptions and our actions. In this respect the perceptual symbol systems theory has much in common with other approaches to categorization that are collectively

Perceptual symbols
Aspects of perceptual memories that stand for events in the world and enter into all forms of symbolic activity.

Category-specific deficits
Selective deficits in
knowledge, resulting from
brain damage.

called *sensory–functional theories* (Cree and McRae, 2003, p. 168). Such approaches have their roots in a study by Warrington and Shallice (1984) of **category-specific deficits** due to brain damage. The four patients they studied had partially recovered from encephalitis and were able to correctly identify inanimate objects. For example, one patient defined a *submarine* as a *ship that goes underneath the sea*. However, they were unable to provide satisfactory definitions for living things; one patient defined *ostrich* as simply *unusual* (Farah & McClelland, 1991, p. 340). To account for this selective impairment, Cree and McRae (2003) proposed that *living things* are understood primarily in terms of their sensory features, while *inanimate objects* are understood primarily in terms of their functions. Thus a *moose* might have *antlers* as one of its most salient features, whereas a *knife* might be defined as something that is *used for cutting* (Cree & McRae, 2003, p. 199). Sensory-functional theories assume that "knowledge of a specific category is located near the sensory-motor areas of the brain that process its instances.... Consequently, a deficit for living things may arise from damage to brain regions that process sensory information, whereas a deficit for manipulable artefacts may arise from damage to regions that implement functional action" (Simmons & Barsalou, 2003, p. 452). The sensory-functional theory accounts for some cases, but not all. It predicts that objects that are equally "sensory" should all be equally affected by a conceptual deficit. For example, a conceptual deficit for *living things* should span all *living things*. Yet some patients with a deficit for *fruits* and *vegetables* show no deficit for *animals* (Martin & Caramazza, 2003, p. 199; Samson & Pilon, 2003). Findings such as these mean that a simple sensory-functional theory can't be the whole story, and that complementary viewpoints need to be taken into account to provide a fuller account of conceptual deficits (Simmons & Barsalou, 2003, p. 454). We will become acquainted with some of these alternative viewpoints in the remainder of this chapter.

CONCEPTS AS METAPHORS

A simile is a figure of speech in which we use the word *like* to draw an analogy between two otherwise unrelated things. A metaphor is much the same, except that it doesn't use *like*: instead, it makes the connection directly, either by stating that one thing *is* the other, or by referring to one thing in language normally associated with the other. Some of the most famous literary metaphors come from Shakespeare: "the world's a stage," "love is blind," "a sea of troubles." As Lakoff and Johnson (1999, p. 46) have argued, however, metaphor is not only or even primarily a literary device. Rather, it arises naturally as a result of connections between sensory-motor and other forms of experience. For example, every time a child pours water into a glass, he or she will see the level of liquid rise. Over time, repetition of this experience leads to the formation of connections between those areas of the brain responsible for representing quantity and those representing verticality. Eventually "more is up" becomes a **primary metaphor**, "pair[ing] subjective experience and judgment with sensorimotor experience" (Lakoff & Johnson, 1999, p. 49). We can then understand and use expressions such as "Prices are down" or "The stock market is high" without thinking the metaphors through.

Primary metaphor
A pairing of subjective
experience with
sensorimotor experience

Another example given by Lakoff and Johnson (1999, p. 50) is the connection between *friendliness* or *affection* and *warmth*. They suggest that this pairing reflects the literal warmth we experience in an affectionate embrace. They also observe that "we first acquire the bodily and spatial understanding of concepts and later understand their metaphorical extensions in abstract concepts" (Johnson & Lakoff, 2002,

THINK TWICE
BOX 8.3

Warm Hands, Warm Heart?

If you were asked to categorize another person's personality, would you use Asch's (1955) approach and focus on "warm" and "cold" words? Perhaps a more interesting question to explore would be whether the direction of this relationship can be reversed. That is, can actual physical "warmth" or "coldness" influence the way you would describe another person? Williams and Bargh (2008) tested this by having participants hold either a hot or cold drink before assessing the personality of someone else. In this clever experiment, each participant took a short elevator ride with a confederate of the experiment who was carrying several things, including a cup of coffee that was either hot or iced. The confederate would then ask the participant to lend a hand and carry the coffee. Amazingly, those who had held the hot coffee later rated a hypothetical person as having a warmer personality than did those who had carried the iced coffee.

Is it really that easy to influence another person's judgment of you? Should you give a hot coffee to everyone you want to have warm feelings for you? And what about countries that naturally have warmer or colder climates? Anecdotal evidence would suggest that people from tropical countries do tend to be very friendly. Still, most Canadians would probably like to think that they have warm personalities even if they are cold for several months of the year. Clearly, more research is needed on this point.

Gibbs (1996, 2004), in concert with Lakoff and Johnson, has argued that our concepts are inherently metaphorical. In his view, metaphors are particularly valuable in the construction of temporary concepts of the sort we discussed above. "The LOVE IS A JOURNEY metaphor might be used to create a particular conceptualization of love in certain situations, while LOVE IS AN OPPONENT might be more appropriate to use forming a concept in other situations" (Gibbs, 1996, p. 314). Nevertheless, as he has pointed out (2004, p. 1196), not all metaphors appear to be equally grounded in sensori-motor experience. For example, if we compare "love is a journey" with "more is up," it's clear that the experiential link between "travel" and "love" is not as straightforward as the one between "more" and "up." It's not always easy to explain how conceptual metaphors are generated from primary metaphors.

p. 254). This is a point first made by Asch (1955, 1958; Asch & Nerlove, 1960), who described the process whereby words are initially applied to physical events and only later used metaphorically to describe persons. Asch (1955) called terms such as *warm* and *cold* **double-function words**. Essentially they refer to physical properties such as temperature, but secondarily they have been paired with the properties of people. Asch and Nerlove (1960) showed that children initially use these words to refer to physical objects, and only later use them psychologically. Thus children may have difficulty answering the question "Is your teacher a warm person?" unless they are able to use the word *warm* metaphorically. Lakoff and Johnson (1999, p. 50) list a number of primary metaphors, such as "Bad is Stinky" and "Help is Support." It would be a useful exercise to work out the sensorimotor basis for these metaphors yourself; you might also come up with some of your own.

Double-function words
Words that refer to both physical and psychological properties (e.g., *warmth*).

Folk Biology

We suggested in Chapter 2 that the mind is composed of specific parts, or *modules*, each of which is responsible for particular cognitive operations. We also noted that there are differences of opinion concerning the extent to which the mind is modular, as

Conceptual module
A module that is responsible for domain-specific knowledge.

Domain-specific knowledge
Knowledge that is handled by a module dedicated exclusively to a particular subject matter.

Folk biology
The concepts that ordinary folk use to understand living things.

Folk taxonomy
A classification system composed of a hierarchy of groups.

well as the number and kind of modules that may exist (e.g., Fodor, 1983; Pinker, 1997; Sperber, 2002). In this section we will explore the possibility that there is a **conceptual module** our naive understanding of biology is dependent on. A conceptual module is one that is responsible for **domain-specific knowledge**: that is, it deals exclusively with a particular subject matter (Hirschfeld & Gelman, 1994). Although the number of domain-specific modules is a subject of considerable controversy, a likely candidate for domain specificity is what has been called **folk biology** (Medin & Atran, 2004): the concepts that ordinary people use to understand living things.

Discussions of folk biology are often introduced by a quotation from Darwin (1859, p. 431) (e.g., Atran, 2005, p. 43):

> From the most remote period in the history of the world organic beings have been found to resemble each other in descending degrees, so that they can be classed into groups under groups. This classification is not arbitrary like the grouping of stars in constellations.

Darwin's hypothesis that people invariably classify living things hierarchically has been borne out in research, beginning with the work of Berlin, Breedlove, and Raven (1974). All cultures have a **folk taxonomy**, or classification system, "composed of a stable hierarchy of inclusive groups of organisms, or taxa, which are mutually exclusive at each level of the hierarchy" (Atran, 1999, p. 316). These levels can be compared to the levels identified by Rosch et al. in Table 8.1, in that there is a superordinate level (*tree*, *bird*), followed by a basic generic species level (*oak*, *robin*), and then a subordinate level (*white oak*, *mountain robin*) (Medin & Atran, 2004, p. 962). The generic species level plays the same role in folk biology that basic-level concepts play in the classification of Rosch et al. However, there are also some important differences, as we will see below.

FOLK BIOLOGY AND THE BRAIN

We saw earlier that some brain-damaged patients display a category-specific deficit in that they are unable to provide satisfactory definitions for living things. This does not necessarily mean that there is a conceptual module that is responsible for folk biology. However, advocates of the domain-specific module theory point to such findings in support of their position (e.g., Medin & Atran, 2004, p. 963). In one such study, Farah and Rabinowitz (2003) reported on a case of a young man who suffered brain damage as a result of meningitis when he was only one day old. Adam (a pseudonym) attended public school and had a normal verbal IQ. However, at age 16, when he was asked to name pictures of living and non-living things, he showed "a relatively selective impairment in knowledge of living things" (p. 404). In another test, he was given a questionnaire consisting of four item types:

1. Visual knowledge of living things (e.g., Do ducks have long ears?)
2. Non-visual knowledge of living things (e.g., Are roses given on Valentine's day?)
3. Visual knowledge of non-living things (e.g., Is a canoe widest in the centre?)
4. Non-visual knowledge of non-living things (e.g., Were wheelbarrows invented before 1920?)

Of a total of 380 questions, Adam correctly answered half in each category *yes*, the rest *no*. Control participants got roughly 80–90 per cent correct in each category. Adam's performance on the non-living things questions was not different from that of

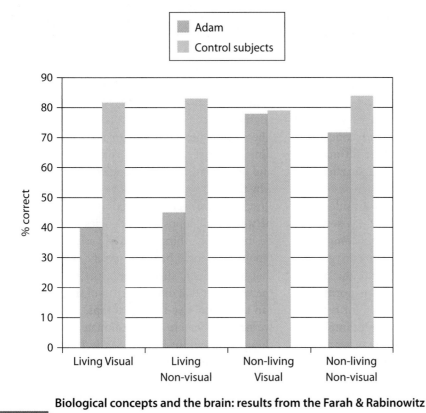

From: Farah, M.J., & Rabinowitz, C. (2003). Genetic and environmental influences on the organization of semantic memory in the brain: Is "living things" an innate category? *Cognitive Neuropsychology, 20*, 401–408.

FIGURE 8.5 Biological concepts and the brain: results from the Farah & Rabinowitz (2003) experiment involving a brain-damaged individual

the controls. However, for both types of living things questions, his performance was only 40–45 per cent (Figure 8.5). Farah and Rabinowitz concluded that Adam's deficit was specific to knowledge of living things. They also drew out the implications of the fact that his brain damage had been present virtually since birth, arguing that "prior to any experience . . . we are destined to represent our knowledge of living and non-living things with distinct neural substrates" (p. 408).

Summary

We use concepts to organize and categorize the events we experience based on their *attributes* and the values we assign to those attributes. Attributes can define concepts in several ways, as seen in examples of *conjunctive*, *disjunctive*, and *relational* concepts. To understand what makes something an instance of a concept, though, we need to determine the attributes that are critical for membership in the concept.

The processes by which we acquire and use concepts have been studied extensively. Classical research by J.S. Bruner used selection and reception tasks to observe and test different strategies used in concept acquisition, such as abstraction, conservative focusing, and successive and simultaneous scanning. However, the classical approach has been criticized for studying artificial concepts constructed in a lab rather than real-world concepts that people actually do acquire and use.

Case Study Wrap-Up

The irrelevance of the classical approach to real-world concept formation becomes clear when we consider the iPad and difficulty that people had in categorizing it. The work of Bruner et al. was concerned with the relations between attributes and concepts, where the concepts can be complex but are ultimately rather clear-cut. The problem is that categorizing an iPad is not so simple, as its features cut across many different types of technologies. Those who consider the iPad to be a kind of laptop notice that it has several of the same attributes: it's a light, portable computer about the size of a textbook. However, if you are going to call an iPad a laptop, then your concept of the latter must be extended to include attributes not normally associated with laptops (e.g., a touch screen for typing instead of physical keys). This would be an example of a disjunctive concept. Unfortunately, those other attributes are central to other concepts, such that of the eReader. And there lies the problem.

Eleanor Rosch has taken a different tack, using the natural concept of colour categories to explore the idea that members of a category share a family resemblance. She finds that with natural concepts there are prototypical instances that are unusually good examples of a particular category. Furthermore, she identifies two principles that govern the way we use natural concepts: cognitive economy and perceived world structure. These principles lead us to organize concepts along two dimensions: vertical (superordinate, basic, subordinate) and horizontal. These ideas may help us to understand why the iPad was so difficult to categorize. For instance, Rosch's notion of cognitive economy recognizes a tension between two opposing tendencies. On one hand, the desire to make things as simple as possible leads us to ignore differences between specific objects or events so that we can lump them all into the same category: thus many devices that differ in terms of size, colour, or brand can all be conceived of as "laptops." On the other hand, we need to be able to discriminate accurately between things that are not in fact identical. After all, there are many critical features that make the iPad unique and valuable that are not captured by the standard attributes of the laptop category. The key is balance: thus the desire to increase the complexity of the category of laptop or portable computer is balanced by the desire to keep things as simple as possible.

? In the Know: Review Questions

1. Outline the procedure that Bruner, Goodnow, and Austin used to study concepts. What were their major conclusions? Briefly criticize their approach.

2. Outline the procedure used by Reber and his colleagues to study complex rules. What was his major conclusion? Criticize Reber's work from the viewpoint of Dulany, Carlson, and Dewey.

3. What innovations did Rosch introduce to the study of concepts? Outline the horizontal and vertical dimensions of the system she used to understand concepts.

4. In what sense is cognition "embodied"?

Key Concepts

category-specific deficits	criterial attribute
cognitive unconscious	domain-specific knowledge
commitment heuristic	double-function words (Asch)
conceptual module	embodied cognition
conservative focusing	family resemblance (Wittgenstein)
correlated attributes	focus gambling

folk biology

folk taxonomy

goal-derived categories (Barsalou)

graded structure

implicit learning versus explicit
  learning

misaligned hierarchies

partist strategy

perceptual symbol systems

primary metaphors

prototypical

reception task

selection task

simultaneous scanning

successive scanning

superordinate, basic, and subordinate
  levels (Rosch)

wholist strategy

Links to Other Chapters

domain-specific knowledge

Chapter 4 (attention capture)

Chapter 11 (social contract theory)

implicit vs explicit learning

Chapter 13 (mere exposure and implicit
  learning)

tacit knowledge

Chapter 6 (procedural memory)

Further Reading

Many experimental paradigms other than Reber's have been used to investigate implicit or incidental learning. A good example is Lacroix, Giguère, and Larochelle (2005).

Perruchet and Vinter explore alternative approaches to the cognitive unconscious.

Do current events have an effect on what we consider to be a typical exemplar of a category? This question is examined in Novick (2003).

Two good examples of neural network approaches to classical concept formation problems are Carbonaro (2003) and Dawson, Medler, McCaughan, Willson, and Carbonaro (2000).

For a clever experiment designed to demonstrate a weakness of embodied cognition theories see Markman and Brendl (2005).

Geary and Huffman (2002) offer an evolutionary perspective on modularity.

Carbonaro, M. (2003). Making a connection between computational modeling and educational research. *Journal of Educational Computing Research, 28*, 63–81.

Dawson, M.R.W., Medler, D.A., McCaughan, D.B., Willson, L., & Carbonaro, M. (2000). Using extra output learning to insert a symbolic theory into a connectionist network. *Minds and Machines, 10*, 171–201.

Geary, D., & Huffman, K. (2002). Brain and cognitive evolution: Forms of modularity and functions of mind. *Psychological Bulletin, 128*, 667–698.

Lacroix, G.L., Giguère, G., & Larochelle, S. (2005). The origin of exemplar effects in rule-driven categorization. *Journal of Experimental Psychology: Learning, Memory, and Cognition, 31*, 272–288.

Markman, A.B., & Brendl, C.M. (2005). Constraining theories of embodied cognition. *Psychological Science, 16*, 6–10.

Novick, L.R. (2003). At the forefront of thought: The effect of media exposure on airplane typicality. *Psychonomic Bulletin & Review, 10*, 971–974.

Perruchet, P., & Vinter, A. (2002). The self-organizing consciousness. *Behavioral and Brain Sciences, 25*, 297–388.

CHAPTER 9

Language

Chapter Contents

Chapter Objectives

- To outline Chomsky's approaches to language.
- To review evidence for the innateness hypothesis and identify the "poverty of the stimulus" argument.
- To examine the process of communication and comprehension.
- To evaluate evidence for linguistic relativity.

Case Study Reading in the "Olden Days"

First published in the late 1870s (and revised substantially over the years), *McGuffey's First Eclectic Reader* was for many years one of the most popular reading textbooks in North America. Whether at school or at home, children who were learning to read did so using the McGuffey series, which included a Primer and a Spelling Book as well as five progressively more difficult readers.

The McGuffey's series was characterized by a rigour that is rarely seen in contemporary reading material for children. For example, by lesson 228 in the Spelling Book, students were learning words such as corymb and terpsichorean. (If you want to develop a truly "erudite" vocabulary, you can look them up.)

ECLECTIC SERIES.

SHORT SOUNDS.

ă, as in ăm.	ŏ, as in ŏdd.
ĕ, " ĕlm.	ŭ, " ŭp.
ĭ, " ĭn.	o͝o, " lo͝ok.

DIPHTHONGS.

oi, as in oil.	ou, as in out.

TABLE OF SUBVOCALS.

b, as in bĭb.	v, as in vălve.
d, " dĭd.	th, " this.
g, " gĭg.	z, " zi̱ne.
j, " jŭg.	z, " ăzure.
n, " nīne.	r, " râre.
m, " māim.	w, " wē.
ng, " hăng.	y, " yĕt.
l, as in lŭll.	

TABLE OF ASPIRATES.

f, as in fīfe.	t, as in tärt.
h, " hĭm.	sh, " shē.
k, " ċāke.	ch, " chăt.
p, " pīpe.	th, " thĭck.
s, " sāme.	wh, " whȳ.

FIGURE 9.1 **A page from *McGuffey's Second Eclectic Reader***

Note the diacritical marks and the proper pronunciation of various letters and letter combinations.

From: *McGuffey's Second Eclectic Reader*, Revised Edition, p. 8. John Wiley & Sons, Inc.

As for the complexity of the readers, take a look at the excerpt from the *Second Eclectic Reader* (p. 8) in Figure 9.1. Students were encouraged to learn how to interpret **diacritical marks**: symbols above letters that indicate their correct pronunciation in a particular word. According to the reader's preface,

> If the pupil is not familiar with the diacritical marks, he should be carefully drilled . . . until the marked letter instantly suggests the correct sound. He is then prepared to study his reading lessons without any assistance from the teacher. (p. iii)

With the help of the diacritical marks, students could teach themselves how to read almost from the start, when learning easy words such as *mine*, *soap*, *was*, and *red*. In a given lesson, such as Lesson IV shown in Figure 9.2, students would be shown a set of new words with the diacritical marks indicating the correct pronunciation. A short reading passage containing the

16 *ECLECTIC SERIES.*

LESSON IV.

a bȯve'	wõrld	därk	ŏft
nĕv'er	spärk	dew	tĭll
dī'a mond	twĭn̲'kle	blāz'ing	

THE LITTLE STAR.

1. Twinkle, twinkle, little star;
How I wonder what you are,
Up above the world so high,
Like a diamond in the sky!

2. When the blazing sun is set,
And the grass with dew is wet,
Then you show your little light;
Twinkle, twinkle, all the night.

3. Then, if I were in the dark,
I would thank you for your spark.
I could not see which way to go,
If you did not twinkle so.

4. And when I am sound asleep,
Oft you through my window peep;
For you never shut your eye,
Till the sun is in the sky.

FIGURE 9.2 **Reading Lesson IV from *McGuffey's Second Eclectic Reader***

From: *McGuffey's Second Eclectic Reader*, Revised Edition, p. 8. John Wiley & Sons, Inc.

new words would follow. Students would be required to practise the passage on their own until they had mastered it and then to read the passage to the teacher.

By the sixth reader students would be learning more complex aspects of reading, such as proper intonation. Intonation was diagrammed as shown in Figure 9.3, with lines set at angles to show how the voice should rise and fall as the sentence is read. Throughout the course of study, students would also be learning the correct interpretation and use of punctuation, as well as **articulation**, defined as the "utterance of the element sounds of a language, and of their combinations" (*McGuffey's Sixth Eclectic Reader*, p. 11). To "acquire the power of uttering those sounds with *distinctness*, *smoothness*, and *force*," students were urged to practise until they had gained "perfect control of [their] organs of speech" (p. 11, italics in the original).

The McGuffey method is quite different from the methods used to teach reading today. Chances are that you were never taught how to interpret diacritical marks, or the art of articulation, and you might wonder how children in grade 2 could have managed it all, mostly on their own. You might also wonder whether teaching complexities such as diacritical marks, intonation, and articulation ultimately led to better results than modern methods.

In this chapter we will discuss some of the main concepts in the cognitive psychology of language. One of the questions we will address is whether the complexity of a teacher's speech can influence the development of speech in children. Before we get there, however, we will begin by considering the main theories of how language is structured.

Articulation
The production of a language's sounds.

Diacritical marks
Symbols that indicate the correct pronunciation of letters in a particular word.

FIGURE 9.3   A lesson on intonation from *McGuffey's Sixth Eclectic Reader*

From: *McGuffey's Sixth Eclectic Reader*, p. 20. John Wiley & Sons (1997).

The Structure of Language

Wilhelm Wundt (1832–1920) is often credited with founding the first laboratory in psychology, but he was also one of the first to do important research into the psychology of language (Blumenthal, 1970; Carroll, 1953). Wundt's view anticipated many contemporary theories regarding the structure of language. One of his most interesting discussions concerned the relation between experience and the words used to describe it. Let's briefly reconsider the structure of our experience.

As we saw in Chapter 4, we are able to attend to "one out of what seem several simultaneously possible objects or trains of thought" (James, 1890, p. 403). Our attention is like a spotlight that highlights some aspects of a situation and leaves others in the background (Treisman, 1986). Nevertheless, all the aspects of a situation to which we could pay attention are available simultaneously. We can shift our attention from one aspect to another, and consider the relationships between the various parts of a situation.

Wundt (1890/1970; Blumenthal, 1970, p. 17) used **tree diagrams** to describe the relationships between different parts of our overall experience of a situation. For example, suppose you are listening to some music. Your experience includes relations between elements that you can put into words and could be diagrammed as in Figure 9.4. Thus the music can be described as the subject of a sentence and its loudness as the predicate, as in "The music is loud." The process of speech proceeds from one level at which a number of relations are simultaneously present to another level at which these relations are ordered serially as a succession of words in a sentence (e.g., subject, predicate). The person who hears "The music is loud" can then reconstruct the speaker's experience by reversing the process and moving from the level of words in succession to the level where the two elements are present simultaneously. Wundt's model of sentence production is similar to more modern notions. In particular they resemble some of Noam Chomsky's early formulations. Although Chomsky's linguistic theories have had a profound impact on cognitive psychology, they have undergone many changes over the years. We will begin with some of his early ideas because they are still part of the way in which many cognitive psychologists think about language. We will then explore some of his more recent approaches.

Tree diagram
A description of a process that proceeds from one level at which a number of relations are simultaneously present to other levels at which those relations are ordered serially.

FIGURE 9.4 A tree diagram of the relation between two elements experienced while listening to music

Transformational Grammar

Chomsky is one of the most important figures in the history of linguistics. His ideas have always been hotly debated, and he has never shrunk from controversy. Chomsky has been "among the ten most-cited writers in all of the humanities (beating out Hegel and Cicero and trailing only Marx, Lenin, Shakespeare, the Bible, Aristotle, Plato, and Freud) and the only living member of the top ten" (Pinker, 1994, p. 23). His fame was not immediate, however. In fact, his doctoral dissertation was considered so unusual that he had difficulty getting it published. A condensed version was published as *Syntactic Structures* (1957). In that book Chomsky considered the way we produce sentences. A sentence is a grammatical utterance and is recognized as such by a native speaker of the language. Chomsky points out that the set of possible sentences in a language is infinite. **Language** is open-ended and consists of all possible sentences, but **speech**, which consists of those sentences that are actually spoken, is only a small subset of language (de Saussure, 1916). This is a very important point, because it means that there must be a set of rules—a *grammar*—that everyone uses to generate sentences in his or her language. This grammar must be capable of producing all possible sentences in the language. From a finite set of rules, the grammar is in principle able to generate an infinite set of sentences. In order to understand the structure of language, we need to understand the structure of this grammar.

Chomsky makes the point that a grammatical utterance need not be a meaningful utterance. His famous example of this is the nonsense sentence "Colourless green ideas sleep furiously" (Chomsky, 1957, p. 15). Although meaningless, the collection of words is still grammatical, at least when compared to the utterance "Furiously sleep ideas green colourless." This observation, and others like it, led Chomsky to make a sharp distinction between *grammar* and *semantics*, the study of meaning. He argued that the processes that made a sentence grammatical are different from the processes that make a sentence meaningful.

Chomsky went on to consider the nature of a grammar for a natural language such as English. He rejected the possibility that a finite state grammar could generate all the sentences in a language. We considered finite state grammars in Chapter 8, when we reviewed Reber's work. You may wish to go over that material again now. For the purposes of the present discussion, a critical feature of a finite state grammar is that every word in a sentence is produced in a sequence starting with the first word and ending with the last. A railroad diagram, which produces several sentences, is given in Figure 9.5. This grammar generates sentences such as *The man comes*, *The old man comes*, *The men come*, and *The old men come*. These are only a few of the possible sentences in English. Can you imagine how vast a railroad diagram would have to be in order to be able to generate 1000 sentences? 10,000? 100,000? There are a great many more possible sentences than these in English. If we had to learn them all using a finite state grammar, we would need to listen to several sentences a second for more than 100 years before we had learned enough sentences to allow us to speak and understand a significant portion of English (G.A. Miller, Galanter, & Pribram, 1960, p. 147).

Chomsky's (1957, p. 21) objection to finite state grammars is that it is impossible to construct one that will generate all and only the grammatical utterances of a natural language. Finite state grammars are too simple to underlie the complexity of natural languages. As an illustration of this complexity, consider the fact that natural languages contain sentences that are embedded within other sentences. This example comes from Chomsky (1957): *The man who said that S is arriving today* (p. 22). The symbol *S* can stand for an unlimited number of possible sentences that could be inserted at that point in the example. *The man who said that the bank will renew our mortgage is arriving today* and *The man who said that Roscoe will become a star is arriving today* are just two out of an indefinite number of possibilities. A grammar must be able to generate such sentences, and Chomsky believed it was impossible for a finite state grammar to do so.

One of the problems with finite state grammars is that they operate at only one level. They generate sentences by a process that moves only from left to right, as it were.

Language
Open-ended verbal communication that consists of all possible sentences.

Speech
Those sentences that are actually spoken; only a small subset of language.

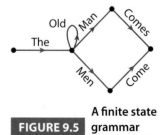

FIGURE 9.5   A finite state grammar

From: Chomsky, N. (1957). *Syntactic structures*. The Hague: Mouton, p. 19. Copyright 1957 by Mouton de Gruyter. Reprinted by permission.

The alternative proposed by Chomsky (1957) is a top-down process that uses phrase structure rules and grammatical transformations. **Phrase structure rules** consist of symbols and rewrite rules. Here is a small set of such rules, adapted from Chomsky (1957, p. 26) and J. Greene (1972, p. 35):

1. Sentence (S) → Noun Phrase (NP) + Verb Phrase (VP)
2. NP → Article (*art*) + Noun (N)
3. VP → Verb (V) + NP
4. *art* → *a, the*
5. N → *girl, car, boy*, etc.
6. V → *drives, likes, helps*, etc.

These rules, which describe the way symbols such as S can be rewritten as other symbols, such as NP and VP, are capable of generating an infinite number of sentences. The derivation of a sentence can be represented using a tree diagram, as in Figure 9.6. Each stage in the process yields a different string (such as NP + VP), and the final sequence of words generated is called a terminal string.

Rewrite rules operate on single symbols, such as NP and VP. However, Chomsky (1957, p. 44) proposed that there are also rules that operate on entire strings to convert them to new strings. He called these rules **grammatical transformations**. An example is the *passive transformation*. Take a sentence with the following underlying form:

$$NP_1 + V + NP_2$$

An example is the sentence *Boswell admired Johnson*. The passive transformation, *Johnson was admired by Boswell*, converts the string underlying the terminal string to produce something like the following (Deese, 1970, p. 26):

$$NP_2 + to\ be + V + by + NP_1$$

This transformation reverses the order of the two noun phrases and inserts a form of the verb *to be* and the word *by* in their proper places. Instead of *Boswell admired Johnson* we now have *Johnson was admired by Boswell*. The passive transformation is an example of an *optional transformation*. It's not necessary for optional transformations to be applied in order to make a sentence grammatical. Chomsky (1957, p. 45) defined *kernel sentences* as those that are produced without optional transformations. This suggests that kernel sentences might be easier to understand and remember because they require fewer transformations. Much psychological research was stimulated by this notion (e.g., Mehler, 1963). However, it was difficult to demonstrate that it was the number of transformations—rather than variables such as sentence length—that determined ease of understanding and recall (J. Greene, 1972, pp. 157ff.). For example, the passive sentence *Johnson was admired by Boswell* has more words than its active counterpart, and may be more difficult to process for that reason.

In the end, interest in the concept of kernel sentences declined as Chomsky revised his theory. Chomsky (1965, 1966, 1967, 1968, 1972) went on to introduce several concepts that became very influential. Among the

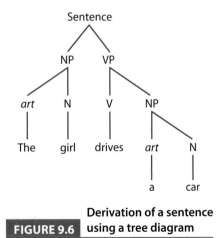

FIGURE 9.6 Derivation of a sentence using a tree diagram

important distinctions he introduced were those between *competence* and *performance* and between *deep structure* and *surface structure*.

COMPETENCE AND PERFORMANCE

Chomsky (e.g., 1967, p. 397) considered what it means to say that a person "has a command" of a language. On the one hand, it means that the person has internalized a system of rules that relates sound to meaning. This internalized system of rules constitutes a basic linguistic **competence**—the basis on which the person is able to understand and to use the language. This competence is not always reflected in the person's actual use of the language. Linguistic **performance** is determined not only by the person's basic linguistic competence, according to Chomsky, but also by cognitive factors such as memory and the person's understanding of his or her situation. In principle, therefore, we can generate extremely long sentences, but such sentences cannot be easily understood because they exceed the attentional capacities of listeners. To take another example, the form that utterances take often depends on the age of the speaker. The same thing might not be said in the same way by an adult and by a young child. Thus even though the grammar of a language is a model of linguistic competence, observations of linguistic performance will not always give us a completely accurate picture of a person's competence.

Chomsky (1967, p. 399) argued that a central problem for psychology is to discover the characteristics of linguistic competence. This would involve specifying the idealized grammar that constitutes this competence. A theory of linguistic performance would specify not only the nature of linguistic competence but also the psychological processes that go into the production of actual sentences.

Competence vs performance
We may have an internalized system of rules that constitutes a basic linguistic competence, but this competence may not always be reflected in our actual use of the language (performance).

DEEP AND SURFACE STRUCTURES

Chomsky believes that linguistic competence has a largely innate internal structure. This innate structure is called *universal grammar*. One aspect of universal grammar is universal syntax, which provides the rules that enable us to transform meaning into words. The meaning is at one level, called the **deep structure**, whereas the words are at another level, called the **surface structure**. The distinction between deep and surface structure allows us to understand a number of interesting linguistic phenomena, including ambiguous sentences.

The reason ambiguous sentences are interesting is often illustrated by sentences like the following (e.g., Bigelow, 1986, p. 379):

1. *Time flies like an arrow.*

2. *Fruit flies like a banana.*

Sentence 1 is usually interpreted as a comparison in which *flies* is a verb and *like* is a preposition: time passes as quickly as an arrow flies through the air. A similar interpretation could be imposed on sentence 2 as well. However, in this case we're more likely to read *flies* as a noun and *like* as a verb.

These examples may seem a bit silly, but they help to make a serious point. From Chomsky's perspective, the existence of ambiguity in language illustrates why we need

Deep and surface structure
The sequence of words that makes up a sentence constitutes a surface structure that is derived from an underlying deep structure.

to make a distinction between deep and surface structure. The same surface structure can be derived from different deep structures. The two different meanings of sentence 1, for example, are carried by two different deep structures. *Meaning* is not given on the surface of a sentence: it is given by the *deep structure* interpretation of the sentence. When we understand a sentence, we transform a surface structure into a deep structure. When we produce a sentence we work the other way: from a deep structure to the construction of a surface structure.

▌ The Innateness Hypothesis

THE "POVERTY OF THE STIMULUS" ARGUMENT

Innateness hypothesis
The hypothesis that children innately possess a language acquisition device that comes equipped with principles of universal grammar.

"Poverty of the stimulus" argument
The argument that the linguistic environment to which a child is exposed is too deficient to enable the child to acquire language on that basis alone.

Language acquisition device (LAD) and universal grammar hypothesis
The hypothesis that children possess a language acquisition device containing general principles that apply to any natural language (universal grammar).

As we noted above, Chomsky believes that linguistic competence is largely innate. Among the arguments for this **innateness hypothesis** is the belief that the speech to which a small child is exposed is an inadequate database from which to abstract the structure of language (e.g., Chomsky, 1972, pp. 13–160). The typical linguistic performance of an adult is too full of errors and too incomplete a sample of language to give children the data they need to generate a natural language grammar on their own. This is called the **"poverty of the stimulus" argument** (Chomsky, 1980a, 1980b; Lightfoot, 1982) because it claims that the stimulus for language (which is other people's language) is too deficient to enable children to use it effectively. Children acquire their first language too rapidly for them to start from scratch. Consequently, children must possess a **language acquisition device**, or **LAD** (McNeill, 1970), that contains principles of **universal grammar**. These are very general principles that apply to any natural language, be it English or Chinese. Among the things that LAD "knows" are the facts that languages contain things such as noun phrases and verb phrases, and that they are arranged in particular ways, such as subject followed by predicate (McNeill, 1970, p. 71). LAD is a theory of language that children use to discover the structure of the particular language community in which they happen to be living. LAD must be a very powerful theory because it enables children to quickly make sense out of the language to which they are exposed. Children come equipped with the tools necessary to enable them to rapidly acquire a facility in their first language.

Support for the innateness hypothesis came in part from the findings of a classic study by R. Brown and Hanlon (1970). According to Pinker (1988), Brown and Hanlon's findings "may be one of the most important discoveries in the history of psychology" (p. 104). The reason Brown and Hanlon's study is so important is that it bears directly on one of the alternatives to the innateness hypothesis. That alternative is usually identified with B.F. Skinner (1957).

Skinner's approach, and others like it, implied that children must learn a language by receiving informative feedback on their utterances. Perhaps language learning takes place when children are given approval for generating grammatical sentences and disapproval for generating ungrammatical ones (R. Brown & Hanlon, 1970, p. 46). However, Brown and Hanlon found no evidence to support that idea. Observing the interactions of mothers and their children, Brown and Hanlon found that mothers not only allowed ungrammatical sentences to go uncorrected, but responded to such utterances in the same way that they responded to grammatical utterances. Approval seemed to depend on whether or not the statement the child was trying to make was true; its grammatical quality was irrelevant. Thus to a child who says *Mama isn't boy, he a girl* the parent says *That's right*. However, to a child who says *And Walt Disney comes on Tuesday* the parent says *No, he does not* (R. Brown & Hanlon, 1970, p. 49).

One implication of studies such as Brown and Hanlon's is that children do not typically receive information that would tell them when they are making an ungrammatical sentence (Rice, 1989, p. 150). In the absence of such feedback, it's not easy to see how the child could learn to eliminate ungrammatical utterances. Yet from the perspective of the innateness hypothesis this does not seem such a big problem. That is because the innateness hypothesis maintains that children come equipped with the kind of knowledge that will ultimately allow them to produce grammatical sentences and avoid ungrammatical ones. As we shall see, however, not everyone accepts the innateness hypothesis. Moreover, even if we accept some version of the innateness hypothesis, we still need to spell out precisely what it is that must be innate in order for children to acquire language, and that is not at all easy.

MINIMALISM

As we noted earlier, Chomsky's theory has undergone considerable modification over time (e.g., Chomsky, 1981, 1995, 2005). The current version is called **minimalism** (Uriagereka, 1998). As the name suggests, the minimalist approach assumes that linguistic competence has only those characteristics that are absolutely necessary, with no added frills. Minimalism operates according to a principle of parsimony (Atran, 2005, p. 58), in that it aims for the simplest possible theory of linguistic competence. The working hypothesis of minimalism is that "the human language faculty might be a computationally perfect solution to the problem of relating sound to meaning" (Lasnik, 2002, p. 434).

A key hypothesis of the current theory is that the acquisition of a particular language involves **parameter setting** (Piatelli-Palmarini, 1989). Chomsky (1981, 1995) proposed that universal grammar contains a variety of switches, which can be set to any of several possible values, or parameters. A parameter is a universal aspect of language that can take on one of a small set of possible values. Here is an example from Hyams (1986, p. 3). In an English verb phrase the verb always comes before its object, as in "take the cheese." A native English speaker would never say "the cheese take." However, in a German verb phrase the verb always follows the object. The position of the verb is a parameter set for a specific language. Chomsky (1995) described parameter-setting as follows:

> A plausible assumption today is that the principles of language are fixed and innate, and that variation is restricted. . . . Each language, then, is . . . determined by a choice of values for lexical parameters: with one array of choices, we should be able to deduce Hungarian; with another Yoruba. . . . The conditions of language acquisition make it plain that the process must be largely inner-directed, as in other aspects of growth, which means that all languages must be close to identical, largely fixed by initial state. (p. 17)

As Piatelli-Palmarini (1989) pointed out, the parameter-setting approach implies that children are not instructed to learn a specific language. Children are not given explicit training on the position of verbs in verb phrases, for example. Rather, a language is selected out of the many possible ones that are supported by universal grammar.

Minimalism
The belief that linguistic competence has only those characteristics that are absolutely necessary.

Parameter-setting hypothesis
The hypothesis that language acquisition involves a universal grammar that contains a variety of switches, which can be set to one of a number of possible values, or parameters. A parameter is a universal aspect of language that can take on one of a small set of possible values.

Through exposure to a particular language, such as English or German, the switches get set to the specific values that characterize that language (Yang, 2004).

Of course, the need for parameter-setting arises because of the variety of languages that children must be prepared to acquire as their native tongues. But why do different languages exist at all? It's possible that different languages arose and developed through a series of historical accidents:

> We find different languages because people move apart and lose touch, or split into factions that hate each other's guts. People always tinker with the way they talk, and as the tinkerings accumulate on different sides of the river, mountain range, or no-man's land, the original language slowly splits into two. To compare two languages is to behold the histories of two peoples, their migrations, conquests, innovations, and daily struggles *to make themselves understood*. (Pinker, 1997, p. 213, italics added)

Concealing function hypothesis
The hypothesis that language is a kind of code, and that the parameters set for one language serve to conceal its meanings from the speakers of another language.

Like Pinker, most theorists assume that the goal of every speaker, regardless of language, is to be able to communicate with others. But what if the goal was to facilitate communication with some people *and not with others*? In other words, what if "the language faculty [had] a **concealing function** as well as a revealing function" (p. 351)? In that case, the parameters that are set for one language would serve to conceal its meanings from the speakers of another language, and vice versa. This would mean that language could usefully be seen as a kind of code. Baker (2003) points out that the US successfully used the Navajo language as a code in the Second World War. In general, it would be advantageous for the members of a particular group to be able to pass information to one another while keeping it secret from the members of another group with whom they were at war, or with whom they were competing in some other way. Since war and other forms of human conflict are extremely common, it may be that linguistic parameters evolved precisely in order to keep open the possibility of creating and learning new languages. This example illustrates the extremely broad range of possible evolutionary explanations for the various features that language possesses. Different theories of the psychology of language are intimately associated with specific theories of the evolution of language. It's virtually impossible to disentangle the psychology of language from the story of its evolution. An exploration of some aspects of the way psychologists have dealt with the evolution of language is given in Box 9.1 (you might want to review the material on Broca's area in Chapter 2 before reading this box).

IS THE STIMULUS FOR LANGUAGE REALLY IMPOVERISHED?

As Pullum and Scholz (2002; Scholz & Pullum, 2002) observed, the "poverty of the stimulus" argument rests on the premise that the data a child needs in order to acquire a language from scratch are unavailable. If that is true, then language cannot be acquired solely by means of data-driven learning. However, the poverty of the stimulus argument would be undermined if one could "identify a set of sentences such that if the learner had access to them, [then] the claim of data driven-learning . . . would be supported" (Pullum & Scholz, 2002, p. 19). Since the Brown and Hanlon (1970) study discussed above, an enormous amount of information has accumulated concerning the kinds of sentences to which children may be exposed (e.g., MacWhinney, 2000). Consequently, investigators now have much richer samples against which to test the "poverty of the stimulus" argument. By examining large samples of sentences, Pullum and Scholz (2002, pp. 24–26) were able to document the existence of many constructions that had been assumed to be either infrequent or absent from the language to which infants would be exposed. For example, consider how children understand irregular constructions such as plurals in noun–noun compounds. The sentence *I put my books on the book shelf* is fine as an English sentence. However, *I put my books on the books shelf* sounds strange, and we can surmise that children are very unlikely to hear it. Nevertheless, children understand that *a new books shelf* means *a shelf for new books*. They don't think it means *a new shelf of books*. Where does this understanding come from? It has been claimed that children understand constructions like this as "another demonstration of knowledge despite 'poverty of the input'" (Pinker, 1994, p. 147). However, the child's knowledge should not be surprising, given the number of constructions such as *rules committee, publications catalogue, letters policy*, or *complaints department* that they will be able to overhear in the speech of adults. Perhaps exposure to these constructions provides all that the child needs in order to use this grammatical form properly.

Pullum and Scholz (2002) render what is called a "Scottish verdict" on the "poverty of the stimulus" argument: not proven. Indeed, Hoff (2004) makes the useful point that it is difficult if not impossible to disprove the poverty of the stimulus argument. No one has given, or perhaps ever can give, a complete account of all the data available to a child that would make language acquisition possible without any innate contribution. Nevertheless, enough evidence has accumulated to suggest that children acquiring language are given much more evidence in support of their efforts than had previously been suspected (MacWhinney, 2004). We have space here to consider only two examples of the evidence contained in the enormous literature on the topic of language acquisition. First, it now appears that children do both receive and make use of corrective feedback on their ungrammatical constructions. Second, the complexity of the speech to which the child is exposed is significantly related to the complexity of the speech that the child then produces. We will now briefly examine representative studies illustrating both of these influences.

ADULT REFORMULATIONS OF CHILD ERRORS

"Children produce many errors during acquisition, and the issue is how they manage to get rid of them" (Chouinard & Clark, 2003, p. 638). Perhaps **parental reformulations** of a child's erroneous utterances play a role. For example, consider the following exchange:

> Child: I want butter mine.
> Father: OK give it here and I'll put butter on it.
> Child: I need butter *on it*. (Chouinard & Clark, 2003, p. 656)

Parental reformulations
Adult reformulations of children's speech. They are negative in that they inform children that they have made a mistake and positive in that they provide examples of correct speech.

The fact that he takes up his father's reformulation suggests that the child realizes two things: that the reformulation means the same thing as his initial erroneous formulation, and that in order to speak correctly he must emulate his father. In general, adult reformulations are negative in that they inform children that they have made a mistake. At the same time they are positive in that they provide models of correct speech.

Chouinard and Clark sampled utterances of five children between the ages of two and four years, the parental responses to these utterances, and the child's next utterance. Their data came from a standard archive called the "Child Language Data

CONSIDER THIS
BOX 9.1

The Evolution of Language

Psychologists have speculated endlessly about the evolution of language. At times the speculation is so rampant that it almost seems reasonable to ban discussion of the topic. Indeed, the French Academy of Sciences did exactly that in 1866. Like most prohibitions, it proved ineffective, and we once again have an abundance of theories. However, one theory in particular is currently attracting more attention than any other. It should come as no surprise that this theory is associated with Noam Chomsky.

Hauser, Chomsky, and Fitch (2002) made a distinction between broad and narrow conceptions of the faculty of language. In its broad sense, the faculty of language has three parts. There is a sensory–motor system that allows us both to perceive and to produce patterns of speech. There is also a conceptual–intentional system that allows us to grasp the meaning of speech. Finally, there is a uniquely human system that mediates between the first two. Let's consider each of these systems in turn.

Sensory–Motor System

Other animals share our ability to perceive and produce speech sounds. For example, vocal imitation occurs in dolphins, parrots, crows, and songbirds. Songbirds are particularly interesting examples. They acquire their songs by listening to other birds of the same species. This input must come during a critical period or their songs will not develop properly. It's much the same with human language acquisition. After a certain age people cannot speak a second language and sound completely like a native. This, along with other similarities between human and animal sensory–motor systems, suggests that there is nothing uniquely human about this aspect of language.

Recursion
A process that refers to itself.

Conceptual–Intentional System

The ability of other animals to represent the world and their place in it may not be as rich as that of humans. However, they are still capable of formulating and acting on relatively complex plans. For example, recall our discussion in Chapter 6 of foraging in scrub jays (Clayton &

Dickinson, 1998). These birds stored both larvae (which they value highly as food but which spoils quickly) and peanuts (which they value less highly as food, but which remain edible for a long time) in different locations. When the birds were allowed to retrieve stored food, their choice depended on the length of the interval between storage and retrieval. If the interval was short, then they retrieved the larvae, but if it was long they went for the peanuts instead. "Individuals often search for food by an optimal strategy, one involving minimal distances, recall of locations searched, and kinds of objects retrieved" (Hauser, Chomsky, & Fitch, 2003, p. 1578). Thus one would be loath to argue that the conceptual–intentional system is peculiar to humans.

Uniquely Human System

What may be unique to humans is the ability to use symbols recursively. We have already seen an example of recursion earlier in this chapter when we considered sentences embedded within other sentences. **Recursion** is a process that refers to itself. Consider the following examples, adapted from Uriagereka (1999, pp. 3–4).

S → You are saying that S
S → You are saying that you are thinking that S
S → You are saying that you are thinking that you are talking to someone that S

In these examples S calls itself, so that each successive example becomes longer. In principle this recursive process could go on indefinitely, but in practice it is limited by what we can keep in working memory (as well as the capacity of the listener or audience to attend to what we are saying).

Morton (1976) gave a witty example of recursion. His article is titled "On recursive reference." The body of the paper consists of one sentence: "Further details of this paper may be found in Morton (1976)." That is, the paper refers to itself, inviting the reader to go back to the beginning and read it over again, and then again, and so on. The paper is not only about recursion, but is an example of a recursive loop in itself.

Hauser, Chomsky, and Fitch (2002) realized that recursive behaviour may yet be found in animals, but they could find no good examples from existing research. They concluded that recursion may be the uniquely human property of the language faculty. Hence the narrow conception of the faculty of language is that it consists of the ability to recursively combine symbols. It enables the construction of an infinite number of possible expressions of the conceptual–intentional system to be realized as sentences produced by the sensory–motor system (Hauser, Chomsky, & Fitch, 2002, p. 1578). In short, it enables us to translate thought into speech.

Chomsky (2005) describes the evolutionary appearance of this narrow faculty of language as follows:

> The simplest account of the "Great Leap Forward" in the evolution of humans would be that the brain was rewired, perhaps by some slight mutation. . . . Perhaps . . . the Great Leap Forward was effectively instantaneous, in a single individual, who was instantly endowed with intellectual capacities far superior to those of others, transmitted to offspring and coming to predominate. . . . (p. 12)

From Gesture to Speech

An alternative account of the evolution of language presents much more specific hypotheses about its emergence. Corballis (2003, 2004a, 2004b) weaves together the following facts:

- Other primates do not have speech, but they do have a relatively sophisticated system of gestural communication.
- The area corresponding to Broca's area in monkeys contains **mirror neurons** that fire not only when the animal makes grasping movements, but also when the monkey observes other animals making those movements.
- A mutation on a gene called foxp2 can cause a severe speech disorder. Functional MRI studies suggest that this disorder may be due to a problem in Broca's area that prevents it from handling speech.
- Around 40,000 years ago there was a rapid increase in the production of tools, decorations, and cave art.

These facts can be combined to form the following narrative. Like other primates, humans originally communicated by means of gesture. Indeed, people still make meaningful gestures while speaking (McNeill, 1980, 1985a, 1985b, 1989). However, at one time we communicated primarily through gesture supplemented by simple vocalizations bearing little resemblance to modern speech. Broca's area was responsible for gestural communication, enabling us not only to regulate our gestures, but also to interpret the gestures of other people. A mutation on foxp2 enabled the recruitment of Broca's area for speech. That is why any further mutation on foxp2 causes a speech disorder. The emergence of speech took the pressure off gesture as a channel of communication, freeing the hands for other tasks. This in turn allowed the development of elaborate tools, decorations, and works of art.

There are other evolutionary narratives, of course (e.g., Pinker & Jackendoff, 2005). All of them are open to debate. However, there is no denying the reciprocal influence between the search for the evolutionary origins of language and the development of the psychology of language.

> **Mirror neurons**
> Broca's area in monkeys contains neurons that fire not only when the animal makes grasping movements, but also when the monkey observes other animals making those movements.

Exchange System" (MacWhinney, 2000). The data set they analyzed was quite large, varying from 730 items for one child to 9187 for another. Chouinard and Clark discovered that reformulations of erroneous utterances occurred between 50 and 70 per cent of the time when the child was about two years old. They also found that the children took up these reformulations as frequently as 50 per cent of the time, as shown by their subsequent repetition of the reformulation. Thus these interactions provide occasions for the child to learn how to speak correctly, and the children take advantage of them. Reformulations decline as children get older, presumably because of ongoing improvements in their speech.

THE IMPACT OF TEACHERS' SPEECH

Huttenlocher, Vasilyeva, Cymerman, and Levine (2002, p. 338) note that "there are substantial variations in the language environments children encounter and . . . these variations may be correlated with differences in development." For example, children's **syntactic development**—their ability to organize words into grammatical sentences—may be influenced by input from speakers other than parental caregivers. Language development is an ongoing process that does not stop at a specific age. After a certain age, much of the speech that children are exposed to comes from teachers. The complexity of kindergarten and first-grade children's syntax develops more between October and April than between April and October (Huttenlocher et al., 2002, p. 343)—the period that includes the summer vacation. A reasonable hypothesis is that exposure to speech at school is the important factor. In order to test this hypothesis, Huttenlocher and her co-workers sampled the speech of different teachers. Huttenlocher et al. recorded preschool teachers' speech during a typical class day. These recordings were analyzed to determine the extent to which individual teachers presented children with challenging examples of speech. A particularly important example is the multi-clause sentence (e.g., *The lamp broke because it fell off the table*). Consequently, Huttenlocher et al. calculated the proportion of multi-clause sentences in each teacher's speech, which turned out to vary between 11 and 32 per cent (Figure 9.7). The children were roughly four years old, attended three different preschools, and came from families that together represented a range of incomes from high to low. The children were tested by means of a comprehension task (illustrated in Figure 9.8) that required them to match each sentence with the correct picture. The test included both multi-clause sentences and sentences with varying numbers of noun phrases.

Each class had the same primary teacher throughout the study. Children were tested both at the beginning and the end of the school year. An average comprehension score for each class was calculated for both the first and second tests. Then the average scores on the first test were subtracted from the average scores on the second test. This gave a measure of how much syntactic growth had taken place *in each class*. This measure was found to be significantly related to the complexity of teacher speech: the more complex the teacher's speech, the greater the syntactic growth in that class. Importantly, "teacher speech was *not* significantly related to children's skill levels at the start of the school year, but *was* significantly related to growth in children's skill levels over the school year" (Huttenlocher et al., 2002, p. 370).

One of the benefits of exposure to complex speech may be that the child learns to represent more complex ways of thinking about things. In this context, Huttenlocher et al. (2002, p. 371) cite Vygotsky's (1934/1986) work on the interaction between language and thought. This is a topic that we will take up later in the chapter.

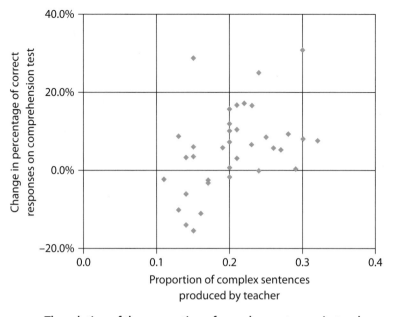

FIGURE 9.7 The relation of the proportion of complex sentences in teacher speech to comprehension scores

From: Huttenlocher, J., Vasilyeva, M., Cymerman, E., & Levine, S. (2002). Language input and child syntax. *Cognitive Psychology, 45*, 337–374. Copyright 2002. Reprinted by permission of Elsevier.

The boy is looking for the girl behind a chair, but she is sitting under the table.

The baby is holding the big ball and the small block.

FIGURE 9.8 The comprehension task

From: Huttenlocher, J., Vasilyeva, M., Cymerman, E., & Levine, S. (2002). Language input and child syntax. *Cognitive Psychology, 45*, p. 363. Copyright 2002. Reprinted by permission of Elsevier.

EVALUATION OF CHOMSKIAN THEORIES

If the value of theories is measured by the amount of research they generate, then Chomsky's various theories have been a smashing success. The degree to which they are true or false has still to be determined. However, two complementary trends seem to have been established. The first is that, in comparison with earlier formulations, innate processes now are believed to play a lesser role in language acquisition (Pinker & Jackendoff, 2005, p. 204). The second is that the linguistic environment of the child is much richer than had been believed. Language acquisition is increasingly acknowledged to be dependent on learning.

▌▌ Communication and Comprehension

Obviously, an important field of inquiry within the psychology of language studies is the way listeners comprehend spoken and/or written speech. When you comprehend spoken or written language, you understand what it means. The context in which listeners or readers receive language is extremely important in determining what interpretations they will extract from the message. As a consequence, speakers or writers must take the audience's context into account.

Given–new contract
A tacit agreement whereby the speaker agrees to connect new information to what the listener already knows.

A useful distinction is made between *given* and *new information* (H.H. Clark & E. Clark, 1977, pp. 32, 92). Speakers and listeners are said to enter into a **given–new contract** (H.H. Clark & Haviland, 1977) whereby the speaker tacitly agrees to connect new information to what the listener already knows. Thus, for example, a sentence may consist of part that is given, or shared between speaker and listener, and a part that is known to the speaker but new to the listener (Bruner, 1985, p. 31). Suppose there is a howling winter storm outside, and you say, "A cold front from Alberta is causing this storm." You are introducing a new piece of information (*a cold front from Alberta*), and relating it to something your listener and you already know (*the storm*). Comprehension would be difficult if not impossible if we simply introduced new information without connecting it to something of which the listener already has some knowledge.

Code model of communication
A model of communication based on the information-processing theory.

Sperber and Wilson's (1986/1995; 2002) theory of the way conversation is conducted and comprehended has been very influential. They contrasted two approaches to communication: the **code model** and the inferential model. The code model derives from information-processing theories such as those we reviewed in Chapter 2. According to this model, the initial stage of communication is a process whereby a speaker's thoughts are encoded in words. When spoken, these words are an acoustic signal that passes through the air and impinges on the listener. The listener must decode the signal to arrive at the thought that the speaker intended to communicate. According to Sperber and Wilson, the code model assumes that both speaker and listener share a great deal of mutual knowledge. Otherwise the listener would not be able to decode the signal properly and arrive at the correct interpretation. As an example, Sperber and Wilson imagined a speaker who says: *Coffee would keep me awake*. This sentence is open to at least two interpretations. One is that the speaker wishes to stay awake, and so wants a cup of coffee, and the other is that the speaker does not wish to stay awake, and so does not want a cup of coffee. To successfully interpret this sentence the listener must share the speaker's understanding of the situation. Sperber and Wilson point out that a drawback of the code model is the difficulty of spelling out how people could come to have enough mutual knowledge to guarantee successful communication.

The **inferential model** derives from the work of Grice (1957/1971, 1975), who analyzed communication in terms of *intentions* and *inferences*. A speaker intends to inform a listener, and the listener infers what the speaker intends. Suppose you're sitting in a room with another person. It's the middle of winter, but you think the room is stuffy and so you open a window. What would you infer if the other person then said, "Were you raised in a barn?" Would you decode this utterance as a simple request for information, and reply sincerely, "No, I was raised in a two-bedroom semi-detached house"? Or might you interpret the utterance as a request that the window be closed, because the speaker is implying that only people raised in primitive conditions would open the window in winter? The meaning of the utterance depends critically on the inferences you make concerning the meaning that the speaker intends. Grice (1957/1971) suggested that to say someone "meant something" by a particular utterance is to say that the speaker intended "to produce some effect in an audience by means of the recognition of this intention" (p. 58). In the example above, when you recognize that your companion "meant something" by asking if you were raised in a barn, you're expected to respond appropriately, most likely by closing the window.

To facilitate the process of communication, most of us follow what Grice called the **co-operative principle**: speakers try to be concise, truthful, relevant, and unambiguous, and listeners take it for granted that this is the case. From this principle Grice derived four rules or **conversational maxims** (Paprotte & Sinha, 1987, p. 205):

1. Say no more than is necessary (*maxim of quantity*);
2. Be truthful (*maxim of quality*);
3. Be relevant (*maxim of relation*); and
4. Avoid ambiguity and be clear (*maxim of manner*).

In turn, according to Grice, listeners assume that speakers are following those maxims, and make inferences, or *implicatures*, based on that assumption.

To illustrate how the inferential model might work in ordinary conversation, let's return to Sperber and Wilson's example of the person who says, "Coffee will keep me awake." Suppose that the speaker and listener are on a road trip, driving nonstop from Winnipeg to Vancouver, and it's the speaker's turn to drive. If both parties are following the co-operative principle, the listener can easily infer that the speaker wants coffee. There's nothing mysterious about this process: it simply involves taking the four conversational maxims for granted and drawing the inferences that make sense in the circumstances. On the other hand, Grice was writing more than half a century ago. Do the people you know follow the co-operative principle? Is the inferential model valid today?

For Sperber and Wilson (1986), communication sometimes follows the coding model and sometimes follows the inferential model. People communicate in ways that blend coding and inference. Under all circumstances, however, the goal of communication is *relevance*. An utterance is relevant to the extent that it is both true and easy to understand (Van der Henst, Carles, & Sperber, 2002, p. 458). Truthfulness and relevance are not always the same. For example, when they are asked the time, many people will round the answer to the nearest five minutes: thus if your watch says 2:18, you might say it's 2:20. In one study, Van der Henst et al. (2002) found that 97 per cent of speakers with analog watches rounded their replies to the nearest five minutes. Perhaps this is because the precise time is more difficult to see on a wrist watch, or is not relevant; or perhaps a rounded time is simply easier for both speaker and listener to process.

Inferential model of communication
A model of communication based on Grice's inferential theory.

Co-operative principle
The assumption that the speaker intends to say something concise, truthful, relevant, and unambiguous.

Conversational maxims
Say no more than is necessary (*maxim of quantity*); be truthful (*maxim of quality*); be relevant (*maxim of relation*); and avoid ambiguity (*maxim of manner*).

Comprehension may require inferences of the sort Grice proposed, but the inferential process need not be a conscious chain of reasoning. Sperber and Wilson (2002) refer to comprehension as "intuitive," meaning that it is an "unreflective process which takes place below the level of consciousness" (p. 9). It's possible that most people have an implicit theory of how other people's minds work, and that they use this theory when they attempt to comprehend what others are saying (Perner, 2000; Sperber & Wilson, 2002, p. 275).

FIGURATIVE LANGUAGE

Figurative language
Various figures of speech, such as metaphor and irony.

Insight into the way communication works can be gained from the study of **figurative language**, which consists of figures of speech such as metaphor and irony (Roberts & Kreuz, 1994). Figurative language may at first seem to be an unusual form of communication. However, it is commonly used in ordinary discourse (Pollio, Smith, & Pollio, 1990), as we saw in Chapter 8, on concepts. In what follows we will focus on *irony* because a great deal of research has been devoted to it. We will see that irony illustrates many facets of communication in everyday life.

IRONY

Irony belongs to a family of concepts that includes *satire* and *sarcasm*. A satirical remark holds something up to ridicule. Sarcasm and irony are vehicles for satire. *The Oxford English Dictionary* defines *sarcasm* as a "sharp, bitter or cutting remark" and *irony* as "a figure of speech in which the intended meaning is the opposite of that expressed by the words used." Irony is sometimes considered to be a form of sarcasm, and ordinary speakers of the language consider the two to be quite similar (Gibbs, 1986).

An ironic statement is intended to communicate the opposite of what it says. Thus you might say of someone you find particularly cold and unfeeling, "He's such a warm person." Given the right context and tone of voice, you can communicate exactly how you feel, even though you are saying the opposite. What are the conditions under which a listener perceives the ironic intent of a speaker?

Pretense theory of irony
When speaking ironically, people are only pretending to mean what they say.

H.H. Clark and Gerrig (1984, p. 121) followed Grice (1978) in arguing that irony involves the use of **pretense**: the speaker is only pretending to mean what he says. They quoted Fowler (1965):

> Irony is a form of utterance that postulates a double audience, consisting of one party that hearing shall hear and shall not understand, and another party that, when more is meant than meets the ear, is aware both of that more and of the outsiders' incomprehension. . . . [It] may be defined as the use of words intended to convey one meaning to the uninitiated . . . and another to the initiated, the delight of it lying in the secret intimacy set up between the latter and the speaker. (pp. 305, 306)

As Clark and Gerrig noted, irony usually involves a particular tone of voice. It's difficult to spell out, but when someone says something like "What a terrific movie" ironically, the tone is unmistakably different from the one that would be used if the speaker really meant the words.

Several authors have described (without necessarily accepting) what is sometimes called the *standard theory of irony* (e.g., Gibbs, 1986; Jorgenson, Miller, & Sperber,

1984; Kreuz & Glucksberg, 1989). According to this theory, listeners initially take the ironic utterance literally, but soon realize that the speaker can't mean it literally. Then the listener reaches the conclusion that the speaker means the opposite of what he or she has just said. Grice's *co-operative principle* (that listeners normally expect speakers to be truthful and relevant) could help to explain the way the listener arrives at this conclusion (Kreuz & Glucksberg, 1989, p. 374). The listener realizes that the speaker cannot be both truthful and relevant and literally mean what he or she says. Thus the listener can infer that the speaker must mean the opposite.

A recurrent issue in the study of irony in particular and of figurative language in general is whether or not the listener must understand the literal meaning of an utterance first before extracting the figurative meaning. Gibbs (1986) presented evidence that people comprehend ironic utterances as quickly as literal ones. Glucksberg (2003) reported that metaphorical utterances (e.g., *My job is a jail*) are also apprehended "as quickly and as automatically as we apprehend literal meanings." Results such as these imply that we don't need to extract the literal meaning of an utterance first. This may be particularly true if speakers and listeners share enough common ground (H.H. Clark & Gerrig, 1984, p. 124) to enable the latter to comprehend the ironic utterance more or less directly (Gibbs, 1986, p. 13). However, when figurative language is unexpected, we may take longer to process it. For example, in many cultures people expect men to make more sarcastic utterances than women. Consequently, comprehension of a sarcastic utterance made by a woman is "delayed as people attempt to integrate" the statement with their expectations (Katz, Blasko, & Kazmerski, 2004, p. 187).

SPEECH DISFLUENCY

It's very common for speakers to pause at various points while they speak. Such **hesitation pauses** have been extensively researched (e.g., Goldman-Eisler, 1968; Deese, 1984). Stanley Schachter and his colleagues (Schachter, Christenfeld, Ravina, & Bilous, 1991; Schachter, Rauscher, Christenfeld, & Crone, 1994) explored hesitation pauses made by university lecturers, focusing on pauses filled by *ums*, *ers*, *uhs*, and *ahs*. No doubt you will have heard many such *speech disfluencies*. Schachter and his colleagues counted the number of filled pauses in the speech of 47 lecturers in 10 departments at Columbia University. These measurements were made unobtrusively by a trained observer sitting in the class. The data showed that more speech disfluencies were more common among lecturers in the humanities and social sciences than among their counterparts in the sciences (Figure 9.9).

Schachter et al. (1991) attributed the difference in hesitation pauses between the disciplines to a difference in vocabulary between the sciences and the arts. Science lecturers are speaking about a subject matter that is well-defined relative to the arts. As Schachter et al. (1994) observed, there are fewer synonyms for scientific terms than there are for concepts in the humanities and social sciences. "There are, for example, no synonyms for *molecule*, or *atom* or *ion*. . . . In contrast, consider the alternatives for *love*, *beauty*, *group structure*, *prejudice*, or *style*" (p. 37). This vocabulary difference means that lecturers in the arts have many more possible words to choose among than do lecturers in the sciences. Hesitation pauses represent points at which the lecturers are choosing among the various possibilities afforded by their respective disciplines. Since science lecturers have fewer choices to make, they produce fewer hesitation pauses.

Hesitation pauses
Pauses in speech, often characterized by disfluencies such as *um* or *uh*.

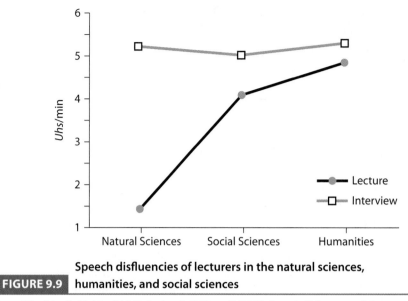

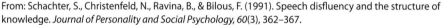

FIGURE 9.9   Speech disfluencies of lecturers in the natural sciences, humanities, and social sciences

From: Schachter, S., Christenfeld, N., Ravina, B., & Bilous, F. (1991). Speech disfluency and the structure of knowledge. *Journal of Personality and Social Psychology, 60*(3), 362–367.

Schachter et al. (1994) suggested that the differences they uncovered are not unique to lecturers, but can be found in speech generally. Someone who produces many speech disfluencies when talking about subjects in the arts or humanities is likely to produce many fewer when talking about a scientific topic.

Clark and Fox Tree (2002) suggested that *uh* and *um* should be seen as English words with specific uses in spontaneous speech. They hypothesized that *uh* is used to signal a short delay in speaking, while *um* is used to signal a longer delay. Clark and Fox Tree examined speech from a variety of sources, ranging from conversations to messages recorded on answering machines. The results were in line with their predictions. Pauses after *um* were longer than pauses after *uh*. The implication of this finding is that speakers are doing two things at the same time. On the one hand, they are planning what they are going to say. On the other, they are monitoring the planning process itself. When they detect an upcoming delay, they insert *uh* or *um*, depending on how long they think the delay will be. Of course, this monitoring process may not be fully or even partly conscious. The following example (Clark & Fox Tree, 2002, p. 84) comes from a study in which participants were asked questions that could be answered in one word (Smith & Clark, 1993).

Questioner: In which sport is the Stanley Cup awarded?
Participant: (Pauses for 1.4 s) Um (Pauses for 1.0 s) hockey.

Not only were pauses after *um* significantly longer than pauses after *uh*, but the length of time from the end of the question until the beginning of the answer was longer with *um* than with *uh*. Participants "were able to estimate how long it would take them to retrieve the answer even before they had retrieved it" (Clark & Fox Tree, 2002, p. 84).

All this leads to the conclusion that *uh* and *um* are not merely speech disfluencies, but also serve a communicative function. They notify the listener that the speaker has detected either a minor (*uh*) or a major (*um*) problem while attempting to produce the appropriate output.

The Social Context of Language

Although L.S. Vygotsky died in the first half of the twentieth century, his ideas have become more influential as time has gone by. One reason is that Vygotsky "provides the still needed provocation to find a way of understanding [the person] as a product of culture as well as a product of nature" (Bruner, 1986, p. 78). As a noted Vygotsky scholar (Wertsch, 1985, p. 231) remarked, "It may strike many as ironic that Vygotsky's ideas should appear so fruitful to people removed from him by time and space. . . . Instead of viewing this as paradoxical, however, it should perhaps be seen as a straightforward example of how human genius can transcend historical, social and cultural barriers."

Originally published in the 1930s, Vygotsky's book *Thought and Language* was not translated into English until 1962 (a newer translation has since become available). Vygotsky (1934/1986, p. 83) was particularly interested in the interaction between thought and speech. Of course, thought and speech can function independently of each other: we can think without speaking just as surely as we can speak without thinking! However, Vygotsky believed that children begin to think about what they say in their second year, and that at that point thought and speech begin to influence each other. Children begin to show a marked increase in curiosity about word meanings around that age (Wertsch, 1985, pp. 99ff.), and vocabulary grows quite rapidly (G.A. Miller, 1986, p. 174).

Vygotsky (1986, p. 226) reanalyzed what Piaget (1923/1948) had called **egocentric speech**. Piaget observed that young children's speech often does not take the listener's viewpoint into account. Egocentric speech declines as the child becomes socialized, and social speech develops in its place. Egocentric speech might be described as speech for oneself, whereas social speech might be described as speech for others (Werner & Kaplan, 1963, p. 318; Vygotsky, 1986, p. 225). Vygotsky argued that egocentric speech does not disappear but becomes **inner speech** (as opposed to external speech) and as such comes to play an important role in regulating thought

The structure and function of inner speech were summarized by Werner and Kaplan (1963, pp. 322ff.) as follows. Because inner speech is silent, it's a rapid medium for thought. It's also a condensed form of representation. Vygotsky (1986, pp. 236ff.) observed that inner speech typically consists of predicates: because it is addressed to oneself, there is no need to specify the subject. In this respect, inner speech resembles the speech that takes place between people who know each other well. Have you ever been part of a three-way conversation in which the other two people know each other intimately and you are barely acquainted with either of them? The two who know each other well can communicate with a single word or gesture, but you need to spell everything out.

In inner speech, one word can contain a great many meanings. Inner speech conveys the personal meaning of words rather than the conventional meaning. This makes inner speech a very rich medium. Sometimes the richness of inner speech can be observed, especially when speech occurs under unusual conditions. Vygotsky (1986) made this point by way of an entry from Dostoyevsky's *Diary of a Writer* for 1873. It told of

> a conversation of drunks that entirely consisted of one unprintable word . . . : "One Sunday night I happened to walk for some fifteen paces next to a group of six drunken young workmen, and I suddenly realized that all thoughts, feelings and even a whole chain of reasoning could be expressed by that one noun, which is moreover extremely short." (Vygotsky, 1986, p. 241)

Egocentric speech
Speech that does not take the listener's perspective into account.

Inner speech
Speech for oneself that regulates thought.

Dostoyevsky then went on to illustrate how the same word can be used to express contempt, doubt, anger, insight, delight, disapproval. (Can you imagine other contexts in which a word can take on many different senses?) In inner speech all these senses are available, allowing thought to proceed along multiple avenues (Werner & Kaplan, 1963, p. 322).

Although inner speech in adults is usually silent, it is occasionally externalized. Goffman (1978) suggested several situations in which people may produce audible speech that is ostensibly for themselves but is actually intended for others. For example, people coming in from the cold sometimes say *brr*. How often have you said *brr* when no one else was around? Isn't it your intention to implicitly communicate your inner state to others? How about saying *oops* when you make a mistake? Do you say *oops* if there's nobody there to hear you? Perhaps the most compelling of Goffman's examples involves people who are reading something in the presence of someone else and suddenly let out an exclamation— *amazing!* or *incredible!* or *unbelievable!* Their eyes may never leave the printed page, but they are still attempting to communicate with the other person. Instead of saying *I've just read something really interesting that I'd like to share with you*, they try to attract the other person's attention without explicitly asking for it. Try not responding the next time you're with someone who says *Interesting!* while reading in your presence; then see what happens.

One function of inner speech that Vygotsky (1986, p. 242) believed to be especially important was the planning of cognitive operations. He compared inner speech to a mental draft that we use to plan and organize our thinking. While we are engaged in a task, whether planning a meal or changing a car tire, inner speech directs us through the operations necessary to complete the task (Benjafield, 1969a; Luria, 1961; Wertsch & Stone, 1985). Switching between tasks is also under the control of inner speech. Emerson and Miyake (2003) found that when participants' inner speech was suppressed by forcing them to repeat the letters *a-b-c*, then their ability to switch between an addition and a subtraction task was impaired. Baddeley (2003, p. 199) suggested that one way inner speech may be articulated is by means of the phonological loop part of working memory (discussed in Chapter 6).

THE ZONE OF PROXIMAL DEVELOPMENT

Zone of proximal development
Defined by Vygotsky as "the distance between the actual developmental level as determined by independent problem-solving and the level of potential development as determined through problem-solving under adult guidance or in collaboration with more capable peers."

Vygotsky (1935/1978) defined the **zone of proximal development** as "the distance between the actual developmental level as determined by independent problem-solving and the level of potential development as determined through problem-solving under adult guidance or in collaboration with more capable peers" (p. 86). The concept of a zone of proximal development draws our attention to the social aspects of cognitive development. "What is in the zone of proximal development today will be the actual developmental level tomorrow—that is, what a child can do with assistance today she will be able to do herself tomorrow" (Vygotsky, 1978, p. 87). As Berk (1994) observed, there is a close relation between the zone of proximal development and the development of inner speech. "When a child discusses a challenging task with a mentor, that individual offers spoken directions and strategies. The child incorporates the language of those dialogues into his or her private speech and then uses it to guide independent efforts" (p. 80).

LITERACY

Literacy means a great many different things to different people (e.g., Heath, 1986, 1989). Before we try to settle on a definition of literacy, it may be useful to consider some work by one of the prominent contemporary literacy researchers, David Olson (e.g., Olson, 1977, 1985, 1986, 1996). We'll begin our consideration of literacy as Olson and Astington (1986b, p. 8) began theirs, by quoting a famous interview of an illiterate man from Uzbekistan by Luria (1976, p. 108). Luria was a student of Vygotsky, and among the most influential of Russian psychologists.

Luria began by presenting the man with a syllogism:

"In the Far North, where there is snow, all bears are white. Novaya Zemlya is in the Far North and there is always snow there. What colour are the bears there?"

The illiterate participant replied, "There are different sorts of bears."

Luria then repeated the syllogism.

The illiterate participant responded with this: "I don't know; I've seen a black bear, I've never seen any others. . . . Each locality has its own animals: if it's white, they will be white; if it's yellow, they will be yellow."

Luria then asked directly, "But what kind of bears are there in Novaya Zemlya?"

The illiterate participant said, "We always speak of what we see; we don't talk about what we haven't seen."

Finally, Luria asked, "But what do my words imply?" and repeated the syllogism.

The illiterate participant had the last word: "Well, it's like this: Our tsar isn't like yours, and yours isn't like ours. Your words can be answered only by someone who was there, and if a person wasn't there he can't say anything on the basis of your words."

The illiterate participant was not willing to draw any conclusions from what Luria said. As Olson and Astington noted, he wanted to talk about real bears, whereas Luria wanted to talk about hypothetical ones. In refusing to discuss the implications of Luria's words, he made it clear that, for him, words were nothing without the reality they referred to. By contrast, in talking about language without worrying about what it referred to (Cazden, 1976; Yaden & Templeton, 1986), Luria was demonstrating **metalinguistic awareness**. Sometimes metalinguistic awareness is described in terms of the ability to make language opaque (Cazden, 1976); that is, "difficult to see through." Usually the language we read or hear is transparent: we don't focus on the words themselves entirely literally, but rather see through the words to the meaning they convey.

> **Metalinguistic awareness**
> The ability to talk about language itself, without worrying about what it refers to.

Ordinarily we use language to talk about other things, but we can also use language to talk about language itself. When we do that, we are using *metalanguage*. For example, to use the word *simile* to refer to a comparison between two things using *like* or *as* is to employ metalanguage. Thus literacy can mean the ability to talk or write about text—to discuss a play by Shakespeare or to write an essay about Whitman's use of language, for example. It can also mean the ability to use metalanguage to discuss the performers in a play or the speech of a politician.

As Olson and Astington (1986b) pointed out, **literacy** in this sense is much broader than the simple ability to read and write. It means "being competent to participate in a certain form of discourse. . . . [Literacy means] competence in talking about talk, about questions, about answers, in a word, competence with a metalanguage" (p. 10). As such, literacy has sometimes been described as a kind of cognitive steroid, enabling us to think in a way that we could not otherwise. Some people experience deficiencies in this regard for a variety of reasons, as discussed in Box 9.2.

> **Literacy**
> The ability to read and write; sometimes extended to include the metalinguistic ability to talk or write about text.

COGNITION IN ACTION BOX 9.2
Deficits in Reading

Reading is an integral part of human communication. This has become even more true with the advent of blogs, text messaging, and text-based forums such as Twitter. What are the processes that underlie reading? A simple model of word reading is shown in Figure 9.10. According to this model, when a reader sees a printed word, he or she processes it as a complete unit and compares it to a mental dictionary (also known as a "lexicon") that contains all the words he or she knows. Once a match is made, the reader recognizes the word and is able to utter it.

Although this simple model seems reasonable, studies of people with **dyslexia**—individuals who have trouble reading printed text for reasons other than poor instruction or problems with seeing or speaking—suggest that it is not the whole story. Consider, for instance, people with a subtype of dyslexia known as **surface dyslexia**. They have trouble pronouncing irregular words such as *yacht* (see Castles & Coltheart, 1993). People with surface dyslexia cannot match a word to a mental dictionary to come up with the right pronunciation. Instead, they have to sound out the word letter-by-letter using a set of rules that convert graphemes (letter shapes) to phonemes (sounds); they then stitch the sounds together when uttering the word. This means that people with surface dyslexia use a different pathway when reading, one that involves translating letters to sounds (see Figure 9.11). Because surface dyslexics can string words together letter-by-letter, they are able to read non-words such as *blost*, even though they have never seen them before (see Castles & Coltheart, 1993).

Thus it is not always the case that reading involves access to a mental dictionary, as our simple model

suggests. Nevertheless, that model is supported by another subtype of dyslexia known as **phonological dyslexia**. People with this deficit cannot read letter-by-letter and can read only by comparing the letter strings to words in their mental dictionaries (see Castles & Coltheart, 1993). Phonological dyslexics can read irregular words by accessing their mental dictionary but are unable to properly read non-words that they have never seen before, since those non-words are not in their dictionaries.

Dyslexia
An impairment in the ability to read that is distinct from difficulties resulting from poor instruction or problems with seeing or speaking.

Surface dyslexia
A form of dyslexia affecting only the ability to recognize words as entire units; the ability to read words letter-by-letter remains intact.

Phonological dyslexia
A form of dyslexia affecting only the ability to read letter-by-letter; the ability to recognize words as entire units remains intact.

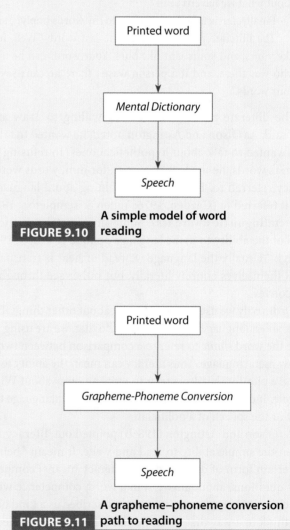

FIGURE 9.10 A simple model of word reading

FIGURE 9.11 A grapheme–phoneme conversion path to reading

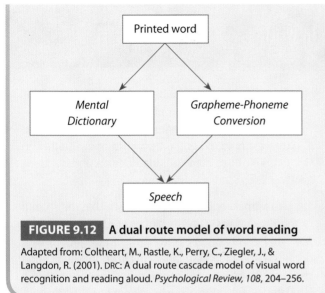

FIGURE 9.12 **A dual route model of word reading**

Adapted from: Coltheart, M., Rastle, K., Perry, C., Ziegler, J., & Langdon, R. (2001). DRC: A dual route cascade model of visual word recognition and reading aloud. *Psychological Review, 108*, 204–256.

The differences between surface and phonological dyslexia have led researchers to postulate a **dual route theory** of reading (Castles & Coltheart, 1993; Coltheart et al., 2001). Essentially, the theory suggests that we are able to read either by accessing a mental dictionary (the lexical route), as in Figure 9.10, or by assigning phonemes to graphemes (the non-lexical route) as in Figure 9.11. The combined model with the "dual routes" is shown in Figure 9.12.

Dual route theory
A theory that posits two separate pathways for reading, one for comparing words to a mental dictionary and another for converting letters to sounds.

Literacy makes it possible to make a distinction between the text (oral or written) and interpretations of it (Olson, 1986, p. 113). Someone who is literate is able to discuss different possible interpretations of a variety of texts: plays, poetry, and novels; biographies and histories; laws and regulations; and so on. As Olson pointed out, such interpretations are seen as subjective. That is, they are understood to be the outcomes of mental processes, rather than objectively given by the text. There is a certain kind of language that is used to describe this kind of mental process. This language includes words such as *interpret* and *infer* (Olson, 1986, p. 120). Such words are a part of the language of literacy: they are used for talking about text (Olson & Astington, 1986b, p. 12).

An implication of the preceding discussion is that our language changes when we become literate. It's likely that a literate person has learned a stock of words to use when talking about text. Not surprisingly, our ability to use the language of literacy improves with age, and we may not master that language until we have had considerable practice with metalinguistic words (Olson & Astington, 1986a, p. 191).

Most of the words people use to talk about talking—words like *assert*, *contradict*, and *remark*—came into the English language relatively late in its history. Olson and Astington (1986a, 1986b) reported that these words typically emerged during or after the sixteenth century. By contrast, words such as *know* and *think*, which are used to describe mental states but are not used to talk about text, are usually much older. Thus the emergence of literacy coincided with the use of a special language designed to refer to language itself.

THE CONSEQUENCES OF PRINT EXPOSURE

Stanovich and Cunningham (1992) pointed out that literacy is not an all-or-nothing state of affairs. Even people who are literate differ widely in their exposure to printed materials and in the degree to which they develop metalanguages. It's possible that variation may be correlated with cognitive skills such as vocabulary and verbal fluency. To assess the strength of the relationship between print exposure and cognitive skills, Stanovich and Cunningham studied 300 undergraduate students from American state universities.

THINK TWICE BOX 9.3 — An Exercise in Writing

Before you read the rest of this box, take a few minutes to write a paragraph about why you decided to go to university and what you plan to do after you graduate. Then ask several friends to do the same.

Now that you and your friends have written your paragraphs, consider the following findings reported by David Snowdon in his fascinating book *Aging with Grace: What the Nun Study Teaches Us About Leading Longer, Healthier and More Meaningful Lives* (2001). In it Snowdon describes how 678 elderly nuns opened their lives and (after death) their brains to science for what is now known as "the Nun Study." Snowdon and his colleagues were interested in understanding what sorts of factors, measured early in life, could predict the onset of cognitive decline (i.e., dementia) later in life. Among the best predictors they found were the short autobiographical essays that all the nuns had written just before entering the convent. Snowdon and his colleagues analyzed these essays and scored them on their "**idea density**"—a measure based on the number of distinct ideas present in a sentence or paragraph.

Idea density
The number of distinct ideas present in a sentence or paragraph.

Here are two examples of sentences written approximately 60 years earlier by two nuns who joined the study in the early 1990s (Snowdon, 2001, p. 110):

I was born in Eau Claire, Wis., on May 24, 1913 and was baptized in St. James Church –Sister Helen.

It was about a half hour before midnight between February twenty-eighth and twenty-ninth of the leap year nineteen-hundred-twelve when I began to live and to die as the third child of my mother, whose maiden name is Hilda Hoffman, and my father, Otto Schmitt –Sister Emma.

No formal coding is required to see that the second of these examples is much higher in idea density than the first. By 1992 Sister Helen had been diagnosed with dementia. The initial assessment of her cognitive function showed it to be severely impaired, and when she died, a year later, examination of her brain confirmed the diagnosis of Alzheimer's disease. On the same test Sister Emma received the maximum score, and she showed no sign of decline a year later.

In short, the idea density of the autobiographies they wrote as young women predicted which of the nuns would show evidence of dementia in their eighties: "Somehow, a one-page writing sample could, fifty-eight years after pen was put to paper, strongly predict who would have cognitive problems" (Snowden, 2001, p. 112).

Now take a look at the paragraphs you and your friends wrote. Are some more densely packed with ideas than others? It could be that whoever wrote the paragraph with the highest idea density will be least likely to develop dementia later in life.

These students were given several tests, including a test of general intelligence as well as tests of cognitive skills such as vocabulary, verbal fluency, spelling, and knowledge of history and literature. In addition, the students' exposure to print was assessed by several measures, including an author recognition test (ART) and a magazine recognition test (MRT). The ART asked students to indicate whether or not they were familiar with a list of book authors, while the MRT did the same for a list of magazines. Stanovich and Cunningham found that scores on the ART and MRT predicted scores on the cognitive skills measures even after general intelligence had been taken into account.

These results suggest that print exposure makes an independent contribution to cognitive skills, over and above general intelligence. It's noteworthy that the ART was a particularly powerful predictor of cognitive skills. The ART is an indirect measure of the degree to which a person reads books. "Relative to magazine reading, exposure to books appears to be more related to positive verbal outcomes. . . . Perhaps there are differences in depth of processing typically associated with different types of reading material, with magazines being more likely to elicit shallow processing" (p. 63).

Language, Cognition, and Culture

LINGUISTIC RELATIVITY

In addition to being one of the most influential linguists of the twentieth century, Benjamin Lee Whorf (1956, p. 135) worked for a fire insurance company. He was responsible for investigating the causes of many fires and explosions, and in the course of his work it became clear to him that many fires were the result of the way people perceived a situation. Moreover, people's perception of that situation was determined by the way they described it. That is, the words they used to label objects shaped their behaviour in relation to those objects. Here is one of Whorf's examples:

> People will exercise great caution around a set of containers labelled "gasoline drums." Because they know that gasoline is flammable, they will be careful about smoking in the vicinity. However, if the containers are labelled "empty gasoline drums," then people will be less cautious. This is because the word *empty* not only suggests that there is no gasoline, but also that the containers are inert and not dangerous. In fact, as Whorf pointed out, empty gasoline drums are very dangerous because they contain gasoline vapour and are extremely flammable. However, the way the drums are labelled may make people perceive them as safe when they are not.

Notice the relation between words and the interpretation of those words that this example brings out. The word *empty* determines that a dangerous situation will be perceived as safe. Whorf gave many other examples of this sort, demonstrating that the way we judge a situation is determined by the words we use to describe it. These examples show how a particular language conditions the way we analyze a situation. Suppose we spoke another language with a different way of describing the very same situation. Might not the way we perceive that situation be different because the language used to describe it leads us to perceive it differently? This kind of question led to the formulation of what is often called the **Sapir–Whorf hypothesis**. Sapir was a linguist with whom Whorf studied, and whose ideas greatly influenced him. Whorf began one of his papers by quoting Sapir (1949) on the relationship between language and experience. This quotation nicely gives the flavour of the Sapir–Whorf hypothesis:

> Human beings do not live in the objective world alone, nor alone in the world of social activity as ordinarily understood, but are very much at the mercy of the particular language which has become the medium of expression for their society. It is quite an illusion to imagine that one adjusts to reality essentially without the use of language and that language is merely an incidental means of solving specific problems of communication or reflection. The fact of the matter is that the "real world" is to a large extent unconsciously built up on the language habits of the group. . . . We see and hear and otherwise experience very largely as we do because the language habits of our community predispose certain choices of interpretation. (p. 162)

Sapir–Whorf hypothesis
The hypothesis that two languages may be so different from one another as to make their native speakers' experience of the world qualitatively different.

The Sapir–Whorf hypothesis is not limited to the way individual words shape our experience of the world. The hypothesis is much more general. Whorf (1956) argued that different languages have different "grammatical categories, such as plurality, gender, and similar classifications (animate, inanimate, etc.), tenses, voices and other verb forms, classifications of the type of parts of speech" (p. 137), which combine to create a particular system of categories that organizes our experience of the world. Whorf's view leads to **linguistic relativity**: the notion that two languages may be so different from each other as to make their native speakers' experience of the world quite different from each other (e.g., Black, 1962, p. 244). Whorf (1956) put it this way: "The linguistic relativity principle . . . means, in informal terms, that users of markedly different grammars are . . . not equivalent as observers but must arrive at somewhat different views of the world" (p. 221).

Linguistic relativity
The notion that two languages may be so different from each other as to make their native speakers' experience of the world quite different from each other.

Whorf grouped together European languages, such as English, French, and German, as standard average European (SAE) languages. He contrasted SAE languages with Amerindian languages such as Hopi, which he believed to have a fundamentally different structure. Here is an example of the sort of basic difference between these languages that Whorf (1956, p. 141) thought was important. In SAE we have a pattern of description that follows the formula *form + substance*. We have names for substances such as *water*, *coffee*, and *meat*. These are called mass nouns. In our system, mass nouns denote formless substances. The word *bread*, for example, does not by itself convey anything about the size or shape of the bread. Bread is a substance existing independently of any particular case. Mass nouns refer to unbounded, or limitless, categories. When we describe a particular case using a mass noun, we must also include a description of its limits. Thus we say *a loaf of bread*, or *a cup of coffee*, or *a glass of water*. We describe a form (e.g., *a glass of*) plus a substance (e.g., *water*). This way of describing things corresponds to the way we think about the world. We believe that the world consists of formless substances that are given a specific form on particular occasions. After describing this pattern of thought, which he said is common to speakers of SAE, Whorf went on to claim that Hopi speakers experience the world differently. In Hopi, all nouns refer to particular occurrences: "'water' means one certain mass or quantity of water, not what we call the substance water" (Whorf, 1956, p. 141). The Hopi speaker experiences the world in terms of specific events. This goes along with a different conception of time. Time is not thought of as existing independent of specific occurrences. Instead of talking about "this summer"—in which the current season, or the one just passed, is to the unbounded category "summer" what "a loaf of" is to "bread"—the Hopi talk only about specific occasions: "summer now" or "summer recently" (Whorf, 1956, p. 143).

Whorf famously cites the number of words that Inuit use for snow. The Inuit, many of whom live in Nunavut, used to be called "Eskimos" but are now called by their own name for themselves: Inuit means "the people" in their language, Inuktitut. Whorf claimed that the Inuit have many different words for *snow*, indicating that their perception of snow is more finely differentiated than ours. This example of the "Whorfian hypothesis" is very widely accepted. According to a document from Canada's Department of Indian and Northern Affairs (2000), there are at least 14 words for snow in Inuktitut, ranging from *apigiannagaut* ("the first snowfall of autumn") to *qiqumaaq* ("snow whose surface has frozen after a light spring thaw"), which would seem to support the Whorfian hypothesis.

Drawing on research by Martin (1986), Pullum (1991) attempted to debunk the more-words-for-snow hypothesis. He approached this project in two ways. First he looked carefully at what some researchers have claimed are Inuit words for snow. For example, *igluksaq* is supposed to be "snow for igloo-making." However, it is actually formed from *iglu* (meaning "house"), and *ksaq* (meaning "material for"). Thus Pullum argued that *igluksaq* really means "house-building material," and "would probably include plywood, nails, perhaps bricks or roofing tiles" (Pullum, 1991, p. 169). However, "would probably" sounds more like a hypothesis than a rigorously researched fact. Furthermore, Pullum's claim assumes adaptation to the post-contact era: if the term was originally part of the pre-contact Inuktitut lexicon, it could not have referred to anything but snow (*ksaq*) suitable for the building of the *iglu*. Second, Pullum pointed out that there are many more English words used to refer to snow than Whorf may have noticed; consider *slush, sleet, blizzard, hardpack, powder, flurry, dusting*, and so on. Pullum claims that the Inuit may perceive many different kinds of snow, but that it's probably not because they have more words for it. Instead he suggests that if the Inuit do indeed perceive more varieties of snow, it's because of their expertise with snow. In this respect they are like other kinds of specialists: "Horse breeders have various names for breeds, sizes, and ages of horses; botanists have names for leaf shapes; interior decorators have names for shades of mauve; printers have many different names for different fonts" and so on (Pullum, 1991, p. 165). The names are the result of their expertise and are not what determines their expertise. In fact, though, while knowledge of snow creates language about snow, that language in turn preserves and even enhances the knowledge of it within a culture or society.

Despite the controversial nature of the Whorfian hypothesis, a milder version of it has attracted favourable attention from some psychologists. For example, Hunt and Agnoli (1991) reviewed evidence suggesting that differences between languages may have effects on cognitive processes that are at least as important as the individual differences in cognitive processes found within a particular language community. That is, not only are there differences in cognitive processes between individuals who speak the same language, but there are equally large differences in cognitive processes between people who speak different languages. For example, there are cases in which two different languages "cause speakers . . . to structure the same experience in different ways" (p. 379). One example of this possibility concerns **polysemy**. A polysemous word has more than one meaning. English words are significantly more polysemous than Italian words. Hunt and Agnoli (1991) pointed out that the English sentence "I went out to buy the pot" is ambiguous because we don't "know whether the speaker spends leisure time in gardening or recreational pharmacology" (p. 382). But the corresponding Italian sentence (*"Uscii a comprare il vaso"*) is not ambiguous. Consequently, it's likely that a native English speaker will need more time to disambiguate such a sentence than a native Italian speaker would. On the basis of examples such as this, Hunt and Agnoli concluded that differences between languages can affect performance, even if it is the case that every sentence in any one language can be translated into a sentence in any other language.

Other lines of investigation are reviving a stronger form of the hypothesis of linguistic relativity (Bloom & Keil, 2001, pp. 356–358). It is to a consideration of these that we now turn.

Polysemy
The existence of multiple meanings for one word.

COLOUR WORDS

Another focus for the study of the relationships between language, thought, and culture has been the relation between colour perception and colour naming (Rosch, 1988, pp. 374ff.). On the one hand, colour names provide distinctive categories such as *red* and *green*. On the other hand, the physical stimulus for colour is continuous: different colours, or *hues*, are elicited by different wavelengths of light. The term *visible spectrum* refers to those wavelengths of light that we can see. Within the visible spectrum, *blue* is elicited by relatively short wavelengths, whereas *red* is elicited by relatively long wavelengths (Ratliff, 1976, p. 313). Do colour names refer to the same parts of the visible spectrum regardless of culture, so that the same wavelength corresponds to *blue* for everyone? Or do different cultures carve up the visible spectrum differently, so that the wavelength for *blue* in one culture is not the same as the wavelength for *blue* in another? Perhaps what we call *blue* strikes people from another culture as more *bluish green* because in their colour-naming system a true blue is located at a different place on the visible spectrum (R. Brown, 1968, p. 238).

A very influential study of the importance of colour names was that of R. Brown and Lenneberg (1956; R. Brown, 1968, pp. 239ff.). They had a group of judges select 24 colours that were representative of the entire range of colours. Of the 24 colours, eight were judged to be "ideal" examples of *red*, *green*, *yellow*, *blue*, *orange*, *purple*, *brown*, and *pink*. With these as the central colours, the others that were not judged to be such good exemplars became the *peripheral* members of their respective colour categories. Brown and Lenneberg then asked their participants, all of whom spoke English as their native language, to name the 24 different colours. There were several differences between responses to the central and peripheral colours. For example, the central colours were named more rapidly. Moreover, when participants were shown an assortment of colours they had seen earlier and colours they had not been exposed to, they recognized the central colours as ones they had seen before. This finding, that colours that can be easily named are also more easily remembered, appeared to be quite reliable (Rosch, 1988, p. 376).

It would be interesting to know whether a culture with different colour names also remembers colours differently. Heider [Eleanor Rosch] and Olivier (1972) studied the Dani, an Indonesian New Guinea people who appeared to have only two colour names. Heider and Olivier reported that memory for colours was similar for both the Dani and the American participants. Having a colour name available in the language did not seem to be a prerequisite for remembering the colour. Moreover, the Dani appeared to remember central colours better than peripheral ones, just as the American participants did. These results implied that colours were not perceived as arbitrary, but that the structure of colour perceptually was similar for everyone. It's possible that central, or focal, colours are more perceptually salient than peripheral colours, and that colour names refer to those aspects of the spectrum that are most readily noticed. Heider and Olivier's findings complemented the results of cross-cultural research conducted by Berlin and Kay (1969), whose remarkable theory we will now discuss.

Berlin and Kay argued that there are 11 **basic colour terms**, and that there appears to be an invariant sequence regulating the emergence of these colour terms in any language. This sequence is diagrammed below and can be described as follows. Although different languages may have different numbers of colour words, there is a particular order in which colour terms emerge in the history of a given language. If a

Basic colour terms hypothesis (Berlin–Kay order)
The hypothesis that there is an invariant sequence regulating the emergence of colour terms in any language.

language has only two colour terms, then those words will be *black* and *white*; those with only three colour terms have words for *black*, *white*, and *red*; those with five colour words have *black*, *white*, *red*, *green*, and *yellow*; and so on.

black	red	green	blue	brown	purple
white		yellow			pink
					orange
					grey

This invariance was claimed to be a consequence of the nature of the visual system (Kay & McDaniel, 1978; Ratliff, 1976; Rosch, 1988). The model of colour perception that was used to explain the Berlin–Kay order derives from Hering (1878/1961). Hering argued that red, green, blue, and yellow are *primary colours*, meaning that they are not experienced as blends of other colours. Hering's theory also attempted to capture the distinction between *achromatic* and *chromatic* colours. Achromatic colours cover the range between black through grey to white, whereas chromatic colours such as red, blue, green, and yellow have hue. Hering invented the **opponent process theory of colour vision** (Hurvich & Jameson, 1957). He imagined that the process of colour vision was based on three pairs of antagonistic colours: yellow–blue, red–green, and white–black, the last being responsible for achromatic colours. In the absence of stimulation, all pairs give rise to the experience of grey, which represents a state of balance between opponent processes. Light acts on each pair so as to yield one of its component colours and inhibit the other. Thus we cannot experience a "reddish-green" because red and green form an antagonistic pair. However, one can experience a "greenish-yellow" or a "reddish-blue," because the colours they are composed of can both be activated at the same time (Hurvich & Jameson, 1957, p. 400). A theory similar to Hering's appears to ground the Berlin–Kay order in the visual system. Perhaps *black*, *white*, *red*, *green*, *yellow*, and *blue* refer not only to basic colours, but also to basic visual processes. If that is the case, these colours will be the first ones that a language will name. Other colour terms, such as *pink*, are blends of primary visual experiences, and consequently less salient and less likely to be named.

Unfortunately, theories of the Hering type do not appear to be standing up to the test of time. Without denying that opponent process cells exist, Saunders and van Brakel, (1997, p. 178) argue that the evidence still does not support the hypothesis for "exactly two pairs of opponent hues nor three pairs of opponent colours." Moreover, the visual system does not appear to process colour separately from other forms of visual information. "There is strong evidence that between retina and cortex, processing of wavelength is intricately mixed with luminosity, form, texture, movement response, and other environmental change" (Saunders & van Brakel, 1997, p. 177). Davidoff (2001, p. 382) concluded that "there is no evidence that neurons respond selectively to any of the four basic colours." In short, there would not appear to be a strong case for the existence of an isomorphism between the Berlin–Kay series and the physiology of the visual system.

Furthermore, there now appears to be some doubt about the universality of the Berlin–Kay series itself. Recall that, in their studies of the Dani, Heider [Eleanor Rosch] and Olivier (1972) found that the lack of a colour name in their language did not seem to prevent the Dani from remembering the colour. In an attempt to replicate the Heider and Olivier result, Roberson, Davies, and Davidoff (2000) studied the

Opponent process theory of colour vision
The hypothesis that colour vision is based on three pairs of antagonistic processes.

Berinmo, another stone-age tribe from Papua New Guinea. The Berinmo language contains five colour terms:

- *wapa*: *white and pale colours*; also means "European person"
- *kel*: *black*; also means "dirty"
- *mehl*: *red*
- *wor*: spans *yellow/orange/brown/khaki*
- *nol*: spans *green/blue/purple*; also means "live"

The participants were 22 Berinmo-speakers and a matched British sample. They all were asked to name 40 different colour chips. They all took a memory task in which they were shown a colour chip for five seconds, then were asked to pick it out of an array of 40 colour chips. The results did not replicate Heider and Olivier's findings. Rather, the pattern of Berinmo colour memory was different from that of the English-speakers, and was in fact related to Berinmo colour names. These results did not support the hypothesis that "the colour space is universally similar and independent of language" (p. 377).

Davidoff, Davies, and Roberson (1999) took advantage of the fact that the Berinmo language does not distinguish between *blue* and *green*, but does make a distinction that is not made in English. Thus *nol* spans *green/blue/purple* and is categorically different from *wor*, which spans *yellow/orange/brown/khaki*. Participants were shown and then asked to remember a colour for 30 seconds. They were then shown a pair of colours and asked to identify the one they had been shown previously. Suppose the participants were first shown a blue colour and then tested with a blue/green pair. This should have been more difficult for the Berinmo than for the English participants, because blue and green are in the same language category for the former but in different categories for the latter. In general, pairs of colours within a category should be more difficult to choose between than pairs of colours from two different categories. This turned out to be true. English participants made relatively more errors when they had to choose between *nol* and *wor* colours, but the Berinmo made relatively more errors when they had to choose between *blue* and *green* colours. What is a qualitative distinction for one culture is a different shade for the other.

In a study that examined the acquisition of colour names in two different languages, Roberson, Davidoff, Davies, and Shapiro (2004) provided more evidence for the linguistic relativity hypothesis. They studied the Himba, "a semi-nomadic cattle-herding tribe in northern Namibia" (p. 555). The Himba have five basic colour terms:

- *serandu*: spans *red*, *orange*, and *pink*
- *dumbu*: spans *beige*, *yellow*, and *light green*
- *zoozu*: spans all dark colours and *black*
- *vapa*: spans all light colours and *white*
- *burou*: spans *green*, *blue*, and *purple*

The acquisition of colour terms was studied for both English and Himba. The participants were children, and they were studied for three years beginning at three or four years of age. One finding was that the English children did not necessarily acquire colour words in the Berlin–Kay order. In both languages, the order in which colour terms were acquired varied quite widely. As the children, both Himba and English, acquired colour terms, the pattern of their memory for colours changed and they began showing superior performance for colours that are focal in their language. The conclusion was that colour categories are not the outcome of an innate unfolding of the visual system, but are acquired within a particular culture.

At least as far as colour words are concerned, the evidence is currently tilting towards the linguistic relativity hypothesis. However, Kay and Regier (2003) still maintained that there are "genuine universal tendencies in colour naming" (p. 9085). They acknowledged considerable variability in colour words between languages. However, based on survey data from more than 100 unwritten languages, they concluded that there are "universally privileged points . . . reflected in the basic colour terms of English" (p. 9089). Only time will tell how this long-standing controversy will play out. Regier and Kay (2004, p. 290) suggested that the "universalist–relativist" dichotomy has outlived its usefulness and that "the field might benefit from its abandonment." However, precisely what might replace it remains unclear.

(a)

LANGUAGE AND SPATIAL FRAMES OF REFERENCE

The linguistic relativity hypothesis is still alive and well in the study of spatial frames of reference. The studies we reviewed in Chapter 7 suggested that we imagine ourselves as upright in a spatial framework that can be described by terms such as *above–below*, *ahead–behind*, and *left–right* (Tversky, 2003). But it's important to note that the *we* in the preceding sentence refers to speakers of English, who are often the only group represented by the participants in psychological studies. What about speakers of other languages? At least three spatial frames of reference can be found in different languages (Levinson, 1996).

The differences between the three can be seen in Figure 9.13a, which is based on an example from Levinson, Kita, Haun, and Rasch (2002, p. 159). If we said that *the man is at the chair's back* we would be using an **intrinsic frame of reference**, based on the relations between the objects being described. But we could also say that *the man is to the right of the chair*. In that case we would be using a **relative frame of reference**, so-called because the man is to the right of the chair *relative to* our position as observers. The relative frame of reference is the one most familiar to speakers of English. Finally, we could say that *the man is to the north of the chair*. In this case the frame of reference is said to be **absolute**, because the relations between the objects are described in terms of an invariant set of coordinates. You might find this last example puzzling; isn't the man standing to the *east* of the chair? In fact, we don't know: we are simply accustomed to thinking of maps, which are typically drawn with north at the top and east on the right *relative to* the observer. In an absolute frame of reference the man could be standing to the north of the chair.

Now imagine yourself walking around behind the picture and looking at it from the other side. What you would see is shown in Figure 9.13b. Describe the relations between the man and the chair from within each frame of reference. The man is still at the chair's *back* and to the *north* of the chair. However, he is now to the *left* of the chair. This illustrates how a change in the observer's position affects the orientation of objects in the relative frame of reference, but leaves the other frames of reference unchanged.

Suppose there were languages that described spatial relations in an intrinsic or absolute frame of reference but not in a relative frame of reference. In fact, there are such languages. For example, Tzeltal (a Mayan language) uses the word *uphill* to

(b)

The man is at the chair's back

FIGURE 9.13

Intrinsic frame of reference
Spatial relations are based solely on the relations between the objects being described.

Relative frame of reference
Spatial relations are described relative to an observer's viewpoint.

Absolute frame of reference
Spatial relations are described in terms of an invariant set of coordinates.

mean approximately *south*, and the word *downhill* to mean approximately *north*. In this language you might say the equivalent of *I left my glasses to the north of the telephone* (Majid, Bowerman, Kita, Haun, & Levinson, 2004, p. 109). Does this different way of speaking correspond to a different way of representing space? In a series of experiments, Levinson and his colleagues (e.g., Levinson, Kita, Haun, & Rasch, 2002; Pederson, Danziger, Wilkins, Levinson, Kita, & Senft, 1998) have demonstrated the effect of language on spatial representation. One example is given in Figure 9.14. Participants are shown a toy figure being moved by the experimenter along the path represented on the viewing table. After a delay of 30 seconds, the participant is then rotated 180° and shown a maze on the testing table. The participant's task is to "choose the path that the toy person . . . followed" (Majid, Bowerman, Kita, Haun, & Levinson, 2004, p. 110). If the participants spoke Tzeltal, they tended to choose a path based on an absolute frame of reference. However, if the participants were Dutch, they overwhelmingly chose a path based on a relative frame of reference. The Dutch language, like English, specializes in a relative linguistic framework. Thus each group's responses were consistent with their habitual frame of reference. The conclusion, based on this and similar experiments, was that the particular language we speak imposes a way of representing space that we must use in order to be able to communicate with others in our linguistic community.

Without endorsing its conclusions, Bloom and Keil (2001, p. 358) considered Levinson's line of research to be "one of the most promising attempts to explore the relationship between the linguistic difference and cognitive differences." Some investigators are prepared to conclude that "Whorf's original idea about how language shapes categories might be right after all" (Yoshida & Smith, 2005). However, there are still those who claim that spatial frames of reference are universal. For example, Gallistel

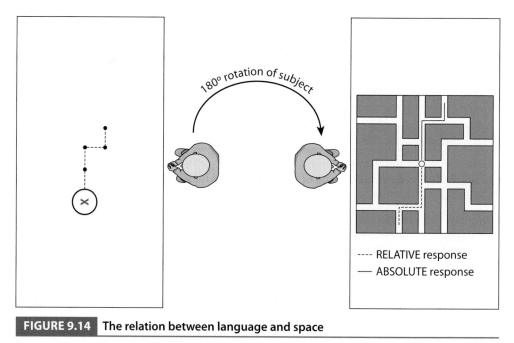

FIGURE 9.14   The relation between language and space

From: Levinson, S.C., Kita, S., Haun, D.B.M., & Rasch, B.H. (2002). Returning the tables: Language affects spatial reasoning. *Cognition, 84*, p. 165. Copyright 2002. Reprinted by permission of Elsevier.

(2002a, 2002b) argued that the brain can represent a number of different spatial frameworks, and that these are available for use quite independent of the language spoken. In a similar vein, Clark (2004) suggested that languages do not obliterate conceptual frameworks that are inconsistent with them. Although different languages highlight certain categories rather than others, we are not fated to think only in the ways that our language provides.

We do not yet know the final verdict on the linguistic relativity hypothesis. Nevertheless, as Barbara Malt has noted, its revival reflects "the kind of cross-cultural work . . . [which] psychologists have traditionally left to linguists and anthropologists." A cognitive psychologist who studies language and thought, Malt went on to express the "hope that [these studies] will inspire more cognitive and developmental psychologists to go into the field and pursue these kinds of comparisons, which are the only way to really find out which aspects of perception and cognition are universal and which are culture and language specific" (Malt, as quoted in Adelson, 2005, p. 26).

Summary

In this chapter we have learned how cognitive psychologists think about language. From the earliest research in the field to more recent work, a relationship between the structure of our experience and the structure of language has been observed. Furthermore, theories of language structure are intimately linked to theories of language acquisition and evolution.

One influential figure in the psychology of language is Noam Chomsky. His concepts of universal grammar, deep structures, and surface structures suggest that a process for learning language is *innate* or present from birth (i.e., the innate hypothesis). The alternative theory, championed by B.F. Skinner, suggests that we learn language as children by making use of informative feedback on our utterances. While their veracity remains undetermined, these theories have inspired researchers to demonstrate the surprising richness of the linguistic environment in which children can learn language.

Other approaches examine the impact of different contexts on aspects of language. For example, the context in which you receive and understand written/spoken language influences specific modes of communication and comprehension (e.g., code and inferential models, figures of speech). More personal contexts include those in which thought appears to be independent of speech, as with inner speech (i.e., speech for oneself) or literacy (i.e., the influence of language on itself). Finally, cultural contexts provide evidence that some aspects of cognition and perception may not be universal, but rather culture-specific. As such, the different languages we learn and the different words we use may shape how we actually experience and perceive the world (linguistic relativity).

Case Study Wrap-Up

We opened this chapter with a look at the McGuffey's series of readers. Clearly, the English that young students were expected to learn 140 years ago was much more complex and difficult than the English that is taught today. Does the simplification of the language that students are exposed to have an impact on adult literacy and general cognitive ability?

That is a tough question to answer. However, several pieces of evidence reviewed in this chapter are relevant to it. For instance, research by Huttenlocher et al. (2002) showed that students' language comprehension ability is influenced by the complexity of their teachers' speech. We also saw that the way parents correct their children's speech affects their speech production (Chouinard & Clark, 2003), and noted that increased exposure to printed language (i.e., reading more) might improve overall intelligence (Stanovich & Cunningham, 1992). Finally, the Nun Study reported by Snowdon (Box 9.3) suggests a strong link between *idea density* early in life and cognitive health in later years.

Together, these findings suggest that (1) language abilities depend on how language is learned early in life, and (2) early language abilities may predict cognitive abilities (and even intelligence) later in life. In the light of these findings, you might want to pick up *McGuffey's Reader* and get to work! You might also want to learn another language: it seems that regular use of two or more languages may stave off the onset of dementia symptoms by roughly four years (see Bialystok, Craik, & Freedman, 2007).

? In the Know: Review Questions

1. Outline the development of Chomsky's various approaches to language, including his views on the evolution of language.

2. Review evidence bearing on the innateness hypothesis, paying particular attention to the "poverty of the stimulus" argument.

3. Discuss the process of communication and comprehension, using figurative language to illustrate the process.

4. Discuss evidence for and against the linguistic relativity hypothesis. Which side of the debate are you on? Why?

Key Concepts

absolute frame of reference	deep and surface structure
articulation	diacritical marks
basic colour terms (Berlin–Kay order)	dual route theory
code model and inferential model of communication	dyslexia
competence and performance	egocentric speech (Piaget)
concealing function	figurative language
conversational maxims	given–new contract
co-operative principle (Grice)	grammatical transformations
	hesitation pauses

idea density
inferential model of communication
innateness hypothesis
inner speech (Vygotsky)
intrinsic frame of reference
language
language acquisition device (LAD) and
   universal grammar
linguistic relativity
literacy
metalinguistic awareness
minimalism
mirror neurons
opponent process theory of colour vision
   (Hering)
parameter setting

parental reformulations
phonological dyslexia
phrase structure rules
polysemy
"poverty of the stimulus" argument
pretense theory of irony
recursion
relative frame of reference
Sapir–Whorf hypothesis
speech
surface dyslexia
syntactic development
tree diagrams
zone of proximal development
   (Vygotsky)

Links to Other Chapters

frames of reference
Chapter 7 (egocentric frame of reference)

innateness hypothesis
Chapter 4 (domain-specific modules)
Chapter 6 (evolution of memory systems)
Chapter 8 (implicit and explicit learning)
Chapter 12 (musical intelligence)
Chapter 13 (emotion and memory)

language acquisition device
Chapter 12 (evolution of *g*)

recursion
Chapter 11 (paradoxes, reasoning, and
   recursion)

Further Reading

D. Bickerton advanced an influential version of the hypothesis that a specific innate faculty contains a model of language. Much of his work is based on fascinating studies of pidgin and creole languages. (A pidgin is a rudimentary language that develops among people who need to communicate but don't share a common language; a creole is a more formal and structured language that develops from a pidgin when children begin to acquire it as their native language.) See Bickerton, D. (1984); Bickerton, D.J. (1988); and Bickerton, D. (2000).

Judgments of grammaticality often rest on the intuitions of native speakers of the language—a rather elusive criterion. Carroll, Bever, and Pollack (1981) spell out just how problematic those intuitions can be.

For a study of individual differences in the use of irony see Ivanko, Pexman, and Olineck (2004).

Eskritt, Lee, and Donald (2001) bring out an intriguing aspect of literacy. More effects of language on categorization are discussed in Sera, Elieff, Forbes, Burch, Rodríguez, and Dubois (2002).

Bickerton, D. (1984). The language bioprogram hypothesis. *Behavioral and Brain Sciences, 7,* 173–221.

Bickerton, D.J. (1988). A two-stage model of the human language faculty. In S. Straus (Ed.), *Ontogeny, phylogeny and historical development* (pp. 86–105). Norwood, NJ: Ablex.

Bickerton, D. (2000). Resolving discontinuity: A minimalist distinction between human and non-human minds. *American Zoologist, 40,* 862–873.

Carroll, J.M., Bever, T.G., & Pollack, C.R. (1981). The non-uniqueness of linguistic intuitions. *Language, 57,* 368–383.

Eskritt, M., Lee, K., & Donald, M. (2001). The influence of symbolic literacy on memory. *Canadian Journal of Psychology, 55,* 39–50.

Ivanko, S., Pexman, P.M., & Olineck, K.M. (2004). How sarcastic are you? *Journal of Language and Social Psychology, 23,* 244–271.

Sera, M.D., Elieff, C., Forbes, J., Burch, M.C., Rodríguez, W., & Dubois, D.P. (2002). When language affects cognition and when it does not: An analysis of grammatical gender and classification. *Journal of Experimental Psychology: General, 131,* 377–397.

CHAPTER 10

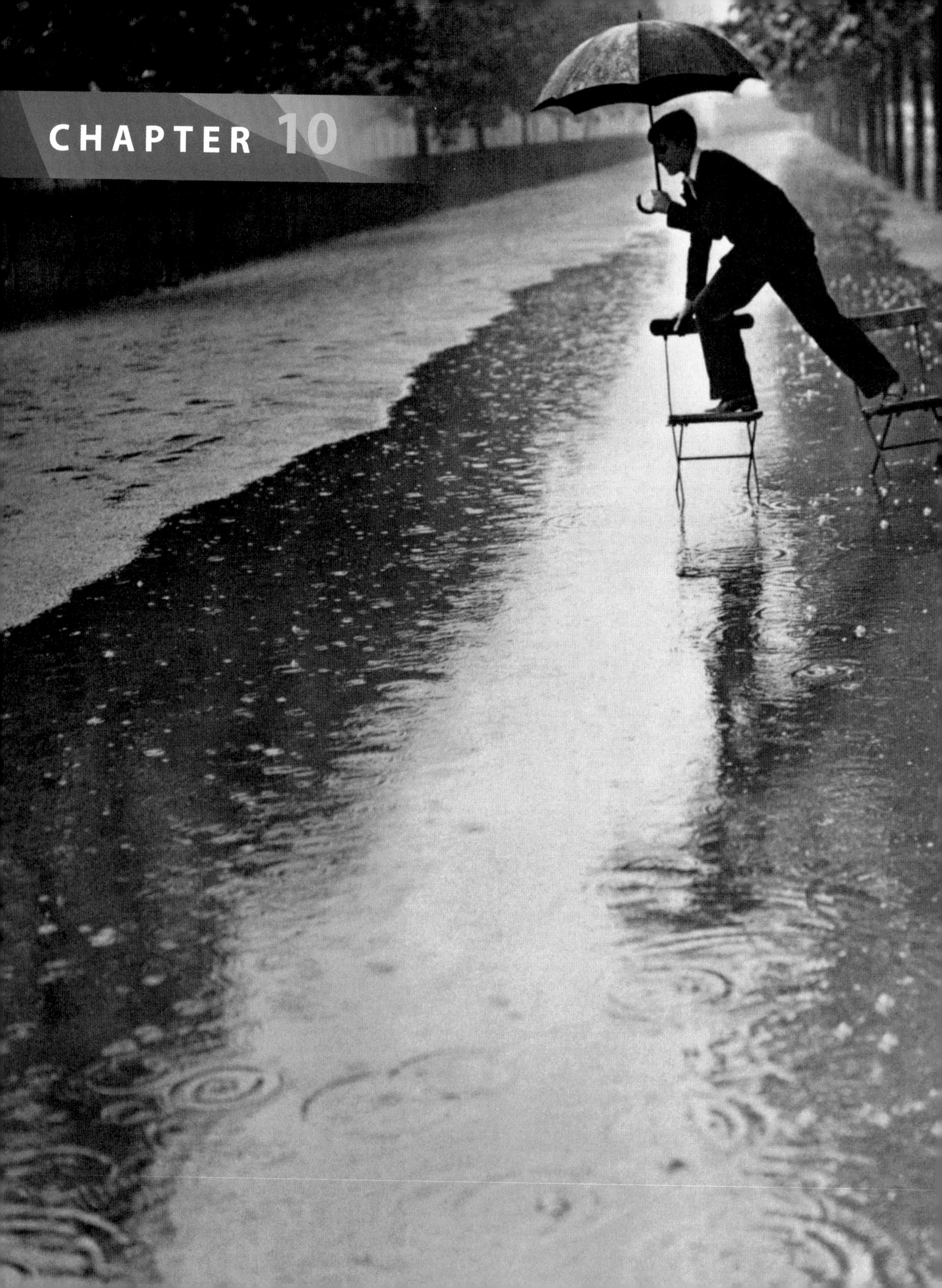

Problem-Solving

Chapter Contents

Chapter Objectives

- To describe the Gestalt approach to insight and problem-solving.
- To consider functional fixedness and how it can hinder problem-solving.
- To examine artificial intelligence approaches to problem-solving and how they resemble the ways humans solve problems.
- To discuss the various approaches to the study of problem-solving in science.

What do the following have in common?

- waterproof clothing
- nonstick pans
- carpet spill protectors
- wire insulation
- lawn mower protectant
- wall paint
- tennis racquets
- cycling lubricants
- skis and snowboards
- windshield wiper blades
- marine coatings

The answer is: Teflon. According to the materials innovation giant DuPont, which discovered it, Teflon can be found in some brands of all the products listed above (http://www2.dupont.com/Teflon/en_US/products/index.html). One of the main properties of Teflon is the fact that its polymer chains leave enough space for air molecules to pass through but not enough for water. Thus many waterproof yet breathable jackets are made of Gore-Tex, which is essentially fabric bonded with Teflon. Another special property of Teflon is its amazing slipperiness, which accounts for its use in everything from non-stick pans to the external hulls of boats (Teflon coating considerably reduces the boat's drag in the water). Interestingly, Teflon also works well as an

insulator; in fact, one of its first uses was as insulation for electrical wires.

The story of Teflon's discovery is a fascinating combination of serendipity and problem-solving. A brief history can be found on the website of the Fluoropolymers Division of the Society of the Plastics Industry, Inc. (http://www.fluoropolymers.org/about/teflon.htm). Another account of the discovery is related by Robinson and Stern (1997) in their book *Corporate Creativity: How Innovation and Improvement Actually Happen*. According to these sources, Teflon came into existence in 1938, when DuPont scientist Roy Plunkett was using a gas, known as tetrafluoroethylene, to make another compound that he thought would be useful for refrigeration. After putting the gas in a container and storing it in a way that put the gas under pressure, Plunkett was surprised to find that the gas had disappeared and the inside of the container had become coated with a solid polymer that came to be known as polytetrafluoroethylene (PTFE) and was eventually named Teflon.

The accidental discovery of Teflon is an interesting story. Even more interesting are the insights that led to Teflon's many applications. One example involves the DuPont scientist Bill Gore, who was on the team of scientists responsible for developing applications for the new material. Here is Robinson and Stern's (1997, p. 177) account of what happened in 1957:

> Knowing Teflon's unique properties as an electrical insulator, Bill Gore had been attempting to find a way to coat wire with it, but nothing seemed to work. Dejectedly, Gore showed some of his failed efforts to his son [Bob Gore: a chemical engineering student]. As he was doing so, Bob Gore happened to notice a roll of 3M sealant tape made of Teflon. He asked his father if, instead of coating wire with Teflon, the wire couldn't be sandwiched between two pieces of tape instead.

Bob Gore's flash of insight, triggered by a seemingly insignificant roll of tape, ultimately led to the solution of his father's problem and the creation of Teflon-insulated ribbon cable, a product that launched the now sizable W.L. Gore & Associates, Inc. Later, Bob Gore had the idea of "stretching" Teflon (see Figure 10.2) and found that the stretched compound was "strong, highly porous and extremely versatile" (http://www.gore.com/timeline/). This discovery, which occurred in 1969, ultimately led to the development of Gore-Tex.

In this chapter we will focus on cognitive studies and theories of problem-solving. As you will see, researchers have long been interested in understanding how insight—as exemplified by the development of Teflon products—actually occurs. Of course, insight is not all there is to problem-solving. However, in keeping with our case study, it seems appropriate to start with the Gestalt perspective on insightful solutions to seemingly complex problems.

FIGURE 10.2   Bob Gore stretching Teflon

Insight Problems and the Gestalt Theory of Thinking

We briefly considered the Gestalt psychologists in Chapters 2 and 3. *Gestalt* means form or configuration. Gestalt psychologists argue that consciousness tends to be organized into a coherent whole or *Gestalt*. As an example, recall the ambiguous bi-stable figures shown in Figure 3.19, such as the one that can be perceived as either an old woman or a young woman. Perception of the two configurations of a bi-stable figure is all-or-nothing. At any given moment you see one organization or the other as whole and complete, never both at the same time. The experience you have when an ambiguous bi-stable figure suddenly changes from one stable configuration (the young woman) to the other (the old woman) is called a **Gestalt switch** (Hanson, 1958; Kuhn, 1970; Searle, 2000; Wright; 1992).

Gestalt switches can also occur in response to verbal material. Consider the following example, from Koffka (1935, p. 640):

> Swimming under a bridge came two ducks in front of two ducks, two ducks behind two ducks, and two ducks in the middle. How many ducks were there in all?

If you're like most people, your spontaneous answer will be *six*, because your representation of the ducks is organized like this.

```
        O       O
        O       O
        O       O
```

The phrase "two ducks" makes you think of a *pair*. But suppose you were told that the ducks were swimming in single file. Now you may realize there is another

Gestalt switch
A sudden change in the way information is organized.

organization that fits the description just as well, but is simpler. The answer is that that there were *four* ducks, organized like this:

O

O

O

O

When you realize that *four ducks* is a simpler solution to the problem, you may experience the sort of Gestalt switch that is characteristic of **insight problems**. An insight problem typically gives us all the information we need to solve it: no additional information is required. However, the way the problem is posed makes it difficult to see the solution; therefore we need to look at in a different way. An insight problem may be defined as one that requires "a re-structuring of the way in which it is represented [i.e., framed in the mind] before [a] solution is possible" (Gilhooly, 2003, p. 478; Weisberg, 1995, p. 161). By no means are all problems insight problems, and we will explore other problem types as we go along. To begin with, however, we will concentrate on insight problems.

The Gestalt theory of insight has been very controversial, but it is still central to problem-solving research. Before we can evaluate contemporary research on insight, we need to be as clear as we can be about what the Gestalt psychologists meant by the term *insight*. To that end, let's review some examples of Gestalt psychologists' work on this topic.

Insight problem
A problem that we must look at from a different angle before we can see how to solve it.

KÖHLER AND THE MENTALITY OF APES

Köhler (1925/1956) was marooned on the island of Tenerife during the First World War. While there he studied the process of problem-solving in chimpanzees. Köhler described his work as concerned with testing "the intelligence of the higher apes . . . whether they do not behave with intelligence and insight under conditions which require such behavior" (Köhler, 1925/1956, p. 3). Chimpanzees were useful partici-pants because they could be placed in an experimental situation and required to solve a problem that they might never have faced before. Köhler described the behaviour of a chimpanzee named Sultan, who was in a cage with fruit outside it, beyond his reach (Figure 10.3). There was a short stick *in* the cage, and a longer stick just *outside* the bars. The longer stick was out of reach, but the short one could be used to drag it nearer. After vainly trying to use first the short stick and then a bit of wire, Sultan stud-ied the whole scene. Finally he used the short stick to obtain the large stick and then used the latter to get the banana. "From the moment his eyes fall upon the long stick, his procedure forms one consecutive whole . . . [and] follows, quite suddenly on an interval of hesitation and doubt" (Köhler, 1925/1956, pp. 155–156). To Köhler, Sultan's behaviour displayed insight, by which he meant the ability to understand how the parts of a situation are related to one another. Insight occurs spontaneously and suddenly, and involves a perceptual restructuring of the situation. The chimpanzee suddenly saw how to solve the problem. Insightful problem-solving was all-or-nothing: either he saw the solution or he did not.

FIGURE 10.3 Sultan performing a problem-solving task

From: Köhler, W. (1925). *The mentality of apes*. London: Routledge & Kegan Paul. Reproduced by permission of Taylor & Francis Books UK.

WERTHEIMER AND PRODUCTIVE THINKING

Wertheimer (1959) is often considered the founder of Gestalt psychology. His book on problem-solving was called *Productive Thinking*. To get a handle on what productive thinking entails, let's consider Wertheimer's (1959, p. 266) *altar window problem*.

The problem is as follows (see also Figure 10.4). A circular altar window is to be surrounded with gold paint. The area to be painted gold is bounded by two parallel vertical lines tangent to the circle and equal in length to the diameter of the circle. These lines are joined by semicircles. To figure out how much paint is required, you need to know the size of the area inside the lines but outside the window.

Wertheimer described several attempts to solve this problem. The accounts from some of his adult participants are particularly instructive. They interpreted the problem in terms of what they had learned from similar problems in the past. Some of them felt certain that they could solve such an apparently simple problem. However, they attempted to apply solution procedures blindly, without any real conception of what the problem required. Thus it was easy for them to find the area of the window itself because they already knew the formula for finding the area of a circle. Similarly, it was easy to see how the area of the semicircles at the top and the bottom of the figure could be calculated, but they couldn't remember any formulas for calculating the area of "the four funny remainders" (Wertheimer, 1959, p. 267).

Enter a child with no mathematical training. His first reaction to the problem is to say that, of course, he doesn't know enough to solve it. (Humility in the face of a problem is always a good way to begin.) Then he looks at the figure for a moment and realizes that the two top and bottom semicircles fit inside the window. Thus the area required is simply the area of a square with sides the same size as the diameter of the circle.

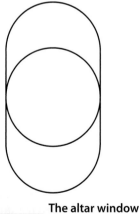

FIGURE 10.4 The altar window problem

From: *Productive Thinking* by Max Wertheimer and edited by Michael Wertheimer. Copyright © 1945, 1959 by Valentin Wertheimer; renewed © 1987 by Michael Wertheimer. Reprinted by permission of HarperCollins Publishers.

Productive thinking
Thinking based on a grasp
of the general principles
that apply in the situation
at hand.

Structurally blind thinking
The tendency to reproduce
thinking appropriate for
other situations, but not for
the current situation.

The child is capable of seeing the relationships between the parts of the whole figure, and that's all he needs to see the solution. Too often, as with Wertheimer's educated participants, superficial learning interferes with the ability to see what might be obvious to someone more naive. As Alexander Pope observed, "a little learning is a dangerous thing."

The altar window example shows why Wertheimer argued that there are two types of thinking. **Productive thinking** reflects a grasp of the general principles that apply in the situation at hand. **Structurally blind thinking** is the kind of thinking shown by those adult participants who reproduced thinking they had done before in other situations, which was inappropriate for this particular situation. Instead of thinking reproductively, the child was sensitive to the structural requirements of the actual problem that he was asked to solve.

In order to think productively, you need to go beyond having a little knowledge that you can misapply: you need to look at the situation with fresh eyes in order to recognize and apply the general principles that are relevant to it. To illustrate, here are some insight problems.

Look at Figure 10.5. Suppose that a is 5 inches long and b is 5½ inches long. The problem is to find the area of the square plus the strip (Wertheimer, 1967b, p. 279). The productive approach to such a problem is to ask, "What general truths do I know that might fit a situation like this?" In order to discover them, you need to perceptually restructure this situation and recognize that the figure can be decomposed into two triangles of base b and height a. Now you can see that the general principle you need is the formula for finding the area of a triangle, which is $\frac{1}{2}(a \times b)$. Because there are two triangles, the required area is $(2 \times \frac{1}{2})(a \times b)$, or just $a \times b$. Thus formulas you have learned in the past can be very useful, but they need to be applied with an understanding of the structural requirements of the situation. That is, they need to be used with insight into the problem's structure.

The tendency to apply previous learning blindly can sometimes lead you to the right answer without your understanding why it is right. Consider the following problem (Wertheimer, 1967b, p. 280). Is the number below divisible by nine?

$$1,000,000,000,000,000,000,000,000,000,000,008$$

Suppose you try dividing 9 into the first two digits and notice that the remainder is 1, so that the same result will recur for all of the division steps up to the final digit. The remainder of 1 at the penultimate step produces a final dividend that is divisible evenly by 9: hence the entire number is evenly divisible by 9. A calculator will confirm this conclusion. To have insight into the problem, however, you need to see that this number can be decomposed into two numbers. Thus:

$$\frac{999,999,999,999,999,999,999,999,999,999,999}{+9}$$
$$1,000,000,000,000,000,000,000,000,000,000,008$$

Because both numbers are divisible by nine, their sum must also be divisible by nine. This insight will hold for any number of the same form.

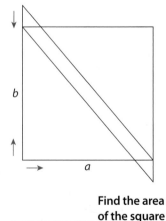

FIGURE 10.5 Find the area of the square plus the strip

From: Wertheimer, M. (1925/1967). The syllogism and productive thinking. In W.D. Ellis (Ed.), *A source book of Gestalt psychology*. New York: Humanities Press, p. 279. Copyright 1967 by Routledge & Kegan Paul.

**THINK TWICE
BOX 10.1**

Can You Solve This Problem?

Karl Duncker's seminal monograph "On Problem-Solving" (Duncker, 1945) has become a classic of the problem-solving literature. In it Duncker presents numerous interesting problems and analyzes how people solve them. Among them is what Duncker (1945, p. 26) calls the "familiar match problem in which four equilateral triangles are to be constructed out of six matches." Can you come up with a solution? If you do, try to relate your problem-solving process to the concepts in this chapter.

DUNCKER AND FUNCTIONAL FIXEDNESS

Duncker (1945) was particularly interested in the effect that previous experience has on problem-solving. When we have a problem, often our first impulse is to ask ourselves, "What did I do in similar situations in the past?" Duncker called this activity **analysis of the situation**, and it involves determining what functions the objects in the situation have and how they could be used to solve the problem. Each object can be seen as potentially capable of performing several different functions. Sometimes, though, we are unable to see beyond the most common function of a particular object and recognize that it could also perform the function we need to solve a problem. When that happens, we have fallen into the trap of **functional fixedness**.

Here is an example of functional fixedness called the coin problem (Simmel, 1953). Suppose you have eight coins and a balance. One of the coins is counterfeit and therefore lighter than the others. How can you find the counterfeit coin by using the balance only twice?

Most people initially think of dividing the coins into two groups of four coins each. One of the two groups will be lighter and so must contain the counterfeit coin. Then you can take the four coins from that group and weigh them two against two. Of course, one of the groups of two will be lighter. But you can't determine which of the two remaining coins is the counterfeit one because you have already used the balance twice.

Before we consider how to approach this problem correctly, let's analyze the previous solution attempt. Why do we initially divide the coins into two groups of four? One reason is that we know that eight things can be evenly divided into two groups of four. One of the functions of the number eight is that it can be divided that way. The fact that 4 + 4 = 8 is a highly available bit of knowledge for us. Because this property of the number eight is so well known, it's the first thing we think of. In fact, when people try to solve this problem, they often keep coming back to the four versus four division. When the obvious way of using materials keeps us from seeing the most appropriate way for the situation at hand, then we are functionally fixed.

The solution to Simmel's coin problem can be very difficult to see. You need to divide the coins in a way that is far from obvious: in three groups of three, three, and two coins. Then you weigh three versus three. If they balance, then the counterfeit coin must be in the group of two coins and you will then weigh them one against one. Alternatively, if you find on your first weighing that one group of three coins is lighter than the other, you can take any two of the three coins from the lighter group and

Analysis of the situation
Determining what functions the objects in the situation have and how they can be used to solve the problem.

Functional fixedness
The inability to see beyond the most common use of a particular object and recognize that it could also perform the function needed to solve a problem; also, the tendency to think about objects based on the function for which they were designed.

weigh them against each other. If they balance, then the third (unweighed) coin must be the counterfeit one. If they don't balance, then you will know that the lighter one is counterfeit. This procedure is guaranteed to find the solution. However, it's much more complex and less familiar than the four-against-four approach.

Finding solutions to problems may require you to overcome functional fixedness. It may be only after you've realized that the obvious ways of tackling a problem don't work that you will be open to a reorganization of the problem that will allow you to see the solution. Variables that may determine the presence or absence of functional fixedness will be considered later in this chapter.

MAIER AND THE CONCEPT OF DIRECTION

N.R.F. Maier was not one of the original Gestalt psychologists, but he adopted many of their ideas in his approach to the study of thinking. He is usually credited with introducing one of the most difficult of all insight problems, known as the nine-dot problem (see Figure 10.6). It requires you to connect all the dots with four straight lines without lifting your pencil from the paper (the solution is given in the second part of the figure). Notice that the solution requires that you extend two lines outside the square formed by the dots. What keeps many people from seeing the solution is the assumption that all their lines must be drawn within the square.

A Gestalt psychologist might say that the problem-solver is fixated by this unnecessary assumption, and that once this fixation is overcome, the problem can be solved. Weisberg and Alba (1981) reasoned that, if participants were told that they could draw lines outside the square area, they should be able to solve the problem more easily than if they were not given that **hint**. However, even with the hint, many participants still did not solve the problem. "The Gestalt view holds that once fixation is broken, the solution either appears whole in a flash of insight or is produced smoothly as one step leads to another" (Weisberg, 1986, p. 45). Because this is not what happens, Weisberg and Alba concluded that there is no evidence to support the Gestalt theory of problem-solving.

Hints
A hint must be consistent with the direction that the person's thinking is taking, and cannot be useful unless it responds to a difficulty that the person has already experienced.

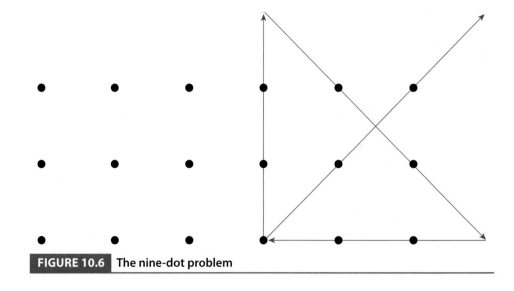

FIGURE 10.6   The nine-dot problem

Weisberg and Alba's conclusion led to a controversy over the nature of insight (e.g., Dominowski, 1981; Ohlsson, 1984). Ellen (1982) tried to show that Weisberg and Alba's account of Gestalt theory was incorrect. To do this he relied on Maier's (1931/1968; 1970) classic explorations of problem-solving in the Gestalt tradition. One of Maier's best-known problems is the two-string problem shown in Figure 10.7. There are two strings hanging from the ceiling. The participant must tie the two strings together, but they are too short for the participant to reach one while holding onto the other. The productive solution is to tie a weight to one of the strings, set it swinging, go and get the second string, walk over to the middle of the room, and wait for the first string to swing over to you. Then you can tie them together.

If participants did not see the solution spontaneously, Maier gave them a hint. He brushed past one of the strings, setting it swinging. After this hint, many participants solved the problem. For several of them the solution appeared suddenly, as a whole. However, few of the latter attributed their discovery to the hint that Maier had given them. Maier (1931/1968) interpreted these results in the Gestalt way:

> Changes in meaning and organization are experienced suddenly . . . it is not surprising to find that the very thing which sets off this combination is unexperienced. Before the solution is found there is disharmony. The reasoner cannot quite see the relation of certain things in the room to the solution of the problem. The next experience is of having an idea. The "transformation" or "organization" stage is not experienced in reasoning any more than in a reversible perspective [recall the bi-stable figures in Chapter 3.] The new organization is suddenly there. It is the dominant experience and covers any factor that just preceded it. (p. 26)

In other words, an insightful experience can mask the hint that gave rise to it.

Maier argued that, in order to be effective, a hint must be consistent with the direction that the person's thinking is taking. It can't be useful unless it responds to a difficulty that the person has already experienced: otherwise it will not be recognized as relevant to the problem. Ellen argued that the hint given by Weisberg and Alba was irrelevant to the direction of their participants' thought, and so was useless to them. That explained why they tended to have no insightful solutions.

INSIGHT IS INVOLUNTARY

Metcalfe and Wiebe (1987) attempted to clarify the distinction between problems that require insight to solve and problems that do not. They pointed out that one of the essential characteristics of an insight problem is that the solution appears suddenly, without warning. We have already considered several examples of insight problems

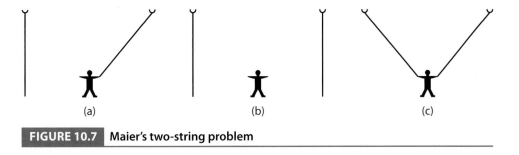

FIGURE 10.7   Maier's two-string problem

with this characteristic. By contrast, problems solved without insight are solved gradually in a stepwise progression. Metcalfe and Wiebe suggested that many arithmetic and algebra problems are of this type. For example, finding the square root of 16 requires not insight but the application of a stepwise solution procedure.

Metcalfe and Wiebe believed that participants should be able to distinguish between these two problem types. As people work on a non-insight problem, they should be able to tell when they are getting closer to the solution. A common way of expressing the feeling you have as you approach the solution is to say that you're "getting warm." That is, for non-insight problems participants should have an awareness of incremental success, or a growing **feeling of warmth**, as they get closer to the solution. This is because non-insight problems are solved step-by-step, and with each step you are "getting warmer." With insight problems, however, there is not a gradual approach to the solution, and so participants should not feel that they are getting warmer until the solution actually appears. If you ask participants to rate their feelings of "warmth" as they solve a non-insight problem in a four-minute interval, feeling-of-warmth ratings should gradually rise as the solution is approached. By contrast, with insight problems feeling-of-warmth ratings should stay more or less level until the solution is reached, at which time they should rise dramatically. In their experiments, Metcalfe and Wiebe found that this was largely the case (Figure 10.8).

Metcalfe and Wiebe also examined ratings for **feeling of knowing**. In this case, participants were asked to rank in order the set of problems they would be working on, from those they thought would be the easiest to handle to those they thought they might not be able to solve. They then tried to solve the problems. For non-insight problems, participants were able to predict fairly accurately which ones they would be able to solve and which ones they would not. For insight problems, however, there was no such predictability. These results are consistent with the hypothesis that participants

Feeling of warmth
The feeling that many people have as they approach the solution to a problem (i.e., "getting warm").

Feeling of knowing
The feeling that you will be able to solve a particular problem.

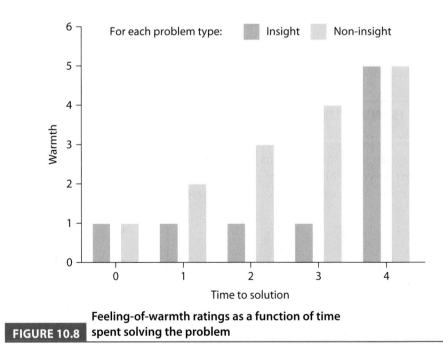

FIGURE 10.8 **Feeling-of-warmth ratings as a function of time spent solving the problem**

Data from: Metcalfe, J., & Wiebe, D. (1987). Intuition in insight and non-insight problem solving. *Memory and Cognition, 15*, 238–246.

COGNITION IN ACTION BOX 10.2

Problem-solving with Red Green!

Since a roll of Teflon tape played a major part in the case study at the start of this chapter, it seems fitting to note that another kind of tape is famous (at least among TV comedy fans) as "the handyman's secret weapon." If you want to see some hilarious examples of creative problem-solving, take a look at *The Red Green Show*, starring the award-winning Canadian comedian Steve Smith. Red is the leader of a men's lodge located somewhere in northern Canada, and almost every episode of his show includes a segment called "Handyman Corner." Here Red demonstrates improbable do-it-yourself projects, virtually all of which involve a roll (sometimes many rolls) of duct tape. One early project was a beer cooler made of duct tape and an old toilet tank. A list of the episodes and links to videos of all 300 episodes can be found at **http://www.redgreen.com/watch.html**. You won't have to watch many episodes to realize that duct tape is not the only key to Red's success at comedic problem-solving: another is his ability to overcome *structurally blind thinking* and *functional fixedness*.

are aware of the procedures they can use to solve non-insight problems. They can predict which ones they will be able to solve based on whether or not they possess the relevant knowledge. By contrast, insight problems are solved by the sudden emergence of knowledge that the participant was not aware of before attempting to solve the problem.

Feelings of knowing and feelings of "warmth" reflect judgments that participants make about their own knowledge. Such judgments are examples of metacognition, or what you know about what you know—how accurately you can assess your own cognitive processes. Metcalfe and Wiebe showed that participants' metacognitive assessments of their performance on non-insight problems were quite accurate. However, their metacognitive assessments of their performance on insight problems were not accurate, because an insight is not something that can be planned. An insight is something that happens to you, not something that you decide to have.

Current Approaches to Insight Problems

Jones (2003) observed that there are two contrasting approaches to the study of insight problems, which he called the progress monitoring theory and the representational change theory. Let's look at each of them in turn.

PROGRESS MONITORING THEORY

Progress monitoring theory is represented by the work of MacGregor, Ormerod, and Chronicle (2001; Ormerod, MacGregor, & Chronicle, 2002; Chronicle, MacGregor, & Ormerod, 2004). They found that participants in their research took what seemed to them to be the most straightforward route to a solution. However, in an insight problem the most straightforward route invariably leads to failure. Only when the participants realized that they had gone down a blind alley did they consider alternative possibilities. The participants monitored their progress on a problem, and when they reached an impasse they were open to an insightful solution.

Progress monitoring theory
The theory that we monitor our progress on a problem, and when we reach an impasse we are open to an insightful solution.

In one experiment participants were given the nine-dot problem with one correct line already drawn. Look again at Figure 10.6. One group of participants was given the problem with a line connecting three dots horizontally and extending outside the area of the square. Another group was given the problem with a diagonal line that did not extend outside the area of the square. Since drawing lines outside the square is crucial to the solution, you might think that the horizontal line would be more effective. However, the diagonal line led to the greatest percentage of participants solving the problem.

The reason the diagonal line is superior is that it leads the participant to reach an impasse more quickly. Participants typically look ahead only one or two moves at a time and try to connect the most dots possible with each line. Given the diagonal line, they can more easily see that if they follow that strategy they will run out of moves before reaching the solution. This realization prompts them to consider alternative strategies, increasing the likelihood of reaching a solution.

REPRESENTATIONAL CHANGE THEORY

Representational change theory
The theory that insight requires a change in the way the participant represents the problem.

Constraint relaxation
An aspect of representational change theory: the removal of assumptions that are blocking problem solution.

Chunk decomposition
An aspect of representational change theory: parts of the problem that are recognized as belonging together are separated into "chunks" and thought about independently.

Representational change theory is represented by the work of Knoblich, Ohlsson, Haider, and Rhenius (1999; Knoblich, Ohlsson, & Raney, 2001). Like the Gestalt psychologists, they argued that insight requires a change in the way we represent the problem to ourselves. Their unique contribution was to hypothesize that achieving representational change depends on two processes: constraint relaxation and chunk decomposition. **Constraint relaxation** is the removal of whatever assumptions are blocking problem solution; for example, the assumption that lines may not extend outside the square area is a constraint that may prevent solution of the nine-dot problem. **Chunk decomposition** means separating the problem into the "chunks" that belong together and thinking about them independently. As an example, Knoblich et al. (1999, p. 1536) pointed to highly skilled chess players who see familiar patterns in the arrangement of chess pieces on the board but can decompose these patterns into individual pieces when necessary.

The role of these two processes in insight problems can be illustrated by way of *matchstick arithmetic problems*. These are equations composed of Roman numerals formed with matchsticks. Here is an example.

$$VI = III + III$$

The equation says that 6 (VI) equals 3 (III) plus 3 (III). Now consider the following:

$$IV = III + III$$

This equation is clearly incorrect, since 4 (IV) does not equal 3 (III) plus 3 (III). However, it can be made correct by moving a single matchstick. Can you tell which one? If not, look again at the first example.

To solve problems like these, people familiar with ordinary arithmetic need to relax constraints that they have learned. For example, in ordinary arithmetic you cannot simply change one number (e.g., 4) into another (e.g., 6). However, as we have just seen, in matchstick arithmetic you *can* change IV into VI by simply moving the matchstick on the left of the V to the right of the V. Another condition for solving matchstick arithmetic problems is that you must be able to decompose chunks. For example, the configuration V is a chunk. Now consider the following equation. What do you need to do to make both sides equal?

$$V = II$$

The V is composed of two matchsticks. If you make both of them vertical, then you will have II = II. Alternatively, you could make the right-hand side of the equation into V by tilting the vertical matchsticks obliquely to one another, which would give you V = V.

Both constraint relaxation and chunk decomposition promote insight by facilitating the construction of novel representations. In one study, Knoblich, Ohlsson, and Raney (2001) monitored eye movements as participants solved matchstick arithmetic problems. Presumably eye movements indicate which parts of the problem the participant is thinking about. The fact that successful solvers spent more time looking at the parts of the problem that required constraint relaxation and/or chunk decomposition supports the hypothesis that these processes lead to changes in the way the problem is represented.

The finding that eye movements can successfully predict insightful solutions has been replicated by Grant and Spivey (2003). They made solutions more likely by highlighting those parts of a problem that participants needed to pay attention to. Guiding the problem-solver's attention may be a useful way of facilitating solutions. "Although it may often seem that attention and eye movements are the result of cognitive processing, it may be that sometimes cognitive processing is the result of attention and eye movements" (p. 466).

Jones (2003, p. 1026) noted that the progress monitoring and representational change theories are not contradictory. The former focuses on the process by which reaching an impasse forces the participant to seek an insightful solution, while the latter focuses on the process that makes it possible to reach an insightful solution. In other words, the two theories address different parts of the problem-solving process and therefore should be seen as complementary.

INSIGHT AND THE BRAIN

In Chapter 4, on attention, we discussed evidence that the anterior cingulate cortex (ACC) detects conflicting response tendencies and facilitates the process whereby we become aware of such conflicts. Luo and Niki (2003; Luo, Niki, & Philips, 2004; Mai, Luo, Wu, & Luo, 2004) have found evidence for ACC involvement in the insight process using both functional magnetic resonance imaging (fMRI) and event-related potential (ERP) techniques. Participants in their studies were given riddles such as *What can move heavy logs but cannot move a small nail?* Most participants came up with answers that they suspected to be incorrect, such as *a crane*. If they could not think of an answer, they were given it. In this case the answer was *a river*. Participants reported having an *Aha!* experience on learning the answer. Corresponding to these insight experiences was activation in the ACC. The authors suggested that the ACC may be involved in detecting the conflict between the way we have been thinking about the problem and the correct way to solve it.

Luo and Niki (2003) also reported hippocampal involvement in the insight process. We discussed the importance of the hippocampus for the consolidation of memories in Chapter 5, on memory traces and memory schemas. Luo and Niki (2003, p. 321) believe that this function of the hippocampus helps to explain its role in insight. "From an evolutionary perspective, the property of responding to the 'insightful' experiences and fixing them in long-term memory can greatly enhance the possibility of an animal's survival. . . . [T]his property of the hippocampus enables the organism to preserve" the sort of information that may facilitate survival sometime in the future. The relation between the hippocampus and insight is also explored in the studies we will examine next.

INSIGHT AND SLEEP

When you have a problem and are uncertain of the solution, you may decide to "sleep on it." Wagner, Gais, Haider, Verleger, and Born (2004) have shown that this may be an excellent strategy. To investigate the relation between sleep and insight, they gave participants a *number reduction task*. This is a demanding task that requires close attention to detail. Participants are given a string of eight numbers, all composed of only three numbers: 1, 4, and 9. They then have to generate a series of responses using two rules. The first, called the *same rule*, stipulates that if there is a sequence of two *identical* numbers, then the response must be one of those numbers. Thus for the sequence 4 4 the response is 4. The second rule, called the *different rule*, stipulates that for a sequence of two *different* numbers, the response is the third number. For example, the response to the sequence 1 4 would be 9. The response to the first two numbers in a string is then compared with the third number in the string. Thus if the first two numbers are 4 and 4, for which the response is 4, this response (4) is then compared to the next number in the string. If that next number is 9, then the correct response is 1. How this works can be seen in the diagram at the bottom of this page.

Comparing 1 and 9, by the second rule, gives you 4 as the first response; then comparing 4 to 1 gives you 9 as the second response, by the same rule; 9 is then compared with 4 so that 1 is the next response, again by the same rule; 1 compared with 9 gives 4, by the same rule. Then 4 compared with 4 gives 4; this is the first time that the first rule comes into play. You can complete the response sequence for yourself. The participant's task is to find the last number in the response sequence. In this case, the last response is 9, and so that is the answer to the problem. Participants are not required to provide any other number: only the last one.

Now examine the response sequence for this sequence of numbers: 4 9 1 4 4 1 9. Notice that the last three numbers are the mirror image of the numbers in the second, third, and fourth positions: 4 1 9 is the mirror image of 9 1 4. The second, third, and fourth responses are the mirror image of the last three responses for all the problems the participant is asked to solve. This means that the required response, which is the last one, is always the same as the second response. Consequently the participant has only to generate the second response in order to have the response the problem requires. This is the insightful solution: you don't need to generate seven responses to find the required response; all you need to find is the second response.

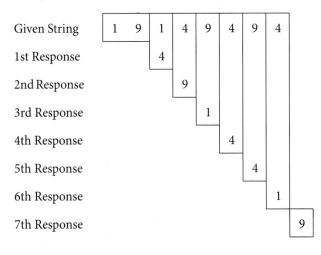

Given String	1	9	1	4	9	4	9	4
1st Response			4					
2nd Response				9				
3rd Response					1			
4th Response						4		
5th Response							4	
6th Response								1
7th Response									9

Even after solving many such problems, few of the participants in the Wagner et al. study achieved an insightful solution, although they did become faster with practice. However, once they gained insight into the problems' structures, their behaviour changed dramatically. They would no longer produce a string of responses, but simply announce the required response immediately after determining the second response. Three groups of participants were given a training period consisting of several number reduction problems, followed by an interval of eight hours during which one group slept and the others did not; then they were tested on additional number reduction problems. One group *slept* between 11 p.m. and 7 a.m.; the second remained *awake* between 11 p.m. and 7 a.m.; and the third remained *awake* between 11 a.m. and 7 p.m. The interesting result was that 59 per cent of the participants who had slept produced insightful solutions when tested. Across both groups of those who had remained awake, only 22 per cent of participants produced insightful solutions. The conclusion drawn by Wagner et al. was that sleep promotes insight. The results of the experiment are shown in Figure 10.9.

The restructuring process that occurs as a result of sleep may be similar to memory consolidation during sleep, "resulting in delayed learning without the need for further practice or task engagement" (Stickgold & Walker, 2004, p. 192). Wagner et al. (2004, p. 354) suggested that, partly through interaction with other neural structures, the hippocampus "not only strengthens memory traces quantitatively, but can also catalyze mental restructuring, thereby setting the stage for the emergence of insight."

Functional Fixedness and the Design of Tools

Although the use of tools is not unique to humans, it is so common among us that we can justifiably be called "the ultimate tool users" (Defeyter & German, 2003, p. 134). Most of the tools we use as adults in a technologically advanced society have only one

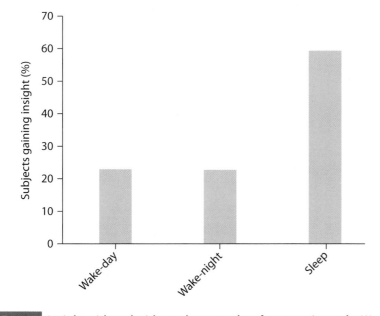

FIGURE 10.9 Insight with and without sleep: results of an experiment by Wagner et al.

From: Wagner, U., Gais, S., Haider, H., Verleger, R., & Born, J. (2004). Sleep inspires insight. *Nature, 427*, 352–355.

function. For example, lawnmowers, garlic presses, and staplers are generally used sole-ly for the purposes for which they were designed. As we saw in our earlier discussion of Duncker and functional fixedness, we are often unable to think of a use for an object other than its intended function.

In a series of experiments, German and Defeyter (2000; Defeyter & German, 2003) have demonstrated that young children may be less functionally fixed than older children. In one study, five-, six-, and seven-year-olds were divided into two groups at each age level and presented with a task that required them to discover that a box they had been given could be used not just as a container but as something to stand on. One group was presented with the *pre-utilization condition*, and the other was presented with the *no-pre-utilization condition*. In the pre-utilization condition, the box was full of things, demonstrating its conventional function as a container. In the no-pre-utilization condition, the box was empty. The amount of time taken by those children who solved the problem is shown in Figure 10.10. Notice that the five-year-olds were equally fast regardless of whether the boxes were full or empty. However, the six- and seven-year-olds performed much worse under the pre-utilization condition.

German and Defeyter (2000; Defeyter & German, 2003) interpreted these and similar results as pointing to the development of a tendency to perceive the function of a tool in terms of the use for which it was designed. By age six or thereabouts, children believe that the function of an object is the one for which it was created, and have difficulty seeing any other use for it. By contrast, children who are five or younger see the function of an object as determined by the goal of the *user* rather than that of the *designer*. If the goal is to find something to stand on, then, to the five-year-old mind a box will do perfectly well.

Is functional fixedness acquired solely in technologically advanced countries where many objects are designed for a single purpose? To explore this question, German and Barrett (2005) examined functional fixedness in the Shuar of the Amazon region in Ecuador. These people have been "exposed only to a small set of manufactured artifacts, and the set of artifacts to which they are exposed tends to be 'low tech' (p. 2). The participants were adolescents and young adults, ranging in age from 12 to 25 years

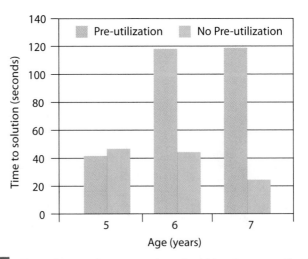

FIGURE 10.10   Effect of pre-utilization on functional fixedness as a function of age

Data from: German, T.P., & Defeyter, M.A. (2000). Immunity to functional fixedness in young children. *Psychonomic Bulletin & Review, 7,* p. 710.

old. One of the tasks they were given was similar to the box problem described above, with one group in the pre-utilization condition and the other in the non-pre-utilization condition. The Shuar participants showed the same effect of pre-utilization as the older children in the earlier experiment. That is, it took them longer to solve the problem when the box's function as a container had been shown to them than when it had not. The researchers' conclusion was that even in a technologically sparse culture, people will develop the idea that an object's function is the one for which it was designed. This leads to the broader conclusion that there may be a universal tendency to think about objects "based on design rather than current use" (German & Barrett, 2005, p. 4). This way of thinking may have evolved because most problems are solved by using tools in the way they were designed to be used. It's usually not necessary to think of alternative uses for a lawnmower, for example. Functional fixedness would then come about as a "costly side effect" of an otherwise efficient system (Defeyter & German, 2003, p. 152).

The Flexibility–Rigidity Dimension

The experiments of the Luchinses (1942; Luchins & Luchins, 1950, 1994a, 1994b) are among the most interesting demonstrations of the way repeating a particular way of solving a problem can leave us unable to see alternative ways of solving the problem. One of the ways the Luchinses showed this was with *water jar problems*. Imagine that you have three jars, labelled A, B, and C, and a supply of water. Your task is to use the jars to obtain a specific amount of water. For example, suppose the three jars had capacities of 21, 127, and 3 litres, respectively. How could you use them to obtain 100 litres of water? Think about it.

The solution to this problem involves four steps. First, fill up the 127-litre container. Second, pour out 21 litres into jar A. Third, pour 3 litres into jar C. Fourth, dump out jar C and pour 3 litres into jar C again. You are left with 100 litres in jar B, and the problem is solved. Now consider this problem. Jar A has a capacity of 14 litres, B a capacity of 163 litres, and C a capacity of 25 litres. Your task is to get 99 litres. This problem can be solved in the same way as the first. Fill jar B, subtract jar A, and subtract jar C twice.

In the Luchinses' experiments, participants were given a series of water jar problems just like the two we have considered. All of them could be solved using the same formula: *B minus A minus 2C*. After solving five problems using that formula, participants had developed a *rigid set*, or **Einstellung effect**. As we saw in Chapter 4, a set facilitates some responses while inhibiting others. In the water jar situation, participants developed a particularly rigid set as shown by their responses to the following problem, which was given next in the series. A, B, and C have capacities of 23, 49, and 3 litres, respectively, and the required amount is 20 litres. Participants typically use the *B minus A minus 2C* formula on this problem, even though a simpler procedure would work just as well. The required amount can be obtained simply by filling A and emptying 3 litres out of it into C. So the simpler formula, A minus C, would work, but participants don't see it because of the Einstellung they have developed on the previous trials.

The Luchinses administered this kind of test to more than 5000 participants. Einstellung effects were very reliable findings. In one of their experiments (Luchins & Luchins, 1950, experiment 3), with sixth-graders, the effects were quite dramatic. The children were told to work as quickly as possible. After initially solving the problems

Einstellung effect
The tendency to respond inflexibly to a particular type of problem; also called a *rigid* set.

using the same method throughout, they were told there was a simpler method for some of the problems and were instructed to find it. However, it was difficult for them to change their approach, and most of them persisted in following the more complicated procedure. There was evidence that the children found the demands of the situation quite stressful. Under pressure to perform quickly, they were locked into a rigid pattern and unable to be flexible.

Woltz, Gardner, and Bell (2000) tested the generality of the Luchinses' findings using a version of the number reduction task that we looked at earlier in this chapter. Recall that number reduction problems have two rules, a *same* rule and a *different* rule. In the problems used by Woltz et al., the three numbers were always 1, 2, and 3, and the given string was four numbers long (e.g., 3213). Participants were trained on number sequences that required them to follow the same sequence of rules over and over. For example, they might be asked to solve problems in which the rules had to be applied in the sequence *same–different–same* or *different–same–different*. They were then tested on problems that required the use of new rule sequences, such as *same–different–different* or *different–same–same*. Those participants who had the most practice during training showed the greatest **negative transfer** when tested with problems requiring a new rule sequence. That is, they kept responding with previously learned rule sequences and their performance levels dropped as a result. Indeed, for highly practised participants errors increased from 20 per cent during training to 60 per cent during testing. Less practised participants also showed negative transfer, but the increase in their error rate was not so dramatic: from 20 per cent errors to 35 per cent. These results clearly showed an Einstellung effect resulting from repetitive practice.

Woltz et al. relate their study to other research into common errors made in everyday life. The Einstellung effect resembles the kinds of errors we all make when we have overlearned a particular routine and continue to follow it when we should do something new. Reason (1990) describes such routines as **strong but wrong** (Reason, 1990). For example, suppose that you always take the bus to and from work but one day you drive instead. There's a good chance that you'll end up leaving your car in the parking lot and taking the bus home.

FLEXIBILITY–RIGIDITY AND THE BRAIN

In Chapter 4, on attention, we noted that prefrontal areas of the brain are thought to provide "a top-down bias that favors the selection of task-relevant information. . . . [S]uch a bias is especially important for exerting control when task-irrelevant information can effectively compete with task-relevant information for priority in processing" (Milham, Banich, & Barad, 2004, p. 212). Then we discussed the fact that the left dorsolateral prefrontal cortex (DLPFC) has been singled out as playing a particularly important role in selecting between alternative response tendencies. In Chapter 6, on memory systems, we reviewed evidence suggesting that the left DLPFC should be seen as an integral part of working memory, monitoring and controlling alternative courses of action.

Colvin, Dunbar, and Grafman (2000) have extended this picture of the role of the left DLPFC in a study of water jar problems done with patients with prefrontal lesions. Solutions to water jar problems require a counterintuitive move—one that appears to take the solver farther away from the goal rather than closer to it. In order to make the

Negative transfer
The tendency to respond with previously learned rule sequences even when they are inappropriate.

Strong but wrong routines
Overlearned response sequences that we follow even when we intend to do something else.

CONSIDER THIS
BOX 10.3   Self-control and Problem-solving

Have you ever noticed that making a hard decision can drain you mentally and even make you feel physically tired? In *Willpower: Rediscovering the Greatest Human Strength* (2011), the social psychologist Roy F. Baumeister and the well-known journalist John Tierney develop the idea that certain demanding tasks can deplete the reserves of willpower that are needed for exercising self-control. They also review recent studies showing that, conversely, performance on demanding tasks (e.g., problem-solving tasks) can be impaired when the resources needed for self-control are depleted.

A good example of how depletion of those resources can lead to poorer problem-solving is provided by Baumeister, Bratslavsky, Muraven, and Tice (1998). In their study, Baumeister and colleagues depleted some participants' self-control resources by having them hold back their emotions while they viewed emotionally impactful videos; then they had them complete a problem-solving task (unscrambling sequences of letters to make meaningful words within a predetermined time limit). Strikingly, those participants who had had to control their emotions formed fewer meaningful words in the allotted time frame than did a control group that had watched the same video without trying to control their emotions. Apparently, exerting self-control drained a resource needed for problem-solving. What is that resource? Evidence suggests that it could be the amount of glucose available to fuel successful brain function (see Baumeister & Tierney, 2011; Gailliot, Baumeister, DeWall, Maner, Plant, Tice, Brewer & Schmeichel, 2007).

counterintuitive move the solver must inhibit the most obvious move. For example, in the first of the Luchinses' problems discussed above, the most obvious strategy is to find a way to put 100 litres *into* the 127-litre jar. The counterintuitive strategy is to find a way to empty 27 litres *out of* the 127-litre jar.

Both frontal lobe lesion patients and normal controls were given water jar problems. The patients solved fewer problems than the controls, and also made fewer counterintuitive moves. When patients were categorized according to the sites of their lesions, those with damage to the left frontal lobe showed the most impairment. It appeared that "intact left dorsolateral prefrontal cortex function is critical for successful" performance on water jar problems (Colvin et al., 2000, p. 1136). Without that function the person is unable to inhibit obvious moves in order to make counterintuitive ones.

MINDLESSNESS

Langer (1989, 2000; Langer & Piper, 1987) proposed that the flexibility–rigidity distinction could be conceptualized in terms of **mindfulness** and **mindlessness**. People who are experiencing Einstellung effects are behaving in a *mindless* way. To behave mindlessly means to act as if a situation has only one possible interpretation. To behave *mindfully* means to actively seek new possibilities. As Langer pointed out, once you have mindfully created a new way of doing something, then you may later use that way mindlessly. This is what happened to the participants in the Luchinses' experiments. After mindfully discovering the "B minus A minus 2C" rule, those participants proceeded to mindlessly apply it to subsequent problems.

Mindfulness vs mindlessness
Openness to alternative possibilities versus the tendency to behave as if the situation had only one possible interpretation.

Langer and Piper reasoned that one way of preventing the development of mindlessness is to encourage people to think about things in a tentative rather than absolute way. For example, describing objects in terms that allowed participants to see that they could have alternative uses might encourage mindfulness, whereas describing them in terms of single uses might not. Langer and Piper did an experiment in which participants were shown three objects: a dog's rubber chew toy, a polygraph pen, and a hairdryer attachment. For half the participants, the objects were described unconditionally as one thing only, as in, "This is a dog's chew toy." For the other half of the participants, the objects were described conditionally, as in, "This could be a dog's chew toy." The experimenter then pretended to need an eraser and asked participants what to do. A mindful response would have been to suggest that the chew toy could be used as an eraser. If the chew toy had been described conditionally, then participants were much more likely to make the mindful response than when it had been described unconditionally.

Responding to new objects and events conditionally appears to be an important aspect of mindfulness. Conditional understanding allows people to avoid rigidity in responding. Although unconditional description offers an economical way of categorizing things, it does so by blinding us to new possibilities.

▮ Artificial Intelligence Approaches to Problem-Solving

Might it be possible to program a computer so that the way it does things is indistinguishable from the way that a person does them? If so, then the computer program might be a good model of human behaviour. Computer simulation approaches to problem-solving have been extremely influential, in large measure because of the work of Nobel Prize winner Herbert Simon. As we shall see, there are computer programs that solve problems in ways that resemble the intelligent human approach to problem-solving. These programs are examples of **artificial intelligence**. Let's look at some examples and see how computer simulation and artificial intelligence work.

The relation between artificial intelligence approaches and other approaches to problem-solving is well illustrated by Newell's (1983) discussion of the work of George Polya. Polya wrote a famous guide to problem-solving called *How to Solve It* (Polya, 1945/1957) based on **heuristics**: problem-solving procedures (typically rules of thumb or shortcuts) that can often be useful but do not always work.

Polya (1945/1957, p. xvi) outlined his heuristic methods as follows. First, to understand the problem you need to formulate it in a way that will allow you to begin thinking about it. For example, you might draw a diagram. Once you think you understand what the problem requires, then you can move on to the next stage: devising a plan. Several methods may be helpful here. You might try to find a similar problem that you know how to solve, for instance, and then see if the methods used to solve that problem will also work for the present problem. When you have formulated a plan for attacking the problem, you can go on to step three, carrying out the plan. This calls for careful attention to detail. Finally, you need to examine the solution obtained. This involves making sure that the result is in fact the one you need, and determining whether or not the methods you used in this case could be used to solve other problems.

Artificial intelligence
The "intelligence" of computer programs designed to solve problems in ways that resemble human approaches to problem-solving.

Heuristic
A problem-solving procedure (typically a rule of thumb or shortcut) that can often be useful but does not guarantee a solution.

As Newell (1983, p. 202) observed, Polya's description of problem-solving has much in common with later artificial intelligence techniques. Artificial intelligence requires as clear and precise a formulation of the problem as possible. In order to make a computer program work, we can't rely on vague hunches and intuitions; we must be able to specify a procedure. Polya tried to present heuristic methods that were clear, precise, and explicit. It is this kind of heuristic method that people working on artificial intelligence have tried to devise.

In programming heuristic problem-solving methods, artificial intelligence researchers use unambiguous solution procedures called **algorithms** (Dietrich, 1999). The rules governing long division are an example of an algorithm: they are unambiguous and a computer can easily be programmed to follow them. Algorithms may be divided into two classes: *systematic* and *non-systematic*. "A systematic algorithm is guaranteed to find the solution if one exists ... [but] non-systematic algorithms ... are not guaranteed to find a solution" (Korf, 1999, p. 373). Since Polya's heuristic methods are not guaranteed to find a solution, they are non-systematic algorithms.

A SIMPLE EXAMPLE OF ARTIFICIAL INTELLIGENCE

Computer programs that play games invented by humans are useful examples of artificially intelligent systems. For example, there are excellent programs that play games such as checkers, Scrabble, backgammon, chess, and bridge, and that solve crossword puzzles (Schaeffer & van den Herik, 2002). A tipping point in the history of artificial intelligence occurred in 1997 when the chess-playing program *Deep Blue* defeated world chess champion Garry Kasparov in a six-game match (Campbell, Hoane, & Hsu, 2002). Interestingly, early research in artificial intelligence centred on creating a chess-playing program (Newell, Shaw, & Simon, 1958; Newell & Simon, 1972, Chap. 11). Chess is a very intricate game, and the programs written to play it are correspondingly complicated. It will be easier for us, and just as useful, if we consider a much simpler game that has also been explored by psychologists (e.g., Eisenstadt & Kareev, 1977). The game is called Go-Moku.

Go-Moku is played on a lattice, a portion of which is shown in Figure 10.11, and is similar to tic-tac-toe. One player tries to place five *Xs* in a line, while the other tries to place five *Os* in a line. The situation in Figure 10.11 is such that the person playing *Xs* is in an unstoppable position. No matter where the person playing *Os* moves, *X* will win on the following move. This situation is called an *open four*, and is obviously one that both players try to create. Meanwhile, the person playing *Os* has created a situation called an *open three*. If you can create two open threes, then you will be in a better position, because if your opponent blocks one of them you can turn the other into an open four on your next move. Thus in addition to the overall goal of making five in a row there are various **subgoals**, such as creating open fours and threes.

If you were writing a computer program to play Go-Moku against an opponent, what sorts of characteristics would your program need to have? First it would need a data structure and an **evaluation function**. The data structure corresponds to what Polya called "understanding the problem." It consists of a representation of the playing board and the possible states of each position on the board, whether *X, O,* or empty. The evaluation function handles all the elements that Polya referred to as "creating a plan, carrying out the plan and evaluating the plan" (Polya, 1945/1957, p. xvi). Given a particular

Algorithm
An unambiguous solution procedure (e.g., the rules governing long division).

Subgoal
A goal derived from the original goal, the solution of which leads to the solution of the problem as a whole.

Evaluation function
The process whereby a plan is created, carried out, and evaluated.

```
+    +    +    +    +    +    +

+    X    +    +    +    +    +

+    +    X    O    +    +    +

+    +    +    X    +    +    +

+    +    +    +    X    +    +

+    O    O    O    +    +    +
```

FIGURE 10.11   A portion of Go-Moku playing surface

position on the board, the program works out all the possible moves. Each of the possibilities is evaluated. For example, a move that makes five in a row has the highest value; one that makes four in a row the next highest; and so on. Defensive moves can also be given a value: blocking five in a row gets the most points; blocking four in a row gets the next most; and so on. The move with the highest value is the one that the program will make.

THE PROBLEM SPACE

In the case of a simple game like Go-Moku, it's possible to have the program evaluate all possible moves at any stage of the game. Thus a successful computer program uses a systematic algorithm to calculate which of all the possible moves would be the best. Current Go-Moku programs will win every time, provided they are allowed to make the first move (Allis, van der Herik, & Huntjens, 1996; Muller, 2001). However, Go-Moku programs typically don't do the sorts of things that more complicated games must. The term **problem space** refers to the representation of the problem, including the goal to be reached and the various ways of transforming the given situation into the solution (Newell & Simon, 1972, p. 59; Keren, 1984). Go-Moku's problem space is very simple, but more complex games such as chess have extremely complicated problem spaces, and they must be analyzed at least two moves in advance. Good chess players need to be able to anticipate not only what their opponents might do in response to their next move, but what moves they might make then, how their opponent might respond, and so on. Thus the possibilities have to be examined two, three, or even more moves in advance. This makes it very difficult to create a systematic algorithm for chess, as we shall see.

A **search tree** represents all the possible moves branching out from the initial state of the problem. As Newell, Simon, and Shaw (1962) pointed out, solving a problem is a bit like making your way through a maze. In a maze such as the one shown in Figure 10.12, you must get from the start (S) to the goal (G), and avoid taking a path that leads to a dead end. From the starting point you are faced with a series of choices, or branches, in the maze. Finding your way through the maze requires you to make the right decision at each choice point. The search tree for a game like chess is enormous, since there are 30 or even 40 legal moves that can be made at any point in the game. If you were to evaluate each alternative to see where it would lead, you would have to examine another 30 or 40 alternatives for each of the first 30 or 40 alternatives.

Problem space
The representation of a problem, including the goal to be reached and the various ways of transforming the given situation into the solution.

Search tree
A representation of all the possible moves branching out from the initial state of the problem.

You can begin to see where this will lead. "If we undertake to look ahead only 5 moves, with 30 legal alternatives at each step, we must consider 1015 positions in order to evaluate a single move" (Newell & Simon, 1972, p. 97). The extremely rapid increase in the number of alternatives that must be considered as you explore the problem space for a complex problem is called a *combinatorial explosion*. Such an explosion cannot be effectively managed by a systematic algorithm. "Even if a computer could examine a million possibilities per second, examining 1015 possibilities would take 31.7 years" (Korf, 1999, p. 372). Since you can't consider all the alternatives, you need non-systematic methods to find the best route through the problem space.

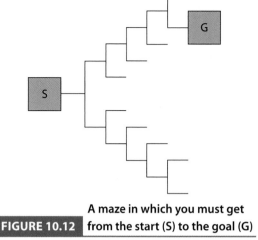

FIGURE 10.12 A maze in which you must get from the start (S) to the goal (G)

GENERAL PROBLEM SOLVER (GPS) AND THE TOWER OF HANOI

One of the most frequently cited computer programs designed to perform that kind of heuristic search was Newell and Simon's (1972; Simon, 1979) **General Problem Solver (GPS)**. To model problem-solving, it's often useful to analyze the structure of **toy problems**. As the name suggests, these are not real-life problems, but the sort of thing you might find in a toy shop. They are useful because they have a known structure and interesting data can be collected from participants as they try to solve them. One of the problems extensively explored by Simon and his co-workers is the *Tower of Hanoi problem* (e.g., Anzai & Simon, 1979; Simon, 1975); see Figure 10.13. In one version of this problem, three concentric rings (small, medium, and large) are placed around one of three posts and the task is to move all the rings from the post labelled A to the post labelled C. The constraints are that only one ring may be moved at a time and no ring may be placed on a ring smaller than itself. Thus you can move the smallest ring to B, but then you can't place the medium-sized ring on top of it.

> **General Problem Solver (GPS)**
> A computer program used to perform non-systematic searches.
>
> **Toy problems**
> Problems used to analyze the problem-solving process.

Before looking at Figure 10.13, which shows the solution to a three-ring problem, try solving it yourself. Although the final goal is to move all the rings from A to C, this goal can be decomposed into a series of subgoals. One subgoal is to move the small and medium rings to post B. This subgoal can be achieved by moving the small ring to C, then the medium ring to B, and finally placing the small ring on top of the medium ring on B. This allows the large ring to be moved to C. The next subgoal is to move the small and medium rings from B to C. First move the small ring to A, then move the medium ring to C, and finally move the small ring to C.

> **Production rules**
> A production rule consists of a condition and an action (C→A).

How can you program a procedure like that on a computer? GPS does it by means of **production rules** (Eisenstadt & Simon, 1997; Simon, 2000). A production rule consists of a condition and an action. The notation that Simon used is C→A, where *C* stands for a condition and *A* stands for an action. Thus one obvious production rule is:

$$\text{Problem solved} \rightarrow \text{halt}$$

If the condition of solving the problem is met, then the problem-solving process is halted. How is it determined that the problem is solved? A problem is solved if there is no difference between the state that has been reached and the goal that was sought. The analysis of differences between the current state and the goal state is an essential part of GPS. At the beginning of the problem-solving process there is a large difference between the current

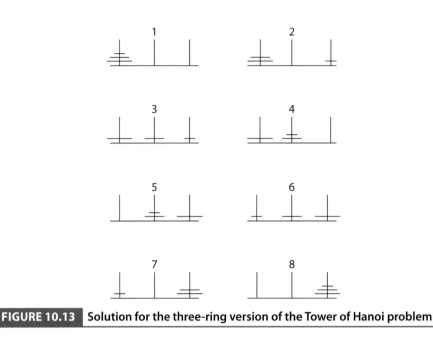

FIGURE 10.13 Solution for the three-ring version of the Tower of Hanoi problem

and goal states. This is in fact the definition of a problem: being in one state and attempting to reach another state (the goal). The heuristic procedure that GPS uses to reduce differences between current and goal states is known as **means–end analysis**.

In order for the problem-solving process to advance, subgoals may have to be substituted for the original goal. For example, if there is no action that would follow from the current condition and lead directly to the goal, there may be a subgoal that can be reached directly from the current state. Once that is accomplished, then the difference between the initial state and the goal state will have been reduced. If necessary another subgoal can then be formulated, and once that is reached, the difference between initial and final states will be further reduced. In analyzing a problem, GPS creates a **goal stack**. The final goal to be reached is on the bottom of the stack, with the subgoals piled on top of it in an order that is the reverse of the one in which they are to be attained. Thus the first subgoal to be reached is on the top of the stack, followed by the next subgoal, and so on.

Notice that the description we have just given is a more general formulation of the specific procedure for solving the Tower of Hanoi problem. Simon (1975) argued that GPS is, as its name implies, a general problem-solving procedure that can be applied to particular problems such as the Tower of Hanoi. The condition–action pairs that would be used to solve the Tower of Hanoi would include rules that recognize when a goal cannot be directly achieved and would then substitute another goal for it, until a legal move can be made. This procedure is applied over and over until the problem is solved.

Thinking Aloud as a Method for Studying Human Problem-Solving

One of the goals of Simon's research was to write computer programs that mimic the procedures participants actually use when solving problems such as the Tower of Hanoi. In order to find out what those procedures are, a technique called **thinking aloud** has

Means–end analysis
The procedure used by General Problem Solver to reduce differences between current and goal states.

Goal stack
The final goal to be reached is on the bottom of the stack, with the subgoals piled on top of it in the reverse of the order in which they are to be attained.

Thinking aloud
Concurrent verbalization: the verbalization of information as the participant is attending to it.

often been used (Ericsson & Simon, 1980, 1993; Newell, 1977). Ericsson and Simon referred to the thinking-aloud method as *concurrent verbalization*: the verbalization of information as the participant is attending to it. By contrast, in *retrospective verbalization* the participant is asked about cognitive processes that occurred at an earlier point in time. Concurrent verbalization relies on short-term memory, whereas retrospective verbalization relies on long-term memory. When participants think aloud, they put into words a process that normally takes place non-verbally. This verbal description of the solution process is called a *protocol*. Although there may be omissions in these protocols, they still contain a great deal of useful information.

Here is a typical example of a protocol generated by a participant while solving the Tower of Hanoi problem, taken from Anzai and Simon (1979, p. 138). The participant is trying to solve a *five*-disk version of the Tower of Hanoi puzzle. You might find it instructive to try this yourself.

1. I'm not sure, but first I'll take 1 from A and place it on B.
2. And I'll take 2 from A and place it on C.
3. And then, I take 1 from B and place it on C. (The interrogator asks, "If you can, tell me why you placed it there.")
4. Because there was no place else to go, I had to place 1 from B to C.
5. Then, next, I placed 3 from A to B.
6. Well . . . , first I had to place 1 to B, because I had to move all disks to C. I wasn't too sure though.
7. I thought that it would be a problem if I placed 1 on C rather than B.
8. Now I want to place 2 on top of 3, so I'll place 1 on A.
9. Then I'll take 2 from C, and place it from A to B.
10. And I'll take 1 and . . . place it from A to B.
11. So then, 4 will go from A to C.
12. And then . . . , um . . . , oh . . . , um . . .

As you can see, there is a lot of information in these protocols. In conjunction with observing the actual behaviour of the participant, these protocols can give the experimenter a reasonably complete description of a psychological process. Obviously, the raw protocol needs to be analyzed carefully. Newell (1977) recommended taking a series of steps to clarify the protocol. First, the protocol should be divided into phrases (descriptions of single acts). Then the experimenter constructs a problem behaviour graph: a concrete description of the way the participant moves around in the problem space. This description can be used as the basis for a production system designed to model the participant's behaviour. Generalizing across a number of participants' descriptions makes it possible to model the kind of system that is eventually embodied in a computer simulation.

Although concurrent verbalization is very widely used, there is evidence suggesting that it may interfere with some aspects of the problem-solving process (Schooler, Ohlsson, & Brooks, 1993). In order to determine the usefulness of thinking-aloud protocols, Weisberg and Fleck (2004) conducted a detailed analysis and comparison of problem-solving behaviour in both verbalization and non-verbalization conditions. They concluded that "instructing participants to verbalize did not adversely affect their thought processes" (p. 1003). It's important that the participants "talk to themselves" rather than to the experimenter. This produces a useful record of the problem-solving process without requiring the participant to communicate to anyone other than him/herself. Protocols obtained in this way resemble inner speech, and may capture some aspects of the process whereby speech regulates thought (Benjafield, 1969a).

Can Computer Programs Experience Insight?

Michael Wertheimer (1985), the son of the Max Wertheimer who wrote *Productive Thinking*, criticized computer simulations of problem-solving from a Gestalt perspective. He argued, as have many others, that insight is nowhere to be found in a computer program. "Missing in such work is the crucial step of *understanding*, that is, grasping both what is crucial in any given problem and why it is crucial. Classical Gestalt analyses of productive thought emphasized precisely this phenomenon of insight" (Wertheimer, 1985, p. 19).

In a reply, Simon (1986, p. 253) argued that there were really two parts to Wertheimer's critique. The first issue is empirical. Can computer programs "represent, and thereby explain, the rich range of learning and problems solving behaviors with which Gestalt psychology has been centrally concerned"? The second issue is whether the concepts of Gestalt psychology can be "sharpened up and made useful to experimental psychology." We'll address each of these issues in turn.

PROGRAMMING INSIGHT

Kaplan and Simon (1990) showed that even a very difficult insight problem can be analyzed in terms compatible with an artificial intelligence approach. The problem they focused on is called the *mutilated checkerboard problem* (see below left). There is a standard 8-by-8 checkerboard, from which two corners have been removed. Participants are asked to imagine placing dominoes on the board. Each domino covers two vertical or two horizontal squares. Dominoes cannot be placed diagonally. There are 62 squares. Can 31 dominoes be placed to cover the 62 squares exactly? If not, why is it not possible for 31 dominoes to cover the 62 squares? Spend a few minutes thinking about this problem.

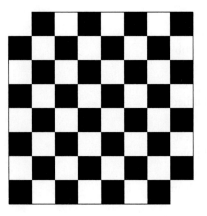

The way that the typical participant initially represents the problem cannot lead to a solution. Participants can imagine placing tiles on the checkerboard for several hours without reaching a solution. At that point the participant will have reached an impasse. The participant may realize "a need to look at the problem in a new way" (Simon, 1995, p. 944). A restructuring of the problem's representation can occur if the participant begins to focus on the number of black and white squares. Notice that both the missing squares are white. This means that there are 32 black squares and 30 white ones. Each domino must cover one black and one white square, and there are 31 dominoes. After covering 30 black and 30 white squares with 30 dominoes, there will still be two black squares left over. Remember that a domino must cover one black and one white square. Therefore, no matter where the two black squares are, they cannot be covered by the single remaining domino. It is not possible for 31 dominoes to cover the 62 squares.

The mutilated checkerboard problem has all the features of an insight problem. First, the way the problem is initially represented leads the solver nowhere. Reaching an impasse, the solver is forced to restructure the problem, focusing on previously unattended elements. This leads the solver to the insight that the problem cannot be solved.

Simon (1995, pp. 943–944) constructed a computational model of insight that was intended to explain the process of restructuring. The program begins searching for a problem solution, following a path that leads to a dead end. When it has been unsuccessful for a certain period of time, a *stop rule* will cause the program to pause and abandon the problem space it has been searching. When the program resumes, it will begin by attending to previously neglected aspects of the problem and represent the problem in a new way. As a result the program takes a new direction, which is more likely to be successful.

This model of insight reflects the behaviour of human problem-solvers. Yet those sympathetic to Gestalt psychology might still say that the program does not capture the richness of the insight experience. This brings us to Simon's second issue: can the concepts of Gestalt psychology be "sharpened up and made useful to experimental psychology"? In Simon's theory of insight, all the explanatory concepts have a definite meaning, and *insight*, insofar as it is a scientific concept, can be modelled just as any other cognitive process can. To modern proponents of the Gestalt perspective who might argue that computer simulation of *insight* and *understanding* requires "twisting these terms out of all semblance to their intended meaning," Simon responds that their concepts may be too distant from empirical science to be meaningful (1986, p. 253–254). In his view, it might be necessary to abandon the language of Gestalt psychology in order to achieve truly scientific explanations.

Solving Problems in Science

Although Simon found it "reasonable that research on human thinking should begin with relatively contentless tasks" such as the Tower of Hanoi, "research in both cognitive psychology and artificial intelligence has been turning more and more to . . . domains that have substantial, meaningful content" (1981, p. 102). Among those domains is problem-solving in science. Klahr and Simon (1999, 2001) observed that there are four complementary approaches to the study of problem-solving in science: **historical accounts**, **observation of ongoing scientific investigations**, **laboratory studies**, and **computational models**.

HISTORICAL ACCOUNTS

Simon (1992, p. 157) recommended studying the history of science as a source of hypotheses concerning the ways in which knowledge is acquired. However, it was Nersessian (1995) who coined the phrase **cognitive history of science**. This endeavour combines "case studies of historical scientific practices" with "scientific investigations of how humans reason, judge, represent, and come to understand" (Nersessian, 1995, p. 195). In other words, case studies of working scientists are informed by the framework that cognitive science provides.

Historical accounts, observation of ongoing scientific investigations, laboratory studies, and computational models
Different methods for studying problem-solving in science.

Cognitive history of science
The study of historically important scientific discoveries in a framework provided by cognitive science.

A landmark in cognitive historical studies was Gruber's (1974/1981; Gruber & Wallace, 2001) reconstruction of the process by which Darwin arrived at his theory of evolution through natural selection. Gruber spent 20 years studying Darwin's notebooks to understand the thinking that led to evolutionary theory. Scientists are often meticulous record-keepers, and this was especially true of Darwin. His notebooks trace the development of his ideas over more than 50 years. Gruber observed that Darwin's enterprise illustrated the strength of the **Zeigarnik effect**: the "quasi-need" to finish incomplete tasks (Zeigarnik, 1927/1967). Although this effect can be detected in a laboratory, its true significance is revealed only when we see someone working on a problem over many years or even decades. This is precisely the sort of lifelong problem-solving that many successful scientists engage in. Giving up is not an option for them, and without such persistence complex scientific problems might never be solved.

Zeigarnik effect
The "quasi-need" to finish incomplete tasks.

Another important strand of research in cognitive history is Tweney's (1991, 1999) analysis of the diaries of the nineteenth-century English physicist Michael Faraday. Faraday's "work revolutionized physics and led directly to both classical field theory and relativity theory" (Williams, 1991, p. 278). Tweney shows that the diaries themselves played an essential role in Faraday's scientific problem-solving. Faraday understood that keeping detailed records of his work was essential because he could not rely on his memory. One reason he could not rely on memory was that he was extraordinarily productive, completing over 30,000 experiments. We have already seen how unreliable memory can be, and Faraday was acutely aware of its failings. Farady's diary served as an external memory aid. However, the diary entries themselves needed to be organized. One way of understanding this necessity is to imagine yourself with an enormous number of files stored on your computer. You need an indexing system not only to find files, but also to remember what the files contain (Tweney, 1991, p. 303). Faraday used a version of the *method of loci*, which we reviewed in Chapter 7, to help him keep track of diary entries. More important, he used paper slips much in the way we might use Post-it notes now. These slips were reminders of diary entries, and he would arrange and rearrange them, looking for patterns, "in effect constructing a larger whole from the separate bits and pieces" (Tweney, 1991, p. 305). The larger whole he sought was the body of scientific laws he eventually came to discover. In Faraday's diaries we can see how important memory is to the process of scientific problem-solving.

THE OBSERVATION OF ONGOING SCIENTIFIC INVESTIGATIONS/ LABORATORY STUDIES

In vivo/in vitro **method**
In the case of scientific problem-solving, *in vivo* research involves the observation of ongoing scientific investigations, while *in vitro* research involves laboratory studies of scientific problem-solving.

Dunbar (2000, 2001; Dunbar & Blanchette, 2001; Fugelsang, Stein, Green, & Dunbar, 2004) pioneered what he called the ***in vivo/in vitro* method** for studying problem-solving in science. *In vivo* means "in the living" and *in vitro* means "in glass." This distinction comes from biology, where it refers to studies of the living organism (*in vivo*) versus studies in an artificial environment (*in vitro*). In psychology it refers to the distinction between ecologically valid research (*in vivo*) and laboratory research (*in vitro*). In the case of scientific problem-solving, *in vivo* research involves the observation of ongoing scientific investigations, while *in vitro* research involves laboratory studies of scientific problem-solving. "A key feature of the *in vivo/in vitro* method is that we can investigate a question in a naturalistic situation and then go back to the psychological laboratory and conduct controlled experiments on what has been identified in the naturalistic settings" (Dunbar, 2001, p. 118).

To set up an *in vivo* study, the investigator needs to find research settings in which successful scientific problem-solving is likely to occur. Dunbar chose to investigate the field of molecular biology because of its attraction for ambitious and high-achieving scientists. By interviewing outstanding figures in the field, including a Nobel Prize winner, Dunbar was able to identify a number of laboratories in which important and innovative research had been and was continuing to be done. He eventually selected eight laboratories to study (Dunbar, 2000, p. 51). Dunbar found that each laboratory held weekly meetings, attended by the head of the lab, post-doctoral and graduate students, and lab technicians. Since a great deal of scientific problem-solving took place at these meetings, Dunbar made extensive video and/or audiotape recordings of them, and these recordings became part of the data with which Dunbar and his colleagues worked. They also built their own molecular genetics laboratory, where participants were first taught about molecular genetics using computer models and then given tasks such as "discovering how genes control other genes" (Dunbar, 2000, p. 50). (The *in vivo/in vitro* method is extremely time-consuming.) These laboratory studies provided a complementary data set. Several findings emerged from Dunbar's studies, but we have space here to deal with only two of them.

Unexpected Findings

Most people resist accepting information that is inconsistent with their expectations. This is a phenomenon we will examine at length in the next chapter, on reasoning. Even now, however, you can easily see that ignoring **unexpected findings** would be fatal to successful scientific problem-solving. Although scientists may initially resist information that disconfirms one of their favourite hypotheses, successful problem-solvers don't persist in trying to confirm their original hypotheses: instead, they set themselves a new goal of explaining the unexpected findings. This is an adaptive strategy in science because unexpected results are so common: Dunbar (2000, p. 52) found that unexpected results occurred 40 to 60 per cent of the time in experiments done across all of the laboratories studied. Always being right is not the hallmark of successful scientists. Rather, success is related to the extent that unexpected findings are made a primary focus of research. This focus leads to the reformulation of scientific models, which can themselves be tested in turn.

> **Unexpected findings**
> Although scientists may initially resist information that disconfirms one of their favourite hypotheses, successful problem-solvers attempt to explain surprising results.

Distributed Reasoning

Scientists in earlier times, including Darwin, may have solved problems largely in isolation, but today successful scientific problem-solving is usually the product of a group effort. Weekly team meetings provide a wealth of information concerning **distributed reasoning** (reasoning done by more than one person). Distributed reasoning is particularly effective in changing problem representations because different people reach different conclusions even when all of them are dealing with the same evidence (Dunbar, 2000, p. 55). Consequently, distributed reasoning is a way of avoiding Einstellung effects and promoting novel lines of investigation instead.

> **Distributed reasoning**
> Reasoning done by more than one person.

COMPUTATIONAL MODELS

Scientific problem-solving can be studied by creating computer programs that simulate well-known discoveries. These programs can derive scientific laws from the relevant data (Simon, Valdéz-Pérez, & Sleeman, 1997). One example is **BACON**, a program that

> **BACON**
> A computer program that has been able to "discover" several well-known scientific laws.

incorporates very general heuristics (Langley, Simon, Bradshaw, & Zytkow, 1987). For example, it searches for patterns in the relations between two variables, such as whether they increase together, or one increases while the other decreases. BACON has "discovered" several well-known scientific laws. Among them was Kepler's third law of planetary motion, which expresses the relation between the length of time it takes a planet to orbit the sun and the distance of that planet from the sun. The closer to the sun a planet is, the less time it takes to complete an orbit. Kepler's third law describes this relation precisely, and was originally derived using data that Kepler got from others. Furthermore, Kepler did not make detailed records of the process whereby he discovered the third law. Thus the heuristics of BACON cannot be compared with a protocol of Kepler's discovery process to see if they are similar. However, Qin and Simon (1990) compared BACON's heuristics with the procedures that students used when confronted with data similar to those used by Kepler. All their participants had experience with physics, calculus, and chemistry. They were told that the experimenters were interested in how scientific laws were discovered. The participants' problem was to "build a formula describing the relationship between two groups of data" (p. 283). Although none of the participants realized that what they had to discover was Kepler's third law, some discovered it nonetheless. The heuristics used by the successful participants were similar to those used by BACON. This research shows that scientific problem-solving may be entirely data-driven, since everything that both BACON and the participants did was determined solely by the data they were given, without any theoretical framework.

Klahr and Simon (1999) noted that each approach to scientific problem-solving has its own strengths and weaknesses. For example, studies of historical records have **face validity** in that they are obviously about scientific problem-solving and not something else. Laboratory studies are not obviously face valid, since true scientific problem-solving cannot carried out in the short time span of a psychological laboratory experiment. However, these studies can provide rigour and precision through control over variables that are hypothesized to be important determinants of scientific problem-solving. Direct observation of ongoing scientific work not only has face validity but may expose new phenomena as well as social factors that other methods may not reveal. Computational modelling is low in face validity, but allows for rigorous testing of models of problem-solving that have been derived from the other methods (Klahr & Simon, 1999, p. 531). No method can replace any other, but all are complementary.

Face validity
Methods that clearly measure what they are supposed to measure are said to be "face valid."

Summary

In this chapter we have discussed how cognitive psychologists approach problem-solving and evaluate contemporary research in the field. First we considered how Gestalt psychologists conceptualize *insight problems*. "Insight" is the sudden, often involuntary, understanding of a complex situation, and Gestalt psychologists stress the importance of understanding how the parts of a situation are related to the whole in the insight process. To solve insight problems we must engage in *productive thinking* and avoid *structurally blind thinking* and *functional fixedness*.

We also considered two approaches to the study of insight problems: the *progress monitoring theory* and the *representational change theory*. Although these theories stand in contrast to one another, they both reflect the idea that there must be a change in the way a problem is represented before an insight problem can be solved.

We reviewed research that supports the involvement of the *anterior cingulate cortex* and the *hippocampus* in the insight process and considered the evidence that sleep promotes insight.

Research on functional fixedness suggests that after the age of about six, people tend to perceive the function of a tool according to its intended function, and that this tendency is found in primitive as well as technologically advanced societies. The term *flexibility–rigidity dimension* refers to the finding that repeatedly taking the same approach to solving a problem can prevent us from considering alternative approaches.

We also considered how computer programs have been used to model human problem-solving behaviour, using Newell and Simon's *General Problem Solver* as an example. Gestalt psychologists have criticized computer simulations of problem-solving for lacking a genuine experience of insight. In response to this criticism, Simon and colleagues have argued that insight problems can be analyzed in ways that are compatible with an artificial intelligence approach, and that Gestalt conceptualizations of insight must be stated in terms that can be studied experimentally.

Finally, this chapter has looked at four complementary approaches to studying problem-solving in science: *historical accounts, observation of ongoing scientific investigation, laboratory studies,* and *computational models*. All these methods are valuable because they highlight different aspects of the problem-solving process.

Case Study Wrap-Up

The story of Teflon illustrates many of the concepts discussed in this chapter. Recall, for instance, how a roll of 3M tape inspired Bob Gore to come up with a way to insulate electrical wire using Teflon. We could say that he experienced a sudden flash of *insight*. He didn't solve the problem *algorithmically*, getting closer to the problem over successive steps with incremental *feelings of warmth* (remember Metcalfe & Wiebe, 1987). It just happened in an instant. Simply seeing the roll of tape enabled him to *restructure* the situation in much the way that the Gestalt psychologist Kohler (1925/1956) described. While his father remained *functionally fixed* on the idea that the wire had to be "coated" with Teflon, Bob Gore's flash of insight led to the realization that it could be "wrapped" or "sandwiched" between two tape-like pieces of Teflon. Weisberg and Alba (1981) might say that the tape served as an effective *hint*, while Knoblich and colleagues (2001) might say that it triggered *constraint relaxation*. Whatever the process that led to it, Bob Gore's insight solved the problem.

? In the Know: Review Questions

1. What is insight? What is responsible for its occurrence? What can be done to facilitate it?
2. What is functional fixedness? Why does it occur?
3. Outline the basic features of GPS. Use the Tower of Hanoi problem to illustrate your answer.
4. Discuss methods for studying problem-solving in science.

Key Concepts

algorithms
analysis of the situation
artificial intelligence
BACON
chunk decomposition
cognitive history of science
computational models
constraint relaxation
distributed reasoning
Einstellung effect (Luchins)
evaluation function
face valid
feeling of knowing
feeling of warmth
functional fixedness (Duncker)
General Problem Solver (GPS)
Gestalt switch
goal stack
heuristic
hints
historical accounts

insight problem
in vivo/in vitro method (Dunbar)
laboratory studies
means–end analysis
mindfulness–mindlessness (Langer)
negative transfer
observation of ongoing scientific
    investigations
problem space
production rules
productive thinking (Wertheimer)
progress monitoring theory
representational change theory
search tree
strong but wrong tendency
structurally blind thinking
subgoals
thinking aloud
toy problems
unexpected findings
Zeigarnik effect

Links to Other Chapters

feeling of knowing
Chapter 6 (butcher-on-the-bus
    phenomenon)

Gestalt switch
Chapter 2 (isomorphism)
Chapter 13 (thinking about persons)

heuristics
Chapter 8 (commitment heuristic)
Chapter 11 (heuristics and biases, repre-
    sentativeness, availability, recognition)
Chapter 13 (warm-glow heuristic)

insight
Chapter 12 (creativity and
    problem-finding)

metacognition
Chapter 5 (elaboration and distinctiveness)

problem space
Chapter 11 (importance of the problem
    space)
Chapter 12 (creativity and
    problem-finding)

Further Reading

Gick and Lockhart (1995) proposed a simple technique for constructing insight problems that you might like to try yourself. They noted that the key to composing a riddle is to get the problem-solver to initially interpret information incorrectly. One way to do this is to use a word that can be interpreted in more than one way. For example, most people interpret the word *lake* to refer to a liquid body of water, but a lake can also be frozen. A riddle can be constructed by requiring the problem-solver to come up with the less common meaning in order to make sense of the situation that the riddle describes. An example of a riddle solution given by Gick and Lockhart is "The stone rested on the surface of the lake for three months, after which it sank to the bottom some 10 metres below." Only when the problem-solver realizes that the lake was initially frozen does the solution to the riddle become clear.

Some criticisms of computer simulation approaches to thinking go even further than the Gestalt critique, arguing that the activities of computer programs don't count as thinking. People who express this belief often ally themselves with the German philosopher Heidegger (1968). For Heidegger, the ability of computer programs to represent the chain of inferences leading from one state to another would not have been the essence of thinking. Computer programs are good at simulating processes such as reasoning and calculation. However, the essence of thinking lies *behind* these processes; it is not reducible to them. Computer programs don't capture the subjective origin of thinking—the concern with the fundamental problem of being alive in the world. Although Heidegger is often difficult to follow, and even more difficult to paraphrase, his ideas about thinking may resonate with many people who have reservations about artificial intelligence.

Computer simulation approaches to psychological processes have often been criticized for what they appear to leave out. Even some cognitive psychologists have suggested that to design a computer program that would simulate emotion would not be a very meaningful exercise; among them is Neisser (1964). Although Simon (1967) attempted to deal with this problem, most work in this area has specialized in cognition, and it is perhaps fair to say that the role of emotion in mental life has been neglected. See also Simon (1995).

For a wonderful example of cognitive history of science see Netz (1999).

Gick, M., & Lockhart, R.S. (1995). Cognitive and affective components of insight. In R.J. Sternberg & J.E. Davidson (Eds.), *The nature of insight* (pp. 197–228). Cambridge, Mass.: MIT Press.

Heidegger, M. (1968). *What is called thinking?* (J. Glen Gray, Trans.). New York: Harper & Row.

Neisser, U. (1964). The multiplicity of thought. *British Journal of Psychology, 54*, 1–14.

Netz, R. (1999). *The shaping of deduction in Greek mathematics: A study in cognitive history*. Cambridge: Cambridge University Press.

Simon, H.A. (1967). Motivational and emotional controls of cognition. *Psychological Review, 74*, 29–39.

Simon, H.A. (1995). The information-processing theory of mind. *American Psychologist, 50*, 507–508.

CHAPTER 11

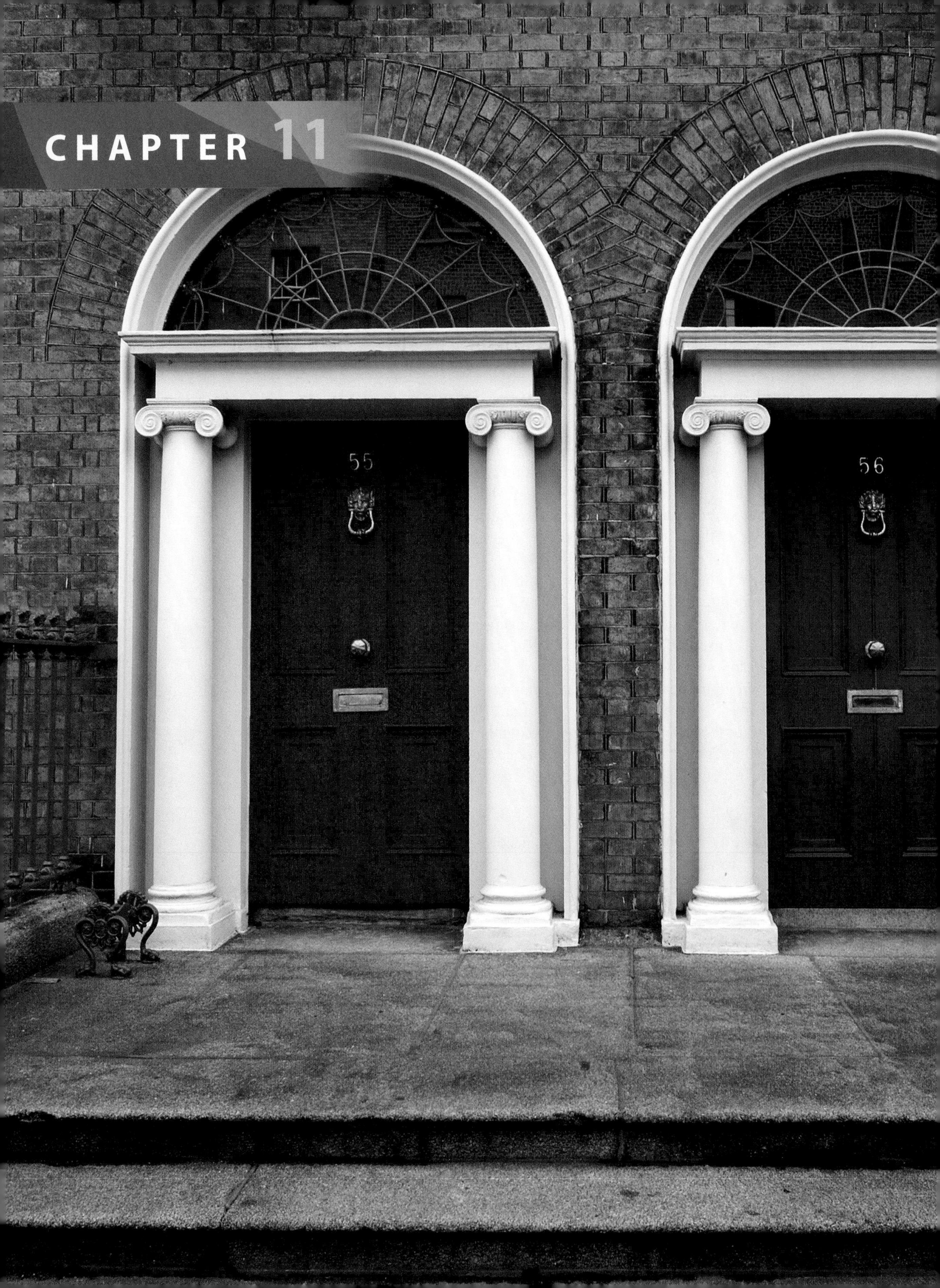

Reasoning, Judgment, and Choice

Chapter Objectives

- To develop an understanding of syllogistic reasoning.
- To review experimental evidence for representativeness, adjustment and anchoring, and availability.
- To identify different approaches to judgment and choice.
- To identify various heuristics and biases that affect decision-making.

Case Study — What a Pain!

Colonoscopy is a painful procedure—at least it was in the days when it was regularly performed without a general anesthetic. Mostly conducted on older people to catch early signs of cancer in the colon and rectum, it begins with the insertion of a flexible tube attached to a camera (a colonoscope) into the anus. As the doctor moves the colonoscope through the intestine, the camera transmits images to a computer screen. (You can read about the procedure in detail on the following websites: http://digestive.niddk .nih.gov/ddiseases/pubs/colonoscopy/ and http:// www.nlm.nih.gov/medlineplus/ency/article/003886 .htm and http://healthfinder.gov/news/newsstory .aspx?docID=662450.) If you are brave (and have a high pain threshold) you can be put under light anesthesia and still be conscious enough to watch images of the inside of your colon on a computer screen. During the procedure, the folds of the intestine have to be straightened out so that its walls can be properly examined. This is achieved by forcing air into the colon to expand it and was particularly painful in the pre-anesthesia days—so much so that many people vowed never again to undergo colonoscopy. For that reason the medical community was very interested in reducing the pain associated with the procedure. This led to the exploration of how it is that people judge pain, and what factors influence their assessments.

One seminal study was conducted by Daniel Kahneman and his colleagues. Over the course of his distinguished career, Kahneman made numerous important contributions to research on attention and perception, many of them while he was a professor at the University of British Columbia from 1978 to 1986 (see http://www.publicaffairs.ubc.ca/ services-for-media/ubc-facts-figures/). In collaboration with his long-term colleague Amos Tversky, Kahneman applied ideas from the fields of attention and perception to the fields of judgment and decision-making, creating an influential research program that ultimately garnered him the 2002 Nobel Prize in Economics (see Kahneman, 2002). We will be discussing quite a few of Kahneman's studies and theories later in this chapter, but here we'll briefly touch on his research into how we judge pain, which is elegantly and lucidly described in his latest book, *Thinking, Fast and Slow* (Kahneman, 2011, p. 378–381). Redelmeir and Kahneman (1996) had patients who were undergoing colonoscopies without anesthesia provide

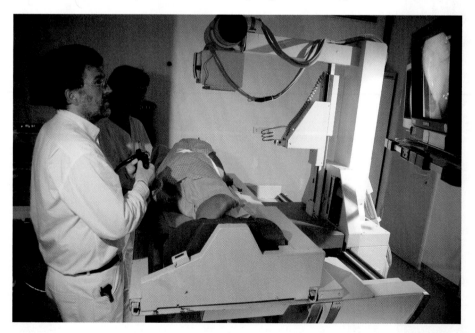

FIGURE 11.1 Colonoscopy

minute-by-minute ratings of the amount of pain they were feeling. The scale ranged from "0" meaning "no pain" to "10" meaning "extreme pain" (see p. 4). Following the colonoscopy, patients were required to retrospectively judge the total amount of discomfort they had felt over the course of the procedure. Redelmeir and Kahneman (1996) centred their discussion of the results on data from two patients (Patient A and Patient B); Figure 11.2 shows their

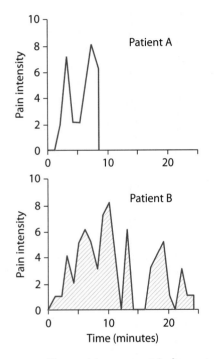

Moment-to-moment judgments of pain from two patients undergoing colonoscopies

FIGURE 11.2

From: Redelmeier, D. A., & Kahneman, D. (1996). Patients' memories of painful medical treatments: real-time and retrospective evaluations of two minimally invasive procedures. *Pain*, 66, 3–8. This figure has been reproduced with permission of the International Association for the Study of Pain® (IASP). The figure may not be reproduced for any other purpose without permission.

minute-by-minute pain ratings. As you can see, Patient B experienced more pain overall than Patient A. Interestingly, however, their retrospective judgments of discomfort did not show the same pattern. How was that possible?

The data strongly suggested that the patients did not base their retrospective judgments of discomfort on the sum of their moment-to-moment experiences of pain. Rather, they formed those judgments by averaging (1) the highest level of pain experienced during the procedure and (2) the level of pain experienced at the end of the procedure. This finding reflects what Kahneman (2011) called the **peak–end rule**. What's even more interesting is that the retrospective judgments of discomfort did not reflect the total duration of the colonoscopy, a phenomenon referred to as **duration neglect** (Kahneman, 2011). These findings led to the counterintuitive conclusion that people will retrospectively feel better about a painful procedure if its duration is extended until the pain has begun to subside (Kahneman, 2011; see also Kahneman, Fredrickson, Schreiber, & Redelmeier, 1993).

> **Peak–end rule**
> Retrospective judgments of the total painfulness of an event are formed by averaging the pain experienced during the most painful moment of the event and that felt at the end of the event.
>
> **Duration neglect**
> The finding that retrospective judgments of the total painfulness of an event are unrelated to the event's duration.

Findings such as those reported by Kahneman (2011) suggest the general conclusion that our judgments are not always based on the objective evidence, although they do follow an interesting variety of rules. In this chapter we will discuss those rules, along with the related topics of reasoning and choice. We begin with studies of reasoning.

Reasoning

SYLLOGISTIC REASONING

There has been a veritable explosion of research in reasoning over the last several years, "turning logic and reasoning into a major field of cognitive psychology" (Evans, 2002, p. 978). One useful definition of **reasoning** is "a process of thought that yields

> **Reasoning**
> A thought process that yields a conclusion from premises.

TABLE 11.1   Four Forms of Syllogistic Reasoning

FORM	EXAMPLES
Universal	All A are B.
Affirmative	All cows are animals. All right angles are 90-degree angles.
Universal	No A are B.
Negative	No tomatoes are animals. No acute angles are 90-degree angles.
Particular	Some A are B.
Affirmative	Some animals are dangerous. Some pigeons are clever.
Particular	Some A are not B.
Negative	Some animals are not cows. Some pigeons are not clever.

Syllogism
A syllogism consists of two premises and a conclusion. Each of the premises specifies a relationship between two categories.

a conclusion from percepts, thoughts, or assertions" (Johnson-Laird, 1999, p. 110). Those "percepts, thoughts, or assertions" are called *premises*. Exactly what makes a conclusion follow logically from the premises is not always an easy question to answer because there are different systems of logic (Evans, 2002, p. 985). The oldest of those systems, Aristotelian or syllogistic logic, has been the subject of much psychological research.

A syllogism consists of two premises and a conclusion. Each of the premises specifies a relationship between two categories. Consequently, **syllogistic reasoning** is sometimes called *categorical reasoning*. Each premise in a syllogism can take any of four different forms (see Table 11.1).

Let's briefly consider each of these premise forms. The *universal affirmative* premise can be represented diagrammatically as shown below for the premise "All A are B." Notice that this premise might refer to a situation in which "All A are B, but some B are not A." This would be the case for a premise such as "All cows are animals," because some animals are not cows. However, sometimes a universal affirmative premise refers to a situation in which "All A are B, and all B are A." This would be true for a statement such as "All right angles are 90-degree angles" (Chapman & Chapman, 1959, p. 224). Thus a universal affirmative premise may be understood in different ways, even though from a logical point of view all possible ways of understanding a premise are equally important.

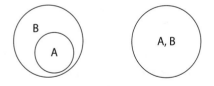

The diagrammatic representation for "No A are B" is completely different. The two circles are separate, meaning that no member of one class is also a member of the other class. An important property of a *universal negative* premise is that its converse also is true. A premise may be converted by reversing the order of the subject and predicate. The converse of "No A is B" is "No B is A." Thus "No tomatoes are animals" also means that "No animals are tomatoes."

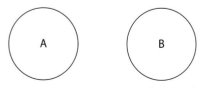

For the *particular affirmative* case illustrated below, in which "Some A are B," there are several possible depictions. Notice that, although "Some A are B," it may still be true that "Some A are not B," or that "Some B are not A." Thus it is true that "Some animals are not dangerous" and that "Some dangerous beings are not animals." Nevertheless, particular affirmative premises may be converted. If "Some A are B," then it is also true that "Some B are A." Finally, as counterintuitive as it may seem, in logic *some* means at least one, and *possibly* all (Ruby, 1960, p. 194); we will explore the challenge that this poses a little later. To reiterate, it's important to recognize that premises such as these may be interpreted in a variety of ways.

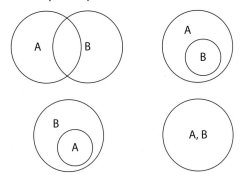

The *particular negative* case is diagrammed below as overlapping circles; however, like the other premise forms, "Some A are not B" is open to a number of specific interpretations. For example, the converse of "Some A are not B" is "Some B are not A." This is an inference that people often accept (Chapman & Chapman, 1959), although it is not necessarily true. It is true that "Some animals are not cows," but it does not follow that "Some cows are not animals." Similarly, people often infer that "Some A are not B" means that "Some A are B" (Ruby, 1960, p. 195). In everyday language, the latter is often the intended meaning. In the case of "Some animals are not cows," it's also empirically true that "Some animals are cows." But consider a statement such as "Some Saudi Arabians are not ice hockey players." Perhaps some Saudi Arabians *are* ice hockey players: we don't know. However, it isn't logically necessary for *some* Saudi Arabians to be ice hockey players just because some of them are not; it may also be the case that *none* of them are.

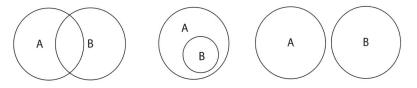

As we have seen, it's possible to interpret the premises of a syllogism in a variety of ways. From the standpoint of logic, all possible ways of understanding a premise are equally important. This situation becomes more complicated when premises are combined to arrive at a conclusion, especially since a valid syllogism requires that the conclusion follows for every possible scenario. Even one exception will render the syllogism invalid.

LOGICISM

At least since Aristotle, many have believed that logical reasoning is an essential part of human nature. This belief is called **logicism**. To illustrate it, logicists point to the practical syllogism (e.g., Thornton, 1982). A **practical syllogism** is one in which two premises point to a conclusion that calls for action (see Henle, 1962/1968, p. 103). Here is an example:

Logicism
The belief that logical reasoning is an essential part of human nature.

Practical syllogism
One in which two premises point to a conclusion that calls for action.

Premise 1:   I need to understand psychology as a whole.

Premise 2:   The only way to understand psychology as a whole is through the study of cognition.

Conclusion: Therefore I need to study cognition.

If you accept the premises, then you will agree that you need to study cognition. Some (e.g., Henle, 1962/1968) have argued that the practical syllogism is a common feature of everyday life. For example: "People who have a virus should act so as not to infect others. I have a virus. Therefore I should act so as not to infect others." Once again, if you accept the premises, then you will act so as not to infect others. For those who believe in the importance of logic in everyday life, the practical syllogism is not an abstraction studied in a cognition course, but "the natural mode of functioning of the conscious mind" (Henle, 1962/1968, p. 103). From this perspective, the ability to reason is what most distinguishes human beings from other forms of life.

One problem for logicism is that untrained participants make logical errors when asked to evaluate the validity of syllogistic arguments. This suggests that processes other than logic determine the conclusions that participants reach. However, it is also true that the same participants do not always make logical errors. Rather, they make logically correct deductions at a level greater than chance (Evans, 2002, p. 992). Consequently, a central concern in reasoning research is to determine the conditions under which participants will reason logically as well as the conditions under which they will reach conclusions in some other way.

THE EFFECT OF CONTENT ON SYLLOGISTIC REASONING

Consider the following syllogism:

All Canadians love snow.
All Mounties are Canadians.
Therefore, all Mounties love snow.

You might object to this syllogism if you happen to know a Canadian who doesn't love snow, and so determine that the first premise is empirically incorrect. However, when it comes to judging the validity of a syllogism, the truth or falsehood of the premises is irrelevant. The validity of a syllogism depends only on whether or not the conclusion necessarily follows from the premises. People often find it difficult to separate the validity of a syllogism from the issue of whether the syllogism is consistent with their experience or beliefs. Thus they may accept an invalid syllogism if they believe that the conclusion is true in the real world (Galotti, 1989, p. 336). However, the effect of believability is greater if the syllogism is invalid (Newstead, Pollard, Evans, & Allen, 1992). To illustrate this point consider the following invalid syllogisms taken from Evans, Handley, and Harper (2001, p. 932).

Premise 1	No addictive things are inexpensive.	No millionaires are hard workers.
Premise 2	Some cigarettes are inexpensive.	Some rich people are hard workers.
Conclusion	Therefore, some addictive things are not cigarettes.	Therefore, some millionaires are not rich people.

Believable but invalid syllogisms like the one on the left were accepted as valid by 71 per cent of participants, while unbelievable and invalid syllogisms like that on the right were accepted by only 10 per cent. The difference in acceptance rate is 61 per cent, showing a very large effect of believability for some invalid syllogism types. Now examine the following valid syllogisms, again taken from Evans, Handley, and Harper (2001, p. 932).

Premise 1	No police dogs are vicious.	No nutritional things are inexpensive.
Premise 2	Some highly trained dogs are vicious.	Some vitamin tablets are inexpensive.
Conclusion	Therefore, some highly trained dogs are not police dogs.	Therefore, some vitamin tablets are not nutritional.

Believable and valid syllogisms like the one on the left were accepted as valid by 89 per cent of participants, while unbelievable but valid syllogisms like that on the right were accepted as valid by 56 per cent. The difference in acceptance rate is only 33 per cent, indicating that believability has a much smaller effect for valid syllogisms. These data are presented graphically in Figure 11.3.

What accounts for the difference in acceptance rates? Evans, Handley, and Harper (2001, p. 955) suggest that participants in a syllogistic reasoning task initially determine whether the conclusion is believable or unbelievable. If it's unbelievable, they then try to find some flaw in the premises that renders the conclusion invalid. However, if the conclusion is believable, they don't try to establish that the syllogism is invalid: instead, they try to find some way of thinking about the premises that renders the conclusion valid. In other words, they set themselves the goal of discovering a syllogism to be invalid only if the conclusion is unbelievable.

THE INTERPRETATION OF "SOME"

The fact that premises are often open to alternative interpretations creates another serious difficulty for participants who are asked to judge the validity of syllogisms. In order to judge whether or not a conclusion is valid, they must consider only those inferences that are consistent with all possible interpretations of a set of premises. Yet people don't always work out *all* the possible interpretations of a set of premises. Consequently, participants reason according to the specific way they interpret the premises (Begg, 1987, p. 63; Begg & Harris, 1982; Ceraso & Provitera, 1971). The way they interpret premises that contain the word *some* provides a good example.

Consider the statement "Some people are human." Although it is a meaningful (and empirically true) statement, it violates our feelings about the proper use of *some* and may even be offensive. The statement "Some people are human" seems to imply that "Some people are not human." Although that is not a logically necessary implication, it seems to be because we ordinarily

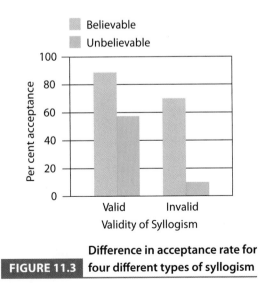

FIGURE 11.3 Difference in acceptance rate for four different types of syllogism

Data from: Newstead, S.E., Pollard, P., Evans, J. St B.T., & Allen, J.L. (1992). The source of belief bias effects in syllogistic reasoning. *Cognition, 45*, p. 262.

interpret *some* to mean "some but not all" (Feeney, Scrafton, Duckworth, & Handley, 2004). Thus according to our usual understanding of *some*, the statement "Some people are human" means that "*Not all* people are human." If you use *some* in this way, you are not using it strictly in the way dictated by logic, in which *some* means "at least one, and *possibly* all" (Ruby, 1960, p. 194). A study by Begg (1987) showed how ubiquitous the ordinary, non-logical use of *some* may be.

In Begg's (1987) experiment, participants were given a description of a set of people and their occupations. For example, they might be told that a group of people consists of 20 artists and 80 writers. Half of each subgroup are men, and the other half are women. Thus subsets of the group can be described using statements such as:

> *Some men are artists; some men are writers.*
> *Some women are artists; some women are writers.*

In one part of the experiment, participants were asked to rate certain statements using the word *some* in terms of how misleading they felt them to be. Statements in which *some* referred to a minority of the group were felt to be less misleading than those that referred to a majority of the group. Thus statements such as "Some men are artists" are considered more easily believed and less misleading than statements such as "Some men are writers" because there are fewer male artists (10) than male writers (40). In other words, for many people the word *some* carries with it the connotation of "less than the whole amount under consideration." The same result was found for "Some women are artists" and "Some women are writers." The former statement is seen as more believable than the latter.

Feeney, Scrafton, Duckworth, and Handley (2004) found that children use *some* in the conversational manner by age seven or eight.

MENTAL MODELS AND DEDUCTIVE REASONING

The most influential current theory of syllogistic reasoning is Phillip Johnson-Laird's (1983, 1988, 2001; Johnson-Laird & Byrne, 1993; Johnson-Laird & Steedman, 1978). According to Johnson-Laird (1988, pp. 277ff.), we construct a mental model of the situation to which a set of premises refers and then draw conclusions that are consistent with the model. There may be several mental models that can be derived from a given set of premises. If a conclusion is consistent with all the models that are constructed, then it is accepted.

What does a mental model look like? From Johnson-Laird's viewpoint, the details of the model, such as whether it makes use of vivid imagery, are irrelevant. The important thing is how the parts of the model go together. A mental model is a mental structure. Let's see how this might work for a premise such as "All whales are strong." We will use the kind of notation employed by Johnson-Laird (1983, Chap. 5; 1988, p. 228). You might first imagine a set of whales, like this:

> whale
> whale

You might form your model from images of whales, or something else entirely. You can represent them in a variety of ways. You can then add to your mental model the information that *whales are strong*.

```
whale = strong
whale = strong
      [strong]
```

The purpose of putting brackets around one of the cases of *strong* is to represent the fact that your model may contain strong things that are not whales. If you then think of Moby Dick, a famous fictional whale, you can add him to your model:

```
Moby Dick = whale = strong
            whale = strong
                  [strong]
```

Having constructed this model, you are in a position to make an inference. You can now see that Moby Dick is strong, a relationship that might not have occurred to you before you constructed your model.

What makes a syllogism difficult is that there may be several alternative mental models. To see why this matters, consider these premises:

No camels are whales.
All whales are endangered animals.

Three mental models can be constructed from these premises. Let's begin with the first model and the first premise, which can be represented like this:

```
camel
camel
_____
          whale
          whale
          [whales]
```

In Johnson-Laird's notation, the line represents the fact that camels and whales belong to different sets. "The two groups are, as it were, fenced off from each other" (Johnson-Laird, 1983, p. 96). The second premise can be incorporated into the model as follows:

```
camel
camel
_____
          whale = endangered animal
          whale = endangered animal
          whale = endangered animal
                [endangered animals]
```

If the reasoner stops here, having constructed only one model, then the most likely conclusion is that "No camels are endangered animals." In fact, Johnson-Laird (1988, p. 229) noted that this as a very common response when participants are given this particular type of premise pair. However, there is a second mental model that can be constructed from these premises, incorporating the possibility that *camels* might be *endangered animals*, too.

camel
camel = endangered animal
_____
    whale = endangered animal
    whale = endangered animal
    [endangered animals]

Johnson-Laird reported that this kind of model can lead to the conclusion that *Some camels are not endangered animals.* However, this conclusion also looks risky if you construct the third mental model:

camel = endangered animal
camel = endangered animal
_____
whale = endangered animal
whale = endangered animal
[endangered animals]

At this point you might want to give up without drawing any conclusion from this pair of premises. Johnson-Laird (1983, Table 5.1; 1988, p. 229) reported that no participants in his experiments drew the valid conclusion that "Some endangered animals are not camels." Drawing this conclusion requires the inspection of the three models from the bottom up, as it were, to see that it is valid in each case. Johnson-Laird's model seems to fit nicely as an explanation for the difficulty that can arise in deductive reasoning.

RELATIONAL REASONING

Relational reasoning
Reasoning involving premises that express the relations between items (e.g., *A is taller than B*).

The scope of mental models theory has expanded considerably over the years (Johnson-Laird, 2001). A good example of its range of applicability is **relational reasoning** (Goodwin & Johnson-Laird, 2005). Of particular interest are *transitive relations* (Strawson, 1952, p. 46), which are usually expressed by comparative sentences such as *A is taller than B*. The relation *taller than* is transitive because if *A is taller than B*, and *B is taller than C*, then *A must also be taller than C*. There are a great many transitive relations; other examples include *wider than* and *deeper than*. Transitive relations typically come in pairs, one of which is the opposite of the other (Clark & Card, 1969; Harris, 1973). Thus *narrower than* is the opposite of *wider than* and *shallower than* is the opposite of *deeper than*.

Three-term series problem
Linear syllogisms consisting of two comparative sentences from which a conclusion must be drawn.

A widely investigated form of reasoning is the *linear syllogism*, or **three-term series problem** (Wason & Johnson-Laird, 1972, Ch. 9). These problems consist of two comparative sentences from which a conclusion must be drawn. Suppose you were told that "B is smaller than A" and "B is larger than C," and then were asked "Which is smallest?" In response to such questions, many people construct a mental model consisting of a horizontal or vertical spatial array (DeSoto, London, & Handel, 1965; Johnson-Laird, 1972). A vertical array could be built by first placing B in the array, and then A above it, like this:

A
|
B

Then you could deal with the second premise by putting C below B.

A
|
B
|
C

By inspecting this imaginary array, you can see that C is the smallest. The conclusion is not required in order to construct the array. Rather, the conclusion emerges once the array has been constructed out of the two premises (B < A; B > C).

This example illustrates the **iconic** nature of mental models: the relations between the parts of the model correspond to the relations between the parts of the situation it represents (Goodwin & Johnson-Laird, 2005, p. 475). It also shows that you can get more out of a mental model than you put into it. Goodwin and Johnson-Laird (2005, p. 476) call this the principle of **emergent consequences**. Once you have constructed a mental model, you can see relationships that were not evident before you constructed it.

Another principle is that of **parsimony**, whereby people tend to construct only one mental model if possible, and the simplest one at that. For example, what mental model would you construct given the following premises? *Ann is a blood relative of Chris* and *Chris is a blood relative of Gordon*. If you're like most people, you will construct a mental model something like this:

Ann
|
Chris
|
Gordon

This mental model leads to the conclusion *Ann is a blood relative of Gordon*. However, treating *blood relative* as a transitive relation leads to an overly simple mental model. It is overly simple because it fails to consider the possibility that Gordon and Ann are the parents of Chris, and thus not blood relatives of one another. Participants given linear syllogisms based on such *pseudotransitive relations* drew the logically incorrect conclusion most of the time. However, when encouraged to think about more complicated examples, such as relationships based on marriage, participants can see the error of their thinking. Once again we see that people may at first behave less than logically, but later can think in a more complex manner.

AN ALTERNATIVE TO THE MENTAL MODELS APPROACH

Another approach to reasoning is based on the idea that there are natural deduction systems (Braine, 1978; Gentzen, 1964; Rips, 1983, 1988, 1994). To begin to understand this approach, let's consider a problem from Smullyan (1978, p. 22). The problem is cast in the form of statements made by the inhabitants of an island, each of whom is either a knight or a knave. Knights always tell the truth, while knaves always lie. Suppose you are told the following (Rips, 1989, p. 86):

Iconic
A characteristic of mental models, according to Johnson-Laird's theory: the relations between the parts of the model correspond to the relations between the parts of the situation it represents.

Emergent consequences
A principle of Johnson-Laird's theory: you can get more out of a mental model than you put into it.

Parsimony
A principle of Johnson-Laird's theory: people tend to construct the simplest mental model possible.

CONSIDER THIS
BOX 11.1

Paradoxes, Reasoning, and Recursion

A process that refers to itself is called *recursive*. Recursion can have interesting effects on reasoning. The first thing to recognize about recursion is that it can sometimes lead to awkward forms of thought. The most famous example is the liar paradox (P. Hughes & Brecht, 1975). There is a very old story about Epimenides the Cretan, who is supposed to have said that *All Cretans are liars*. Because Epimenides is a Cretan, he is including himself when he says that *All Cretans are liars*. Suppose that Epimenides is telling the truth. That means that *All Cretans are liars* and that Epimenides, being a Cretan, is himself a liar. But if Epimenides is a liar, then he cannot be telling the truth and all Cretans are not liars. Thus the assumption that he is telling the truth leads to the conclusion that he is not telling the truth.

What happens if we begin by assuming that Epimenides is lying? That means that his statement *All Cretans are liars* is a lie. If some Cretans tell the truth, then Epimenides' behaviour is merely one example of the state of affairs on Crete. Thus the assumption that he is a liar leads to the conclusion that he exemplifies the truth while lying. We may conclude that if Epimenides exemplifies truth when he lies, then in some sense when he is lying he is expressing a truth. As Hughes and Brecht pointed out, this kind of reasoning can make your head swim.

We have three inhabitants, A, B, and C, each of whom is a knight or a knave. Two people are said to be of the same type if they are both knights or both knaves. A and B make the following statements:

A: B is a knave.
B: A and C are of the same type.
What is C?

Knight–knave problems always have solutions. What do you think the solution to this one is? We know that A is either a knight or a knave. If we assume that A is a knight, and is therefore telling the truth, "B is a knave" must be a true statement. And since knaves are liars, B's statement that A and C are of the same type is false. A and C must be of different types. If A is a knight, then C must be a knave. What happens if we begin by assuming that A is a knave and therefore lying? That means that "B is a knave" is a false statement and B is a knight. Because knights tell the truth, B's statement that A and C are of the same type must be true. If A is a knave, then C must be a knave as well. Thus if we begin by assuming that A is a knight, then we conclude that C is a knave, and if we begin by assuming that A is a knave, then we also conclude that C is a knave. C must be a knave.

Other reasoning problems only look as if they have solutions. We can waste a lot of time trying to solve those insoluble problems. This issue is explored in Box 11.1.

NATURAL DEDUCTION SYSTEMS

Natural deduction system
A reasoning system made up of propositions and deduction rules that are used to draw conclusions from these propositions.

When Rips (1989) asked undergraduate participants to think aloud while solving knight–knave problems, he found that they appeared to follow what he called natural deduction rules. A **natural deduction system** makes use of propositions stored in working memory. Propositions are statements structured around connectives such as *if . . . then*, *and*, *or*, and *not*. The system uses deduction rules to draw conclusions from these propositions. When one proposition follows from another, the first proposition can be said to *entail* the second. Among the rules belonging to a natural deduction system are the following, where *p* and *q* are propositions (Rips, 1989, p. 94):

1. *p* AND *q* entail *p, q*

This rule means that if you have a proposition of the form *p* AND *q* in working memory, then you can derive *p* and *q* as separate propositions. Thus from the proposition "A is a knight AND B is a knight" you can infer the two propositions "A is a knight" and "B is a knight."

2. *p* OR *q* and NOT *p* entails *q*

For example, if you have the propositions "A is a knight OR B is a knight" and "A is NOT a knight" in working memory, then you can infer the proposition "B is a knight."

These are not the only rules in the system, but they are probably enough to give you the general idea. A natural deduction system consists of psychologically basic inference rules. These are "elementary inference principles" (Rips, 1989, p. 94) that participants rely on to solve reasoning problems. Rips showed that the number of errors and the time taken to solve the knight–knave problem depend on the number of inferences required.

The natural deduction approach to reasoning is different from Johnson-Laird's mental models approach. "According to the natural deduction model, people carry out deduction tasks by constructing mental proofs. They represent the problem information, make further assumptions, draw inferences, and come to conclusions on the basis of this derivation" (Rips, 1989, p. 107).

Johnson-Laird and Byrne (1990; Johnson-Laird, 1997a, 1997b) proposed a mental models alternative to Rips's theory. However, Rips (1990, 1997) argued that his data showed no evidence that people construct mental models to solve reasoning puzzles such as knight–knave problems. Gallotti, Baron, and Sabini (1986) studied the solution procedures of participants who had been asked to solve a set of syllogisms and concluded that some of them seemed to take a mental models approach, whereas others used strategies that were more consistent with the sort of rule-following theory suggested by Rips. Nevertheless, it's unlikely that the two approaches can be easily reconciled (e.g., Johnson-Laird, 1997a, 1997b; Rips, 1997).

WASON'S PUZZLES

Syllogisms were not invented for the purpose of psychological research. Studies of syllogistic reasoning are just one example of research that focuses on a task familiar to a discipline other than psychology in the hope that it will shed light on psychological processes. Another approach to the study of reasoning is to invent reasoning tasks that directly tap interesting aspects of reasoning. No one was more inventive in the design of psychologically interesting reasoning tasks than Wason (Evans & Johnson-Laird, 2003). His puzzles have been used in hundreds of studies. We will review research springing from two of his inventions: the generative problem and the card selection task.

THE GENERATIVE PROBLEM

According to Wason (1960, 1977a, 1978; Wason & Johnson-Laird, 1972), a generative problem is one in which people do not passively receive information about a problem,

Generative problem
Participants are told that
the three numbers 2, 4,
6 conform to a simple
relational rule that the
experimenter has in
mind, and that their task
is to discover the rule by
generating sequences
of three numbers. The
experimenter tells them
each time whether the rule
has been followed.

but must generate their own information in order to solve it. Wason apparently discovered this problem in a dream. Participants in an experiment using Wason's (1966) **generative problem** were told that "the three numbers 2, 4, 6 conformed to a simple relational rule which the experimenter had in mind, and that their task was to discover the rule by generating sequences of three numbers, the experimenter telling them each time whether the rule held" (p. 139) for the sequence they generated. At each trial, participants would also write down a hypothesis about the rule. When participants felt highly confident that they had discovered the rule, they were allowed to propose it. If they were not correct, they were told so and then would continue with the task until they discovered the rule.

Participants in such experiments tend to think that the task is more straightforward than it often turns out to be. For example, one of Wason's (1966, p. 140) participants generated the numbers 8, 10, 12, and was told that this sequence was consistent with the rule that Wason had in mind. At that point, the participant had the hypothesis that two are added to each previous number. Then the participant generated another sequence, 14, 16, 18, and was told that it too was consistent with the rule. After generating some other sequences, such as 20, 22, 24, and 1, 3, 5, and learning that they too were consistent with the rule, the participant proposed that *starting with any number, two is added each time to form the next number*—but this was not the rule Wason had in mind. The participant went on to propose several other sequences, such as 2, 6, 10, and other rules, such as *the difference between two numbers next to each other is the same*. This was not the correct rule either. Many of Wason's participants gave up before discovering the rule.

The rule Wason had in mind was *any increasing series of numbers*. Thus all the sequences proposed in the preceding paragraph were consistent with it (as are 1, 2, 3, or 1, 4, 9; in fact, the number of possible sequences is infinite). If you are ever a participant in a similar experiment, you might want to keep in mind that proposing sequences that are consistent with your hypothesis is not an effective strategy: rather, you should propose a sequence that is *inconsistent* with your hypothesis.

To see why this is so, consider the following example. Suppose you believe that *starting with any number, two is added each time to form the next number*. What will happen if you propose a sequence such as 1, 2, 3, which is inconsistent with your hypothesis? You will be told that it is consistent with the rule that the experimenter has in mind. You can then conclude that your hypothesis is false.

Eliminative strategy
A strategy based on
attempting to falsify your
hypotheses, in order to
eliminate incorrect beliefs.

Finding out that your hypothesis is false may not strike you as particularly useful, but in fact that is all you can ever discover with certainty in this task. The appropriate strategy is to attempt to falsify your hypotheses, and thus eliminate incorrect beliefs. In other words, you can arrive at the correct rule by means of what Wason (1966, p. 141) called an **eliminative strategy**.

Confirmation bias
The tendency to seek
confirmatory evidence for a
hypothesis.

As influential philosophers of science (e.g., Popper, 1959) have pointed out, formulating a hypothesis and then attempting to falsify it is a key aspect of scientific inquiry. From that viewpoint, participants in Wason's task were not behaving like scientists. Instead they persisted in seeking confirmatory evidence for their hypotheses. As we noted in the last chapter, even successful scientists may at first resist evidence that disconfirms a favourite hypothesis. Certainly Wason's experiments show that ordinary people are prone to a **confirmation bias**. We will explore this subject in more detail as we go along.

Selection task (Wason)
A four-card problem based
on conditional reasoning.

Wason's (1966, p. 145; Wason & Evans, 1975) most influential invention is his **selection task**. It has given rise to an enormous amount of research. Like the generative problem considered above, this problem can appear deceptively simple, leading participants to believe that they know the answer when in fact they are mistaken. If you have not seen this problem before, you might like to try it yourself. Participants are shown four cards, each of which has a number on one side and a letter on the other side. Suppose you were shown the cards below and told by the experimenter that if a card has a vowel on one side, then it has an even number on the other side. Which cards must you turn over in order to determine whether or not the experimenter is telling the truth?

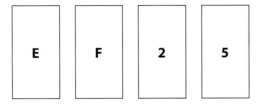

If you concluded that you need to turn over the E and the 2, or just the E, then you are in good company. Those are the most common types of response to this task. Johnson-Laird and Wason (1970) reported that of 128 participants given the selection task, 59 chose the alternatives corresponding to turning over the E and the 2, and another 42 participants chose just the alternative corresponding to turning over the E. However, these responses are not entirely correct. In order to see why there is another answer, we must explore the logical structure of this task more carefully.

Think again about the rule given by the experimenter: if a card has a vowel on one side, then it has an even number on the other side. Suppose that the backs of the four cards you have already seen were as follows:

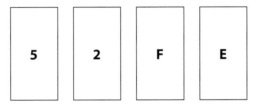

Thus if you turned over the E, you would find the number 5. This discovery clearly falsifies the rule and tells you that the experimenter was not telling the truth. Therefore you would have been correct to want to turn over the E, because the odd number on its back would tell you that the rule was false. Now consider the second card. Because F is not a vowel, it doesn't matter that there is an even number on the other side. Whatever might be on the other side, it can't tell you anything about the rule, so you don't need to turn this card over. The result for the third card is also irrelevant, because the rule does not say that an even number on one side *requires* a vowel on the other. If there were a vowel on the other side it would be consistent with the rule, but a consonant does not falsify the rule. So you don't need to turn over the third card either. The result for the fourth card, however, is particularly informative. If you turn over the 5, you find the letter E on the other side. Notice that this falsifies the rule, because there is a card with a vowel on one side and an odd number on the other. In general, you need to turn over cards displaying odd numbers, because they can falsify the rule.

Initially, the results of experiments using the selection task were taken to support the operation of a confirmation bias. If participants choose a card showing a vowel and a card showing an even number, they are deliberately choosing cards that could confirm the rule rather than disconfirm it. Oakhill and Johnson-Laird (1985) argued that actively seeking information that will disconfirm a rule is one of the characteristics of rational thought:

CONSIDER THIS
BOX 11.2

Conditional Reasoning

Wason's selection task illustrates what is called **conditional reasoning**. Conditional reasoning uses conditional statements—that is, statements with an IF . . . THEN . . . form: IF one condition occurs, THEN another condition occurs. A conditional statement has two parts, the *antecedent* and the *consequent*. The antecedent comes after the word "if," and the consequent comes after the word "then." The rule in the selection task is an example of a conditional statement: *IF a card has a vowel on one side, THEN it has an even number on the other side*. The antecedent of this rule comes after IF, as in: *IF a card has a vowel on one side*. The consequent comes after the word THEN, as in: *THEN it has an even number on the other side*. In general, we can say that conditional statements have the form **IF p, THEN q**, where *p* refers to the antecedent, and *q* refers to the consequent.

Conditional reasoning
Reasoning that uses conditional ("if . . . then")—statements.

Truth tables
A way of presenting the various combinations of the constituents of logical statements.

Truth tables were invented by Wittgenstein (1921/1974, p. 32) as a way of presenting the various combinations of the constituents of logical statements. In the truth table to the right are listed the possible truth values for an antecedent (*p*) and a consequent (*q*). The truth value of *p* can be either true (T) or false (F), as can the truth value of *q*. When both *p* and *q* are true, then obviously the conditional statement *IF p THEN q* is also true. When *p* is true but *q* is false, then *IF p THEN q* is false. This case corresponds to a card with a vowel on one side but an odd number on the other. If *p* is false but *q* is true, then *IF p, THEN q* is still true. This case corresponds to a card with a consonant on one side and an even number on the other; it does not falsify the rule. To drive this point home, consider a statement such as *If it rains, then the match will be cancelled* (Strawson, 1952, p. 82). The match might be cancelled for a variety of reasons other than rain, and that would not falsify the statement. Finally, if both *p* and *q* are false, then that does not falsify *IF p, THEN q*. If it does not rain, and the match is not cancelled, then the rule still stands.

p	q	If p then q
T	T	T
T	F	F
F	T	T
F	F	T

Rationality depends on the search for counterexamples. If, say, you hold the prejudice that women are bad drivers, and your curiosity is only provoked by cases of bad driving, then you will never be shaken from your bias; if a bad driver turns out to be a woman, your prejudice is confirmed; if a bad driver turns out to be a man your prejudice is not disconfirmed since you don't believe that only women are bad drivers. Unless you somehow are able to grasp the potential relevance of *good* drivers to your belief, then the danger is that you will never be disabused of it, and will never understand the force of counterexamples. (p. 93)

However, subsequent research has shown that the selection task is heavily influenced by the content of the cards (Johnson-Laird, 1983, pp. 31ff.). For example, Wason and Shapiro (1971) showed that a more realistic version of the task was much easier to solve. Suppose that the rule is: *Every time I go to Toronto, I travel by plane*. In a task such as this, the majority of participants see that they need to turn over the card with *car* on it. This is because (as you should have guessed by now) if they turn over the *car* card and it has *Toronto* on the other side, then the rule will have been falsified.

THE SELECTION TASK AND DOMAIN-SPECIFIC REASONING

Cosmides (1989) pointed out that there is little evidence to support the hypothesis that people reason in accordance with the rules of a single logical system. If we did use a single system, our reasoning processes should not be affected by the content of the problem. However, as we have just seen, performance on logical tasks such as Wason's selection task is heavily influenced by content. The inferences that people make with a concrete version of the task are different from the inferences they make with an abstract version. According to Cosmides, the evidence is compelling that people do not use the same reasoning processes across different tasks, and consequently there is no single "psychologic" that we use when we reason.

Cosmides (1989; Cosmides & Tooby, 1994; Fiddick, Cosmides, & Tooby; 2000) proposed an evolutionary account of human reasoning. "It is advantageous to reason adaptively, instead of logically, when this allows one to draw conclusions that are likely to be true but cannot be inferred by strict adherence" to formal logic (Cosmides, 1989, p. 193). Natural selection would tend to produce inference procedures for solving "important and recurrent adaptive problems" (Cosmides, 1989, p. 193). What constitutes adaptive reasoning may differ from one type of problem to another. Consequently, different types of problem may require the use of different, *domain-specific* inference procedures.

One kind of adaptive problem that humans must solve involves "social exchange—co-operation between two or more individuals for mutual benefit" (Cosmides, 1989, p. 195). People make **social contracts**. They agree to arrangements in which they give something up in order to gain something else. A social contract specifies the relation between the costs and the benefits of such an arrangement. It would be very important to be able to detect cheaters—individuals who violate social contracts—because they would attempt to have the benefit without paying the cost (Cosmides, 1989, p. 197). Cosmides hypothesized that inference procedures have evolved that allow us to pay particular attention to such cases.

Social contract theory
The theory that inference procedures have evolved to deal with social contracts in which people give something up in order to gain something else.

With this background in mind, consider the inferences required in the Wason selection task. This task can be used to represent a social contract, as shown below. The standard social contract can be stated in the form of the rule *If you take the benefit, then you pay the cost*. Obviously, in order to see if the rule is being followed, you would choose the *Cost not paid* and *Benefit accepted* cards. The other two cards are irrelevant to the detection of rule violations.

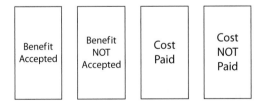

A "switched" social contract has a different structure: *If you pay the cost, then you take the benefit*. How would you detect violations of this rule? If you are behaving logically, then you must choose the *Benefit not accepted* and the *Cost paid* cards. For a switched social contract, the logically correct choices are the two cards that should not be chosen for a standard social contract. Yet Cosmides hypothesized that people will tend to follow a procedure for detecting cheaters (i.e., violators of a social contract).

In order to detect cheaters, you should choose the *Cost not paid* and *Benefit accepted* cards even in the switched version of the social contract problem. In this case the logically correct choice and the social contract choice are not the same. Cosmides presented evidence that participants given social contract and switched social contract problems make choices that are consistent with social contract theory.

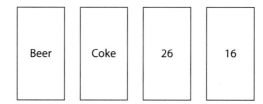

In general, Cosmides argued that in a selection task that has the content of a social contract people will make inferences consistent with social contract theory. However, a selection task that does not have such content does not elicit such inferences. Thus the abstract version of the Wason selection task does not embody a social contract, and does not elicit the same inferences as the concrete social contract version shown above, which was invented by Griggs and Cox (1982). In this example, each card has a beverage on one side and an age on the other side. The rule is: *If a person is drinking beer, then he must be over 21 years old.* The benefit, such as it is, is permission to drink beer. The cost is waiting until one is 21. In order to detect cheaters, you should turn over the Beer card and the 16 card, and this is in fact what participants do when asked to solve this problem.

Cosmides' results were replicated with similar problems by Gigerenzer and Hug (1992). They have also been replicated in a culture quite remote from Harvard, where Cosmides (1989) gathered her original data. Sugiyama, Tooby, and Cosmides (2002) studied the Shiwiar, who are hunter-horticulturalists living in the Ecuadorian Amazon. Sugiyama et al. (2002) hypothesized that a domain-specific reasoning process such as cheater detection would be a cross-cultural universal, since natural selection would have ensured that such a functional process could not be disrupted by "cultural or environment variability" (p. 11538). Because most tests of the existence of a domain-specific cheater detection module had been conducted in literate, industrialized societies, it was important to see if the same sort of reasoning process existed in a much more isolated cultural context. Of course, a selection task involving legal drinking age was not an appropriate research tool for the Shiwiar, and so the task was modified to be culturally relevant. The standard social contract was *If you eat an aphrodisiac, then you must be married.* The switched social contract was *If you give me a basket of fish when you return from fishing, then you may use my motorboat.* Given these tasks, the Shiwiar chose the cheater detection response at a rate almost identical to that of Harvard students. Sugiyama et al. (2002, p. 11541) concluded that the reasoning governing social contracts is "a reliably developing, universal feature of the human cognitive architecture, functioning as an evolutionarily stable strategy."

Cosmides' theory of reasoning holds that there are specialized inference procedures that we use to think about different kinds of problems, although precisely how many inference procedures there may be is an open question. Cosmides argued against the view that people use the same reasoning procedures across all domains. Rather, there may be several different *domain-specific modules* that operate in different ways on problems with different content (Cosmides & Tooby, 1994).

Judgment and Choice

Thus far we have looked at reasoning tasks that involve evaluating or arriving at a conclusion based solely on given information. In what follows we look at what happens when we are forced to go beyond the given information and make judgments and choices between possible, often uncertain, outcomes.

Judgment and choice are two sides of the same coin. Good judgment is a prerequisite for good decision-making. Someone who is able to make good judgments will be able to choose appropriately between alternative courses of action. The circumstances under which we make good or bad judgments have been extensively explored. A parallel line of investigation concerns the nature of good judgment itself.

HEURISTICS AND BIASES

The study of judgment and choice has been strongly influenced by the collaboration of Amos Tversky and Daniel Kahneman, who established a research program devoted to heuristics and biases (Gilovich & Griffin, 2002). A heuristic, as we noted in Chapter 10, is a rule of thumb or shortcut that works in some situations but can mislead us in others, while a **bias** is a predisposition to see a particular type of situation in a particular way. Psychologists such as Tversky and Kahneman have uncovered several biases associated with particular heuristics. In what follows we examine some of the biases that arise in situations that require us to make judgments and/or decisions.

Bias
A predisposition to see a particular type of situation in a particular way.

INTUITIVE STATISTICS

What happens when people try to estimate the chances that a particular event will occur? Suppose someone asked you to predict how often an unbiased coin will come up heads in a series of four tosses. Obviously, the best guess would be two out of four: since the coin is unbiased, you would expect it to come up heads 50 per cent of the time. However, you would probably not be surprised to see no heads at all in any particular series of four tosses. In general, the events that make up a particular sample can't be expected to mirror the proportions of those events in the total population. Thus an unbiased coin will come up heads 50 per cent of the time in the long run, but may come up heads in other proportions in the short run. This fact is called the **law of large numbers**.

One of the misconceptions surrounding the law of large numbers is its relation to what is commonly called the law of averages (Newman, 1956, pp. 1450ff.). The law of large numbers allows us to believe that a particular proportion will obtain in the long run. Now suppose that after 10 tosses a coin still has not come up heads. The common belief in the **law of averages** may lead you to believe that it's now more likely that the next toss will come up heads. People appear to believe that because there will be an equal number of heads and tails in the long run, at some point there must be more heads to compensate for the tails that have already come up.

That this conclusion is incorrect can be seen from the following hypothetical example, adapted from Schuh (1968, pp. 211ff.). It could be that after an initial run of 10 tails there are even numbers of heads and tails over the next 1000 tosses. This would

Law of large numbers
The larger the sample, the closer a statistic will be to the true value.

Law of averages
A fallacy based on the assumption that events of one kind are always balanced by events of another kind.

mean that there were 510 tails and 500 heads after 1000 tosses of the coin. This is pretty close to a 50–50 split; in fact, it is a 50–50 split to two decimal places. All the law of large numbers requires is that the proportion of heads or tails increasingly approximate 0.50 after a sufficiently large number of tosses. The law of large numbers does not require that this proportion actually be 0.50 after some arbitrary number of tosses (say, 1000). At no point in the sequence of tosses, regardless of how many there are, do the odds of throwing a head or a tail differ from 50–50. The odds on any particular coin toss are independent of any other coin toss. To believe otherwise is to accept what is called the **gambler's fallacy**. In reality, your chances of throwing heads are no better after a sequence of tails than after any other sequence.

REPRESENTATIVENESS AND THE BELIEF IN THE LAW OF SMALL NUMBERS

We noted above that the events that make up a particular sample may not reflect the proportions of those events in the entire population. Suppose that half the students at a university are men, the other half women. That does not mean that a small, random sample of ten students will contain five men and five women. Nevertheless, people often seem to believe in what Tversky and Kahneman (1971) called the **law of small numbers**. This is the belief that a small sample should be representative of the population from which it is drawn. This belief is reflected in use of the **representativeness heuristic**, a rule of thumb according to which we make inferences on the assumption that small samples resemble one another and the population from which they are drawn. The following example comes from Kahneman & Tversky (1972):

> There are two programs in a high school. Boys are a majority (65 per cent) in program A, and a minority (45 per cent) in program B. There are equal numbers of classes in each of the two programs.
>
> You enter a class at random, and observe that 55 per cent of the students are boys. What is your best guess—does the class belong to program A or program B? (p. 431)

People will tend to guess that the class belongs to program A, because it has a majority of boys and is therefore more *representative* of program A than of program B.

The same kind of representativeness heuristic operates when people are asked to judge whether or not a particular sequence of events was produced by a random process. Tversky and Kahneman discussed research showing that a sequence of coin tosses such as T T H H T T H H does not strike us as truly random because it has a pattern, and patterns are intuitively unlikely if a process is not operating according to some rule.

Lopes (1982) pointed out that even very sophisticated thinkers with a lot of mathematical training have difficulty specifying what distinguishes random from non-random processes. She noted that there is a difference between a random process and a random product. A random process, such as tossing an unbiased coin, may generate sequences that don't appear to be random. Thus even though it is perfectly possible for an unbiased coin to generate the sequence T T H H T T H H, most of us will feel that this sequence is not one we would choose to represent randomness.

Gambler's fallacy
The mistaken belief that an event that has not occurred on several independent trials is more likely to happen on future trials.

Law of small numbers
The mistaken belief that a small sample should be representative of the population from which it is drawn.

Representativeness heuristic
Making inferences on the assumption that small samples resemble one another and the population from which they are drawn.

ADJUSTMENT AND ANCHORING

Which of the following produces the larger number?

$8 \times 7 \times 6 \times 5 \times 4 \times 3 \times 2 \times 1$

$1 \times 2 \times 3 \times 4 \times 5 \times 6 \times 7 \times 8$

Students who were given five seconds to come up with an estimate consistently judged the second sequence to yield a much smaller product than the first (Tversky & Kahneman, 1974). The average estimate for the first sequence was 2250; for the second, 512. In fact, both sequences yield 40,320. Why even the higher estimate was so far off the mark would be interesting to explore; however, what concerns us here is the difference between the two estimates. This discrepancy arose because the participants **adjusted** their estimates depending on the starting value of the sequence. Because the first sequence started with a larger number than the second, it appeared to yield a larger product than the second. In other words, the two sequences were **anchored** by different values, and those anchors created the illusion that the sequences yielded different outcomes.

In general, when people are asked to judge the magnitude of something, their judgment will be biased by the initial value to which they are exposed (Chapman & Johnson, 2002, p. 121). In another study cited by Kahneman and Tversky (1974), different groups of participants were asked to estimate the percentage of African countries in the United Nations. Before answering, each group was given a random number and instructed to indicate whether that number was higher or lower than their estimate. Those participants initially given a low number (e.g., 10) subsequently estimated the percentage of African countries in the UN to be significantly lower than did those who were given a higher number (e.g., 65). This result suggests that our judgment is not simply a function of what we know, or think we know. Rather, judgment can be biased by aspects of the situation in which the judgment is made.

> **Adjustment and anchoring**
> People's judgments of magnitude are biased (i.e., adjusted) by the initial value to which they are exposed (i.e., the anchor).

AVAILABILITY

Some experiences are more easily recalled than others. We could say that those experiences are more *available* than others (Asch & Ebenholtz, 1962). In general, **availability** refers to the ease with which something can be brought to mind (Horowitz, Norman, & Day, 1966; Tversky & Kahneman, 1974; Schwartz & Vaughn, 2002). Obviously, availability plays a central role in the way we recall previous experiences. There may be many things we have experienced that do not come readily to mind. Tversky and Kahneman have shown how availability influences our judgment.

For example, suppose you were asked to judge how frequently an event of a particular class occurs. Tversky and Kahneman (1973a) asked people to judge the relative frequency with which the letter *R* occurs in different positions in words—specifically, whether it occurs more frequently as the first letter or the third. They found that approximately 69 per cent of participants judged *R* to occur more frequently in the first position. In fact, *R* is more often the third letter.

Why do so many people believe that *R* occurs more frequently in the first position than in the third? In order to judge the frequency of the two classes of words, you might try to recall words of each type. But the letter *R* is a better cue for words beginning with *R* than for words with *R* in the third position. Thus you would be more likely to think

> **Availability**
> The ease with which something can be brought to mind.

COGNITION IN ACTION BOX 11.3

Is There a Hot Hand in Basketball?

A controversial example of the way the representative-ness heuristic works was presented by Gilovich, Vallone, and Tversky (1985). Many fans of men's professional basketball perceive a player who has shot a run of baskets as having a **hot hand**. In fact, Gilovich et al. (1985) found that 91 per cent of fans believed that a player has "a better chance of making a shot after having just made his last two or three shots than he does after having just missed his last two or three shots" (p. 297). In other words, most fans believe that success on any particular shot is not random.

Gilovich et al. analyzed 48 home games played by the Philadelphia 76ers in the 1980–1 season. They could find no evidence that players were more likely to shoot a basket after making one, two, or three baskets than they were after missing one, two, or three. Thus the chance of hitting a shot was not greater after a sequence of hits than it was after a sequence of misses. For example, if a player made 50 per cent of his shots, then the probability of his hitting a shot was not greater than 50 per cent

after a hit, nor was it lower than 50 per cent after a miss. There was no evidence that either hits and/or misses were clustered. Sequences of hits and misses occurred no more frequently than would be expected on a purely random basis.

Another interesting finding was that most of the Philadelphia 76ers the researchers interviewed appeared to share their fans' belief that hits were more likely following hits than following misses. Players and fans alike tended to perceive any sequence of shots as a "streak," even though the probability of making a basket is completely independent of the outcome of preceding shots.

Many people disputed Gilovich et al.'s conclusion, and the hot-hand belief may in fact be true for some sports (e.g., Gilden & Wilson, 1995). And even though statistically sophisticated observers now generally accept that the hot-hand belief is false in the case of basketball, it may still be useful for players to behave as if it were true. Burns (2004) distinguishes between hot-hand belief and **hot-hand behaviour** and points out that even if the belief is false, it may benefit the team if it means that better shooters get the ball more often. Hence, Burns (2004) concludes, it is not always the case that a belief must be true in order to lead to adaptive behaviour.

Hot-hand belief
The belief that a player who has just made two or three shots is on a streak and will likely make the next shot.

Hot-hand behaviour
A bias that leads the teammates of a player who has just scored a basket to let him take the next shot.

---

of a word such as *runner* or *rain* than *carpet* or *berry*. In this situation, words beginning with *R* are more available. Because they are more easily recalled, we believe there are more of them. We confuse the frequency with which we can remember something with how frequently it actually occurs.

ILLUSORY CORRELATION

Illusory correlation
The mistaken belief that events go together when in fact they do not.

Intuitive concept
A concept that is easily acquired and used by almost all adults.

Availability may also be responsible for the phenomenon called **illusory correlation** (Chapman & Chapman, 1969). Sometimes people believe that events go together when in fact they do not. Tversky and Kahneman (1974) suggested that judgments of how frequently two events occur together depend on availability. If thinking of one kind of event makes you remember the other kind of event, then you may infer that the two events tend to occur together in the real world.

Shweder (1977) conducted an extensive review of this kind of thinking. As he pointed out, correlation is not an intuitive concept. **Intuitive concepts** are relatively easy to acquire, and are used by almost all adults. Among Shweder's examples were the concept of an external world, the idea that one thing can be a part of something else, and the notion that one word can be synonymous with another. No formal education is needed to acquire concepts of this kind. However, many other concepts are not so easily learned. Statistical concepts, for example, are not acquired without formal instruction and willingness to learn. Often the proper use of such non-intuitive concepts requires fairly detailed calculations. Consider the following problem: "A piece of paper is folded in half. It is folded in half again, and again. . . . After 100 folds, how thick will it be?" (Shweder, 1977, p. 638). When you first hear this problem, you might intuitively think of a large book and estimate a thickness of 3 or 4 inches. In fact, the thickness is over 200,000 *miles*. You have to actually work out what happens when you fold the paper in order to see why the thickness becomes so great.

Correlation is a very good example of a non-intuitive concept. To explain why the concept of correlation is so difficult to acquire, Shweder used an example taken from Smedslund (1963). Consider the data in Table 11.2.

Smedslund's participants, who were nurses, generally inferred from those data that there was a connection between having the symptom and having the disease. The reason most often given for this conclusion was that the largest number of cases occurs in the cell showing the presence of both the disease and the symptom. That is, the nurses focused on instances that were consistent with the hypothesis that the disease and the symptom are correlated. This experiment is important in part because it is another illustration of confirmation bias. However, it also shows how the tendency to pay attention to confirming instances and ignore disconfirming instances facilitates illusory correlation.

In order to properly determine whether or not the data in Table 11.2 demonstrate a correlation between the symptom and the disease, you must also consider those cases in which the symptom is absent but the disease is present. In fact, the data show that of the 70 people who have the symptom only 37 (53 per cent) have the disease, whereas of the 30 who do not have the symptom 57 per cent have the disease. Thus you can see that the symptom is not a very good predictor of who has the disease and who does not. Therefore you should not say that the symptom and the disease are correlated. On the contrary, on the basis of these data you should conclude that the two events—symptom and disease—are unrelated.

Redelmeier and Tversky (1996) provided a good example of a common, real-world illusory correlation. The belief that arthritis pain is correlated with changes in the weather goes back thousands of years. Many doctors as well as patients still believe in this relationship. However, research on the subject has failed to find good evidence for it. Redelmeier and Tversky obtained data for 18 arthritis patients twice a month for 15 months. Sixteen of those patients believed in the weather/arthritis pain correlation. Patients' assessments of their pain on particular days were correlated with the local weather as measured by barometric pressure, temperature, or humidity. The average of these correlations was .01. Since correlations can vary from −1 to +1, with .00 denoting a complete absence of correlation, this result

| TABLE 11.2 | Relationship between a Symptom and a Disease in a Sample of 100 Cases | | |

	DISEASE		
SYMPTOM	PRESENT	ABSENT	TOTAL
Present	37	33	70
Absent	17	13	30
Total	54	46	100

From: Shweder, R.A. (1977). Likeness and likelihood in everyday thought. *Current Anthropology*, 18, 637–658. Copyright 1977 by the University of Chicago. Reprinted by permission.

means that there is no evidence whatsoever that arthritis pain and the weather are related. Some patients believed that there might be a lag between the weather and their symptoms, so correlations were also computed between arthritis pain and the weather on two days before and two days after the day on which pain data was recorded. The average of these correlations was .00.

Given that it is extremely unlikely that weather and arthritis pain actually have anything to do with one another, what is it that prompts so many people to believe in a causal relation? Redelmeier and Tversky suggest that people may focus on days when they experience extreme pain and look for changes in the weather at those times, ignoring times when the weather changes but their pain remains the same. "A single day of severe pain and extreme weather might sustain a lifetime of belief in a relation between them" (Redelmeier & Tversky, 1996, p. 2896).

REGRESSION TOWARDS THE MEAN

Another way in which the concept of correlation is sometimes misused involves the phenomenon of regression towards the mean. To understand how this works, consider two variables that are in fact correlated: the average height of parents and the average height of their children. However, the correlation is not perfect. For purely mathematical reasons, whenever two variables are not perfectly correlated, extreme values on one variable tend to yield less extreme values on the other variable. Thus very tall parents tend to have somewhat shorter offspring, and very short parents tend to have somewhat taller offspring. The relation between these two variables in a sample gathered by Galton (1886) is shown in Figure 11.4. The average, or mean, values for both parents and children are about the same (roughly 68 inches). The figure can be used to predict the height of children on the basis of their parents' height. Notice how, for any value of parents' height, the predicted value of children's height is closer to the average, or mean, than is that of their parents. Thus parents whose combined heights average out to less than 65 inches tend to have children who are almost 66 inches tall, whereas parents

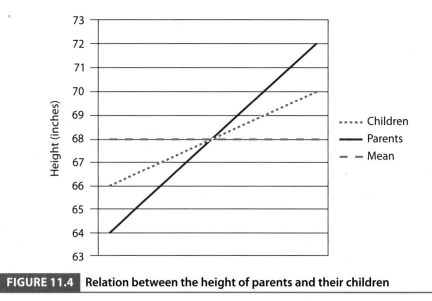

FIGURE 11.4 **Relation between the height of parents and their children**

whose heights average to 72 inches tend to have children who are less than 71 inches tall. This phenomenon is called **regression to the mean**. To regress means to return: thus parents (the "extreme value" variable) tend to have children (the less extreme variable) who regress to the mean.

In general, for two variables that are not perfectly correlated, high values on the first variable are related to lower values on the second, and low values on the first are related to higher values on the second. This means that when you use the values of one variable to predict the values of the other, you will find that the predicted values of the second variable are somewhat closer to the mean, or average, of the second variable. Keep in mind that this occurs for purely mathematical reasons. Galton (1889, as cited by Walker, 1943, and Senders, 1958), who first discovered regression to the mean, put it this way:

> The law of Regression tells heavily against the full hereditary transmission of any gift. Only a few out of many children would be likely to differ as widely as the more exceptional of the two parents. The more bountifully the Parent is gifted by nature, the more rare will be his good fortune if he begets a son who is endowed yet more largely. But the law is even-handed: it levies an equal succession-tax on the transmission of badness as of goodness. If it discourages the extravagant hopes of a gifted parent that his children will inherit all his powers, it no less discountenances extravagant fears that they will inherit all his weakness and disease. (p. 106)

Regression to the mean occurs in a great many situations beyond the one that intrigued Galton. Tversky and Kahneman (1974) gave several examples. Suppose that some students perform much better on a particular examination than would normally be expected of them. What would you predict for their next examination? If you follow the logic of regression towards the mean, you would predict that their next examination would be closer to their average level of performance. Similarly, a dismal score on an exam should predict a better outcome next time.

There is no need for causal explanations of this variability. Yet a causal explanation is often precisely what we want. After a poor performance is succeeded by a better one, we may attribute the difference to the fact that we worked harder the second time, or that the exam was easier. Such explanations may account for some of the variability in our performance, but some variability will remain unexplained. It is just this uncertainty that people find hard to accept. Because we are anxious to understand the reasons for our successes and failures, we sometimes impose unwarranted interpretations.

Tversky and Kahneman pointed out the relevance of regression to the mean for understanding the role that reward and punishment may, or may not, play in changing behaviour. For example, if a child performs exceptionally well on some task, then it's tempting for parents to offer praise. Those same parents might be disappointed when, on a subsequent occasion, the child's performance is not so good. If they punish the child and (as is likely) the performance improves the next time around, the parents may be tempted to credit the punishment. Yet these varying results may have nothing to do with the fact that the child's behaviour was rewarded or punished: they may come about purely as a consequence of regression to the mean. As Tversky and Kahneman (1973b) observed, "the human condition is such that, by chance alone, one is most often rewarded for punishing others and most often punished for rewarding them" (p. 251).

Regression to the mean
For purely mathematical reasons, whenever two variables are not perfectly correlated, extreme values on one variable tend to be related to values on the other variable that are closer to (i.e., regressed to) the mean of that variable.

THINK TWICE
BOX 11.4

Assessing Your Own Reasoning Abilities

How good are your reasoning and decision-making skills? One popular test was developed by Frederick (2005). Known as the Cognitive Reflection Test, or CRT, it consists of the three following problems. Without looking at the answers below, try to answer them as quickly as you can.

The answers are as follows: (1) 5 cents; (2) 5 minutes; and (3) 47 days. Chances are that you missed at least one of them. Why? Although the questions look easy, they are actually the sort of "trick questions" you hope never to see on a test or exam. Each one is designed in such as way as to lead you to think of an "intuitive" answer very quickly. For instance, when answering the third question, you think about covering *half* the lake, and this immediately leads you to think it should take *half* the time. Half the patch, half the time, right? Wrong! What often gets missed

is the fact that it would have taken 47 days of doubling for the patch to reach half of its final extent: on day 47 it would have been half the size that it would be on the final, 48th day.

Fredrick (2005) notes that to be successful on questions like these, you have to (a) recognize that the first answer you think of is wrong, (b) put it aside, and (c) continue to apply rigorous reasoning. This test is often used to distinguish between decision-making done by a fast, intuitive system (which in this case gives you the wrong answer), and a much slower, more effortful rational system (which in this case provides the right answer). This distinction is captured in the title of Kahneman's *Thinking Fast and Slow*, which we mentioned at the beginning of this chapter.

(1) A bat and a ball cost $1.10 in total. The bat costs $1.00 more than the ball. How much does the ball cost? _____ cents

(2) If it takes 5 machines 5 minutes to make 5 widgets, how long would it take 100 machines to make 100 widgets? _____ minutes

(3) In a lake, there is a patch of lily pads. Every day, the patch doubles in size. If it takes 48 days for the patch to cover the entire lake, how long would it take for the patch to cover half of the lake? _____ days

FIGURE 11.5 The three-question CRT

From: Frederick, S. (2005). Cognitive reflection and decision making. *Journal of Economic Perspectives, 19*, 25-42.

Training in Statistical Reasoning

THE IMPORTANCE OF THE PROBLEM SPACE

We considered the problem space within which reasoning takes place in Chapter 10. As we noted then, the problem space consists of the way the problem is represented, including the goal to be reached and the various ways in which the situation might be transformed into the solution (Newell & Simon, 1972, p. 59). Keren (1984) has analyzed how misunderstanding of the problem space leads to the use of inappropriate heuristics. Consider the following problem:

> Three coins are to be given to two children (Dan and Mike) using the following rule. An ordinary deck of cards is shuffled and cut. If the top card is red, Dan gets a coin, but if it is black, Mike gets a coin. The deck is shuffled again, and the next coin is assigned using the same procedure. Finally, the third coin is allocated, again following the same method. What is more likely to occur:
>
> a. One child will get three coins; the other will get none.
> b. One child will get two coins; the other one.
> c. Both possibilities (a) and (b) are equally likely.

The correct answer is (b), but more than 40 per cent of participants chose the incorrect but intuitively reasonable alternative (c). In order to see why (b) is correct, examine Figure 11.6. It is a tree diagram of the various possible outcomes. Notice that there are eight possibilities, and that in six of them one child gets two coins and the other child gets one. Thus alternative (b) is the most likely outcome. If you think through the problem in this way, you then they will get the right answer.

However, there is at least one other way of thinking about the problem, which leads to the wrong answer. Participants might imagine only the possible ways in which the coins could be divided, without thinking about how these divisions come about. When the problem is so construed, then there appear to be only four possible outcomes. Mike could get 3, and Dan 0; Mike could get 2 and Dan 1; Mike could get 1 and Dan 2; and Mike could get 0 and Dan 3. If the participant assumes that these alternatives are equally likely, then alternative (c) appears to be correct. Half the time one child gets 3 coins and the other 0; and the other half of the time one child gets 2 coins and the other gets 1.

By considering the different ways in which participants can represent a problem, we can understand why some answers seem more reasonable than others. Different problem spaces provide different *frames* within which a problem can be understood or misunderstood (Kahneman & Tversky, 1984). As Tversky and Kahneman (1983) have noted, "because we normally do not have adequate formal models for computing the probabilities of such events, intuitive judgment is often the only practical method for

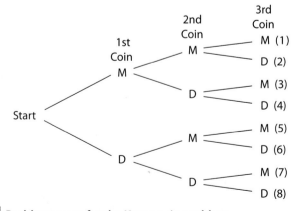

FIGURE 11.6 **Problem space for the Keren coin problem**

From: Keren, G. (1984). On the importance of identifying the correct "problem space". *Cognition, 16*, 121–128. Copyright 1984 by Elsevier Science Publishers. Reprinted by permission.

assessing uncertainty" (p. 293). In the Keren coin problem on the previous page, people who don't think through the problem may rely on the more intuitive solution procedure and end up making an incorrect inference. However, as Nisbett, Krantz, Jepson, and Kunda (1983) have observed, proper training in statistics may enable us to think more appropriately about problems like these.

As Nisbett et al. pointed out, some situations make it more likely that even untrained people will use the appropriate reasoning procedures. Nisbett et al. proposed that three factors determine when people will use the appropriate reasoning procedures:

1. Clarity of the problem space. In the Keren problem it's important to be aware of all the alternatives. This is true of any problem that calls for statistical reasoning. Some problem spaces are easier to grasp than others. When the problem space is poorly understood, errors may result.

2. Recognition of the operation of chance. It's easier to see chance at work in some situations than in others. In sports the operation of chance factors such as weather and injuries is relatively obvious, and the effect these factors have on the outcome of games is clear. Yet as we saw in our discussion of the hot-hand fallacy people often perceive chance phenomena as orderly even when they know better. Nevertheless, we may be more likely to use sound reasoning procedures when we are aware that chance is a factor.

3. Cultural prescription. People may reason better if they come from a culture that values statistical reasoning and provides the appropriate training.

In one of their studies Nisbett et al. (1983) gave participants two problems. The first involved a football coach who typically finds two or three exciting prospects at the beginning of each season, but finds that they seldom go on to perform as well as he had expected. Participants are asked to explain why the coach has to revise his opinion of players he originally thought were brilliant.

The second problem involved a director of a theatre company who is initially enthusiastic about the stage presence of some novice actors but is eventually disappointed by their performances. Participants were asked to explain why the director has to revise her opinion of actors who showed such promise at first.

Both these problems require at least an intuitive understanding of the concept of regression to the mean, and the explanation is the same in both cases: the novices performed at an exceptionally high level at the tryouts, and after that their performance returned to its usual level. Causal explanations such as "The boys who did well at tryout slacked off to avoid making their teammates jealous" were not relevant.

Nisbet et al. (1983) found that participants who had some experience with the field of activity mentioned in the problem were more likely to reason appropriately about it. Thus people who had played team sports in high school or college were more likely to recognize a regression effect in the first problem than were those who did not have such experience. Similarly, participants with acting experience were more likely to recognize a regression effect in the second problem.

Nisbett et al. interpreted these results to mean that expertise in a particular area may lead to greater use of appropriate statistical reasoning procedures. They also pointed out that becoming an expert in a particular area means becoming a member of its subculture (e.g., football players, actors), and that the process of enculturation may require the acquisition of the reasoning procedures appropriate to that domain. In that case, some of the heuristics that people use may be *domain-specific*. Nevertheless, the fact that we can learn to use the correct inference procedures in specific areas suggests that we can be trained to use statistical reasoning in almost any context. Nisbett et al. (1983) believed that such training was becoming the norm in our culture, and that in time we might see a general rise in the ability to reason statistically.

It's important to remember, however, that training in the methods of one field does not tell you anything about appropriate reasoning procedures in other fields. Lehman, Lempert, and Nisbett (1988) reviewed the reasoning ability of people in various fields who had received training in the reasoning procedures specific to their disciplines. Graduate students in psychology who had been trained in statistical reasoning were able to generalize their training to problems in everyday life. However, training in chemistry did not provide that kind of benefit: "chemistry provides no improvement in statistical or methodological reasoning. . . . [T]here is little need to differentiate among the various types of causal relations because chemistry deals primarily with necessary-and-sufficient causes. . . . [T]he luxury of not being confronted with messy problems that contain a substantial uncertainty and a tangled web of causes means that chemistry does not teach some rules that are relevant to everyday life" (Lehman, Lempert, & Nisbett, 1988, p. 441). Thus training in a discipline such as psychology may help a student cope with reasoning problems in everyday life in a way that training in a discipline such as chemistry cannot. Mill, Gray, and Mandel (1994, p. 247) further explored Lehman and Nisbett's (1990) claim that "undergraduate training in the social sciences, particularly psychology, does lead students to apply statistical and methodological reasoning skills to a range of everyday situations." Mill, Gray, and Mandel (1994) recruited participants from undergraduate research methods and statistics courses in psychology and tested their ability to apply what they were being taught to situations in everyday life. For example, they were asked to evaluate the claim of a pharmaceutical company that its new drug led to recovery from illness in 75 per cent of patients who received it. Of course, such a claim is meaningless unless you know what percentage of people recover without taking the drug. It turned out that students who had taken methods and statistics courses did no better on "critical thinking" items than students who had not taken such courses. Only students who had taken additional tutorials in critical thinking showed improvement. Thus undergraduate training in research methods does not necessarily mean that students will be able to apply what they have been taught. Recall Kahneman's (2002, p. 451) observation that reason is not very vigilant, and "allows many intuitive judgments to be expressed, including some that are erroneous." To apply what you have learned about statistical reasoning to problems in everyday life is hard work, and sometimes people may prefer to forgo the effort.

Ecological Rationality

Tversky and Kahneman's work has not gone unchallenged. For example, Gigerenzer and Goldstein (1996, p. 651) argued that heuristics and biases research suggests that people are "hopelessly lost in the face of real-world complexity, given their supposed inability to reason according to the canon of classical rationality, even in simple laboratory experiments." By contrast, Gigerenzer and Goldstein proposed that people usually make good decisions by using simple heuristics that rely on ecologically valid cues. For example, consider what Goldstein and Gigerenzer (2002) call the **recognition heuristic**:

Recognition heuristic
When choosing between two objects (according to some criterion), if one is recognized and the other is not, then select the former.

When choosing between two objects (according to some criterion), if one is recognized and the other is not, then select the former. For instance, if deciding at mealtime between Dr. Seuss's famous menu choices of green eggs and ham (using the criterion of being good to eat), this heuristic would lead one to choose the recognized ham over the unrecognized odd-colored eggs. (Todd & Gigerenzer, 2000, p. 732)

The recognition heuristic relies on the fact than people are very good at telling the difference between events they have experienced previously and those they have not. The classic demonstration of this discriminatory behaviour was an experiment by Shepard (1969), who allowed participants to examine 612 photographs for as long as they liked. They were then given 68 pairs of photographs. One member of each pair was from the previous set and one was new. Participants were able to tell which was which about 99 per cent of the time. But the recognition heuristic will not work unless two conditions are met. First, the person must recognize some of the alternatives between which a choice must be made, but not all of them. Second, the alternatives that are recognized must also be the correct choices. Under those conditions the recognition heuristic is ecologically valid and using it is **ecologically rational**. A heuristic is ecologically rational if it "produces useful inferences by exploiting the structure of information in the environment" (Todd, Fiddick, & Krauss, 2000, p. 375).

Gigerenzer and his colleagues (Goldstein & Gigerenzer, 2002) have shown how the recognition heuristic works in a series of demonstrations. One such demonstration required participants to decide which of two US cities was larger. When the two cities were San Diego and San Antonio, American students correctly chose San Diego two-thirds of the time. However, German students correctly chose San Diego 100 per cent of the time. This result is counter-intuitive because we would expect that American students would know more about American cities than would German students. The explanation is that the American students recognized both San Antonio and San Diego as American cities, and therefore were unable to use the recognition heuristic to distinguish between them. Thus American students could not know which city was larger unless they had that knowledge in their memory to be recalled. The German students, however, didn't need to know which city was larger in order to make the correct choice: they simply picked San Diego because they recognized it and rejected San Antonio because they did not recognize it. Recognition is ecologically valid in a situation like this because people are more likely to have heard of large cities than small ones. Therefore the recognition heuristic is *ecologically rational* in this case.

This example illustrates the difference between the recognition heuristic and the *availability heuristic*, which we considered earlier in this chapter. The availability heuristic inclines the participant to decide in favour of the most easily recallable alternative. By contrast, the recognition heuristic doesn't require participants to recall anything. They don't need to *recall* the population of San Diego or San Antonio. All they need to do is *recognize* one of the two choices.

One of the implications of the recognition heuristic is that people who know less may sometimes be able to make better judgments than people who know more. Here is an example modelled on one used by Goldstein and Gigerenzer (2002, p. 79). Imagine three American sisters, each of whom must take a test on the relative size of Canadian cities. One of the Americans is housebound and knows nothing about Canada. The second knows only what she has read in the press and seen on television. The third has been studying Canadian geography and history. Who will do better on the test? Goldstein & Gigerenzer would predict that the second sister would do better than

Ecological rationality
A heuristic is ecologically rational if it produces useful inferences by exploiting the structure of information in the environment.

the others, because "she is the only one who can use the recognition heuristic" (2002, p. 79). The third sister knows *too much* to be able to use it, and the first sister knows *too little*. This outcome is called the **less-is-more effect**.

CRITICISMS OF THE ECOLOGICAL RATIONALITY APPROACH

Gigerenzer and his colleagues have proposed the existence of an *adaptive toolbox* containing a variety of heuristics, of which the recognition heuristic is usually a component. However, some have argued that the recognition heuristic is much more limited in its generality than Gigerenzer and his group suggest (e.g., Oppenheimer, 2003; Newell, 2005). Others have suggested that simple heuristics might work well for some relatively unimportant decisions, but that they can't be applied to truly important decisions such as choosing a mate or raising a child:

> Mate selection does not just involve the self and the partner. It usually also involves the interests of parents, friends, members of reference groups, and so forth. A career decision, too, often involves many different parties, as do union–management negotiations, international negotiations, and the like. . . . I suspect that many others seeking decision rules for the high stakes decisions they encounter in their lives will not find that [these] rules . . . make their decisions all that easy. (Sternberg, 2000a, p. 764)

For their part, Kahneman and Tversky (1996) argued that Gigerenzer had exaggerated the difference between his work and theirs. There is no reason why the recognition heuristic couldn't be studied within the framework of heuristics and biases research (Kahneman & Frederick, 2002, pp. 58–59). It's possible that, over time, these two approaches will become more complementary than antagonistic.

▮ Summary

In this chapter we have seen how logic and reasoning can shed light on psychological processes. Different systems of logic vary in their answers to the question of what makes a conclusion follow logically from a set of assertions or *premises*.

Syllogistic or categorical reasoning examines the relation between two premises and a conclusion and takes several forms. One influential theory of syllogistic reasoning proposes that we construct a *mental model* of the situation to which a set of premises refers and then draw conclusions that are consistent with the model. Another, *natural deduction systems* theory, holds that we use deduction rules to draw conclusions from various propositions—statements structured around connectives such as *if . . . then*, *and*, *or*, and *not*—that are stored in working memory. *Wason's puzzles* represent an alternative approach, focusing not on syllogistic reasoning but on a variety of tasks that directly tap interesting aspects of reasoning (*generative problem*, *eliminative strategy*, *the selection task*).

All three of the above research approaches examine the more or less formal reasoning we do when we are given certain information and draw conclusions from it. In many cases, however, the information required for that kind of reasoning is not available. In those cases we must rely on judgment. Good judgment is the ability to choose appropriately between alternative courses of action. Much research has been conducted on the factors that influence judgment for good or ill, including heuristics and biases, statistical reasoning, and ecological rationality.

Case Study Wrap-Up

We began this chapter with a discussion of how people judge the pain they experience during colonoscopies. It seems that retrospective judgments of pain are not based on the total amount of moment-to-moment pain experienced during an event (Kahneman, 2011). Rather, such judgments are based on the most salient and easily recallable moments. After reading the chapter, you will recognize that judgments of pain involve the use of *heuristics* and *biases*. How we assess our pain depends on the *availability* of the experience. Because the two moments that come to mind most readily are the most painful moment and the most recent one, those are the moments on which people base their retrospective judgments, neglecting most of the other moments and even the duration of the procedure.

The striking point is that human judgment and decision-making are rarely if ever fully rational. Instead of applying logical reasoning, we make judgments on the fly, based on fragments of information, and often give less weight to the validity of an argument than to its fit with our own biases. As Kahneman (2011, p. 45) notes, failure to do the slow, deliberate work of rational thinking often leads to "embarrassing" results.

? In the Know: Review Questions

1. Discuss possible sources of difficulty in syllogistic reasoning, paying particular attention to content bias and the meaning of *some*.

2. Outline Johnson-Laird's mental models approach to syllogistic reasoning. Compare it to natural deduction theory.

3. What do experiments conducted using Wason's puzzles suggest about what makes a reasoning problem difficult?

4. Define and give examples of each of the following: representativeness; adjustment and anchoring; availability. In each case, briefly describe a relevant experiment.

5. Do you believe in the hot hand? Give reasons for your answer. In what other situations might the hot hand be a true or a false belief?

6. Define and give examples of illusory correlation and regression to the mean. In your answer, include a discussion of the effect of statistical training on these phenomena.

7. What is rational about the recognition heuristic? Can you think of any situations other than those identified in the text in which it might work?

Key Concepts

adjustment and anchoring
availability
conditional reasoning
confirmation bias
duration neglect
ecologically rational

eliminative strategy
emergent consequences
gambler's fallacy
generative problem (Wason)
heuristics and biases (Tversky & Kahneman)

hot-hand belief and hot-hand behaviour
iconic (mental models)
illusory correlation
intuitive concept
law of averages
law of large numbers
law of small numbers
less-is-more effect
logicism
natural deduction system (Rips)
parsimony
peak–end rule

practical syllogism
reasoning
recognition heuristic (Gigerenzer)
regression to the mean (Galton)
relational reasoning
representativeness heuristic
selection task (Wason)
social contract theory (Cosmides)
syllogistic reasoning
three-term series problem
truth tables

Links to Other Chapters

mental models
Chapter 7 (cognitive maps and mental
  models)

emergent properties
Chapter 2 (Sperry)
Chapter 7 (imagery and ambiguous
  figures)

heuristics
Chapter 8 (commitment heuristic)
Chapter 13 (warm-glow heuristic)

availability
Chapter 13 (warm-glow heuristic)

Further Reading

Suppose that the following assertions apply to a specific hand of cards:

> If there is a king in the hand then there is an ace in the hand or if there is a queen in
> the hand then there is an ace in the hand.
> There is a king in the hand.
> What, if anything, follows?

If you think there *must* be an ace in the hand, then you should read Johnson-Laird and Savary (1999). If you find paradoxes interesting, read Sainsbury (1988). For a novel approach to the study of reasoning based on the centrality of linguistic processes see Polk and Newell (1995).

Research interest in the selection task has been intense. As a consequence, there are too many alternative explanations to fully cover in this text. For an account of the selection task based on relevance theory see Sperber and Girotto (2002). For a connectionist approach see Leighton and Dawson (2001). Atran (2001) argues that the selection task does not require a domain-specific interpretation.

Josephs, Giesler, and Silvera (1994) proposed a heuristic called the *quantity principle*. In one experiment, participants were asked to write an essay that they believed would earn them a very high grade. Those who used a small font for their essays tended to write more than those who chose a larger font, even though no restrictions were placed on the length of the essay. Since a small font requires more words to produce the same number of pages as a larger font, it appeared that quantity was the important variable influencing participants' judgment of the quality of their essays. The saying "more is better" describes the principle that is consistent with the *quantity principle*, a heuristic that tends to make us confuse quality with quantity. Have you known any professors who seemed to believe that good essays have more pages than poor ones?

For some marvellous illustrations of how meaningful coincidences can mislead us, see Eco (1989).

Over (2000) provides a good brief critique of the ecological rationality issue.

Atran, S. (2001). A cheater detection module? Dubious interpretations of the Wason selection task and logic. *Evolution and Cognition, 7*, 1–7.

Eco, U. (1989). *Foucault's pendulum.* New York: Knopf.

Johnson-Laird, P.N., & Savary, F. (1999). Illusory inferences: A novel class of erroneous deductions. *Cognition, 71*, 191–229.

Josephs, R.A., Giesler, R.B., & Silvera, D.H. (1994). Judgment by quantity. *Journal of Experimental Psychology: General, 123*, 21–32.

Leighton, J.P., & Dawson, M.R.W. (2001). A parallel distributed processing model of Wason's selection task. *Journal of Cognitive Systems Research, 2*, 207–231.

Over, D.E. (2000). Ecological issues: A reply to Todd, Fiddick, & Krauss. *Thinking and Reasoning, 6*, 385–388.

Polk, T.A., & Newell, A. (1995). Deduction as verbal reasoning. *Psychological Review, 102*, 533–566.

Sainsbury, R.M. (1988). *Paradoxes.* Cambridge: Cambridge University Press.

Sperber, D., & Girotto, V. (2002). Use or misuse of the selection task? Rejoinder to Fiddick, Cosmides, and Tooby. *Cognition, 85*, 277–290.

Intelligence and Creativity

Chapter Objectives

- To examine the various ways that cognitive psychologists have conceptualized intelligence and how these conceptualizations have changed over time.
- To describe the Flynn effect and look at possible explanations for it.
- To review and evaluate Robert Sternberg's theory of successful intelligence.
- To critically consider Howard Gardner's theory of multiple intelligences.
- To identify the factors related to the development of *expertise*.
- To explain the processes involved in *creativity*.

prodigy may be defined as a person with outstanding ability in some capacity. Child prodigies display abilities well beyond those of the average adult, let alone child. They are extremely rare, but they do exist. A recent example is the chess player Sergey Karjakin (b. 1990), who was awarded the title of Grandmaster—the second highest honour in the chess world—when he was just 12. Another outstanding child prodigy was Kim Ung-Yong.

Born in 1962, Kim was listed in the *Guinness Book of World Records* as having the world's highest IQ, 210. Keep in mind that an average IQ is 100 and that to be

considered a genius a person generally needs an IQ of at least 130 (the exact definition of genius still eludes researchers). Kim's extraordinary talents began to surface shortly after birth. It was reported that he began speaking at the age of 2 months and was able to converse fluently by 6 months. By contrast, most children only begin to produce simple words such as *dada* around 12 months of age and don't start speaking in short two- or three-word sentences until about 18 months. By the time he turned 4 Kim was able to read not only in his own language (Korean), but also in Japanese, German, and English, and he demonstrated his proficiency in these languages as well as Chinese, Spanish, Vietnamese, and Tagalog on Japanese television before he turned 5.

Kim's talents did not end with his linguistic ability. Whereas most kids in North America begin learning algebra around the age of 13, Kim was able to understand algebraic and calculus concepts before his first birthday. Later, also on Japanese television, he demonstrated this talent and solved complicated calculus problems. Having audited physics courses in Korea between the ages of 4 and 7, he was invited to the United States by NASA and went on to complete his doctoral studies in physics at the age of 15. He then began a career working with NASA. In 1978, however, he chose to return to Korea. We will look at the reasons behind that decision at the end of this chapter.

FIGURE 12.1 Kim Ung-Yong

The Concept of Intelligence: Historical Background

Perhaps no concept has been more central to the development of psychology as a discipline than the concept of intelligence. For more than a century, intelligence has typically been measured using intelligence tests (Anastasi, 1965). The makers of these tests have patterned their work on the example set by Binet in France (Fraisse & Piaget, 1963, pp. 40–43).

THE BINET–SIMON TEST

One of the best-known contemporary researchers in the field, Robert J. Sternberg (1992, p. 134), noted that "the intelligence test of today is quite similar to that of Alfred Binet." That is, despite variations in form and content, intelligence tests tend to be similar to the one that Binet, in collaboration with Théophile Simon (Binet & Simon, 1905a/1965), devised in response to a request from French educational authorities who wanted a way of assessing the benefit of schooling for children. The test they created was designed to distinguish between children of normal and subnormal intelligence. Binet and Simon (1905b/1965) defined **intelligence** as:

> a fundamental faculty, the alteration or lack of which is of the utmost importance for practical life. This faculty is judgment, otherwise called good sense, practical sense, initiative, the faculty of adapting oneself to circumstances. To judge well, to comprehend well, to reason well, these are the essential activities of intelligence. (p. 38)

Notice the *practical* emphasis of that definition: intelligence is "practical sense," "the faculty of adapting oneself to circumstances," and consists of "activities" such as reasoning and comprehension. Some examples from the Binet and Simon (1911/1915) test are given in Table 12.1. Binet and Simon were careful to base their scale on a substantial body of empirical research, arranging their items "in a real order of increasing difficulty" (Binet & Simon, 1908/1965), to permit comparison in terms of *mental age*. Of "203 children studied individually" 103 performed at "exactly the mental level that we attribute[d] to their age"; 44 were advanced and 56 were below their age level (Binet & Simon, 1908/1965, p. 44).

The Binet–Simon scale seemed to be just the sort of thing that many people in the United States were looking for. Lewis M. Terman (1877–1956) developed the most successful adaptation of the scale for the American context. Because Terman did this work at Stanford University, his version of the Binet test was called the *Stanford–Binet*. Based on a suggestion by the German psychologist William Stern (1912/1967, p. 453) that a useful measure of intelligence could be obtained by dividing a child's mental age (MA) by his or her chronological age (CA), Terman proposed the following equation for what came to be known as the intelligence quotient (IQ):

$$IQ = \frac{MA}{CA} \times 100$$

This formula means that a "normal" child will have an IQ of 100. Terman (1916/1948, p. 489) obtained Stanford–Binet IQ scores for 905 children between the ages of 9 and 14, and reported that their distribution was approximately normal. The fact that there was a significant relationship between IQ and variables such as teachers' estimates of children's intelligence suggested that the test had some validity. Partly for this reason, the Stanford–Binet test came to be very widely accepted.

CHARLES SPEARMAN

It's not easy to decide whether the word *intelligence* should be taken to refer to one ability or to many different abilities. If the latter, it's not easy to determine precisely how these abilities are related to one another. We can begin to appreciate some of these problems if we consider the work of Charles Spearman

> **Intelligence (Binet and Simon's 1905 definition)**
> A fundamental faculty, the alteration or lack of which is of the utmost importance for practical life.

TABLE 12.1 Example of Binet and Simon's Items

AGE	ITEM
3	Give family name
4	Repeat three numbers
5	Compare two weights
6	Distinguish morning and afternoon
7	Describe a picture
8	Give a day and date
9	Name months of the year in order
10	Criticize absurd statements
12	Describe abstract words
15	Give three rhymes for a word in one minute
Adult	Give three differences between a president and a king

Factor analysis
A statistical procedure that derives a number of underlying factors that may explain the structure of a set of correlations.

(1863–1945), who laid the groundwork for what became **factor analysis** (Lovie & Lovie, 1993). Factor analysis begins with a set of correlations between several measures, such as different mental tests. Then statistical procedures are used to derive a number of underlying variables ("factors") that may explain the structure of the set of correlations. As a result of his analysis of the pattern of correlations between different tests of mental abilities, Spearman (1904, 1927/1965) proposed what came to be called the *two-factor theory of intelligence*. This theory held that:

> every individual measurement of every ability . . . can be divided into two independent parts. . . . The one part has been called the "general factor" and denoted by the letter *g*; it is so named because, although varying freely from individual to individual, it remains the same for any one individual. . . . The second part has been called the "specific factor" and denoted by the letter *s*. It not only varies from individual to individual, but even for any one individual from each ability to another. (Spearman, 1932/1970, p. 75)

The two-factor theory is illustrated in Figure 12.2. As you can see, it's a hierarchical model in which **general intelligence**, or *g*, is the primary factor on which various specific factors (*s*) depend. In Figure 12.2, those specific factors are represented by abilities in four specific school subjects (French, English, mathematics, and music). Spearman found that those specific abilities were all correlated with each other, such that people who did well in one specific area tended to do well in the others, and vice versa. Still, the inter-correlation between specific abilities was not perfect. Each specific ability was seen as determined in part by *g* and in part by circumstances specific to that ability. Thus someone could have a high level of *g*, but varying specific abilities. This formulation continues to be a subject of controversy. When it came to estimating the effect of education on intelligence, Spearman concluded that heredity was more important in determining *g*, but that the specific factors could be shaped by schooling.

General intelligence (*g*)
The part of intelligence that is common to all abilities.

Spearman was able to devise a statistical criterion that allowed him to estimate the amount of *g* that contributed to each specific ability. Still, any attempt to interpret the correlations between scales that purport to measure different abilities calls for great caution (Loehlin, 1989, 1992, pp. 18–23; Neisser et al., 1996, p. 81). Spearman believed that *g* represented the amount of *mental energy* available to an individual. This was a general, non-specific energy that could be directed towards the specific abilities, which were seen as engines driven by *g*.

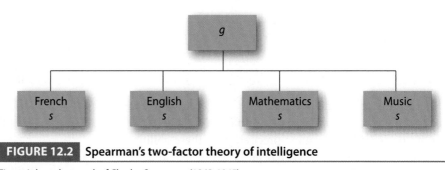

FIGURE 12.2 Spearman's two-factor theory of intelligence

Figure is based on work of Charles Spearman (1863-1945)

Spearman exercised considerable influence on the way succeeding generations of psychologists have regarded intelligence. Despite the controversy that surrounds his view, it is widely supported (e.g., Johnson, Bouchard, Krueger, McGue, & Gottesman, 2004). Many would agree with Jensen (1972, p. 77) that "when the term intelligence is used it should refer to *g*, the factor common to all tests of complex problem solving."

General Intelligence (*g*)

In a review of research done over the 100 years since Spearman (1904), Lubinski (2004) argued that, if anything, general intelligence is more important in the twenty-first century than ever before. General intelligence predicts academic achievement and work performance. However, it accounts for only about half of the variability in performance. As Lubinski points out, even highly intelligent people must work hard if they are to fulfill their goals, and they must work even harder if they are to become outstanding in their field. On this point Lubinski cites Simonton (1994), whose work we will consider later in the chapter. Ambitious students would do well to heed Simonton's words:

> Making it big [becoming a star] is a career. People who wish to do so must organize their whole lives around a single enterprise. They must be monomaniacs, even megalomaniacs, about their pursuits. They must start early, labor continuously, and never give up the cause. Success is not for the lazy, procrastinating or mercurial. (1994, p. 181)

FLUID INTELLIGENCE AND *g*

A distinction is often made between fluid and crystallized intelligence (Cattell, 1963). **Crystallized intelligence** consists of things we have learned, and may increase throughout life. By contrast, **fluid intelligence** is the ability to think flexibly, and although it may increase while we are young, it levels off as we mature. Fluid intelligence and general intelligence are often thought to be highly similar if not identical (Lubinsky, 2004, p. 98). Thus tests of general intelligence typically assess the ability to grasp unfamiliar relationships, rather than the content of a person's knowledge. Spearman's word for the ability that underlies *g* was **eduction**, from the Latin meaning *to draw out*. Thus general intelligence may be measured by the ability to draw out the known relationships that apply in a novel situation. A set of measures known as the **Raven Progressive Matrices** (Carpenter, Just, & Shell, 1990; J.C. Raven, Styles, & J. Raven, 1998) was explicitly designed to measure a central aspect of what Spearman meant by general intelligence (J. Raven, 2000).

For examples of problems similar to those in the Raven test, see Figure 12.3. Each matrix contains nine configurations, the last of which is left blank. You must decide which of the eight alternatives presented under each matrix is the correct one to fill in the blank. Make a note of your answer to each of the three matrix problems in the figure before you read the answers at the end of the chapter. You will see that the reasoning required can be quite subtle and varied. Spearman called this sort of reasoning *eduction of relations and correlates*: the ability to grasp how things are related to one another and what goes with what.

Crystallized intelligence
The body of what someone has learned; may continue to increase throughout life.

Fluid intelligence
The ability to think flexibly; may increase in youth but levels off as we mature.

Eduction
Literally, *drawing out*. General intelligence may be the ability to draw out the relationships that apply in a novel situation.

Raven Progressive Matrices
A set of problems that constitutes the most widely accepted test of *g*.

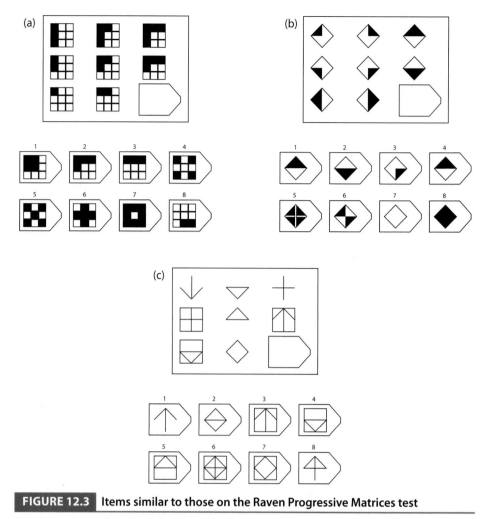

FIGURE 12.3   Items similar to those on the Raven Progressive Matrices test

From: Carpenter, P.A., Just, M.A., & Shell, P. (1990). What one intelligence test measures: A theoretical account of the processing in the Raven Progressive Matrices Test. *Psychological Review, 97*, p. 409. Copyright 1990 by the American Psychological Association.

WORKING MEMORY AND *g*

Working memory capacity
The theory that working memory capacity and *g* are closely related.

It has been suggested that **working memory capacity** may be not only an important aspect of *g*, but even synonymous with it (Conway, Kane, & Engle, 2003; Engle, Tuholski, Laughlin, & Conway, 1999). One reason is that Spearman's concept of *mental energy* is intuitively similar to the *central executive function* of working memory (Ackerman, Beier, & Boyle, 2005). As you may recall from Chapter 6, the central executive selects and integrates information, constituting a workspace within which solutions to problems are formulated (Baars, 2002). Now look again at Figure 6.11, which distinguishes between *fluid* and *crystallized* systems. As Baddeley (2000b) put it, the former are "themselves unchanged by learning," while the latter are "cognitive systems capable of accumulating long-term knowledge" (p. 421). Thus the central executive appears to perform a function similar to that ascribed to fluid intelligence and, by extension, to *g*.

Even so, the fact that there seems to be an intuitive relationship between general intelligence and the central executive function of working memory doesn't mean that there is an empirical one. If there were an empirical relationship, then scores on a test of individual differences in working memory capacity would be correlated with scores on a test of *g*. One way of testing working memory capacity is to have people continue to work on a task in the face of distraction (Conway, Kane, & Engle, 2003, p. 551). For example, the *operation span task* measures the ability to remain goal-oriented and not allow extraneous information to interfere with the problem at hand (Engle, Tuholski, Laughlin, & Conway, 1999, p. 315). Participants are shown an arithmetic problem that requires a yes/no answer; for example, "Does (8/4) – 1 = 1?" Once the participants have responded, a word (e.g., *tree*) appears on the screen and they read it aloud. Then another arithmetic problem is presented, followed by another word. This sequence may be repeated as many as six times. During the testing phase, the participants are shown the arithmetic problems again and asked to pair each one with the word that had followed it. Thus they must not only solve arithmetic problems, but at the same time keep track of the relationship between each problem and the corresponding word. The participant's score is the number of words correctly recalled in the correct order.

Tests of working memory capacity do correlate positively with tests such as the Raven. But the correlation is far from perfect. After reviewing dozens of studies, Ackerman et al. (2005, p. 51) concluded that working memory capacity and *g* are not the same. In fact, measures of working memory capacity show some correlation not only with *g* but with many different measures of intellectual ability. Barrett, Tugade, and Engle (2004) argued that working memory capacity is related to the ability to regulate attention. If that is the case, it would play an important role in bringing cognitive processes under voluntary control.

NEURAL PLASTICITY AND *g*

Garlick (2002, 2003) pointed out that Spearman's concept of *mental energy* is no longer a useful explanatory concept in the context of current neuroscientific theories. Rather, he advanced the hypothesis that **neural plasticity** underlies *g*. *Plasticity* is the ability of an organism to adapt to changes in the environment. *Neural* plasticity

> is an experience dependent change in neuronal circuitry that occurs throughout life, though on a larger scale during infancy, childhood, and adolescence. . . . During this early part of life, long-term changes that may occur include the rewiring of existing networks and the establishment of new sets of connections, the results of which include increased capacity and improved efficiency. (Petrill, Lipton, Hewitt, Plomin, Cherny, Corley, & Defries, 2004, p. 811)

Individual differences in neural plasticity reflect differences in the ability to adapt to a changing environment by forming and/or altering connections between neurons. Individual differences in neural plasticity are likely due to genetic variation (Petrill et al., 2004, p. 811). However, the precise mechanisms whereby genes determine plasticity are as yet unknown. Garlick's (2002, p. 121) hypothesis is that people vary in the extent to which their brains were "able to adapt their neural circuitry to environmental stimulation during childhood." The hallmark of neural plasticity is the ability to adapt to any circumstances with which we are confronted, although there are obvious limits to this ability. Such a mechanism would not only "mean that children would be able to learn to read and write" even if their ancestors lacked those skills, but would also "allow the person to adapt and function intelligently no matter what the environmental requirements" (Garlick, 2002, p. 120). However, children low in neural plasticity would be

Neural plasticity
Plasticity is the ability of an organism to adapt to changes in the environment. *Neural* plasticity reflects changes in neuronal circuitry as a function of experience.

less able to adapt to environmental change, and even children high in neural plasticity would develop intellectually only to the extent that they were exposed to appropriate environmental stimulation.

THE EVOLUTION OF *g*

Dedicated intelligence
Intelligence associated with domain-specific modules that would have evolved to solve recurring problems.

Improvisational intelligence
Flexible intelligence that would have evolved to deal with relatively unique, unpredictable problems.

A theory of the evolution of *g* has been advanced by Kanazawa (2004). Central to this theory is a distinction made by Cosmides and Tooby (2002) between **dedicated intelligence** and **improvisational intelligence**. They associate the former with the domain-specific modules that are hypothesized to have evolved to solve recurring problems; two examples that we have considered in this book are the *cheater detection module* (Chapter 11) and the *language acquisition device* (Chapter 9). By contrast, improvisational intelligence would have evolved to deal with relatively unique, unpredictable problems. The ability to deal with surprises such as a bush fire or a flash flood may have enabled survival and thus been selected for. As Kanazawa pointed out, unexpected problems by definition cannot be solved by dedicated, preprogrammed mechanisms. Rather, what is required is the flexibility that general intelligence affords. Thus Kanazawa argues that *g* and improvisational intelligence are the same.

As we have seen, our current circumstances are radically more novel and complex than those faced by prehistoric people. Kanazawa (2004, p. 515) pointed out that very few things in the environment of a technologically advanced society "existed 10,000 years ago . . . virtually everything you see around you today in your natural environment (books, computers, telephones, televisions, automobiles, etc.) is evolutionarily novel." Dedicated mechanisms are of limited use in such an environment. What is required is general intelligence (Gottfredson, 1997).

One implication of Kanazawa's theory is that general intelligence is valuable only in evolutionarily novel situations. For example, mating is certainly not an evolutionarily novel situation, and so we would not expect high *g* to be advantageous in that context. Not only do people high in general intelligence not have more children than those low in *g*, but in our era *g* is *negatively* correlated with number of offspring (Kanazawa, 2004, p. 517). One possible explanation might be that the use of contraceptive methods varies with *g*. Birth control may help to solve the evolutionarily novel problem of no longer being able to rely on infant mortality to control the number of our dependants (Kanazawa, 2004, p. 521).

▌ The Flynn Effect

J.R. Flynn (1984, 1987, 1999, 2003) created a firestorm of controversy when he discovered that IQ scores had been rising over time in every industrialized country he examined. These increases were not trivial. For example, Americans had gained 14 IQ points between 1932 and 1978. Samples of members of the military of the Netherlands, Israel, Norway, and Belgium show an average gain of six IQ points per decade between 1952 and 1982 (Flynn, 1999, p. 6). This last result is particularly noteworthy because it is based on Raven scores. Since the Raven is acknowledged to be the best measure of *g* (Neisser, 1997, p. 441), it would appear that *g* has been increasing over time. A few decades are far too short a time for evolution to have worked its magic. Consequently, the rapid rise in *g* must be due to environmental factors. Notice that this does not mean that *g* is completely determined by environmental factors, for the following reason. Suppose that g depends on neural plasticity. Variations in neural plasticity may be inherited. However, as we observed earlier, neural plasticity requires environmental stimulation in order to actualize its potential. An individual's actual level of g will depend on the interaction of neural plasticity with environmental conditions (Garlick, 2003, p. 188). Thus the **Flynn effect** could be the result of an enriched environment that enables potential g to become actual g (cf. Dickens & Flynn, 2001).

A great deal of attention has been devoted to trying to figure out which environmental changes have produced the Flynn effect (e.g., Neisser, 1998). Among the possible candidates are improvements in nutrition and health.

Flynn effect
An increase in IQ scores over historical time.

NUTRITION AND HEALTH

Lynn (1998) summarized the evidence that nutrition has improved in industrialized countries since the 1930s and suggested that "Improvements in nutrition have increased the growth of the brain, and probably also its neurological development, and this has increased intelligence" (p. 211). Daley, Whaley, Sigman, Espinosa, and Neumann (2003) have shown that the Flynn effect can also occur in a developing country. They examined children's IQs in rural Kenya in 1984 and 1998. They also measured nutritional levels in both years. On the Raven, IQ scores were 26.3 points higher in 1998 than in 1984. They also found that children's caloric intake had improved substantially by 1998, and that the numbers of children infested with hookworm, which can cause anemia, had decreased. Thus improvements in nutrition and health may have contributed to the IQ gains.

Parasitic infections can have deleterious cognitive effects. Although such infections are rare in industrialized countries, they are extremely common in the developing world. Sternberg, Powell, McGrane, and Grantham-McGregor (1997) studied schoolchildren in Jamaica who were infected with whipworm, which has been associated with deficient cognitive functioning. After treatment for whipworm, the previously infected children did not improve as much as had been expected. Sternberg et al. observed that the infected children tended to come from families with lower socio-economic status than did the non-infected children. They suggested that simply removing the infection is insufficient to produce significant gains in cognitive abilities. Such children also need "academic remediation and enrichment to enable them to attain the level of acculturation achieved by other individuals" (p. 74).

EDUCATION

Williams (1998) pointed out that people in the United States in the 1930s completed on average eight or nine years of schooling. By the 1990s that average had increased to 14 years. In addition, Blair, Gamson, Thorne, and Baker (2005) have presented evidence that American mathematics curricula became more demanding after the mid-twentieth century. Almost all children in the US were enrolled in primary schools by the 1950s. However, IQ gains after that time must have had a source other than mere exposure to school. That's where mathematics comes in. By analyzing the curriculum in early primary grades from the 1890s to the 1990s, Blair et al. showed that there was almost no mathematics education in the early 1900s, but that by the 1960s mathematics was offered in all grades. Mathematics education may be expected to heighten fluid intelligence. Indeed, many of the tasks given to primary school children are similar to the reasoning tasks that make up tests like the Raven.

ENVIRONMENTAL COMPLEXITY

Coincident with changes in nutrition, health, and education, the environment in which children are raised has become increasingly complex over the last 100 years, especially in industrialized countries (Schooler, 1998). Neisser (1997) pointed out that the twentieth century witnessed a phenomenal increase in exposure to visual media. A short list includes photographs, movies, computers, and television. Neisser hypothesized that

> Exposure to complex visual media has produced genuine increases in a significant form of intelligence. This hypothetical form of intelligence might be called "visual analysis." Tests such as Raven's may show the largest Flynn gains because they measure visual analysis rather directly. . . .(p. 447)

Green and Bavelier (2003) studied the effects of playing video games in a group of 18–23-year-olds who had played games such as *Grand Theft Auto* and *Halo* for at least one hour per day for the previous six months. This group showed superior performance on a number of standard attention tasks when compared with a group that had no video game experience. Moreover, training naive participants on video games for as little as 10 days led to gains on standard attention tasks such as the flanker task and the attentional blink task (both of which we encountered in Chapter 4). Although this study did not investigate the possibility that intelligence increases as a result of complex visual experience, it did show that such experience may enhance basic cognitive processes.

Whether any or all of these variables are crucial to the Flynn effect is impossible to say. As Williams (1998) pointed out, several other variables could also have played a role in the rise in IQ. What do you think some of those variables might be?

■■■ Sternberg's Theory of Successful Intelligence

There are other approaches to intelligence that de-emphasize the importance of *g* in order to highlight alternative aspects of intelligence. Two of the most influential are those of Robert J. Sternberg and Howard Gardner. We will consider Sternberg's theory first.

Instead of analyzing intelligence in terms of factors, Sternberg focused on what have been referred to as **intellectual components**. Whereas factors define the *structure* of intelligence, components describe the *processes* of intelligence. A component is "an elementary information process that operates upon internal representations of objects or symbols" (Sternberg, 1980, p. 574). We represent events to ourselves by means of cognitive processes such as perception and memory. We then manipulate these representations in a variety of ways. We can think about things, imagine them from different perspectives, remember similar things, and so on. The different ways in which we transform cognitive representations are the components of intelligence. For example, you can represent the object in which you are now sitting as a chair and then think of the superordinate category for that concept (*chair* is a member of the class *furniture*). People vary in the speed and accuracy with which they can carry out such operations, and these variations are part of what we recognize as individual differences in intelligence.

Sternberg (1984b) identified three kinds of components: *metacomponents*, *performance components*, and *knowledge acquisition components*. These components are found in all aspects of intelligence, and so may be said to be universal (Sternberg, 1998, 1999a, 1999b).

Intellectual components Elementary information processes that operate on internal representations of objects or symbols.

METACOMPONENTS

Metacomponents are "higher order processes used in planning, monitoring, and decision making in task performance" (Sternberg, 2009, p. 57). These are the components that control the execution of other components. Before you attempt to solve a problem, you must make some decisions about the kind of problem it is and how you will tackle it; it's at this stage that metacomponents come into play. Many intelligence test items are timed, and in that context a speedy response is often taken to be more indicative of intelligence than a slow, considered one. Yet the most intelligent approach to solving a particular problem may not be the fastest approach. In many situations, careful consideration of the nature of the problem, thorough planning of the solution procedure, and monitoring of that operation as it proceeds will lead to better results than "shooting from the hip." Emphasizing the distinction between reflective and impulsive approaches to problem-solving, Sternberg suggested that in most situations what matters is not speed but "intelligent allocation of one's time to the various . . . problems at hand" (2009, p. 60).

> **Metacomponents**
> Executive processes used in planning, monitoring, and decision-making in task performance.

PERFORMANCE COMPONENTS

Performance components—"the processes that are used in the execution of a task" (Sternberg, 1984a, p. 166)—are used at every stage of the solution process. These stages include encoding the various aspects of the problem situation, comparing the different parts of the problem, and generating the appropriate response. The running example used by Sternberg (e.g., 1980, p. 576) is the procedure for solving analogies. When asked to solve the analogy *fish is to water as worm is to: (a) earth or (b) hook*, you must first encode each term to determine its meaning. Then you can compare the parts of the analogy to find similarities (e.g., *fish* and *worm* are both living creatures). Mapping is a very important process whereby past knowledge is related to ("mapped onto") the present situation. You already know the relation between *fish* and *water*: fish live in the water. You can then map this relation onto the pairs *worm, earth* and *worm, hook*. The relation of "lives in" certainly fits the first pair better than the second. Worms live in the earth, but they die on hooks. After finding the solution you can then give the appropriate response (*earth*).

> **Performance components**
> The processes that are used in the execution of a task.

KNOWLEDGE ACQUISITION COMPONENTS

As the name suggests, **knowledge acquisition components** are the processes used for "learning new information and storing it in memory" (Sternberg, 1983, p. 5). The key aspect of these components is selectivity. It's impossible to learn everything; you must be able to filter out the irrelevant and pick up the relevant information. Information so acquired must then be retained in a meaningful form so that it can be used later. An expert is someone who has acquired and is able to use information specific to a particular class of tasks.

> **Knowledge acquisition components**
> Processes concerned with learning and storing new information.

THE TRIARCHIC THEORY

The components just described are universal in that they enter into all intelligent behaviour. However, intelligent behaviour has three different content areas: analytical, creative, and practical. All three make use of the same components, but they vary with respect to the "mental contents and representations" they use (Sternberg,

COGNITION IN ACTION
BOX 12.1

Can Colour Help Us Solve Problems?

When we want to get to know someone, we'll ask a variety of questions: Where are you from? Where did you go to school? Do you have any siblings? And so on. As we get to know the person better we'll start to ask more intimate questions about things like childhood memories or favourite colours. Remarkably, psychologists have only recently begun to study the relationship between colours and human cognition. Recent research suggests that simply viewing a particular colour can either enhance or diminish performance on simple tasks. For example, Stone (2003) claimed to show evidence that performance on an easier task diminished over time in a blue environment but remained steady in a red environment However, the advantage for red over blue was reversed in other research (see Elliot, Maier, Moller, Friedman, & Meinhardt, 2007). To address these contradictory findings, Mehta and Zhu (2009) explored how different colours could affect cognitive performance on a number of tasks.

You might be wondering how it is possible that a change of colour could lead to a change in performance. One reason could be that we learn to make associations between colours and certain experiences (e.g., environments, ideas, tasks, moods). For example, you might have learned to associate red with danger or mistakes (what colour does your professor use to highlight errors on papers and exams?). By contrast, blue is often associated with peace and relaxation (think of a calm sea or a cloudless sky). Mehta and Zhu used this framework to propose that red could be associated with *avoidance* of danger and mistakes, together with heightened vigilance and enhanced performance on tasks requiring attention to detail. The reverse was hypothesized for blue, which should be associated with *approach* and lead to enhanced performance on tasks requiring innovative solutions to problems.

Using tasks designed to test their conceptualizations of avoidance (red) and approach (blue), Mehta and Zhu (2009) found that these colours did in fact have the hypothesized effects. Their procedure was relatively straightforward: participants were asked to complete different tasks on a computer with the background coloured either red or blue (or a neutral control condition). In one of the experiments participants were required to solve a series of 12 anagrams. For six of these the target words related to either approach (e.g., *adventure*) or avoidance (e.g., *prevent*), and for six the target words were neutral. As hypothesized, response times were fastest when the background colour matched the orientation associated with the target word (approach or avoidance). A second study required participants to rate various brands of products such as toothpaste that were described in terms that emphasized either positive aspects (whitens teeth: approach) or negative aspects (cavity prevention: avoidance). Again, when accompanied by the blue background the approach condition was favoured over the avoidance condition, and vice versa.

While these first two studies are interesting, neither really tested whether the background colour for a particular type of task—red for detail-oriented (avoidance) tasks; blue for creative tasks (approach)—enhanced performance. This was precisely what the remaining experiments in the Mehta and Zhu (2009) study were designed to do. The first, a word-recall task performed against either a red or a blue background, showed that performance was better in the red condition (i.e., participants were able to remember more words). The final experiment gave participants one minute to list as many uses for a brick as they could think of (see p. 399). Although participants came up with equal numbers of uses, regardless of colour condition, the uses suggested by those in the blue condition were judged to be more creative.

What can we learn from this research? We may not yet fully understand the relationship between art and human cognition, but research such as Mehta and Zhu's shows that we are making significant strides towards understanding the influence of colour. Perhaps you should try changing the background colour on your computer, depending on the kind of assignment you're working on.

Castejón, Prieto, Hautamäki, & Grigerenko, 2001, p. 2). As we note in Box 12.2, Sternberg's **triarchic theory** has a surprising parallel with another, much older theory of intelligence.

Analytical Intelligence

For Sternberg, **analytical intelligence** is the closest to what conventional intelligence tests measure. To the extent that *g* is important, it is with respect to analytical intelligence. Tests such as the Raven are good measures of analytical intelligence.

Creative Intelligence

Creative intelligence is the ability to reason using novel concepts (Sternberg, 1999a, p. 304). A familiar situation allows people to use what Sternberg (1982) called **entrenched concepts**; these strike us as natural and are easy to reason with. By contrast, unfamiliar or novel situations may require the use of **non-entrenched concepts** that strike us as unnatural and are difficult to reason with. Following are examples of these two types of concept, which Sternberg adapted from Goodman (1955). The colour concepts *blue* and *green* are natural concepts. Robins' eggs have been blue ever since we can remember, and we expect that they will remain blue forever. Emeralds are always green, and we expect them to remain so in the future. However, we do not ordinarily possess colour concepts that refer to objects that change colour over time. For example, freshly picked bananas are often green and turn yellow only as they ripen. We could invent a concept called *grellow* to describe objects that are green now, but later turn yellow. Similarly, there could be a novel concept *bleen* to describe objects that are blue now, but will turn green later. To reason with concepts such as *grellow* and *bleen* would be to reason in a novel conceptual system.

Sternberg invented several problems to measure people's ability to think with novel concepts such as *grellow* and *bleen*. For example, can there be an object to which the concept *blue* was applied in the year 2000, but to which the concept *green* properly applies in 2013? It's tempting to answer "Yes," but what do you think? The proper answer, given the possibility of *bleen*, is "No." If an object changes colour from green to blue, then it must be a *bleen* object in the year 2013. Conceptualizing it as *blue* in 2000 turns out to have been a mistake. When the object turns green in the year 2013, it becomes clear that it was really a *bleen* object all along.

The ability to reason with novel concepts allows us to explore problem spaces that otherwise would remain closed to us. This increases the range of problems we can approach successfully.

Practical Intelligence

Sternberg (1999a, p. 305; Sternberg & Wagner, 1986, 1994) saw **practical intelligence** as important in familiar situations of a non-academic sort. He stressed the necessity of studying intelligence in real-world settings. To illustrate the difference between practical intelligence and IQ, Sternberg (1998, p. 494) cited the work of Silvia Scribner (1986, 1993; Herman, 1993). Scribner used the *ethnographic method* in her investigations, approaching the study of practical cognition in the same way that an anthropologist would approach the study of a particular culture or subculture. This method relies

---

Triarchic theory of intelligence
Sternberg's theory consisting of analytic, practical, and creative intelligence.

Analytical intelligence
The ability to solve relatively straightforward problems; considered to be general intelligence.

Creative intelligence
The ability to reason using novel concepts.

Entrenched vs non-entrenched concepts
Entrenched concepts strike us as natural and easy to reason with, whereas non-entrenched concepts strike us as unnatural and difficult to reason with.

Practical intelligence
The ability to find problem solutions in real-world, everyday situations.

CONSIDER THIS BOX 12.2

An Ancient Parallel to Sternberg's Theory of Intelligence

The similarity of Sternberg et al's theory to Aristotle's classical theory of intelligence was pointed out by Tigner and Tigner (2000). They observed that Aristotle (384–323 BC) also recognized three kinds of intelligence. The first is theoretical intelligence, which corresponds to what most people now think of as "intelligence." It is the ability to understand subjects such as mathematics and science and to acquire and analyze various metalanguages such as those involved in language analysis, literary criticism, or the analysis of history and government (what we now call political science). Aristotle's second kind of intelligence is practical; here, the focus is on the ability to choose a wise course of action. Finally, productive intelligence is reflected in the ability to make things and is perhaps best exemplified in the arts.

As Tigner and Tigner (2000) pointed out, Aristotle's system has strong similarities to the triarchic theory of intelligence proposed by Sternberg (1988). Although Sternberg used different labels for them (analytical,

practical, and creative), his three kinds of intelligence are essentially the same as Aristotle's. Sternberg did not copy Aristotle's system, but arrived at it using the empirical methods of contemporary psychology. Thus one reason for believing that Aristotle's system has merit is that it has been independently verified by an investigator using different methods in a very different era.

Sternberg (2000b) made the sage observation that the similarity between his theory and Aristotle's illustrates the importance of revisiting historically important approaches to psychology. "If both philosophical and psychological analysis support an idea, the idea gains credibility by virtue of the overlap in substantive findings across methods of analysis. . . . Tigner and Tigner's (2000) analysis shows how important it is to study the history and philosophy of psychology. There are many alternative paths to knowledge and understanding about the human mind" (Sternberg, 2000b, p. 178).

on naturalistic observation in the field, and should be seen as a part of the ecological approach to psychology (Scribner, 1993). A good example of the ethnographic method in action is Scribner's (1986) study of dairy workers.

A common stereotype of work in highly mechanized contexts such as assembly lines (Figure 12.4) is that it does not engage the worker's cognitive processes at a very high level. There may be some truth to this, but perhaps not as much as is commonly believed. Scribner (1986, p. 15) defined practical thinking as "mind in action . . . thinking that is embedded in the larger purposive activities of daily life and that functions to achieve the goals of these activities." One of the contexts she investigated was a modern dairy. "The dairy is a prototypical industrial system in which many occupational activities involve standardized and repetitive duties performed under highly constrained conditions" (Scribner, 1986, p. 21).

Scribner observed workers performing a variety of functions. For example, delivery truck drivers developed their own ways of working out the cost of a delivery. Scribner reported that experienced drivers made virtually no computational errors in on-the-job calculations. However, they made many errors in pencil and paper tests of arithmetic. It may be concluded that the pencil and paper test, which was similar to the sort of test that might be given in school, did not predict their on-the-job behaviour very well.

Sternberg and Kaufman (1998, p. 495) argued that Scribner's study shows the independence of practical intelligence from "measures of academic skills, including intelligence test scores, arithmetic test scores, and grades."

FIGURE 12.4 **Assembly-line worker**

THE STERNBERG TRIARCHIC ABILITIES TEST

Sternberg, Castejón, Prieto, Hautamäki, and Grigorenko (2001) collected data from three international samples to validate the Sternberg Triarchic Abilities Test (STAT). This test contains items intended to measure the three content areas of intelligence identified in the triarchic theory. Sternberg et al. argued that the data supported the hypothesis that the three content areas were distinct factors. However, the results were not unambiguous, and (as we shall see below) they lend themselves to alternative interpretations.

SUCCESSFUL INTELLIGENCE

For Sternberg (1999a, 1999b; Sternberg & Kaufman, 1998, pp. 493–496), all three aspects of intelligence are important, each in its own way. Seldom will an individual be strong in all three. People need to make the most of their individual strengths while at the same time recognizing their weaknesses. Someone strong in analytical intelligence may find the most success in an academic career. Someone high in creative intelligence may become a successful entrepreneur. Practical intelligence may enable someone to "work effectively in an environment" without being "explicitly taught" what is required (Sternberg, 1999a, p. 305). People who are strong in all these intelligences will perform well in a greater variety of contexts than those who are not.

CRITICISMS OF STERNBERG'S THEORY

Although Sternberg's approach has been extremely influential, it is not without its critics. For example, Brody (2003a, 2003b) observed that the STAT measures of analytical, practical, and creative intelligences are correlated; he concluded that the three are "substantially related to one another" (p. 341). In a similar vein, Gottfredson (2003a, 2003b) argued that there was no evidence unequivocally supporting the independent existence of a practical intelligence. Indeed, Gottfredson suggested that Sternberg underplayed the importance of g in practical affairs. The thrust of these criticisms is that the STAT adds nothing to existing measures of *g*, and that the triarchic theory is superfluous, given the wealth of evidence supporting *g* theory. In response to his critics, Sternberg (2003a, 2003b) observed that the triarchic theory is relatively recent compared to *g* theory and expressed the hope that future research will fulfill the promise of the former.

◼ Howard Gardner and the Theory of Multiple Intelligences

Multiple intelligences
The hypothesis that intelligence consists not of one underlying ability but of many different abilities.

For Gardner (1983, 1993a) intelligence is not one thing but many. Rejecting the idea that there is an underlying ability common to all intelligent activity, he argued that there are **multiple intelligences**, or "relatively autonomous human intellectual competences" (1983, p. 8). He played down the importance of *general intelligence* (*g*), arguing that it emerges only as a result of sampling too narrow a range of abilities (Walters & Gardner, 1986, p. 177).

Gardner traced his approach in part to the nineteenth-century phrenology of Gall and Spurzheim, which we discussed in Chapter 2. The basic idea behind phrenology was that particular areas of the brain have unique functions, similar to the faculties we considered in Chapter 2. The phrenologists proposed that basic differences in abilities between people arose because the areas of the brain that were responsible for controlling these functions were differentially developed. If we translate the basic phrenological insight about brain organization into a statement about intelligence, then we could say, with Gardner (1983, p. 55), that there are several distinctive intelligences, each of which is supported by specific parts of the brain. Although a complex task, such as playing the violin, may draw on several parts of the brain, not all parts are equally involved in all forms of intelligence. In fact, this is one of Gardner's arguments for the existence of separate intelligences: "To the extent that a particular faculty can be destroyed, or spared in isolation, as a result of brain damage, its relative autonomy from other human faculties seems likely" (Gardner, 1983, p. 63). Research with neuroimaging techniques has lent some support to Gardner's "distinction among domains in terms of the separable anatomical networks they activate" (Posner, 2004, p. 25). However, these networks do not operate in complete isolation: they interact with one another.

In all, Gardner (1983, p. 63) listed eight criteria for the identification of a separate intelligence. Three of the most interesting are as follows. First, a separate intelligence will have a **symbol system** for representing what we know. Usually we think of knowledge as being represented in a language of some kind. For instance, this textbook uses English to represent information about cognitive psychology, while a calculus textbook would use, in addition to English, mathematical formulae. But these are not the only symbolic forms available to us.

Symbol systems
Different forms of representation, such as drawing, music, and mathematics, that express different forms of intelligence.

If you had to tell someone how to get to your place, for instance, you could use words to describe the route; in that case you would be creating a cognitive map. But you could also use a pencil and paper to draw a literal map. Similarly, if someone asked you to describe your mood, you could use words to explain; but you might also play a piece of music that you feel expresses your state of mind. So here we have, in drawing and music, at least two additional *symbolic forms* (Cassirer, 1953–1959), or ways of representing events. Language, pictures, music, and mathematics are examples of symbol systems that are used around the world and are all, in different contexts, important for adaptation and survival. Gardner investigated the possibility that each of these symbolic forms expresses a separate intelligence.

Gardner's second "sign" of a separate intelligence is an association with exceptional individuals such as *prodigies*. The existence of these rare cases cannot be easily explained by a general theory of intelligence. Furthermore, why is it that prodigies appear in certain disciplines, such as mathematics and chess, and rarely if ever in others, such as literature (Gardner, 1983, p. 29)? The symbolic forms in which prodigies specialize may be the separate intelligences that underlie competence in other areas. By contrast, competence in a discipline such as history may require the interplay of several specific intelligences, as well as long-term study.

Third, a separate intelligence will have a distinctive *developmental history* (Gardner, 1983, p. 64). There should be a characteristic way in which expertise develops, with everyone beginning in the same way and some, though not all, reaching very high levels of competence. To describe an intelligence in this way is to assume that it is possible to objectively define what constitutes the expert use of a particular symbolic form. The study of the development of expertise is a significant part of the study of specific intelligences.

Here is Gardner's original list of intelligences, with one or two outstanding examples of each type: musical intelligence (Mozart, Louis Armstrong), bodily–kinesthetic intelligence (Babe Ruth, Wayne Gretzky), linguistic intelligence (Shakespeare, T.S. Eliot), logico-mathematical intelligence (Isaac Newton, Albert Einstein), spatial intelligence (London taxi drivers; Polynesian sailors who navigate over vast distances), and personal intelligence (Annie Sullivan, the teacher who found a way to communicate with the young Helen Keller). Gardner (2004) did not consider this list to be final, and other candidates are always considered. Gardner's unique contribution has been to focus our attention on symbol systems that are not always seen as central to the concept of intelligence.

Gardner's (1980, 1982) work has had the salutary effect of drawing attention to neglected but extremely important aspects of intelligence. In the next two sections we will look at the typical developmental patterns in two symbol systems, visual and musical. Then we will consider how these symbolic forms express themselves in exceptional cases, such as prodigies.

DRAWING

Our ability to make pictures is one facet of what Gardner (1983) called *spatial intelligence*. The development of this ability is not linear. It's not as if the preschool child were a bad artist, the school-age child a better artist, and the trained adult a superior artist. Rather, Gardner and Winner (1982; Winner, 1982, p. 175) suggest that artistic skills, and perhaps many others, follow a pattern of **U-shaped development** in which "aesthetic pleasingness" is initially quite high, then declines for a time before rising again (see Figure 12.5). As Siegler (2004) observed, U-shaped development is particularly interesting because it contradicts the widespread assumption that performance always improves with age. In U-shaped development, "performance is initially relatively good, . . . subsequently becomes worse, and . . . eventually improves" (p. 3).

A child's early drawings are relatively high in what might be called *aesthetic pleasingness* because of their vitality (Gardner, 1980, pp. 94ff.). Preschoolers' artwork is called *preconventional* for several reasons. There are only passing attempts to use realistic colour or to organize objects in the way they are actually organized in space; objects appear to float on top of the page (Winner, 1982, p. 152), and there is no attempt at perspective. According to Winner (1982, p. 169) the "golden age of children's drawing"

U-shaped development
The hypothesis that the development of many symbolic forms initially is delightfully pre-conventional, then descends to the merely conventional, but ultimately may achieve the integration of the post-conventional.

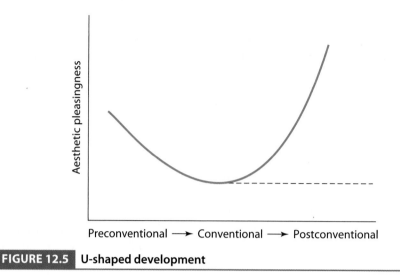

FIGURE 12.5 U-shaped development

is characterized by use of bright colours, freedom from the constraints of realism, absence of stereotyped forms, and willingness to explore and experiment.

When children go to school, however, their artwork enters a *conventional period*. According to Gardner and Winner, the dip in the U comes about not so much because children have lost the freedom of self-expression as because they are preoccupied with learning the rules and conventions that underpin expertise in drawing. Ultimately, those who master the rules will be able to use them in a creative way. When they are no longer entirely bound by convention, their work can move into a *postconventional* phase in which it may be admired for its vitality as well as its mastery. A well-known example is the work of Picasso.

Many professional artists have admired preschoolers' art. Mature artists' work often shows the freedom from constraint by conventional norms that characterizes young children's art. But they are doing something very different from what preschoolers do. They are trying to achieve what children achieve, but in a skillful way. The mature artist knows how to achieve intentionally what the child achieves without thinking (Winner, 1982, p. 175). However, Winner emphasizes that it is rare to advance this far along the developmental curve, at least in our culture. Once we descend to the conventional level (the dotted line in Figure 12.5), most of us are content to stay there.

MUSIC

The development of musical intelligence is similar in some respects to the development of drawing. During the first few years of life, children spontaneously do a number of musical things. "Toddlers commonly invent songs before they can reproduce conventional songs" (Trehub, 2003, p. 669). They sing tunes and beat rhythmic patterns. Dowling and Harwood (1986, pp. 144ff.) have reviewed some of the musical phenomena of the preschool years. The emergence of early musical activity, such as singing, may require that the child have older models, such as parents and siblings, to imitate. In any case, when children reach their second year, they begin to produce what adults will accept as something resembling singing.

Some theorists, notably Bernstein (1976, p. 16), have argued that young children typically produce a particular melodic pattern spontaneously, and that this pattern is evidence of an innate musical knowledge. Bernstein maintained that the kinds of sound patterns that children use to tease each other ("Nya-Nya-Nya-Nya-Nya") or call each other by name ("A-lice," "Tom-my") reflect this innate musical knowledge.

Gardner (1982, pp. 144ff.) examined the possibility that there is a basic melody that all children would spontaneously sing as their first song. He concluded that there is not much evidence that such an **ur-song**, (*ur* means original or earliest) actually exists, but it is an intriguing speculation all the same (see also Dowling & Harwood, 1986, p. 147).

Ur-song
The hypothetical first song that all children would spontaneously sing.

By the end of the third year, children begin reproducing conventional, culturally provided song models such as the "Alphabet Song," "Twinkle, Twinkle Little Star," or "Old MacDonald Had a Farm." Like drawing, singing does not typically develop during the school years the way that linguistic skills do; the latter, of course, are honed through schooling. But Gardner (1983, p. 111) observed that there are wide cross-cultural variations in this respect. In cultures that put a higher value on musical competence than North America does, such as those of some European or African countries, musical intelligence typically progresses much further. Here again we can see the role that culture plays in encouraging the development of particular intelligences.

There has been widespread speculation concerning the possibility that music lessons enhance IQ. One of the most persuasive studies was done by Schellenberg (2004). For one year, four different groups of six-year-olds were exposed to keyboard lessons, voice lessons, drama lessons, or no lessons. The IQ scores of all groups improved, probably as a result of starting schooling in general. However, the two groups exposed to music lessons showed greater IQ gains than the other two groups. This suggests that particular kinds of music in school curricula might have beneficial effects on IQ. Shellenberg speculates that chess lessons or science lessons might also have a beneficial effect. Such activities may provide instruction in a wide range of abilities (e.g., spatial, mathematical) that are transferrable to other contexts.

Bamberger's (1982, 1986) studies of the development of musical knowledge indicate that it varies along the tacit–explicit dimension, which we considered in our Chapter 8 discussion of concepts. When we reviewed Reber's work we noted that people can have tacit knowledge without being able to say what it is that they know. Bamberger's observations of musically gifted children suggest that their knowledge is initially of this tacit kind. For example, a child's ability to imitate a well-known older performer appears to reflect a feeling for the task as a whole, rather than a careful analysis of the model.

About the tacit nature of young people's musical ability, Bamberger (1986) said, "Indeed, exposing it to scrutiny is almost to be feared: . . . 'it won't work if you think about it'" (p. 393). However, as these students become adolescents, they inevitably become more reflective about their music, as they do about other aspects of their life. They feel an inconsistency between their increasingly explicit understanding of music and the earlier, spontaneous, non-reflective understanding (and love) of music they had as children. Bamberger referred to this phase as the **mid-life crisis of the musician** because gifted musicians typically begin studying music very early in their lives (often before the age of five), and so are well into their musical careers by adolescence. Winner (2000) observed that gifted children may feel they are studying music more for their parents or teachers than for themselves. She noted that many music students give up their studies at this point.

Mid-life crisis of the musician
As music students become adolescents, they may feel a tension between their increasingly explicit understanding of music and the spontaneous love of music they had as children.

Bamberger's analysis may hold true for less than gifted music students as well. How many people do you know who stopped taking music lessons around the age of 14? How many of them loved the music, but hated the lessons? Integrating the tacit and explicit aspects of music is a difficult task, but necessary if the student is to achieve adult mastery of this symbolic form (Gardner, 1982, p. 111).

PRODIGIES

As we noted earlier, one of Gardner's "signs" of a separate intelligences is the existence of prodigies in that area. **Prodigies** perform at an expert level at a much earlier age would normally be expected (Feldman, 1986, Gardner, 1993b). One type of prodigy about which we know a good deal is the musical prodigy (Figure 12.6). How do you recognize a prodigy? Consider the following example, given by Ruthsatz and Detterman (2003, p. 514):

> The subject was a 6-year-old musical prodigy. At the time of testing, the subject had played in numerous concerts, appeared several times on national television, and been in two movies. He had released two musical CDs in which he sings in two languages and plays several musical instruments. Unlike the mechanical flat performance often reported in the savant literature, his performance was expressive. He is able to entertain large paying audiences with his musical skill. He is capable of many instruments but prefers the piano and accordion. He is the only child of an intact family from the Southern United States. No one in his immediate family reported any knowledge of accelerated musical ability. However, his mother has played the piano. The young music prodigy, Derek, has not engaged in structured musical lessons but masters his music by listening to other performers and improvising his own musical pieces.

Derek (a pseudonym) was given the Stanford–Binet IQ test, which includes several subscales such as verbal reasoning, abstract/visual reasoning, quantitative reasoning, and short-term memory. He scored above average on all scales.

FIGURE 12.6   **The musical prodigy**

Prodigies
Children who perform at an expert level at a much earlier age than would normally be expected.

However, his most striking score was on short-term memory, where he scored 158 (the average is 100). "Derek seems to compensate for an absence of formal training and deliberate practice by his enhanced ability to remember melodies and recreate them" (Ruthsatz & Detterman, 2003, p. 517).

Although Derek had not yet devoted time to lessons and practice, most prodigies eventually must do so in order to fully develop their prodigious skills. Feldman (1986, Chap. 5) notes that a critical part of the cultural support that a prodigy requires is the nurturance provided by the family. In most of the cases that Feldman studied, the family played a major role in fostering the development of a prodigiously gifted child. Although it may not be this way in other cultures, in North America the family of such a child must be prepared to shoulder a significant burden. Parents soon realize that they cannot do the job that is required. They must then decide how much control of their child's life they will give up to teachers and coaches, how much money they will spend on developing their child's gift, how much familial dislocation they will tolerate for the sake of developing it. For example, a phenomenally talented young hockey player may be asked to move far from home to get expert coaching. This might involve considerable strain for all members of the family, including the child.

CRITICISMS OF MULTIPLE INTELLIGENCE THEORY

Walters and Gardner (1986) reviewed some of the early objections to the theory of multiple intelligences. One criticism was that what the theory calls "intelligences" are more properly called "talents" or "gifts." But Walters and Gardner saw no reason to reserve "intelligence" for the kind of logical/mathematical or linguistic skills that are most valued by our culture. Certainly, Gardner's approach has had considerable influence on parents' and educators' belief that "people differ in their abilities to solve problems and make contributions to society in diverse ways" (Cuban, 2004).

A persistent criticism is that the theory of multiple intelligences is not grounded in scientific data (Chen, 2004). This criticism has much truth to it. However, the theory does have support from case studies (e.g., Gardner, 1993b). Gardner (1999, 2004) has consistently argued that the study of intelligence is by nature interdisciplinary and should be approached from a variety of perspectives, including those of the humanities and the arts as well as the sciences.

Expertise

We noted that one of Gardner's criteria for a separate intelligence was that it be possible to define what constitutes expertise in that area. Independent of Gardner's theory, there has been a great deal of interest in understanding what it takes to make someone an expert. The classic study of expertise was undertaken by Chase and Simon (1973), who extended earlier work by de Groot (1965). They compared the ability of chess masters and novices to remember the positions of chess pieces they had been shown arranged on a chessboard. Memory was tested by having participants reproduce the positions they had seen. Chess masters remembered the positions better than novices, particularly if the arrangement they were shown was one that had been reached in an actual game. The relations between the pieces in such an arrangement are meaningful to chess experts, whereas a random placement of pieces is relatively meaningless to experts and novices alike. Experts are only slightly superior to novices in their ability to remember a random arrangement of pieces (Gobet & Simon, 1996).

Chase and Simon suggested that experts perceive game position arrangements in larger units, or chunks, than novices, who don't know enough to recognize the meaning of pieces' positions. Because novices are not able to "chunk" the information, they must remember the position of each individual piece, and this constraint makes the task more difficult for them than for the experts, particularly when the situation to be remembered is one that could occur in an actual game. Gobet and Simon (1996, p. 31) observed that "chess players have seen thousands of positions, and for expert players, most positions they see readily remind them of positions or types of positions they have seen before."

Ericsson and Charness (1994) reviewed the literature on expert performance and concluded that its most important determinant is *practice*. They downplayed the importance of innate talent and emphasized the degree to which becoming a world-class expert in any area depends on "extended intense training" (p. 730). Whether the goal is to become a chess master or an Olympic medallist, at least 10 years of full-time practice are required. This **10-year rule** (Rossano, 2003, p. 210) works out to roughly 10,000 hours. The quality of the practice also matters: in music, for instance, morning practice appears to be best. At the same time it is important not to practise too much, to avoid the risk of "burn-out" (Ericsson & Charness, 1994, p. 742).

No evidence has been found to suggest that there are anatomical differences between the brains of novices and experts, at least in the case of expert memorizers. Maguire, Valentine, Wilding, and Kapur (2003) compared top-level participants at the World Memory Championships with a group of non-expert participants matched for age and intelligence. MRI images revealed no structural differences in the brains of the two groups. However, the expert memorizers reported using the *method of loci* for tasks such as remembering strings of digits. As we saw in Chapter 7, this method involves a mental walk through a series of images, and in fact fMRI scans revealed that parts of the brain associated with navigation, such as the hippocampus, were more active in the expert memorizers than in the novices. In other words, although there was no *anatomical* difference between the two groups, there was a *functional* difference in the parts of the brain that were active. By contrast, the brain scans of London taxi drivers and a control group (Chapter 7) did show an *anatomical* difference (enlargement of the posterior part of the hippocampus). The difference between expert memorizers and taxi drivers probably reflects the fact that the memorizers had learned to employ the same strategy—the method of loci—for different materials, whereas the taxi drivers had had to acquire their knowledge of London's streets by sheer repetition. Ericsson (2003) noted that the Maguire et al. study (2000) supports the view that there is nothing innately different about the brains of experts. Rather, years of practice shape the brain and make true expertise possible.

Creativity

It's no easier to find a consensus concerning the meaning of **creativity** than it is to find a consensus for the meaning of *intelligence*. However, one definition that has been widely accepted holds that creativity involves "the production of novel, socially valued products" (Mumford & Gustafson, 1988, p. 28). The reference to social value suggests that

10-year rule
The hypothesis that roughly 10 years of intense practice is necessary in order to become an expert in a domain.

Creativity
The production of novel, socially valued products.

creativity entails not just originality but what Vinacke (1974) called appropriateness (p. 354). To qualify as creative, a product must not only be original: it must also provide a "solution to a significant social problem" (Mumford & Gustafson, 1988, p. 28). This definition is quite broad, and allows for a variety of research approaches. Some studies have focused on the processes responsible for original behaviours, without really addressing the question of appropriateness. Others have more thoroughly explored the social context within which creative behaviour is evaluated.

CREATIVITY AND PROBLEM-FINDING

Psychologists exploring creativity and original thinking have been especially interested in **problem-finding** (Runco, 2004, p. 675). The best-known researcher associated with this topic was Getzels (1975). He observed that problem-finding may strike some people as a luxury. Aren't there already enough problems to go around? Why would we need more people finding problems? The answer is that the quality of a solution often depends on the way the problem is formulated. To make this point Getzels (1975) quoted Einstein:

> The formulation of a problem is often more essential than its solution, which may be merely a matter of mathematical or experimental skill. To raise new questions, new possibilities, to regard old questions from a new angle, requires creative imagination and marks real advance in science. (p. 12)

However, science is not the only context in which problem-finding is valuable. Getzels (1975, p. 15) gave the following example of problem-finding in the real world. Suppose you have a flat tire on a deserted country road. You need to change the tire, but you don't have a jack, and so you define the problem as getting a jack. In that case you would probably start walking back to town. However, someone else might define the problem as raising the car. This is a more productive approach because it allows you to see the potential relevance of things other than jacks to the solution of your problem. In Getzels's example, the person who defines the problem as raising the car notices that there is a pulley attached to the hay loft of a nearby barn. If you push the car over to the barn, you can use the pulley to raise it while you change the tire. The creative solution is made possible by the way the problem is formulated.

Getzels (1975) contrasted problem-finding with other forms of cognition in three respects: the way the problem is stated, the method used to solve the problem, and the solution itself. In many cognitive processes all three of these elements are simply given to us. For example, suppose a group of students have been asked to multiply 1232 by 54,762. In this case (a) the problem is provided by the teacher to the students; (b) the solution procedure is known by the teacher (and, we hope, by the students); and (c) the students simply generate a solution, which the teacher can evaluate as either right or wrong. In this case the students do not discover anything in the course of solving the problem: they simply apply the rules they have already learned. Of course, it is possible to present students with problems in a way that allows them to discover something in the course of problem-solving. Sometimes the teacher knows the correct method for approaching a problem, but allows the students to discover the method on their own. Many of the "insight" problems (e.g., the nine-dot problem) that we considered in Chapter 10 are problems of this sort. The person to whom the problem is given does not know how to solve it initially, but discovers the correct method in the course of attempting a solution.

Problem-finding
The ability to discover new problems, their methods and solutions.

Even in this case, however, the person does not discover the problem: rather, it is given to him or her. True problem-finding does not occur unless the same person formulates the problem, devises the method, and reaches the solution, all of which are unknown to anyone else. This kind of problem-finding occurs in all areas of endeavour. According to Csikszentmihalyi (2002), Getzels's

> most generative idea has been the concept of "problem finding"—the notion that whereas most approaches to understanding creativity focus on its problem-solving aspects, what really differentiates a creative thought from a less original one is that it deals with an issue no one had seen as problematic before. Thus, it is the formulation of a hitherto unperceived problem, rather than its solution, that is the hallmark of creativity. (Csikszentmihalyi, 2002, p. 290)

CREATIVITY AS EVOLUTION IN MINIATURE

Blind variation and selective retention
The generation of alternative problem solutions without foresight, and the retention of those that work in a particular context.

An influential theory of the creative process was advanced by Campbell (1960), who applied Darwinian evolutionary theory to the process of knowledge acquisition. As Campbell saw it, there are two key aspects to the evolutionary process. One is **blind variation**, in which we explore alternatives without knowing in advance which one will have the desired consequences. An example of blind variation is trial and error, of the sort that was perhaps first described by the comparative psychologist C. Lloyd Morgan (1894). Morgan noted that his dog had learned how to escape from the fenced-in yard by lifting the latch on the gate. This was not the product of any insight on the dog's part: rather, it was the result of a process in which the animal explored his environment and by chance hit on an action that would free him.

Other forms of blind variation allow the organism to pick up information from the environment without actually moving around in it. As an example Campbell pointed to *echolocation*—the system that species such as bats use to navigate and find prey. The bat will emit a sound that bounces off objects in the environment, producing an echo that serves as a cue to the location of objects. The animal can then behave appropriately on the basis of the feedback it gets from the sound it emits. People can also learn to echolocate, and it seems that many blind people do so.

Many years ago, one of the authors of this text was a participant in an echolocation experiment (Taylor, 1966). The layout of the experiment is given below (Figure 12.7). He sat blindfolded at the table, and a rectangular metal target was placed at one of the positions on the table. His task was to move his head from left to right and back again, saying "Where is it? Where is it?" and to reach for the target when he thought he knew where it was. When he did hit it, the target would then be placed at another randomly determined position. (A white noise generator was turned on to mask the sound of the repositioning.) Although he felt foolish at first, after numerous trials on several subsequent days, he began to sense vaguely where

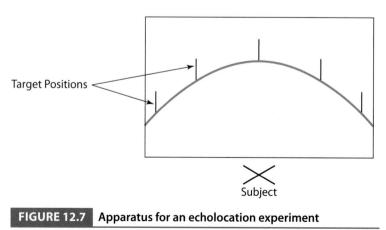

Target Positions

Subject

FIGURE 12.7   **Apparatus for an echolocation experiment**

the target was, even though he could not see it. At the same time his ability to hit the target on the first try increased, although a sense of the target's position was not necessary in order to hit it. The words "Where is it?" were apparently enough to produce an echo from the target, and the echo was a cue that could be learned and used to determine the target's position.

Campbell's point about echolocation is that it is a *blind* process, both literally and figuratively: the sound that is emitted is not sent in any particular direction. In order for echolocation to work properly, all locations must have an equal chance of being sampled. It's the feedback from the environment that tells us which direction is the correct one. The environment provides the selection criterion for a correct action. Without blind variation, we won't get any information from the environment, and we won't learn anything new.

Creative thinking, from Campbell's viewpoint, involves blind variation on a symbolic level. We can imagine various alternative courses of action, as well as the selection criterion for an appropriate action. We may have a fairly clear idea of the sort of solution that a given problem requires, and may then vary our thinking until an idea occurs that fits the requirements. The variation is *blind* in that we have no idea what the answer will be, so that any idea is a potential candidate. There is no restriction on the ideas this process may generate. Of course, most of the ideas generated will be of little or no value (Campbell, 1960, p. 393). But eventually the process of generating alternative ideas may result in a successful one. The key mechanism of creative thinking is *serendipity*—accidental discovery. Alternatives that turn out to meet the selection criteria, whatever they happen to be, are then retained for future use in similar contexts.

All the foregoing can be summarized in terms of Simonton's (1984, 1988, 1993, 1994, 2003) version of Campbell's theory. Simonton stated three "core propositions":

1. Creative solutions to problems require some process of variation. These variations are **chance permutations** of mental elements. Permutations are different combinations of cognitive units such as ideas and concepts.

2. Variations are selected on the basis of a set of criteria.

3. Variations that meet the criteria are retained.

Chance permutations
Different combinations of mental elements produced according to no set rule.

Some combinations of mental elements are more stable and better organized than others; these are called *configurations*. Some configurations will meet the requirements of a particular problem situation. These requirements may be of various sorts. Some are conventional: thus a novel should at least be grammatical, and a symphony should meet conventional criteria for music. Others might be related to the satisfaction that comes from combining simpler configurations to form higher order units. Simonton argued that people seek to create stable, well-organized, inclusive mental structures.

If a configuration is to become culturally relevant, obviously it must be communicated to others. The process of communication may lead to further alterations in the configuration, as it must be put in a format that others can assimilate. As you may have noticed with your own essays, having a good idea is one thing; writing a paper about it is quite another, and ensuring that your paper will be well received is something else again. Communication of a configuration shifts the selection criteria from the personal to the social realm. In order to survive, the configuration must be seen as useful by other people. If it meets whatever social criteria are in force at the time, then it may eventually become a cultural norm. Today's successful innovation is tomorrow's tradition.

Price's law
The hypothesis that half of all contributions in a field will be produced by the square root of the total number of workers in the field.

Creative potential
The ability to generate useful configurations of ideas.

Not all workers contribute equally to creativity in a particular discipline. In fact, most of the important contributions to an area are made by relatively few people. **Price's law** (Price, 1963) is an approximate description of the way productivity is distributed. It holds that half of all contributions in a field will be produced by the square root of the total number of workers in the field. Thus if there are 100 workers in all, then 10 of them will produce half the contributions. If there are 10,000 workers, 100 of them will account for half of the creative work, and so on. Simonton presented evidence suggesting that this "law" is roughly true not only for scientific disciplines, but also for fields such as classical music, literature, and legislation.

Simonton interpreted the way that productivity is distributed in terms of the chance permutation process. He argued that productive people have available to them a greater number of mental elements. The more mental elements are available, the more combinations of these elements are possible. It turns out that, as the number of mental elements increases, the number of permutations of these elements increases much faster. A few people with a large number of mental elements to work with can generate vastly more permutations of these elements than can the great majority of people who have fewer elements. Those few people make the greatest contribution simply because they are much more likely to generate useful configurations. We could say that those few people have the greatest **creative potential**.

What are the determinants of creative potential? Simonton (1988) noted the importance of a "diversified, enriching environment" (p. 107). This general statement can be broken down into several developmental antecedents of creative potential. We will discuss only a few of these, to give you a sense of the sort of variable that is important. Among the antecedents of creative potential, family background is obviously an important variable. Simonton reviewed research suggesting that parental loss is associated positively with creative potential, perhaps because it heightens the individual's sense of independence, which might be associated with a willingness to try out new combinations of ideas. But of course it is not necessary to be orphaned in order to be creative.

In particular cases, the cultural stimulation provided by the household into which the person is born can also be important. Interestingly, formal education is not related to creative potential in a simple way. Simonton presented evidence that people who are acknowledged to be creative in their fields have neither too much nor too little education. In general, they had completed an undergraduate degree, but did not have doctorates. Some training is clearly needed in order to instill a sufficient quantity of mental elements. Apparently, though, too much formal education inhibits the chance permutation process. Of course, the optimal level of education will vary with different disciplines. The optimal level in the sciences, for instance, may be higher than in the humanities. In any case, if you're thinking of quitting school to avoid constraining your creative potential, you should probably think again.

CREATIVITY AND REMOTE ASSOCIATIONS

In Simonton's view (2003, p. 483), one characteristic of creative individuals is the ability to generate remote (i.e., uncommon) associations. Given a word association task, most adults will produce common associations. For example, when asked to name the first word they think of when they hear "chair," they will tend to say "table"; and when they hear "body," they will most often say "mind" (Deese, 1965). We may think of words and objects as having a hierarchy of associations attached to them. In the case of objects, these associations involve possible uses. An example of such a hierarchy is given in Figure 12.8. This kind of structure is sometimes called a *divergent hierarchy* because it consists of a set of associations that diverge from a single object (Berlyne, 1965, p. 88). Associations that are low in the hierarchy are less obvious and less available to most of us as responses. The availability of responses is related to the frequency of their occurrence in the person's experience: the most frequently used sit at the top of the hierarchy.

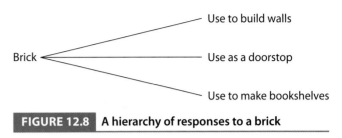

FIGURE 12.8 **A hierarchy of responses to a brick**

One of the difficulties that may arise when we want to solve a problem is that the response we need is low in the hierarchy of associations available to us. If I want to build a bookcase and have a supply of bricks at hand, but don't think of bricks as possible components of a bookcase, then I will miss one possible solution to the problem. As we saw in Chapter 10, it's easy to be functionally fixed: that is, to be unable to see anything beyond the familiar or obvious uses for things. Functional fixedness is the opposite of originality. In fact, a widely used test of original thinking is the **alternate uses test** (Barron, 1963; Vartanian, Martindale, & Kwiatkowski, 2003), in which people are asked to list as many uses as possible for common objects. The more unusual the uses suggested, the higher the score.

Mednick (1962) suggested that an individual's creativity is a reflection of his or her **associative hierarchy**. Most of us have only a few associations arranged in a steep hierarchy and therefore see only the most obvious uses for things. By contrast, creative people have many associations arranged in a "flat" hierarchy and hence are just as likely to see unusual uses as more obvious ones. As Simonton (2003, p. 483) observed, "a flat associative hierarchy means that for any given stimulus, the creative person has many associations available, all with roughly equal probabilities of retrieval." This means that the associations of creative people are relatively unpredictable (cf. Mohr, Graves, Gianotti, Pizzagalli, & Brugger, 2001). This variability leads creative people to generate a wide variety of ideas that can be subjected to selection criteria.

Mednick (1967) invented a widely used test of originality called the **remote associations test (RAT)**. It requires the person to come up with a single association to link three apparently unrelated words. Consider these three words: *soda, buffalo, fall*. Can you think of one word that is associated with all three of them? How about *water* (*soda water, water buffalo, water fall*)? Here are a number of other examples that are similar to RAT items, although they are not taken from the RAT. Some are much easier than others, depending on how strongly associated the answer is with one or more of the three words. (Answers are at the end of the chapter.)

Alternate uses test
A test that asks people to list uncommon uses for common objects.

Associative hierarchy
The idea that the associations used for problem-solving are arranged in a hierarchy, and that creative people not only have more associations than most, but have them arranged in "flatter" hierarchies: thus they are more likely than most to recognize alternative possibilities.

Remote associations test (RAT)
A test that asks the participant to come up with a single association to link three apparently unrelated words.

worm	*juice*	*blossom*
fish	*gun*	*up*
head	*sick*	*port*
blood	*grass*	*eyes*
guard	*blow*	*some*
log	*ship*	*boy*
sugar	*man*	*hard*
foot	*rat*	*course*

time	end	fare
new	good	leap
craft	broom	hunt
man	air	black
chase	work	news
name	poison	pig

The RAT purports to measure the individual's ability to produce associations between words that at first do not appear to be strongly related. However, it has been criticized on the grounds that its results do not correlate well with those of independent measures of the ability to produce remote associations (Perkins, 1981, p. 252). The role of remote associations in creative thinking remains unclear, especially if we define creativity in terms of the production of material that is not only novel, but socially valued. Remote associations may play a part in the production of novel ideas, but their role in the production of socially relevant ideas is less obvious.

THINK TWICE BOX 12.3 — Creative Thinking

What is the hallmark of a highly intelligent person? Is it just the ability to remember large numbers of facts? Could the ability to think creatively be linked to intelligence? These are questions that many researchers have addressed, and it does appear that creativity and intelligence are linked. Some of you may remember the television show *MacGyver* (a movie spoof was recently made, called *MacGruber*). In every episode MacGyver would face some seemingly impossible predicament, yet he would always find a solution by using nearby materials in unorthodox ways. For example, in one episode he managed to create a "rocket-powered" harpoon gun and zip line using only materials found in an old attic: cleaning fluid, a telescope, moth balls, rope, and a pulley. The capacity for creative problem-solving is not limited to humans. For example, chimpanzees will use different-sized sticks to dig out an ant or termite nest, and crows will drop nuts on the road, then wait for a car to drive by and crack open the shells.

Today more than ever, creative thinking is seen as central to intelligence. In many situations we actually have all the information we need to solve a problem stored in our long-term memory, but can't access it because of the way the problem is framed. It takes flexible and creative thinking to come up with the right answer. Are you interested in testing your own ability to think creatively? One common test involves thinking of unusual ways to use a brick (see p. 399). Another takes familiar phrases involving numbers and asks you to identify them on the basis of the numbers and the first letters of the words: thus *24 H in a D* would mean *24 hours in a day*. Here are a few more examples (answers are at the end of the chapter):

5 T on a F
9 L of a C
12 M in a Y
52 C in a P (WJs)
13 L in a B D

From: http://www.experts-exchange.com/other/puzzles_riddles/q_21793289.html.

Summary

In this chapter we have discussed the ways in which psychologists have conceptualized *intelligence*. Many conceptualizations rest on the notion of a single *general intelligence* (*g*) that is common to all types of intelligence and underlies more specific abilities. General intelligence appears to be a useful construct, as research has shown that it can predict academic achievement and work performance. We also considered the importance of working memory, neural plasticity, and evolution in relation to general intelligence.

An important finding in research on intelligence is the *Flynn effect*, which indicates that IQ scores have been increasing in industrialized nations over time. Since increases in IQ have been occurring too quickly for evolution to account for them, researchers have looked to environmental factors such as improvements in nutrition, health, and education, and increasing environmental complexity.

While many theories emphasize the importance of general intelligence, several others focus on different aspects of intelligence. Robert Sternberg's theory of *successful intelligence* proposes that three different types of components or processes underlie all aspects of intelligence: *metacomponents*, *performance components*, and *knowledge acquisition components*. Sternberg also outlined three different content areas of intelligence—*analytical*, *creative*, and *practical*—and suggested that individuals will vary across the three types. Similarly, Howard Gardner's theory of *multiple intelligences* proposes that intelligence does not consist of one ability but rather of many different abilities. An important contribution of this theory is the emphasis it places on the use of *symbol systems*, such as drawing and music, in intelligent behaviour.

Research on *expertise* indicates that practice is the most important factor in the development of expertise. Innate talent or anatomical differences in brain structure do not appear to be critical in the development of expertise.

Like the study of intelligence, there are numerous conceptualizations of *creativity*; nevertheless, cognitive psychologists agree that creativity involves the production of novel, socially valued products. Concepts such as *problem-finding*, *blind variation*, and *remote associations* are considered instrumental to understanding creativity.

Case Study Wrap-Up

Kim Ung-Yong, the child prodigy who was the subject of the case study that opened this chapter, was estimated by the Stanford–Binet test to have an IQ of 210. How Kim would score on the Raven test of *g* (general intelligence) we don't know, but according to Spearman's two-factor theory of intelligence (Figure 12.2) he would probably have a very high *g*. We can likely make the same assumption with respect to Sternberg's concept of analytical intelligence, since it has been argued that *g* and analytical intelligence are largely the same. Where Kim would score on Spearman's variable *s* (specific ability: the variable ability within an individual for different abilities) or Sternberg's practical intelligence is not clear. However, we may find a partial answer in Kim's own reflections on his life.

As we saw, Kim completed his PhD at the age of 15 and then went to work for NASA—the agency that had invited him to study in the US at the age of 8. But after only 10 years the loneliness of his life there led him to leave NASA and move back to Korea. Although he eventually established a successful career in business planning, the choice to return attracted considerable attention, and some media critics judged him a failure. In 2010 Kim told the *Korea Herald* that "People expected me to become a high-ranking official in the government or a big company, but I don't think just because I chose not to become the expected it gives anyone a right to call anyone's life a failure."

Fortunately, Kim now says he is happy. Although his exceptional intelligence has helped him in life, he feels that too much importance is attached to a high IQ: "If there is a long spectrum of categories with many different talents, I would only be a part of the spectrum. I'm just good in concentrating on one thing, and there are many others who have different talents." Thus by his own assessment it seems likely that Kim would have a relatively high *g*, but varying specific abilities.

You have probably noticed that one of the messages of this chapter is that there are many kinds of intelligence. A high *g* does not necessarily mean that someone will be intelligent across all domains, or act in the most intelligent manner in all situations. There may be many supposed geniuses who don't have a creative bone in their bodies. Kim's story may lend credence to Gardner's theory of multiple intelligences. In any event, his modest appraisal of his own abilities may give hope to the rest of us. Even if you aren't an expert in calculus, as he was, there are likely some other types of intelligence in which you excel.

⟨?⟩ In the Know: Review Questions

1. Discuss the nature and evolution of general intelligence.

2. What is the Flynn effect? Which explanation of it do you find most plausible? Why?

3. First discuss the triarchic theory of intelligence and then briefly criticize Sternberg's approach to the study of intelligence.

4. Discuss Gardner's criteria for identifying a separate intelligence. Then outline his approach to the study of a particular symbol system, such as drawing or music. Briefly state a criticism of this approach.

5. Do you prefer Sternberg's or Gardner's approach? Why?

6. What makes someone an expert? Take into account the properties of expertise outlined in the text.

7. What is problem-finding? Why is it important in the creative process?

8. Discuss the role of associations in the creative process. In your answer, discuss at least two measures of creativity.

Key Concepts

alternate uses test (Barron)
analytical intelligence
associative hierarchy
blind variation and selective retention
   (Campbell)

chance permutations
creative intelligence
creative potential
creativity
crystallized intelligence

dedicated intelligence

eduction (Spearman)

entrenched and non-entrenched concepts

factor analysis

flat hierarchies

fluid intelligence

Flynn effect

general intelligence (*g*)

improvisational intelligence

intellectual components (Sternberg)

intelligence (Binet and Simon)

knowledge acquisition components (Sternberg)

metacomponents (Sternberg)

mid-life crisis of musicians (Bamberger)

multiple intelligences (Gardner)

neural plasticity

performance components (Sternberg)

practical intelligence

Price's law

problem-finding (Getzels)

prodigies

Raven Progressive Matrices

remote associations test—RAT (Mednick)

symbol systems

10-year rule

triarchic theory of intelligence

ur-song

U-shaped development

working memory capacity

Links to Other Chapters

blind variation and selective retention
Chapter 6 (evolution of memory systems)

fluid and crystallized intelligence
Chapter 6 (working memory)

neural plasticity
Chapter 5 (phantom limbs and the body schema)

remote associations test
Chapter 13 (cognition and emotion)

working memory capacity
Chapter 6 (working memory)

Further Reading

For a wealth of material associated with the study of intelligence, go to http://www.indiana.edu/~intell/.

There is not enough room in a textbook to discuss the challenges of studying group differences in intelligence. If you wish to investigate this topic in the context of American culture, you could begin by reading Chapter 5 of Cand Sternberg (2004). Herrnstein & Murray (1994) took a contentious approach to the topic, touching off a controversy that is the subject of Jacoby and Glauberman (1995). For an alternative to Herrnstein and Murray's viewpoint see Gould (1996).

Sternberg and Lubart (1992) explore the relation between problem-finding and risk-taking.

Both Gardner and Winner belong to Project Zero, the mission of which "is to understand and enhance learning, thinking, and creativity in the arts, as well as humanistic and scientific disciplines, at the individual and institutional levels"; for more information go to http:// www.pz.harvard.edu/.

For a useful overview of multiple intelligences theory see Shearer (2004). And for more on the psychology of music see Lewis (2002) and Moore, Burland, and Davidson (2003). The evolution of intelligence is further explored by Roth and Dicke (2005).

Ciancialo, A.T., & Sternberg, R.J. (2004). *Intelligence: A brief history*. Oxford: Blackwell.

Gould, S.J. (1996). *The mismeasure of man* (2nd ed.). New York: Norton.

Herrnstein, R.J., & Murray, C. (1994). *The bell curve: Intelligence and class structure in American life*. Glencoe, Ill.: Free Press.

Jacoby, R., & Glauberman, N. (1995). *The bell curve debate*. New York: Times Books. Ill.: Free Press.

Lewis, P.A. (2002). Musical minds. *Trends in Cognitive Sciences, 6*, 364–366.

Moore, D.G., Burland, K., & Davidson, J.W. (2003). The social context of musical success: A developmental account. *British Journal of Psychology, 94*, 529–549.

Roth, G., & Dicke, U. (2005). Evolution of the brain and intelligence. *Trends in Cognitive Sciences, 9*, 250–257.

Shearer, B. (2004). Multiple intelligences theory after 20 years. *Teacher's College Record, 106*, 2–16.

Sternberg, R.J., & Lubart, T.I. (1992). Buy low and sell high: An investment approach to creativity. *Current Directions in Psychological Science, 1*, 1–5.

http:// www.indiana.edu/~intell/.

http:// www.pz.harvard.edu/.

Answers to Problems

Raven Progressive Matrices problems.

Problem a: The number of black squares in the top of each row increases by one from the first to the second and the second to the third column. The number of black squares along the left stays the same within a row but changes between rows from 3 to 2 to 1. Answer: 3.

Problem b: The figures in the first two columns (or rows) combine to form the figure in the third column (or row). Answer: 8.

Problem c: In each row, look for three elements—for example, horizontal line, vertical line, and V—each of which occurs only twice in that row. Answer: 5.

Answers to the remote association items on pp. 399–400 *apple, blow, air, blue, body, cabin, candy, race, zone, year, witch, mail, paper, pen.*

Answers to the creative thinking items in Box 12.3: 5 toes on a foot, 9 lives of a cat, 12 months in a year, 52 cards in a pack (without jokers), 13 loaves in a baker's dozen.

CHAPTER 13

Personal Cognition

Chapter Contents

Chapter Objectives

- To describe and evaluate theories of the relation between cognition and emotion.
- To outline different experimental approaches to the study of emotion and memory.
- To explain how cognitive processes shape our concept of the self.
- To explore autobiographical memory.
- To explain the "bump" in autobiographical memories from the years between 10 and 30.
- To look at how we form impressions of other people and resolve conflicting information about them.

Imagine that you are returning to your childhood home for a quick vacation. When you arrive, two people who look like your parents are waiting to greet you at the door. Yet you can't help feeling that they aren't *really* your parents. Physically, they are identical. In fact, you can't see any difference between these doppelgängers and your true parents. Nevertheless you are certain that they are imposters. How can this be? You fear that something is dreadfully wrong.

In fact, this far-fetched tale is grounded in reality. In 1923 French psychiatrist Joseph Capgras described the astonishing case of a woman who claimed that her entire family had been replaced by doubles (Capgras & Reboul-Lachaux, 1923). Since then a number of similar cases have been identified. This scenario can have dire consequences both for the individual with what has come to be known as Capgras delusion and for those within his or her social network.

Take the case of Blazej Kot. A former doctoral student at Cornell University, Kot married a postdoctoral researcher named Caroline Coffey in 2008. Within a few months he developed severe mental disturbances, including depression and paranoia, both associated with Capgras delusion. In fact, Capgras delusion was the defence presented to the court after Kot was charged with murdering his wife in June 2009.

The prosecution claimed that Kot had attacked Coffey on a nature trail in central New York and then set fire to their home in an attempt to cover up evidence. The defence argued that Kot was not responsible for his actions as he suffered from Capgras delusion and thought his wife was an imposter. Whether or not you believe Kot's defence (we'll return to his case at the end of the chapter), there is no doubt that our emotions are strongly linked to cognition. The way we perceive (or misperceive) things can influence our emotions and ultimately our behaviour. Conversely, our emotional state can also affect the way we perceive things. Someone who is seriously depressed, for example, would be unlikely to find a light comedy very entertaining.

In this chapter we will take a closer look at the more personal forms of cognition that we have only touched on in previous chapters. In particular, we will focus on studies of personal cognition that relate to aspects of the cognitive processes we have explored in earlier chapters. Topics such as memory, implicit learning, and concept formation are all relevant to understanding personal aspects of cognition. Two areas of personal cognition that have been extensively investigated are the relation between emotion and memory, and the nature of the self.

As William James (1890/1983, pp. 220–221) observed, "every thought is part of a personal consciousness. . . . My thought belongs with my other thoughts, and your thoughts with your other thoughts." What makes our thoughts personal is their "quality of warmth and intimacy and immediacy" (p. 232). Our feelings and thoughts are intimately bound together as complementary aspects of our selves. Thus it makes sense to begin a discussion of personal cognition by exploring the relation between cognition and emotion.

Cognition and Emotion

Cognitive psychologists have long understood that emotion influences our cognitive processes in important ways. "Emotional experience is an essential aspect of the process of cognition and must be considered in any adequate description of it" (Blumenthal, 1977, p. 101). We will not deal with general theories of emotion here: only with those that focus on emotion as it relates to cognition. In what follows we will consider some of the ways in which cognition and emotion interact. We begin by examining studies that demonstrate a connection between emotion and the kind of creative behaviour we examined in Chapter 12.

POSITIVE AFFECT AND COGNITION

Isen, Daubman, and Nowicki (1987) presented evidence that performance on a test of creative thinking was influenced by how the participants felt when they took the test. In one study, participants were given a bag of candy before taking a version of the Remote Associations Test (RAT) of creativity. This group performed better on the RAT than did participants who were not given anything before they took the test. In another experiment, participants who saw an amusing film before taking the RAT performed better than did those who did not see the film, or who exercised prior to taking the test. Other experiments conducted by Isen and her co-workers indicated that inducing positive feelings improved creative problem-solving, whereas inducing negative feelings (e.g., by showing a sad film) did not. Overall, there is impressive evidence that feeling good facilitates creative thinking. Isen (1984) argued that cognitive processes generally vary with *affect* (i.e., moods and feelings). Mildly positive affect appears to enable us to think more flexibly.

Ashby, Isen, and Turken (1999; Ashby & Casale, 2003) have hypothesized that positive affect influences cognition through the action of the neurotransmitter **dopamine**. Neurotransmitters are chemicals that modify communication between neurons (LeDoux, 2003, pp. 45–49). The process whereby positive affect increases cognitive flexibility has at least two parts. First, positive affect is associated with heightened dopamine levels. Second, heightened dopamine levels in the anterior cingulate cortex (ACC; see Chapter 4) facilitate switching from one set to another, "increas[ing] the flexibility of the executive-attention system" (Ashby et al., 1999, p. 540).

As evidence for their hypothesis, Ashby et al. observed that patients with Parkinson's disease, who suffer from reduced dopamine levels, typically show impaired performance on tasks requiring a change in task selection or set (e.g., learn a changing rule when sorting cards with different geometric shapes and colours). It's important to note that the effects of dopamine are complex and not fully understood (LeDoux, 2003, p. 246). Dreisbach and Goschke (2004) agreed with Ashby et al. (1999) that positive affect acts through dopamine to heighten flexibility in cognitive tasks. However, they also presented evidence that positive affect increases the risk of distraction by irrelevant information. In other words, positive affect tips the balance between stability and flexibility in favour of the latter: "Adaptive action requires a dynamic, context-dependent balance between maintenance and switching of goals, cognitive sets and behavioral dispositions" (Dreisbach & Goschke, 2004, p. 352). The presence of positive affect may be a signal that all is well, and that we can afford to let our attention wander while we are considering novel ideas.

UNCERTAINTY AND COGNITION

Berlyne (1965, Chap. 9; 1971, pp. 68ff.) believed that an important determinant of cognitive activity was what he called the *collative* (i.e., comparative) *properties of stimuli*. **Collative stimulus variables** are properties of a stimulus that become apparent through comparison with other stimuli. For example, to identify a particular stimulus

Dopamine
A neurotransmitter that is intimately involved in the reward and pleasure centres of the brain. Thus an increase in dopamine levels can give rise to an increase in positive affect.

Collative stimulus variables
Properties of a stimulus that are perceived through comparison with other stimuli.

as novel, or complex, or surprising, we must compare it with other stimuli. One of Berlyne's most important contributions was to begin investigating this kind of variable (Cupchik, 1988; Loewenstein, 1994, p. 85).

Collative stimulus variables can be related to uncertainty. For example, the more novel a stimulus is, the more uncertain we will be about how to respond to it. The same can be said for surprising or complex stimuli. When confronting a novel, complex, or surprising situation, we tend to experience what Berlyne (1965, p. 256) called **conceptual conflict** between the new information it presents us with and what we understood in the past. By contrast, in a highly familiar, very simple, or totally predictable situation there is no uncertainty, complexity, or surprise, and therefore no conflict.

When we experience conceptual conflict, we seek to reduce our uncertainty by engaging in what Berlyne called **specific exploration**. This is a kind of problem-solving activity in which we explore the situation for alternatives to eliminate or resolve the conflict. By contrast, a highly predictable situation poses the risk of boredom, in which case we may seek to increase our uncertainty by engaging in **diversive exploration**. Daydreaming and various forms of entertainment are examples of diversive exploration.

In order to represent the relationship between conflict and affect (positive or negative), Berlyne (1971) revived a nineteenth-century model known as the **Wundt curve** (Figure 13.1). On the vertical axis is plotted the affect experienced in a particular situation—what Wundt called "pleasantness" and Berlyne called "hedonic value." On the horizontal axis is plotted what Wundt called "stimulus intensity" and Berlyne referred to variously as "uncertainty," "novelty," "complexity," and so on. For the purposes of our discussion, this axis represents conflict. The neutral emotional state (neither positive nor negative) at the far left of the horizontal axis reflects the absence of uncertainty or conflict associated with a highly familiar situation, but as the intensity of the stimulus increases, hedonic value begins to rise. It continues rising for some time, but eventually the stimulus intensity reaches a point where it is no longer pleasant, and at that point hedonic value begins to fall (hence the inverted U). At the far end of the continuum, totally unfamiliar events are highly conflicting, and as a result hedonic value may cross the line into negative territory. Thus the greatest pleasure or hedonic value is associated with moderate conflict.

Does the idea that we get the most pleasure from things that give rise to a moderate degree of conceptual conflict—that is, complex things—mean that once we have understood something, we no longer find it interesting? As has often been pointed out (e.g., Kreitler & Kreitler, 1972), things that are enduringly interesting have multiple levels of meaning to encourage further exploration. Something deeply interesting is, in a sense, inexhaustible because there are always new levels to explore. With truly interesting things, increasing familiarity opens up new ways of thinking about them. Complex works of art, such as Shakespeare's plays, may remain at the midpoint of the Wundt curve no matter how familiar they become. Repeated exposure does not diminish the gratification they offer. The more complex something is, the more possibilities it affords and the greater its potential to continue giving you pleasure indefinitely.

Even with something that has the potential to give you that kind of pleasure, however, the initial period during which you must become somewhat familiar with

Conceptual conflict
Conflict provoked by a novel, complex, or surprising situation.

Specific vs diversive exploration
Specific exploration reduces uncertainty, while diversive exploration increases it.

Wundt curve
A graph of the relationship between arousal and affect (positive–negative).

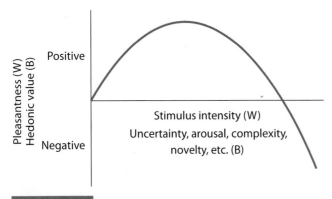

FIGURE 13.1   **The Wundt–Berlyne curve**

Figure is based on the ideas originally put forth by Wundt in the nineteenth century

it can be fairly unpleasant. This period is described by the far-right portion of the Wundt curve, which dips down below the horizontal axis into the region of unpleasant feelings. The initial stages of acquiring a complex skill or subject matter (such as playing the piano or learning mathematics) may be so full of false starts that we give up before we have a chance to experience the pleasure that comes from moving to the left on the Wundt curve.

Although Berlyne cited several experimental studies that supported the inverted-U theory of the relation between complexity and what he called hedonic value (i.e., pleasantness), there are other studies that contradict it. For example, Heinrichs (1984) had participants rate 36 human figure paintings on a series of scales, including collative stimulus properties (e.g., simple vs complex; familiar vs unfamiliar), and hedonic value (e.g., pleasing vs displeasing). He found no evidence of an inverted-U relationship between collative stimulus properties and pleasantness. Rather, simple, familiar paintings were rated as more pleasant than complex, unfamiliar ones. Thus it is unlikely that the Wundt curve accurately describes the relation between familiarity and liking (Konečni, 1996; Martindale, Moore, & Borkum, 1988). Nevertheless, collative stimulus properties continue to be the focus of research interest (Silvia, 2005, p. 99). We now turn to a very different view of the relationship between familiarity and pleasantness.

MERE EXPOSURE AND COGNITION

According to Zajonc (1968), positive adjectives are used more frequently than negative ones because they tend to be applied to events that are common or normal, whereas negative adjectives tend to be applied to events that are uncommon or deviant. Zajonc found that the more often people were exposed to something, the more they liked it. This finding, which is also called the **mere exposure effect**, could be summed up as "familiarity breeds liking."

A very influential series of experiments dealing with the effects of mere exposure was conducted by Moreland and Zajonc (1977, 1979). In one case they showed slides of Japanese ideographs (characters) to 25 pairs of American participants who were presumably unfamiliar with Japanese. There were only 10 ideographs, but some of them were repeated more than once—up to 27 times for one of them. After viewing all the slides, one member of each pair of participants rated the ideographs for recognizability (new vs old), whereas the other participant rated them for likability (like vs dislike). This is called a *yoked participants design*: two participants at a time receive identical stimuli, but respond to them on different scales.

The recognizability scale gives a measure of subjective familiarity (the extent to which the participant feels that the stimulus is one that he or she has seen before). The results showed that ideographs rated as more familiar were also rated as more likable. However, the ideographs presented more often were also rated as more likable. It's possible that repeated exposure increases subjective familiarity, which in turn increases liking. However, repeated exposure and subjective familiarity were not perfectly correlated: some frequently exposed slides were not rated as highly recognizable. Moreland and Zajonc's analysis of their data suggested that subjective familiarity and repeated exposure had separate effects on liking. Even for stimuli rated as unfamiliar, those exposed more often were liked more than those exposed less often (Zajonc, 1980, p. 161). This implies that mere exposure has an effect on liking that is not due to subjective familiarity.

The importance of Moreland and Zajonc's analysis and others like it (e.g., Tuohy, 1987) lies in the model of the relation between affect and cognition that it implies. Liking is a measure of the affective reaction to a stimulus, whereas familiarity is a

Mere exposure effect
The more often people are exposed to something, the more they like it.

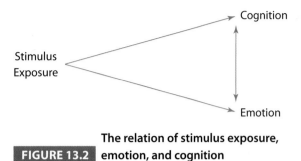

FIGURE 13.2 The relation of stimulus exposure, emotion, and cognition

measure of the cognitive response to it (because it depends on the ability to recognize the stimulus as one that has been seen before). The Moreland and Zajonc results seem to be consistent with a model such as the one shown in Figure 13.2, which is based on the model presented by Zajonc (1980).

In this model emotion and cognition are separate systems that interact with each other but can also receive stimuli independently. In other words, stimuli can have a direct effect on the emotional system without first going through the cognitive system (Zajonc, 1984, p. 117). As Zajonc (1980, p. 172) observed, this view of the cognition–emotion relation implies that emotional responses can take place unconsciously, without regulation by cognition.

Many psychologists took issue with Zajonc's theory of the emotion–cognition relation (e.g., J.O. Brooks & Watkins, 1989). Some, such as Birnbaum and Mellers (1979), argued for a simpler model, in which stimulus exposure has a cognitive effect before it has an emotional one. This would mean, for example, that some form of cognitive appraisal of a situation occurs before it has an emotional impact (Lazarus, 1984). From this latter viewpoint, what a situation *means* to a person determines how he or she will feel about it. However, in a review of 208 experiments bearing on this issue, Bornstein (1989) found generally strong support for the mere exposure effect. In this connection, an interesting result was obtained by Bornstein and D'Agostino (1992), who varied the duration of exposure to stimuli between 5 milliseconds and 500 milliseconds. Repetition of the briefly exposed stimuli caused a greater increase in "liking" ratings than did repetition of stimuli exposed for a longer duration. Since it's likely that participants were not aware of the briefly exposed stimuli, this finding is consistent with the view that "subliminal stimuli produce significantly larger mere exposure effects than stimuli that are clearly recognized" (p. 549). The vast majority of studies have tended to confirm Zajonc's (2001, p. 224) position that "no cognitive mediation, rational or otherwise," is necessary in order for mere exposure to produce liking.

Although the mere exposure effect occurs when people are repeatedly exposed to a stimulus, it also turns out that if a stimulus elicits a feeling of liking you will tend to conclude that you have seen it before, whether or not this is actually the case. Monin (2003, p. 1037) calls this the **warm-glow heuristic**, and defines it as the tendency for liking to be "taken as an indicator of mere exposure." The warm-glow heuristic may lead you to falsely conclude that you have seen someone or something before.

Warm-glow heuristic
The tendency to interpret a liking for something as a sign of previous exposure, even when no such exposure has occurred.

MERE EXPOSURE AND IMPLICIT LEARNING

Gordon and Holyoak (1983) have related the mere exposure effect to implicit learning. As you may recall from Chapter 8, Reber found that simply showing participants strings of letters was sufficient to enable them to learn the grammar underlying the strings. In addition, he argued that learning the grammar did not require that the participant be aware of that learning. Thus implicit learning may take place unintentionally, as a consequence of exposure alone.

Gordon and Holyoak repeated Reber's implicit learning procedure. After exposing participants to a series of letter strings, they showed them a new set of strings, some of which followed the grammar underlying the first set and some of which did not. When participants rated these new strings for both grammatical correctness and liking, they

COGNITION IN ACTION BOX 13.1 — Do Banner Ads Work?

This section has focused on the mere exposure effect. Can you think of any practical applications of the principle behind this effect?

Perhaps the most obvious answer is in advertising. One of the main goals of any advertiser is to get the client's message out to as many people as possible as often as possible. But does this strategy work? When the very first banner ad appeared on HotWired.com, in 1994, it had a click rate of 78 per cent; yet by 2003 the click rate on such ads had dropped to a mere 0.28 per cent (Li & Leckenby, 2010).

Given what we know about the mere exposure effect, it's still possible that banner ads increase the likelihood that people will have a positive impression of the companies that use them. Surprisingly, little research has been done to explore this question. However, in one notable study researchers asked participants to read an online article in the expectation of later answering some questions on the content (Fang, Singh, & Ahluwalia, 2007). As they were reading, banner ads would appear on the screen at varying intervals. Unbeknownst to the participants, one of those ads was the real focus of the experiment. After reading the article they underwent a series of tests designed to measure their recognition of the target ad and how much they liked or disliked it. Although recognition rates were similar regardless of exposure, assessments of the ad showed an interesting pattern: participants in the high exposure group not only responded to the ad more quickly than those in the low exposure group: they also evaluated it more positively, consistent with the mere exposure effect.

If this result suggests that our buying habits are in fact controlled by advertisers, keep in mind that you're the one who makes the final decisions about what to buy . . . aren't you?

gave higher ratings to grammatically correct strings, indicating that they had learned something about grammar in the first phase of the experiment. Participants also *liked* grammatical strings more than ungrammatical ones. Mere exposure to a set of grammatical strings in the first part of the experiment had led to a liking for novel strings that exemplified correct grammar. Gordon and Holyoak interpreted this result to mean that "affective consequences of mere exposure were dependent on the cognitive process of implicit learning" (Gordon & Holyoak, 1983, p. 498).

Zizak and Reber (2004) not only replicated Gordon and Holyoak's findings but also extended them in important ways. In one experiment using strings of unfamiliar Japanese Kana characters, participants learned the underlying grammar, but this did not increase their liking for grammatical strings. However, when familiar letters were used to make up the strings, then a mere exposure effect was found for grammatical strings. Zizak and Reber call this a **structural mere exposure effect**. Apparently mere exposure is enough to induce liking for an underlying structure, and such exposure is most effective when people are not aware of it.

> **Structural mere exposure effect**
> We can learn to like an underlying structure (e.g., a particular musical or artistic form) through mere exposure.

Emotion and Memory

MOOD AND MEMORY

The study of the relation between emotion and memory has made extensive use of network models (Blaney, 1986, p. 229; Levine & Pizarro, 2004, p. 537). Among those models are those created by Anderson, Collins and Quillian, and Collins and Loftus (1975), which we examined in Chapter 6, on memory systems. Figure 6.8 shows a typical network model of memory.

Bower (1981; Gilligan & Bower, 1984) theorized that emotions are units, or nodes, in a network. Although emotion units are largely innate, over time they become connected to other units in the network that represent non-emotional events. When activated, emotion nodes are capable of activating other units in the network more strongly than are non-emotional units. When an emotion occurs, it can colour subsequent thoughts (Gilligan & Bower, 1984, p. 572). Emotional activation can spread throughout a network and become a part of what we retain from an experience.

This view of emotion predicts a phenomenon called **mood-dependent recall**. Many studies have shown that memory is better when the context within which recall takes place is similar to the context in which the information to be recalled was learned; this phenomenon is known as *context-dependent recall* (Baddeley, 1987b). If we consider mood to be an aspect of the context—that is, a part of the network within which the list is stored— then mood congruence between learning and recall sessions should facilitate recall. In fact, several studies have suggested that this is the case, but the effect is not always found (Blaney, 1986; Eich & Forgas, 2003, pp. 70–72).

Another phenomenon that has been extensively studied is the effect of **mood congruence** on "learning of affective material" (Gilligan & Bower, 1984, p. 557). For example, if you are in a sad mood and listen to a story containing both happy and sad episodes, will you later remember more sad episodes than someone who was happy when listening to the story? Gilligan and Bower reported that mood does in fact appear to affect the kind of material that we learn. Blaney (1986, p. 236) summarized the results of 29 studies that generally supported the effect of mood congruence.

DEPRESSION AND MEMORY

The study of how mood affects memory is important because of its relevance to phenomena such as depression (Ellis, 1990). A series of experiments by Hertel and Hardin (1990) investigated the relation between depressed mood and memory using an experimental procedure similar to those we discussed in Chapter 6. Briefly, it involves presenting participants with homophones—words that sound like other words with different meanings (e.g., *pear* and *pair*). In the Hertel and Hardin studies, participants heard homophones embedded in questions (*What colour is a pear?*). The context in which the homophone was presented always favoured the less common spelling of the homophone (*pear* rather than *pair*). Then participants were asked to spell a series of words that included some of the homophones they had heard in the previous phase of the experiment, as well as some homophones they had not heard before and some non-homophones. Finally, they were given a recognition test, in which they were read all the homophones used in the questions, mixed with other words, including some that were in the spelling test but had not been in the original set used in the questions. Participants were asked to indicate for each word whether or not it had been heard in the questions asked in the first phase of the experiment.

In all their experiments Hertel and Hardin used a mood-induction procedure. A depressed mood was induced in some participants by having them read a set of depressive statements (e.g., *I am feeling sad today*). Other participants read a set of neutral

Mood-dependent recall
The hypothesis that mood congruence between learning and recall sessions should facilitate recall.

Mood congruence
The idea that mood might cause selective learning of affective material.

THINK TWICE
BOX 13.2

Mood-dependent Memory

We discussed the notions of encoding specificity and context-dependent learning in Chapter 6. If you're having trouble remembering that discussion, perhaps it would help if you put yourself back in the same environment where you first read it. The concept of context-dependent learning reflects the finding that recall of a particular memory is enhanced when the environment matches the one in which the memory was formed. Thus if you generally study in the library, you would probably perform better on an exam if you could write it in the library. We also briefly discussed how the encoding principle works with respect to different physiological or mental states. Therefore it should not be a surprise to learn that the same principle applies to *mood*. That is, memory is better if you are in the same emotional state at the time of retrieval as at the time when you first encoded the material.

Eich (1995) proposed a number of conditions that might lead to an increase in the strength of mood dependent memory. At the most basic level, if the individual is in the same mood at the time of recall as at the time of encoding (e.g., happy both times), then memory should be better than if there is a mismatch in mood (e.g., happy at the time of encoding, but sad at the time of retrieval). Having said that, there are additional factors that can affect the strength of the mood-dependent memory. For example, memories that are internally driven (e.g., those that you generate yourself, driven by thought, reasoning, imagination, etc.) are more likely to be affected by mood than are external memories (e.g., a list of words to be memorized given to you by an experimenter). This concept was highlighted by Slamecka and Graf (1978), who asked one group of participants to read a target word

(*valley* in the following example) that was paired with a specific category and exemplar (e.g., *natural earth formation: river-valley*) and a second group to generate the word when primed with the first letter (e.g., *natural earth formation: river-v____*). During the encoding session the experimenters manipulated participants' mood to be either very pleasant or unpleasant. At the time of the retrieval test, mood was again manipulated either to match or not to match the mood at encoding. The results showed not only that matching moods led to better recall, but that the effect was greater for words that had been generated by the individual than for words that had been provided by the experimenter.

A second version of the experiment added a new condition at the retrieval stage. Using the same approach outlined above, Eich and Metcalfe (1989) had some participants generate (recall) the target words and others merely recognize them. Their results showed that mood did play a role when participants were required to generate the words; however, no mood-related differences were apparent when participants simply had to decide whether the words they were shown had been presented to them before. The strength of the emotion also played a role, with stronger emotions leading to stronger mood-dependent memories.

In short, the state you are in—physically, emotionally—can have a significant influence on how well you encode and retrieve information. If you want do your best on an exam, therefore, you should try to ensure that both the physical environment and your emotional state are congruent with the conditions in which you learned the material.

statements (e.g., *There are 26 breeds of cats*). Hertel and Hardin found that the initial exposure to homophones led participants to adopt the less common spelling on the spelling test, regardless of mood. This meant that the questions did lead all participants to learn something about the homophones used in the questions. Importantly, however, the mood-induction procedure also had an effect on the number of words recognized: participants in a depressive mood recognized fewer words than did those in a neutral mood.

The deficit shown by participants in a depressive mood could be eliminated by giving them explicit strategies for recognizing the homophones. For example, telling

Initiative and depression
The hypothesis that
depressed people lack
the initiative to learn and
remember information.

participants to try to remember if the word was on the spelling test gave them another source of information about whether or not a particular word was in a question in the first phase of the experiment. Hertel and Hardin suggested that non-depressed participants spontaneously used a strategy for remembering, but that depressed participants had to be explicitly given a strategy before they would use it. This implies that the memory deficits associated with depression might be due to a lack of **initiative**. In other words, depression may prevent people from using strategies that they are in principle fully capable of employing.

Hertel and Hardin (1990) suggested that people who are depressed be given well-organized tasks that require little initiative to complete successfully. For instance, Hertel and Rude (1991) showed both depressed and non-depressed participants a word (e.g., *artist*) followed by a sentence frame (e.g., *The young man's portrait was painted by the* ———). Participants had to decide whether or not the word fit into the sentence frame. Sometimes the participants had to pay close attention to the word because it disappeared from the computer screen before the sentence frame appeared. At other times the word and the frame were presented together, so that participants did not have to focus so closely on the word. Then participants were given an unexpected test of memory for the words. The depressed participants recalled words better if they had been forced to pay attention to them, an effect that was not as pronounced for non-depressed participants. This suggested that unless depressed people are required to focus on a task, their attention may wander and their learning may suffer. Depressed people may be *competent* to learn and remember new material, but fail to *perform* at a level consistent with this competence unless their attention is properly focused.

DEPRESSION AND FORGETTING

Hertel and Gerstle (2003, p. 573) observe that "anyone who has experienced heartbreak, remorse, or failure can imagine the benefits of forgetting." However, depressed people seem to ruminate about their troubles, and this only serves to deepen their depression. It may be that depressed people not only learn new material less well than non-depressed people, but are less able to forget material they have already learned.

To investigate the relation between depression and forgetting, Hertel and Gerstle had participants fill out scales measuring levels of depression and the tendency to ruminate about sad events. People who score high on both these measures are said to be *dysphoric*, meaning ill at ease. Participants then learned a set of 40 adjective–noun pairs. Some pairs were relatively positive (e.g., *wedding dress* or *cozy chair*), while others were relatively negative (e.g., *funeral dress* or *electric chair*). After learning the adjective–noun pairs, participants were shown 15 of the adjectives and asked to try to "avoid saying or thinking anything" about the noun that had been paired with it. That is, they were to suppress their responses for these items. Participants then took a final memory test in which they were given all 40 adjectives and asked to recall the corresponding nouns.

The interesting result was that the more dysphoric participants recalled more items for the set they been told to suppress than did the other participants. This result could be attributable to either dysphoria or faulty attentional control. Certainly depression appears to weaken our ability to focus on the task at hand, whether that task involves remembering or forgetting.

Cognition and the Self

Neisser (1988, 1993) suggested that cognition is not solely a function of events in the nervous system: rather, it is a function of "the whole person who perceives, acts, and is responsible" (p. 3). Thus "a self is not a special part of a person (or of a brain); it is a whole person considered from a particular point of view" (p. 4). Depending on the point of view, different selves, or aspects of the person, become important. (For a different approach to the self, see Box 13.3.)

Neisser (1993) drew attention to two fundamental selves, ecological and interpersonal. The **ecological self**, as Gibson (1979) and Neisser (1976, p. 115) observed, is the self that we perceive directly as we move around in the environment. In the course of that movement, what we experience in the environment changes. Walking down a corridor, for example, provides a continually changing pattern of stimulation. This continually changing pattern provides information not only about the environment, but also about ourselves in relation to it. Moving towards something, such as a car, makes that object an increasingly large part of what we perceive. This gives us information not only about the car, but also about our location relative to it. We don't need to make inferences about where our ecological self is located, because we perceive it directly. The ecological self involves "awareness of where we are, what we are doing, and what we have done" (Neisser, 1993, p. 9).

> **Ecological self**
> The self that we experience in the environment; involves awareness of where we are, what we are doing, and what we have done.

The interpersonal self comes into play when we take part in a social interaction. For Neisser, human beings are intrinsically social, and the perception of other people is as fundamental as the perception of physical events: "Without the special contribution of interpersonal experience, normal human forms of knowing could not exist" (1993, p. 12). Neisser (1993, p. 10) realized that what he meant by the **interpersonal self** was similar to what William James (1890) called the *social self*. "No more fiendish punishment could be devised, were such a thing physically possible, than that one should be turned loose in society and remain absolutely unnoticed by all the members thereof" (James, 1890, p. 293). James made a shrewd observation when he noted that "we have as many social selves as there are people who know us" (p. 294), implying that each of us shows different sides of our selves depending on the company we keep. Thus our social self seeks to present itself in as good a light as possible to those whose opinions we value. The process of self-presentation has been extensively researched, and we will now examine one aspect of it.

> **Interpersonal self**
> The self that comes into play when we take part in a social interaction.

THE PRESENTATION OF SELF

We may see how people want to present themselves when they sit for a portrait. Nicholls, Clode, Wood, and Wood (1999) hypothesized that we show the left side of the face when we want to express emotion and the right side when we want to show our ability to control emotion. They tested this hypothesis by asking people to pose under two conditions. In the first condition, participants were asked to imagine that they were "warm-hearted and affectionate" people having their portraits done as gifts for their loving families. In the second condition, they were asked to imagine that they

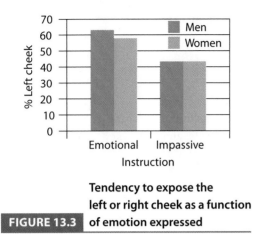

Tendency to expose the left or right cheek as a function of emotion expressed

FIGURE 13.3

Data from: Nicholls, M.E.R., Clode, D., Wood, S.J., & Wood, A.G. (1999). Laterality of expression in portraiture: Putting your best cheek forward. *Proceedings of the Royal Society of London, Series B, 266*, p. 1521.

were "cool-headed, calm and reasonable" people seeking to present an impression of intelligence in portraits intended for the Royal Society (a prestigious group of scientists). All participants were seated in front of a video camera and instructed not to look directly into it. The experimenter, who was unaware of the condition each participant had been assigned to, recorded whichever side of the face was turned towards the camera.

The results are shown in Figure 13.3. The "emotional" condition elicited a bias for the left cheek, while the "impassive" condition elicited a bias for the right cheek. This was true for both men and women. Nicholls et al. concluded that we show the left side of our face when we want to *display* emotion and the right side when we want to *conceal* emotion. This interpretation was reinforced in another study by Nicholls, Wolfgang, Clode, and Lindell (2002), who showed that participants rated faces displaying either the left cheek or both cheeks as more emotionally expressive than faces displaying the right cheek alone. Only when the left cheek was concealed were faces perceived as lacking emotional expressiveness. Interestingly, when Benjafield and Segalowitz (1993) asked participants to rate a sample of Leonardo da Vinci's drawings, the faces showing the right side were judged to be stronger and more active than those showing the left side.

Nichols et al. (1999, 2002) pointed out that there is no evidence that use of the left side of the face to portray emotion is a learned behaviour. Rather, they suggested that it may be an innate tendency (cf. Ekman, 1999). In any case, "if you want to make an emotional impact on the person you are talking to, try turning your left cheek towards them" (Ogilvie, 2002, p. 234).

FIGURE 13.4   Rembrandt van Rijn, *Portrait of Ephraim Bueno* (1647)

FIGURE 13.5 Francisco de Goya y Lucientes, *The Clothed Maja* (c. 1803)

FIGURE 13.6 Leonardo da Vinci, *Head of a Young Woman* (c. 1510)

CONSIDER THIS
BOX 13.3

Are We Losing Our Selves?

Most people believe themselves capable of regulating their own behaviour. Willpower and self-control are promoted as ways of leading a better life. But can we actually choose (for example) to eat less and exercise more, or is our conscious will an illusion (e.g., Wegner, 2003)?

Farah (2005a, 2005b; Gillihan & Farah, 2005) suggests that some people increasingly believe that our behaviour is determined by the brain rather than by a conscious self. She argues that neuroscience is rapidly replacing traditional methods for controlling and changing behaviour. Instead of relying on will power, people who want to modify their behaviour are increasingly turning to substances and techniques that modify brain processes.

A striking example of Farah's point is the use of the drugs Ritalin and Adderall to treat people diagnosed with attention deficit hyperactivity disorder (ADHD). People diagnosed with ADHD, the majority of whom are children, are extremely inattentive, hyperactive, and impulsive. Between 1987 and 1997 the number of doses of Ritalin administered per day in the US went from a little over 50 million to more than 350 million. Furthermore, Farah observed that some people who had not been diagnosed with any disorder were taking drugs such as Ritalin to boost their memory and executive function performance. These practices raise serious ethical questions. Should authorities in schools and other institutions be coercing parents into using medication to control their children? Is it fair to allow healthy individuals to use performance-enhancing drugs in competitive situations such as university or college (see, for example, Sahakian & Morein-Zamir, 2007)? What do you think?

Whatever the outcome of the ethical debate, Farah observed that advances in neuroscience and related fields may be undermining belief in the distinction between things and persons. "With brain images adorning our websites and magazine articles on everything from children's learning to compulsive gambling, neuroscience is gradually being incorporated into people's understanding of human behavior" (Farah, 2005a, p. 39). If purely neuroscientific explanations of behaviour come to be universally accepted, as Farah argued they will, then the concept of personal moral responsibility for our behaviour may disappear.

In a comment on Farah (2005a), Jedliça (2005) pointed out that the belief that "we are nothing else but a pack of neurons" leaves out the reality of conscious experience. Farah (2005b, p. 173) responded by acknowledging that "no matter how good neuroscience gets at reducing functional psychological mechanisms to neural mechanisms . . . it will not necessarily ever explain or dispense with" consciousness.

The problem that consciousness poses for a purely materialistic view of mind has been widely discussed. Montero (1999, p. 183) framed the issue as follows: "Are mental properties, such as the property of being in pain or thinking about the higher orders of infinity, actually physical properties?" More generally, what does it mean when we say that something is physical? Montero called this question the body problem. As Farah conceded, our current understanding of what the body is like has no place for conscious experience. Therefore we might conclude that our current conception of what it means for something to be a physical entity is incomplete. Science may be able to develop a more inclusive conception of the physical in which "concepts such as consciousness and free will could end up being part of physics proper" (Farah, 2005b, p. 173).

It's far too early to conclude that we are witnessing the demise of the self. Indeed, other approaches to and conceptions of neuroscience support the idea of the autonomous self. Unforeseen developments in science may lead to the eventual unification of what may now seem to be irreconcilable phenomena (Jedliça, 2005, p. 172).

AUTOBIOGRAPHICAL MEMORY

In addition to presenting ourselves to other people, we construct life stories for ourselves (Fivush & Hayden, 2003). The story of a person's life is made up of memories of the events of which he or she has been a part. **Autobiographical memories** are episodic memories of events recalled in terms of the time in our lives when each one occurred. Research into autobiographical memory benefited from the technique invented by Crovitz and Schiffman (1974), which we introduced in Chapter 6. They gave participants a list of 20 words and asked them to attach a personal memory to each one. The participants then dated these memories in terms of how long ago they occurred. The words were common nouns such as *hall* and *oven*, which occur frequently in English and easily elicit a mental image in most people. The units that the participants in the Crovitz and Schiffman experiment used to date their memories were the usual categories of minutes, hours, days, weeks, months, and years. The procedure was similar to one invented by Galton (1879a, 1879b), who used to take note of the personal memories cued by each object he came across in the course of a walk. (This is a very simple task, and we would encourage you to try it. Make a list of memories as you experience on your walk; then later work out when the remembered events occurred.)

Crovitz and Schiffman found that there was a regular decline in the frequency of episodic memories as the length of time since the events increased. Crovitz, Schiffman, and Apter (1991) attempted to determine the number of autobiographical memories to which we typically have access. They found that their subjects generally recalled about 220 autobiographical episodes, which they called **Galton's number**, from the last 20 years. However, Crovitz and Schiffman noted that it was difficult to generalize from their findings to all persons. As we shall see, autobiographical memories take different forms for different people.

CHILDHOOD AMNESIA

One factor that may have an effect on autobiographical memory is **childhood amnesia**. There appear to be fewer memories from the first few years of life than would be expected if memory decayed smoothly over time. Wetzler and Sweeney (1986) examined a series of studies of early memories and concluded that childhood amnesia sets in sometime before age five. Rubin (2000) reviewed 10 studies that used four different methods to sample early childhood memories. In addition to the Crovitz and Schiffman technique, there was the *exhaustive search technique*, in which participants spent several hours trying to recall childhood memories; the *focused method*, in which people were asked to recall events from a particular period of childhood; and the *intensive personal interview method*. Combining data from all these studies, Rubin (2000) found that the first three years accounted for only 1.1 per cent of all memories from the first 10 years of life. After age three, the percentage of childhood memories in each year begins to increase rapidly. Rubin noted that these data were collected from Americans, and that children in other cultures may show a different pattern (cf. Fivush & Nelson, 2004).

The fact that not all memories formed before the age of three are lost has been observed in studies by Usher and Neisser (1993) and Eacott and Crawley (1998). The accuracy of such memories (e.g., being told that your mother was going to have a baby) was often confirmed by the mothers of the participants. This led Neisser (2004) to conclude that there may be no definite age before which there are no autobiographical memories.

Autobiographical memories
Episodic memories of events recalled in terms of the time in our life when they occurred.

Galton's number
The number of autobiographical episodes from the preceding 20 years recalled by participants in Crovitz, Schiffman, and Apter's (1991) study: about 220.

Childhood amnesia
Inability to retrieve episodic memories from early in one's life, e.g., before the age of 5 years.

Despite the uncertainty surrounding childhood amnesia, it's clear that the way children experience events will change as they develop the ability to describe them using language (Neisser, 1962; Fivush & Nelson, 2004). As children begin to use different means for representing events in memory, they may lose contact with early memories (Schactel, 1947). Neisser (1962) suggested that any discontinuity in development will tend to produce amnesia for events prior to the change. The rapid development of language is certainly one of the more profound discontinuities in a child's development, and memories formed before and after that change should be expected to differ radically. A similar discontinuity would occur for bilinguals who learned one language as children and then another after moving to another country. For example, Marian and Neisser (2000) studied Cornell students who had immigrated to the United States from Russia around the age of 14. Two sets of English cue words (e.g., *summer*, *neighbours*) were constructed. Half the participants were given the first list, followed by a Russian translation of the second list. The other half were given a Russian translation of the second list, followed by the first list. The participants produced autobiographical memories to each cue word. Russian cue words elicited more "Russian memories," meaning that everyone in the event recalled spoke only Russian. English cue words tended to elicit "English memories," meaning that everyone in the event recalled spoke only English. That is, each language tends to elicit autobiographical memories originally experienced in the context of that language. As Shrauf and Rubin (2003, p. 141) put it, "insofar as memory is language specific, it makes sense to think of the bilingual immigrant as inhabiting different worlds and having the experience of language-specific selves."

THE MEMORY BUMP

Rubin, Wetzler, and Nebes (1986) examined data from several studies that employed the Crovitz and Schiffman technique with a wide range of age groups. They summarized the data concerning autobiographical memory as follows. First, childhood amnesia makes very early memories largely inaccessible. Second, there is a general tendency (discussed in Chapter 5) for memories to become increasingly unavailable as time passes: thus things that happened many years ago are generally less recallable than things that happened just a short time ago. Third, despite this general tendency for memories to decay with time, people over the age of about 50 tend to have significantly more memories from their teens and twenties than would be expected if memories decayed smoothly over time (Rubin, 2000). These three tendencies combine to produce the curve shown in Figure 13.7. There is a distinct **memory bump** for the years between the ages of 10 and 30.

Although the bump is a reliable phenomenon, its magnitude depends to a certain extent on the way autobiographical memories are elicited. Usually such cues are verbal. However, Chu and Downs (2000) showed that using odours as cues produced a different pattern of recall. The novelist Marcel Proust is famous for describing the power of taste and smell as autobiographical memory cues, so this could be called a **Proust effect**. Chu and Downs demonstrated the Proust effect using a variety of spices (e.g., cloves, mint), beverages (e.g., coffee, whisky), and other common materials (e.g., paint, baby powder) as cues. Participants ranged in age from 65 to 83. Some were given each substance in a bottle and asked, after sniffing it, to report any autobiographical events that occurred to them. These participants had their eyes closed and were not told the name of the substance. Other participants were given only the name of the substance and did not sniff it. The verbal cue condition produced the expected bump in

Memory bump
An increase in the number of memories between 10 and 30 years of age over what would be expected if memories decayed smoothly over time.

Proust effect
The power of odours as autobiographical memory cues.

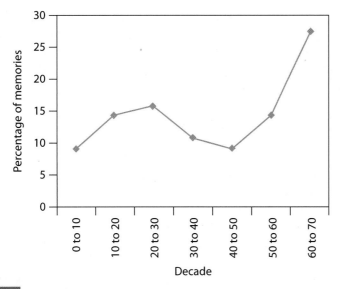

FIGURE 13.7   Percentage of autobiographical memories in different decades

Data from: Chu, S., & Downs, J.J. (2000). Long live Proust: The odour-cued autobiographical memory bump. *Cognition, 75*, p. B43.

autobiographical memories. However, the odour cue produced more memories from between ages 6 and 10 than did the verbal cue. Thus odours may bypass verbally coded memories and make contact with earlier non-verbally coded memories.

Theories of the Bump

Even though the magnitude of the bump depends to some extent on the method used to elicit autobiographical memories, it is still a sufficiently robust phenomenon to require an explanation. One theory (Erikson, Erikson, & Kivnick, 1986) is based on Erik Erikson's (1959) theory concerning the role of identity in the life cycle. People who are now over 50 probably made their most important choices (marriage, career, etc.) several decades earlier, in late adolescence and young adulthood. Therefore it's not surprising that when they engage in reminiscence and reflection on what they have done with their lives, the focus tends to be on the periods when they were making particularly formative decisions (Boylin, Gordon, & Nehrke, 1976; Mackavey, Malley, & Stewart, 1991, p. 52).

As a test of this theory, Mackavey, Malley, and Stewart (1991) did a content analysis of the autobiographies of 49 well-known psychologists (31 men and 18 women) written at various ages between 54 and 86 years; the average age was 72. They found that approximately 80 per cent of the **autobiographically consequential experiences** (ACEs) reported in these accounts occurred between the ages of 18 and 35. This result is consistent with the hypothesis that it is their importance in the formation of a person's identity that makes experiences occurring between 10 and 30 particularly memorable (Conway & Pleydell-Pearce, 2000, p. 280).

Erikson's theory is not the only proposed explanation for the memory bump, however (Rubin, Rahhal, & Poon, 1998). Another theory emphasizes the importance of *life scripts* as culturally provided narratives that guide autobiographical memories (Berntsen & Rubin, 2002, 2004; Rubin & Berntsen, 2003). We briefly considered this hypothesis in Chapter 5. To refresh your memory, life scripts prescribe the age norms for important events in an individual's life. Life scripts are "handed down from older

Autobiographically consequential experiences
Pivotal experiences in a person's life, typically occurring between the ages of 18 and 35.

generations, from stories, and from observations of the behavior of other, typically older, people within the same culture" (Berntsen & Rubin, 2004, p. 429).

One reason for thinking that life scripts may be important is that the bump becomes evident when older people are asked to recall their most positive and important memories but not when they are asked for their saddest or most negative memories (Berntsen & Rubin, 2002); as you might expect, memories of the latter kind—the deaths of loved ones, for instance—tend to occur later in life. Since life scripts are structured mainly around positive events, such as falling in love and getting a job, the life script schema favours the recall of events that took place during the bump period. The net result is that when older people recall their lives, most of the stories they tell are relatively happy; the more difficult times are often excluded (Rubin & Berntsen, 2003, p. 12).

Yet another theory of the bump is based on the action of basic cognitive processes (Rubin, 2005). In earlier discussions of *distinctiveness* (Chapters 5 and 7) we observed that relatively novel events will tend to be remembered better than events that are similar to one another. The second and third decades of life are a period when people are likely to experience a number of distinctive events (Rubin, 2000, p. 173): falling in love for the first time, having their first child, and so on. The first time an event occurs, it is distinctive not only because of its novelty but because we pay more attention to details that we will have learned to ignore by the time it occurs again (Rubin, Rahhal, & Poon, 1998, p. 14).

Of course, all these explanations are compatible with one another. Autobiographically consequential experiences and those prescribed by life scripts are distinctive almost by definition. Each explanation simply highlights different aspects of what may very well be the same underlying process of development during a particularly important period of life.

SELF-DECEPTION?

People often overestimate their performance in a wide variety of situations (Metcalfe, 1998). A good example can be seen in Bahrick, Hall, and Berger's (1996) study of the accuracy of recall for grades (marks) achieved in school. University students were asked to recall their grades in high school, and these were then checked against their high school transcripts. Recall accuracy declined from 89 per cent correct for A grades to 29 per cent correct for D grades. This is consistent with the hypothesis that we remember pleasant events better than unpleasant ones. It is also consistent with the existence of a bias for reconstructing past events as more positive than they actually were.

Metcalfe (1998) documented a number of situations illustrating the **overconfidence effect**. Among them was a study by Metcalfe and Wiebe (1987) that we encountered in Chapter 10. Not only were people unable to predict when they *would* solve an insight problem, but when they thought that they were on the verge of reaching a solution they were most often about to produce an error. The tip-of-the-tongue effect, which we considered in Chapter 6, is another example. Suppose you were asked a question such as "What is the last name of the only woman who signed the Declaration of Independence?" Of course, no woman signed the Declaration of Independence, but you might still experience a tip-of-the-tongue state because you feel as if you do know something that you cannot possibly know. The Moses illusion, which we encountered in Chapter 6, illustrates a similar phenomenon. When people answer *two* to the question *How many animals did Moses take on the Ark?* they are either assuming they know something that cannot be known or (perhaps more likely) just not paying close attention to the question.

Overconfidence effect
People tend to overestimate their performance in a wide variety of situations.

Errors of this sort might be seen as a result of self-deception if we simply persuaded ourselves that we knew something that we did not know. However, Metcalfe argued that this is not the case: people in this situation are not trying to make themselves look better, whether in their own eyes or in others'. Rather, Metcalfe suggested, people retrieve whatever information is easiest to retrieve in the current situation, and "everything retrieved is assumed to be correct" (p. 106). In other words, there is a tendency to assume that whatever you can remember is the information that you need.

As Metcalfe observed, there is a similarity between the overconfidence effect and the various heuristics and biases we discussed in Chapter 11 on judgment and choice. Like them, the overconfidence effect happens more or less automatically. To minimize the risk of the overconfidence effect, try not to respond too quickly: take your time and think things through.

Thinking about Persons

The literature on social cognition is vast and we will not attempt to review it here. Rather, in this section we will look at some of the work of Solomon Asch, a pioneering cognitive psychologist who did seminal research in the field (Leyens & Corneille, 1999; Rock, 1990). We have already come across some of Asch's work in Chapter 8, where we discussed his observation that words such as *warm* and *cold* are used first to describe physical states, and later used metaphorically to describe personal characteristics.

Asch used the Gestalt concept as a guide in his research. As we noted in Chapter 2, *Gestalt* means "form" or "configuration". Asch's (1946; Asch & Zukier, 1984) studies of social cognition are consistent with a basic premise of Gestalt psychology, which is that we tend to experience events as coherent and related to one another. The corresponding premise in the social sphere is that we experience people as psychological units. That is, we don't perceive others as merely the sum of their parts: we treat their individual attributes as parts of an overall Gestalt. One of Asch's (1946) experiments will illustrate the point. Participants were presented with one of two lists of traits. One group heard a person described as "intelligent, skillful, industrious, *warm*, determined, practical and cautious," while another group heard a person described as "intelligent, skillful, industrious, *cold*, determined, practical and cautious." The two lists were identical except for one word: *warm* in the first list and *cold* in the second. Yet the impressions formed by the two groups of participants were strikingly different. The group given the *warm* list formed an impression of the target person as "wise, humorous, popular, and imaginative," while the group given the *cold* list formed an impression of someone lacking those qualities. Thus "a change in one quality produces a fundamental change in the entire impression" (Asch, 1952, p. 210). We do not form impressions of others simply by adding up pieces of information about them. If that were the way we formed impressions, then changing one attribute would not alter the entire impression. Rather, we appear to relate personal qualities to each other as parts to a whole. In general, people tend to experience aspects of other people as coherent and related to one another.

Asch and Zukier (1984) pointed out that some attributes seem to go together more easily than others; for example, *warm* and *humorous* seem to fit together, whereas *generous* and *vindictive* seem to clash. Asch and Zukier examined the process whereby, faced with a pair of discordant attributes (referred to below as a variation in "fitness"), we resolve the contradiction. In their experiment, Asch and Zukier asked the question, "How do we integrate attributes which lack fitness and still preserve a unitary impression of a person?"

Participants were given a series of word pairs labelling attributes of a person and asked to evaluate each pair for fitness. The criteria for discordant pairs were that they were rated as incongruent, did not imply each other, and neither term brought the other term to mind. Fitting pairs were ones that met the opposites of these criteria (i.e., were rated as congruent, implied each other, and each term brought the other to mind). The result of this exercise was an estimate of the extent to which the various pairs were either congruent (e.g., *intelligent* and *witty*) or discordant (e.g., *sociable* and *lonely*). For each pair, participants were then asked to describe what such a person might be like and to explain how the two attributes might be related.

In almost every case, participants were able to form a unitary impression with an incongruent pair just as easily as with a congruent one. They used a variety of strategies to harmonize discordant attributes. Sometimes they would regard one attribute as reflecting a deeper aspect of the person, whereas the other attribute was more superficial. Given the pair *sociable–lonely*, for instance, one participant said that a person might appear sociable on the surface but be "unable to form deep relations, so that he feels lonely" (Asch & Zukier, 1984, p. 1234).

Asch and Zukier (1984) concluded that their participants brought with them a "fundamental premise or intuition" that "a person is a psychological unit," and that this underlying "premise of unity" was reflected in their explanations of the interactions between attributes (1984, p. 1239–1240). Asch and Zukier's interpretation was representative of a well-established tradition in the study of social cognition, going back at least as far as F. Heider (1958). This tradition maintains that interpersonal cognition tends towards coherence and internal consistency. However, as Asch and Zukier pointed out, this does not mean that our impressions of others must be simple. As the example above illustrates, even an impression based on just two attributes can allow for a measure of complexity.

Hampson (1998; Casselden & Hampson, 1990) replicated and extended Asch and Zukier's findings using Peabody's (1990) distinction between the *evaluative* and *descriptive* aspects of personal descriptors. To illustrate this distinction, consider the four terms in the table below, adapted from Peabody (1990, p. 59). Both *generous* and *thrifty* are evaluatively positive, even though the behaviours they describe differ significantly. Similarly, both *extravagant* and *stingy* are evaluatively negative, even though the behaviours they describe are opposite in kind.

Evaluative distinction

Descriptive	generous	extravagant
Distinction	thrifty	stingy

To describe someone as *generous but thrifty* would appear to be behaviourally inconsistent. However, to say that someone is *generous but extravagant* would appear to be evaluatively inconsistent. Which type of inconsistency is the most difficult for participants to resolve? In one experiment (Hampson, 1998) participants were given pairs of traits and asked to rate their accuracy as descriptions both of themselves and of three other people they knew. Descriptive inconsistencies (e.g., *generous but thrifty*) were judged to be accurate more often than evaluative inconsistencies (e.g., *generous but extravagant*). Participants explained the descriptive inconsistencies in terms of behaviours that could be appropriate in particular situations. For example, the participant might argue that in some specific situations it is good to be generous, even if we ought to be thrifty in general. By contrast, the evaluative dimension is conserved across situations (e.g., both generous and thrifty are evaluatively positive).

Hampson concluded that although we can easily explain behavioural inconsistencies, we seek consistency when it comes to evaluation, whether of ourselves or of others. "Thus, the use of descriptive inconsistencies is an excellent strategy for maintaining overall evaluative coherence (*Jane is a nice person*), while allowing for situationally limited behavioral weaknesses (*Jane is extravagant as well as generous*)" (Hampson, 1998, p. 116).

Summary

In this chapter we have examined more personal forms of cognitive processes such as memory, learning, and concepts. Research on personal cognition has focused extensively on the study of emotion and the nature of the self.

Cognitive psychologists have shown that cognition varies with affect, and that positive affect is particularly associated with more flexible, creative thinking. It seems that the neurotransmitter dopamine plays an important role in the interaction of emotion and cognition. We also examined different explanatory models (e.g., collative properties of stimulus, mere exposure effect, and warm-glow heuristic). The interplay between the cognitive and emotional systems, whether these are defined as separate or interconnected, involves a relation between familiarity/uncertainty and pleasantness that is ultimately important for decision-making, implicit learning, and social interaction.

Studies of the relation between emotion and memory have focused mainly on network models of memory. Emotional activation spreads throughout a network when emotional units become connected to non-emotional units. This is the basis for memory-related phenomena such as mood-dependent recall and mood congruence. The study of mood and memory has been particularly revealing with respect to the impact of depression on both learning and forgetting. Perhaps not surprisingly, mood is more relevant to the recall of internally generated events, especially autobiographical memories, than of external events.

Neisser argued that the self is "a whole person considered from a particular point of view." After a brief discussion of two particular "selves" identified by Neisser (the ecological self and the interpersonal self) we looked at two aspects of self-presentation: the way we present our faces to the world in portraits and the way we present our lives to ourselves in the form of autobiographical memories. Autobiographical memories do not decay steadily over time. Most if not all memories of the earliest years are lost by about the age of 5 ("childhood amnesia"), while the years between 10 and 30 account for a large proportion of memories. In terms of memory across the lifespan, this heightened recall of events during the second and third decades of life produces a reliable curve called the memory bump. Theories explaining the bump reflect different accounts of what makes the events associated with that phase of life so memorable.

Finally, we examined social cognition. In an important experiment, Asch and Zukier found that when we form our impressions of other people, we assume that every individual is a coherent whole.

Case Study Wrap-Up

Those of you who have skipped ahead to find out the verdict in the Blazej Kot case may or may not be surprised to learn that he was found guilty of murder and sentenced to 25 years in prison. But what about those of you who have already read the chapter? Now that you understand more about the interaction between emotions and cognition, are you surprised at the verdict? If Kot did indeed suffer from Capgras delusion, do you think he should have been held responsible for his actions?

Whether or not you agree with the jury's decision, it's obvious that human cognition and emotion are closely linked. Indeed, as we have seen, a single previous exposure to a particular item can lead us to feel fonder of it than of something comparable that we have not been exposed to before. And this can happen even if we aren't aware of the earlier exposure (i.e., implicit perception). The "coffee" experiment described in Chapter 8 (Box 8.3: Think Twice, p. 257) was another example of the way our emotions can be affected by the subtlest influences. As you may recall, Williams and Bargh (2008) gave participants a cup of coffee to hold while taking a brief elevator ride with a research assistant. The only experimental manipulation involved the temperature of the coffee. Subsequent ratings of the research assistant were more positive (i.e., "warmer") if the coffee was hot than if it was cold. The authors attributed this effect to an increase in interpersonal warmth due to an increase in perceived physical warmth. This experiment reflected the profound influence that Asch's work has had in the field of social cognition.

In conclusion, it's clear that while our cognition can have many effects on our emotions (seeing someone else crying or smiling can often make us feel sad or happy, and so on), this is not a one-way street. Emotions too can affect cognition and behaviour (road rage is an obvious example). The linkage between cognition and emotion, which is an important part of everyday experience, should give us pause to think about what is driving our thoughts, feelings, and actions in different situations.

? In the Know: Review Questions

1. Consider the theories of the relation between emotion and cognition advanced by Berlyne and Zajonc. In what respects are they similar? How do they differ? Which approach do you prefer? Why?

2. Discuss the relation between mere exposure and cognition. Include in your answer a discussion of the warm-glow heuristic.

3. Discuss some of the possible relations between emotion and memory. Cite relevant experiments where appropriate.

4. Do you think we are losing our selves?

5. What accounts for the "bump" in autobiographical memory?

6. How do we resolve conflicting information about other people? Which kind of conflicts are the easiest to resolve?

Key Concepts

autobiographically consequential
  experiences
autobiographical memories
childhood amnesia
collative stimulus variables (Berlyne)
conceptual conflict
dopamine
ecological self (Neisser)
Galton's number
initiative and depression
interpersonal self

memory bump
mere exposure effect (Zajonc)
mood congruence
mood-dependent recall (Bower)
overconfidence effect
Proust effect
specific vs diversive exploration
structural mere exposure effect
warm-glow heuristic
Wundt curve

Links to Other Chapters

autobiographical memories
Chapter 6 (episodic memory)

Berlyne
Chapter 12 (remote associations and
  creativity)

internally generated items
Chapter 5 (source monitoring)

life scripts
Chapter 5 (scripts)

Further Reading

For further discussion of the interaction of cognition and emotion see Ochsner and Gross (2005). Two good overviews of some of the relevant literature on mood and memory are Walter, Kiefer, and Erk (2002) and Lewis and Critchley (2003). Oatley (1999) discusses the importance of reading fiction as a way of simulating the interaction of cognition and emotion. More on the philosophical implications of the self can be found in Gallagher (2000).

According to ten Cate (2002), scientists tend to present the right side of their faces in portraits.

Neisser (1981) pioneered the detailed analysis of a single case of autobiographical memory with his study of John Dean, who had been one of President Nixon's lawyers prior to the Watergate scandal in 1974. Edwards and Potter (1992) suggest that the accuracy of autobiographical memories is beside the point: when we remember the events of our lives, we aren't trying to be accurate. Rather, autobiographical memories are shaped by the goals we are trying to achieve. It's not that we deliberately lie; it's simply that "truth" is irrelevant.

Finally, in addition to personal memories, our autobiographies contain memories of the important historical events that influenced and gave meaning to the episodes of our lives. N.R. Brown found that for Americans a historical period corresponds to the term of a US president. Perhaps in the UK or Canada the meaningful unit of a historical period is the reign of a sovereign or the term of a prime minister. What do you think?

Brown, N.R. (1990). Organization of public events in long-term memory. *Journal of Experimental Psychology: General, 119,* 297–314.

Edwards, D., & Potter, J. (1992). The Chancellor's memory: Rhetoric and truth in discursive remembering. *Applied Cognitive Psychology, 6,* 187–215.

Gallagher, S. (2000). Philosophical conceptions of the self: Implications for cognitive science. *Trends in Cognitive Sciences, 4,* 14–21.

Lewis, P.A., & Critchley, H.D. (2003). Mood-dependent memory. *Trends in Cognitive Sciences, 7,* 431–433.

Neisser, U. (1981). John Dean's memory: A case study. *Cognition, 9,* 1–22.

Oatley, K. (1999). Why fiction may be twice as true as fact: Fiction as cognitive and emotional simulation. *Review of General Psychology, 3,* 101–117.

Ochsner, K.N., & Gross, J.J. (2005). The cognitive control of emotion. *Trends in Cognitive Science, 9,* 242–249.

ten Cate, C. (2002). Posing as professor: Laterality in posing orientation for portraits of scientists. *Journal of Nonverbal Behavior, 26,* 175–192.

Walter, H., Kiefer, M., & Erk, S. (2002). Content, context and cognitive style in mood-memory interactions. *Trends in Cognitive Sciences, 7,* 433–434.

Glossary

Absolute frame of reference: Spatial relations are described in terms of an invariant set of coordinates.

Abstraction: The hypothesis that we tend to remember only the gist, not the entirety, of what we experience.

Action slips: The kind of behavioural errors that often occur in everyday life.

Adjustment and anchoring: People's judgments of magnitude are biased (i.e., adjusted) by the initial value to which they are exposed (i.e., the anchor).

Affordances: The potential functions or uses of stimuli (i.e., objects and events) in the real world.

Algorithm: An unambiguous solution procedure (e.g., the rules governing long division).

Alternate uses test: A test that asks people to list uncommon uses for common objects.

Ambient optical array (AOA): All the visual information that is present at a particular point of view.

Analog form of representation hypothesis: The hypothesis that a mental image embodies the essential relationships of the thing it represents.

Analysis of the situation: Determining what functions the objects in the situation have and how they can be used to solve the problem.

Analytical intelligence: The ability to solve relatively straightforward problems; considered to be general intelligence.

Anoetic, noetic, autonoetic: Three levels of consciousness corresponding to the procedural, semantic, and episodic memory systems.

Anterior cingulate cortex (ACC): An area of the brain that may detect conflicting response tendencies of the sort that the Stroop task elicits.

Apoptosis: Programmed pruning of neurons.

Apparent-distance theory: An explanation for the moon illusion; it posits that

the moon on the horizon appears larger because "distance" cues lead the observer to perceive it as being farther away than the zenith moon.

Articulation: The production of a language's sounds.

Artificial intelligence: The "intelligence" of computer programs designed to solve problems in ways that resemble human approaches to problem-solving.

Associative deficit hypothesis: The hypothesis that older adults have a deficiency in creating and retrieving links between single units of information.

Associative hierarchy: The idea that the associations used for problem-solving are arranged in a hierarchy, and that creative people not only have more associations than most, but have them arranged in "flatter" hierarchies: thus they are more likely than most to recognize alternative possibilities.

Atomistic: Focusing on the features or components of objects.

Attention capture: The diversion of attention by a stimulus so powerful that it compels us to notice it even when our attention is focused on something else.

Attentional blink: Failure to notice the second of two stimuli presented within 550 milliseconds of each other.

Autobiographical memories: Episodic memories of events recalled in terms of the time in our life when they occurred.

Autobiographically consequential experiences: Pivotal experiences in a person's life, typically occurring between the ages of 18 and 35.

Availability: The ease with which something can be brought to mind.

Backward masking: Presenting a stimulus, called the target, to the participant and then covering, or masking, the target with another stimulus.

BACON: A computer program that has been able to "discover" several well-known scientific laws.

Basic colour terms hypothesis (Berlin–Kay order): The hypothesis that there is an invariant sequence regulating the emergence of colour terms in any language.

Bias: A predisposition to see a particular type of situation in a particular way.

Bi-stable figures: Images from which two separate percepts can be formed.

Bit: Short for "binary digit"; the most basic unit of information. Every event that occurs in a situation with two equally likely outcomes provides one "bit" of information.

Blind spot: A region in the eye that does not contain any photoreceptors and so the visual system cannot process visual stimulation that falls in that region.

Blind variation and selective retention: The generation of alternative problem solutions without foresight, and the retention of those that work in a particular context.

Blindsight: A condition in which patients with damage to the primary visual cortex are able to make accurate judgments about objects presented to their blind area even though they report no conscious experience of the objects and believe they are only guessing.

Body schema or body image: The individual's schematic representation of his or her body.

Bottom-up influences: The influence of the stimulus on the resulting perceptual experience.

Broca's aphasia: A deficit in the ability to produce speech as a result of damage to Broca's area.

Broca's area: The area of the brain's left hemisphere that is responsible for how words are spoken.

Brown–Peterson task: An experimental paradigm in which subjects are given a set of items and then a number. Subjects immediately begin counting backward by threes from the number and, after a specific interval, are asked to recall the original items.

Butcher-on-the-bus phenomenon: The feeling of knowing a person without being able to remember the circumstances of any previous meeting or anything else about him or her.

Capacity model: The hypothesis that attention is like a power supply that can support only a limited amount of attentional activity.

Categorical distance: The number of units traversed during mental scanning: for instance, landmarks on an island map, rooms in a building, or counties in a state.

Category-specific deficits: Selective deficits in knowledge, resulting from brain damage.

Central bottleneck: The hypothesis that there is only one path along which information can travel, and it is so narrow that the most it can handle at any one time is the information relevant to one task.

Central executive: The function of the brain that coordinates information received from among the three subsystems.

Ceteris paribus: A Latin phrase meaning "other things being equal."

Chance permutations: Different combinations of mental elements produced according to no set rule.

Change blindness: The failure to consciously detect an obvious change in a scene.

Channel capacity: The maximum amount of information that can be transmitted by an information-processing device.

Childhood amnesia: Inability to retrieve episodic memories from early in one's life, e.g., before the age of five years.

Chromesthesia: Coloured hearing.

Chronesthesia: Our subjective sense of time.

Chunk decomposition: An aspect of representational change theory: parts of the problem that are recognized as belonging together are separated into "chunks" and thought about independently.

Cocktail party phenomenon: The ability to attend to one conversation when many other conversations are going on around you.

Code model of communication: A model of communication based on the information-processing theory.

Cognitive dedifferentiation: Fusion of perceptual processes that typically function independently.

Cognitive demon: A feature detector in the pandemonium model that decides whether the stimulus matches its pattern.

Cognitive ethology: A new research approach that links real-world observations with laboratory-based studies.

Cognitive history of science: The study of historically important scientific discoveries in a framework provided by cognitive science.

Cognitive map: Information from the environment that is "worked over and elaborated . . . into a tentative, cognitive-like map . . . indicating routes and paths and environmental relationships" (Tolman, 1948, p. 193).

Cognitive unconscious hypothesis: The hypothesis that implicit learning represents an evolutionarily primitive form of unconscious cognition.

Collative stimulus variables: Properties of a stimulus that are perceived through comparison with other stimuli.

Commission error: Failure to withhold a response to the infrequent digit in the SART.

Commitment heuristic: A strategy in which we commit ourselves to the belief that something is true when it is only likely to be true.

Competence vs performance: We may have an internalized system of rules that constitutes a basic linguistic competence, but this competence may not always be reflected in our actual use of the language (performance).

Concealing function hypothesis: The hypothesis that language is a kind of code. The parameters that are set for one language conceal its meanings from the speakers of another language.

Conceptual conflict: Conflict provoked by a novel, complex, or surprising situation.

Conceptual module: A module that is responsible for domain-specific knowledge.

Concreteness (Paivio's sense): The degree to which a word refers to something that can be experienced by the senses (i.e., heard, felt, smelled, or tasted).

Concurrent: The synesthetic response itself.

Conditional reasoning: Reasoning that uses conditional ("if . . . then") statements.

Confirmation bias: The tendency to seek confirmatory evidence for a hypothesis.

Connectionism: A theory that focuses on the way cognitive processes work at the physiological/neurological (as opposed to information-processing) level. It holds that the brain consists of an enormous number of interconnected neurons and attempts to model cognition as an emergent process of networks of simple units (e.g., neurons) communicating with one another.

Conservative focusing: A concept formation strategy of actively formulating hypotheses and selecting instances to see if your hypotheses are correct by focusing on one attribute at a time and by selecting instances that vary only in that attribute.

Consolidation theory: The classic theory that memory traces of an event are not fully formed immediately after that event, but take some time to consolidate.

Constraint relaxation: An aspect of representational change theory: the removal of assumptions that are blocking problem solution.

Context effects: The influence of proximate stimuli and the situation on the perceptual experience of a stimulus.

Contrast energy: The relative ease with which a stimulus can be distinguished from the background against which it is displayed.

Controlled vs automatic processes: Processes that demand attention if we are to carry them out properly versus processes that operate without requiring us to pay attention to them.

Conversational maxims: Say no more than is necessary (*maxim of quantity*); be truthful (*maxim of quality*); be relevant (*maxim of relation*); and avoid ambiguity (*maxim of manner*).

Co-operative principle: The assumption that the speaker intends to say something concise, truthful, relevant, and unambiguous.

Correlated attributes: The hypothesis that some combinations of attributes tend to occur more frequently than other combinations.

Covert attention: Attending to something without eye movement.

Creative intelligence: The ability to reason using novel concepts.

Creative potential: The ability to generate useful configurations of ideas.

Creativity: The production of novel, socially valued products.

Criterial attribute: An attribute that is required in order for something to qualify as an instance of a concept.

Cross-modal effects: The ability to appreciate that the sensations of one modality can be similar to those in another modality.

Crystallized intelligence: The body of what someone has learned; may continue to increase throughout life.

Crystallized systems: Cognitive systems that accumulate long-term knowledge.

Decision demon: A feature detector in the pandemonium model that determines which pattern is being recognized.

Dedicated intelligence: Intelligence associated with domain-specific modules that would have evolved to solve recurring problems.

Deep and surface structure: The sequence of words that makes up a sentence constitutes a surface structure that is derived from an underlying deep structure.

Default network: A set of brain areas that are active when an individual does not have a specific task to do and is absorbed in internal thought.

Déjà vu: The impression of having previously experienced the situation in which one finds oneself, accompanied by the sense that this is not actually the case.

Denotivity: The degree to which an object is meaningful and familiar to an individual observer.

Diacritical marks: Symbols that indicate the correct pronunciation of letters in a particular word.

Dichotic listening: Participants are exposed to two verbal messages simultaneously and are required to answer questions posed in only one of the messages.

Diffusion tensor imaging (DTI): An MRI-based neuroimaging technique that makes it possible to visualize the white-matter tracts within the brain.

Direct vs indirect measures: Participants' reports that they have seen a stimulus, as opposed to the effects of an undetected stimulus on a subsequent task.

Disconnection syndrome: Amnesic patients may be able to acquire new information and yet not be aware that learning has taken place.

Dissociation paradigm: An experimental strategy designed to show that it is possible to perceive stimuli in the absence of any conscious awareness of them.

Distinctiveness: The precision with which an item is encoded.

Distinctiveness hypothesis: The hypothesis that the more distinctive the item is, the easier it will be to recall.

Distributed reasoning: Reasoning done by more than one person.

Divided attention: The ability to attend to more than one thing at a time.

Domain-specific knowledge: Knowledge that is handled by a module dedicated exclusively to a particular subject matter.

Domain-specific modules: The hypothesis that parts of the brain may be specialized for particular tasks, such as recognizing faces.

Dopamine: A neurotransmitter that is intimately involved in the reward and pleasure centres of the brain. Thus an increase in dopamine levels can give rise to an increase in positive affect.

Dorsolateral prefrontal cortex (DLPFC): An area of the brain that may exert a top-down bias that favours the selection of task-relevant information.

Double-function words: Words that refer to both physical and psychological properties (e.g., *warmth*).

Dual route theory: A theory that posits two separate pathways for reading, one for comparing words to a mental dictionary and another for converting letters to sounds.

Dual-coding theory: The theory that there are two ways of representing events, verbal and non-verbal.

Duration neglect: The finding that retrospective judgments of the total painfulness of an event are unrelated to the event's duration.

Dyslexia: An impairment in the ability to read that is distinct from difficulties resulting from poor instruction or problems with seeing or speaking.

Early selection: The hypothesis that attention prevents early perceptual processing of distractors.

Echo: When a probe goes out from primary to secondary memory, memory traces are activated to the extent that they are similar to the probe.

Ecological approach: A form of psychological inquiry that reflects conditions in the real world.

Ecological approach to the study of memory: An approach that emphasizes real-world complexities in its investigations to discover general principles.

Ecologically valid: Generalizable to conditions in the real world.

Ecological rationality: A heuristic is ecologically rational if it produces useful inferences by exploiting the structure of information in the environment.

Ecological self: The self that we experience in the environment; involves awareness of where we are, what we are doing, and what we have done.

Eduction: Literally, *drawing out*. General intelligence may be the ability to draw out the relationships that apply in a novel situation.

Egocentric frame of reference: Using information available from our current perspective to orient ourselves.

Egocentric perspective transformations: You imagine yourself moving, while the objects in the environment remain still.

Egocentric speech: Speech that does not take the listener's perspective into account.

Eidetic imagery: Images projected onto the external world that persist for a minute or more even after the stimulus (e.g., a picture) is removed.

Einstellung effect: The tendency to respond inflexibly to a particular type of problem; also called a *rigid set*.

Elaboration: Adding to or enriching information by relating it to other information.

Eliminative strategy: A strategy based on attempting to falsify your hypotheses, in order to eliminate incorrect beliefs.

Embodied: Existing within a body; the term reflects the general view that cognition depends not only on the mind but also on the physical constraints of the body in which the mind exists.

Embodied cognition: The role of cognition is to facilitate successful interaction with the environment.

Emergent causation: In Sperry's sense, causation brought about by an emergent property. Once the "mind" emerges from the brain, it has the power to influence lower-level processes.

Emergent consequences: A principle of Johnson-Laird's theory: you can get more out of a mental model than you put into it.

Emergent properties: New properties that emerge when a mental image is constructed.

Emergent property: In Sperry's sense, a property that "emerges" as a result of brain processes, but is not itself a component of the brain. In the case of the mind, this means that consciousness is neither reducible to, nor a property of, a particular brain structure or region.

Empirical theory of colour vision: The theory that colour perception involves not only the processing of wavelengths of light but also the influence of prior experiences with the way different surrounding objects and different lighting conditions affect the appearance of objects.

Encoding: The process of transforming information into one or more forms of representation.

Entrenched vs non-entrenched concepts: Entrenched concepts strike us as natural and easy to reason with, whereas non-entrenched concepts strike us as unnatural and difficult to reason with.

Entry points: The locations to which we direct our eyes before starting to read a section in a piece of complex material such as a newspaper.

Epiphenomenalism: "Mind" is a superfluous by-product of bodily functioning.

Episodic buffer: The mechanism that moves information to and from episodic and long-term memory.

Episodic memory: The memory system concerned with personally experienced events.

Errorless learning: Subjects in a learning situation are taught in such a way that they never have the opportunity to make errors.

Evaluation function: The process whereby a plan is created, carried out, and evaluated.

Event-related potential (ERP): An electrical signal emitted by the brain after the onset of a stimulus.

Excitatory and inhibitory connections: Connections that either enhance or diminish the associations between the units that make up a neural network.

Explicit knowledge: Knowing that something is the case.

Face validity: Methods that clearly measure what they are supposed to measure are said to be "face valid."

Factor analysis: A statistical procedure that derives a number of underlying factors that may explain the structure of a set of correlations.

Family resemblance: Instances of concepts that possess overlapping features, without any features being common to all.

Feature: A component or characteristic of a stimulus.

Feature binding: The combining of visual features to form whole objects; a process that takes place when attention is directed at a particular location.

Feature detection theory: Detecting patterns on the basis of their features or properties.

Feature integration theory (FIT): Before we can attend to objects in the world we must extract the features that constitute them.

Feeling of knowing: The feeling that you will be able to solve a particular problem.

Feeling of warmth: The feeling that many people have as they approach the solution to a problem (i.e., "getting warm").

Figurative language: Various figures of speech, such as metaphor and irony.

Figure–ground segmentation: Perceptual organization of a scene such that one element becomes the foreground (figure) and the other element(s) become(s) the background (ground).

Filter: A hypothetical mechanism that would admit certain messages and block others.

Filter model: A theory based on the idea that information-processing is restricted by channel capacity.

Fixation: Holding the eye relatively still in order to maintain an image on the fovea.

Flanker task: An experiment in which participants may be influenced by an irrelevant stimulus beside the target.

Flashbulb memories: Vivid, detailed memories of significant events.

Fluid intelligence: The ability to think flexibly; may increase in youth but levels off as we mature.

Fluid systems: Cognitive processes that manipulate information.

Flynn effect: An increase in IQ scores over historical time.

Focus gambling: The concept formation strategy of selecting instances that vary from the first positive instance in more than one attribute.

Folk biology: The concepts that ordinary folk use to understand living things.

Folk psychology: An umbrella term for various assumptions and theories based on the everyday behaviour of ourselves and others.

Folk taxonomy: A classification system composed of a hierarchy of groups.

Forgetting curve: Ebbinghaus's finding that the rate at which information is forgotten is greatest immediately after the information has been acquired, and declines more gradually over time.

Fovea: The central region of the retina where photoreceptors are most densely packed.

Functional fixedness: The inability to see beyond the most common use of a particular object and recognize that it could also perform the function needed to solve a problem; also, the tendency to think about objects based on the function for which they were designed.

Functional magnetic resonance imaging (fMRI): A non-radioactive, magnetic procedure for detecting the flow of oxygenated blood to various parts of the brain.

Galton's number: The number of auto-biographical episodes from the preceding 20 years recalled by participants in Crovitz, Schiffman, and Apter's (1991) study: about 220.

Gambler's fallacy: The mistaken belief that an event that has not occurred on several independent trials is more likely to happen on future trials.

General intelligence (g): The part of intelligence that is common to all abilities.

General Problem Solver (GPS): A computer program used to perform non-systematic searches.

Generative problem: Participants are told that the three numbers 2, 4, 6 conform to a simple relational rule that the experimenter has in mind, and that their task is to discover the rule by generating sequences of three numbers. The experimenter tells them each time whether the rule has been followed.

Geons: The set of 36 basic three-dimensional shapes from which all real-world objects can be constructed.

Gestalt psychology: A branch of psychology that focuses on wholes as opposed to parts.

Gestalt switch: A sudden change in the way information is organized.

Gestaltist's error: The assumption that whole objects will always dominate over the elements of an image.

Given–new contract: A tacit agreement whereby the speaker agrees to connect new information to what the listener already knows.

Goal stack: The final goal to be reached is on the bottom of the stack, with the sub-goals piled on top of it in the reverse of the order in which they are to be attained.

Goal-derived category: A category invented for a specific purpose on a particular occasion.

Graded structure: Describes a concept in which some members of the category are better examples of it than others and the boundaries of the category are vague.

Gradient of texture density: Incremental changes in the pattern on a surface, which provide information about the slant of the surface.

Grammatical transformations: Rules operating on entire strings of symbols to convert them to new strings.

Grand illusion of perception: The illusion that what we see in our visual field is a clear and detailed picture of the world.

Grouping: The combination of individual elements to form a perceptual whole object.

Hebb rule: A connection between two neurons takes place only if both neurons are firing at approximately the same time.

Hesitation pauses: Pauses in speech, often characterized by disfluencies such as *um* or *uh*.

Heuristic: A problem-solving procedure (typically a rule of thumb or shortcut) that can often be useful but does not guarantee a solution.

Hints: A hint must be consistent with the direction that the person's thinking is taking, and cannot be useful unless it responds to a difficulty that the person has already experienced.

Hippocampus: A site in the brain that plays a crucial role in the consolidation of memory traces.

Historical accounts, observation of on-going scientific investigations, laboratory studies, and computational models: Different methods for studying problem-solving in science.

Höffding function: The process whereby an experience makes contact with a memory trace, resulting in recognition.

Holistic: Focusing on the whole configuration of an object.

Hot-hand behaviour: A bias that leads the teammates of a player who has just scored a basket to let him take the next shot.

Hot-hand belief: The belief that a player who has just made two or three shots is on a streak and will likely make the next shot.

Icon: The initial, brief representation of the information contained in a visual stimulus.

Iconic: A characteristic of mental models in Johnson-Laird's theory: the relations between the parts of the model correspond to the relations between the parts of the situation it represents.

Idea density: The number of distinct ideas present in a sentence or paragraph.

Illusory correlation: The mistaken belief that events go together when in fact they do not.

Image as anticipation hypothesis: The hypothesis that an image is a readiness to perceive something.

Imagens: The units containing information that generate mental images; the components of the non-verbal system.

Imagery (Paivio's sense): The ease with which something such as a word can elicit a mental image.

Implicit memory: Memory without episodic awareness; the expression of previous experience without conscious recollection of the prior episode.

Implicit perception: The effect on a person's experience, thought, or action of an object in the current stimulus environment in the absence of, or independent of, conscious perception of that event.

Implicit vs explicit learning: Learning that takes place unintentionally versus learning that takes place intentionally.

Improvisational intelligence: Flexible intelligence that would have evolved to deal with relatively unique, unpredictable problems.

***In vivo/in vitro* methods:** In the case of scientific problem-solving, *in vivo* research involves the observation of on-going scientific investigations, while *in vitro* research involves laboratory studies of scientific problem-solving.

Inattentional blindness: Failure to attend to events that we might be expected to notice.

Inducer: The cue that elicits a synesthetic experience.

Inferential model of communication: A model of communication based on Grice's inferential theory.

Information pickup: The process whereby we perceive information directly.

Information theory: The theory that the information provided by a particular event is inversely related to the probability of its occurrence.

Initiative and depression: The hypothesis that depressed people lack the initiative to learn and remember information.

Innateness hypothesis: The hypothesis that children innately possess a language acquisition device that comes equipped with principles of universal grammar.

Inner speech: Speech for oneself that regulates thought.

Insight problem: A problem that we must look at from a different angle before we can see how to solve it.

Integration: The hypothesis that we abstract the meaning of an event and then put that meaning together with the rest of our knowledge to form a coherent, consistent whole.

Intellectual components: Elementary information processes that operate on internal representations of objects or symbols.

Intelligence (Binet and Simon's 1905 definition): A fundamental faculty, the alteration or lack of which is of the utmost importance for practical life.

Interactionism: Mind and brain are separate substances that interact with and influence each other.

Interhemispheric transfer: Communication between the brain's hemispheres, enabled in large part by the corpus callosum.

Interpersonal self: The self that comes into play when we take part in a social interaction.

Interpretation: The hypothesis that we interpret information by making inferences, and then remember the inferences as part of the original information.

Intrinsic frame of reference: Spatial relations are based solely on the relations between the objects being described.

Introspection: "Looking inward" to observe one's own thoughts and feelings.

Intuitive concept: A concept that is easily acquired and used by almost all adults.

Involuntary semantic memory ("mind popping"): A semantic memory that pops into your mind without episodic context.

Isomorphism: Mental events and neural events share the same structure.

Jost's law of forgetting: Of two memory traces of equal strength, the younger trace will decay faster than the older one.

Jumbled word effect: The ability to raed wdors in steentnces dsepite hvinag mexid-up ltteers in teh mlidde of smoe of the wrods. (The ability to read words in sentences even when the letters in the middle of some of the words are mixed up.)

Knowledge acquisition components: Processes concerned with learning and storing new information.

Korsakoff's syndrome: A form of amnesia affecting the ability to form new memories, attributed to thiamine deficiency and often (though not exclusively) seen in chronic alcoholics.

Lab-based approach to memory research: An approach that emphasizes controlled laboratory (as opposed to real-world) research in the search for general principles.

Language: Open-ended verbal communication that consists of all possible sentences.

Language acquisition device (LAD) and universal grammar hypothesis: The hypothesis that children possess a language acquisition device containing general principles that apply to any natural language (universal grammar).

Late selection: The hypothesis that we perceive both relevant and irrelevant stimuli, and therefore must actively ignore the irrelevant stimuli in order to focus on the relevant ones.

Law of averages: A fallacy based on the assumption that events of one kind are always balanced by events of another kind.

Law of equipotentiality: Even though some areas of the cortex may become specialized for certain tasks, any part of an area can (within limits) do the job of any other part of that area.

Law of large numbers: The larger the sample, the closer a statistic will be to the true value.

Law of mass action: Learning and memory depend on the total mass of brain tissue remaining rather than the properties of individual cells.

Law of progressions and pathologies: A "last in, first out" principle referring to the possibility that the last system to emerge is the first to show the effects of degeneration.

Law of small numbers: The mistaken belief that a small sample should be representative of the population from which it is drawn.

Left and right hemispheres theory: The theory that the left hemisphere of the brain controls speech and is better at processing verbal material than the right hemisphere, which is better at non-verbal tasks.

Less-is-more effect: Sometimes the person who knows less is able to make a better judgment than the person who knows more but is unable to use that knowledge in the situation at hand.

Levels of processing: A continuum that ranges from registering an event purely in terms of its physical characteristics to analyzing it in terms of its relationship to other things that you know.

Lexical decision task: A task in which participants must indicate whether or not a stimulus is a word.

Life script: A cultural narrative that guides autobiographical memories and prescribes the age norms for important events in an individual's life.

Limen: Threshold.

Linguistic relativity: The notion that two languages may be so different from each other as to make their native speakers' experience of the world quite different from each other.

Literacy: The ability to read and write; sometimes extended to include the meta-linguistic ability to talk or write about text.

Localization of function: The idea that there is a direct correspondence between specific cognitive functions and specific parts of the brain.

Location-suppression hypothesis: A two-stage explanation for the Quiet Eye phenomenon: in the preparation stage, the Quiet Eye maximizes information about the target object; then, during the location stage, vision is suppressed to optimize the execution of an action or behaviour.

Logicism: The belief that logical reasoning is an essential part of human nature.

Logogens: The units containing the information underlying our use of a word; the components of the verbal system.

Magnetoencephalography (MEG): A non-invasive brain imaging technique that directly measures neural activity.

McGurk effect: The auditory experience of the syllable "da" when seeing a mouth silently saying "ga" while at the same time hearing a voice say "ba."

Means–end analysis: The procedure used by General Problem Solver to reduce differences between current and goal states.

Memory bump: An increase in the number of memories between 10 and 30 years of age over what would be expected if memories decayed smoothly over time.

Memory trace: The trace that an experience leaves behind in memory.

Mental chronometry: Measuring how long cognitive processes take.

Mental model theory: The theory that we construct a mental model of a given situation, on the basis of which we understand, reason, and draw conclusions about it.

Mental rotation: Imagining an object in motion and viewing it from different perspectives.

Mere exposure effect: The more often people are exposed to something, the more they like it.

Metacognition: Knowledge about the way that cognitive processes work; understanding of our own cognitive processes.

Metacomponents: Executive processes used in planning, monitoring, and decision-making in task performance.

Metalinguistic awareness: The ability to talk about language itself, without worrying about what it refers to.

Metamemory: Beliefs about how memory works.

Method of loci: A mnemonic technique based on places and images.

Method of opposition: Pits conscious (explicit) and unconscious (implicit) tendencies against one another.

Method of repeated reproduction: One participant is given multiple opportunities to recall a story over time.

Method of serial reproduction: One participant, A, writes down what he or she can recall of a previously read story. A's version is given to a second participant, B, who reads it and then tries to reproduce it. B's version in turn is given to C, and so on.

Method of vanishing cues: Amnesic patients learned the meaning of computer commands by being presented with definitions of the commands and fragments of the commands' names. Additional letters were presented until the patient guessed the word. Then letters were progressively removed until the patient was able to give the name of the command when presented with its definition.

Mid-life crisis of the musician: As music students become adolescents, they may feel a tension between their increasingly explicit understanding of music and the spontaneous love of music they had as children.

Mind wandering: A shift of mental resources away from the task at hand and towards internal thoughts.

Mindfulness vs mindlessness: Openness to alternative possibilities versus the tendency to behave as if the situation had only one possible interpretation.

Minimalism: The belief that linguistic competence has only those characteristics that are absolutely necessary.

Mirror neurons: Broca's area in monkeys contains neurons that fire not only when the animal makes grasping movements, but also when the monkey observes other animals making those movements.

Misaligned hierarchies: Judgments made with respect to one level suggest one conclusion while judgments made at another level suggest a contrasting conclusion.

Misinformation effect: The hypothesis that misleading post-event information can become integrated with memory for the original event.

Mnemonic techniques: Procedures used to aid memory.

Modules: Different parts of the brain, each of which is responsible for particular cognitive operations.

Mood congruence: The idea that mood might cause selective learning of affective material.

Mood-dependent recall: The hypothesis that mood congruence between learning and recall sessions should facilitate recall.

Moon illusion: The tendency for the moon to appear different in size depending on where it is in the sky.

Moses illusion: The tendency to answer the question *How many animals of each kind did Moses take on the Ark?* with *Two*, either because you assume that the person who posed the question meant to say *Noah* rather than *Moses*, or because you didn't notice the error.

Moving window technique: A method of determining how much visual information can be taken in during a fixation, in which the reader is prevented from seeing information beyond a certain distance from the current fixation.

Multiple intelligences: The hypothesis that intelligence consists not of one underlying ability but of many different abilities.

Multiple-trace memory model: Traces of each individual experience are recorded in memory. No matter how often a particular kind of event is experienced, a memory trace of the individual event is recorded each time.

Mystic writing pad model: A model of memory based on a toy writing tablet that retains fragments of old messages even after they have been "erased." In time, these fragments accumulate and begin to overlap, so that they become increasingly hard to read.

Natural deduction system: A reasoning system made up of propositions and deduction rules that are used to draw conclusions from these propositions.

Negative transfer: The tendency to respond with previously learned rule sequences even when they are inappropriate.

Neural network: Neurons that are functionally related or connected.

Neural plasticity: *Plasticity* is the ability of an organism to adapt to changes in the environment. *Neural* plasticity reflects changes in neuronal circuitry as a function of experience.

Nonsense syllables: Nonsense "words" consisting of a consonant followed by a vowel followed by a consonant.

Now Print! theory: The theory that especially significant experiences are immediately "photocopied" and preserved in long-term memory.

Number forms: Automatically generated images of numbers in various spatial layouts external to an individual.

Nystagmus: Small but continuous movements made by the eye during fixation.

Objective and subjective thresholds: The point at which participants can detect a stimulus at a chance level versus the point at which they say they did not perceive it.

Objective distance: The true distance between objects in the real world, which are preserved in our mental images.

Opponent process theory of colour vision: The hypothesis that colour vision is based on three pairs of antagonistic processes.

Optic ataxia: Patients with this condition can identify objects but are unable to successfully reach for them, especially when the object is presented to their peripheral vision.

Optic flow field: The continually changing (i.e., transforming) pattern of information that results from the movement of either objects or the observer through the environment.

Organizational principles: The rules (or laws) that govern how whole objects or events are perceived from a collection of individual elements.

Overconfidence effect: People tend to overestimate their performance in a wide variety of situations.

Overt attention: Attending to something with eye movement.

Pandemonium: A model of pattern recognition consisting of three levels: data, cognitive demons, and decision demon.

Parallel distributed processing (PDP): A model of perception according to which different features are processed at the same time by different "units" (simple processing elements) connected together in a network.

Parallel mental activity: Thinking about something other than the task at hand.

Parallel processing: Many neural connections may be active at the same time.

Parallelism: "Mind" and brain are two aspects of the same reality and flow in parallel.

Parameter-setting hypothesis: The hypothesis that language acquisition involves a universal grammar that contains a variety of switches, which can be set to one of a number of possible values, or parameters. A parameter is a universal aspect of language that can take on one of a small set of possible values.

Parental reformulations: Adult reformulations of children's speech. They are negative in that they inform children that they

have made a mistake and positive in that they provide examples of correct speech.

Parsimony: A principle of Johnson-Laird's theory: people tend to construct the simplest mental model possible.

Partist strategy: A concept formation strategy, used in reception tasks, in which you initially hypothesize that only some attributes are members of the concept.

Path integration: The process whereby our position in relation to an important location is continuously updated as we move through the environment.

Pattern recognition: The ability to recognize an event as an instance of a particular category of event.

Peak–end rule: Retrospective judgments of the total painfulness of an event are formed by averaging the pain experienced during the most painful moment of the event and that felt at the end of the event.

Penfield homunculus: A map of the sensory cortex that shows where the various parts of the body are represented; the size of each part is proportional to the area of the cortex that represents it.

Percept: The visual experience of sensory information.

Perception: The processing of sensory information in such a way that it produces conscious experiences and guides action in the world.

Perception without awareness: A stimulus has an effect even though it is below the participant's subjective threshold of awareness.

Perceptual completion (filling-in): The incorrect impression that a stimulus occupies a section of the visual scene when in fact it occupies only the surrounding region.

Perceptual cycle: The process whereby our schemata guide our exploration of the world and in turn are shaped by what is found there.

Perceptual representation system (PRS): A memory system containing very specific representations of events that is hypothesized to be responsible for priming effects.

Perceptual symbols: Aspects of perceptual memories that stand for events in the world and enter into all forms of symbolic activity.

Performance components: The processes that are used in the execution of a task.

Permastore: Bahrick's term for the state of relative permanence in which he found that some kinds of memory can be retained over very long periods of time.

Phantom limb: The feeling, following the sudden loss of a body part, that it is still present.

Phonological dyslexia: A form of dyslexia affecting only the ability to read letter-by-letter; the ability to recognize words as entire units remains intact.

Phonological loop and visuo-spatial sketchpad: Temporary stores of linguistic and non-verbal information, respectively.

Photoreceptors: Receptor cells in the retina that help transform energy from photons (light) into neural signals.

Phrase structure rules: Rules describing the way symbols can be rewritten as other symbols.

Phrenology: The study of the shape, size, and protrusions of the cranium in an attempt to discover the relationships between parts of the brain and various mental activities and abilities.

Plasticity: Flexibility.

Polysemy: The existence of multiple meanings for one word.

Positron emission tomography (PET): An imaging technique in which a participant is injected with a radioactive substance that mingles with the blood and circulates to the brain. A scanner is then used to detect the flow of blood to particular areas of the brain.

"Poverty of the stimulus" argument: The argument that the linguistic environment to which a child is exposed is too deficient to enable the child to acquire language on that basis alone.

Practical intelligence: The ability to find problem solutions in real-world, everyday situations.

Practical syllogism: One in which two premises point to a conclusion that calls for action.

Preattentive processing: The unconscious extraction of features that must take place before we can perceive an object.

Prefrontal leucotomy: A surgical procedure, now abandoned, in which the connections between the prefrontal lobes and other parts of the brain were severed; also known as prefrontal lobotomy.

Pretense theory of irony: When speaking ironically, people are only pretending to mean what they say.

Price's law: The hypothesis that half of all contributions in a field will be produced by the square root of the total number of workers in the field.

Primary memory: What we are aware of in the "immediately present moment"; often termed "immediate memory" or "short-term memory."

Primary metaphor: A pairing of subjective experience with sensorimotor experience.

Priming: The tendency for some initial stimuli to make subsequent responses to related stimuli more likely.

Principle of closed forms: Visual elements that form the edges of closed shapes are grouped to form a whole.

Principle of common movement: Visual elements that move simultaneously and in the same way are grouped to form a whole.

Principle of encoding specificity: The way an item is retrieved from memory depends on the way it was stored in memory.

Principle of experience: Visual elements are grouped together based on the prior experience and knowledge of the observer.

Principle of good contour: Visual elements that form the most direct continuation of each other are grouped together.

Principle of proximity: Visual elements that are close to one another are grouped to form a whole.

Principle of similarity: Visual elements that are similar are grouped together.

Probe: A "snapshot" of information in primary memory that can activate memory traces in secondary memory.

Problem space: The representation of a problem, including the goal to be reached and the various ways of transforming the given situation into the solution.

Problem-finding: The ability to discover new problems, their methods and solutions.

Procedural memory: The memory system concerned with knowing how to do things.

Process dissociation procedure: An experimental technique that requires participants *not* to respond with items they have observed previously.

Prodigies: Children who perform at an expert level at a much earlier age than would normally be expected.

Production rules: A production rule consists of a condition and an action (C→A).

Productive thinking: Thinking based on a grasp of the general principles that apply in the situation at hand.

Progress monitoring theory: The theory that we monitor our progress on a problem, and when we reach an impasse we are open to an insightful solution.

Propositional knowledge hypothesis: The hypothesis that knowledge about the world is stored in memory in the form of propositions.

Prospective memory: The intention to remember to do something at some future time.

Prototypical: Representative of a pattern or category.

Proust effect: The power of odours as autobiographical memory cues.

"Quiet Eye": Sustained and steady eye gaze prior to an action or behaviour.

Rapid serial visual presentation (RSVP): The presentation of a series of stimuli in quick succession.

Rationalization: The attempt to make memory as coherent and sensible as possible.

Raven Progressive Matrices: A set of problems that constitutes the most widely accepted test of *g*.

Reappearance hypothesis: The hypothesis that the same memory can reappear, unchanged, again and again.

Reasoning: A thought process that yields a conclusion from premises.

Recency bias vs primacy bias: A tendency to recall experiences from the recent past versus a tendency to recall experiences from the relatively distant past.

Reception task: A concept formation task in which the instances presented to the participant are chosen by the experimenter.

Recognition by components (RBC): The theory that we recognize objects by breaking them down into their fundamental geometric shapes.

Recognition heuristic: When choosing between two objects (according to some criterion), if one is recognized and the other is not, then select the former.

Reconsolidation: The hypothetical process whereby a memory trace is revised and reconsolidated.

Recursion: A process that refers to itself.

Regression to the mean: For purely mathematical reasons, whenever two variables are not perfectly correlated, extreme values on one variable tend to be related to values on the other variable that are closer to (i.e., regressed to) the mean of that variable.

Regressions: Right to left movements of the eyes during reading, directing them to previously read text.

Relational reasoning: Reasoning involving premises that express the relations between items (e.g., *A is taller than B*).

Relative frame of reference: Spatial relations are described relative to an observer's viewpoint.

Remote associations test (RAT): A test that asks the participant to come up with a single association to link three apparently unrelated words.

Representational change theory: The theory that insight requires a change in the way the participant represents the problem.

Representativeness heuristic: Making inferences on the assumption that small samples resemble one another and the population from which they are drawn.

Retina: Tissue at the back of the eye that is filled with photoreceptors.

Retroactive interference: A decline in the recall of one event as a result of a later event.

Ribot's law of retrograde amnesia: Older memories are less likely to be lost as a result of brain damage than are newer memories.

Saccades: The rapid, jerky movements made as the eye scans an image.

Sapir–Whorf hypothesis: The hypothesis that two languages may be so different from one another as to make their native speakers' experience of the world qualitatively different.

Scatter-reflection: The degree to which light scatters when reflected from a surface.

Schema: An expectation concerning what we are likely to find as we explore the world; plural "schemas" or "schemata."

Schema (Bartlett): An active mass of organized past reactions that provides a setting that guides our behaviour.

Script: A set of expectations concerning the actions and events that are appropriate in a particular situation.

Search tree: A representation of all the possible moves branching out from the initial state of the problem.

Secondary memory: Knowledge acquired at an earlier time that is stored indefinitely, and is absent from awareness; also called "long-term memory."

Selection: The hypothesis that we select information both as we receive it and as we recall it.

Selection task: A concept formation task in which the participant selects instances from those presented by the experimenter.

Selection task (Wason): A four-card problem based on conditional reasoning.

Selective attention: Attending to relevant information and ignoring irrelevant information.

Selective looking: Occurs when we are exposed to two events simultaneously, but attend to only one of them.

Semantic memory: The memory system concerned with knowledge of words, concepts, and their relationships.

Sequential attention hypothesis: A hypothesis about the relationship between overt and covert attention that posits a tight relationship between the two whereby covert attention is shifted first and overt eye movement follows.

Serial processing: Only one neural activity may take place at any one time.

Set: A temporary, top-down organization in the brain that facilitates some responses while inhibiting others, in order to achieve a certain goal; also referred to as a "mental set."

Shadowing task: A task in which the subject is exposed to two messages simultaneously and must repeat one of them.

Simultaneous scanning: The concept formation strategy that keeps in mind all possible hypotheses and tries to eliminate as many as possible with each instance selection.

Smooth pursuit movements: Movements of the eye that, because they are not jerky, enable the viewer to maintain fixation on a moving object.

Social contract theory: The theory that inference procedures have evolved to deal with social contracts in which people give something up in order to gain something.

Source monitoring framework: A theory of the reason people sometimes fail to distinguish between a real and an imagined event.

Spatial framework: An imaginary space with one vertical (*above–below*) and two horizontal dimensions (*ahead–behind* and *left–right*).

Special places strategy: Choosing a storage location that other people will not think of; the problem is that you may not think of it either when the time comes to retrieve the item.

Specific and general levels of representation: As people age they tend to forget specific details but to remember deeper, more general meanings.

Specific vs diversive exploration: Specific exploration reduces uncertainty, while diversive exploration increases it.

Speech: Those sentences that are actually spoken; only a small subset of language.

Split brain: A condition created by severing the corpus callosum.

Spreading activation: The idea that activation of the paths that make up a semantic network spreads from the node at which the search begins.

Squelching: The tendency of the nervous system to inhibit the processing of unclear features.

Stimulus: An entity in the external environment that can be perceived by an observer.

Stimulus onset asynchrony (SOA): The temporal delay between the first stimulus and a masking stimulus.

Strong but wrong routines: Overlearned response sequences that we follow even when we intend to do something else.

Strong synesthetes: People who are susceptible to an inducer in one sensory modality (e.g., a sound) producing a concurrent image in another sensory modality (e.g., a colour).

Stroop task: A naming task in which colour names are printed in colours other than the colours they name.

Structural limits: The hypothesis that attentional tasks interfere with one another to the extent that they involve similar activities.

Structural mere exposure effect: We can learn to like an underlying structure (e.g., a particular musical or artistic form) through mere exposure.

Structurally blind thinking: The tendency to reproduce thinking appropriate for other situations, but not for the current situation.

Subgoal: A goal derived from the original goal, the solution of which leads to the solution of the problem as a whole.

Subliminal perception: Also known as unconscious perception, subliminal perception occurs when an observer is unaware of perceiving a stimulus, yet the stimulus can still have an impact on his or her behaviour.

Successive scanning: The concept formation strategy that involves formulating a single hypothesis and testing it by selecting instances until the correct hypothesis emerges.

Superordinate, basic, and subordinate levels: Levels of inclusiveness of a concept, as in *tree*, *oak*, and *live oak*.

Supervenient: In Sperry's sense, describes mental states that may simultaneously influence neuronal events and be influenced by them.

Surface dyslexia: A form of dyslexia affecting only the ability to recognize words as entire units; the ability to read words letter-by-letter remains intact.

Sustained attention to response task (SART): A continuous response task in which digits (e.g., 0 to 9) are sequentially presented on a computer screen and participants are asked to press a button in response to all but one of them (e.g., the infrequent digit 3); response to this infrequent digit is supposed to be withheld (see Robertson et al., 1997).

Switch cost: The finding that performance declines immediately on switching tasks.

Syllogism: A syllogism consists of two premises and a conclusion. Each of the premises specifies a relationship between two categories.

Symbol systems: Different forms of representation, such as drawing, music, and mathematics, that express different forms of intelligence.

Synesthesia: The condition in which a stimulus appropriate to one sense (e.g., a sound) triggers an experience appropriate to another sense (e.g., a colour).

Syntactic development: Development of the ability to organize words into grammatical sentences.

Tacit knowledge: Knowing how to do something without being able to say exactly what it is that you know.

Task-related knowledge: An observer's knowledge of the goals and the task at hand as it guides the eyes during a visual task.

Task switching: Changing from working on one task to working on another; usually studied in situations in which the switch is involuntary.

Teachable language comprehender (TLC): A computer program that is a model of semantic memory.

Template-matching theory: The hypothesis that the process of pattern recognition relies on the use of templates or prototypes.

10-year rule: The hypothesis that roughly 10 years of intense practice is necessary in order to become an expert in a domain.

Theory of ecological optics: The proposition that perception is based on direct contact of the sensory organs with stimulus energy emanating from the environment and that an important goal of perception is action.

Thinking aloud: Concurrent verbalization: the verbalization of information as the participant is attending to it.

Three-term series problem: Linear syllogisms consisting of two comparative sentences from which a conclusion must be drawn.

Time spaces: The visual experience of time units such as days of the week or months of the year as occupying spatial locations outside the body.

Tip-of-the-tongue phenomenon: Knowing that you know something without quite being able to recall it.

Top-down influences: The influence of context and an observer's knowledge, expectations, and high-level goals on perceptual experience.

Topological breakage: The discontinuity created by the intersection of two texture gradients.

Toy problems: Problems used to analyze the problem-solving process.

Transformation: In the theory proposed by Gibson (1966), the change of optical information hitting the eye when the observer moves through the environment.

Tree diagram: A description of a process that proceeds from one level at which a number of relations are simultaneously present to other levels at which those relations are ordered serially.

Triarchic theory of intelligence: Sternberg's theory consisting of analytic, practical, and creative intelligence.

Truth tables: A way of presenting the various combinations of the constituents of logical statements.

Unexpected findings: Although scientists may initially resist information that disconfirms one of their favourite hypotheses, successful problem-solvers attempt to explain surprising results.

Ur-song: The hypothetical first song that all children would spontaneously sing.

U-shaped development: The hypothesis that the development of many symbolic forms initially is delightfully pre-conventional, then descends to the merely conventional, but ultimately may achieve the integration of the post-conventional.

Visual agnosia: An inability to identify objects visually even though they can be identified using other senses (e.g., touch).

Vividness of visual imagery: The degree to which images are clear and lively, resembling actual percepts.

Von Restorff effect: If one item in a set is different from the others, it is more likely to be recalled.

Warm-glow heuristic: The tendency to interpret a liking for something as a sign of previous exposure, even when no such exposure has occurred.

Weak synesthetes: People who can appreciate cross-modal associations without having strong synesthetic experiences.

Wernicke's aphasia: A deficit in the ability to comprehend speech as a result of damage to Wernicke's area.

Wernicke's area: Area of the brain's left hemisphere that is responsible for processing the meaning of words.

Wholist strategy: A concept formation strategy, used in reception tasks, in which you initially hypothesize that all attributes are members of the concept.

Word superiority effect: It's easier to identify a letter (e.g., "P") if it appears in a word (e.g., "WARP") than if it appears alone.

Working memory: The system that allows for the temporary storage and manipulation of information that is necessary for various cognitive activities.

Working memory capacity: The theory that working memory capacity and g are closely related.

Wundt curve: A graph of the relationship between arousal and affect (positive–negative).

Zeigarnik effect: The urge to finish incomplete tasks.

Zone of proximal development: Defined by Vygotsky (1935/1978, p. 86) as "the distance between the actual developmental level as determined by independent problem-solving and the level of potential development as determined through problem-solving under adult guidance or in collaboration with more capable peers."

References

Abraham, C. (2004, Dec. 4). Marooned in the moment. *Globe and Mail*, pp. F1, F4–F5.

Ackerman, P.L., Beier, M.E., & Boyle, M.O. (2005). Working memory and intelligence: The same or different constructs? *Psychological Bulletin, 31*, 30–60.

Adelson, R. (2005). Hues and views: A cross-cultural study reveals how language shapes color perception. *Monitor on Psychology, 36*. Retrieved March 23, 2005, from APA Online, at: www.apa.orgmonitor/feb05/hues.html.

Alaimo, C. (1996a, December 2). No ordinary sales pitch. *St. Catharines Standard*, p. B1.

Alaimo, C. (1996b, November 4). A rags to fishes story. *St. Catharines Standard*, p. D1.

Alba, J.W., & Hasher, L. (1983). Is memory schematic? *Psychological Bulletin, 93*, 203–231.

Allen, R., & Reber, A.S. (1980). Very long term memory for tacit knowledge. *Cognition, 8*, 175–186.

Allis, L.V., van den Herik, H.J., & Huntjens, H.J. (1996). Go-Moku solved by new search techniques. *Computational Intelligence, 12*, 7–23.

Allport, D.A. (1980). Attention and performance. In G. Claxton (Ed.), *New directions in cognitive psychology* (pp. 26–64). London: Routledge & Kegan Paul.

Allport, D.A., Styles, E.A., & Hsieh, S. (1994). Shifting intentional set: Exploring the dynamic control of tasks. In C. Umiltà & M. Moscovitch (Eds.), *Attention and performance XV: Conscious and unconscious information processing* (pp. 421–452). Cambridge, Mass.: MIT Press.

Altmann, G.T.M. (2001). The language machine: psycholinguistics in review. *British Journal of Psychology, 92*, 129–170.

Anastasi, A. (1965). *Individual differences*. New York: Wiley.

Anderson, C.A., & Bushman, B.J. (1997). External validity of "trivial" experiments: The case of laboratory aggression. *Journal of General Psychology, 1*, 19–41.

Anderson, J.R. (1976). *Language, memory and thought*. Hillsdale, NJ: Erlbaum.

Anderson, J.R. (1978). Arguments concerning representations for mental imagery. *Psychological Review, 85*, 249–277.

Anderson, J.R. (1983). *The architecture of cognition*. Cambridge, Mass.: Harvard University Press.

Anderson, J.R. (1984). Spreading activation. In J.R. Anderson & S.M. Kosslyn (Eds.), *Tutorials in learning and memory* (pp. 61–90). San Francisco: Freeman.

Anderson, J.R., Bothell, D., & Douglass, S. (2004). Eye movements do not reflect retrieval processes. *Psychological Science, 15*, 225–231.

Anderson, J.R., & Bower, G.H. (1973). *Human associative memory*. Washington: Hemisphere Press.

Anderson, J.R., & Reder, L.M. (1999). The fan effect: New results and new theories. *Journal of Experimental Psychology: General, 128*, 186–197.

Anderson, R.C., & Pichert, J.W. (1978). Recall of previously unrecallable information following a shift in perspective. *Journal of Verbal Learning and Verbal Behavior, 17*, 1–12.

Andrews, P.W., Gangestad, S.W., & Matthews, D. (2002). Adaptationism—how to carry out an exaptationist program. *Behavioral and Brain Sciences, 25*, 489–553.

Anstis, S.M. (1974). A chart demonstrating variations in acuity with retinal position. *Vision Research, 14*, 589–592.

Anzai, Y., & Simon, H.A. (1979). The theory of learning by doing. *Psychological Review, 86*, 124–140.

Armstrong, S.L., Gleitman, L.R., & Gleitman, H. (1983). What some concepts might not be. *Cognition, 13*, 263–308.

Arrington, C.M., & Logan, G.D. (2004). The cost of a voluntary task switch. *Psychological Science, 15*, 610–615.

Asch, S.E. (1946). Forming impressions of personality. *Journal of Abnormal and Social Psychology, 41*, 258–290.

Asch, S.E. (1955). On the use of metaphor in the description of persons. In H. Werner (Ed.), *On expressive language* (pp. 29–38). Worcester, Mass.: Clark University Press.

Asch, S.E. (1958). The metaphor: A psychological inquiry. In R. Tagiuri & L. Petrillo (Eds.), *Person perception and interpersonal behavior* (pp. 86–94). Stanford, Calif.: Stanford University Press.

Asch, S.E. (1969). A reformulation of the problem of associations. *American Psychologist, 24*, 92–102.

Asch, S.E., & Ebenholtz, S.M. (1962). The principle of associative symmetry. *Proceedings of the American Philosophical Society, 106*, 135–163.

Asch, S.E., & Nerlove, H. (1960). The development of double function terms in children. In H. Wapner & B. Kaplan (Eds.), *Perspectives in psychological theory* (pp. 41–60). New York: International Universities Press.

Asch, S.E., & Zukier, H. (1984). Thinking about persons. *Journal of Personality and Social Psychology, 6*, 1230–1240.

Ashby, F.G., & Casale, M.B. (2003). A model of dopamine modulated cortical activation. *Neural Networks, 16*, 973–984.

Ashby, F.G., Isen, A.M., & Turken, A.U. (1999). A neuropsychological theory of positive affect and its influence on cognition. *Psychological Review, 106*, 529–550.

Atkinson, R.C., & Shiffrin, R.M. (1968). Human memory: A proposed system and its control processes. In K.W. Spence & J.T. Spence (Eds.), *The psychology of learning and motivation*. (Vol. 2, pp. 89–105). New York: Academic Press.

Atkinson, R.C., & Shiffrin, R.M. (1971). The control of short-term memory. *Scientific American, 225*, 82–90.

Atran, S. (1999). Folk biology. In R. Wison & F. Keil (Eds.), *The MIT encyclopedia of the cognitive sciences* (pp. 316–317). Cambridge, Mass.: MIT Press.

Atran, S. (2005). Adaptationism for human cognition: Strong, spurious or weak? *Mind and Language, 20*, 39–67.

Atran, S., Medin, D., & Ross, N. (2004). Evolution and evolution of knowledge: A tale of two biologies. *Journal of the Royal Anthropological Institute, 10,* 395–420.

Attance, C.M., & O'Neill, D.K. (2001). Episodic future thinking. *Trends in Cognitive Sciences, 5,* 533–539.

Azzopardi, P., & Cowey, A. (1993). Preferential representation of the fovea in the primary visual cortex. *Nature, 361,* 719–721.

Baars, B.J. (1986). *The cognitive revolution in psychology.* New York: Guilford Press.

Baars, B.J. (1992). *Experimental slips and human error: Exploring the architecture of volition.* New York: Plenum Press.

Baars, B.J. (2002). The conscious access hypothesis: Origins and recent evidence. *Trends in Cognitive Sciences, 6,* 47–52.

Bach, P., & Tipper, S. P. (2006). Embodying the motor skills of famous athletes. *Quarterly Journal of Experimental Psychology, 59,* 2033-2039.

Baddeley, A.D. (1978). The trouble with levels: A re-examination of Craik and Lockhart's framework for memory research. *Psychological Review, 85,* 139–152.

Baddeley, A.D. (1986). *Working memory.* Oxford: Oxford University Press.

Baddeley, A.D. (1987a). Amnesia. In R.L. Gregory (Ed.), *The Oxford companion to the mind* (pp. 20–22). Oxford: Oxford University Press.

Baddeley, A.D. (1987b). Memory and context. In R.L. Gregory (Ed.), *The Oxford companion to the mind* (pp. 463–464). Oxford: Oxford University Press.

Baddeley, A.D. (1989). The psychology of remembering and forgetting. In T. Butler (Ed.), *Memory: History, culture and mind* (pp. 36–60). Oxford: Blackwell.

Baddeley, A.D. (2000a). Short-term and working memory. In E. Tulving & F.I.M. Craik (Eds.), *The Oxford handbook of memory* (pp. 77–92). New York: Oxford University Press.

Baddeley, A.D. (2000b). The episodic buffer: A new component of working memory? *Trends in Cognitive Sciences, 11,* 417–423.

Baddeley, A.D. (2001). The concept of episodic memory. *Philosophical Transactions of the Royal Society (Series B), 356,* 1345–1350.

Baddeley, A.D. (2002a). Fractionating the central executive. In D.T. Stuss and R.T. Knight (Eds.), *Principles of frontal lobe function* (pp. 246–260). New York: Oxford University Press.

Baddeley, A.D. (2002b). Is working memory still working? *European Psychologist, 7,* 85–97.

Baddeley, A.D. (2003a). Working memory and language: An overview. *Journal of Communication Disorders, 36,* 189–203.

Baddeley, A.D. (2003b). Working memory: Looking back and looking forward. *Nature Reviews Neuroscience, 4,* 829–839.

Baddeley, A.D., & Andrade, J. (2000). Working memory and the vividness of imagery. *Journal of Experimental Psychology: General, 129,* 126–145.

Baddeley, A.D., & Hitch, G.J. (1974). Working memory. In G. Bower (Ed.), *Recent advances in learning and motivation* (Vol. 8, pp. 47–89). New York: Academic Press.

Bahrick, H.P. (1984). Semantic memory in permastore: Fifty years of memory for Spanish learned in school. *Journal of Experimental Psychology: General, 113,* 1–31.

Bahrick, H.P. (2000). Long-term maintenance of knowledge. In E. Tulving & F.I.M. Craik (Eds.). *The Oxford handbook of memory* (pp. 347–362). New York: Oxford University Press.

Bahrick, H.P., & Hall, L.K. (1991). Lifetime maintenance of high school mathematics content. *Journal of Experimental Psychology: General, 120,* 20–33.

Bahrick, H.P., & Hall, L.K. (2005). The importance of retrieval failures to long-term retention: A metacognitive explanation of the spacing effect. *Journal of Memory and Language, 52,* 566–577.

Bahrick, H.P., Hall, L.K., & Berger, S.A. (1996). Accuracy and distortion in memory for high school grades. *Psychological Science, 5,* 265–271.

Bailey, M.E.S., & Johnson, K.J. (1997). Synaesthesia: Is genetic analysis feasible? In S. Baron-Cohen & J.E. Harrison (Eds.), *Synaesthesia: Classic and contemporary readings* (pp. 182–207). Oxford: Blackwell.

Baker, M.C. (2003). Linguistic differences and language design. *Trends in Cognitive Sciences, 7,* 349–353.

Baldwin, J.M. (1897). *Mental development of the child and the race* (2nd ed.). New York: Macmillan.

Ballard, P.B. (1913). Oblivescence and reminiscence. *British Journal of Psychology Monograph Supplements, 1,* 1–82.

Bamberger, J. (1982). Growing up prodigies: The mid-life crisis. In D.H. Feldman (Ed.), *Developmental approaches to giftedness* (pp. 61–77). San Francisco: Jossey-Bass.

Bamberger, J. (1986). Cognitive issues in the development of musically gifted children. In R.J. Sternberg & J. Davidson (Eds.), *Conceptions of giftedness* (pp. 388–413). New York: Cambridge University Press.

Banaji, M.R., & Crowder, R.G. (1989). The bankruptcy of everyday memory. *American Psychologist, 44,* 1185–1193.

Bar, M. (2004). Visual objects in context. *Nature Reviews Neuroscience, 5,* 617–629.

Barber, P. (1988). *Applied cognitive psychology.* New York: Methuen.

Barnard, P.J., Scott, S., Taylor, J., May, J., & Knightley, W. (2004). Paying attention to meaning. *Psychological Science, 15,* 179–186.

Barrett, L.F., Tugade, M.M., & Engle, R.W. (2004). Individual differences in working memory capacity and dual-process theories of mind. *Psychological Review, 130,* 553–573.

Barron, F. (1963). The disposition toward originality. In C.W. Taylor & F. Barron (Eds.), *Scientific creativity: Its recognition and development* (pp. 139–152). New York: Wiley.

Barron, S. (2005, July 24). R we D8ting? *New York Times.* Accessed July 24, 2005.

Barsalou, L.W. (1983). Ad hoc categories. *Memory & Cognition, 11,* 211–227.

Barsalou, L.W. (1987). The instability of graded structure: Implications for the nature of concepts. In U. Neisser (Ed.), *Concepts and conceptual development* (pp. 101–140). Cambridge: Cambridge University Press.

Barsalou, L.W. (1999). Perceptual symbol systems. *Behavioral and Brain Sciences, 22,* 577–660.

Barsalou, L.W. (2003). Abstraction in perceptual symbol systems. *Philosophical*

Transactions of the Royal Society of London (Series B), 358, 1177–1187.

Barsalou, L.W., Simmons, W.K., Barbey, A.K., & Wilson, C.D. (2003). Grounding conceptual knowledge in modality-specific systems. *Trends in Cognitive Sciences, 7,* 84–91.

Barsalou, L.W., Solomon, K.O., & Wu, L.L. (1999). Perceptual simulation in conceptual tasks. In M.K. Hiraga, C. Sinha, & S. Wilcox (Eds.), *Cultural, typological, and psychological perspectives in cognitive linguistics: The proceedings of the 4th conference of the International Cognitive Linguistics Association: Vol. 3* (pp. 209–228). Amsterdam: John Benjamins.

Bartlett, F.C. (1932). *Remembering.* Cambridge: Cambridge University Press.

Bartlett, F.C. (1958). *Thinking: An experimental and social study.* New York: Basic Books.

Baumeister, R.F. (1984). Choking under pressure: Self-consciousness and paradoxical effects of incentives on skillful performance. *Journal of Personality and Social Psychology, 46,* 610–620.

Baumeister, R.F., Bratslavsky, E., Finkenhauer, C., & Vohs, K.D. (2001). Bad is stronger than good. *Review of General Psychology, 5,* 323–370.

Baumeister, R. F., Bratslavsky, E., Muraven, M., & Tice, D. M. (1998). Ego depletion: Is the active self a limited resource? *Journal of Personality and Social Psychology, 74,* 1252-1265.

Baumeister, R.F., & Tierney, J. (2011). *Willpower.* Penguin Press: New York.

Bavalier, D., Corina, D., Jezzard, P., Padmanabhan, S., Clark, V.P., Karni, A., Prinster, A., Braun, A., Lalwani, A., Rauschecker, J.P., Turner, R., & Neville, H. (1997). Sentence reading: A functional MRI study at 4 Tesla. *Journal of Cognitive Neuroscience. 9,* 664–686.

Beck, J. (Ed.). (1982). *Organization and representation in perception.* Hillsdale, NJ: Erlbaum.

Begg, I. (1982). Imagery, organization and discriminative processes. *Canadian Journal of Psychology, 36,* 273–290.

Begg, I. (1987). Some. *Canadian Journal of Psychology, 41,* 62–73.

Begg, I., & Denny, J.P. (1969). Empirical reconciliation of atmosphere and conversion interpretations of syllogistic reasoning errors. *Journal of Experimental Psychology, 81,* 351–354.

Begg, I., & Harris, G. (1982). On the interpretation of syllogisms. *Journal of Verbal Learning and Verbal Behavior, 21,* 595–620.

Beilock, S. L., & Holt, L. E. (2007). Embodied preference judgments: Can likeability be driven by the motor system? *Psychological Science, 18,* 51-57.

Benjafield, J. (1969a). Evidence that "thinking aloud" constitutes an externalization of inner speech. *Psychonomic Science, 15,* 83–84.

Benjafield, J. (1969b). Logical and empirical thinking in a problem-solving task. *Psychonomic Science, 14,* 285–286.

Benjafield, J. (1983). Some psychological hypotheses concerning the evolution of constructs. *British Journal of Psychology, 74,* 47–59.

Benjafield, J. (1987). An historical, social analysis of imagery and concreteness. *British Journal of Social Psychology, 26,* 155–164.

Benjafield, J., & Adams-Webber, J. (1976). The Golden Section hypothesis. *British Journal of Psychology, 67,* 11–15.

Benjafield, J., & Giesbrecht, L. (1973). Context effects and the recall of comparative sentences. *Memory & Cognition, 1,* 133–136.

Benjafield, J., & Green, T.R.G. (1978). Golden Section relations in interpersonal judgement. *British Journal of Psychology, 69,* 25–35.

Benjafield, J., & Segalowitz, S. (1993). Left and right in Leonardo's drawings of faces. *Empirical Studies of the Arts, 11,* 25–32.

Benjamin, A.S., Bjork, R.A., & Schwartz, B.L. (1998). The mismeasure of memory: When retrieval fluency is misleading as a metamnemonic index. *Journal of Experimental Psychology: General, 127,* 55–68.

Benson, D.F., & Greenberg, J.P. (1969). Visual form agnosia: A defect in visual discrimination. *Archives of Neurology, 20,* 82–89.

Bergman, E.T., & Roediger, H.L. (1997). Can Bartlett's repeated reproduction experiments be replicated? *Memory & Cognition, 27,* 937–947.

Berk, L.E. (1994, November). Why children talk to themselves. *Scientific American, 271,* 78–83.

Berlin, B., Breedlove, D.E., & Raven, P.H. (1973). General principles of classification and nomenclature in folk biology. *American Anthropologist, 89,* 914–920.

Berlin, B., & Kay, P. (1969). *Basic color terms: Their universality and evolution.* Berkeley: University of California Press.

Berlyne, D.E. (1965). *Structure and direction in thinking.* New York: Wiley.

Berlyne, D.E. (1971). *Aesthetics and psychobiology.* New York: Appleton-Century-Crofts.

Bernstein, L. (1976). *The unanswered question.* Cambridge, Mass.: Harvard University Press.

Berntsen, D., & Rubin, D.C. (2002). Emotionally charged autobiographical memories across the life span: The recall of happy, sad, traumatic, and involuntary memories. *Psychology and Aging, 17,* 636–652.

Berntsen, D., & Rubin, D.C. (2004). Cultural life scripts structure recall from autobiographical memory. *Memory & Cognition, 32,* 427–442.

Berry, D.C., & Dienes, Z. (1991). The relationship between implicit memory and implicit learning. *British Journal of Psychology, 82,* 359–373.

Best, J.B. (2001). Conditional reasoning processes in a logical deduction game. *Thinking and Reasoning, 7,* 235–254

Betsch, T., Haberstroh, S., Molter, B., & Glöckner, A. (2004). Oops, I did it again—relapse errors in routinized decision-making. *Organizational Behavior and Human Decision Processes, 93,* 62–74.

Bialystok, E., Craik, F.I.M., & Freedman, M. (2007). Bilingualism as a protection against the onset of symptoms of dementia. *Neuropsychologia, 45,* 459-464.

Bianchi, M. (2002). Novelty, preferences, and fashion: When goods are unsettling. *Journal of Economic Behavior & Organization, 47,* 1–18.

Biederman, I. (1987). Recognition-by-components: A theory of human image understanding. *Psychological Review, 94*(2), 115–147.

Biederman, I., Ju, G., & Clapper, J. (1985). The perception of partial objects. Unpublished manuscript, State University of New York at Buffalo.

Bielock, S.L., Carr, T.H., MacMahon, C., & Starkes, J.L. (2002). When paying attention becomes counterproductive: Impact of divided versus skill-focused attention on novice and experienced performance of sensorimotor skills. *Journal of Experimental Psychology: Applied, 8*, 6–16

Bigelow, P. (1986). The indeterminability of time in "Sein und Zeit." *Philosophy and Phenomenological Research, 46*, 357–379.

Binet, A., & Simon, T. (1965). New methods for the diagnosis of the intellectual level of subnormals. In A. Anastasi (Ed.), *Individual differences* (pp. 35–41). New York: Wiley. (Original work published 1905b).

Binet, A., & Simon, T. (1965). The development of intelligence in the child. In A. Anastasi (Ed.), *Individual differences* (pp. 41–44). New York: Wiley. (Original work published 1908).

Binet, A., & Simon, T. (1965). Upon the necessity of establishing a scientific diagnosis of inferior states of intelligence. In A. Anastasi (Ed.), *Individual differences* (pp. 30–34). New York: Wiley. (Original work published 1905a).

Binet, A., & Simon, T. (1915). *A method of measuring the development of the intelligence of young children* (C.H. Town, Trans.). Chicago: Chicago Medical Books. (Original work published 1911).

Binkofski, F., Amunts, K., Stephan, K.M., Posse, S., Schormann, T., Freund, H.J., Zilles, K., & Seitz, R.J. (2000). Broca's region subserves imagery of motion: A combined cytoarchitectonic and fMRI study. *Human Brain Mapping, 11*, 273–285.

Birnbaum, M.H., & Mellers, B.A. (1979). Stimulus recognition may mediate exposure effects. *Journal of Personality and Social Psychology, 37*, 391–394.

Birnboim, S. (2003). The automatic and controlled information-processing dissociation: Is it still relevant? *Neuropsychology Review, 13*, 19–31.

Bjork, R.A., & Richardson-Klavehn, A. (1989). On the puzzling relationship between environmental context and memory. In C. Izawa (Ed.), *Current issues in cognitive processes* (pp. 313–344). Hillsdale, NJ: Erlbaum.

Black, M. (1962). Linguistic relativity: The views of Benjamin Lee Whorf. In M. Black (Ed.), *Models and metaphors* (pp. 244–257). Ithaca, NY: Cornell University Press.

Blair, C., Gamson, D., Thorne, S., & Baker, D. (2005). Rising mean IQ: Cognitive demand of mathematics education for young children, population exposure to formal schooling, and the neurobiology of the prefrontal cortex. *Intelligence, 33*, 96–106.

Blaney, P.H. (1986). Affect and memory: A review. *Psychological Bulletin, 99*, 229–246.

Bloom, A. (1981). *The linguistic shaping of thought.* Hillsdale, NJ: Erlbaum.

Bloom, P., & Keil, F.C. (2001). Thinking through language. *Mind & Language, 16*, 351–367.

Blumenthal, A.L. (1970). *Language and psychology.* New York: Wiley.

Blumenthal, A.L. (1977). *The process of cognition.* Englewood Cliffs, NJ: Prentice-Hall.

Bodner, G.E., & Masson, M.E.J. (2003). Beyond spreading activation: An influence of relatedness proportion on masked semantic priming. *Psychonomic Bulletin & Review, 10*, 645–652.

Bohannon, J.N. (1988). Flashbulb memories for the space shuttle disaster: A tale of two theories. *Cognition, 29*, 179–196.

Borges, B., Goldstein, D.G., Ortmann, A., & Gigerenzer, G. (1999). Can ignorance beat the stock market? In G. Gigerenzer, P.M. Todd, & the ABC Research Group (Eds.), *Simple heuristics that make us smart* (pp. 59–72). New York: Oxford University Press.

Borges, J. (1966). *Other inquisitions.* New York: Washington Square Press.

Bornstein, R.F. (1989). Exposure and affect: Overview and meta-analysis of research, 1968–1987. *Psychological Bulletin, 106*, 265–289.

Bornstein, R.F., & D'Agostino, P.R. (1992). Stimulus recognition and the mere exposure effect. *Journal of Personality and Social Psychology, 63*, 545–552.

Boucher, J., & Osgood, C.E. (1969). The Pollyanna hypothesis. *Journal of Verbal Learning and Verbal Behavior, 8*, 1–8.

Bourne, L.E. (1966). *Human conceptual behavior.* Boston: Allyn & Bacon.

Bower, G.H. (1970a). Analysis of a mnemonic device. *American Scientist, 58*, 496–510.

Bower, G.H. (1970b). Imagery as a relational organizer in paired-associate learning. *Journal of Verbal Learning and Verbal Behavior, 9*, 529–533.

Bower, G.H. (1981). Mood and memory. *American Psychologist, 26*, 129–148.

Bower, G.H., & Morrow, D.G. (1990). Mental models in narrative comprehension. *Science, 247*, 44–48.

Boylin, W., Gordon, S.K., & Nehrke, M.F. (1976). Reminiscing and ego integrity in institutionalized elderly males. *Gerontologist, 16*, 118–124.

Bradley, D.R., & Petry, H.M. (1977). Organizational determinants of subjective contour: The subjective Necker cube. *American Journal of Psychology, 90*, 253–262.

Braine, M.D.S. (1978). On the relation between the natural logic of reasoning and standard logic. *Psychological Review, 85*, 1–21.

Brandimonte, M.A., & Gerbino, W. (1993). Mental reversal and verbal recoding: When ducks become rabbits. *Memory & Cognition, 21*, 23–33.

Bransford, J.D., & Franks, J. (1971). The abstraction of linguistic ideas. *Cognitive Psychology, 2*, 331–350.

Brefczynski, J.A., & Yoe, E.A. (1999). A physiological correlate of the "spotlight" of visual attention. *Nature Neuroscience, 2*, 370–374.

Bregman, A.S. (1977). Perception and behavior as compositions of ideals. *Cognitive Psychology, 9*, 250–292.

Brentano, F.C. (1874). *Psychologie von dem Empirischen Standpunkt* [Psychology from an empirical standpoint]. Leipzig: Duncker & Humblot.

Broadbent, D.E. (1954). The role of auditory localization in attention and memory span. *Journal of Experimental Psychology, 47*, 191–196.

Broadbent, D.E. (1956). Successive responses to simultaneous stimuli. *Quarterly Journal of Experimental Psychology 8*, 145–52.

Broadbent, D.E. (1957). A mechanical model for human attention and immediate memory. *Psychological Review, 64*, 205–215.

Broadbent, D. (1958). *Perception and Communication.* London: Pergamon Press.

Broadbent, D.E. (1980). Donald E. Broadbent. In L. Gardner (Ed.), *A history of psychology in autobiography* (vol. 7, pp. 39–73). San Francisco: W.H. Freeman.

Broadbent, D.E. (1980). The minimization of models. In A.J. Chapman & D.M. Jones (Eds.), *Models of man* (pp. 113–128). Leicester: British Psychological Society.

Broadbent, D.E. (1984). The Maltese cross: A new simplistic model for memory. *Behavioral and Brain Sciences, 7*, 55–94.

Broadbent, D.E. (1990). A problem looking for solutions. *Psychological Science, 1*, 240–246.

Broadbent, D.E. (1992). Listening to one of two synchronous messages. *Journal of Experimental Psychology, General, 121*, 51–55. (Original work published 1952).

Broca, P. (1966). Paul Broca on the speech center. In R. Herrnstein & E. Boring (Eds.), *A source book in the history of psychology* (pp. 223–229). Cambridge, Mass.: Harvard University Press. (Original work published 1861).

Brockmole, J.R., Wang, R.F., & Irwin, D.E. (2002). Temporal integration between visual images and visual percepts. *Journal of Experimental Psychology: Human Perception and Performance, 28*, 315–334.

Brody, N. (2003a). Construct validation of the Sternberg Triarchic Abilities Test: Comment and reanalysis. *Intelligence, 31*, 319–324.

Brody, N. (2003b). What Sternberg should have concluded. *Intelligence, 31*, 339–342.

Brokate, B., Hildebrandt, H., Eling, P., Fichtner, H., Runge, K., & Timm, C. (2003). Frontal lobe dysfunctions in Korsakoff's syndrome and chronic alcoholism: Continuity or discontinuity? *Neuropsychology, 17*, 420–428.

Brooks, J.O., & Watkins, M.J. (1989). Recognition memory and the mere exposure effect. *Journal of Experimental Psychology: Learning, Memory, and Cognition, 15*, 968–976.

Brooks, L.R. (1968). Spatial and verbal components of the act of recall. *Canadian Journal of Psychology, 22*, 349–368.

Brown, A.S. (1991). A review of the tip-of-the-tongue experience. *Psychological Bulletin, 109*, 204–223.

Brown, A.S. (2003). A review of the déjà vu experience. *Psychological Bulletin, 129*, 394–413.

Brown, A.S., Bracken, E., Zoccoli, S., Douglas, K. (2004). Generating and remembering passwords. *Applied Cognitive Psychology, 18*, 641–651.

Brown, J. (1958). Some tests of the decay theory of immediate memory. *Quarterly Journal of Experimental Psychology, 10*, 12–21.

Brown, R. (1968). *Words and things*. New York: Free Press.

Brown, R. (1973). *A first language*. Cambridge, Mass.: Harvard University Press.

Brown, R., & Hanlon, C. (1970). Derivational complexity and the order of acquisition in child speech. In J.R. Hayes (Ed.), *Cognition and the development of language* (pp. 11–53). New York: Wiley.

Brown, R., & Kulik, J. (1977). Flashbulb memories. *Cognition, 5*, 73–99.

Brown, R., & Lenneberg, E. (1956). A study in language and cognition. *Journal of Abnormal and Social Psychology, 49*, 454–462.

Brown, R., & McNeill, D. (1966). The "tip of the tongue phenomenon." *Journal of Verbal Learning and Verbal Behavior, 5*, 325–337.

Brown, S.C., & Craik, F.I.M. (2000). Encoding and retrieval of information. In E. Tulving & F.I.M. Craik (Eds.), *The Oxford handbook of memory* (pp. 93–107). New York: Oxford University Press.

Bruce, D. (1985). The how and why of ecological memory. *Journal of Experimental Psychology: General, 114*, 78–90.

Bruce, D. (1986). Lashley's shift from bacteriology to neuropsychology, 1910–1917, and the influence of Jennings, Watson, and Franz. *Journal of the History of the Behavioral Sciences, 22*, 27–43.

Bruce, D., & Bahrick, H.P. (1992). Perceptions of past research. *American Psychologist, 47*, 319–328.

Bruner, J.S. (1983). *Child's talk*. New York: Norton.

Bruner, J.S. (1985). Vygotsky: A historical and conceptual perspective. In J. Wertsch (Ed.), *Culture, communication and cognition* (pp. 21–34). Cambridge: Cambridge University Press.

Bruner, J.S., Goodnow, J.J., & Austin, G.A. (1956). *A study of thinking*. New York: Wiley.

Brunswik, E. (1956). *Perception and the representative design of experiments*. Berkeley: University of California Press.

Bruyer, R., Laterre, C., Seron, X., Feyereisen, P., Strypstein, E., Pierrard, E., & Rectem, D. (1983). A case of prosopagnosia with some preserved covert remembrance of familiar faces. *Brain and Cognition, 2*, 257–284.

Bryant, D.J., Tversky, B., & Franklin, N. (1992). Internal and external spatial frameworks for representing described scenes. *Journal of Memory and Language, 31*, 74–98.

Bryson, B. (2003). *A short history of nearly everything*. New York: Broadway Books.

Burke, D.M., MacKay, D.G., Worthley, J.S., & Wade, E. (1991). On the tip of the tongue: What causes word finding failures in young and older adults? *Journal of Memory and Language, 30*, 542–579.

Burns, B.D. (2004). Heuristics as beliefs and behaviors: The adaptiveness of the "hot hand." *Cognitive Psychology, 48*, 295–331.

Burns, B.D., & Weith, M. (2004). The collider principle in causal reasoning: Why the Monty Hall dilemma is so hard. *Journal of Experimental Psychology: General, 133*, 414–449.

Cabeza, R., & Nyberg, L. (2003). Special issue on functional neuroimaging of memory. *Neuropsychologia, 41*, 241–244.

Cacioppo, J.T., Berntson, G.G., Lorig, T.S., Norris, C.J., Rickett, E., & Nusbaum, H. (2003). Just because you're imaging the brain doesn't mean you can stop using your head: A primer and set of first principles. *Journal of Personality and Social Psychology, 85*, 650–661.

Calvo-Merino, B., Glaser, D. E., Grezes, J., Passingham, R. E., & Haggard, P. (2005). Action observation and acquired motor skills: An fMRI study with expert dancers. *Cerebral Cortex, 15*, 1243-1249.

Calvo-Merino, B., Grezes, J., Glaser, D. E., Passingham, R. E., & Haggard, P. (2006). Seeing or doing? Influence of visual or motor familiarity in action observation. *Current Biology, 16*, 1905-1910.

Campbell, D.T. (1960). Blind variation and selective retention in creative thought as in other knowledge processes. *Psychological Bulletin, 67,* 380–400.

Campbell, M., Hoane, A.J., & Hsu, F. (2002). Deep Blue. *Artificial Intelligence, 134,* 57–83.

Caplan, D., Alpert, N., Waters, G., & Olivieri, A. (2000). Activation in Broca's area by syntactic processing under conditions of concurrent articulation. *Human Brain Mapping, 9,* 65–71.

Card, S.K., English, W.K., Burr, B.J. (1978). Evaluation of mouse, rate controlled isometric joystick, step-keys, and text keys for selection on a CRT. *Ergonomics, 21,* 601–613.

Carpenter, P.A., Just, M.A., & Shell, P. (1990). What one intelligence test measures: A theoretical account of the processing in the Raven Progressive Matrices Test. *Psychological Review, 97,* 404–431.

Carroll, J.B. (1953). *The study of language.* Cambridge, Mass.: Harvard University Press.

Carroll, J.M. (1997). Human-computer interaction: Psychology as a science of design. *International Journal of Human-Computer Studies, 46,* 501–522.

Carroll, J.M., Bever, T.G., & Pollack, C.R. (1981). The non-uniqueness of linguistic intuitions. *Language, 57,* 368–383.

Carroll, J.M., Kellogg, W.A., & Rosson, M.B. (1991). The task-artifact cycle. In J.M. Carroll (Ed.), *Designing interaction: Psychology at the human-computer interface* (pp. 74–102). New York: Cambridge University Press.

Carter, J.R., & Irons, M.D. (1991). Are economists different, and if so, why? *Journal of Economic Perspectives, 5,* 171–177.

Casselden, P.A., & Hampson, S.E. (1990). Forming impressions from incongruent traits. *Journal of Personality and Social Psychology, 59,* 353–362.

Cassirer, E. (1953–1959). *The philosophy of symbolic forms* (3 vols.). New Haven: Yale University Press.

Castles, A., & Coltheart, M. (1993). Varieties of developmental dyslexia. *Cognition, 47,* 149–180.

Cattell, J. McK. (1903). Statistics of American psychologists. *American Journal of Psychology, 14,* 310–328.

Cattell, R.B. (1963). Theory of fluid and crystallized intelligence: A critical experiment. *Journal of Educational Psychology, 54,* 1–22.

Cazden, C.B. (1976). Play with language and metalinguistic awareness. In J.S. Bruner, A. Jolly, & K. Sylva (Eds.), *Play: Its role in development and evolution* (pp. 603–608). London: Penguin.

Ceraso, J., & Provitera, A. (1971). Sources of error in syllogistic reasoning. *Cognitive Psychology, 2,* 400–410.

Chalmers, P.A. (2003). The role of cognitive theory in human computer interface. *Computers in Human Behavior, 19,* 593–607.

Chambers, D., & Reisberg, D. (1985). Can mental images be ambiguous? *Journal of Experimental Psychology: Human Perception and Performance, 11,* 317–328.

Chambers, D., & Reisberg, D. (1992). What an image depicts depends on what an image means. *Cognitive Psychology, 24,* 145–174.

Chang, T.M. (1986). Semantic memory: Facts and models. *Psychological Bulletin, 99,* 199–220.

Chapman, G.B., & Johnson, E.J. (2002). Incorporating the irrelevant: Anchors in judgments of belief and value. In T. Gilovich, D. Griffin, & D. Kahneman (Eds.), *Heuristics and biases: The psychology of intuitive judgment* (pp. 120–138). Cambridge: Cambridge University Press.

Chapman, L.J., & Chapman, J.P. (1959). Atmosphere effect re-examined. *Journal of Experimental Psychology, 55,* 220–226.

Chapman, L.J., & Chapman, J.P. (1969). Illusory correlation as an obstacle to the use of valid psychodiagnostic signs. *Journal of Abnormal Psychology, 74,* 271–280.

Chase, W.G., & Simon, H.A. (1973). Perception in chess. *Cognitive Psychology, 4,* 55–81.

Chaytor, N., & Schmitter-Edgecomb, M. (2003). The ecological validity of neuropsychological tests: A review of the literature on everyday cognitive skills. *Neuropsychological Review, 13,* 181–197.

Cheesman, J., & Merikle, P.M. (1986). Distinguishing conscious from unconscious perceptual processing. *Canadian Journal of Psychology, 40,* 343–367.

Chen, J.-Q. (2004). Theory of multiple intelligences: Is it a scientific theory? *Teacher's College Record, 106,* 17–23.

Cherniak, C. (1984). Prototypicality and deductive reasoning. *Journal of Verbal Learning and Verbal Behavior, 23,* 625–642.

Cherry, E.C. (1953). Some experiments on the recognition of speech with one and with two ears. *Journal of the Acoustical Society of America, 25,* 975–979.

Chomsky, N. (1957). *Syntactic structures.* The Hague: Mouton.

Chomsky, N. (1959). Review of Skinner's verbal behavior. *Language, 35,* 26–58.

Chomsky, N. (1965). *Aspects of the theory of syntax.* The Hague: Mouton.

Chomsky, N. (1966). *Cartesian linguistics.* New York: Harper & Row.

Chomsky, N. (1967). The formal nature of language. In E. Lenneberg, *Biological foundations of language* (pp. 397–442). New York: Wiley.

Chomsky, N. (1968). *Language and mind.* New York: Harcourt, Brace & World.

Chomsky, N. (1972). *Language and mind* (Enlarged ed.). New York: Harcourt Brace Jovanovich.

Chomsky, N. (1980a). *Rules and representations.* New York: Columbia University Press.

Chomsky, N. (1980b). Rules and representations. *Behavioral and Brain Sciences, 3,* 1–61.

Chomsky, N. (1981). *Lectures on government and binding.* Dordrecht, the Netherlands: Fortis.

Chomsky, N. (1995). Language and nature. *Mind, 104,* 1–61.

Chomsky, N. (2005). Three factors in language design. *Linguistic Inquiry, 36,* 1–22.

Chouinard, M.M., & Clark, E.V. (2003). Adult reformulations of child errors as negative evidence. *Journal of Child Language, 30,* 637–669.

Christian, J., Bickley, W., Tarka, M., & Clayton, K. (1978). Measures of free recall of 900 English nouns. *Memory & Cognition, 6,* 379–390.

Christoff, K., Gordon, A.M., Smallwood, J., Smith, R., & Schooler, J.W. (2009). Experience sampling during fMRI reveals default network and executive system contributions to mind wandering. *Proceedings of the National Academy of Sciences, 106* (21), 8719–8724.

Chronicle, E.P., Ormerod, T.C., & MacGregor, J.N. (2004). What makes an insight problem? The roles of heuristics, goal conception, and solution recoding in knowledge-lean problems. *Journal of Experimental Psychology: Learning, Memory, and Cognition, 30,* 14–27.

Chu, S., & Downs, J.J. (2000). Long live Proust: The odour-cued autobiographical memory bump. *Cognition, 75,* B41–B50.

Chwilla, D.J., & Kolk, H.H.J. (2002). Three-step priming in lexical decision. *Memory & Cognition, 30,* 217–225.

Claparède, E. (1951). Recognition and "me-ness." In D. Rapaport (Ed.), *Organization and pathology of thought* (pp. 58–75). New York: Columbia University Press. (Original work published 1911).

Clark, E.V. (2004). How language acquisition builds on cognitive development. *Trends in Cognitive Sciences, 8,* 472–478.

Clark, H.H. (1969). Linguistic processes in deductive reasoning. *Psychological Review, 76,* 387–404.

Clark, H.H. & Card, S.K. (1969). The role of semantics in remembering comparative sentences. *Journal of Experimental Psychology, 82,* 545–553.

Clark, H.H., & Clark, E. (1977). *The psychology of language.* New York: Harcourt Brace Jovanovich.

Clark, H.H., & Fox Tree, J.E. (2002). Using *uh* and *um* in spontaneous speaking. *Cognition, 84,* 73–111.

Clark, H.H., & Gerrig, R. (1984). On the pretense theory of irony. *Journal of Experimental Psychology: General, 113,* 121–126.

Clark, H.H., & Haviland, S.E. (1977). Comprehension and the given-new contract. In R.O. Freedle (Ed.), *Discourse production and comprehension* (pp. 1–40). Norwood, NJ: Ablex.

Clark, J.M., & Paivio, A. (1989). Observational and theoretical terms in psychology: A cognitive perspective on scientific language. *American Psychologist, 44,* 500–512.

Clayton, N.S., & Dickinson, A. (1998). Episodic-like memory during cache recovery by scrub jays. *Nature, 395,* 272–278.

Cleeremans, A., Destrebecqz, A., & Boyer, M. (1998). Implicit learning: News from the front. *Trends in Cognitive Sciences, 2,* 406–416.

Clifford, B.R. (2004). Celebrating levels of processing. *Applied Cognitive Psychology, 18,* 486–489.

Cofer, C. (1973). Constructive processes in memory. *American Scientist, 61,* 537–543.

Cole, W.G., & Loftus, E.F. (1979). Incorporating new information into memory. *American Journal of Psychology, 92,* 413–425.

Collins, A.M., & Loftus, E.F. (1975). A spreading-activation theory of semantic processing. *Psychological Review, 82,* 407–428.

Collins, A.M., & Quillian, M.R. (1972). Experiments on semantic memory and language comprehension. In L.W. Gregg (Ed.), *Cognition in learning and memory* (pp. 117–137). New York: Wiley.

Colman, A.M. (2003). Cooperation, psychological game theory, and limitations of rationality in social interaction. *Behavioral and Brain Sciences, 26,* 139–198.

Coltheart, M., Rastle, K., Perry, C., Ziegler, J., & Langdon, R. (2001). DRC: A dual route cascade model of visual word recognition and reading aloud. *Psychological Review, 108,* 204–256.

Colvin, M.K., Dunbar, K., & Grafman, J. (2000). The effects of frontal lobe lesions on goal achievement in the water jug task. *Journal of Cognitive Neuroscience, 13,* 1129–1147.

Conway, A.R.A., Kane, M.J., & Engle, R.W. (2003). Working memory capacity and its relation to general intelligence. *Trends in Cognitive Sciences, 7,* 547–552.

Conway, M.A., & Pleydell-Pearce, C.W. (2000). The construction of autobiographical memories in the self-memory system. *Psychological Review, 107,* 261–288.

Corballis, M.C. (1997). Mental rotation and the right hemisphere. *Brain and Language, 57,* 100–121.

Corballis, M.C. (2003). From mouth to hand: Gesture, speech and the evolution of right handedness. *Behavioral and Brain Sciences, 26,* 199–260.

Corballis, M.C. (2004a). The origin of modernity: Was autonomous speech the critical factor? *Psychological Review, 111,* 543–552.

Corballis, M.C. (2004b). FOXP2 and the mirror system. *Trends in Cognitive Sciences, 8,* 95–96.

Coren, S., & Girgus, J.S. (1980). Principles of perceptual organization and spatial distortion: The Gestalt illusions. *Journal of Experimental Psychology: Human Perception and Performance, 6,* 404–412.

Cosmides, L. (1989). The logic of social exchange: Has natural selection shaped how humans reason? Studies with the Wason selection task. *Cognition, 31,* 187–276.

Cosmides, L., & Tooby, J. (1994). Origins of domain specificity: The evolution of functional organization. In L.A. Hirschfeld & S.A. Gelman (Eds.), *Mapping the mind: Domain specificity in cognition and culture* (pp. 85–116). New York: Cambridge University Press.

Cosmides, L., & Tooby, J. (2002). Unraveling the enigma of human intelligence: Evolutionary psychology and the multimodular mind. In R.J. Sternberg & J.C. Kaufman (Eds.), *The evolution of intelligence* (pp. 145–198). Mahwah, NJ: Erlbaum.

Cowan, N. (1988). Evolving conceptions of memory storage, selective attention, and their mutual constraints within the human information-processing system. *Psychological Review, 104,* 163–191.

Craik, F.I.M. (1980). *Cognitive views of human memory* (Cassette Recording). Washington: American Psychological Association.

Craik, F.I.M. (2002). Levels of processing: Past, present . . . and future? *Memory, 10,* 305–318.

Craik, F.I.M., & Grady, C.L. (2002). Aging, memory, and frontal lobe functioning. In D.T. Stuss and R.T. Knight (Eds.), *Principles of frontal lobe function* (pp. 528–540). New York: Oxford University Press.

Craik, F.I.M., & Lockhart, R.S. (1972). Levels of processing: A framework for memory research. *Journal of Verbal Learning and Verbal Behavior, 11,* 671–684.

Crawford, L.E., & Cacioppo, J.T. (2002). Learning where to look for danger: Integrating affective and spatial information. *Psychological Science, 13,* 449–453.

Cree, G.S., & McRae, K. (2003). Analyzing factors underlying the structure and computation of the meaning of *Chipmunk, Cherry, Chisel, Cheese,* and *Cello* (and many other such concrete nouns). *Journal of Experimental Psychology: General, 132,* 163–201.

Crovitz, H.F. (1970). *Galton's walk.* New York: Harper & Row.

Crovitz, H.F., & Schiffman, H. (1974). Frequency of episodic memories as a function of their age. *Bulletin of the Psychonomic Society, 4,* 517–518.

Crovitz, H.F., Schiffman, H., & Apter, A. (1991). Galton's number. *Bulletin of the Psychonomic Society, 29,* 331–332.

Csikszentmihalyi, M. (1990). *Flow: The psychology of optimal experience.* New York: Harper & Row.

Csikszentmihalyi, M. (2002). Jacob Warren Getzels (1912–2001). *American Psychologist, 57,* 290–291.

Csikszentmihalyi, M., & Beattie, O.V. (1979). Life themes: A theoretical and empirical exploration of their origins and effects. *Journal of Humanistic Psychology, 19,* 46–63.

Csikszentmihalyi, M., & Getzels, J. (1973). The personality of young artists: An empirical and theoretical exploration. *British Journal of Psychology, 64,* 91–104.

Cuban, L. (2004). Assessing the 20-year impact of multiple intelligences on schooling. *Teacher's College Record, 106,* 140–146.

Cui, X., Jeter, C.B., Yang, D., Montague, P.R.,& Eagleman, D.M. (2007). Vividness of mental imagery: Individual variability can be measured objectively. *Vision Research, 47,* 474–478.

Cupchik, G.C. (1988). The legacy of Daniel E. Berlyne. *Empirical Studies of the Arts, 6,* 171–186.

Curran, T. (2001). Implicit learning revealed by the method of opposition. *Trends in Cognitive Sciences, 5,* 503–504.

Curtis, C.E., & D'Esposito, M. (2003). Persistent activity in the prefrontal cortex during working memory. *Trends in Cognitive Sciences, 7,* 415–423.

Cytowic, R.E. (2002). *Synaesthesia: A union of the senses* (2nd ed.). Cambridge, Mass.: MIT Press.

Daley, T.C., Whaley, S.E., Sigman, M.D., Espinosa, M.P., & Neumann, C. (2003). IQ on the rise: The Flynn effect in rural Kenyan children. *Psychological Science, 14,* 215–219.

Damasio, A.R., & Benton, A.L. (1979). Impairment of hand movements under visual guidance. *Neurology, 29,* 170.

D'Andrade, R. (1987). A folk model of the mind. In D. Holland & N. Quinn (Eds.), *Cultural models in language and thought* (pp. 112–148). Cambridge: Cambridge University Press.

Darwin, C. (1859). *On the origins of species by means of natural selection.* London: Murray.

Davidoff, J. (2001). Language and perceptual categorization. *Trends in Cognitive Sciences, 5,* 382–387.

Davidoff, J., Davies, I., & Roberson, D. (1999). Colour categories in a stone-age tribe. *Nature, 398,* 203–204.

Dawes, R.M. (1988). *Rational choice in an uncertain world.* San Diego: Harcourt Brace Jovanovich.

Dawes, R.M. (1993). Prediction of the future versus understanding of the past: A basic asymmetry. *American Journal of Psychology, 106,* 1–24.

Dawes, R.M. (1994). *House of cards: Psychology and psychotherapy built on myth.* New York: Free Press.

Dawes, R.M. (1999). A message from psychologists to economists: Mere predictability doesn't matter like it should (without a good story appended to it). *Journal of Economic Behavior & Organization, 39,* 29–40.

Dawkins, R. (1976). *The selfish gene.* Oxford: Oxford University Press.

Dawkins, R. (1988). *The blind watchmaker.* London: Penguin.

Dawson, M.R.W. (2005). *Connectionism: A hands-on approach.* Malden, Mass.: Blackwell.

Debner, J.A., & Jacoby, L.L. (1994). Unconscious perception: Attention, awareness, and control. *Journal of Experimental Psychology: Learning, Memory, and Cognition, 20*(2), 304–317.

DeDreu, C.K.W., & Boles, T.L. (1998). Share and share alike or winner take all? The influence of social value orientation upon the choice and recall of negotiation heuristics. *Organization Behavior and Human Decision Processes, 76,* 253–276.

Deese, J. (1965). *The structure of associations in language and thought.* Baltimore: Johns Hopkins University Press.

Deese, J. (1970). *Psycholinguistics.* Boston: Allyn & Bacon.

Deese, J. (1984). *Thought into speech: The psychology of a language.* New York: Prentice-Hall.

Deese, J., & Hamilton, H.W. (1974). Marking and propositional effects in associations to compounds. *American Journal of Psychology, 87,* 1–15.

Defeyter, M.A., & German, T.P. (2003). Acquiring an understanding of design: Evidence from children's insight problem-solving. *Cognition, 89,* 133–155.

de Groot, A.D. (1965). *Thought and choice in chess.* The Hague: Mouton.

Dehaene, S. (2003). The neural basis of the Weber-Fechner law: A logarithmic mental number line. *Trends in Cognitive Science, 7,* 145–147.

De Lisi, R., & Wolford, J.L. (2002). Improving children's mental rotation accuracy with computer game playing. *Journal of Genetic Psychology, 163*: 272–282.

Denis, M., & Kosslyn, S.M. (1999). Scanning visual mental images: A window on the mind. *Current Psychology of Cognition, 18,* 409–465.

Dennett, D. (1991). *Consciousness explained.* Boston: Little, Brown.

Dennett, D. (1995). *Darwin's dangerous idea.* New York: Simon & Schuster.

Dennett, D. (2003). The Baldwin effect: A crane, not a skyhook. In B.H. Weber & D.J. Depew, *Evolution and learning: The Baldwin effect reconsidered* (pp. 69–80). Cambridge, Mass.: MIT Press.

Depew, D.J. (2003). Baldwin and his many effects. In B.H. Weber & D.J. Depew, *Evolution and learning: The Baldwin effect reconsidered* (pp. 3–31). Cambridge, Mass.: MIT Press.

de Saussure, F. (1916). *Cours de linguistique generale* [Course in general linguistics]. Paris: Bally & Sechehaye.

DeSoto, C.B., London, M., & Handel, S. (1965). Social reasoning and spatial paralogic. *Journal of Personality and Social Psychology, 2,* 513–521.

Di Carlo, A., Baldereschi, M., Amaducci, L., Lepore, V., Bracco, L., Maggi, S., Bonaiuto, S., Perissinotto, E., Scarlato, G., Farchi, G., & Inzitari, D. (2002). Incidence of dementia, Alzheimer's disease, and vascular dementia in Italy. The ILSA Study. *Journal of the American Geriatric Society, 50,* 41–48.

Dickens, W.T., & Flynn, J.R. (2001). Heritability estimates versus large environmental effects: The IQ paradox resolved. *Psychological Bulletin, 108,* 346–369.

Dietrich, E. (1999). Algorithm. In R.A. Wilson, & F.C. Keil, (Eds.), *The MIT encyclopedia of the cognitive sciences* (pp. 11–12). Cambridge, Mass.: MIT Press.

DiLiilo, V., Kawahara, J.-I., Zuvic, S.M., & Visser, T.A.W. (2001). The preattentive emperor has no clothes: A dynamic redressing. *Journal of Experimental Psychology: General, 130,* 479–492.

DiPellegrino, G., Fadiga, L., Fogassi, L., Gallese, V., Rizzolatti, G. (1992). Understanding motor events: A neurophysiological study. *Experimental Brain Research, 91,* 176-189.

DiSessa, A. (1983). Phenomenology and the evolution of intuition. In D. Gentner & A.L. Stevens, (Eds.), *Mental models* (pp. 15–33). Hillsdale, NJ: Erlbaum.

Dixon, M.J., Smilek, D., Cudahy, C., & Merikle, P.M. (2000). Five plus two equals yellow. *Nature, 406, 365.*

Dixon, N.F. (1971). *Subliminal perception: The nature of a controversy.* London: McGraw-Hill.

Dixon, R.M.W. (1982). *Where have all the adjectives gone?* Berlin: Walter de Gruyter.

Dominowski, R.L. (1981). Comment on "An examination of the alleged role of 'fixation' in the solution of several 'insight' problems by Weisberg and Alba." *Journal of Experimental Psychology: General, 110,* 199–203.

Dowling, W.J., & Harwood, D.L. (1986). *Music cognition.* New York: Academic Press.

Downing, P.E., Bray, D., Rogers, J., & Childs, C. (2004). Bodies capture attention when nothing is expected. *Cognition, 93,* B27–B38.

Downs, R.M., & Stea, D. (1977). *Maps in minds: Some reflections on cognitive mapping.* New York: Harper & Row.

Dreisbach, G., & Goschke, T. (2004). How positive affect modulates cognitive control: Reduced perseveration at the cost of increased distractibility. *Journal of Experimental Psychology: Learning, Memory, and Cognition, 30,* 343–353

Dudai, Y. (2004). The neurobiology of consolidations, or, how stable is the engram? *Annual Review of Psychology, 55,* 51–86.

Dulany, D., Carlson, R., & Dewey, G. (1984). A case of syntactical learning and judgment: How conscious and how abstract? *Journal of Experimental Psychology: General, 113,* 541–555.

Dulany, D., Carlson, R., & Dewey, G. (1985). On consciousness in syntactic learning and judgment: A reply to Reber, Allen and Regan. *Journal of Experimental Psychology: General, 114,* 25–32.

Dunbar, K. (2000). How scientists think in the real world: Implications for science education. *Journal of Applied Developmental Psychology, 21,* 49–58.

Dunbar, K. (2001). What scientific thinking reveals about the nature of cognition. In K. Crowley & C.D. Schunn (Eds.), *Designing for science: Implications from everyday, classroom, and professional settings* (pp. 115–140). Mahwah, NJ: Erlbaum.

Dunbar, K., & Blanchette, I. (2001). The *in vivo/in vitro* approach to cognition: The case of analogy. *Trends in Cognitive Sciences, 5,* 334–339.

Duncker, K. (1945). On problem-solving. *Psychological Monographs, 58* (5, Whole No. 270).

Dupré, J. (1987). *The latest on the best: Essays on evolution and optimality.* Cambridge, Mass.: MIT Press.

Durgin, F.H. (1999). The (illusory) perception of visual detail: Texture and faces. *Perception, 28* (Suppl.), 43.

Eacott, M.J., & Crawley, R.A. (1998). The offset of childhood amnesia: Memory for events that occurred before age 3. *Journal of Experimental Psychology: General, 127,* 22–33.

Eagle, M., Wolitzky, D.L., & Klein, G.S. (1966). Imagery: The effect of a concealed figure in a stimulus. *Science, 151,* 837–839.

Ebbinghaus, H. (1964). *Memory: A contribution to experimental psychology.* New York: Dover. (Original work published 1885).

Eco, U. (1989). *Foucault's pendulum.* New York: Knopf.

Edgerton, S. (1975). *The Renaissance rediscovery of linear perspective.* New York: Basic Books.

Edmonds, E.A., & Green, T.R.G. (Eds.). (1984). Ergonomics of the user interface (Special Issue). *Behaviour and Information Technology, 3*(2).

Edwards, D., & Potter, J. (1992). The Chancellor's memory: Rhetoric and truth in discursive remembering. *Applied Cognitive Psychology, 6,* 187–215.

Egan, J.P., Carterette, E.C., & Thwing, E.J. (1954). Some factors affecting multichannel listening. *Journal of the Acoustical Society of America, 26,* 774–782.

Eich, E. (1984). Memory for unattended events: Remembering with and without awareness. *Memory & Cognition, 12,* 105–111.

Eich, E. (1995). Searching for mood dependent memory. *Psychological Science, 6,* 67–75.

Eich, E., & Forgas, J.P. (2003). Mood, cognition, and memory. In A.F. Healy & R.W. Proctor (Eds.), *Handbook of psychology: Vol 4. Experimental psychology* (pp. 61–83). Hoboken, NJ: Wiley.

Eich, E., & Macaulay, D. (2000). Are real moods required to reveal mood-congruent and mood-dependent memory? *Psychological Science, 11,* 244–248.

Eich, E., Macaulay, D., & Ryan, L. (1994). Mood-dependent memory for events of the personal past. *Journal of Experimental Psychology: General, 123,* 201–215.

Eich, E., & Metcalfe, J. (1989). Mood-dependent memory for internal versus external events. *Journal of Experimental Psychology: Learning, Memory, and Cognition, 15,* 443–455.

Einstein, G.O., & McDaniel, M.A. (1987). Distinctiveness and the mnemonic benefits of bizarre imagery. In M.A. McDaniel & M. Pressley (Eds.), *Imagery and related mnemonic processes: Theories, individual differences and applications* (pp. 78–102). New York: Springer-Verlag.

Einstein, G.O., McDaniel, M.A., & Lackey, S. (1989). Bizarre imagery, interference, and distinctiveness. *Journal of Experimental Psychology: Learning, Memory, and Cognition, 15,* 137–146.

Einstein, G.O., McDaniel, M. A., Smith, R.E., & Shaw, P. (1998). Habitual prospective memory and aging: Remembering intentions and forgetting actions. *Psychological Science, 9,* 284–288.

Einstein, G.O., McDaniel, M.A., Williford, C.L., Pagan, J.L., & Dismukes, R.K. (2003). Forgetting of intentions in demanding situations is rapid. *Journal of Experimental Psychology: Applied, 9,* 147–162.

Eisenstadt, M., & Kareev, Y. (1977). Perception in game playing. In P.N. Johnson-Laird & P.C. Wason (Eds.), *Thinking* (pp. 548–564). Cambridge: Cambridge University Press.

Eisenstadt, S.A., & Simon, H.A. (1997). Logic and thought. *Minds and Machines, 7,* 365–385.

Ekman, P.D. Facial expressions. (1999). In T. Dalgleish & M. Power (Eds.),

Handbook of cognition and emotion (pp. 45–60). New York: Wiley.

Ellen, P. (1982). Direction, past experience, and hints in creative problem-solving. *Journal of Experimental Psychology: General, 111*, 316–325.

Ellis, H.C. (1990). Depressive deficits in memory: Processing initiative and resource allocation. *Journal of Experimental Psychology: General, 119*, 60–62.

Ellis, M.B., & Lewis, H.D. (2001). Capgras delusion: A window on face recognition. *Trends in Cognitive Sciences, 5*(4), 149–156.

Emerson, M.J., & Miyake, A. (2003). The role of inner speech in task switching: A dual-task investigation. *Journal of Memory and Language, 48*, 148–168.

Engle, R.W., Tuholski, S.W., Laughlin, J.E., & Conway, A.R.A. (1999). Working memory, short-term memory, and general fluid intelligence: A latent variable approach. *Journal of Experimental Psychology: General, 128*, 309–331.

Enns, J.T. (2004). Object substitution and its relation to other forms of visual masking. *Vision Research Special Issue: Visual Attention, 44*(12), 1321–1331.

Enns, J.T. (2004). *The thinking eye, the seeing brain: Explorations in visual cognition.* New York: Norton.

Erdelyi, M.H. (1970). Recovery of unavailable perceptual input. *Cognitive Psychology, 1*, 99–113.

Erdelyi, M.H. (1985). *Psychoanalysis: Freud's cognitive psychology.* New York: Freeman.

Erdelyi, M.H. (2004). Subliminal perception and its cognates: Theory, indeterminacy, and time. *Consciousness and Cognition, 13*, 73–91.

Erdelyi, M.H., & Becker, J. (1974). Hypermnesia for pictures: Incremental memory for pictures but not for words in multiple recall trials. *Cognitive Psychology, 6*, 159–171.

Erdelyi, M.H., & Kleinbard, J. (1978). Has Ebbinghaus decayed with time? The growth of recall (hypermnesia) over days. *Journal of Experimental Psychology: Human Learning and Memory, 4*, 275–289.

Erdmann, E., & Stover, D. (2000). *Beyond a world divided: Human values in the brain-mind science of Roger Sperry.*

San Jose, Calif.: Authors Choice Press. (Originally published 1991).

Erickson, T.D., & Mattson, M.E. (1981). From words to meaning: A semantic illusion. *Journal of Verbal Learning and Verbal Behavior, 20*, 540–551.

Ericsson, K.A. (2003). Exceptional memorizers: Made, not born. *Trends in Cognitive Sciences, 7*, 233–235.

Ericsson, K.A., & Charness, N. (1994). Expert performance: Its structure and acquisition. *American Psychologist, 49*, 725–747.

Ericsson, K.A., & Simon, H.A. (1980). Verbal reports as data. *Psychological Review, 87*, 215–251.

Ericsson, K.A, & Simon, H.A. (1993). *Protocol analysis.* Cambridge, Mass.: MIT Press.

Eriksen, C.W., Azuma, H., & Hicks, R. (1959). Verbal discrimination of pleasant and unpleasant stimulus prior to specific identification. *Journal of Abnormal and Social Psychology, 59*, 114–119.

Erikson, E.H. (1959). Identity and the life cycle. *Psychological Issues, 1*, 50–100.

Erikson, E.H., Erikson, J., & Kivnick, H.Q. (1986). *Vital involvement in old age.* New York: Norton.

Evans, G.W. (1980). Environmental cognition. *Psychological Bulletin, 88*, 259–287.

Evans, J. St B.T. (1980). Current issues in the psychology of reasoning. *British Journal of Psychology, 71*, 227–239.

Evans, J. St B.T. (1982). *The psychology of deductive reasoning.* London: Routledge & Kegan Paul.

Evans, J. St B.T. (2002). Logic and human reasoning: An assessment of the deduction paradigm. *Psychological Bulletin, 128*, 978–996.

Evans, J. St B.T. (2003). In two minds: Dual process accounts of reasoning. *Trends in Cognitive Sciences, 7*, 454–459.

Evans, J. St B.T., & Johnson-Laird, P.N. (2003). Editorial obituary: Peter Wason (1924–2003). *Thinking and Reasoning, 9*, 177–184.

Evans, J. St B.T., Handley, S.J., & Harper, C.N.J. (2001). Necessity, possibility and belief: A study of syllogistic reasoning. *Quarterly Journal of Experimental Psychology, 54*, 935–958.

Falk, R. (1989). Judgment of coincidences: Mine versus yours. *American Journal of Psychology, 102*, 477–493.

Farah, M.J. (1989). Mechanisms of imagery-perception interaction. *Journal of Experimental Psychology: Human Perception and Performance, 15*, 203–211.

Farah, M.J. (1990) *Visual agnosia: Disorders of object recognition and what they tell us about normal vision.* Cambridge, Mass.: MIT Press.

Farah, M.J. (1996). Is face recognition "special"? Evidence from neuropsychology. *Behavioural Brain Research, 76*, 181–189.

Farah, M.J. (2005a). Neuroethics: The practical and the philosophical. *Trends in Cognitive Sciences, 9*, 34–40.

Farah, M.J. (2005b). Reply to Jedliça: Neuroethics, reductionism and dualism. *Trends in Cognitive Sciences, 9*, 173.

Farah, M.J., & McClelland, J.L. (1991). A computational model of semantic impairment: Modality specificity and emergent category specificity. *Journal of Experimental Psychology: General, 120*, 339–357.

Farah, M.J., & Rabinowitz, C. (2003). Genetic and environmental influences on the organization of semantic memory in the brain: Is "living things" an innate category? *Cognitive Neuropsychology, 20*, 401–408.

Faulkner, X., & Culwin, F. (2005). When fingers do the talking: A study of text messaging. *Interacting with Computers, 17*, 167–185.

Fechner, G.T. (1876). *Vorschule der Aesthetik.* Leipzig: Breitkopf und Hartel.

Feeney, A., Scrafton, S., Duckworth, A., & Handley, S.J. (2004). The story of *some*: Everyday pragmatic inference by children and adults. *Canadian Journal of Experimental Psychology, 58*, 121–132

Feldman, D.H. (1986). *Nature's gambit.* New York: Basic Books.

Feldman, J. (2003). The simplicity principle in human concept learning. *Current Directions in Psychological Science, 12*, 227–232.

Fellbaum, C., & Miller, G.A. (1990). Folk psychology or semantic entailment? *Psychological Review, 97*, 565–570.

Fendrich, R., Wessinger, C.M., & Gazzaniga, M.S. (1992). Residual vision in a scotoma: Implications for blindsight. *Science, 258*, 1489–1491.

Feng, J., Spence, I., & Pratt, J. (2007). Playing an action video game reduces gender differences in spatial cognition. *Psychological Science, 18*, 850–855.

Ferber, S., Humphrey, G.K., & Vilis, T. (2003). The lateral occipital complex subserves the perceptual persistence of motion-defined groupings. *Cerebral Cortex, 13*, 716–721.

Fernandez-Duque, D., & Johnson, M.L. (2002). Cause and effect theories of attention: The role of conceptual metaphors. *Review of General Psychology, 6*, 153–165.

Fiddick, L., Cosmides, L., & Tooby, J. (2000). No interpretation without representation: The role of domain-specific representations and inferences in the Wason selection task. *Cognition, 77*, 1–79.

Fiebach, C.J., & Friederici, A.D. (2003). Processing concrete words: fMRI evidence against a specific right hemisphere involvement. *Neuropsychologia, 42*, 62–70.

Findlay, C.S., & Lumsden, C.J. (1988). Thinking creatively about creative thinking. *Journal of Social and Biological Structures, 11*, 165–175.

Findlay, J.M. & Gilchrist, I.D. (2003). *Active vision: The psychology of looking and seeing.* Oxford: Oxford University Press.

Finger, S. (1994). *Origins of neuroscience: A history of explorations into brain function.* New York: Oxford University Press.

Finger, S. (2000). *Minds behind the brain: A history of the pioneers and their discoveries.* New York: Oxford University Press.

Finke, R.A. (1996). Imagery, creativity, and emergent structure. *Consciousness and Cognition, 5*, 381–393.

Finke, R.A., Pinker, S., & Farah, M.J. (1989). Reinterpreting visual patterns in mental imagery. *Cognitive Science, 13*, 51–78.

Fitts, P.M. (1992). The information capacity of the human motor system in controlling the amplitude of movement. *Journal of Experimental Psychology: General, 121*, 262–269. (Original work published 1954).

Fivush, R., & Hayden, C.A. (Eds.). (2003). *Autobiographical memory and the construction of a narrative self.* Mahwah, NJ: Erlbaum.

Fivush, R., & Nelson, K. (2004). Culture and language in the emergence of autobiographical memories. *Psychological Science, 15*, 573–577.

Flavell, J. (1979). Metacognition and cognitive monitoring. *American Psychologist, 34*, 906–911.

Fleck, J., & Weisberg, R.W. (2004). The use of verbal protocols as data: An analysis of insight in the candle problem. *Memory & Cognition, 32*, 990–1006.

Flynn, J.R. (1984). The mean IQ of Americans: Massive gains 1932 to 1978. *Psychological Bulletin, 95*, 29–51.

Flynn, J.R. (1987). Massive IQ gains in 14 nations: What IQ tests really measure. *Psychological Bulletin, 101*, 171–191.

Flynn, J.R. (1999). Searching for justice: The discovery of IQ gains over time. *American Psychologist, 54*, 5–20.

Flynn, J.R. (2003). Movies about intelligence: The limitations of *g*. *Current Directions in Psychological Science, 12*, 95–99.

Fodor, J.A. (1983). *The modularity of mind: An essay in faculty psychology.* Cambridge, Mass.: MIT Press.

Fodor, J.A. (2000). *The mind doesn't work that way.* Cambridge, Mass.: MIT Press.

Fowler, H.W. (1965). *A dictionary of modern English usage* (2nd ed.). Oxford: Oxford University Press.

Fraisse, P., & Piaget, J. (1963). *Experimental psychology: History and method.* New York: Basic Books.

Frank, H. (1959). *Grundlagenprobleme der Informations-sthetik und erste Anwendung auf die mime pure.* Schnelle: Quickborn.

Frank, H. (1964). *Kybernetische Analysen Subjektiver Sachverhalte.* Schnelle: Quickborn.

Frank, R.H., Gilovich, T., & Regan, D.T. (1993). Does studying economics inhibit cooperation? *Journal of Economic Perspectives, 7*, 159–171.

Frank, R.H., Gilovich, T., & Regan, D.T. (1996). Do economists make bad citizens? *Journal of Economic Perspectives, 10*, 187–192.

Franklin, N., & Tversky, B. (1991). Searching imagined environments. *Journal of Experimental Psychology: General, 119*, 63–76.

Franz, S.I. (1912). New phrenology. *Science, 35*, 321–328.

Frase, L.T., & Kamman, R. (1974). Effects of search criterion upon unanticipated free recall of categorically related words. *Memory & Cognition, 2*, 181–184.

Frazer, J.G. (1959). *The golden bough* (abridged). New York: Doubleday (Ed.

T.H. Gaster, 1922). (Original work published 1911).

Frederick, S. (2005). Cognitive reflection and decision making. *Journal of Economic Perspectives, 19*, 25–42.

Freeman, W., & Watts, J.W. (1968). Prefrontal lobotomy. In W.S. Sahakian (Ed.), *History of psychology: A source book in systematic psychology* (pp. 377–379). Itaska, Ill.: Peacock. (Originally published 1950).

French, C.C., & Richards, A. (1993). Clock this! An everyday example of a schema-driven error in memory. *British Journal of Psychology, 84*, 249–253.

French, R.M. (2000). The Turing test: The first 50 years. *Trends in Cognitive Sciences, 4*, 115–122.

Frenkel, K.A. (1989). The next generation of interactive technologies. *Communications of the ACM, 32*, 872–881.

Freud, S. (1961). A note upon the mystic writing pad. In J. Strachey (Ed. & Trans.), *The standard edition of the complete psychological works of Sigmund Freud* (Vol. 19). London: Hogarth Press. (Original work published 1925).

Freud, S. (1977). *Introductory lectures on psychoanalysis* (J. Strachey, Trans.). New York: Norton. (Original work published 1916).

Fugelsang, J.A., Stein, C.B., Green, A.E., & Dunbar, K.N. (2004). Theory and data interactions of the scientific mind: Evidence from the molecular and the cognitive laboratory. *Canadian Journal of Experimental Psychology, 58*, 86–95.

Gailliot, M.T., Baumeister, R.F., DeWall, C.N., Maner, J.K., Plant, E.A., Tice, D.M., Brewer L.E., & Schmeichel, B.J. (2007). Self-control relies on glucose as a limited energy source: Willpower is more than a metaphor. *Journal of Personality and Social Psychology, 92*, 325-336.

Gallistel, C.R. (2002a). Language and spatial frames of reference in mind and brain. *Trends in Cognitive Sciences, 6*, 321–322.

Gallistel, C.R. (2002b). Conception, perception and the control of action. *Trends in Cognitive Sciences, 6*, 504.

Gallotti, K.M. (1989). Approaches to studying formal and everyday reasoning. *Psychological Bulletin, 105,* 331–351.

Gallotti, K.M., Baron, J., & Sabini, J. (1986). Individual differences in syllogistic reasoning: Deduction rules or mental models? *Journal of Experimental Psychology: General, 115,* 16–25.

Galton, F. (1879a). Psychometric experiments. *Brain, 2,* 148–160.

Galton, F. (1879b). Psychometric facts. *The Nineteenth Century,* 425–433.

Galton, F. (1886). Regression toward mediocrity in hereditary stature. *Journal of the Anthropological Institute, 15,* 246–263.

Galton, F. (1908/1973). *Inquiries into human faculty and its development.* New York: E.P. Dutton.

Gardiner, J.M. (2001). Episodic memory and autonoetic consciousness: A first-person approach. *Philosophical Transactions of the Royal Society (Series B), 356,* 1351–1361.

Gardiner, J.M., & Richardson-Klavehn, A. (2000). Remembering and knowing. In E. Tulving & F.I.M.Craik, (Eds.), *The Oxford handbook of memory* (pp. 229–244). New York: Oxford University Press.

Gardner, H. (1980). *Artful scribbles.* New York: Harper & Row.

Gardner, H. (1982). *Art, mind and brain.* New York: Basic Books.

Gardner, H. (1983). *Frames of mind: The theory of multiple intelligences.* New York: Basic Books.

Gardner, H. (1985). *The mind's new science.* New York: Basic Books.

Gardner, H. (1993a). *Multiple intelligences: The theory in practice.* New York: Basic Books.

Gardner, H. (1993b). *Creating minds.* New York: Basic Books.

Gardner, H. (1999) *The disciplined mind: What all students should understand.* New York: Simon & Schuster.

Gardner, H. (2004). Audiences for the theory of multiple intelligences. *Teacher's College Record,* 212–220.

Gardner, H., & Winner, E. (1982). First intimations of artistry. In S. Straus (Ed.), *U-shaped behavioral growth* (pp. 147–168). New York: Academic Press.

Garlick, D. (2002). Understanding the nature of the general factor of intelligence: The role of individual differences in neural plasticity as an explanatory mechanism. *Psychological Review, 109,* 116–136.

Garlick, D. (2003). Integrating brain science research with intelligence research. *Current Directions in Psychological Science, 12,* 185–192.

Garner, W.R. (1962). *Uncertainty and structure as psychological concepts.* New York: Wiley.

Gauthier, I., Curran, T., Curby, K.M., & Collins, D. (2003). Perceptual interference supports a non-modular account of face processing. *Nature Neuroscience, 6,* 428–432.

Gauthier, I., Skudlarski, P., Gore, J.C., & Anderson, A.W. (2000). Expertise for cars and birds recruits brain areas involved in face recognition. *Nature Neuroscience, 3,* 191–197.

Gazzaniga, M.S., Fendrich, R., & Wessinger, C.M. (1994). Blindsight reconsidered. *Current Directions in Psychological Science, 3,* 93–96.

Gelman, S.A. (2004). Psychological essentialism in children. *Trends in Cognitive Sciences, 8,* 404–409.

Gelman, S.A., & Welman, H.M. (1991). Insides and essences: Early understandings of the non-obvious. *Cognition, 38,* 213–244.

Gentner, D. (1983). Structure-mapping: A theoretical framework for analogy. *Cognitive Science, 7,* 155–170.

Gentner, D. (2002). Mental models. In N.J. Smelser & P.B. Bates (Eds.), *International Encyclopedia of the Social and Behavioral Sciences* (pp. 9683–9687). Amsterdam: Elsevier Science.

Gentner, D., & Gentner, D.R. (1983). Flowing waters or teeming crowds: Mental models of electricity. In D. Gentner & A.L. Stevens (Eds.), *Mental models* (pp. 99–129). Hillsdale, NJ: Erlbaum.

Gentzen, G. (1964). Investigations into logical deduction. *American Philosophical Quarterly, 1,* 288–306.

German, T.P., & Barrett, H.C. (2005). Functional fixedness in a technologically sparse culture. *Psychological Science, 16,* 1–5.

German, T.P., & Defeyter, M.A. (2000). Immunity to functional fixedness in young children. *Psychonomic Bulletin & Review, 7,* 707–712.

Getzels, J.W. (1975). Problem finding and the inventiveness of solutions. *Journal of Creative Behavior, 9,* 12–18.

Getzels, J.W., & Csikszentmihalyi, M. (1972). Concern for discovery in the creative process. In A. Rothenberg & C. Hausman (Eds.), *The creativity question* (pp. 161–165). Durham, NC: Duke University Press.

Getzels, J.W., & Csikszentmihalyi, M. (1976). *The creative vision: A longitudinal study of problem finding in art.* New York: Wiley.

Ghiselin, M.T. (1981). Categories, life and thinking. *Behavioral and Brain Sciences, 4,* 269–313.

Gibbs, R.W. (1986). On the psycholinguistics of sarcasm. *Journal of Experimental Psychology: General, 115,* 3–15.

Gibbs, R.W. (1996). Why many concepts are metaphorical. *Cognition, 61,* 309–319.

Gibbs, R.W. (2004). Metaphor is grounded in embodied experience. *Journal of Pragmatics, 36,* 1189–1210.

Gibson, E.J., & Spelke, E.S. (1983). The development of perception. In P.H. Mussen (Ed.), *Handbook of child psychology, vol. 3, Cognitive development* (pp. 1–76). New York: Wiley.

Gibson, J.J. (1941). A critical review of the concept of set in contemporary experimental psychology. *Psychological Bulletin, 38,* 781–817.

Gibson, J.J. (1950). *The perception of the visual world.* Boston: Houghton Mifflin.

Gibson, J.J. (1959). Perception as a function of stimulation. In Sigmund Koch (Ed.), *Psychology, a study of a science: Sensory, perceptual, and physiological formulations.* New York: McGraw-Hill.

Gibson, J.J. (1961). Ecological optics. *Vision Research, 1,* 253–262.

Gibson, J.J. (1966). *The senses considered as perceptual systems.* Boston: Houghton Mifflin.

Gibson, J.J. (1969). Outline of a theory of direct visual perception. Paper presented at the Conference on the Psychology of Knowing, Edmonton, Alberta.

Gibson, J.J. (1977). The theory of affordances. In R. Shaw & J. Bransford (Eds.), *Perceiving, acting and knowing* (pp. 67–82). Hillsdale, NJ: Erlbaum.

Gibson, J.J. (1979). *The ecological approach to visual perception.* Boston: Houghton Mifflin.

Gigerenzer, G., & Edwards, A. (2005). Simple tools for understanding risks: From innumeracy to insight. *British Medical Journal, 327,* 741–744.

Gigerenzer, G., & Goldstein, D.G. (1996). Reasoning the fast and frugal way: Models of bounded rationality. *Psychological Review, 103*, 650–669.

Gigerenzer, G., & Hug, K. (1992). Domain-specific reasoning: Social contracts, cheating, and perspective change. *Cognition, 43*, 127–171.

Gilden, G.L., & Wilson, S.G. (1995). Streaks in skilled performance. *Psychonomic Bulletin & Review, 2*, 260–265.

Giles, G.M., & Clark-Wilson, J. (1988). Functional skills training in severe brain injury. In I. Fussey & G.M. Giles (Eds.), *Rehabilitation of the severely brain-injured adult* (pp. 69–101). London: Croom Helm.

Gilhooly, K. (2003). Problems in problem-solving. *Trends in Cognitive Science, 7*, 477–478.

Gilligan, S.G., & Bower, G.H. (1984). Cognitive consequences of emotional arousal. In C. Izard, J. Kagan, & R. Zajonc (Eds.), *Emotions, cognition and behavior* (pp. 547–588). New York: Cambridge University Press.

Gillihan, S.J., & Farah, M.J. (2005). Is self special? A critical review of evidence from experimental psychology and cognitive neuroscience. *Psychological Bulletin, 131*, 76–97.

Gilovich, T., & Griffin, D. (2002). Introduction-heuristics and biases: Then and now. In T. Gilovich, D. Griffin, & D. Kahneman (Eds.), *Heuristics and biases: The psychology of intuitive judgment* (pp. 1–19). Cambridge: Cambridge University Press.

Gilovich, T., Mevec, V.H., & Chen, S. (1995). Commission, omission, and dissonance reduction: Coping with regret in the "Monty Hall" problem. *Personality and Social Psychology Review, 21*, 182–190.

Gilovich, T., Vallone, R., & Tversky, A. (1985). The hot hand in basketball: On the misperception of random sequences. *Cognitive Psychology, 17*, 295–314.

Gil-White, F. (2001). Are ethnic groups biological "species" to the human brain? *Current Anthropology, 42*, 515–554.

Giroux, L., & Larochelle, S. (1988). *The cognitive ergonomics of computer systems.* Laval, Que.: Canadian Automation Research Centre.

Glenberg, A. (1997). What memory is for. *Behavioral and Brain Sciences, 20*, 1–55.

Glenberg, A., Smith, S.M., & Green, C. (1977). Type I rehearsal: Maintenance and more. *Journal of Verbal Learning and Verbal Behavior, 16*, 339–352.

Glicksohn, J., Steinbach, I., & Elimalac-Malmilyan, S. (1999). Cognitive dedifferentiation in eidetics and synaesthesia: Hunting for the ghost once more. *Perception, 28*, 109–120.

Glisky, E.L., & Schacter, D.L. (1989). Extending the limits of complex learning in organic amnesia: Computer training in a vocational domain. *Neuropsychologia, 27*, 107–120.

Glosser, G., & Friedman, R.B. (1991). Lexical but not semantic priming in Alzheimer's disease. *Psychology and Aging, 6*, 522–527.

Glucksberg, S (2003). The psycholinguistics of metaphor. *Trends in Cognitive Sciences, 7*, 92–96.

Godden, D., & Baddeley, A.D. (1975). Context-dependent memory in two natural environments: On land and underwater. *British Journal of Psychology, 66*, 325–331.

Goffman, E. (1978). Response cries. *Language, 54*, 787–815.

Gold, I., & Stoljar, D. (1999). A neuron doctrine in the philosophy of neuroscience. *Behavioral and Brain Sciences, 22*, 809–869

Goldinger, S.D. (1998). Echoes of echoes? An episodic theory of lexical access. *Psychological Review, 105*, 251–279.

Goldman-Eisler, F. (1968). *Psycholinguistics: Experiments in spontaneous speech.* London: Academic Press.

Goldstein, D.G., & Gigerenzer, G. (2002). Models of ecological rationality: The recognition heuristic. *Psychological Review, 109*, 75–90.

Gonsalves, B., Reber, P.J., Gitelman, D.R., Parrish, T.B., Mesulam, M.-M., & Paller, K.A. (2004). Neural evidence that vivid imagining can lead to false remembering. *Psychological Science, 15*, 655–660.

Goodale, M.A., Milner, A.D., Jakobson, L.S., & Carey, D.P. (1991). A neurological dissociation between perceiving objects and grasping them. *Nature, 349*, 154–156.

Goodman, N. (1955). *Fact, fiction and forecast.* Cambridge, Mass.: Harvard University Press.

Goodwin, G.P., & Johnson-Laird, P.N. (2005). Reasoning about relations. *Psychological Review, 112*, 468–493.

Gordon, I.E. (1974). Left and right in Goya's portraits. *Nature, 249*, 197–198.

Gordon, P.C., & Holyoak, K.J. (1983). Implicit learning and the "mere exposure" effect. *Journal of Personality and Social Psychology, 45*, 492–500.

Gorfein, D.S., & Hoffman, R.R. (1987). *Memory and learning: The Ebbinghaus centennial conference.* Hillsdale, NJ: Erlbaum.

Gorman, M.E. (1986). How the possibility of error affects falsification on a task that models scientific problem-solving. *British Journal of Psychology, 77*, 85–96.

Gorman, M.E. (1989). Error, falsification and scientific evidence. *Quarterly Journal of Experimental Psychology, 41 A*, 385–412.

Gottfredson, L.S. (1997). Why g matters: The complexity of everyday life. *Intelligence, 24*, 79–132.

Gottfredson, L.S. (2003a). Dissecting practical intelligence theory: Its claims and evidence. *Intelligence, 31*, 343–397.

Gottfredson, L.S. (2003b). On Sternberg's 'Reply to Gottfredson'. *Intelligence, 31*, 415–424.

Gottschaldt, K. (1967). Gestalt factors and repetition. In W.D. Ellis (Ed.), *A source book of Gestalt psychology* (pp. 109–135). New York: Humanities Press. (Original work published 1926).

Gould, S.J. (1985). *The flamingo's smile.* New York: Norton.

Gould, S.J., & Lewontin, R.C. (1979). The spandrels of San Marco and the Panglossian paradigm: A critique of the adaptationist programme. *Proceedings of the Royal Society of London (Series B), 205*, 581–98.

Gould, S.J., & Vrba, E.S. (1982). Exaptation: A missing term in the science of form. *Paleobiology, 8*, 4–15.

Graf, P., & Schacter, D.L. (1985). Implicit and explicit memory for new associations in normal and amnesic subjects. *Journal of Experimental Psychology: Learning, Memory, and Cognition, 11*, 501–518.

Grainger, J., & Whitney, C. (2004). Does the human mind raed wrods as a wlohe? *Trends in Cognitive Sciences, 8*, 58–59.

Grant, E.R., & Spivey, M.J. (2003). Eye movements and problem-solving. *Psychological Science, 14*, 462–466.

Gray, R. (2004). Attending to the execution of a complex sensorimotor skill: Expertise differences, choking, and slumps. *Journal of Experimental Psychology: Applied, 10*, 42–54.

Green, C.S., & Bavelier, D. (2003). Action video game modifies visual selective attention. *Nature, 423*, 534–537.

Green, T.R.G. (1982). Pictures of programs and other processes, or how to do things with lines. *Behaviour and Information Technology, 1*, 3–36.

Green, T.R.G., & Payne, S. (1982). The wooly jumper: Typographic problems of concurrency in information display. *Visible Language, 16*, 391–403.

Green, T.R.G., & Payne, S.J. (1984). Organization and learnability in computer languages. *International Journal of Man-Machine Studies, 21*, 7–18.

Green, T.R.G., Payne, S.J., & van der Veer, G.C. (Eds.). (1983). *The psychology of computer use*. London: Academic Press.

Greenberg, D.L. (2004). President Bush's false "flashbulb" memory of 9/11/01. *Applied Cognitive Psychology, 18*, 363–370.

Greenberg, J.H. (1966). *Language universals*. The Hague: Mouton.

Greene, J. (1972). *Psycholinguistics: Chomsky and psychology*. Baltimore: Penguin.

Greene, R.L. (1987). Effects of maintenance rehearsal on human memory. *Psychological Bulletin, 102*, 403–413.

Greeno, J.G. (1994). Gibson's affordances. *Psychological Review, 101*, 336–342.

Greenstein, J.S., & Arnaut, L.Y. (1987). Human factors aspects of manual computer input devices. In G. Salvendy (Ed.), *Handbook of human factors* (pp. 1450–1489). New York: Wiley.

Grice, H.P. (1971). Meaning. In D. Steinberg & L. Jakobovits (Eds.), *Semantics: An inter-disciplinary reader* (pp. 53–59). Cambridge: Cambridge University Press. (Original work published 1957).

Grice, H.P. (1975). Logic and conversation. In P. Cole & J.P. Morgan (Eds.), *Syntax and semantics: Vol. 3. Speech acts* (pp. 41–58). New York: Academic Press.

Grice, H.P. (1978). Further notes on logic and conversation. In P. Cole (Ed.), *Syntax and semantics: Vol. 9. Pragmatics*. New York: Academic Press.

Griggs, R.A., & Cox, J.R. (1982). The elusive thematic materials effect in Wason's selection task. *British Journal of Psychology, 73*, 407–420.

Griggs, R.A., & Newstead, S.E. (1983). The source of intuitive errors in Wason's THOG problem. *British Journal of Psychology, 74*, 451–459.

Groen, G.J., & Parkman, J.M. (1972). A chronometric analysis of simple addition. *Psychological Review, 79*, 329–342.

Gross, L. (1983, March). Why Johnny can't draw. *Arts Education*, 74–77.

Gross, S.R., & Miller, N. (1997). The "golden section" and bias in perceptions of social consensus. *Personality and Social Psychology Bulletin, 1*, 241–271.

Grossenbacher, P.G., & Lovelace, C.T. (2001). Mechanisms of synesthesia: Cognitive and physiological constraints. *Trends in Cognitive Sciences, 5*, 36–41.

Gruber, H.E. (1981). *Darwin on man: A psychological study of scientific creativity* (2nd ed.). Chicago: University of Chicago Press. (Original work published 1974).

Gruber, H.E., & Wallace, D.B. (2001). Creative work: The case of Charles Darwin. *American Psychologist, 56*, 346–349.

Grudin, J. (1989). The case against user interface consistency. *Communications of the ACM, 32*, 1164–1173.

Guastello, S.J., Traut, M., & Korienek, G. (1989). Verbal versus pictorial representations of objects in a human-computer interface. *International Journal of Man-Machine Studies, 31*, 99–120.

Guiard, Y., & Beaudoin-Lafon, M. (2004). Fitts' law 50 years later: Applications and contributions from human-computer interaction. *International Journal of Human-Computer Studies, 61*, 747–750.

Guilford, J. (1967). *The nature of human intelligence*. New York: McGraw-Hill.

Haber, R.N. (1979). Twenty years of haunting eidetic imagery: Where's the ghost? *Behavioral and Brain Sciences, 2*, 583–629.

Haber, R.N. (1983). The impending demise of the icon: A critique of the concept of iconic storage in visual information processing. *Behavioral and Brain Sciences, 6*, 1–13.

Haines, R.F. (1991). A breakdown in simultaneous information processing.

In G. Obrecht & L.W. Stark (Eds.), *Presbyopia research* (pp. 171–175). New York: Plenum Press.

Halper, F. (1997). The illusion of *The Future*. *Perception, 26*, 1321–1322.

Halpern, S. (2002, Aug. 15). Heart of darkness. *New York Review of Books, 49*, 16–22.

Hamilton, H.W., & Deese, J. (1971). Does linguistic marking have a psychological correlate? *Journal of Verbal Learning and Verbal Behaviour, 10*, 707–714.

Hampson, S.E. (1998). When is an inconsistency not an inconsistency? Trait reconciliation in personality description and impression formation. *Journal of Personality and Social Psychology, 74*, 102–117.

Hampton, R.R., & Schwartz, B.L. (2004). Episodic memory in nonhumans: What, and where, is when? *Current Opinion in Neurobiology, 14*, 192–197.

Hanson, N.R. (1969). *Patterns of discovery*. Cambridge: Cambridge University Press.

Harle, S.K., & Vickers, J.N. (2001). Training quiet eye improves accuracy in the basketball free throw. *Sport Psychologist, 15*, 289–305.

Harris, J. (1984). Methods of improving memory. In B.A. Wilson & N. Moffat (Eds.), *Clinical management of memory problems* (pp. 46–62). Rockville, Md: Aspen Publications.

Harris, R.J. (1973). Answering questions containing marked and unmarked adjectives and adverbs. *Journal of Experimental Psychology, 97*, 399–401.

Harrison, J. (2001). *Synaesthesia: The strangest thing*. Oxford: Oxford University Press.

Harshman, R.A., & Paivio, A. (1987). "Paradoxical" sex differences in self-reported imagery. *Canadian Journal of Psychology, 41*, 287–302.

Hatfield, G. (1992). Empirical, rational, and transcendental psychology: Psychology as science and as philosophy. In P. Guyer (Ed.), *The Cambridge companion to Kant* (pp. 200–227). Cambridge: Cambridge University Press.

Hatfield, G. (1998). Kant and empirical psychology in the 18th century. *Psychological Science, 9*, 423–428.

Hatfield, G., & Epstein, W. (1987). The status of the minimum principle in the theoretical analysis of visual perception. *Psychological Bulletin, 97*, 155–186.

Hauser, M.D., Chomsky, N., & Fitch, W.T. (2002). The faculty of language: What is it, who has it, and how did it evolve? *Science, 298*, 1569–1579.

Hayman, C.A., & Tulving, E. (1989). Contingent dissociation between recognition and fragment completion: The method of triangulation. *Journal of Experimental Psychology: Learning, Memory, and Cognition, 15*, 228–240.

Hazeltine, E., Teague, D., & Ivry, R.B. (2002). Simultaneous dual-task performance reveals parallel response selection after practice. *Journal of Experimental Psychology: Human Perception and Performance, 28*, 527–545.

Heath, S.B. (1986). The functions and uses of literacy. In S. de Castell, A. Luke, & K. Egan (Eds.), *Literacy, society and schooling* (pp. 15–26). Cambridge: Cambridge University Press.

Heath, S.B. (1989). Oral and literate traditions among black Americans living in poverty. *American Psychologist, 44*, 367–373.

Hebb, D.O. (1949). *The organization of behavior.* New York: Wiley.

Heckhausen, H., & Beckmann, J. (1990). Intentional action and action slips. *Psychological Review, 97*, 36–48.

Heider, E.R. [Eleanor Rosch]. (1971a). Focal color area and the development of color names. *Developmental Psychology, 4*, 447–455.

Heider, E.R. [Eleanor Rosch]. (1971b). On the internal structure of perceptual and semantic categories. Paper presented at the Conference on Developmental Psycholinguistics, Buffalo, NY.

Heider, E.R. [Eleanor Rosch], & Olivier, D. (1972). The structure of the color space in naming and memory for two languages. *Cognitive Psychology, 3*, 337–354.

Heider, F. (1958). *The psychology of interpersonal relations.* New York: Wiley.

Heim, S., Opitz, B., Friederici, A.D. (2003). Distributed cortical networks for syntax processing: Broca's area as the common denominator. *Brain and Language, 85*, 402–408.

Heinrichs, R.W. (1984). Verbal responses to human figure paintings: A test of the uncertainty hypothesis. *Canadian Journal of Psychology, 38*, 512–518.

Hejmadi, A.H., Rozin, P., & Siegal, M. (2004). Once in contact, always in contact: Contagious essence and conceptions of purification in American and Hindu Indian children. *Developmental Psychology, 40*, 467–476.

Henderson, J.M. (1992). Object identification in context: The visual processing of natural scenes. *Canadian Journal of Psychology, 46*(3), 319–341.

Henderson, J.M. (2003). Human gaze control during real-world scene perception. *Trends in Cognitive Sciences, 7*, 498–504.

Henderson, J.M., Pollatsek, A., & Rayner, K. (1989). Covert visual attention and extrafoveal information use during object identification. *Perception & Psychophysics, 45*, 196–208.

Henle, M. (1968). Deductive reasoning. In P.C. Wason & P.N. Johnson-Laird (Eds.), *Deductive reasoning* (pp. 93–107). Baltimore: Penguin. (Original work published 1962).

Henle, M. (1987). Koffka's principles after fifty years. *Journal of the History of the Behavioral Sciences, 25*, 14–21.

Hering, E. (1961). Principles of a new theory of the color sense. In R.C. Teevan & R.C. Birney (Eds.), *Color vision* (pp. 28–31). New York: Van Nostrand. (Original work published 1878).

Herrmann, D.J. (1993). The ethnographic method and the investigation of memory. *Applied Cognitive Psychology, 7*, 184.

Herrmann, D.J., & Neisser, U. (1979). An inventory of everyday memory experiences. In M.M. Gruneberg & P.E. Morris (Eds.), *Applied problems in memory*. London: Academic Press.

Hertel, P.T., & Gerstle, M. (2003). Depressive deficits in forgetting. *Psychological Science, 14*, 573–578.

Hertel, P.T., & Hardin, T.S. (1990). Remembering without awareness in a depressed mood: Evidence of deficits in initiative. *Journal of Experimental Psychology: General, 119*, 45–59.

Hertel, P.T., & Rude, S.S. (1991). Depressive deficits in memory: Focusing attention improves subsequent recall. *Journal of Experimental Psychology: General, 120*, 301–309.

Heyes, C. (2003). Four routes of cognitive evolution. *Psychological Review, 110*, 713–727.

Hick, W.E. (1952). On the rate of gain of information. *Quarterly Journal of Experimental Psychology, 4*, 11–26.

Hilgard, E.R. (1980). The trilogy of mind: Cognition, affection and conation. *Journal of the History of the Behavioral Sciences, 16*, 107–117.

Hilgard, E.R. (1987). *Psychology in America: An historical survey.* New York: Harcourt Brace Jovanovich.

Hintzman, D.L. (1986). "Schema abstraction" in a multiple-trace memory model. *Psychological Review, 93*, 411–428.

Hintzman, D.L., Curran, T., & Oppy, B. (1992). Effects of similarity and repetition on memory: Registration without learning? *Journal of Experimental Psychology: Learning, Memory, and Cognition, 18*(4), 667–690.

Hirschfeld, L.A., & Gelman, S.A. (1994). *Mapping the mind: Domain specificity in cognition and culture.* Cambridge: Cambridge University Press.

Hirschfeld, L.A., & Gelman, S.A. (1997). What young children think about the relationship between language variation and social difference. *Cognitive Development, 12*, 213–238.

Hirst, W. (1986). The psychology of attention. In J. LeDoux and W. Hirst (Eds.), *Mind and brain: Dialogues in cognitive neuroscience* (pp. 105–141). New York: Cambridge University Press.

Hirst, W., & Kalmar, K. (1987). Characterizing attentional resources. *Journal of Experimental Psychology: General, 116*, 68–81.

Hirst, W., & Levine, E. (1985). Ecological memory reconsidered: A comment on Bruce's "The how and why of ecological memory." *Journal of Experimental Psychology: General, 114*, 269–271.

Hirst, W., Neisser, U., & Spelke, E. (1978). Divided attention. *Human Nature, 1*, 54–61.

Hirst, W., Spelke, E.S., Reaves, C.C., Caharack, G., & Neisser, U. (1980). Dividing attention without alteration or automaticity. *Journal of Experimental Psychology: General, 109*, 98–117.

Hoc, J.M. (2001). Towards ecological validity of research in cognitive ergonomics. *Theoretical Issues in Ergonomic Science, 2*, 278–288.

Hodges, J.R. (2000). Memory in the dementias. In E. Tulving & F.I.M. Craik

(Eds.), *The Oxford handbook of memory* (pp. 645–648). New York: Oxford University Press.

Hodges, J.R., Salmon, D.P., & Butters, N. (1992). Semantic memory impairment in Alzheimer's disease: Failure of access or degraded knowledge? *Neuropsychologia, 30*, 301–314.

Hoff, E. (2004). Progress, but not a full solution to the logical problem of language acquisition. *Journal of Child Language, 31*, 923–926.

Hoffman, R.R., & Deffenbacher, K.A. (1992). A brief history of applied cognitive psychology. *Applied Cognitive Psychology, 6*, 1–48.

Hofstadter, D. (1979). *Godel, Escher, Bach: An eternal golden braid.* New York: Basic Books.

Hofstadter, D. (1982). Meta-font, metamathematics, and metaphysics: Comments on Donald Knuth's "The concept of a meta-font." *Visible Language, 16*, 309–338.

Hollins, M. (1985). Styles of mental imagery in blind adults. *Neuropsychologia, 23*, 561–566.

Holloway, C. (1978). *Cognitive psychology: Units 22–23.* Milton Keynes, UK: Open University.

Holmberg, N., Holsanova, J., & Holmqvist, K. 2006. Using eye movement measures to describe readers' visual interaction with newspapers, Proceedings, EARLI SIG 2 conference, "Text and Graphics Comprehension," University of Nottingham, 30 Aug.–1 Sept.

Hoptman, M.J., & Davidson, R.J. (1994). How and why do the two cerebral hemispheres interact? *Psychological Review, 116*, 195–219.

Horowitz, L.M., Norman, S.A., & Day, R.S. (1966). Availability and associative symmetry. *Psychological Review, 73*, 1–15.

Horstmann, G. (2002). Evidence for attentional capture by a surprising color singleton in visual search. *Psychological Science, 13*, 499–505.

Howard, D.V., Fry, A., & Brune, C. (1991). Aging and memory for new associations: Direct versus indirect measures. *Journal of Experimental Psychology: Learning, Memory, and Cognition, 17*, 779–792.

Howe, M.L., & Courage, M.L. (1993). On resolving the enigma of infantile amnesia. *Psychological Bulletin, 113*, 305–326.

Huettel, S.A., Mack, P.B., & McCarthy, G. (2002). Perceiving patterns in random series: Dynamic processing of sequence in prefrontal cortex. *Nature Neuroscience, 5*, 485–490.

Hughes, G. (1988). *Words in time.* Oxford: Blackwell.

Hughes, P., & Brecht, G. (1975). *Vicious circles and infinity.* New York: Penguin.

Humphrey, G. (1963). *Thinking: An introduction to its experimental psychology.* New York: Wiley. (Original work published 1951).

Humphrey, N.K., & McManus, C. (1973). Status and the left cheek, *New Scientist, 59*, 437–439.

Hunt, E.B., & Agnoli, F. (1991). The Whorfian hypothesis: A cognitive psychology perspective. *Psychological Review, 98*, 377–389.

Hunt, E.B., & Hovland, C.I. (1960). Order of consideration of different types of concept. *Journal of Experimental Psychology, 59*, 220–225.

Hunt, R.R. (1995). The subtlety of distinctiveness: What von Restorff really did. *Psychonomic Bulletin and Review, 2*, 105–112.

Hunt, R.R., & Lamb, C.A. (2001). What causes the isolation effect? *Journal of Experimental Psychology: Learning, Memory, and Cognition, 27*, 1359–1366.

Hunter, I.M.L. (1977). An exceptional memory. *British Journal of Psychology, 68*, 155–164.

Hunter, I.M.L. (1979). Memory in everyday life. In M.M. Gruneberg & P.E. Morris (Eds.), *Applied problems in memory.* London: Academic Press.

Hurvich, L., & Jameson, D. (1957). An opponent-process theory of color vision. *Psychological Review, 64*, 384–390.

Hutchins, E. (1983). Understanding Micronesian navigation. In D. Gentner & A.L. Stevens (Eds.), *Mental models.* Hillsdale, NJ: Erlbaum.

Huttenlocher, J., & Higgins, E.T. (1971). Adjectives, comparatives and syllogisms. *Psychological Review, 78*, 487–504.

Huttenlocher, J., Vasilyeva, M., Cymerman, E., & Levine, S. (2002). Language input and child syntax. *Cognitive Psychology, 45*, 337–374.

Hyams, N.M. (1986). *Language acquisition and the theory of parameters.* Dordrecht, the Netherlands: Reidel.

Hyman, I.E., & Neisser, U. (1991). *Reconstructing mental images: Problems of method* (Emory Cognition Project Tech. Rep. No. 19). Atlanta: Emory University.

Iacoboni, M., Freedman, J., Kaplan, J., Jamieson, K.H., Freedman, T., Knapp, B., & Fitzgerald, K. (2007, Nov. 11). This is your brain on politics. *New York Times* Op-Ed.

Indian and Northern Affairs Canada (2000). *Nunavut, Canada's third territory "North of 60."* Retrieved March 21, 2005, from Indian and Northern Affairs Canada. http:// www.ainc-inac.gc.ca/ks/pdf/nunavu_e.pdf.

Innocence Project (2009). Reevaluating lineups: Why witnesses make mistakes and how to reduce the chance of a misidentification. Benjamin N. Cardozo School of Law, Yeshiva University. http://www.innocenceproject.org/docs/Eyewitness_ID_Report.pdf.

Isen, A.M. (1984). Toward understanding the role of affect in cognition. In R.S. Wyer & T.K. Srull (Eds.), *Handbook of social cognition* (pp. 174–236). Hillsdale, NJ: Erlbaum.

Isen, A.M., Daubman, K.A., & Nowicki, G.P. (1987). Positive affect facilitates creative problem-solving. *Journal of Personality and Social Psychology, 52*, 1122–1131.

Ivry, R., & Knight, R.T. (2002). Making order from chaos: The misguided frontal lobe. *Nature Neuroscience, 5*, 394–396.

Jack, A.I., & Shallice, T. (2001). Introspective physicalism as an approach to the science of consciousness. *Cognition, 79*, 161–196.

Jack, A.I., & Roepstorff, A. (2002). Introspection and cognitive brain mapping: From stimulus-response to script report. *Trends in Cognitive Sciences, 6*, 333–339.

Jackson, M.A., & Simpson, K.H. (2004). Pain after amputation. *Continuing Education in Anaesthesia, Critical Care & Pain, 4*, 20–23.

Jacoby, L.L. (1999). Ironic effects of repetition: Measuring age-related differences in memory. *Journal of Experimental Psychology: Learning, Memory, and Cognition, 25*, 3–22.

Jacoby, L.L., & Dallas, M. (1981). On the relationship between autobiographical memory and perceptual learning.

Journal of Experimental Psychology: General, 110, 306–340.

Jacoby, L.L., & Hollingshead, A. (1990). Reading student essays may be hazardous to your health. *Canadian Journal of Psychology, 44,* 345–358.

Jacoby, L.L., & Kelley, C.M. (1994). A process-dissociation framework for investigating unconscious influences: Freudian slips, projective tests, subliminal perception, and signal detection theory. *Current Directions in Psychological Science, 1,* 174–179.

Jacoby, L.L., & Witherspoon, D. (1982). Remembering without awareness. *Canadian Journal of Psychology, 36,* 300–324.

James, T., Soroka, L., & Benjafield, J. (2001). Are economists rational, or just different? *Social Behavior and Personality, 29,* 359–364.

James, W. (1983). *Principles of psychology.* Cambridge, Mass.: Harvard University Press. (Original work published 1890).

Jaynes, J. (1977). *The origins of consciousness in the breakdown of the bicameral mind.* Boston: Houghton Mifflin.

Jaynes, J. (1979). Paleolithic cave paintings as eidetic images. *Behavioral and Brain Sciences, 2,* 605–607.

Jedliça, P. (2005). Neuroethics: Reductionism and dualism. *Trends in Cognitive Sciences, 9,* 172.

Jenkins, J.G., & Dallenbach, K.M. 1924. Obliviscence during sleep and waking. *American Journal of Psychology, 35,* 605–612.

Jenkins, J.J. (1974). Remember that old theory of memory? Well, forget it! *American Psychologist, 29,* 785–795.

Jensen, A.R. (1972). *Genetics and education.* New York: Harper & Row.

Jersild, A. (1927). Mental set and shift. *Archives of Psychology, 14* (Whole No. 89), 5–82.

Johnson, C.J., Paivio, A., & Clark, J.M. (1996). Cognitive components of picture naming. *Psychological Bulletin, 120,* 113–139.

Johnson, M., & Lakoff, G. (2002). Why cognitive linguistics requires embodied realism. *Cognitive Linguistics, 13,* 245–263.

Johnson, M.K. (1985). The origin of memories. In P.C. Kendall (Ed.), *Advances in cognitive-behavioral research and therapy* (Vol. 4, pp. 1–27). New York: Academic Press.

Johnson, M.K. (1988). Reality monitoring: An experimental phenomenological approach. *Journal of Experimental Psychology: General, 117,* 390–394.

Johnson, M.K., Hashtroudi, S., & Lindsay, D.S. (1993). Source monitoring. *Psychological Review, 114,* 3–28.

Johnson, M.K., & Raye, C.L. (1981). Reality monitoring. *Psychological Review, 88,* 67–85.

Johnson, M.K., & Raye, C.L. (1998). False memories and confabulation. *Trends in Cognitive Sciences, 2,* 137–145.

Johnson, W., Bouchard, T.J., Krueger, R.F., McGue, M., & Gottesman, I.J. (2004). Just one *g*: Consistent results from three test batteries. *Intelligence, 32,* 95–107.

Johnson-Laird, P.N. (1972). The three-term series problem. *Cognition, 1,* 57–82.

Johnson-Laird, P.N. (1983). *Mental models.* Cambridge, Mass.: Harvard University Press.

Johnson-Laird, P.N. (1988). *The computer and the mind.* Cambridge, Mass.: Harvard University Press.

Johnson-Laird, P.N. (1997a). Rules and illusions: A critical study of Rips's *The psychology of proof. Minds and Machines, 7,* 387–407.

Johnson-Laird, P.N. (1997b). An end to the controversy: A reply to Rips. *Minds and Machines, 7,* 425–432.

Johnson-Laird, P.N. (1999). Deductive reasoning. *Annual Review of Psychology, 50,* 109–135.

Johnson-Laird, P.N. (2001). Mental models and deduction. *Trends in Cognitive Sciences, 5,* 434–442.

Johnson-Laird, P.N., & Byrne, R.M.J. (1990). Meta-logical problems: Knights, knaves, and Rips. *Cognition, 36,* 69–84.

Johnson-Laird, P.N., & Byrne, R.M.J. (1993). Precis of "deduction." *Behavioral and Brain Sciences, 16,* 323–380.

Johnson-Laird, P.N., Herrmann, D.J., & Chafin, R. (1984). Only connections: A critique of semantic networks. *Psychological Bulletin, 96,* 292–315.

Johnson-Laird, P.N., Legrenzi, P., Girotto, V., Legrenzi, M.S., & Caverni, J.P. (1999). Naïve probability: A mental model theory of extensional reasoning. *Psychological Review, 106,* 62–88.

Johnson-Laird, P.N., & Steedman, M. (1978). The psychology of syllogisms. *Cognitive Psychology, 10,* 64–99.

Johnson-Laird, P.N., & Wason, P.C. (1970). A theoretical analysis of insight into a reasoning task. *Cognitive Psychology, 1,* 134–148.

Johnston, E.B. (2001). The repeated reproduction of Bartlett's "Remembering." *History of Psychology, 4,* 341–366.

Johnston, W.A., & Dark, V.J. (1986). Selective attention. In M. Rosenzweig & L. Porter (Eds.), *Annual Review of Psychology* (pp. 43–75). Palo Alto, Calif.: Annual Reviews.

Jones, G. (2003). Testing two cognitive theories of insight. *Journal of Experimental Psychology: Learning, Memory, and Cognition, 29,* 1017–1027.

Jones, W.P., & Hoskins, J. (1987, October). Back propagation: A generalized delta learning rule. *Byte Magazine,* pp. 155–162.

Jonides, J., Badre, D., Curtis, C., Thompson-Schill, S.L., & Smith, E.E. (2002). Mechanisms of conflict resolution in prefrontal cortex. In D.T. Stuss & R.T. Knight (Eds.), *Principles of frontal lobe function* (pp. 233–245). New York: Oxford University Press.

Jorgenson, J., Miller, G.A., & Sperber, D. (1984). Test of the mention theory of irony. *Journal of Experimental Psychology: General, 113,* 112–120.

Judson, H.F. (1984). Century of the sciences. *Science 84,* 41–43.

Jung, C.G. (1950). Foreword. In *The I Ching or book of changes* (C.F. Baynes, Trans.). Princeton, NJ: Princeton University Press.

Jung, C.G. (1973). *Synchronicity: An acausal connecting principle.* Princeton, NJ: Princeton University Press.

Kahneman, D. (1973). *Attention and effort.* Englewood Cliffs, NJ: Prentice-Hall.

Kahneman, D. (2002). Maps of bounded rationality: A perspective on intuitive judgment and choice. In Tore Frängsmyr (Ed.), *Les Prix Nobel/The Nobel Prizes 2002.* Stockholm: Nobel Foundation. Retrieved 2 May 2005, from http://nobelprize.org/economics/laureates/2002/kahnemann-lecture.pdf.

Kahneman, D. (2003). A perspective on judgment and choice: Mapping bounded rationality. *American Psychologist, 58*, 697–720.

Kahneman, D., & Frederick, S. (2002). Representativeness revisited: Attribute substitution in intuitive judgement. In T. Gilovich, D. Griffin, & D. Kahneman (Eds.), *Heuristics and biases: The psychology of intuitive judgment* (pp. 49–81). Cambridge: Cambridge University Press.

Kahneman, D., & Miller, D.T. (1986). Norm theory: Comparing reality to its alternatives. *Psychological Review, 93*, 136–153.

Kahneman, D., & Treisman, A. (1984). Changing views of attention and automaticity. In R. Parasuraman & D.R. Davies (Eds.), *Varieties of attention* (pp. 29–61). Orlando, Fla: Academic Press.

Kahneman, D., & Tversky, A. (1972). Subjective probability: A judgment of representativeness. *Cognitive Psychology, 3*, 430–454.

Kahneman, D., & Tversky, A. (1979). Prospect theory: An analysis of decision under risk. *Econometrica, 47*, 263–271.

Kahneman, D., & Tversky, A. (1984). Choices, values, and frames. *American Psychologist, 39*, 341–350.

Kahneman, D., & Tversky, A. (1996). On the reality of cognitive illusions. *Psychological Review, 103*, 582–591.

Kanazawa, S. (2004). General intelligence as a domain-specific adaptation. *Psychological Review, 111*, 512–523.

Kanizsa, G. (1979). *Organization in vision: Essays on Gestalt perception.* New York: Praeger.

Kanouse, D.E., & Hanson, L.R. (1971). Negativity in evaluations. In E.E. Jones (Ed.), *Attribution: Perceiving the causes of behavior.* Morristown, NJ: General Learning Press.

Kant, I. (1929). *Critique of pure reason* (N.K. Smith, Trans.). New York: St Martin's Press. (Original work published 1781).

Kanwisher, N., McDermott, J., & Chun, M. (1997). The fusiform face area: A module in human extrastriate cortex specialized for face perception. *Journal of Neuroscience, 17*, 4302–4311.

Kaplan, C.A., & Simon, H.A. (1990). In search of insight. *Cognitive Psychology, 22*, 374–419.

Kapur, N., Glisky, E.L., & Wilson, B.A. (2002). External memory aids and computers in memory rehabilitation. In A.D. Baddeley, M.D. Kopelman, & B.A. Wilson (Eds.), *The handbook of memory disorders* (pp. 757–783). New York: Wiley.

Katz, A.N., Blasko, D.G., & Kazmerski, V.A. (2004). Saying what you don't mean: Social influences on sarcastic language processing. *Current Directions in Psychological Science, 13*, 186–189.

Katz, A.N., Paivio, A., Marschark, M., & Clark, J.M. (1988). Norms for 204 literary and 260 non-literary metaphors on 10 psychological dimensions. *Metaphor and Symbolic Activity, 3*, 191–214.

Katz, D. (1951). *Gestalt psychology: Its nature and significance.* London: Methuen.

Katz, J. (1993). Phantom limb experience in children and adults: Cognitive and affective contributions. *Canadian Journal of Behavioural Science, 25*, 335–354.

Kaufman, L., & Kaufman, J.H. (1999). Explaining the moon illusion. *Proceedings of the National Academy of Sciences, 97*, 1, 500–505.

Kaufman, L., & Rock, I. (1962). The moon illusion. Part I. *Science, 136*, 953–961.

Kay, P., & McDaniel, C.K. (1978). The linguistic significance of the meanings of basic color terms. *Language, 54*, 610–646.

Kay, P., & Regier, T. (2003). Resolving the question of color naming universals. *Proceedings of the National Academy of Sciences, 100*, 9085–9089.

Kay, R.H. (1989). A practical and theoretical approach to assessing computer attitudes: The Computer Attitude Measure (CAM). *Journal of Research on Computing Education, 21*, 456–463.

Kay. R.H. (1993). An exploration of theoretical and practical foundations for assessing attitudes towards computers: The Computer Attitude Measure (CAM). *Computers in Human Behavior, 9*, 371–386.

Kelley, C.M., & Jacoby, L.L. (2000). Recognition and familiarity; process dissociation. In E. Tulving & F.I.M. Craik (Eds.), *The Oxford handbook of memory* (pp. 215–228). New York: Oxford University Press.

Kennedy, H., Batardiere, A., Dehay, C., & Barone, P. (1997). Synaesthesia: Implications for developmental neurobiology. In S. Baron-Cohen & J.E. Harrison (Eds.), *Synaesthesia: Classic and contemporary readings* (pp. 243–256). Oxford: Blackwell.

Keren, G. (1984). On the importance of identifying the correct "problem space." *Cognition, 16*, 121–128.

Kihlstrom, J.F. (1987). The cognitive unconscious. *Science, 237*, 1335–1552.

Kihlstrom, J.F. (1995). Memory and consciousness: An appreciation of Claparède and "Recognition et Moitié." *Consciousness and Cognition, 4*, 379–386.

Kihlstrom, J.F. (2004). Availability, accessibility, and subliminal perception. *Consciousness and Cognition, 13*, 92–100.

Kinder, A., Shanks, D.R., Cock, J., & Timney, R.J. (2003). Recollection, fluency, and the explicit/implicit distinction in artificial grammar learning. *Journal of Experimental Psychology: General, 132*, 551–565.

Kingstone, A., Smilek, D., Eastwood, J.D. (2008). Cognitive ethology: A new approach for studying human cognition. *British Journal of Psychology, 99*(3), 317–345.

Kingstone, A., Smilek, D., Ristic, J., Friesen, C.K., & Eastwood, J.D. (2003). Attention researchers! It's time to take a look at the real world. *Current Directions in Psychological Science, 12*, 176–180.

Kinsbourne, M., & Wood, F. (1975). Short-term memory processes and the amnesic syndrome. In D. Deutsch & J.A. Deutsch (Eds.), *Short-term memory.* New York: Academic Press.

Kirasic, K. (1991). Spatial cognition and behavior in young and elderly adults: Implications for learning new environments. *Psychology and Aging, 6*, 10–18.

Klahr, D., & Simon, H.A. (1999). Studies of scientific discovery: Complementary approaches and convergent findings. *Psychological Bulletin, 125*, 524–543.

Klahr, D., & Simon, H.A. (2001). What have psychologists (and others) discovered about the process of scientific discovery? *Current Directions in Psychological Science, 10*, 75–79.

Klatzky, R.L., Clark, E.V., & Macken, M. (1971). Asymmetries in the acquisition of polar adjectives. *Journal of*

Experimental Child Psychology, 16, 32–46.

Klauer, K.C., Mierke, J., & Musch, J. (2003). The positivity proportion effect: A list context effect in masked affective priming. *Memory & Cognition, 31,* 953–967.

Klein, R.M., & Pontefract, A. (1994). Does oculomotor readiness mediate cognitive control of visual attention? Revisited! In C. Umiltà and M. Moscovitch (Eds.), *Attention and performance 15: Conscious and non-conscious information processing* (pp. 333–350). Cambridge, Mass.: MIT Press.

Klein, S.B., Cosmides, L., Tooby, J., & Chance, S. (2002). Decisions and the evolution of memory: Multiple systems, multiple functions. *Psychological Review, 109,* 306–329.

Klein, S.B., Loftus, J., & Kihlstrom, J.F. (1996). Self-knowledge of an amnesic patient: Toward a neuropsychology of personality and social psychology. *Journal of Experimental Psychology: General, 125,* 250–260.

Knoblich, G., Ohlsson, S., Haider, H., & Rhenius, D. (1999). Constraint relaxation and chunk decomposition in insight problem-solving. *Journal of Experimental Psychology: Learning, Memory, and Cognition, 25,* 1534–1555.

Knoblich, G., Ohlsson, S., & Raney, G.E. (2001). An eye movement study of insight problem solving. *Memory & Cognition, 29,* 1000–1009.

Koenig, C.S., & Griggs, R.A. (2001). Elementary my dear Wason: The role of problem representation in the THOG task. *Psychological Research, 65,* 289–293.

Koenig, C.S., & Griggs, R.A. (2004a). Analogical transfer in the THOG task. *Quarterly Journal of Experimental Psychology, 57A,* 557–570.

Koenig, C.S., & Griggs, R.A. (2004b). Facilitation and analogical transfer in the THOG task. *Thinking and Reasoning, 10,* 355–370.

Koffka, K. (1922). Perception: An introduction to the Gestalt-Theorie. *Psychological Bulletin, 19*(10), 531–585.

Koffka, K. (1935). *Principles of Gestalt psychology.* New York: Harcourt, Brace.

Köhler, W. (1925). *The mentality of apes.* London: Routledge & Kegan Paul.

Köhler, W. (1929). *Gestalt psychology.* New York: Liveright.

Köhler, W. (1940). *Dynamics in psychology.* New York: Liveright.

Köhler, W. (1956). *The mentality of apes.* New York: Vintage. (Original work published 1925).

Köhler, W. (1969). *The task of Gestalt psychology.* Princeton, NJ: Princeton University Press.

Komatsu, L.K. (1992). Recent views of conceptual structure. *Psychological Bulletin, 112,* 500–526.

Konečni, V.J. (1996). Daniel E. Berlyne (1924–1976): Two decades later. *Empirical Studies of the Arts, 14,* 129–142.

Korf, R. (1999). Heuristic search. In R.A. Wilson & F.C. Keil (Eds.), *The MIT encyclopedia of the cognitive sciences* (pp. 372–373). Cambridge, Mass.: MIT Press.

Koriat, A. (2000). Control processes in remembering. In E. Tulving & F.I.M. Craik (Eds.), *The Oxford handbook of memory* (pp. 333–346). New York: Oxford University Press.

Koriat, A., & Bjork, R.A. (2005). Illusions of competence in monitoring one's knowledge during study. *Journal of Experimental Psychology: Learning, Memory, and Cognition, 31,* 187–194.

Koriat, A., & Goldsmith, M. (1996). Memory metaphors and the real life/laboratory controversy: Correspondence versus storehouse conceptions of memory. *Behavioral and Brain Sciences, 19,* 167–228.

Koriat, A., Goldsmith, M., & Pansky, A. (2000). Toward a psychology of memory accuracy. *Annual Review of Psychology, 51,* 481–537.

Kornmeier, J., & Bach, M. (2004). Early neural activity in Necker-cube reversal: Evidence for low-level processing of a gestalt phenomenon, *Psychophysiology, 41,* 1–8.

Korsakoff, S.S. (1899). Étude médico-psychologique sur une forme des malades de la mémoire [Medical-psychological study of a form of diseases of memory]. *Revue Philosophique, 28,* 501–530.

Kosslyn, S.M. (1980). *Image and mind.* Cambridge, Mass.: Harvard University Press.

Kosslyn, S.M. (1983). *Ghosts in the mind's machine.* New York: Norton.

Kosslyn, S.M., Ball, T.M., & Reiser, B.J. (1978). Visual images preserve metric spatial information: Evidence from studies of image scanning. *Journal of Experimental Psychology: Human Perception and Performance, 4,* 47–60.

Kosslyn, S.M., Ganis, G., & Thompson, W.L. (2003). Mental imagery: Against the null hypothesis. *Trends in Cognitive Sciences, 7,* 109–111.

Kosslyn, S.M., Ganis, G., & Thompson, W.L. (2001). Neural foundations of imagery. *Nature Reviews Neuroscience, 2,* 635–642.

Kosslyn, S.M., Thompson, W.L., & Ganis, G. (2002). Mental imagery doesn't work like that. *Behavioral and Brain Sciences, 25,* 198–201.

Kraus, S., & Wang, X.T. (2003). The psychology of the Monty Hall problem: Discovering psychological mechanisms for solving a tenacious brain teaser. *Journal of Experimental Psychology: General, 132,* 3–22.

Krech, D. (1962). Cortical localization of function. In L. Postman (Ed.), *Psychology in the making.* New York: Wiley.

Krech, D., & Crutchfield, R.S. (1958). *Elements of psychology.* New York: Knopf.

Kreitler, H., & Kreitler, S. (1972). *The psychology of the arts.* Durham, NC: Duke University Press.

Kreuz, R.J., & Glucksberg, S. (1989). How to be sarcastic: The echoic reminder theory of verbal irony. *Journal of Experimental Psychology: General, 118,* 374–386.

Kristol, A. (1980). Color systems in southern Italy: A case of regression. *Language, 56,* 137–145.

Kuhn, D. (1989). Children and adults as intuitive scientists. *Psychological Review, 96,* 674–689.

Kuhn, D. (1991). Thinking as argument. *Harvard Educational Review, 62,* 155–178.

Kuhn, T.S. (1970). *The structure of scientific revolutions* (2nd ed.). Chicago: University of Chicago Press.

Kunda, Z., & Nisbett, R.E. (1986). The psychometrics of everyday life. *Cognitive Psychology, 18,* 195–224.

Kvavilashvili, L., & Mandler, G. (2004). Out of one's mind: A study of involuntary semantic memories. *Cognitive Psychology, 48,* 47–94.

LaBerge, D.L. (1990). Attention. *Psychological Science, 1,* 156–162.

Lachter, J., & Bever, T.G. (1988). The relationship between linguistic structure and associative theories of language learning: A constructive critique of some connectionist learning models. *Cognition, 28*, 195–247.

Lagnado, D.A., & Shanks, D.R. (2003). The influence of hierarchy on probability judgement. *Cognition, 89*, 157–178.

Lakatos, I. (1970). Falsification and the methodology of scientific research programmes. In I. Lakatos & A. Musgrave (Eds.), *Criticism and the growth of knowledge* (pp. 91–195). Cambridge: Cambridge University Press.

Lakoff, G. (1987). *Women, fire and dangerous things*. Chicago: University of Chicago Press.

Lakoff, G., & Johnson, M. (1980). *Metaphors we live by*. Chicago: University of Chicago Press.

Lakoff, G., & Johnson, M. (1999). *Philosophy in the flesh*. New York: Basic Books.

Langer, E.J. (1989). *Mindlessness/mindfulness*. Reading, Mass.: Addison-Wesley.

Langer, E.J. (2000). Mindful learning. *Current Directions in Psychological Science, 9*, 220–223.

Langer, E.J., & Piper, A.I. (1987). The prevention of mindlessness. *Journal of Personality and Social Psychology, 53*, 280–287.

Langley, P., Simon, H.A., Bradshaw, G.L., & Zytkow, J.M. (1987). *Scientific discovery: Computational explorations of the creative process*. Cambridge, Mass.: MIT Press.

Lashley, K.S. (1929). *Brain mechanisms and intelligence*. Chicago: University of Chicago Press.

Lashley, K.S. (1978). Basic neural mechanisms in behavior. In E.R. Hilgard (Ed.), *American psychology in historical perspective* (pp. 265–283). Washington: American Psychological Association. (Original work published 1930).

Lasnik, H. (2002). The minimalist program. *Trends in Cognitive Sciences, 6*, 432–437.

Laughlin, P., Lange, R., & Adamopoulos, J. (1982). Selection strategies for "Master-mind" problems. *Journal of Experimental Psychology: Learning, Memory, and Cognition, 8*, 475–483.

Lavery, J.J. (1962). Retention of simple motor skills as a function of type of

knowledge of results. *Canadian Journal of Psychology, 16*, 300–311.

Lavie, N., Hirst, A., Fockert, J.W. de, & Viding, E. (2004). Load theory of selective attention and cognitive control. *Journal of Experimental Psychology: General, 133*, 339–354.

Lavie, N., Ro, T., & Russell, C. (2003). The role of perceptual load in processing distractor faces. *Psychological Science, 14*, 510–515.

Lazarus, R.S. (1984). On the primacy of cognition. *American Psychologist, 39*, 124–129.

Lazarus, R.S., & McCleary, R. (1951). Autonomic discrimination without awareness: A study of subception. *Psychological Review, 58*, 113–122.

LeDoux, J. (2003). *Synaptic self*. New York: Penguin.

Lee, D.N. (1980). The optic flow field: The foundation of vision. *Philosophical Transactions of the Royal Society B, 290*, 169–179.

Lefebvre, V.A. (1985). The Golden Section and an algebraic model of ethical cognition. *Journal of Mathematical Psychology, 29*, 289–310.

Lefebvre, V.A., Lefebvre, V.D., & Adams-Webber, J. (1986). Modeling an experiment on construing self and others. *Journal of Mathematical Psychology, 30*, 317–330.

Lehar, S. (2003). Gestalt isomorphism and the primacy of subjective conscious experience: A gestalt bubble model. *Behavioral and Brain Sciences, 26*, 375–444.

Lehman, D.R., & Nisbett, R.E. (1990). A longitudinal study of the effects of undergraduate training on reasoning. *Developmental Psychology, 26*, 952–960.

Lehman, D.R., Lempert, R.O., & Nisbett, R.E. (1988). The effects of graduate training on reasoning. *American Psychologist, 43*, 431–442.

Lemmons, P. (1982, November). A short history of the keyboard. *Byte Magazine*, pp. 386–387.

Levine, L.J., & Pizarro, D.A. (2004). Emotion and memory research: A grumpy overview. *Social Cognition, 22*, 530–554.

Levinson, S.C. (1996). Language and space. *Annual Review of Anthropology, 25*, 353–382.

Levinson, S.C., Kita, S., Haun, D.B.M., & Rasch, B.H. (2002). Returning the

tables: Language affects spatial reasoning. *Cognition, 84*, 155–188.

Levy, D.A., Stark, C.E.L., & Squire, L.R. (2004). Intact conceptual priming in the absence of declarative memory. *Psychological Science, 15*, 680–686.

Lévy-Schoen, A. (1981). Flexible and/or rigid control of oculomotor scanning behavior. In D.F. Fisher, R.A. Monty, & J.W. Senders (Eds.), *Eye movements: Cognition and visual perception* (pp. 299–314). Hillsdale, NJ: Erlbaum.

Leyens, J.-P., & Corneille, O. (1999). Asch's social psychology: Not as social as you may think. *Personality and Social Psychology Review, 3*, 345–357.

Liebowitz, S., & Margolis, S.E. (1996). Typing errors. *Reason, 28*, 28–36.

Lightfoot, D. (1982). *The language lottery: Toward a biology of grammars*. Cambridge, Mass.: MIT Press.

Lindsay, D.S. (1993). Eyewitness suggestibility. *Current Directions in Psychological Science, 2*, 86–88.

Lindsay, D.S., & Johnson, M.K. (1989). The eyewitness suggestibility effect and memory for source. *Memory & Cognition, 17*, 349–358.

Lindsay, D.S., & Johnson, M.K. (2001). False memories and the source monitoring framework: Reply to Reyna and Lloyd (1997). *Learning and Individual Differences, 12*, 145–161.

Lindsay, D.S., Hagen, L., Read, J.D., Wade, K.A., & Garry, M. (2004). True photographs and false memories. *Psychological Science, 15*, 149–154.

Link, S. (1994). Rediscovering the past: Gustav Fechner and signal detection theory. *Psychological Science, 5*, 335–340.

Lissauer, H. (1890/1988). A case of visual agnosia with a contribution to theory (M. Jackson, Trans.). *Cognitive Neuropsychology, 5*, 153–192.

Livingston, R. (1967). Reinforcement. In G. Quarton, T. Melenchuk, & F. Schmidt (Eds.), *The neurosciences: A study program* (pp. 499–514). New York: Rockefeller University Press.

Lockhart, R.S., & Craik, F.I.M. (1990). Levels of processing: A retrospective commentary on a framework for memory research. *Canadian Journal of Psychology, 44*, 87–112.

Loehlin, J.C. (1989). Partitioning environmental and genetic contributions to behavioral development. *American Psychologist, 44*, 1285–1292.

Loehlin, J.C. (1992). *Latent variable models: An introduction to factor, path and structural analysis* (2nd ed.). Hillsdale, NJ: Erlbaum.

Loftus, E.F. (1991). The glitter of everyday memory . . . and the gold. *American psychologist, 46*, 16–18.

Loftus, E.F. (1992). When a lie becomes memory's truth: Memory distortion after exposure to misinformation. *Current Directions in Psychological Science, 1*, 121–123.

Loftus, E.F. (2003). Make-believe memories. *American Psychologist, 58*, 867–873.

Loftus, E.F. (2004). Memories of things unseen. *Current Directions in Psychological Science, 13*, 145–147.

Loftus, E.F., & Hoffman, H.G. (1989). Misinformation and memory: The creation of new memories. *Journal of Experimental Psychology: General, 118*, 100–104.

Loftus, E.F., & Loftus, G.R. (1980). On the permanence of stored information in the human brain. *American Psychologist, 35*, 409–420.

Loftus, E.F., & Palmer, J.C. (1974). Reconstruction of automobile destruction: An example of the interaction between language and memory. *Journal of Verbal Learning and Verbal Behavior, 13*, 585–589.

Loftus, E.F., & Yuille, J.C. (1984). Departures from reality in human perception and memory. In H. Weingartner & E.S. Parker (Eds.), *Memory consolidation: Psychobiology of cognition* (pp. 163–184). Mahwah, NJ: Erlbaum.

Lopes, L.L. (1982). Doing the impossible: A note on induction and the experience of randomness. *Journal of Experimental Psychology: Learning, Memory, and Cognition, 8*, 626–636.

Lorayne, H., & Lucas, J. (1976). *The memory book*. London: Allen.

Lovie, A.D., & Lovie, P. (1993). Charles Spearman, Cyril Burt, and the origins of factor analysis. *Journal of the History of the Behavioral Sciences, 29*, 308–321.

Lowenstein, G. (1994). The psychology of curiosity: A review and reinterpretation. *Psychological Bulletin, 116*, 75–98.

Lubart, T.I. (2001). Models of the creative process: Past, present and future. *Creativity Research Journal, 13*, 295–308.

Lubinski, D. (2004). Introduction to the special section on cognitive abilities: 100 years after Spearman's (1904) "'General intelligence' objectively determined and measured." *Journal of Personality and Social Psychology, 86*, 96–111.

Luce, R.D. (2003). Whatever happened to information theory in psychology? *Journal of General Psychology, 7*, 183–188.

Luchins, A.S. (1942). Mechanization in problem-solving. *Psychological Monographs, 54*, Whole No. 248.

Luchins, A.S., & Luchins, E.H. (1950). New experimental attempts at preventing mechanization in problem-solving. *Journal of General Psychology, 42*, 279–297.

Luchins, A.S., & Luchins, E.H. (1994a). The water jar experiments and einstellung effects. Part I: Early history and surveys of textbook citations. *Gestalt Theory, 16*, 101–121.

Luchins, A.S., & Luchins, E.H. (1994b). The water jar experiments and einstellung effects. Part II: Gestalt psychology and past experience. *Gestalt Theory, 16*, 205–270.

Luncageli, D., Tressoldi, P.E., Bendotti, M., Bonaomi, M., & Siegel, L.S. (2003). Effective strategies for mental and written arithmetic calculation from the third to the fifth grade. *Educational Psychology, 23*, 507–520.

Luo, J., & Niki, K. (2003). Function of hippocampus in "insight" of problem-solving. *Hippocampus, 13*, 316–323.

Luo, J., Niki, K., & Philips, S. (2004). Neural correlates of the "Aha!" reaction. *Neuroreport, 15*, 2013–2017.

Luria, A.R. (1961). *The role of speech in the regulation of normal and abnormal behavior*. New York: Liveright.

Luria, A.R. (1976). *Cognitive development: Its cultural and social foundations*. Cambridge, Mass.: Harvard University Press.

Lyddy, F. (2002). Interpreting visual images, individually. *Trends in Cognitive Sciences, 6*, 500.

Lynch, K. (1960). *The image of the city*. Cambridge, Mass.: MIT Press.

Lynn, R. (1998). In support of the nutrition theory. In U. Neisser (Ed.), *The rising curve* (pp. 207–218). Washington: American Psychological Association.

Maas, S. (1983). Why systems transparency? In T.R.G. Green, S.J. Payne, & G.C. van der Veer (Eds.), *The psychology of computer use*. London: Academic Press.

McClelland, J.L. (1979). On the time relations of mental processes: An examination of systems of processes in a cascade. *Psychological Review, 86*, 287–330.

McClelland, J.L. (1981). Retrieving general and specific knowledge from stored knowledge of specifics. Proceedings of the Third Annual Conference of the Cognitive Science Society, Berkeley, Calif.

McClelland, J.L. (2000). Connectionist models of memory. In E. Tulving & F.I.M. Craik (Eds.), *The Oxford handbook of memory* (pp. 583–596). New York: Oxford University Press.

McClelland, J.L., & Rumelhart, D.E. (1981). An interactive activation model of context effects in letter perception. Part I. An account of basic findings. *Psychological Review, 88*, 375–407.

McClelland, J.L., & Rumelhart, D.E. (1986a). A distributed model of memory. In J.L. McClelland & D.E. Rumelhart (Eds.), *Parallel distributed processing* (Vol. 2, pp. 170–215). Cambridge, Mass.: MIT Press.

McClelland, J.L., & Rumelhart, D.E. (Eds.). (1986b). *Parallel distributed processing: Explorations in the microstructure of cognition: Vol. 2. Psychological and biological models*. Cambridge, Mass.: MIT Press.

McClelland, J.L., & Rumelhart, D.E. (1988). *Explorations in parallel distributed processing: A handbook of models, programs and exercises*. Cambridge Mass.: MIT Press.

McClelland, J.L., Rumelhart, D.E., & Hinton, G.E. (1986). The appeal of PDP. In D.E. Rumelhart & J.L. McClelland (Eds.), *Parallel distributed processing* (Vol. 1, pp. 33–44). Cambridge, Mass.: MIT Press.

McCloskey, M., Wible, C.G., & Cohen, N.J. (1988). Is there a special flashbulb-memory mechanism? *Journal of Experimental Psychology: General, 117*, 171–181.

McConkie, G.W., & Rayner, K. (1975). The span of the effective stimulus during a fixation in reading. *Perception and Psychophysics, 17*(6), 578–586.

McDaniel, M.A., DeLosh, E.L., & Merritt, P. (2000). Order information and retrieval distinctiveness: Recall of common versus bizarre material. *Journal of Experimental Psychology: Learning, Memory, and Cognition, 26*, 1045–1056.

McDaniel, M.A., Einstein, G.O., DeLosh, E.L., May, C.P., & Brady, P. (1995). The bizarreness effect: It's not surprising, it's complex. *Journal of Experimental Psychology: Learning, Memory, and Cognition, 21*, 422–435.

McGurk, H., & MacDonald, J. (1976). Hearing lips and seeing voices. *Nature, 264*, 746–748.

Mack, A. (2003). Inattentional blindness: Looking without seeing. *Current Directions in Psychological Science, 12* (5), 180–184.

Mack, A., Pappas, Z., Silverman, M., & Gay, R. (2002). What we see: Inattention and the capture of attention by meaning. *Consciousness and Cognition, 11*, 488–506.

Mack, A., & Rock, I. (1998). *Inattentional blindness*. Cambridge, Mass.: MIT Press.

Mackavey, W.R., Malley, J.E. & Stewart, A.J. (1991). Remembering autobiographically consequential experiences: Content analysis of psychologists' accounts of their lives. *Psychology and Aging, 6*, 50–59.

McKelvie, S.J. (1995). *Vividness of visual imagery: Measurement, nature, function and dynamics*. New York: Brandon House.

Mackworth, N. (1965). Originality. *American Psychologist, 20*, 51–66.

McLean, J.R., & Hoffman, E.R. (1973). The effects of restricted preview on driver steering control and performance. *Human Factors, 15*, 421–430.

MacLeod, C.M. (1991). Half a century of research on the Stroop effect: An integrative review. *Psychological Bulletin, 109*, 163–203.

MacLeod, C.M. (1992). The Stroop task: The "gold standard" of attentional measures. *Journal of Experimental Psychology: General, 121*, 12–15.

MacLeod, C.M., & MacDonald, P.A. (2000). Interdimensional interference in the Stroop effect: Uncovering the cognitive and neural anatomy of attention. *Trends in Cognitive Sciences, 4*, 382–391.

MacLeod, C.M., & Sheehan, P.W. (2003). Hypnotic control of attention in the Stroop task: A historical footnote. *Consciousness and Cognition, 12*, 347–353.

McManus, I.C. (1983). Basic colour terms in literature. *Language and Speech, 26*, 247–252.

McNamara, T.P. (1992). Priming and constraints it places on theories of memory and retrieval. *Psychological Review, 99*, 650–662.

McNamara, T.P., Rump, B., & Werner, S. (2003). Egocentric and geocentric frames of reference in memory of large-scale space. *Psychonomic Bulletin & Review, 10*, 589–595.

McNeill, D. (1970). *The acquisition of language*. New York: Harper & Row.

McNeill, D. (1980). *Conceptual basis of language activity* (cassette recording). Washington: American Psychological Association.

McNeill, D. (1985a). Language viewed as action. In J. Wertsch (Ed.), *Culture, communication and cognition* (pp. 258–270). Cambridge: Cambridge University Press.

McNeill, D. (1985b). So you think gestures are nonverbal? *Psychological Review, 92*, 350–371.

McNeill, D. (1989). A straight path—to where? Reply to Butterworth and Hadar. *Psychological Review, 96*, 175–179.

McRae, K., & Boisvert, S. (1998). Automatic semantic similarity priming. *Journal of Experimental Psychology: Learning, Memory, and Cognition, 24*, 558–572.

MacWhinney, B. (2000). *The CHILDES project: Tools for analyzing talk*. Mahwah, NJ: Erlbaum.

MacWhinney, B. (2004). A multiple process solution to the logical problem of language acquisition. *Journal of Child Language, 31*, 883–914.

Maess, B., Koelsch, S., Gunter, T.C., & Friederici, A.D. 2001. Musical syntax is processed in Broca's area: An MEG study. *Nature Neuroscience, 4*, 540–545.

Maguire, E.A., Gadian, D.G., Johnsrude, I.S., Good, C.D., Ashburner, J., Frackowiak, R.S.J., & Frith, C.D. (2000). Navigation-related structural change in the hippocampi of taxi drivers. *Proceedings of the National Academy of Science, 2000*, 4398–4403.

Maguire, E.A., Valentine, E.R., Wilding, J.M., & Kapur, N. (2003). Routes to remembering: The brains behind superior memory. *Nature Neuroscience, 6*, 90–95.

Mai, X.-Q., Luo, J., Wu, J.-H., & Luo, Y.-J. (2004). "Aha!" effects in a guessing riddle task: An event-related potential study. *Human Brain Mapping, 22*, 261–270.

Maier, N.R.F. (1968). Reasoning in humans: II. The solution of a problem and its appearance in consciousness. In P.C. Wason & P.N. Johnson-Laird (Eds.), *Thinking and reasoning* (pp. 17–27). (Original work published 1931).

Maier, N.R.F. (1970). *Problem-solving and creativity in individuals and groups*. Belmont, Calif.: Wadsworth.

Majid, A., Bowerman, M., Kita, S., Haun, D.B.M., & Levinson, S.C. (2004). Can language restructure cognition? The case for space. *Trends in Cognitive Sciences, 8*, 108–114.

Mandler, G. (2002). Organization: What levels of processing are levels of. *Memory, 10*, 333–338.

Marcel, A.J. (1983a). Conscious and unconscious perception: Experiments on visual masking and word recognition. *Cognitive Psychology, 15*, 197–237.

Marcel, A.J. (1983b). Conscious and unconscious perception: An approach to the relations between phenomenal experience and perceptual processes. *Cognitive Psychology, 15*, 238–300.

Marcel, A.J., Katz, L., & Smith, M. (1974). Laterality and reading proficiency. *Neuropsychologia, 12*, 131–139.

Marian, V., & Neisser, U. (2000). Language-dependent recall of autobiographical memories. *Journal of Experimental Psychology: General, 129*, 361–368.

Marks, D.F. (1972). Individual differences in the vividness of visual imagery and their effect on function. In P.W. Sheehan (Ed.), *The function and nature of imagery* (pp. 83–108). New York: Academic Press.

Marks, D.F. (1999). Consciousness, mental imagery and action. *British Journal of Psychology, 90*, 567–585.

Marks, L.E. (1978). *The unity of the senses: Interrelations among the modalities*. New York: Academic Press.

Marks, L.E. (1982). Bright sneezes and dark coughs, loud sunlight and soft moonlight. *Journal of Experimental Psychology: Human Perception and Performance, 8*, 177–193.

Marschark, M., Richman, C.L., Yuille, J.C., & Hunt, R.R. (1987). The role of imagery in memory: On shared and distinctive information. *Psychological Bulletin, 102*, 28–41.

Marshall, J.C., & Fink, G.R. (2003). Cerebral localization, then and now. *NeuroImage, 20*, S2–S7.

Martin, A., & Caramazza, A. (2003). Neuropsychological and neuroimaging perspectives on conceptual knowledge: An introduction. *Cognitive Neuropsychology, 20*, 195–212.

Martin, L. (1986). Eskimo words for snow: A case study in the genesis and decay of an anthropological example. *American Anthropologist, 88*, 418–423.

Martindale, C. (1981). *Cognition and consciousness*. Homewood, Ill.: Dorsey Press.

Martindale, C. (1984). The pleasures of thought: A theory of cognitive hedonics. *Journal of Mind and Behavior, 5*, 49–80.

Martindale, C., Moore, K., & West, A. (1988). Relationship of preference judgments to typicality, novelty, and mere exposure. *Empirical Studies of the Arts, 6*, 79–96.

Martino, G., & Marks, L.E. (2001). Synesthesia: Strong and weak. *Current Directions in Psychological Science, 10*, 61–65.

Maslow, A.H. (1946). Problem-centering versus means-centering in science. *Philosophy of Science, 13*, 326–331.

Mast, F.W., and Kosslyn, S.M. (2002) Visual mental images can be ambiguous: Insights from individual differences in spatial transformation abilities. *Cognition, 86*, 57–70.

Maurer, D. (1997). Neonatal synaesthesia: Implications for the processing of speech and faces. In S. Baron-Cohen & J.E. Harrison (Eds.), *Synaesthesia: Classic and contemporary readings* (pp. 224–242). Oxford: Blackwell.

Mayer, E. (1991). The ideological resistance to Darwin's theory of natural selection. *Proceedings of the American Philosophical Society, 135*, 123–139.

Mayer, R.E. (2004). Teaching of subject matter. *Annual Review of Psychology, 55*, 715–744.

Mayer, U. (2004). Conflict, consciousness and control. *Trends in Cognitive Sciences, 8*(4), 145–148.

Medin, D.L. (1989). Concepts and conceptual structure. *American Psychologist, 44*, 1469–1481.

Medin, D.L., & Atran, S. (2004). The native mind: Biological categorization and reasoning in development and across cultures. *Psychological Review, 111*, 960–983.

Mednick, S.A. (1962). The associative basis of the creative process. *Psychological Review, 69*, 220–227.

Mednick, S.A. (1967). *The remote associations test*. Boston: Houghton Mifflin.

Mehta, R., & Zhu, R.J. (2009), Blue or Red? Exploring the Effect of Color on Cognitive Task Performances. *Science, 323*, 1226–1229.

Mehler, J. (1963). Some effects of grammatical transformations: On the recall of English sentences. *Journal of Verbal Learning and Verbal Behavior, 2*, 560–566.

Meiran, N., Hommel, B., Bibi, U., & Lev, I. (2001). Consciousness and control in task switching. *Consciousness and Cognition, 11*, 10–33.

Merikle, P.M. (1992). Perception without awareness: Critical issues. *American Psychologist, 47*, 792–795.

Merikle, P.M., & Daneman, M. (2000). Conscious vs. unconscious perception. In M.S. Gazzaniga (Ed.), *The new cognitive neurosciences* (2nd ed.) (pp. 1295–1303). Cambridge, Mass.: MIT Press.

Merikle, P.M., & Joordens, S. (1997). Measuring unconscious influences. In J.D. Cohen & J.W. Schooler (Eds.), *Approaches to consciousness* (pp. 109–123). Hillsdale, NJ: Erlbaum.

Merikle, P.M., & Reingold, E.M. (1998). On demonstrating unconscious perception: Comment on Draine and Greenwald. *Journal of Experimental Psychology: General, 127*(3), 304–310.

Merikle, P.M., Smilek, D., & Eastwood, J.D. (2001). Perception without awareness: Perspectives from cognitive psychology. *Cognition, 79*, 115–134.

Messick, D.M. (1987). Egocentric biases and the golden section. *Journal of Social and Biological Structures, 10*, 241–247.

Metcalfe, J. (1998). Cognitive optimism: Self-deception or memory-based heuristics? *Personality and Social Psychology Review, 2*, 100–110.

Metcalfe, J. (2002). Is study time allocated selectively to a region of proximal learning? *Journal of Experimental Psychology: General, 131*, 349–363.

Metcalfe, J., & Kornell, N. (2003). The dynamics of learning and allocation of study time to a region of proximal learning. *Journal of Experimental Psychology: General, 132*, 530–542.

Metcalfe, J., & Kornell, N. (2005). A region of proximal learning model of study time allocation. *Journal of Memory and Language, 52*, 463–477.

Metcalfe, J., & Wiebe, D. (1987). Intuition in insight and non-insight problem-solving. *Memory & Cognition, 15*, 238–246.

Meyer, D.E., & Schvaneveldt, R.W. (1976). Meaning, memory structure, and mental processes. In C. Cofer (Ed.), *The structure of human memory* (pp. 54–89). San Francisco: Freeman.

Meyer, G.E. & Hilterbrand, K. (1984). Does it pay to be "Bashful"? The seven dwarfs and long-term memory. *American Journal of Psychology, 97*, 47–55.

Milgram, R.M., & Rabkin, L. (1980). Developmental test of Mednick's associative hierarchies of original thinking. *Developmental Psychology, 16*, 157–158.

Milham, M.P., Banich, M.T., & Barad, V. (2003). Competition for processing increases prefrontal cortex's involvement in top-down control: An event-related fMRI study of the Stroop task. *Cognitive Brain Research, 17*, 212–222.

Milivojevic, B., Johnson, B.W., Hamm, J.P., & Corballis, M.C. (2003). Non-identical neural mechanisms for two types of mental transformation: Event-related potentials during mental rotation and mental paper folding. *Neuropsychologia, 41*, 1345–1356.

Mill, D., Gray, T., & Mandel, D.R. (1994). Influence of research methods and statistics courses on everyday reasoning, critical abilities, and belief in unsubstantiated phenomena. *Canadian Journal of Behavioural Science, 26*, 246–258.

Miller, D.R. (1999). The norm of self-interest. *American Psychologist, 54*, 1053–1060.

Miller, G.A. (1953). What is information measurement? *American Psychologist, 8,* 3–11.

Miller, G.A. (1956). The magical number seven, plus or minus two. *Psychological Review, 63,* 81–97.

Miller, G.A. (1986). Dictionaries in the mind. *Language and Cognitive Processes, 1,* 171–185.

Miller, G.A., Galanter, E., & Pribram, K. (1960). *Plans and the structure of behavior.* New York: Holt, Rinehart & Winston.

Milner A.D., & Goodale, M.A. (1995). *The visual brain in action.* Oxford: Oxford University Press.

Milner, P. (2003). A brief history of the Hebbian learning rule. *Canadian Psychology, 44,* 5–9.

Minsky, M., & Papert, S. (1969). *Perceptrons.* Cambridge, Mass.: MIT Press.

Mischel, T. (1967). Kant and the possibility of a science of psychology. *The Monist, 51,* 599–622.

Mischel, T. (1969). Scientific and philosophical psychology: An historical introduction. In T. Mischel (Ed.), *Human action* (pp. 1–40). New York: Academic Press.

Mitchell, D.B. (1989). How many memory systems are there? Evidence from aging. *Journal of Experimental Psychology: Human Learning and Memory, 15,* 31–49.

Mitchell, D.B., & Bruss, P.J. (2003). Age differences in implicit memory: Conceptual, perceptual or methodological? *Psychology and Aging, 18,* 807–822.

Mitchell, G. (2004). Case studies, counterfactuals, and causal explanations. *University of Pennsylvania Law Review, 152,* 1517–1608.

Mitchell, K.J., & Johnson, M.K. (2000). Source monitoring: Attributing mental experiences. In E. Tulving & F.I.M. Craik (Eds.). *The Oxford handbook of memory* (pp. 179–195). New York: Oxford University Press.

Moeser, S.D. (1982). Memory integration and memory interference. *Canadian Journal of Psychology, 36,* 165–188.

Mohr, C., Graves, R.E., Gianotti, L.R.R., Pizzagalli, D., & Brugger, P. (2001). Loose but normal: A semantic association study. *Journal of Psycholinguistic Research, 30,* 475–483.

Monin, B. (2003). The warm glow heuristic: When liking leads to familiarity. *Journal of Personality and Social Psychology, 85,* 1035–1048.

Moniz, E. (1968). Prefrontal leucotomy. In W.S. Sahakian (Ed.), *History of psychology: A source book in systematic psychology* (pp. 372–377). Itaska, Ill.: Peacock. (Original work published 1954).

Monsell, S. (2003). Task switching. *Trends in Cognitive Sciences, 7,* 134–140.

Montero, B. (1999). The body problem. *Noûs, 33,* 183–200.

Moray, N. (1959). Attention and dichotic listening: Affective cues and the influence of instructions. *Quarterly Journal of Experimental Psychology, 11,* 56–60.

Moreland, R.L., & Zajonc, R.B. (1977). Is stimulus recognition a necessary condition for the occurrence of exposure effects? *Journal of Personality and Social Psychology, 35,* 191–199.

Moreland, R.L., & Zajonc, R.B. (1979). Exposure effects may not depend on stimulus recognition. *Journal of Personality and Social Psychology, 37,* 1085–1089.

Morgan, C.L. (1894). *Introduction to comparative psychology.* London: Walter Scott.

Morris, N., & Jones, D.M. (1990). Memory updating in working memory: The role of the central executive. *British Journal of Psychology, 81,* 111–121.

Morris, P.E., Jones, S., & Hampson, P. (1978). An imagery mnemonic for the learning of people's names. *British Journal of Psychology, 69,* 335–336.

Morton, J. (1969). Interaction of information in word recognition. *Psychological Review, 76,* 165–176.

Morton, J. (1976). On recursive reference. *Cognition, 4,* 309.

Muller, M. (2001). Global and local tree game searches. *Information Sciences, 135,* 187–206.

Mullin, P., & Egeth, H.E. (1989). Capacity limitations in visual word processing. *Journal of Experimental Psychology: Human Perception and Performance, 15,* 111–123.

Mumford, M.D., & Gustafson, S.B. (1988). Creativity syndrome: Integration, application and innovation. *Psychological Bulletin, 103,* 27–43.

Murphy, G.L. (2003). The downside of categories. *Trends in Cognitive Sciences, 7,* 513–514.

Murray, D.J. (1993). A perspective for viewing the history of psychophysics. *Behavioral and Brain Sciences, 16,* 115–186.

Nadel, L., & Hardt, O. (2004). The spatial brain. *Neuropsychology 18*(3), 473–476.

Nader, K. (2003). Memory traces unbound. *Trends in Neurosciences, 26,* 65–72.

Nappe, G.W., & Wollen, K.A. (1973). Effects of instructions to form common and bizarre mental images on retention. *Journal of Experimental Psychology, 100,* 6–8.

Natsoulas, T. (1978). Consciousness. *American Psychologist, 33,* 906–914.

Naveh-Benjamin, M. (2000). Adult age differences in memory performance: Tests of an associative deficit hypothesis. *Journal of Experimental Psychology: Learning, Memory, and Cognition, 26,* 1170–1187.

Naveh-Benjamin, M., Guez, J., Kilb, A., & Reedy, S. (2004). The associative memory deficit of older adults: Further support using face-name associations. *Psychology and Aging, 19,* 541–546.

Naveh-Benjamin, M., Hussain, Z., Guez, J., & Bar-On, M. (2003). Adult age differences in episodic memory: Further support for an associative deficit hypothesis. *Journal of Experimental Psychology: Learning, Memory, and Cognition, 29,* 826–837.

Necker, L.A. (1964). On an apparent change of position in a drawing or engraved figure of a crystal. In W. Dember (Ed.), *Visual perception: The nineteenth century* (pp. 78–83). New York: Wiley. (Original work published 1832).

Neisser, U. (1962). Cultural and cognitive discontinuity. In T.E. Gladwin & W. Sturtevant (Eds.), *Anthropology and human behavior.* Washington: Anthropological Society of America.

Neisser, U. (1963). Decision-time without reaction-time: Experiments in visual scanning. *American Journal of Psychology, 76,* 376–385.

Neisser, U. (1967). *Cognitive psychology.* New York: Appleton-Century-Crofts.

Neisser, U. (1970). Visual imagery. In J. Antrobus (Ed.), *Cognition and affect* (pp. 159–178). Boston: Little, Brown.

Neisser, U. (1976). *Cognition and reality: Principles and implication of cognitive psychology.* New York: W.H. Freeman/Times Books/Henry Holt & Co.

Neisser, U. (1978a). Anticipations, images, and introspection. *Cognition, 6,* 169–174.

Neisser, U. (1978b). Memory: What are the important questions? In M.M. Gruneberg, P.M. Morris, & R.N. Sykes (Eds.), *Practical aspects of memory* (pp. 3–24). London: Academic Press.

Neisser, U. (1979). Tracing eidetic imagery. *Behavioral and Brain Sciences, 2,* 612–613.

Neisser, U. (1980). *Toward a realistic cognitive psychology* (cassette recording). Washington: American Psychological Association.

Neisser, U. (1981). John Dean's memory: A case study. *Cognition, 9,* 1–22.

Neisser, U. (1982a). Snapshots or benchmarks? In U. Neisser (Ed.). *Memory observed: Remembering in natural contexts* (pp. 43–48). San Francisco: Freeman.

Neisser, U. (Ed.). (1982b). *Memory observed: Remembering in natural contexts.* San Francisco: Freeman.

Neisser, U. (1983). Components of intelligence or steps in routine procedures? *Cognition, 15,* 189–197.

Neisser, U. (1985). The role of theory in the ecological study of memory: Comment on Bruce. *Journal of Experimental Psychology: General, 114,* 272–276.

Neisser, U. (Ed.). (1986). *The school achievement of minority children.* Hillsdale, NJ: Erlbaum.

Neisser, U. (1988). Five kinds of self-knowledge. *Philosophical Psychology, 1,* 35–59.

Neisser, U. (1988). What is ordinary memory the memory of? In U. Neisser & E. Winograd (Eds.), *Remembering reconsidered: Ecological and traditional approaches to the study of memory* (pp. 356–373). New York: Cambridge University Press.

Neisser, U. (1991). A case of misplaced nostalgia. *American Psychologist, 46,* 34–36.

Neisser, U. (1993). The self perceived. In U. Neisser (Ed.), *The perceived self* (pp. 3–21). New York: Cambridge University Press.

Neisser, U. (1997). Rising scores on intelligence tests. *American Scientist, 85,* 440–447.

Neisser, U. (1997). The ecological study of memory. *Proceedings of the Royal Society of London (Series B), 352,* 1697–1701.

Neisser, U. (Ed.). (1998). *The rising curve.* Washington: American Psychological Association.

Neisser, U. (2003). New directions for flashbulb memories: Comments on the *Applied Cognitive Psychology* special issue. *Applied Cognitive Psychology, 17,* 1149–1155.

Neisser, U. (2004). Memory development: New questions and old. *Developmental Review, 24,* 154–158.

Neisser, U., & Becklen, R. (1975). Selective looking: Attending to visually specified events. *Cognitive Psychology, 7,* 480–494.

Neisser, U., Boodoo, G., Bouchard, T.J., Boykin, A.W., Brody, N., Ceci, S.J., et al. (1996). Intelligence: Knowns and unknowns. *American Psychologist, 51,* 77–101.

Neisser, U., & Weene, P. (1962). Hierarchies in concept attainment. *Journal of Experimental Psychology, 64,* 640–45.

Nelson, K., & Gruendel, J. (1981). Generalized event representations: Basic building blocks of cognitive development. In M.E. Lamb & A.L. Brown (Eds.), *Advances in developmental psychology* (pp. 131–158). Hillsdale, NJ: Erlbaum.

Nersessian, N.J. (1995). Opening the black box: Cognitive science and the history of science. *Osiris, 10,* 194–211.

Newell, A. (1977). On the analysis of human problem-solving protocols. In P.N. Johnson-Laird & P. Wason (Eds.), *Thinking: Readings in cognitive science* (pp. 46–61). Cambridge: Cambridge University Press.

Newell, A. (1983). The heuristic of George Polya and its relation to artifical intelligence. In R. Groner & M. Groner (Eds.), *Methods of heuristics* (pp. 195–243). Hillsdale, NJ: Erlbaum.

Newell, A. (1985). Duncker on thinking: An inquiry into progress in cognition. In S. Koch & D. Leary (Eds.), *A century of psychology as science: Retrospections and assessments* (pp. 392–419). New York: McGraw-Hill.

Newell, A., & Simon, H.A. (1972). *Human problem-solving.* Englewood Cliffs, NJ: Prentice-Hall.

Newell, A., Shaw, J.C., & Simon, H.A. (1958). Chess-playing programs and the problem of complexity. *IBM Journal of Research and Development, 2,* 320–335.

Newell, A., Simon, H., & Shaw, J.C. (1962). The processes of creative thinking. In H.E. Gruber, G. Terrell, & M. Wertheimer (Eds.), *Contemporary approaches to creative thinking* (pp. 63–119). New York: Atherton.

Newell, B.R. (2005). Re-visions of rationality? *Trends in Cognitive Sciences, 9,* 11–15.

Newman, J.R. (1956). *The world of mathematics.* New York: Simon & Schuster.

Newstead, S.E., Pollard, P., Evans, J. St B.T., & Allen, J.L. (1992). The source of belief bias effects in syllogistic reasoning. *Cognition, 45,* 257–284.

Nicholls, M.E.R., Clode, D., Wood, S.J., & Wood, A.G. (1999). Laterality of expression in portraiture: Putting your best cheek forward. *Proceedings of the Royal Society of London (Series B), 266,* 1517–1522.

Nicholls, M.E.R., Wolfgang, B.J., Clode, D., & Lindell, A.K. (2002). The effect of left and right poses on the expression of facial emotion. *Neuropsychologia, 40,* 1662–1665.

Nichols, S. (2004). Folk concepts and intuitions: From philosophy to cognitive science. *Trends in Cognitive Science, 8,* 514–518.

Nickerson, R.S. (1996). Ambiguities and un-stated assumptions in probabilistic reasoning. *Psychological Review, 120,* 410–433.

Nicolson, R.I., & Gardner, P.H. (1985). The QWERTY keyboard hampers school-children. *British Journal of Psychology, 76,* 525–531.

Nisbett, R.E., Krantz, D.H., Jepson, C., & Kunda, Z. (1983). The use of statistical heuristics in everyday inductive reasoning. *Psychological Review, 90,* 339–363.

Noble, C.E. (1952). An analysis of meaning. *Psychological Review, 59,* 421–430.

Noë, A., Pessoa, L., & Thompson, E. (2000). Beyond the grand illusion: What change blindness really teaches us about vision. *Visual Cognition, 7,* 93–106.

Noë, A., & Thompson, E. (2004). Are there neural correlates of consciousness? *Journal of Consciousness Studies, 11,* 3–28

Noice, H. (1991). The role of explanations and plan recognition in the learning of theatrical scripts. *Cognitive Science, 15,* 425–460.

Noice, H. (1992). Elaborative memory strategies of professional actors. *Applied Cognitive Psychology, 6,* 417–427.

Noice, H. (1993). Effects of rote versus gist strategy on the verbatim retention of theatrical scripts. *Applied Cognitive Psychology, 7,* 75–84.

Norman, D.A. (1981). Categorization of action slips. *Psychological Review, 88,* 1–15.

Norman, D.A. (1983). Some observations on mental models. In D. Gentner & A.L. Stevens (Eds.), *Mental models* (pp. 7–14). Hillsdale, NJ: Erlbaum.

Norman, D.A. (1992). *Turn signals are the facial expressions of automobiles.* Reading, Mass.: Addison-Wesley.

Norman, D.A. (1993). *Things that make us smart.* Reading, Mass.: Addison-Wesley.

Norman, D.A. (1998). *The invisible computer.* Cambridge, Mass.: MIT Press.

Norman, D.A. (2002). *The psychology of everyday things.* New York: Basic Books. (Original work published 1988).

Norman, D.A., & Bobrow, D.G. (1976). Active memory processes in perception and cognition. In C. Cofer (Ed.), *The structure of human memory* (pp. 114–132). San Francisco: Freeman.

Norman, D.A., & Draper, S.W. (1986). *User-centered system design.* Hillsdale, NJ: Erlbaum.

Norman, D.A., & Fisher, D. (1982). Why alphabetic keyboards are not easy to use: Keyboard layout doesn't much matter. *Human Factors, 24,* 509–519.

Noveck, I.A. (2001). When children are more logical than adults: Experimental investigations of scalar implications. *Cognition, 78,* 165–188.

Noyes, J., & Garland, K. (2005). Students' attitudes toward books and computers. *Computers and Human Behavior, 21,* 233–241.

Nyberg, L. (2002). Levels of processing: A view from functional brain imaging. *Memory, 10,* 345–348.

Oakhill, J.V., & Johnson-Laird, P.N. (1985). Rationality, memory and the search for counterexamples. *Cognition, 20,* 79–94.

Oakhill, J.V., Johnson-Laird, P.N., & Garnham, A. (1989). Believability and syllogistic reasoning. *Cognition, 31,* 117–140.

O'Brien, D.P., Noveck, I.A., Davidson, G.M., Fusch, S.M., Lea, R.B., & Freitag, J. (1990). Sources of difficulty in deductive reasoning: The THOG task. *Quarterly Journal of Experimental Psychology, 42A,* 329–351.

O'Brien, E.J., & Wolford, C.R. (1982). Effect of delay of testing on retention of plausible versus bizarre mental images. *Journal of Experimental Psychology: Learning, Memory, and Cognition, 8,* 148–152.

Ogilvie, J. (2002). Turn the other cheek. *Trends in Cognitive Sciences, 6,* 234.

Ohlsson, S. (1984). Restructuring revisited. *Scandinavian Journal of Psychology, 25,* 65–78.

O'Keefe, J., & Nadel, L. (1978). *The hippocampus as a cognitive map.* Oxford: Oxford University Press.

Olivers, C.N.L., & Nieuwenhuis, S. (2005). The beneficial effect of concurrent task-irrelevant mental activity on temporal attention. *Psychological Science, 16,* 265–269.

Olson, D.R. (1977). From utterance to text: The bias of language in speech and writing. *Harvard Educational Review, 47,* 257–281.

Olson, D.R. (Ed.). (1985). *Literacy, language and learning: The nature of reading and writing.* New York: Cambridge University Press.

Olson, D.R. (1986). The cognitive consequences of literacy. *Canadian Psychology, 27,* 109–121.

Olson, D.R. (1996). Towards a psychology of literacy: On the relations between speech and writing. *Cognition, 60,* 83–104.

Olson, D.R., & Astington, J.W. (1986a). Children's acquisition of metalinguistic and metacognitive verbs. In W. Demopoulos & A. Marras (Eds.), *Language learning and concept acquisition* (pp. 184–199). Norwood, NJ: Ablex.

Olson, D.R., & Astington, J. (1986b). Talking about text: How literacy contributes to thought. Paper presented to the Boston University Conference on Language Development, Boston.

Olson, G.M., & Olson, J.S. (2003). Human-computer interaction: Psychological aspects of the human use of computing. *Annual Review of Psychology, 54,* 491–516.

Oppenheimer, D.M. (2003). Not so fast! (and not so frugal!): Rethinking the recognition heuristic. *Cognition, 90,* B1–B9.

O'Regan, J.K. (1992). Solving the "real" mysteries of visual perception: The world as an outside memory. *Canadian Journal of Psychology, 46,* 461–488.

Ormerod, T.C., MacGregor, J.N., & Chronicle, E.P. (2002). Dynamics and constraints in insight problem-solving. *Journal of Experimental Psychology: Learning, Memory, and Cognition, 28,* 791–799

Osgood, C.E. (1979). From Yang and Yin in cross-cultural perspective. *International Journal of Psychology, 14,* 1–35.

Osgood, C.E., & Richards, M.M. (1973). From Yang and Yin to "and" or "but." *Language, 49,* 380–412.

Ost, J., & Costall, A. (2002). Misremembering Bartlett: A study in serial reproduction. *British Journal of Psychology, 93,* 243–255.

Paige, J.M., & Simon, H.A. (1966). Cognitive processes in solving algebra word problems. In B. Kleinmuntz (Ed.), *Problem-solving* (pp. 51–119). New York: Wiley.

Paivio, A. (1965). Abstractness, imagery and meaningfulness in paired-associate learning. *Journal of Verbal Learning and Verbal Behavior, 4,* 32–38.

Paivio, A. (1969). Mental imagery in associative learning and memory. *Psychological Review, 76,* 241–263.

Paivio, A. (1971). *Imagery and verbal processes.* New York: Holt, Rinehart & Winston.

Paivio, A. (1983). The empirical case for dual coding. In J. Yuille (Ed.), *Imagery, memory and cognition: Essays in honor of Allan Paivio* (pp. 307–332). Hillsdale, NJ: Erlbaum.

Paivio, A. (1986). *Mental representations.* Oxford: Oxford University Press.

Paivio, A. (1991). Dual coding theory: Retrospect and current status.

Canadian Journal of Psychology, 45, 255–287.

Paivio, A., & Begg, I. (1981). *The psychology of language.* Englewood Cliffs, NJ: Prentice-Hall.

Paivio, A., Khan, M., & Begg, I. (2000). Concreteness and relational effects on recall of adjective-noun pairs. *Canadian Journal of Experimental Psychology, 54,* 149–159.

Paivio, A., Walsh, M., & Bons, T. (1994). Concreteness effects on memory: When and why? *Journal of Experimental Psychology: Learning, Memory, and Cognition, 20,* 1196–1204.

Paivio, A., Yuille, J., & Madigan, S. (1968). Concreteness, imagery and meaningfulness values for 925 nouns. *Journal of Experimental Psychology Monograph Supplement, 76*(1), Pt. 2.

Palmer, C.F., Jones, R.K., Hennessy, B.L., Unze, M.G., & Pick, A.D. (1989). How is a trumpet known? The "basic object level" concept and the perception of musical instruments. *American Journal of Psychology, 102,* 17–37.

Palmer, S.E. (1992). Common region: A new principle of perceptual grouping. *Cognitive Psychology, 24,* 436–447.

Palmer, S.E. (1999). *Vision science: Photons to phenomenology.* Cambridge, Mass.: MIT Press.

Pani, J.F., & Chariker, J.H. (2004). The psychology of error in relation to medical practice. *Journal of Surgical Oncology, 88,* 130–142.

Papanicolauo, A.C. (1998). *Fundamentals of functional brain imaging.* Lisse: Swets & Zeitlinger.

Paprotte, W., & Sinha, C. (1987). A functional perspective on early language development. In M. Hickmann (Ed.), *Social and functional approaches to language and thought* (pp. 203–222). New York: Academic Press.

Parker, A.J., Krug, K., & Cumming, B.G. (2003). Neuronal activity and its links with the perception of multistable figures. In A. Parker, A. Derrington, & C. Blakemore (Eds.), *The physiology of cognitive processes* (pp. 139–156). Oxford: Oxford University Press.

Parkin, A.J., & Hunkin, N.M. (2001). British memory research: A journey through the 20th century. *British Journal of Psychology, 92,* 37–52.

Pashler, H. (1994). Dual-task interference in simple tasks: Data and theory. *Psychological Bulletin, 116*(2), 220–244.

Pashler, H. (1998). *The psychology of attention.* Cambridge, Mass.: MIT Press.

Pashler, H., Johnston, J.C., & Ruthruff, E. (2001). Attention and performance. *Annual Review of Psychology, 52,* 629–651.

Paul, I.H. (1967). The concept of schema in memory theory. In R.R. Holt (Ed.), *Motives and thought: Psychoanalytic essays in honor of David Rapaport* (pp. 215–258). New York: International Universities Press.

Payne, S.J., & Green, T.R.G. (1989). The structure of command languages: An experiment on task-action grammar. *International Journal of Man-Machine Studies, 30,* 213–234.

Peabody, D. (1990). The role of evaluation in impressions of persons. In I. Rock (Ed.), *The legacy of Solomon Asch* (pp. 57–75). Hillsdale, NJ: Erlbaum.

Pederson, E., Danziger, E., Wilkins, D., Levinson, S., Kita, S., & Senft, G. (1998). Semantic typology and spatial conceptualization. *Language, 74,* 557–589.

Peeters, G., & Czapinski, J. (1990). Positive-negative asymmetry in evaluations: The distinction between affective and informational negativity effects. In W. Stroebe & M. Hewstone (Eds.), *European Review of Social Psychology* (Vol. 1). Chichester: Wiley.

Pelli, D.G. (1999). Close encounters—An artist shows that size affects shape. *Science, 285,* 844–846.

Pelli, D.G., Farell, B., & Moore, D.C. (2003). The remarkable inefficiency of word recognition. *Nature, 423,* 752–756.

Perkins, D.N. (1981). *The mind's best work.* Cambridge, Mass.: Harvard University Press.

Perner, J. (2000). Memory and theory of mind. In E. Tulving & F.I.M. Craik (Eds.), *The Oxford handbook of memory* (pp. 297–312). New York: Oxford University Press.

Pessoa, L., Kastner, S., & Ungerleider, L.G. (2003). Neuroimaging studies of attention: From modulation of sensory processing to top-down control. *Journal of Neuroscience, 23,* 3990–3998.

Pessoa, L., Thompson, E., & Noë, A. (1998). Finding out about filling-in: A guide to perceptual completion for visual science and the philosophy of perception. *Behavioral and Brain Sciences, 21*(6), 723–802.

Peterson, L.R., & Peterson, M.J. (1959). Short-term retention of individual verbal items. *Journal of Experimental Psychology, 58,* 193–198.

Peterson, M.A., & Gibson, B.S. (1993). Shape recognition inputs to figure–ground organization in three-dimensional displays. *Cognitive Psychology, 25,* 383–429.

Peterson, M.A., Kihlstrom, J.F., Rose, P.M., & Glisky, M.L. (1992). Mental images can be ambiguous: Reconstruals and reference-frame reversals. *Memory & Cognition, 20,* 107–123.

Petrill, S.A., Lipton, P.A., Hewitt, J.K., Plomin, R., Cherny, S.S., Corley, R., & Defries, J.C. (2004). Genetic and environmental contributions to general cognitive ability through the first 16 years of life. *Developmental Psychology, 40,* 805–812.

Petry, S., & Meyer, G. (1987). *The perception of illusory contours.* New York: Springer.

Pheasant, S. (1986). *Bodyspace: Anthropometry, ergonomics and design.* London: Taylor & Francis.

Piatelli-Palmarini, M. (1989). Evolution, selection and cognition: From "learning" to parameter setting in biology and in the study of language. *Cognition, 31,* 1–44.

Pikas, A. (1966). *Abstraction and concept formation.* Cambridge, Mass.: Harvard University Press.

Pillemer, D.B. (1990). Clarifying the flashbulb memory concept. *Journal of Experimental Psychology: General, 119,* 92–96.

Pinker, S. (1988). Learnability theory and the acquisition of a first language. In F. Kessel (Ed.), *The development of language and language researchers: Essays in honor of Roger Brown* (pp. 97–119). Hillsdale, NJ: Erlbaum.

Pinker, S. (1994). *The language instinct.* London: Penguin.

Pinker, S. (1997). *How the mind works.* New York: Norton.

Pinker, S. (1999). *Words and rules.* New York: HarperCollins.

Pinker, S., & Finke, R.A. (1980). Emergent two-dimensional patterns in images rotated in depth. *Journal of Experimental Psychology: Human*

Perception and Performance, 6, 244–264.

Pinker, S., & Jackendoff, R. (2005). The faculty of language: What's special about it? *Cognition, 95,* 201–236.

Pirolli, P. (2005). Rational analyses of information foraging on the web. *Cognitive Science, 29,* 343–373.

Pirolli, P., & Card, S. (1999). Information foraging. *Psychological Review, 106,* 643–675.

Podgorny, P., & Shepard, R.N. (1978). Functional representations common to visual perception and imagination. *Journal of Experimental Psychology: Human Perception and Performance, 4,* 21–35.

Poeppel, D., & Hickock, G. (2004). Introduction: Towards a new functional anatomy of language. *Cognition, 92,* 1–12.

Poincaré, H. (1960). *Science and method.* New York: Dover. (Original work published 1924).

Polanyi, M. (1958). *Personal knowledge.* Chicago: University of Chicago Press.

Pollio, H.R., Barlow, J.M., Fine, H.J., & Pollio, M.R. (1972). *Psychology and the poetics of growth.* Hillsdale, NJ: Erlbaum.

Pollio, H.R., Smith, M.K., & Pollio, M.R. (1990). Figurative language and cognitive psychology. *Language and Cognitive Processes, 5,* 141–167.

Polya, G. (1957). *How to solve it.* New York: Anchor. (Original work published 1945).

Popper, K.R. (1959). *The logic of scientific discovery.* New York: Basic Books.

Posner, M.I. (1969). Abstraction and the process of recognition. In G.H. Bower & J.T. Spence (Eds.), *The psychology of learning and motivation* (Vol. 3, pp. 44–100). New York: Academic Press.

Posner, M.I. (1973). *Cognition: An introduction.* Glenview, Ill.: Scott, Foresman.

Posner, M.I. (1986). *Chronometric explorations of mind.* Oxford: Oxford University Press.

Posner, M.I. (2004). Neural systems and individual differences. *Teacher's College Record,* 24–30.

Posner, M.I., Goldsmith, R., & Welton, K.E., Jr. (1967). Perceived distance and the classification of distorted patterns. *Journal of Experimental Psychology, 73*(1), 28–38.

Posner, M.I., & Keele, S.W. (1968). On the genesis of abstract ideas. *Journal of Experimental Psychology, 77,* 353–363.

Posner, M.I., & Keele, S.W. (1970). Retention of abstract ideas. *Journal of Experimental Psychology, 83,* 304–308.

Postman, L., Bruner, J., & McGinnis, E. (1948). Personal values as selective factors in perception. *Journal of Abnormal and Social Psychology, 43,* 142–154.

Price, D. (1963). *Little science, big science.* New York: Columbia University Press.

Puente, A.E. (1995). Roger Wolcott Sperry (1913–1994). *American Psychologist, 50,* 940–941.

Pullum, G.K. (1991). *The great Eskimo vocabulary hoax, and other irreverent essays on the study of language.* Chicago: University of Chicago Press.

Pullum, G.K., & Scholz, B.C. (2002). Empirical assessment of stimulus poverty arguments. *Linguistic Review, 19,* 9–50.

Purves, D., & Lotto, R.B. (2003). *Why we see what we do: An empirical theory of vision.* Sunderland, Mass.: Sinaur Associates.

Pylyshyn, Z.W. (1973). What the mind's eye tells the mind's brain: A critique of mental imagery. *Psychological Bulletin, 80,* 1–24.

Pylyshyn, Z.W. (2002). Mental imagery: In search of a theory. *Behavioral and Brain Sciences, 25,* 157–238.

Pylyshyn, Z.W. (2003a). Explaining mental imagery: Now you see it, now you don't. *Trends in Cognitive Sciences, 7,* 111–112.

Pylyshyn, Z.W. (2003b). Return of the mental image: Are there really pictures in the brain? *Trends in Cognitive Sciences, 7,* 113–118.

Qin, Y., & Simon, H.A. (1990). Laboratory replication of scientific discovery processes. *Cognitive Science, 14,* 281–312.

Quillian, R. (1969). The teachable language comprehender: A simulation program and theory of language. *Communications of the* ACM, *12,* 459–476.

Quinlan, P.T. (2003). Visual feature integration theory: Past, present, and future. *Psychological Bulletin, 129,* 643–673.

Rabbitt, P. (1990). Applied cognitive gerontology: Some problems,

methodologies and data. *Applied Cognitive Psychology, 4,* 225–246.

Radvansky, G.A., Gibson, B.S., & McNerney, M.W. (2011). Synesthesia and memory: Color congruency, von Restorff, and false memory effects. *Journal of Experimental Psychology: Learning, Memory and Cognition, 37,* 219–229.

Raichle, M.E. (2003). Functional brain imaging and human brain function. *Journal of Neuroscience, 23,* 3959–3962.

Ramachandran, V.S. (1993). Filling in gaps in perception: Part II: Scotomas and phantom limbs. *Current Directions in Psychological Science, 2,* 56–65.

Ramachandran, V.S. (2004). *A brief tour of consciousness.* New York: Pi Press.

Ramachandran, V.S., & Hirstein, W. (1998). The perception of phantom limbs: The D.O. Hebb lecture. *Brain, 121,* 1603–1630.

Ramachandran, V.S., & Rogers-Ramachandran, D. (2005). *Scientific American: Mind, 14(5),* 99–100.

Ramachandran, V.S., Rodgers-Ramachandran, D., & Cobb, S. (1995). Touching the phantom limb. *Nature, 377,* 489–490.

Rastle, K.G., & Burke, D.M. (1996). Priming the tip of the tongue: Effects of prior processing on word retrieval in young and older adults. *Journal of Memory and Language, 25,* 586–605.

Ratliff, F. (1976). On the psychophysiological bases of universal color terms. *Proceedings of the American Philosophical Society, 120,* 311–330.

Ratneshwar, S., Barsalou, L.W., Pechmann, C., & Moore, M. (2001). Goal-derived categories: The role of personal and situational goals in category representations. *Journal of Consumer Psychology, 10,* 147–157.

Raven, J. (2000). The Raven's progressive matrices: Change and stability over culture and time. *Cognitive Psychology 41,* 1–48.

Raven, J.C., Styles, I., & Raven, M.A. (1998). *Raven's progressive matrices: SPM plus test booklet.* Oxford: Oxford Psychologists Press/San Antonio, Tex.: Psychological Corporation.

Rawson, K.A., & Kintsch, W. (2005). Rereading effects depend on time of test. *Journal of Educational Psychology, 97,* 70–80.

Rayner, K. (1998). Eye movements in reading and information processing: 20 years of research. *Psychological Bulletin, 124*(3), 372–422.

Rayner, K., Rotello, C.M., Stewart, A.J., Keir, J., & Duffy, S.A. (2001). Integrating text and pictoral information: Eye movements when looking at print advertisements. *Journal of Experimental Psychology: Applied, 7*(3), 219–226.

Rayner, K., White, S.J., Johnson, R.L., & Liversedge, S.P. (2006). Raeding wrods with jubmled lettres: There is a cost. *Psychological Science, 17*(3), 192–193.

Raz, A., Landzberg, K.S., Schweizer, H.R., Zephrani, Z.R., Shapiro, T., Fan, J., & Posner, M.I. (2003). Posthypnotic suggestion and the modulation of Stroop interference under cycloplegia. *Consciousness and Cognition, 12*, 332–346.

Reason, J. T. (1979). Actions not as planned: The price of automatization. In G. Underwood & R. Stevens (Eds.), *Aspects of consciousness, Vol. 1: Psychological issues.* London: Wiley.

Reason, J.T. (1984). Lapses of attention in everyday life. In R. Parasuraman & D.R. Davies (Eds.), *Varieties of attention* (pp. 515–549). Orlando, Fla: Academic Press.

Reason, J.T. (1990). *Human error.* New York: Cambridge University Press.

Reber, A.S. (1967). Implicit learning of artificial grammars. *Journal of Verbal Learning and Verbal Behavior, 5*, 855–863.

Reber, A.S. (1985). *The Penguin dictionary of psychology.* London: Penguin.

Reber, A.S. (1989). Implicit learning and tacit knowledge. *Journal of Experimental Psychology: General, 118*, 219–235.

Reber, A.S. (1990). On the primacy of the implicit: Comment on Perruchet and Pacteau. *Journal of Experimental Psychology: General, 119*, 340–342.

Reber, A.S. (1997). Implicit ruminations. *Psychonomic Bulletin & Review, 4*, 49–55.

Reber, A.S., & Allen, R. (1978). Analogy and abstraction strategies in synthetic grammar learning: A functionalist interpretation. *Cognition, 6*, 189–221.

Reber, A.S., Allen, R., & Regan, S. (1985). Syntactical learning and judgment, still unconscious and still abstract: Comment on Dulany, Carlson and Dewey. *Journal of Experimental Psychology: General, 114*, 17, 24.

Reber, A.S., Kassin, S.M., Lewis, S., & Cantor, G. (1980). On the relationship between implicit and explicit modes in the learning of a complex rule structure. *Journal of Experimental Psychology: Human Learning and Memory, 8*, 492–502.

Reber, A.S., & Lewis, S. (1977). Implicit learning: An analysis of the form and structure of a body of tacit knowledge. *Cognition, 5*, 333–362.

Reber, A.S., Walkenfeld, F.F., & Hernstadt, R. (1991). Implicit and explicit learning: Individual differences and IQ. *Journal of Experimental Psychology: Human Learning and Memory, 17*, 888–896.

Rebok, G.W. (1987). *Life-span cognitive development.* New York: Holt, Rinehart & Winston.

Redelmeier, D. A., & Kahneman, D. (1996). Patients' memories of painful medical treatments: Real-time and retrospective evaluations of two minimally invasive procedures. *Pain, 66*, 3–8.

Redelmeier, D.A., & Tversky, A. (1996). On the belief that arthritis pain is related to the weather. *Proceedings of the National Academy of Sciences, 93*, 2895–2896.

Reder, L. (1980). The role of elaboration in the comprehension and retention of prose. *Review of Educational Research, 50*, 5–53.

Reder, L.M., & Kusbit, G.W. (1991). Locus of the Moses illusion: Imperfect encoding, retrieval or match? *Journal of Memory and Language, 30*, 385–406.

Regan, D. (2000). *Human perception of objects.* Sunderland, Mass.: Sinauer Associates.

Regier, T., & Kay, P. (2004). Color naming and sunlight. *Psychological Science, 15*, 289–290.

Reicher, G.M. (1969). Perceptual recognition as a function of meaningfulness of stimulus material. *Journal of Experimental Psychology, 81*, 275–280.

Reisberg, D., Pearson, D.G., & Kosslyn, S.M. (2003). Intuitions and introspections about imagery: The role of imagery experience in shaping an investigator's theoretical views. *Applied Cognitive Psychology, 17*, 147–160.

Rensink, R.A., O'Regan, J.K., & Clark, J.J. (1997). To see or not to see: The need for attention to perceive changes in scenes. *Psychological Science, 8*, 368–373.

Rhodes, G., Byatt, G., Michie, P.T., & Puce, A. (2004). Is the fusiform face area specialized for faces, individuation, or expert individuation? *Journal of Cognitive Neuroscience, 16*, 189–203.

Rice, M.L. (1989). Children's language acquisition. *American Psychologist, 44*, 149–156.

Richeson, J.A., et al. (2003). An fMRI investigation of the impact of interracial contact on executive function. *Nature Neuroscience, 6*, 1323–1328.

Richman, C.L. (1994). The bizarreness effect with complex sentences: Temporal effects. *Canadian Journal of Experimental Psychology, 48*, 444–450.

Rigdon, M.A., & Epting, F. (1982). A test of the Golden Section hypothesis with elicited constructs. *Journal of Personality and Social Psychology, 43*, 1080–1087.

Rinck, M., & Denis, M. (2004). The metrics of spatial distance traversed during mental imagery. *Journal of Experimental Psychology: Learning, Memory, and Cognition, 30*, 1211–1218.

Rips, L.J. (1983). Cognitive processes in propositional reasoning. *Psychological Review, 90*, 38–71.

Rips, L.J. (1988). Deduction. In R.J. Sternberg & E.E. Smith (Eds.), *The psychology of human thought* (pp. 116–152). Cambridge: Cambridge University Press.

Rips, L.J. (1989). The psychology of knights and knaves. *Cognition, 31*, 85–116.

Rips, L.J. (1990). Paralogical reasoning: Evans, Johnson-Laird, and Byrne on liar and truth-teller puzzles. *Cognition, 36*, 291–314.

Rips, L.J. (1994). *The psychology of proof: Deductive reasoning in human thinking.* Cambridge, Mass.: MIT Press.

Rips, L.J. (1997). Goals for a theory of deduction: Reply to Johnson-Laird. *Minds and Machines, 7,* 409–424.

Rips, L.J., & Conrad, F.G. (1989). Folk psychology of mental activities. *Psychological Review, 96,* 187–207.

Rips, L.J., & Conrad, F.G. (1990). Parts of activities: Reply to Fellbaum and Miller. *Psychological Review, 97,* 571–575.

Rizzolatti, G., Riggio, L., Dascola, I., & Umiltà, C. (1987). Reorienting attention across the horizontal and vertical meridians: Evidence in favor of a premotor theory of attention. *Neuropsychologia: Special Issue: Selective Visual Attention, 25*(1-A), 31–40.

Rizzolatti, G., Riggio, L., & Sheliga, B.M. (1994). Space and selective attention. In C. Umiltà and M. Moscovitch (Eds.), *Attention and Performance 15: Conscious and Nonconscious Information Processing* (pp. 232–265). Cambridge, Mass.: MIT Press.

Ro, T., Russell, C., & Lavie, N. (2001). Changing faces: A detection advantage in the flicker paradigm. *Psychological Science, 12,* 94–99.

Roberson, D., Davidoff, J., Davies, I.R.L., & Shapiro, L.R. (2004). The development of color categories in two languages: A longitudinal study. *Journal of Experimental Psychology: General, 133,* 554–571.

Roberson, D., Davies, I., & Davidoff, J. (2000). Color categories are not universal: Replications and new evidence from a stone-age culture. *Journal of Experimental Psychology: General, 129,* 369–398.

Roberts, R.M., & Kreuz, R.J. (1994). Why do people use figurative language? *Psychological Science, 5,* 159–163.

Robinson, D. A. (1965). The mechanics of human smooth pursuit eye movements. *The Journal of Physiology, 180,* 569-591.

Rock, I. (1983). *The logic of perception.* Cambridge, Mass.: MIT Press.

Rock, I. (1984). *Perception.* New York: Freeman.

Rock, I. (Ed.). (1990). *Legacy of Solomon Asch: Essays in cognition and social psychology.* Hillsdale, NJ: Erlbaum.

Rock, I., & Ceraso, J. (1964). A cognitive theory of associative learning. In C. Scheerer (Ed.), *Cognition* (pp. 110–146). New York: Harper & Row.

Rock, I., & Kaufman, L. (1962). The moon illusion. Part II. *Science, 136*(3521), 1023–1031.

Rock, I., Wheeler, D., & Tudor, L. (1989). Can we imagine how objects look from other viewpoints? *Cognitive Psychology, 21,* 185–210.

Roediger, H.L. (1997). Remembering. *Contemporary Psychology, 42,* 488–492.

Roediger, H.L., III, & Blaxton, T.A. (1987). Effects of varying modality, surface features, and retention interval on priming in word fragment completion. *Memory & Cognition, 15,* 379–388.

Roediger, H.L., Gallo, D.A., & Geraci, L. (2002). Processing approaches to cognition: The impetus from the levels-of-processing framework. *Memory, 10,* 319–332.

Roediger, H.L., & McDermott, K.B. (1993). Implicit memory in normal human subjects. In F. Boller & J. Grafman (Eds.), *Handbook of neuropsychology* (Vol. 8, pp. 63–131). Amsterdam: Elsevier.

Ronan, K.R., & Kendall, P.C. (1997). Self-talk in distressed youth: States of mind and content specificity. *Journal of Clinical Child Psychology, 26,* 330–337.

Rosch, E.H. (1975). Cognitive representations of semantic categories. *Journal of Experimental Psychology: General, 104,* 192–233.

Rosch, E.H. (1978). Principles of categorization. In E. Rosch & B. Lloyd (Eds.), *Cognition and categorization* (pp. 27–48). Hillsdale, NJ: Erlbaum.

Rosch, E.H. (1988). Coherences and categorization: A historical view. In F. Kessel (Ed.), *The development of language and language researchers: Essays in honor of Roger Brown* (pp. 373–392). Hillsdale, NJ: Erlbaum.

Rosch, E.H., & Mervis, C.B. (1975). Family resemblances: Studies in the internal structure of categories. *Cognitive Psychology, 7,* 573–605.

Rosch, E.H., Mervis, C.B., Gray, W.D., Johnson, D.M., & Boyes-Braem, P. (1976). Basic objects in natural categories. *Cognitive Psychology, 8,* 382–439.

Rosenholtz, R., & Malik, J. (1997). Surface orientation from texture: Isotropy or homogeneity (or both)? *Vision Research, 37,* 2283–2293.

Rosnow, R.L., & Rosenthal, R. (1989). Statistical procedures and the justification of knowledge in psychological science. *American Psychologist, 44,* 1276–1284.

Rossano, M.J. (2003). Expertise and the evolution of consciousness. *Cognition, 89,* 207–236.

Rouse, W.B., & Morris, N.M. (1986). On looking into the black box: Prospect and limits in the search for mental models. *Psychological Bulletin, 100,* 349–363.

Rozin, P., & Fallon, A.E. (1987). A perspective on disgust. *Psychological Review, 94,* 23–41.

Rozin, P., Fallon, A., & Augustoni-Ziskind, M. (1985). The child's conception of food: The development of contamination sensitivity to "disgusting" substances. *Developmental Psychology, 21,* 1075–1079.

Rozin, P., Markwith, M., & Ross, B. (1990). The sympathetic magical law of similarity, nominal realism and neglect of negatives in response to negative labels. *Psychological Science, 1,* 383–384.

Rozin, P., Millman, L., & Nemeroff, C. (1986). Operation of the laws of sympathetic magic in disgust and other domains. *Journal of Personality and Social Psychology, 50,* 703–712.

Rozin, P., & Nemeroff, C. (2002). Sympathetic magical thinking: The contagion and similarity "heuristics." In T. Gilovich, D. Griffin, & D. Kahneman (Eds.), *Heuristics and biases: The psychology of intuitive judgment* (pp. 201–216). Cambridge: Cambridge University Press.

Rozin, P., & Royzman, E.B. (2001). Negativity bias, negativity dominance, and contagion. *Personality and Social Psychology Review, 5,* 296–320.

Rubens, A.B., & Benson, D.F. (1971). Associative visual agnosia. *Archives of Neurology, 24*(4), 305–316.

Rubin, D.C. (1975). Within word structure in the tip-of-the-tongue phenomenon. *Journal of Verbal Learning and Verbal Behavior, 14,* 392–397.

Rubin, D.C. (2000). The distribution of early childhood memories. *Memory,* 265–269.

Rubin, D.C. (2002). Autobiographical memory across the lifespan. In P. Graf & N. Ohta (Eds.), *Lifespan development of human memory* (pp. 159–184). Cambridge, Mass.: MIT Press.

Rubin, D.C. (2005). A basic-systems approach to autobiographical memory. *Current Directions in Psychological Science, 11*, 79–83.

Rubin, D.C., & Berntsen, D. (2003). Life scripts help to maintain autobiographical memories of highly positive, but not highly negative, events. *Memory & Cognition, 31*, 1–14.

Rubin, D.C., & Friendly, M. (1986). Predicting which words get recalled: Measures of free recall, availability, goodness, emotionality, and pronounceability for 925 nouns. *Memory & Cognition, 14*, 79–94.

Rubin, D.C., Rahhal, T.A., & Poon, L.W. (1998). Things learned early in adulthood are remembered best. *Memory & Cognition, 26*, 3–19.

Rubin, D.C., Wetzler, S.E., & Nebes, R.D. (1986). Autobiographical memory across the lifespan. In D.C. Rubin (Ed.), *Autobiographical memory* (pp. 202–221). Cambridge: Cambridge University Press.

Ruby, L. (1960). *Logic: An introduction.* New York: Lippincott.

Rugg, M.D. (1995). Event-related potential studies of memory. In M.D. Rugg & M.G.H. Coles (Eds.), *Electrophysiology of mind* (pp. 132–170). New York: Oxford University Press.

Rugg, M.D. (2002). Functional neuroimaging of memory. In A.D. Baddeley, M.D. Kopelman, & B.A. Wilson (Eds.), *The handbook of memory disorders* (pp. 57–80). Chichester: Wiley.

Rugg, M.D., Otten, L.J., & Henson, R.N.A. (2003). The neural basis of episodic memory: Evidence from functional neuroimaging. In A. Parker, A. Derrington, & C. Blakemore (Eds.), *The physiology of cognitive processes* (pp. 211–233). Oxford: Oxford University Press.

Rumelhart, D.E., & McClelland, J.L. (Eds.). (1986). *Parallel distributed processing: Explorations in the microstructure of cognition: Vol. I Foundations.* Cambridge, Mass.: MIT Press.

Runco, M.A. (2004). Creativity. *Annual Review of Psychology, 55*, 657–687.

Rundus, D. (1977). Maintenance rehearsal and single-level processing. *Journal of Verbal Learning and Verbal Behavior, 16*, 665–681.

Ruthruff, E., Johnston, J.C., Van Selst, M., Whitsell, S., & Remington, R. (2003). Vanishing dual-task interference after practice: Has the bottleneck been eliminated or is it merely latent? *Journal of Experimental Psychology: Human Perception and Performance, 29*, 280–289.

Ruthsatz, J., & Detterman, D.K. (2003). An extraordinary memory: The case of a musical prodigy. *Intelligence, 31*, 509–518.

Ryle, G. (1949). *The concept of mind.* London: Hutchison.

Sachs, J. (1967). Recognition memory for syntactic and semantic aspects of connected discourse. *Perception and Psychophysics, 2*, 437–442.

Sadoski, M., & Paivio, A. (2001). *Imagery and text: A dual-coding theory of reading and writing.* Mahwah, NJ: Erlbaum.

Sahakian, B., & Morein-Zamir, S. (2007). Professor's little helper. *Nature, 450*, 1157–1159.

Sainsbury, R.M. (1988). *Paradoxes.* Cambridge: Cambridge University Press.

Salmon, D.P., Butters, N., & Chan, A.S. (1999). The deterioration of semantic memory in Alzheimer's disease. *Canadian Journal of Experimental Psychology, 53*, 108–116.

Samson, D., & Pilon, A. (2003). A case of impaired knowledge for fruit and vegetables. *Cognitive Neuropsychology, 20*, 373–400.

Sapir, E. (1949). *Selected writings of Edward Sapir.* Berkeley: University of California Press.

Sarter, M., Berntson, G.G., & Cacioppo, J.T. (1996). Brain imaging and cognitive neuroscience. *American Psychologist, 51*, 13–21.

Saslow, M.G. (1967). Effects of components of displacement-step stimuli upon latency for saccadic eye movement. *Journal of the Optical Society of America, 57*, 1024–1029.

Saunders, B.A.C., & van Brakel, J. (1997). Are there nontrivial constraints on colour categorization? *Behavioral and Brain Sciences, 20*, 167–228.

Schachter, S.S., Christenfeld, N., Ravina, B., & Bilous, F. (1991). Speech disfluency and the structure of knowledge. *Journal of Personality and Social Psychology, 60*, 362–367.

Schachter, S.S., Rauscher, F., Christenfeld, N., & Crone, K.T. (1994). The vocabularies of academia. *Psychological Science, 5*, 37–41.

Schactel, E. (1947). On memory and childhood amnesia. *Psychiatry, 10*, 1–26.

Schacter, D.L. (1987). Implicit memory: History and current status. *Journal of Experimental Psychology: Learning, Memory, and Cognition, 13*, 501–518.

Schacter, D.L. (1992). Understanding implicit memory. *American Psychologist, 47*, 559–569.

Schacter, D.L. (1999). The seven sins of memory: Insights from psychology and cognitive neuroscience. *American Psychologist, 54*, 182–203.

Schacter, D.L., & Dodson, C.S. (2001). Misattribution, false recognition and the sins of memory. *Philosophical Transactions of the Royal Society (Series B), 356*, 1385–1393.

Schacter, D.L., & Graf, P. (1986). Effects of elaborative processing on implicit and explicit memory for new associations. *Journal of Experimental Psychology: Learning, Memory, and Cognition, 12*, 432–444.

Schacter, D.L., & Tulving, E. (1994). What are the memory systems of 1994? In D.L. Schacter & E. Tulving (Eds.), *Memory systems 1994* (pp. 1–38). Cambridge, Mass.: MIT Press.

Schacter, D.L., Wagner, A.D., & Buckner, R.L. (2000). Memory systems of 1999. In E. Tulving & F.I.M. Craik (Eds.). *The Oxford handbook of memory* (pp. 627–643). New York: Oxford University Press.

Schaeffer, J., & van den Herik, H.J. (2002). Games, computers, and artificial intelligence. *Artificial Intelligence, 134*, 1–7.

Schank, R.C. (1982a). Depths of knowledge. In B. de Gelder (Ed.), *Knowledge and representation* (pp. 170–216). London: Routledge & Kegan Paul.

Schank, R.C. (1982b). *Dynamic memory.* New York: Cambridge University Press.

Schank, R.C., & Abelson, R.P. (1975). *Scripts, plans and knowledge.* Proceedings of the Fourth International Joint Conference on Artificial Intelligence. Tbilisi, USSR.

Schank, R.C., & Abelson, R.P. (1977). *Scripts, plans, goals and understanding.* Hillsdale, NJ: Erlbaum.

Schellenberg, E.G. (2004). Music lessons enhance IQ. *Psychological Science, 15*, 511–514.

Schlenker, B.R., & Leary, M.R. (1982). Social anxiety and self-presentation:

A conceptualization and model. *Psychological Bulletin, 92,* 641–669.

Schmidt, R.A., & Bjork, R.A. (1992). New conceptualizations of practice: Common principles in three paradigms suggest new concepts for training. *Psychological Science, 3,* 207–217.

Schmidt, S.R. (2002). The humour effect: Differential processing and privileged retrieval. *Memory, 10,* 127–138.

Schmidt, S.R., & Williams, A.R. (2001). Memory for humorous cartoons. *Memory & Cognition, 29,* 305–311.

Schmuckler, M.A. (2001). What is ecological validity: A dimensional analysis. *Infancy, 2,* 419–436.

Schneider, W. (1987). Connectionism: Is it a paradigm shift for psychology? *Behavior Research Methods, Instruments, & Computers, 19,* 73–83.

Schneider, W., & Chein, J.M. (2003). Controlled and automatic processing: Behavior, theory, and biological mechanisms. *Cognitive Science, 27,* 525–559.

Scholz, B.C., & Pullum, G.K. (2002). Searching for arguments to support linguistic nativism. *Linguistic Review, 19,* 185–223.

Schooler, C. (1998). Environmental complexity and the Flynn effect. In U. Neisser (Ed.), *The rising curve* (pp. 67–79). Washington: American Psychological Association.

Schubotz, R.I., & von Cramon, D.Y. 2001. Interval and ordinal properties of sequences are associated with distinct premotor areas. *Cerebral Cortex, 11,* 210–222.

Schuh, F.C. (1968). *The masterbook of mathematical recreations.* New York: Dover.

Schwartz, N., & Vaughn, L.A. (2002). The availability heuristic revisited: Ease of recall and content of recall as distinct sources of information. In T. Gilovich, D. Griffin, & D. Kahneman (Eds.), *Heuristics and biases: The psychology of intuitive judgment* (pp. 103–119). Cambridge: Cambridge University Press.

Schwartz, R.M. (1997). Consider the simple screw: Cognitive science, quality improvement, and psychotherapy. *Journal of Consulting and Clinical Psychology, 65,* 970–983.

Schwartz, R.M., & Garamoni, G.L. (1986). A structural model of positive and negative states of mind:

Asymmetry in the internal dialogue. In P.C. Kendall (Ed.), *Advances in cognitive-behavioral research and therapy* (Vol. 5, pp. 1–62). New York: Academic Press.

Schwartz, R.M., & Michelson, L. (1987). States of mind model: Cognitive balance in the treatment of agoraphobia. *Journal of Consulting and Clinical Psychology, 55,* 557–565.

Schweich, M., van der Linden, M., Bredart, S., Bruyer, R., Nelles, B., & Schils, J.-P. (1992). Daily life difficulties reported by young and elderly subjects. *Applied Cognitive Psychology, 6,* 161–172.

Scott, S.K. (2004). The neural representation of concrete nouns: What's right and what's left? *Trends in Cognitive Sciences, 8,* 151–153.

Scribner, S. (1986). Thinking in action: Some characteristics of practical thought. In R.J. Sternberg & R.K. Wagner (Eds.), *Practical intelligence* (pp. 13–30). New York: Cambridge University Press.

Scribner, S. (1993). An activity theory approach to memory. *Applied Cognitive Psychology, 7,* 185–190.

Searle, J. (2000). Consciousness. *Annual Review of Neuroscience, 23,* 557–578.

Sedgwick, H.A. (1980). The geometry of spatial layout in pictorial representation. In M.A. Hagen (Ed.), *The perception of pictures* (pp. 33–90). New York: Academic Press.

Selfridge, O. (1959). Pandemonium: A paradigm for learning. In *Symposium on the mechanization of thought processes* (513–526). London: Her Majesty's Stationery Office.

Semon, R. (1923). *Mnemic psychology* (B. Duffy, Trans.). London: George Allen & Unwin. (Original work published 1909).

Senders, V.L. (1958). *Measurement and statistics.* New York: Oxford University Press.

Sévigny, S., Cloutier, M., Pelletier, M.-F., & Ladouceur, R. (2005). Internet gambling: Misleading payout rates during the "demo" period. *Computers in Human Behavior, 21,* 153–158.

Shafto, M., & MacKay, D.G. (2000). The Moses, mega-Moses, and Armstrong illusions: Integrating language comprehension and semantic memory. *Psychological Science, 11,* 372–378.

Shalit, B. (1980). The Golden Section relation in the evaluation of environmental relations. *British Journal of Psychology, 71,* 39–42.

Shams, L., Kamitani, Y., & Shimojo, S. (2004). Modulations of visual perception by sound. In G. Calvert, C. Spence, & B.E. Stein (Eds.), *The Handbook of Multisensory Processes* (pp. 26–32). Cambridge, Mass.: MIT Press.

Shanks, D.R. (2004). Implicit learning. In K. Lamberts & R. Goldstone (Eds.), *Handbook of cognition* (pp. 202–220). London: Sage.

Shannon, C.E. (1948). A mathematical theory of communication. *Bell System Technical Journal* 27 (1948): 379–423, 623–656.

Shannon, C.E., & Weaver, W. (1949). *The mathematical theory of communication.* Urbana: University of Illinois Press.

Shapiro, K.L., Arnell, K.M., & Raymond, J.E. (1997). The attentional blink. *Trends in Cognitive Sciences, 1,* 291–296.

Shepard, R.N. (1966). Learning and recall as organization and search. *Journal of Verbal Learning and Verbal Behavior, 5,* 201–204.

Shepard, R.N. (1967). Recognition memory for words, sentences, and pictures. *Journal of Verbal Learning and Verbal Behavior, 6,* 156–163.

Shepard, R.N. (1978). The mental image. *American Psychologist, 33,* 125–137.

Shepard, R.N. (1984). Ecological constraints on internal representation: Resonant kinematics of perceiving, imagining, thinking, and dreaming. *Psychological Review, 91,* 417–447.

Shepard, R.N., & Cooper, L.A. (1982). *Mental images and their transformations.* Cambridge, Mass.: MIT Press.

Shepard, R.N., & Metzler, J. (1971). Mental rotation of three-dimensional objects. *Science, 171,* 701–703.

Shettleworth, S.J. (2004). Review of B.H. Weber & D.J. Depew, "Evolution and learning: The Baldwin effect reconsidered." *Evolutionary Psychology, 2,* 105–107.

Shiffrin, R.M., & Atkinson, R.C. (1969). Storage and retrieval processes in long-term memory. *Psychological Review, 76,* 179–193.

Shiffrin, R.M., & Schneider, W. (1977). Controlled and automatic human information processing: II. Perceptual learning, automatic attending and a general theory. *Psychological Review, 84,* 127–190.

Shipp, S. (2004). The brain circuitry of attention. *Trends in Cognitive Sciences, 8,* 223–230.

Shneiderman, B. (1998). *Designing the user interface* (3rd ed.). Reading, Mass.: Addison-Wesley.

Sholl, M.J. (1987). Cognitive maps as orienting schemata. *Journal of Experimental Psychology: Learning, Memory, and Cognition, 13,* 615–628.

Shrauf, R.W., & Rubin, D.C. (2003). On the bilingual's two sets of memories. In R. Fivush & C.A. Hayden (Eds.), *Autobiographical memory and the construction of a narrative self* (pp. 121–146). Mahwah, NJ: Erlbaum.

Shweder, R.A. (1977). Likeness and likelihood in everyday thought. *Current Anthropology, 18,* 637–658.

Siegler, R.S. (2004). U-shaped interest in U-shaped development—and what it means. *Journal of Cognition and Development, 5,* 1–10.

Silvia, P.J. (2005). What is interesting? Exploring the appraisal structure of interest. *Emotion, 5,* 89–102.

Sime, M.E., & Coombs, M.J. (Eds.). (1983). *Designing for human computer communication.* London: Academic Press.

Simmel, M.L. (1953). The coin problem: A study in thinking. *American Journal of Psychology, 66,* 229–241.

Simmel, M.L. (1956). Phantoms in patients with leprosy and in elderly digital amputees. *American Journal of Psychology, 69,* 529–545.

Simmons, W.K., & Barsalou, L.W. (2003). The similarity in topography principle: Reconciling theories of conceptual deficits. *Cognitive Neuropsychology, 20,* 451–486.

Simon, H.A. (1969*). The sciences of the artificial.* Cambridge, Mass.: MIT Press.

Simon, H.A. (1975). The functional equivalence of problem-solving skills. *Cognitive Psychology, 7,* 268–288.

Simon, H.A. (1979). *Models of thought.* New Haven: Yale University Press.

Simon, H.A. (1981). *The sciences of the artificial* (2nd ed.). Cambridge, Mass.: MIT Press.

Simon, H.A. (1986). The information-processing explanation of Gestalt phenomena. *Computers in Human Behaviour, 2,* 241–255.

Simon, H.A. (1992). What is an "explanation" of behavior? *Psychological Science,* 150–161.

Simon, H.A. (1995). Explaining the ineffable: AI on the topics of intuition, insight and inspiration. *Proceedings of the Fourteenth International Joint Conference on Artificial Intelligence,* 939–948.

Simon, H.A. (2000). Artificial intelligence. In A.E. Kazlin (Ed.), *American Psychological Association encyclopedia of psychology* (vol. 1, pp. 248–255). New York: Oxford University Press.

Simon, H.A., Valdéz-Pérez, R.E., & Sleeman, D.H. (1997). Scientific discovery and simplicity of method. *Artificial Intelligence, 91,* 177–181.

Simons, D.J. (2000). Attentional capture and inattentional blindness. *Trends in Cognitive Sciences, 4,* 147–155.

Simons, D.J., & Chabris, C.F. (1999). Gorillas in our midst: Sustained inattentional blindness for dynamic events. *Perception, 28,* 1059–1074.

Simons, D.J., & Levin, D.T. (1997). Change blindness. *Trends in Cognitive Science, 1*(7), 261–267.

Simons, D.J., & Levin, D.T. (1998). Failure to detect changes to people during a real-world interaction. *Psychonomic Bulletin & Review, 5*(4), 644–649.

Simons, D.J., & Rensink, R.A. (2005). Change blindness: Past, present, and future. *Trends in Cognitive Sciences, 9*(1), 16–20.

Simonton, D.K. (1984). *Genius, creativity and leadership.* Cambridge, Mass.: Harvard University Press.

Simonton, D.K. (1988). *Scientific genius.* New York: Cambridge University Press.

Simonton, D.K. (1993). Genius and chance: A Darwinian perspective. In J. Brockman (Ed.), *Creativity* (pp. 176–201). New York: Simon & Schuster.

Simonton, D.K. (1994). *Greatness: Who makes history and why.* New York: Guilford.

Simonton, D.K. (2003). Scientific creativity as constrained stochastic behavior: The integration of product, person, and process perspectives. *Psychological Bulletin, 129,* 475–494.

Sinha, P. (2002). Recognizing complex patterns. *Nature Neuroscience Special Issue: Beyond the Bench: The Practical Promise of Neuroscience, 5,* 1093–1097.

Skinner, B.F. (1957). *Verbal behavior.* New York: Appleton-Century-Crofts.

Skinner, B.F. (1964). Behaviorism at fifty. In T.W. Wann (Ed.), *Behaviorism and phenomenology* (pp. 79–97). Chicago: University of Chicago Press.

Skinner, B.F. (1989). The origins of cognitive thought. *American Psychologist, 44,* 13–18.

Slamecka, N. (1985). Ebbinghaus: Some associations. *Journal of Experimental Psychology, 11,* 414–435.

Slamecka, N., & Graf, P. (1978). The generation effect: Delineation of a phenomenon. *Journal of Experimental Psychology: Human Learning and Memory, 4,* 592–604.

Sloboda, J. (1981). Space in musical notation. *Visible Language, 15,* 86–110.

Sloman, S.A. (1996). The empirical case for two systems of reasoning. *Psychological Bulletin, 119,* 3–22.

Sluckin, W., Colman, A.M., & Hargreaves, D.J. (1980). Liking words as a function of the experienced frequency of their occurrence. *British Journal of Psychology, 71,* 163–169.

Smedslund, J. (1963). The concept of correlation in adults. *Scandinavian Journal of Psychology, 4,* 165–173.

Smilek, D., Callejas, A., Dixon, M.J., & Merikle, P.M. (2007). Ovals of time: time-space associations in synaesthesia. *Consciousness and Cognition, 16,* 507–519.

Smilek, D., Dixon, M.J., Cudahy, C., & Merikle, P.M. (2002). Synesthetic color experiences influence memory. *Psychological Science, 13,* 548–552.

Smilek, D., Rempel, M.I., & Enns, J.T. (2006). The illusion of clarity: Image segmentation and edge attribution without filling-in. *Visual Cognition, 14,* 1–36.

Smith, N.K., Cacioppo, J.T., Larsen, J.T., & Chartrand, T.L. (2003). May I have your attention, please: Electrocortical responses to positive and negative stimuli. *Neuropsychologia, 41,* 171–183.

Smith, V.L., & Clark, H.H. (1993). On the course of answering questions. *Journal of Memory and Language, 32,* 25–38.

Smullyan, R.M. (1978). *What is the name of this book? The riddle of Dracula and other logical puzzles.* Englewood Cliffs, NJ: Prentice-Hall.

Smyth, M.M., & Clark, S.E. (1986). My half-sister is a THOG: Strategic processes in a reasoning task. *British Journal of Psychology, 77*, 275–287.

Sohn, M., Anderson, J.R., Reder, L.M., & Goode, A. (2004). Differential fan effect and attentional focus. *Psychonomic Bulletin and Review, 11*, 729–734.

Sokal, M. (2001). Practical phrenology as psychological counseling in the 19th-century United States. In C. Green, M. Shore, & T. Teo (Eds.), *The transformation of psychology: The influences of 19th-century natural science, technology, and philosophy* (pp. 21–44). Washington: American Psychological Association.

Soukoreff, R.W., & Mackenzie, I.S. (2004). Toward a standard for pointing device evaluation, perspectives on 27 years of Fitts' law research in HCI. *International Journal of Human-Computer Studies, 61*, 751–789.

Sparrow, B., Liu, J., and Wegner, D.M. (2011). Google effects on memory: cognitive consequences of having information at our fingertips. *Science 333* (6043), 776–778.

Spearman, C. (1904). "General intelligence" objectively determined and measured. *American Journal of Psychology, 15*, 201–292.

Spearman, C. (1965). The abilities of man: Their nature and measurement. In A. Anastasi (Ed.), *Individual differences* (pp. 51–57). New York: Wiley. (Original work published 1927).

Spearman, C. (1970). *The abilities of man: Their nature and measurement.* New York: AMS Press. (Original work published 1932).

Spelke, E., Hirst, W., & Neisser, U. (1976). Skills of divided attention. *Cognition, 4*, 215–230.

Spence, D.P. (1973). Analog and digital descriptions of behavior. *American Psychologist, 28*, 479–497.

Sperber, D. (2002). In defense of massive modularity. In E. Dupoux (Ed.), *Language, brain and cognitive development: Essays in honor of Jacques Mehler* (pp. 47–57). Cambridge, Mass.: MIT Press.

Sperber, D., & Hirschfeld, L.A. (2004). The cognitive foundations of

cultural stability and diversity. *Trends in Cognitive Sciences, 8*, 40–48.

Sperber, D., & Wilson, D. (1995). *Relevance: Communication and cognition* (2nd ed.). Oxford: Blackwell.

Sperber, D., & Wilson, D. (2002). Pragmatics modularity and mind-reading. *Mind & Language, 17*, 3–23.

Sperling, G. (1960). The information available in brief visual presentations. *Psychological Monographs, 74*, No. 11.

Sperry, R. (1987). Consciousness and causality. In R.L. Gregory (Ed.), *The Oxford companion to the mind* (pp. 164–166). Oxford: Oxford University Press.

Sperry, R. (1988). Psychology's mentalist paradigm and the religion/science tension. *American Psychologist, 43*, 607–613.

Sperry, R.W. (1964, January). The great cerebral commissure. *Scientific American, 210*, 42–52.

Squire, L.R. (2004). Memory systems of the brain: A brief history and current perspective. *Neurobiology of Learning and Memory, 82*, 171–177.

Squire, L.R., & McKee, R. (1992). Influence of prior events on cognitive judgments in amnesia. *Journal of Experimental Psychology: Learning, Memory, and Cognition, 18*, 106–115.

Srivastava, I. (2005). Mobile phones and the evolution of social behavior. *Behavior and Information Technology, 24*, 111–129.

Stanovich, K.E. (2004). *The robot's rebellion: Finding meaning in the age of Darwin.* Chicago: University of Chicago Press.

Stanovich, K.E., & Cunningham, A.E. (1992). Studying the consequences of literacy within a literate society: The cognitive correlates of print exposure. *Memory & Cognition, 20*, 51–68.

Stanovich, K.E., & West, R.F. (1998). Individual differences in rational thought. *Journal of Experimental Psychology: General, 127*, 161–188.

Stanovich, K.E., & West, R.F. (2000). Individual differences in reasoning: Implications for the rationality debate? *Behavioral and Brain Sciences, 23*, 645–726.

Stanovich, K.E., & West, R.F. (2003a). The rationality debate as a progressive research program. *Behavioral and Brain Sciences, 26*, 531–534.

Stanovich, K.E., & West, R.F. (2003b). Evolutionary versus instrumental goals: How evolutionary psychology misconceives human rationality. In D.E. Over (Ed.), *Evolution and the psychology of thinking: The debate.* Hove, UK: Psychology Press.

Steering Committee of the Physicians' Health Study Research Group. (1988). Preliminary report: Findings from the aspirin component of the ongoing physicians' health study. *New England Journal of Medicine, 318*, 262–264.

Stein, B., Bransford, J., Franks, J., Owings, R., Vye, N., & McGraw, W. (1982). Differences in the precision of self-generated elaborations. *Journal of Experimental Psychology: General, 111*, 399–405.

Stern, W. (1966). On the mental quotient. In R.J. Herrnstein & E. Boring (Eds.), *A source book in the history of psychology* (pp. 450–453). Cambridge, Mass.: Harvard University Press. (Original work published 1912).

Sternberg, R.J. (1980). Sketch of a componential subtheory of intelligence. *Behavioral and Brain Sciences, 3*, 573–614.

Sternberg, R.J. (1982). Natural, unnatural, and supernatural concepts. *Cognitive Psychology, 14*, 451–488.

Sternberg, R.J. (1983). Components of human intelligence. *Cognition, 15*, 1–48.

Sternberg, R.J. (1984a). Mechanisms of cognitive development: A componential approach. In R.J. Sternberg (Ed.), *Mechanisms of cognitive development* (pp. 163–209). San Francisco: Freeman.

Sternberg, R.J. (2009). Toward a triarchic theory of human intelligence. In J.C. Kaufman and E.L. Grigorenko (Ed.) *The Essential Sternberg* (pp. 33–70). New York: Springer. .

Sternberg, R.J. (1988). *The triarchic mind: A new theory of human intelligence.* New York: Viking.

Sternberg, R.J. (1992). Ability tests, measurements, and markets. *Journal of Educational Psychology, 84*, 134–140.

Sternberg, R.J. (1999a). The theory of successful intelligence. *Review of General Psychology, 3*, 292–316.

Sternberg, R.J. (1999b). Successful intelligence: Finding a balance. *Trends in Cognitive Sciences, 3*, 436–442.

Sternberg, R.J. (2000a). Damn it, I still don't know what to do! *Behavioral and Brain Sciences, 23,* 764.

Sternberg, R.J. (2000b). Cross-disciplinary verification of theories: The case of the triarchic theory. *History of Psychology, 3,* 177–179.

Sternberg, R.J. (2003a). Issues in the theory and measurement of successful intelligence: A reply to Brody. *Intelligence, 31,* 331–337.

Sternberg, R.J. (2003b). Our research program validating the triarchic theory of successful intelligence: Reply to Gottfredson. *Intelligence, 31,* 399–413.

Sternberg, R.J., Castejón, J.L., Prieto, M.D., Hautamäki, J., & Grigorenko, E.L. (2001). Confirmatory factor analysis of the Sternberg triarchic abilities test in three international samples. *European Journal of Psychological Assessment, 17,* 1–16.

Sternberg, R.J., & Kaufman, J.C. (1998). Human abilities. *Annual Review of Psychology, 49,* 479–502.

Sternberg, R.J., Powell, C., McGrane, P., & Grantham-McGregor, S. (1997). Effects of a parasitic infection on cognitive functioning. *Journal of Experimental Psychology: Applied, 3,* 67–76.

Sternberg, R.J., & Wagner, R.K. (1986). *Practical intelligence.* New York: Cambridge University Press.

Sternberg, R.J., & Wagner, R.K. (1994*). Mind in context: Interactionist perspectives on human intelligence.* New York: Cambridge University Press.

Stevens, A., & Coupe, P. (1978). Distortions in judged spatial distances. *Cognitive Psychology, 10,* 422–437.

Stevens, G.C. (1983). User-friendly computer systems? A critical examination of the concept. *Behaviour and Information Technology, 2,* 3–16.

Stich, S. (1983). *From folk psychology to cognitive science: The case against belief.* Cambridge, Mass.: MIT Press.

Stickgold, R., & Walker, M. (2004). To sleep, perchance to gain creative insight? *Trends in Cognitive Sciences, 8,* 191–192.

Stone, N.J. (2003). Environmental view and color for a simulated telemarketing task. *Journal of Environmental Psychology, 23,* 63–78.

Stover, D., & Erdmann, E. (2000). *A mind for tomorrow: Facts, values, and the future.* Westport, Conn.: Praeger.

Strawson, P.F. (1952). *Introduction to logical theory.* London: Methuen.

Strayer, D., & Drews, F. (2007) Cell-phone-induced driver distraction. *Current Directions in Psychological Science, Vol. 16, No. 3,* 128-131.

Strayer, D.L., Drews, F.A., & Johnston, W.A. (2003). Cell phone-induced failures of visual attention during simulated driving. *Journal of Experimental Psychology: Applied, 9,* 23–52.

Strayer, D.L., & Johnston, W.A. (2001). Driven to distraction: Dual-task studies of simulated driving and conversing on a cellular phone. *Psychological Science, 12,* 462–466.

Strohmeyer, C.F. (1982). An adult eidetiker. In U. Neisser (Ed.), *Memory observed: Remembering in natural contexts* (pp. 399–404). San Francisco: Freeman. (Original work published 1970).

Stroop, J.R. 1935. Studies of inference in serial verbal reactions. *Journal of Experimental Psychology, 18*(6), 643–662. Reprinted 1992 in *Journal of Experimental Psychology: General, 121,* 15–23.

Suddendorf, T., & Busby, J. (2003). Mental time travel in animals? *Trends in Cognitive Sciences, 7,* 391–396.

Sugiyama, L.S., Tooby, J., & Cosmides, L. (2002). Cross-cultural evidence of cognitive adaptations for social exchange among the Shiwiar of Ecuadorian Amazonia. *Proceedings of the National Academy of Sciences, 99,* 11537–11542.

Suzuki, R., & Arita, T. (2004). Interactions between learning and evolution: The outstanding strategy generated by the Baldwin effect. *BioSystems, 77,* 57–71.

Swanson, L.W. (2003). *Brain architecture: Understanding the basic plan.* New York: Oxford University Press.

Talarico, J.M., & Rubin, D.C. (2003). Confidence, not consistency, characterizes flashbulb memories. *Psychological Science, 14,* 455–461.

Talland, G.A. (1968). *Disorders of memory and learning.* Baltimore: Penguin.

Tammet, D. (2009). *Embracing the wide sky: A tour across the horizons of the mind.* Free Press: New York.

Taylor, H.A., & Tversky, B. (1992). Descriptions and depictions of environments. *Memory & Cognition, 20,* 483–496.

Taylor, J.G. (1966). Perception generated by training echolocation. *Canadian Journal of Psychology, 20,* 64–81.

Terman, L.M. (1948).The measurement of intelligence. In W. Dennis (Ed.), *Readings in the history of psychology* (pp. 485–496). New York: Appleton-Century-Crofts. (Original work published 1916).

Terrace, H.S. (1985). In the beginning was the "Name." *American Psychologist, 40,* 1011–1028.

The Oxford English Dictionary [compact disk] (1992). Oxford: Oxford University Press.

The Right Stuff. (1983, December), *Psychology Today, 17*(12), 58–63.

Thomas, J.C., Jr. (1974). An analysis of behaviour in the hobbits-orcs problem. *Cognitive Psychology, 6,* 257–269.

Thompson, C.P. (1997). Schematic and social influences on memory. *Contemporary Psychology, 42,* 492–493.

Thorndike, E.L. (1898). Animal intelligence: An experimental study of the associative processes in animals. *Psychological Review Monograph Supplement, 2(8).*

Thornton, M.T. (1982). Aristotelian practical reason. *Mind, 91,* 57–76.

Tibbetts, P.E. (2001). The anterior cingulate cortex, akinetic mutism, and human volition. *Brain and Mind, 2,* 323–341.

Tierney, J. (1991, July 21). Behind Monty Hall's doors: Puzzle, debate and answer? *New York Times,* pp. 1, 20.

Tigner, R.B., & Tigner, S.S. (2000). Triarchic theories of intelligence: Aristotle and Sternberg. *History of Psychology, 3,* 168–176.

Titchener, E.B. (1966). From "A text-book of psychology." In R.J. Herrnstein & E. Boring (Eds.), *A source book in the history of psychology* (pp. 599–605). Cambridge, Mass.: Harvard University Press. (Original work published 1910).

Todd, P.M., Fiddick, L., & Krauss, S. (2000). Ecological rationality and its contents. *Thinking and Reasoning, 6,* 375–384.

Todd, P.M., & Gigerenzer, G. (2000). Précis of "Simple heuristics that make us smart." *Behavioral and Brain Sciences, 23*, 737–780.

Todd, P.M., & Gigerenzer, G. (2003). Bounding rationality to the world. *Journal of Economic Psychology, 24*, 143–165.

Toglia, M., & Battig, W. (1978). *Handbook of semantic word norms*. Hillsdale, NJ: Erlbaum.

Tolman, E.C. (1948). Cognitive maps in rats and men. *Psychological Review, 55*, 189–208.

Tolman, E.C. (1959). Principles of purposive behavior. In S. Koch (Ed.), *Psychology: A study of a science* (pp. 92–157). New York: McGraw-Hill.

Toppino, T.C. (2003). Reversible-figure perception: Mechanisms of intentional control. *Perception & Psychophysics, 65*, 1285–1295

Toth, J.P. (2000). Nonconscious forms of human memory. In E. Tulving & F.I.M. Craik (Eds.), *The Oxford handbook of memory* (pp. 245–261). New York: Oxford University Press.

Townsend, J.T. (1990). Serial vs. parallel processing: Sometimes they look like Tweedledum and Tweedledee but they can and should be distinguished. *Psychological Science, 1*, 46–54.

Trachtenberg, L., Streumer, J., & van Zolingen, S. (2002). Career counseling in the emerging post-industrial society. *International Journal for Educational and Vocational Guidance, 2*, 85–99.

Tranel, D., & Damasio, A.R. (1985). Knowledge without awareness: An autonomic index of facial recognition by prosopagnostics. *Science, 228*(4706), 1453–1454.

Trehub, S.E. (2003). The developmental origins of musicality. *Nature Neuroscience, 6*, 669–673.

Treisman, A. (1969). Strategies and models of selective attention. *Psychological Review, 76*, 282–299.

Treisman, A. (1986). Features and objects and visual processing. *Scientific American, 255*(5), 114–125.

Treisman, A. (1996). The binding problem. *Current Opinion in Neurobiology, 6*, 171–178.

Treisman, A. (1996). Selection for perception for selection for action. *Visual Cognition, 3*(4), 353–357.

Treisman, A., & Gelade, G. (1980). A feature-integration theory of attention. *Cognitive Psychology, 12*, 97–136.

Treisman, A., & Gormican, S. (1988). Feature analysis in early vision: Evidence from search asymmetries. *Psychological Review, 95*, 15–48.

Tucker, M., & Ellis, R. (1998). On the relations between seen objects and components of potential actions. *Journal of Experimental Psychology-Human Perception and Performance, 24*(3), 830-846.

Tulving, E. (1972). Episodic and semantic memory. In E. Tulving & W. Donaldson (Eds.), *Organization of memory* (pp. 382–403). New York: Academic Press.

Tulving, E. (1983). *Elements of episodic memory*. Oxford: Clarendon Press.

Tulving, E. (1984). Relations among components and processes of memory. *Behavioral and Brain Sciences, 7*, 257–268.

Tulving, E. (1985). Memory and consciousness. *Canadian Psychology, 26*, 1–12.

Tulving, E. (1986). What kind of a hypothesis is the distinction between episodic and semantic memory? *Journal of Experimental Psychology: Learning, Memory, and Cognition, 12*, 307–311.

Tulving, E. (2000). Concepts of memory. In E. Tulving & F.I.M. Craik (Eds.), *The Oxford handbook of memory* (pp. 33–43). New York: Oxford University Press.

Tulving, E. (2001a). The origin of autonoesis in episodic memory. In H.L. Roediger, J.S. Nairne, I. Neath, & A.I. Surprénant (Eds.), *The nature of remembering* (pp. 17–34). Washington: American Psychological Association.

Tulving, E. (2001b). Episodic memory and common sense: How far apart? *Philosophical Transactions of the Royal Society (Series B), 356*, 1505–1515.

Tulving, E. (2002a). Episodic memory: From mind to brain. *Annual Review of Psychology, 53*, 1–25.

Tulving, E. (2002b). Chronesthesia: Conscious awareness of subjective time. In D.T. Stuss and R.T. Knight (Eds.), *Principles of frontal lobe function* (pp. 311–325). New York: Oxford University Press.

Tulving, E., & Donaldson, W. (Eds.). (1972). *Organization of memory*. New York: Academic Press.

Tulving, E., & Schacter, D. (1990). Priming and human memory systems. *Science, 247*, 301–306.

Tulving, E., & Thomson, D.M. (1973). Encoding specificity and retrieval processes in episodic memory. *Psychological Review, 80*, 352–373.

Tulving, E., & Wiseman, S. (1975). Relation between recognition and recognition failure of recallable words. *Bulletin of the Psychonomic Society, 6*, 79–82.

Tunney, R.J., & Shanks, D.R. (2003). Subjective measures of awareness and implicit cognition. *Memory & Cognition, 31*, 1060–1071.

Tuohy, A.P. (1987). Affective asymmetry in social perception. *British Journal of Psychology, 78*, 41–51.

Tuohy, A.P., & Stradling, S.G. (1987). Maximum salience vs golden section proportions in judgemental asymmetry. *British Journal of Psychology, 78*, 457–464.

Tuohy, A.P., & Stradling, S.G. (1992). Positive-negative asymmetry in normative data. *European Journal of Social Psychology, 22*, 483–496.

Turing, A. (1950). Computing machinery and intelligence. *Mind, 59*, 433–450.

Tversky, A., & Kahneman, D. (1971). Belief in the law of small numbers. *Psychological Bulletin, 76*, 105–110.

Tversky, A., & Kahneman, D. (1973a). Availability: A heuristic for judging frequency and probability. *Cognitive Psychology, 5*, 207–232.

Tversky, A., & Kahneman, D. (1973b). On the psychology of prediction. *Psychological Review, 80*, 237–251.

Tversky, A., & Kahneman, D. (1974). Judgement under uncertainty: Heuristics and biases. *Science, 185*, 1124–1131.

Tversky, A., & Kahneman, D. (1983). Extensional versus intuitive reasoning: The conjunctive fallacy in probability judgement. *Psychological Review, 90*, 293–314.

Tversky, A., & Kahneman, D. (2000). Rational choice and the framing of decisions. In D. Kahneman & A. Tversky (Eds.), *Choices, values, and frames* (pp. 209–223). Cambridge: Cambridge University Press.

Tversky, B. (2003). Structures of mental spaces: How people think about space. *Environment and Behavior, 35*, 66–80.

Tweney, R.D. (1991). Faraday's notebooks: The active organization of creative science. *Physics Education, 26*, 301–306.

Tweney, R.D. (1999). Toward a cognitive psychology of science: Recent research and its implications. *Current Directions in Psychological Science, 7*, 150–154.

Uhr, L. (1966). Pattern recognition. In L. Uhr (Ed.), *Pattern recognition* (pp. 365–381). New York: Wiley.

Ullmann, S. (1957). *The principles of semantics: A linguistic approach to meaning* (2nd ed.). Cambridge, Mass.: MIT Press.

Uriagereka, J. (1998). *Rhyme and reason: An introduction to minimalist syntax.* Cambridge, Mass.: MIT Press.

Usher, J.A., & Neisser, U. (1993). Childhood amnesia and the beginnings of memory for four early life events. *Journal of Experimental Psychology: General, 122*, 155–165.

Uttal, W.R. (2001). *The new phrenology: The limits of localizing cognitive processes in the brain.* Cambridge, Mass.: MIT Press.

Van der Henst, J.B., Carles, L., & Sperber, D. (2002). Truthfulness and relevance in telling the time. *Mind and Language, 17*, 457–466.

Vartanian, O., Martindale, C., & Kwiatkowski, J. (2003). Creativity and inductive reasoning: The relationship between divergent thinking and performance on Wason's 2-4-6 task. *Quarterly Journal of Experimental Psychology, 56*, 1–15.

Vendler, Z. (1972). *Res cogitans: An essay in rational psychology.* Ithaca, NY: Cornell University Press.

Vicente, K.J., & Brewer, W.F. (1993). Reconstructive remembering of the scientific literature. *Cognition, 46*, 101–128.

Vickers, J.N. (1996). Visual control when aiming at a far target. *Journal of Experimental Psychology: Human Perception and Performance, 22*, 342–354.

Vickers, J.N. (2004). The Quiet Eye: It's the difference between a good putter and a poor one, here's proof. *Golf Digest* (Jan.), 96–101.

Vinacke, W.E. (1974). *The psychology of thinking.* New York: McGraw-Hill.

von Restorff, H. (1933). Über die Wirkung von Bereichsbildungen im Spurenfeld. *Psychologische Forschung, 18*, 299–342.

Vos Savant, M. (1990a, September 9). Ask Marilyn. *Parade Magazine,* p. 15.

Vos Savant, M. (1990b, December 2). Ask Marilyn. *Parade Magazine,* p. 25.

Vos Savant, M. (1991, February 17). Ask Marilyn. *Parade Magazine,* p. 12.

Vygotsky, L.S. (1986). *Thought and language* (A. Kozulin, Trans.). Cambridge, Mass.: MIT Press. (Original work published 1934).

Vygotsky, L.S. (1978). *Mind in society.* Cambridge, Mass.: Harvard University Press. (Original work published 1935).

Wagenaar, W.A., Hudson, P.T.W., & Reason, J.T. (1990). Cognitive failures and accidents. *Applied Cognitive Psychology, 4*, 273–294.

Wagner, U., Gais, S., Haider, H., Verleger, R., & Born, J. (2004). Sleep inspires insight. *Nature, 427*, 352–355.

Wainer, H., & Velleman, P.F. (2001). Statistical graphics: Mapping the pathways of science. *Annual Review of Psychology, 52*, 305–335.

Walker, H.M. (1943). *Elementary statistical methods.* New York: Holt.

Wallas, G. (1926). *The art of thought.* London: Cape.

Walters, J.M., & Gardner, H. (1986). The theory of multiple intelligences: Some issues and answers. In R.J. Sternberg (Ed.), *Practical intelligence* (pp. 163–182). New York: Cambridge University Press.

Wang, R.F., & Spelke, E.S. (2000). Updating egocentric representations in human navigation. *Cognition, 77*, 215–250.

Wang, R.F., & Spelke, E.S. (2002). Human spatial representation: Insights from animals. *Trends in Cognitive Sciences, 6*, 375–382.

Ward, J., & Simner, J. (2003). Lexical gustatory synaesthesia: Linguistic and conceptual factors. *Cognition, 89*, 237–261.

Warrington, E., & Weiskrantz, L. (1982). Amnesia: A disconnection syndrome? *Neuropsychologia, 20*, 233–248.

Warrington, E.K., & Shallice, T. (1984). Category specific semantic impairments. *Brain, 107*, 829–854.

Wason, P.C. (1960). On the failure to eliminate hypotheses in a conceptual task. *Quarterly Journal of Experimental Psychology, 12*, 129–140.

Wason, P.C. (1966). Reasoning. In B.M. Foss (Ed.), *New horizons in psychology* (pp. 135–151). Harmondsworth, UK: Penguin.

Wason, P.C. (1977a). "On the failure to eliminate hypotheses . . .": A second look. In P.N. Johnson-Laird & P.C. Wason (Eds.), *Thinking: Readings in cognitive science* (pp. 307–314). Cambridge: Cambridge University Press.

Wason, P.C. (1977b). Self-contradictions. In P.N. Johnson-Laird & P.C. Wason (Eds.), *Thinking: Readings in cognitive science* (pp. 114–128). Cambridge: Cambridge University Press.

Wason, P.C. (1978). Hypothesis testing and reasoning. In *Cognitive Psychology* (Block 4, Unit 25, pp. 17–56). Milton Keynes, UK: Open University Press.

Wason, P.C., & Brooks, P.G. (1979). THOG: The anatomy of a problem. *Psychological Research, 41*, 79–90.

Wason, P.C., & Evans, J. St B.T. (1975). Dual processes in reasoning? *Cognition, 3/2*, 141–154.

Wason, P.C., & Johnson-Laird, P.N. (1972). *Psychology of reasoning: Structure and content.* London: Batsford.

Wason, P.C., & Shapiro, D. (1971). Natural and contrived experience in a reasoning problem. *Quarterly Journal of Experimental Psychology, 23*, 63–71.

Watson, J. M. & Strayer, D. L. (2010). Supertaskers: Profiles in extraordinary multi-tasking ability. *Psychonomic Bulletin & Review, 17*, 479–485.

Waugh, N.C., & Norman, D.A. (1965). Primary memory. *Psychological Review, 72*, 89–104.

Weaver, C.A. III. (1993). Do you need a flash to form a flashbulb memory? *Journal of Experimental Psychology: General, 122*, 39–46.

Webster, J.C., & Thompson, P.O. (1953). Some audio considerations in air control towers. *Journal of the Audio Engineering Society, 1*(2), 171–175.

Webster, J.C., & Thompson, P.O. (1954). Responding to both of two overlapping messages. *Journal of the Acoustical Society of America 26*(3), 396–402.

Wegner, D.M. (2003). The mind's best trick: How we experience conscious will. *Trends in Cognitive Sciences, 7*, 65–69.

Weidman, N. (1994). Mental testing and machine intelligence: The Lashley-Hull debate. *Journal of the History of the Behavioral Sciences, 30*, 162–180.

Weisberg, R.W. (1986). *Genius, creativity and other myths.* New York: Freeman.

Weisberg, R.W. (1994). Genius and madness? A quasi-experimental test of the hypothesis that manic-depression increases creativity. *Psychological Science, 5,* 361–367.

Weisberg, R.W. (1995). Prolegomena to theories of insight in problem-solving: A taxonomy of problems. In R.J. Sternberg & J. Davidson (Eds.) *The nature of insight.* Cambridge, Mass.: MIT Press.

Weisberg, R.W., & Alba, J.W. (1981). An examination of the role of fixation in the solution of several insight problems. *Journal of Experimental Psychology: General, 110,* 169–192.

Weiskrantz, L. (2000). Epilogue: The story of memory and the memory of a story. In E. Tulving & F.I.M. Craik (Eds.), *The Oxford handbook of memory* (pp. 645–648). New York: Oxford University Press.

Weitzenhooffer, A.M., & Hilgard, E.R. (1962). *Stanford Hypnotizability Scale Form C.* (Revised by J. Kihlstrom). Retrieved October 5, 2004, from http://ist-socrates.berkeley. edu/~kihlstrm/PDFfiles/Hypnotizability/SH SSC%20 Script.pdf.

Werner, H. (1961). *Comparative psychology of mental development.* New York: Science editions. (Original work published 1948).

Werner, H., & Kaplan, B. (1963). *Symbol formation.* New York: Wiley.

Wertheimer, M. (1959). *Productive thinking.* New York: Harper.

Wertheimer, M. (1967a). Laws of organization in perceptual forms. In W.D. Ellis (Ed.), *A source book of Gestalt psychology* (pp. 71–88). New York: Humanities Press. (Original work published 1923).

Wertheimer, M. (1967b). The syllogism and productive thinking. In W.D. Ellis (Ed.), *A source book of Gestalt psychology* (pp. 274–282). New York: Humanities. (Original work published 1925).

Wertheimer, Michael (1985). A Gestalt perspective on computer simulations of cognitive processes. *Computers in Human Behaviour, 1,* 19–33.

Wertsch, J.V. (Ed.). (1985). *Vygotsky and the social function of mind.* Cambridge, Mass.: Harvard University Press.

Wertsch, J.V., & Stone, C. (1985). The concept of internalization in Vygotsky's account of the genesis of higher mental functions. In J.V. Wertsch (Ed.), *Culture, communication and cognition* (pp. 162–179). Cambridge: Cambridge University Press.

Wetzler, S.E., & Sweeney, J.A. (1986). Childhood amnesia: An empirical demonstration. In D.C. Rubin (Ed.), *Autobiographical memory* (pp. 191–201). Cambridge: Cambridge University Press.

Wheeler. M.A. (2000). Episodic memory and autonoetic awareness. In E. Tulving & F.I.M. Craik (Eds.), *The Oxford handbook of memory* (pp. 597–608). New York: Oxford University Press.

Wheeler, M.A., Stuss, D.T., & Tulving, E. (1997). Toward a theory of episodic memory: The frontal lobes and autonoetic consciousness. *Psychological Bulletin, 121,* 331–354.

Whitehead, D. (2003). Review of Sadoski & Paivio, "Imagery and text: A dual coding theory of reading and writing." *Reading and Writing: An Interdisciplinary Journal, 16,* 159–262.

Whorf, B.L. (1956). *Language, thought and reality.* Cambridge, Mass.: MIT Press.

Wickelgren, W.A. (1979). *Cognitive psychology.* Englewood Cliffs, NJ: Prentice-Hall.

Wickens, C.D. (1984). Processing resources in attention. In R. Parasuraman & D.R. Davies (Eds.), *Varieties of attention* (pp. 63–102). Orlando, Fla: Academic Press.

Wickens, D.D. (1970). Encoding categories of words: An empirical approach to meaning. *Psychological Review, 77,* 1–15.

Williams, L.E., & Bargh, J. A. (2008). Experiencing physical warmth influences interpersonal warmth. *Science, 322,* 606–607.

Williams, L.P. (1991). Michael Faraday's chemical notebook: Portrait of the scientist as a young man. *Physics Education, 26,* 278–283.

Williams, R. (1976). *Keywords: A vocabulary of culture and society.* New York: Oxford University Press.

Williams, W.M. (1998). Are we raising smarter children today? School and home-related influences on IQ. In U. Neisser (Ed.), *The rising curve* (pp. 125–154). Washington: American Psychological Association.

Wilson, B.A. (2002). Management of remediation of memory problems in brain-injured adults. In A.D. Baddeley, M.D. Kopelman, & B.A. Wilson (Eds.), *The handbook of memory disorders* (pp. 655–682). New York: Wiley.

Wilson, B.A., & Moffat, N. (1984). *Clinical management of memory problems.* Rockville, Md: Aspen Publications.

Wilson, B.A., & Patterson, K. (1990). Rehabilitation for cognitive impairment: Does cognitive psychology apply? *Applied Cognitive Psychology, 4,* 247–260.

Wilson, M. (2002). Six views of embodied cognition. *Psychonomic Bulletin & Review, 9,* 625–636.

Winner, E. (1982). *Invented worlds.* Cambridge, Mass.: Harvard University Press.

Winner, E. (2000). The origins and ends of giftedness. *American Psychologist, 55,* 159–169.

Winograd, E., & Soloway, R. (1986). On forgetting the locations of things stored in special places. *Journal of Experimental Psychology: General, 115,* 366–372.

Winograd, T., & Flores, F. (1986). *Understanding computers and cognition: A new foundation for design.* Norwood, NJ: Ablex.

Witkowski, S.R., & Brown, C.H. (1983). Marking reversals and cultural importance. *Language, 59,* 569–582.

Wittgenstein, L. (1953). *Philosophical investigations.* Oxford: Blackwell.

Wittgenstein, L. (1974). *Tractatus logico-philosophicus.* London: Routledge & Kegan Paul. (Original work published 1921).

Wixted, J.T. (2004a). The psychology and neuroscience of forgetting. *Annual Review of Psychology, 55,* 235–269.

Wixted, J.T. (2004b). On common ground: Jost's (1897) law of forgetting and Ribot's (1881) law of retrograde amnesia. *Psychological Review, 111,* 864–879.

Wolfe, J.M. (2003). Moving towards solutions to some enduring controversies in visual search. *Trends in Cognitive Sciences, 7,* 70–76.

Wolff, P., Medin, D.L., & Pankratz, C. (1999). Evolution and devolution of folk biological knowledge. *Cognition, 73*, 177–204.

Woltz, D.J., Gardner, M.K., & Bell, B.G. (2000). Negative transfer errors in sequential cognitive skills: Strong-but-wrong sequence application. *Journal of Experimental Psychology: Learning, Memory, and Cognition, 26*, 601–625.

Wong, C.K., & Read, J.D. (2011). Positive and negative effects of physical context reinstatement on eyewitness recall and identification. *Applied Cognitive Psychology, 25* (1), 2–11.

Wood, N., & Cowan, N. (1995). The cocktail party phenomenon revisited: Attention and memory in the classic selective listening procedure of Cherry (1953). *Journal of Experimental Psychology: General, 124*, 243–262.

Woodworth, R.S. (1940). *Psychology* (4th ed.). New York: Holt.

Wright, E. (1992). Gestalt switching: Hanson, Aronson, and Harre. *Philosophy of Science, 59*, 480–486.

Wundt, W. (1970). The psychology of the sentence. In A.L. Blumenthal (Ed.), *Language and psychology* (pp. 9–33). New York: Wiley. (Original work published 1890).

Yaden, D.B., & Templeton, S. (Eds.). (1986). *Metalinguistic awareness and beginning literacy: Conceptualizing what it means to read and write.* Portsmouth, NH: Heinemann.

Yang, C.D. (2004). Universal grammar, statistics or both? *Trends in Cognitive Sciences, 8*, 451–456.

Yarbus, A.L. (1967). *Eye movements and vision.* Trans. L.A. Riggs. New York: Plenum Press.

Yates, F.A. (1966). *The art of memory.* Chicago: University of Chicago Press.

Yeung, N., & Monsell, S. (2003). The effects of recent practice on task switching. *Journal of Experimental Psychology: Human Perception and Performance, 29*, 919–936.

Yoshida, H., & Smith, L.B. (2005). Linguistic cues enhance the learning of perceptual cues. *Psychological Science, 16*, 90–95.

Yovel, G., & Paller, K.A. (2004). The neural basis of the butcher-on-the-bus phenomenon: When a face seems familiar but is not remembered. *NeuroImage, 21*, 789–800.

Yuille, J. (1968). Concreteness without imagery in PA learning. *Psychonomic Science, 11*, 55–56.

Zacks, J.M., Mires, J., Tversky, B., & Hazeltine, E. (2000). Mental spatial transformations of objects and perspective. *Spatial Cognition and Computation, 2*, 315–332.

Zajonc, R.B. (1968). Attitudinal effects of mere exposure. *Journal of Personality and Social Psychology Monograph, 9* (2, Pt. 2), 1–28.

Zajonc, R.B. (1980). Feeling and thinking: Preferences need no inferences. *American Psychologist, 35*, 151–175.

Zajonc, R.B. (1984). On the primacy of affect. *American Psychologist, 39*, 117–123.

Zajonc, R.B. (2001). Mere exposure: A gateway to the subliminal. *Current Directions in Psychological Science, 10*, 224–228.

Zangwill, O.L. (1972). Remembering revisited. *Quarterly Journal of Experimental Psychology, 24*, 123–138.

Zeigarnik, B. (1967). On finished and unfinished tasks. In W.D. Ellis (Ed.), *A source book of Gestalt psychology* (pp. 300–315). New York: Humanities Press. (Original work published 1927.)

Zhai, S., Kristensson, P.O., & Smith, B.A. (2005). In search of effective text input interfaces for off the desktop computing. *Interacting with Computers, 17*, 229–250.

Zimler, J., & Keenan, J. (1983). Imagery in the congenitally blind: How visual are visual images? *Journal of Experimental Psychology: Learning, Memory, and Cognition, 9*, 269–282.

Zizak, D.M., & Reber, A.S. (2004). Implicit preferences: The role(s) of familiarity in the structural mere exposure effect. *Consciousness and Cognition, 13*, 336–362.

Photo Credits

Index